Drivers of Environmental Change in Uplands

The uplands are a crucial source of ecosystem services, such as water pro-vision, carbon retention, maintenance of biodiversity, provision of recreation value and cultural heritage. This makes them the focus of environmental and social scientists as well as of practitioners and land managers. This volume brings together a wealth of knowledge of the British uplands from diverse but inter-related fields of study, clearly demonstrating their importance in twenty-first-century Britain, and indicating how we may through interdiscip-linary approaches meet the challenges provided by past and future drivers of environmental change.

The upland environments are subject to change. They face imminent threats as well as opportunities from pressures such as climate change, changes in land management and related changes in fire risk, increases in erosion and water colour, degradation of habitats, altered wildlife and recreational value, as well as significant changes in the economy of these marginal areas. This book presents up-to-date scientific background information, addresses policy-related issues and lays out pressing land management questions. A number of world-class experts provide a review of cutting-edge natural and social science and an assessment of past, current and potential future management strategies, policies and other drivers of change. After appraisal of key con-cepts and principles, chapters provide specific examples and applications by focusing on UK upland areas and specifically on the Peak District National Park as a key example for other highly valuable upland regions.

With its strong interdisciplinary approach, this book will be of interest to a wide range of students, researchers and practitioners in the field, includ-ing those engaged with Environmental Economics, Conservation and Land Management, Rural Development, Environmental Management and Phys-ical Geography.

Aletta Bonn is Research Manager for the Moors for the Future Partnership in the Peak District National Park. **Tim Allott** is Reader in Physical Geo-graphy at the University of Manchester and co-leader of the Upland Environ-ments Research Unit. **Klaus Hubacek** is Reader in Ecological Economics at the School of Earth and Environment, University of Leeds. **Jon Stewart** is a Team Leader with Natural England working in the Peak District.

Routledge Studies in Ecological Economics

Sustainability Networks

Cognitive tools for expert collaboration in social–ecological systems
Janne Hukkinen

Drivers of Environmental Change in Uplands
Edited by Aletta Bonn, Tim Allott, Klaus Hubacek and Jon Stewart

Drivers of Environmental Change in Uplands

Edited by Aletta Bonn, Tim Allott,
Klaus Hubacek and Jon Stewart

Routledge
Taylor & Francis Group

LONDON AND NEW YORK

First published 2009 by Routledge
2 Park Square, Milton Park, Abingdon, Oxon, OX14 4RN

Simultaneously published in the USA and Canada
by Routledge
270 Madison Avenue, New York, NY 10016

Routledge is an imprint of the Taylor & Francis Group, an informa business

Typeset in 10/12pt Times New Roman by Graphicraft Limited,
Hong Kong
Printed and bound in Great Britain by TJ International Ltd, Padstow, Cornwall

British Library Cataloguing in Publication Data
A catalogue record for this book is available from the British Library

Library of Congress Cataloging-in-Publication Data
Drivers of environmental change in uplands / Aletta Bonn . . . [et al.].
p. cm.
Includes bibliographical references and index.
ISBN 978–0–415–44779–9 (hb) — ISBN 978–0–203–88672–4 (eb) 1. Land
use—Environmental aspects—Great Britain. 2. Environmental protection—
Great Britain. 3. Uplands—Great Britain. I. Bonn, Aletta.
HD596.D75 2008
333.73—dc22
2008023480

ISBN10: 0-415-44779-8 (hbk)
ISBN10: 0-203-88672-0 (ebk)

ISBN13: 978-0-415-44779-9 (hbk)
ISBN13: 978-0-203-88672-4 (ebk)

Contents

Foreword by John Lee   viii
Acknowledgements   x
List of tables   xii
List of figures   xv
List of contributors   xx

**1 Introduction: Drivers of change in upland environments:
    concepts, threats and opportunities**   1
    ALETTA BONN, TIM ALLOTT, KLAUS HUBACEK AND JON STEWART

**PART I
Processes and policy – the overarching drivers of change**   11

2 Natural changes in upland landscapes   13
    MARTIN EVANS

**3 Threats from air pollution and climate change to upland
    systems: past, present and future**   34
    SIMON J. M. CAPORN AND BRIDGET A. EMMETT

4 Policy change in the uplands   59
    IAN CONDLIFFE

**PART II
Ecosystem services and drivers of change**   91

5 The carbon budget of upland peat soils   93
    FRED WORRALL AND MARTIN G. EVANS

6 Upland hydrology   113
    JOSEPH HOLDEN

7 The state of upland freshwater ecosystems 135
TIM ALLOTT

8 Condition of upland terrestrial habitats 156
ALISTAIR CROWLE AND FAY MCCORMACK

9 Burning issues: the history and ecology of managed fires
in the uplands 171
ADRIAN R. YALLOP, BEN CLUTTERBUCK AND
JONATHAN I. THACKER

10 Moorland management with livestock: the effect of policy
change on upland grazing, vegetation and farm economics 186
SARAH M. GARDNER, TONY WATERHOUSE AND C. NIGEL R. CRITCHLEY

11 International importance and drivers of change of upland bird
populations 209
JAMES W. PEARCE-HIGGINS, MURRAY C. GRANT, COLIN M.
BEALE, GRAEME M. BUCHANAN AND INNES M. W. SIM

12 Mammals in the uplands 228
DEREK W. YALDEN

13 Managing uplands for game and sporting interests:
an industry perspective 241
NICK SOTHERTON, RICHARD MAY, JULIE EWALD,
KATHY FLETCHER AND DAVID NEWBORN

14 Moors from the past 261
BILL BEVAN

15 Leisure in the landscape: rural incomes and public benefits 277
NIGEL CURRY

PART III
Social change, land management and conservation:
driving change 291

16 Description of the upland economy: areas of outstanding
beauty and marginal economic performance 293
KLAUS HUBACEK, KATHARINA DEHNEN-SCHMUTZ, MUHAMMAD
QASIM AND METTE TERMANSEN

17 The future of public goods provision in upland regions:
learning from hefted commons in the Lake District, UK 309
ROB J. F. BURTON, GERALD SCHWARZ, KATRINA M. BROWN, IAN T.
CONVERY AND LOIS MANSFIELD

18 The economic value of landscapes in the uplands of England 323
NICK HANLEY AND SERGIO COLOMBO

19 Landscape as an integrating framework for upland management 339
CARYS SWANWICK

20 Using scenarios to explore UK upland futures 358
KATHRYN ARBLASTER, MARK S. REED, EVAN D. G. FRASER AND
CLIVE POTTER

21 Effective policy-making in the uplands: a case study in the
Peak District National Park 376
STEVE CONNELLY AND TIM RICHARDSON

22 How class shapes perceptions of nature: implications for
managing visitor perceptions in upland UK 393
NATALIE SUCKALL, EVAN FRASER AND CLAIRE QUINN

23 Moorland wildfire risk, visitors and climate change: patterns,
prevention and policy 404
JULIA MCMORROW, SARAH LINDLEY, JONATHAN AYLEN,
GINA CAVAN, KEVIN ALBERTSON AND DAN BOYS

24 Moorland restoration: potential and progress 432
PENNY ANDERSON, MATT BUCKLER AND JONATHAN WALKER

25 Ecosystem services: a new rationale for conservation of upland
environments 448
ALETTA BONN, MICK REBANE AND CHRISTINE REID

26 Conclusions: Managing change in the uplands – challenges
in shaping the future 475
ALETTA BONN, TIM ALLOTT, KLAUS HUBACEK AND JON STEWART

List of acronyms 495
Index 498

Foreword

John Lee

It is nearly sixty years since W. H. Pearsall's classic text *Mountains and Moorlands* appeared. At the time, and for at least two decades afterwards, it was arguably the best English ecological text, providing an unrivalled description of the ecology of the British uplands. Pearsall had known the uplands intimately since he was a boy in the last years of the nineteenth century, and had pursued distinguished ecological research there during an academic career begun at the Victoria University of Manchester and continued at the Universities of Leeds and Sheffield and at the University College London. Among the many important observations in the book, Pearsall emphasised that the British uplands had been subjected to continuous change since the last glaciation, although the cause and nature of this change had altered over time. In the intervening years since *Mountains and Moorlands* appeared there has been a number of books devoted to upland ecology and at least one devoted to ecological change, but the present volume is perhaps the first to adopt a wide-ranging interdisciplinary approach incorporating science, policy and management considerations.

The fact that change in the uplands has been continuous but that the drivers have changed over time makes predictions about the future problematic. One can immediately see this by reading the last chapter of *Mountains and Moorlands*, which is devoted to the future as Pearsall saw it in 1950. To take but one example, Pearsall could not have foreseen the massive overgrazing problems of the last few decades of the twentieth century conditioned by the European Union's Common Agricultural Policy, one of the largest drivers of change in the uplands. Few can doubt today the importance of the link between science, policy and management when considering the viability of upland farming, very much a major current concern. The interdisciplinary approach as exemplified in many of the chapters in this book is very much to be applauded.

A major preoccupation of environmental scientists, managers, policy-makers and indeed the general public today is that of human-made global climate change, and many of the authors in this volume refer to it as a major driver of change. They are of course right to do so, given the over-riding importance of climate in determining ecological processes. In helping us to predict the effects of climate change scenarios on the uplands we are in a much stronger position now than in Pearsall's day. The last fifty years have seen a great increase in environmental research in the British uplands, much of which is documented in the chapters of this book. We have now knowledge based on considerable careful experimentation as well as on observation to guide managers and policy-makers into the future. However, we still have an imperfect understanding of how upland ecosystems respond in the longer term to environmental perturbations and restoration practices, and this is likely to be the focus of much further research to help us anticipate future challenges.

The huge economic and social value of ecosystems as a source of goods and services for people has become much more widely recognised in recent years, notably through the Millennium Ecosystem Assessment launched in 2001. For many years the uplands have been used as a source of water for lowland cities and towns as well as a place of recreation for their inhabitants. However, until recently, very little emphasis has been placed on the connections between upland and lowland Britain. One topical example of these connections is to what extent the management of upland catchments for agriculture or game birds may influence lowland flooding and water quality. Similarly, it is only recently that peatlands have been valued for their potential long-term carbon storage as atmospheric concentrations of carbon dioxide continue to rise. Peatlands play an important role in both the water and carbon economies of upland Britain and of some other parts of the world, but have been badly neglected in the past. The neglect and the environmental problems this has caused are well documented in this volume, as are attempts to rectify the situation through reclamation practices.

The uplands have provided, and continue to provide, many benefits to society. Perhaps these benefits have not been as widely appreciated by policy-makers and the population at large as they should have been. This volume brings together a wealth of knowledge of the British uplands from diverse but inter-related fields of study. It clearly demonstrates their importance in twenty-first century Britain, and indicates how we may through interdisciplinary approaches meet the challenges provided by past and future drivers of environmental change.

John Lee
Department of Animal and Plant Sciences
The University of Sheffield

Acknowledgements

This book has been a great collaborative project by all authors involved. The inter-disciplinary nature of this project brought together social and natural scientists as well as key experts and representatives from upland policy and management. The collation has been a stimulating and productive process, and we are grateful to all contributors. Similarly, we are indebted to all reviewers, both scientists and practitioners, who examined the contents with a critical eye and provided many constructive comments that enhanced the book. Special thanks to Joanna Collins, Dabo Guan and Yuan Guan for editorial assistance. We are also grateful to the Routledge publishing team for their advice and guidance.

The project developed out of a productive upland research forum in the Peak District National Park, UK, a platform for cross-disciplinary upland research. The forum is fostered by the Moors for the Future Partnership, a public–private partnership dedicated to restoration, awareness-raising and research. The partnership aims to develop and share expertise of how to protect upland environments and adapt to change in the future (www.moorsforthefuture.org.uk). The first phase of the programme was supported by the Heritage Lottery Fund, and past and current partners include: Peak District National Park Authority, Natural England, National Trust, Department for Environment, Food and Rural Affairs (Defra), Environment Agency, United Utilities, Severn Trent Water, Yorkshire Water, Sheffield City Council, Derbyshire County Council, Moorland Association, Country Land and Business Association, National Farmers Union as well as private moorland owners. We would very much like to thank staff and members of these organisations and individuals, whose vital support facilitated many of the case studies reported in this book.

Two of the editors and several authors (Hubacek, Bonn, Boys, Fraser, Holden, Quinn, Reed, Termansen and Worrall) are involved in the research consortium project 'Sustainable uplands: learning to manage future change' RES-224-25-0088, funded through the Rural Economy and Land Use (RELU) Programme, co-sponsored by UK research councils ESRC, NERC and BB SRC and UK agencies Defra and SEERAD.

The editors have used their best endeavours to ensure URLs provided for external websites are correct and active at the time of going to press. However, the publisher has no responsibility for websites and cannot guarantee that contents will remain live or appropriate.

List of tables

2.1 Classification of the major agents of Holocene change in
     upland landscapes   14
3.1 The main primary and secondary pollutants emitted to
     the atmosphere that have a role in environmental
     toxicology and climate change   36
3.2 Radiative forcing (global warming potential), average
     concentrations and trends of anthropogenic greenhouse
     gases and other components in 2005   42
3.3 Comparison of climatic variables averaged over two time
     periods at Moor House in the English North Pennines   44
3.4 Summary of selected UK climate change scenarios   46
4.1 Milestones in UK and European policy affecting upland
     agriculture   62
4.2 Comparison of recent uptake of agri-environment schemes
     in Less Favoured Areas (LFA) and non-LFA in England   84
5.1 Summary of carbon exports and inputs for the Trout
     Beck catchment at Moor House   95
5.2 Summary of carbon export and input ranges used for
     calculation of carbon budget of British peats   98
6.1 Percentage runoff collected in automated throughflow
     troughs from peat layers on hillslopes in Upper
     Wharfedale, December 2002–December 2004   117
6.2 Mean summary hydrological characteristics for two sites
     with and without grazing during 2005   124
8.1 European interest features in the UK uplands   158
8.2 Areas on Sites of Special Scientific Interest (SSSIs) where
     burning can result in the land being recorded as in
     unfavourable condition   166
9.1 Summary of guidance on burning for grouse management   176
10.1 Grazing regimes used in the economics and vegetation
     change modelling studies   188
10.2 Responses to questions about changes in farm policy,
     past and future, from hill sheep farmers in mid-Wales,

the Scottish Highlands, the Lake District and the Peak
District in 2006   191
10.3 Preferred strategies for future hill farming   191
10.4 Model predictions for abundance of three key species in
mat grass heath at ADAS Pwllpeiran   201
10.5 Comparison of ranks of Best and Worst grazing regimes
for vegetation management and economic viability for the
sites at ADAS Redesdale and ADAS Pwllpeiran   202
11.1 The latest UK population estimates of upland bird
populations, and assessments of conservation importance   210
11.2 Variation in the distribution, abundance, survival,
productivity or population trends of upland bird species
as a function of dwarf shrub cover and vegetation density   214
11.3 Summary of the likely impacts of grouse moor
management on upland bird density, breeding success
or population change   216
11.4 Summary of the likely impacts of afforestation on the
density, breeding success or population changes of upland
birds on adjacent moorland   218
13.1 Comparison in the density of moorland birds of
conservation concern on areas managed for grouse-
shooting within the Peak District National Park in 1990
and 2004   250
13.2 Percentage losses in breeding range of three moorland
birds   251
13.3 The costs of a grouse moor in the Peak District   257
15.1 Main reasons for not visiting the countryside in England
in 2005   281
18.1 Attributes and attribute levels used in the choice
experiment   327
18.2 Example card – Yorkshire and Humberside sample   328
18.3 Random parameters logit model coefficients for each
region   330
18.4 Explanation of variable abbreviations and coding in
Table 18.3   331
18.5 Willingness to Pay estimates (implicit prices) and their
95 per cent confidence intervals   332
18.6 Predictions of the change in the landscape attributes
under the four policy scenarios   333
18.7 Compensating surplus estimates for three policy options   334
18.8 Compensating surplus aggregated across all households
resident in SDA regions   335
19.1 Joint Character Areas allocated to three broad 'upland'
landscape types   345
20.1 Overview of UK upland scenario studies   362

20.2   Methods used to develop and evaluate scenarios of
       upland change in eight UK studies   364
20.3   UK upland scenarios developed by eight studies, not
       including Business as Usual scenarios   366
23.1   Probit estimation results for Peak District National
       Park reported moorland wildfires, 1 February 1978 to
       1 August 2004   415
23.2   Contingency table for Peak District National Park
       moorland wildfires temporal model for (a) probit model
       training data and (b) test data   416
23.3   Factors and associated datasets considered in the multi-
       criteria (MCE) spatial model of the risk of wildfire
       occurrence in the Peak District National Park   419
24.1   Upland management problems and some solutions   435
25.1   Ecosystem services provided by the uplands   450

List of figures

1.1	Linkages between ecosystem services and human well-being	2
1.2	Britain at night. Satellite imagery depicting light pollution in 2000 as one indicator for tranquillity	8
2.1	The post-glacial spread of key upland tree taxa across Britain	15
2.2	Chemical evolution of lake basins in Glacier Bay	16
2.3	Dynamic equilibrium of upland landscapes	18
2.4	LiDAR imagery of the Cowms Rocks Landslide Complex	21
2.5	Representation of the water budget of ombrotrophic peatlands	22
2.6	Water table and runoff data from the Trout Beck catchment of the Moor House National Nature Reserve in the North Pennines, UK	23
2.7	The peat land-system representing the potential range and connectivity of geomorphological features found on a typical eroding mire	24
2.8	A conceptual model of sediment delivery in eroding peatlands	25
2.9	The blanket peat erosion mosaic	26
3.1	Drivers, responses and effects of air pollution in ecosystems	35
3.2	UK total emissions of NO_x, SO_2 and NH_3	37
3.3	Diurnal pattern in ozone concentrations on 2 July 2006 during a hot summer at an upland (Great Dun Fell) and a lowland (Glazebury) site in northern England	39
3.4	Measured total deposition of nitrogen compounds	40
3.5	Central England temperatures from 1659 to 2007 shown as a five-year running average	43
3.6	Accumulative snow cover in Snowdonia, north Wales, 1979–2006	45
3.7	Annual average temperatures from the central England Temperature data set (CET) at a South Pennine site at Holme Moss and Moor House in the North Pennines from 1992 to 2006	47

3.8	Exceedance of nutrient nitrogen critical loads for dwarf shrub heath by total N (NO_x + NH_y) deposition for 2001–3.	49
3.9	Pollutant concentrations in rainwater at Wardlow Hay Cop, 1988–2000	52
3.10	Increase in the number of species of *Sphagnum*, other mosses and liverworts in open plots at Holme Moss in the South Pennines between 1983–5 and 2005–6	52
4.1	Total livestock numbers in Derbyshire and Devon, UK	67
4.2	Spatial coverage of Less Favoured Areas (LFA) in England	68
4.3	Diagram of Defra's agri-environment strategy	82
4.4	Farm business income 2006–7, LFA Grazing Livestock	86
5.1	Schematic diagram of the carbon uptake and release pathways that control the carbon budget of an upland peat soil	94
5.2	Location of the Moor House study site	97
6.1	Discharge from Oughtershaw Moss, a peatland catchment in the Yorkshire Dales, over a six-month period	114
6.2	Main hillslope runoff pathways	115
6.3	Water-table depth for an undisturbed peat soil, Upper Wharfedale, UK, January–June 2004	117
6.4	Submerged soil pipe surrounded by cracked peat	118
6.5	Mean water-table depth and percentage occurrence of overland on bi-weekly monitored plots, October 2002 to October 2004	122
6.6	Gully erosion in the Peak District	125
7.1	The critical loads concept	138
7.2	Critical loads exceedance maps for UK freshwaters in 1995–7 and 2010	139
7.3	The 2004 Peak District Moorland Stream Survey (PD-MSS) sampling points, distributions of key chemical variables, critical loads and exceedances	141
7.4	Differences in macro-invertebrate species richness between sites exceeding and not exceeding their critical acidity load in the 2004 Peak District Moorland Stream Survey (PD-MSS)	142
7.5	Streamwater chemistry trends for the river Etherow 1988–2006	145
7.6	MAGIC model hindcasts and forecasts of the distribution of acid neutralising capacity (ANC) in South Pennine reservoirs for the years 1850, 1970, 2000, 2010 and 2100	146
8.1	Condition of upland SSSIs in England, December 2007	162
8.2	Condition of upland SSSI habitat in England, December 2007	163

8.3   Moor burning, overgrazing and drainage on upland heath
       and bogs in England, December 2007   164
8.4   Top fifteen reasons for adverse condition on upland SSSIs
       in England, December 2007   164
9.1   An example of rapid increase in extent of management
       burning over the previous fifty years from aerial
       photography for an upland catchment in the South
       Pennines, UK   174
9.2   Illustrative relationship between aerial photograph
       interpretation (API) of growth following burning in
       Calluna vulgaris   176
9.3   Burn exhibiting poor recovery on a blanket bog SSSI in
       the Peak District National Park   178
9.4   Relationship between area of new *Calluna* burn on deep
       peat soils and winter dissolved organic carbon (DOC)
       concentrations from thirteen sub-catchments within three
       Pennine drinking-water supply catchments   181
10.1   Predicted net margins for different grazing regimes for
       upland moor at ADAS Redesdale with (a) no Single
       Payment Scheme (SPS) or Higher Level Stewardship
       (HLS) payments and (b) with SPS and basic HLS
       payments included   194
10.2   Income sources for the different grazing regimes listed in
       Table 10.1   195
10.3   Effect of summer cattle and reduced all-year sheep on the
       predicted abundance of heather and purple moor grass at
       ADAS Redesdale   200
10.4   Variation between the six plant communities at ADAS
       Redesdale in the predicted change in abundance of heather
       and purple moor grass after twenty years of summer cattle
       or all-year sheep grazing   200
10.5   Comparison of field and model estimates of abundance for
       heather, purple moor grass and mat grass under reduced
       sheep-stocking at ADAS Redesdale 1990–2000   201
12.1   Mountain hare distribution in the Peak District National
       Park   233
13.1   Percentage heather cover on moorland in Scotland where
       grouse moor management has either been retained or
       abandoned in the 1940s, 1970s and 1980s   245
13.2   Map of the North Pennines Special Protection Area (SPA)
       showing the extent of moorland managed and not
       managed for red grouse   247
13.3   Breeding pairs of birds observed on 320 upland kilometre
       squares with similar vegetation types but separated into those
       managed for red grouse or those that were not managed   248

13.4   Percentage habitat composition of four vegetation types
       on moorland in the Peak District National Park on estates
       managed or not managed for red grouse   249
13.5   Percentage of pairs fledging young on the four plots in
       the Game and Wildlife Conservation Trust's Upland
       Predation Experiment, 2002–6   253
14.1   Hope woodlands township and Howden farmholding
       (Derbyshire) in the early seventeenth century   266
14.2   Post-medieval farmsteads, peat cuts and trackways   267
14.3   Post-medieval features in the Upper Derwent   272
14.4   The Mass Trespassers on their way to Kinder Scout in 1932   274
17.1   Location map of upland areas in Cumbria   312
17.2   Upland farm in Lake District   313
17.3   Structure of a traditional upland farm   313
19.1   Landscape as the interaction of people and place   341
19.2   Upland, upland fringe and moorland Joint Character
       Areas in England   344
19.3   A local landscape character assessment from the White
       Peak Vision Project   346
19.4   A spectrum of landscape-centred approaches   348
20.1   Scenarios grouped according to levels of support for a
       pro-environment policy agenda and varying levels of
       financial support for farmers   368
21.1   The effective deliberation framework   379
21.2   The framework applied: deliberation in practice   388
22.1   Likert mean scores assigned to groups of photographs
       depicting a botanical garden, a moorland, an urban park
       and a shopping mall by students from two economically
       distinct schools   399
23.1   Climate scenarios for summer maximum temperature for
       the UK   409
23.2   Conceptual model of the relationships between climate
       change, visitors, ecosystems and wildfires   410
23.3   Climate scenarios for summer rainfall for the PDNP, with
       1978–2004 wildfires overlaid   412
23.4   Temporal distribution of reported wildfires in the PDNP
       and its relationship to precipitation   413
23.5   Relationship of probability of a wildfire in the PDNP on
       a Spring Bank Holiday Monday and daily maximum
       temperature   417
23.6   (*a*) Example of derivation of empirical habitat scores for
       PDNP MCE model; (*b*) stakeholder views from the online
       survey of the importance of five broad habitats for
       explaining fire risk in the PDNP   420

23.7   Average wildfire risk-of-occurrence scores for the two
       most statistically robust wildfire models   421
23.8   Results of 'what-if' scenario for relocation of the southern
       portion of the Pennine Way in the PDNP   422
23.9   The trade-off between reliability and effectiveness of
       fighting moorland wildfires   425
24.1   Vegetation cover on Bleaklow Plateau (Peak District
       National Park) in 2006 on unrestored site and a site
       restored three years previously   441
25.1   Strategies to deliver visions   462
26.1   Temporal and spatial effects of selected drivers of
       environmental change in uplands   477
26.2   Constraints to experimental design   481

List of contributors

Kevin Albertson is a Principal Lecturer in Economics at the Manchester Metropolitan University. He has fifteen years experience as an applied forecaster and has particular interests in the areas of seasonality and time-series modelling.

Tim Allott is Reader in Physical Geography at the University of Manchester and co-leader of the Upland Environments Research Unit. His research interests include upland environmental change, the impacts of air pollution on freshwater and peatland systems, and the restoration of degraded upland systems.

Penny Anderson is Managing Director of Penny Anderson Associates, a long-established ecological consultancy, which has developed special expertise in the moorland environment. Penny has over twenty-five years experience of practical moorland restoration, assessment and management, especially in the Peak District and the South Pennines.

Kathryn Arblaster is a Researcher at the Centre for Environmental Policy, Imperial College London. Her current research area is biodiversity protection and agri-environmental transition in the new EU member states. Kathryn previously worked as an Agriculture and Rural Development Policy Analyst at the Institute for European Environmental Policy.

Jonathan Aylen is a Director of Manchester Institute of Innovation Research within Manchester Business School. He began his career researching the cost–benefit analysis of historic building restoration. A paper on scrap recycling with co-author Kevin Albertson won the Williams Award of the Institute of Materials, Minerals and Mining in 2007.

Colin Beale is a Spatial Ecologist at the Macaulay Land Use Research Institute in Aberdeen. His research interests are focused upon gaining a deeper understanding of how species and individuals are distributed at a range of spatial scales.

Bill Bevan is Interpretation Project Officer for the Peak District Interpretation Partnership, having spent twelve years as Survey Archaeologist for the Peak District National Park Authority. His research interests include landscape archaeology, long-term social change, the Iron Age and the application of photography to convey sense of place at archaeological monuments.

Aletta Bonn is Research Manager for the Moors for the Future Partnership in the Peak District National Park, which fosters an active upland research forum to address drivers of change in collaboration with national research consortia. Her background is in biodiversity and conservation science, and she is research associate with the University of Sheffield.

Dan Boys is Moor Care Project Officer for the Moors for the Future Partnership in the Peak District National Park. He works in interpretation and conservation, and his responsibilities include raising awareness of the severe threats to moorland ecosystems posed by issues such as dogs and summer fires.

Katrina M. Brown is a Cultural Geographer based at the Macaulay Institute, Aberdeen. She investigates how people assert and secure claims over particular rural spaces, places and landscapes, and how the process is negotiated and contested between particular social groups through various mobilities, representations and identities.

Graeme Buchanan is a Research Biologist with the Royal Society for the Protection of Birds (RSPB), now working on the application of Earth Observation to conservation problems, especially habitat monitoring in Africa. He formerly worked on upland research, including studies on declining bird species and the habitat associations of upland birds.

Matt Buckler is Conservation Works Manager for the Moors for the Future Partnership, which undertakes and develops best practice in moorland restoration in the Peak District National Park.

Rob Burton is a Senior Researcher for Agresearch, New Zealand. His key research interest is agricultural land use change. Recently he has been investigating how culture influences farmer response to agri-environmental policy drivers and the implications for policy formulation in the EU.

Simon Caporn is a Reader in Environmental Ecology at Manchester Metropolitan University where he lectures and researches in Environmental Science and Ecology. He has a particular interest in plants, soils and their responses to atmospheric pollution.

Gina Cavan is a Researcher in the School of Environment and Development, University of Manchester. Her research interests lie in exploring human–environment interactions, particularly in climate change impacts and adaptation, and relationships between climate change, tourism and landscape capacity.

Ben Clutterbuck is a Senior Researcher at Cranfield University working primarily on the development and application of airborne and satellite remote sensing techniques for monitoring habitats. His other research interests include the role of land management in determining peat condition and water quality in the uplands.

Sergio Colombo is Researcher at the Agricultural Economics Department of IFAPA, Andalusian Government, Spain. His main research areas are environmental economics and policy. He advised government on quantifying the landscape impacts of upland agriculture and the social value of public right of way.

Ian Condliffe is an independent Land Management and Agri-environment Consultant. He is the UK independent LFA technical adviser to the European Commission and a research associate of the Countryside and Community Research Institute, University of Gloucestershire. For many years he was the national technical adviser to Defra for environmental and agricultural upland policy and research.

Steve Connelly's research focuses on the implications for sustainability and democracy of governance through partnerships and participation, in the UK and Africa. He lectures on environmental policy and spatial planning in the global South at the University of Sheffield's Department of Town and Regional Planning.

Ian Convery is Senior Lecturer at the National School of Forestry, University of Cumbria. His recent research includes sense of place in northern England, animal disease and rural communities and the integration and governance of the RDPE in Cumbria. His background is rural health and community development.

Nigel Critchley is a Senior Research Scientist for ADAS UK Ltd, based in Northumberland. He is a plant ecologist carrying out research at the interface between agriculture and conservation with a special interest in vegetation management and plant community dynamics in upland and lowland landscapes.

Alistair Crowle is a National Specialist with Natural England. He provides advice in relation to land management, site protection, biodiversity and condition assessment in the English uplands, and commissions research and projects to support these areas of work.

Nigel Curry is Professor of Countryside Planning and Director of the Countryside and Community Research Institute, a joint Institute of the Universities of Gloucestershire and the West of England. His research interests are in access to the countryside, the planning system in rural areas and rural decision-making.

Katharina Dehnen-Schmutz is a Research Fellow at the University of Warwick. She is an ecologist with particular interests in interdisciplinary ecological–economic research. Her main research areas are biological invasions and their links with human activities.

Bridget Emmett is Head of Site at the Centre for Ecology and Hydrology (CEH) Bangor. She has been working on the impacts of climate change, air pollution and land management on the biogeochemistry and ecosystem function of upland systems for over twenty years.

Martin Evans is Reader in Geomorphology in the Upland Environments Research Unit at the University of Manchester. He works on upland sediment systems and particularly on peatland geomorphology and the interaction between geomorphological change and peatland function.

Julie Ewald is Head of Geographical Information Science at the Game and Wildlife Conservation Trust in Hampshire, southern England. She is involved in research examining the effect of management decisions, in both moorland habitats and agricultural ecosystems, on wildlife resources.

Kathy Fletcher is a Senior Scientist with the Game and Wildlife Conservation Trust based in Teesdale, County Durham. She is currently leading a project investigating the impact of grouse moor management techniques on biodiversity in the uplands.

Evan Fraser is a Senior Lecturer and ESRC Research Fellow at the School of Earth and Environment, University of Leeds, who specialises in issues surrounding the rural economy and land use.

Sarah Gardner has twenty years experience in moorland ecology. Her work focuses on the development of modelling tools to evaluate the drivers of habitat change and the effects of land management policy and practice on biodiversity and ecosystem services. Formerly a Principal Research Scientist with ADAS, she is an independent consultant.

Murray Grant is a Senior Research Biologist with the Royal Society for the Protection of Birds (RSPB), leading on a range of upland research, encompassing studies on declining bird species and on the effects of land use and management on upland birds. His main interests concern effects of land use and environmental changes on bird populations and their habitats.

Nick Hanley is a Professor of Environmental Economics at the University of Stirling, where he heads up the Environmental Economics Research Group. Most of Nick's work at present is in the areas of environmental cost–benefit analysis and agri-environmental policy design. He is a member of Defra's Academic Panel.

Joseph Holden is Chair of Physical Geography at the University of Leeds and Director of Water@Leeds. He specialises in peatland hydrology and environmental change and has published over a hundred research papers, reports and book chapters.

Klaus Hubacek is Reader in Ecological Economics at the School of Earth and Environment, University of Leeds. His research interests include ecologic–economic modelling, land-use change and rural development, governance and sustainable consumption and production.

Sarah Lindley is a Lecturer in GIS in the School of Environment and Development, University of Manchester and Co-Director of the Centre for Urban and Regional Ecology. Her research interests include air pollution, climate risk assessment and adaptation, environmental GIScience and decision-support for sustainable development.

Fay McCormack is a National Specialist working in Natural England's Science Services Team. She is responsible for producing reports and analysis on designated sites data and provides evidence to support the Government's SSSI Target 2010.

Julia McMorrow is Senior Lecturer in Remote Sensing, School of Environment and Development, University of Manchester. Julia is a geographer, specialising in hyperspectral remote sensing of peatland vegetation and soils and GIS analysis of wildfire risk. She leads the FIRES trans-disciplinary seminar series on relationships between moorland fire risk, ecosystem services and climate change.

Lois Mansfield is a Principal Lecturer in Environmental Management working in the International Centre for the Uplands at the University of Cumbria. Her research interests include upland agriculture and the environment, footpath erosion and countryside management.

Richard May is Regional Chairman of the Moorland Association and of the Moorland Biodiversity Action Plan for the Peak District, and has had a lifetime's interest in field sports and conservation. He is a private moorland owner involved in active heather restoration and the introduction of black grouse and red grouse.

David Newborn is a Senior Project Scientist in the Upland Research Group of the Game and Wildlife Conservation Trust. His research interests include upland moorland management, the impact of parasites on red grouse populations and development of parasite management techniques to reduce their impact on grouse populations.

James Pearce-Higgins is a Research Biologist with the Royal Society for the Protection of Birds (RSPB), working on climate change and upland research. Specific projects include developing a mechanistic understanding of climate change impacts, understanding ring ouzel and black grouse declines, investigating the impacts of grazing and disturbance on upland birds, and modelling effects of wind farm development.

Clive Potter is Reader in Environmental Policy at Imperial College London and visiting professor at the University of Exeter. His research interests include the socio-environmental effects of agricultural restructuring and the implications of trade liberalisation for biodiversity and landscapes.

Muhammad Qasim is a Researcher at the School of Earth and Environment, University of Leeds, and scientific officer with the Pakistan Agricultural Research Council. His research interest includes economic land-use modelling, land-use change and its environmental implications, upland agriculture and livelihoods.

Claire Quinn is a Social-Environmental Scientist working on the RELU project 'Sustainable Uplands' in the School of Earth and Environment, University of Leeds. Her research in both the UK and Africa focuses on the links between ecology, livelihoods and institutions for management, and the opportunities for adaptation to environmental change.

Mick Rebane is a Senior National Specialist for Natural England. He is responsible for the provision of advice on the ecology, land management and research priorities of upland ecosystems, including those SSSIs and sites of European importance within the English uplands.

Mark Reed is a Senior Lecturer in Participatory Conservation at the School of Earth and Environment, University of Leeds. He has led research projects focusing on land degradation, sustainability indicators and participatory processes in the UK, Southern Europe and Southern and Eastern Africa, and works closely with government agencies on upland issues.

Christine Reid is Upland Futures Project Manager with Natural England. The project is seeking to develop a shared vision for the English uplands and an action plan to achieve it. She has worked on various conservation policy issues over the years including ancient woodland and forestry, CAP reform, agri-environment schemes and the rural development.

Tim Richardson is Professor in Urban and Mobility Studies at Aalborg University, Denmark, and Visiting Professor at the Royal Institute of Technology, Stockholm. His research examines the treatment of mobility in spatial planning, and the theorisation of power in planning.

Gerald Schwarz is a Rural Policy Analyst at the Macaulay Institute with a background in agricultural economics. His main research interests are the implementation and evaluation of rural development programmes in the EU and the impact of rural policy changes on land management in uplands.

Innes Sim is a Research Biologist with the Royal Society for the Protection of Birds (RSPB), currently investigating the causes of ring ouzel declines. He has previously been involved with national surveys of hen harrier and black grouse, and led on the recent Repeat Upland Bird Surveys project.

Nick Sotherton is Director of Research at the Game and Wildlife Conservation Trust in Hampshire, southern England. His research interests include problem-solving at the interface of Agriculture and Wildlife, Integrated Pest Management, and Wildlife Ecology and Conservation.

Jon Stewart is a Team Leader with Natural England working in the Peak District. He has extensive experience of working on uplands for nature conservation agencies in England and Scotland. He is involved in regional coordination and partnership working on upland restoration and conservation and advises on best practice.

Natalie Suckall is a Social Scientist at the School of Earth and Environment, University of Leeds. Her research focuses on the interaction between human societies and the natural environment.

Carys Swanwick is Professor of Landscape in the Department of Landscape at the University of Sheffield. She has been instrumental in developing UK approaches to landscape character and was the lead author of the guidance on Landscape Character Assessment for England and Wales published in 2002.

Mette Termansen is a Senior Lecturer in Ecological Economics at the School of Earth and Environment, University of Leeds. Her research interests include ecologic–economic modelling, valuation of ecosystem services, and biodiversity impacts of land use and climate change.

Jonathan Thacker is Visiting Fellow in the Department of Natural Resources at Cranfield University with research interests in ecology, invertebrate population dynamics, upland biodiversity and the application of geostatistics in vegetation mapping. He works as a consultant with both CS Conservation Survey and Hopkins Invertebrate Survey.

Jonathan Walker is Research Manager for the Moors for the Future Partnership in the Peak District National Park. He is an ecologist with research interests in conservation biology and sustainable agriculture.

Tony Waterhouse is Head of the Hill and Mountain Research Centre at the Scottish Agricultural College (SAC), with a research focus on interactions between upland farming systems and environmental issues using both bioeconomic modelling and participative research with land managers and stakeholders. He has considerable practical experience of upland land use, managing SAC's upland research farms.

Fred Worrall is Reader in Environmental Chemistry, Department of Earth Sciences, University of Durham. He has led the way in developing carbon budget monitoring and modelling in peat ecosystems, and manages a range of carbon storage projects in both lowland and upland settings.

Derek Yalden was Reader in Vertebrate Zoology, School of Life Sciences, University of Manchester, until his retirement in 2005, and remains an Honorary Reader there. He is President of the Mammal Society, UK, and an active Peak District naturalist.

Adrian Yallop is a Senior Research Fellow in spatial ecology in the Integrated Environmental Sciences Institute at Cranfield University. His primary areas of research are in conservation ecology, the application of advance techniques for habitat mapping, upland biodiversity and water quality.

1 Introduction

Drivers of change in upland environments: concepts, threats and opportunities

Aletta Bonn, Tim Allott, Klaus Hubacek and Jon Stewart

Introduction

Uplands are globally a crucial source of ecosystem services, such as provision of food and fibre, water supply, climate regulation, maintenance of biodiversity, as well as providing opportunities for recreation, inspiration and cultural heritage (see Box 1.1). They are often of exceptional natural beauty, centres of species distinctiveness and richness, and historically have been extensively managed for food production owing to difficult terrain and thus low productivity. This is reflected in the fact that most upland regions in Europe, as well as globally, receive national and international conservation designations. In addition, the uplands provide livelihoods and homes for local residents, but often in marginal economies with associated social, economic and demographic problems. Owing to their natural beauty, uplands often provide opportunities for recreational and educational activities for visitors, contributing major direct or indirect income streams for local communities and regions. An example of the impact of reduced tourism on rural economies has most dramatically been demonstrated by the effects of access closures during the foot-and-mouth disease outbreak in Britain in 2001 (see Curry, this volume).

However, upland environments face threats and sometimes competing challenges from pressures such as climate change, atmospheric pollution deposition, policy and funding direction, land management and anthropogenic disturbance. These in turn drive related changes in fire risk, increases in erosion and water colour, degradation of habitats, loss of biodiversity and recreational value, as well as significant demographic shifts and changes in the economy of these marginal areas. In the past fifty years the uplands have seen increasing pressures to meet growing demands for food, timber and opportunities for recreation. These changes have helped to improve the livelihood of some, but at the same time have weakened nature's ability to deliver other key ecosystems services (MA, 2005). Less tangible but sometimes extremely important benefits to society have tended to take second place to the

Box 1.1. Upland ecosystem services

Environmental, socio-economic and political drivers all impact directly or indirectly on the ability of ecosystems to provide important ecosystem services. The concept of ecosystem services has been developed to aid the understanding of the human use and management of natural resources. Ecosystem services are the processes by which the environment produces or regulates resources utilised by humans such as clean air, water, food and materials that are indispensable to our health and well-being. The Millennium Ecosystem Assessment (MA, 2005) identifies four major categories of ecosystem services that directly affect human well-being (Figure 1.1). For the uplands this means:

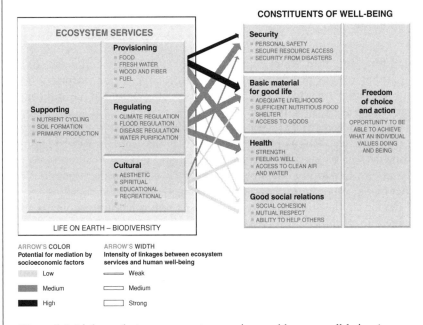

Figure 1.1 Linkages between ecosystem services and human well-being (reproduced by kind permission of the Millennium Ecosystem Assessment: MA, 2005).

- *Provisioning services* deliver important ecosystem products. Upland ecosystem products include food (livestock, game, crops), hay for livestock, timber for building material, fuel such as peat or wood, and minerals used in industry and construction. Most notably, upland catchments provide over 70 per cent of fresh water in Britain. Uplands can also provide a source for hydro-electricity or wind power.

- *Regulating services* in the uplands include air-quality regulation through atmospheric deposition and cooling. UK uplands actively contribute to climate regulation. As 50–60 per cent of UK soil carbon is stored in peatlands, most of this in uplands, the maintenance, enhancement through further carbon sequestration, or degradation of these stores can affect the local climate and contribute to global climate change. Further examples of regulating services include erosion and wildfire regulation as well as water regulation, affecting water quality and quantity.
- *Cultural services* include non-material benefits people obtain from uplands, such as enjoyment of landscape aesthetics, biodiversity and cultural heritage. Uplands are considered some of the most natural ecosystems and typically have low population densities, therefore providing invaluable opportunities for recreation, spiritual enrichment and education. It is not surprising that they are a major tourist destination.
- *Supporting services* are those services that are necessary for the production of all other ecosystem services. Uplands and their habitats and species play a major role in nutrient and water cycling, as well as in soil formation.

People vitally depend on these services. Healthy upland ecosystems can normally maintain a sustainable flow of these services, even when affected by change and disturbance (for a detailed list, see Table 25.1, this volume). The full benefits people gain from these services are difficult to measure, as are the costs when these are lost. However, by unsustainable management we may risk losing these upland services for present and future generations.

more immediate and sometimes short-term benefits. Considering the added challenges posed by climate change, these issues are thrown into sharper focus. In fact, uplands have been identified as particularly vulnerable with respect to climate change (IPCC, 2007), and profound changes are likely to both environments and societies in upland regions and beyond.

The aim of this book is therefore to identify and discuss some key directions and drivers of change in upland environments, how ecosystem services are affected by them and can become drivers in their own rights. It provides insights into how future management and conservation options might address the challenge of sustaining ecosystem services.

The book provides up-to-date scientific background information and lays out pressing land-management questions, the answers to which are needed to address policy-related issues. Our goal is to showcase examples of high-quality research from a wide range of disciplines reflecting the need to understand the complex environmental, social and economic interactions that characterise the uplands. We aim thus to provide relevant information to help inform discussions between organisations, scientists and practitioners relating to sustainable management of uplands. We hope this book appeals to students in environmental and social sciences, researchers, environmental practitioners, land managers, policy-makers, and others with an interest in the functioning and management of fragile upland environments and economic marginal areas. Most of the papers draw heavily on UK experience but are of wider applicability to uplands around the world, especially those experiencing relatively intensive pressures. Many of the themes have applications beyond upland regions.

Definition of uplands

It takes a brave person to make a definitive claim as to what constitutes the uplands. There is some discussion on definitions in relation to the English uplands in *The Upland Management Handbook* (English Nature, 2001). As stated there, the distinction between uplands and lowlands is blurred. It will also tend to vary depending on the factors being considered. Taking a habitat lead, uplands can be considered as areas above the upper limits of enclosed farmland (Ratcliffe and Thompson, 1988). However, there is a very strong link between the open land above the limit of enclosure and the more intensively managed farmland. As a boundary for the uplands we use the term *Less Favoured Areas* (LFA; see Figure 4.2, Condliffe, this volume) developed by the European Union. Although originally introduced primarily as a socio-economic designation, LFA does tie in well with upland habitats. LFA describes an area where farming becomes marginal and less profitable because of natural handicaps (such as harsh climate, short crop season and low soil fertility), or that is mountainous or hilly, as defined by its altitude and slope, or that is remote. Uplands can therefore be defined by climatic conditions that affect plant growth, and altitudinal demarcations can vary in different regions (Fielding and Haworth, 1999).

Drivers of change

As drivers of change are multi-faceted and multi-dimensional, the book has a strong interdisciplinary scope. It is important to identify the nature of the drivers and distinguish between their source, their duration, their impact and their interactions as well as their direct or indirect nature.

Direct drivers influence ecosystem processes explicitly, and can usually be recorded and measured with differing degrees of reliability. They can be natural short-term drivers, such as extreme weather events leading to floods or erosion, or natural long-term drivers, such as changes in climate influencing blanket bog formation. Important anthropogenic drivers include land use and management leading to desired or unintentional habitat and ecosystem service change, overexploitation (e.g. excessive grazing), fragmentation, degradation (e.g. drainage or intensive burning) and disturbance (e.g. wildfire and visitors). All of these drivers are local and internal to the ecosystem affected, and can be addressed by a change in management. External short-term and long-term anthropogenic drivers include pollution through atmospheric deposition or runoff, as well as acceleration of natural levels of climate change. Furthermore, some natural drivers such as invasion by alien species or pest species are also often triggered by human activity (e.g. intentionally or unintentionally introduced species becoming naturalised). Direct drivers are relatively well recognised and documented, although their effects and interactions are not always clearly understood.

In contrast, indirect drivers operate by altering the level or rate of change of one or more direct drivers and include demographic, socio-political, economic, technological and cultural factors. For example, the recent change of US and EU policies with regard to biofuels or weather-induced reductions in crop outputs have implications for lowland and subsequently upland agriculture patterns with implications for the continued provision of upland ecosystem services. Such links between indirect drivers and their effects on upland environments are not always clear and are often subject to time delays. They are often external to the affected ecosystem, and complex interactions with a multitude of other indirect and direct drivers make them less easy to measure or to predict. Important indirect drivers of change include changes in population (e.g. size and age structure of farming communities), changes in policies and legislation, economic incentives (e.g. Common Agricultural Policy Pillars 1 and 2), and shifts in socio-cultural values (e.g. leisure patterns). As awareness grows of the important links between how uplands are managed and their role in providing ecosystem services such as carbon storage, water provision and downstream water-flows, these services are starting to drive change through policy, legislation and economic incentives.

Book structure

The first section addresses the broad external and long-term drivers over which local practitioners have little influence. These include natural processes (Evans) as well as anthropogenic drivers such as climate change and air pollution (Caporn and Emmett). The policy drivers that tend to steer land management in the short and longer term are outlined (Condliffe).

The second section considers a variety of upland ecosystem services that can be both driven by and drive change. It addresses past, present and anticipated future processes, and identifies options for responses to these different drivers of change. Major ecosystem services provided by the uplands include carbon storage and flux (Worrall and Evans), water yield and flood protection (Holden), provision of freshwater (Allott) and terrestrial habitats

(Crowle and McCormack; Yallop, Clutterbuck and Thacker). Land management and changes in land use, with grazing and burning as the dominating forms of land use, are discussed with regard to their direct effects on habitat characteristics and farm economy (Gardner, Waterhouse and Critchley). Moorland wildlife services are covered as exemplified by birds (Pearce-Higgins, Grant, Beale, Buchanan and Sim), mammals (Yalden), and game and shooting interests (Sotherton, May, Ewald, Fletcher and Newborn). The effect of past management and cultural heritage for the upland landscapes today is discussed (Bevan), and the importance of recreation in uplands for human well-being and rural economies reviewed (Curry).

The third section of the book considers changing upland institutional, social and economic systems, and how these might influence the choices we make for ecosystem service provision from the uplands. This section provides informed visions and advice for future management of public goods. First, an overarching analysis of the changing economic circumstances of the uplands is provided (Hubacek, Dehnen-Schmutz, Qasim and Termansen). Next, potential future trends and approaches to farming – arguably the most important direct influence on upland ecosystems – are explored in relation to commons and farm integrity (Burton, Schwarz, Brown, Convery and Mansfield) and at the landscape scale (Hanley and Colombo). Developing the landscape-scale approach, the value of landscape character as a framework for policy is discussed (Swanwick). Landscape is very much concerned with the relationship of people and place, and the next chapter investigates how visions for multiple benefits of land use can be achieved through scenario-building and participatory approaches involving all relevant stakeholders (Arblaster, Reed, Fraser and Potter). Following, these ideas are developed in discussing whether sustainable governance of public goods can be achieved by public participation and how different approaches vary in success (Connelly and Richardson). The next chapter takes a particular aspect of public engagement and addresses the influence of social barriers and class on the enjoyment of these landscapes (Suckall, Fraser and Quinn). Another aspect of the role of the public is considered in looking at the threats from wildfires (McMorrow, Lindley, Aylen, Cavan, Albertson and Boys). The authors model spatial and temporal risks to develop mitigation strategies, such as informed recreation planning and fire prevention measures. In areas of past inappropriate management or damaging wildfires, the health of upland ecosystems and habitats can be severely negatively impacted and prime ecosystem functioning can be lost. In such areas restoration may help to re-establish ecosystem functions and services (Anderson, Buckler and Walker). Given the role of conservation in helping restore ecosystem health, it is fitting that the last chapter of this section looks at upland conservation. Informed by clear visions and strategies to deliver, conservation has to meet new and sometimes not so new challenges such as climate change, continuing land-use change and achieving multiple objectives. The ecosystem approach can help to driver these (Bonn, Rebane and Reid).

Finally, the conclusion chapter in the book attempts to synthesise the wide range of material presented, highlighting key issues for the sustainable management of our uplands and presenting an outlook for the future.

The Peak District National Park as case study

After reviewing the general background, key concepts and principles, most chapters provide specific examples and applications by focusing on UK upland area case studies. Many chapters use the Peak District National Park as a key example for highly valuable upland regions (PDNPA, 2006). The Peak District forms the oldest national park in Britain, established in 1951 as a result of the access movement culminating in the Mass Trespass on Kinder Scout in 1932, demanding the public right to access and recreation in the uplands (Bevan, this volume). The National Park covers 1,438 km^2 with 509 km^2 of upland moorlands, most of which are under national and international conservation designations as a Site of Special Scientific Interest (SSSI), a Special Area of Conservation (SAC) and a Special Protection Area (SPA). Today, the Peak District continues to be at the centre of social change with 38,000 local residents and 16 million people living within sixty minutes travelling time in surrounding conurbations – roughly a quarter of the UK population (see Figure 1.2.). At the heart of the UK, the Peak District uplands provide valuable ecosystem goods and services to local and surrounding populations, including:

- *Provision of food and fibre:* 79 per cent of the Peak District National Park is farmed land for livestock, with sheep contributing to around 80 per cent of all livestock numbers. Crop production on less than 2 per cent of the area is negligible, and water companies and the Forestry Commission manage some woodlands, mainly around reservoirs.
- *Water provision:* There are 55 reservoirs of over 2 hectares in the Peak District. These supply 450 million litres of water a day to surrounding cities and towns.
- *Carbon storage:* The Peak District moorlands store up to 30–40 Mt carbon and additionally have the potential to sequester up to 41,000 t of carbon per year (Worrall, unpublished data).
- *Recreational value and cultural heritage:* With 600 km of Public Rights of Ways (PROW footpaths), 500 km^2 of open-access land and well in excess of 10 million leisure visits a year, the Peak District is one of the most visited national parks in the country. To support field sports activities, 65 per cent of the upland moorlands are managed for red grouse *Lagopus lagopus scoticus* (Sotherton *et al.*, this volume).

The Peak District is also a landscape arguably subject to extreme historic and current environmental change. Situated at the southern climatic border of blanket bog distribution, and subject to a legacy of air pollution from

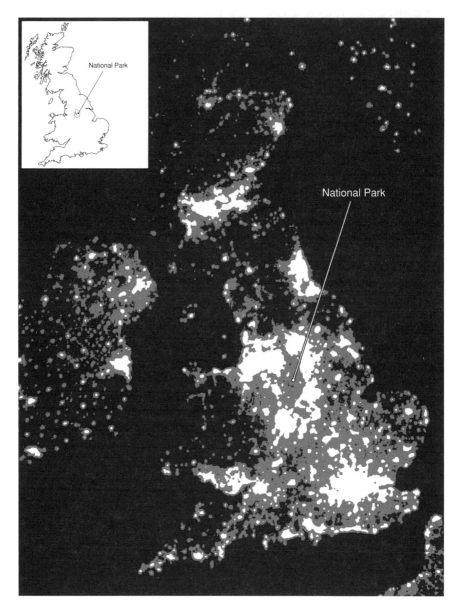

Figure 1.2 Britain at night. Satellite imagery depicting light pollution in 2000 as one indicator for tranquillity. The Peak District National Park is surrounded by major cities, with 16 million people living within 1 hour's drive. While providing valuable ecosystem goods and services to urban communities, such as agricultural products, drinking water, carbon storage, wildlife and recreation opportunities, the Peak District uplands are affected by external drivers, such as climate change, atmospheric pollution and visitors, bringing opportunities and threats (reproduced by kind permission of the Campaign to Protect Rural England: CPRE, www.cpre.org.uk).

surrounding industries, present and historic since the birth of the industrial revolution, as well as today's traffic fumes, the Peak District uplands are among the most significantly impacted by air pollution and acidification within the UK (Caporn and Emmett, this volume). Such external pressures have been compounded by intensive land use. For example, livestock farming has become much more intensive and specialised in the Peak District since around the middle of the last century in common with other upland areas in the UK. In addition, driven grouse-moor management with its structured regimes has been a feature of the last 150 years in the UK. The upland ecosystems are fragile and already subject to environmental degradation in some areas, manifested for example in high levels of erosion and subsequent water discolouration, wildfire incidences, and impoverished flora and fauna. In contrast, recent developments and conservation efforts mean that many moorlands are now excluded from grazing pressure, and large-scale restoration projects in the Peak District have been implemented to restore the fragile moorlands (Anderson *et al.*, this volume). Despite the trends of intensifying land use, however, the Peak District upland hill farming community has remained one of the poorest in the UK (PDRDF, 2004), whereas at the same time converted farmhouses are in high demand by high-income commuters from surrounding cities.

The Peak District offers a unique focus of national and international relevance. Our focus on this region as a case study highlights different perspectives and an in-depth consideration of rural socio-economic and environmental changes, with implications beyond the boundaries of the National Park, and with important lessons for other such areas.

Outlook

Writing this book has been an interesting and challenging project bringing together scientists from a wide variety of backgrounds, practitioners and policy-makers, all with a strong interest in uplands. We hope it demonstrates how drivers clearly influence the ability to prioritise and maintain ecosystem services, and how this interaction directly and indirectly affects rural economies, livelihoods and well-being. The chapters contribute to documenting and understanding the driving forces and their effects in the past, the present and potentially the future. Based on these assessments, we provide guidance for developing strategies to better anticipate, respond to and harness change. We hope this book will serve as a source and stimulus for discussion and debate in the development of management, policy and science to sustain the future of our precious uplands.

Acknowledgements

We are grateful for comments by Paul Adam, Andy Cooper, Chris Dean and Des Thompson that improved the text.

References

English Nature (2001) *The Upland Management Handbook*. English Nature. http://www.english-nature.gov.uk/pubs/Handbooks/upland.asp?id=1

Fielding, A. H. and Haworth, P. F. (1999) *Upland Habitats*. London: Routledge.

IPCC (2007) *Intergovernmental Panel on Climate Change. Fourth Assessment Report.* http://www.ipcc.ch/

MA (2005) *Millennium Ecosystem Assessment. Ecosystems and Human Well-being: Synthesis.* Washington, DC: Island Press. http://www.millenniumassessment.org/

PDNPA (2006) *Peak District National Park 2006–11 Management Plan. Peak District National Park Authority, Bakewell.* http://www.peakdistrict.org/index/looking-after/plansandpolicies/npmp.htm

PDRDF (2004) *Hard Times: A Report into Hill Farming and Farming Families in the Peak District.* Peak District Rural Deprivation Forum, Hope Valley, Derbyshire. http://pdrdf.org/hillfarmingreport.htm

Ratcliffe, D. A. and Thompson, D. B. A. (1988) The British uplands: their ecological character and international significance. *Ecological Change in the Uplands* (ed. M. B. Usher and D. B. A. Thompson), pp. 9–36. Oxford: Blackwell Scientific Publications.

Part I

Processes and policy – the overarching drivers of change

2 Natural changes in upland landscapes

Martin Evans

Introduction

Upland landscapes in Britain are often perceived as the last wild lands on an increasingly overcrowded island. Whilst the uplands undoubtedly play an important recreational role as an escape from the urban experience, further enhanced recently by increased access under the Countryside Rights of Way Act, the notion of a wild land is untenable. The common classification of the British uplands as semi-natural ecosystems acknowledges the important role of human activity in creating and maintaining contemporary upland landscapes. In 2001, during the UK outbreak of foot-and-mouth disease, concern was expressed that the loss of hefted flocks of Herdwick sheep (flocks habituated to a particular upland area) would lead to dramatic reductions in grazing pressure and scrub invasion, causing the loss of the 'landscapes of Wordsworth' (BBC News, 2001). At the same time the counter view that the 'scrub invasion' represented the precursor to a desirable return to natural woodland was also advanced (Holdgate, 2001). Central to this discussion is the fact that the upland landscapes of Britain represent a delicate balance of the processes of natural ecosystem change and both intended and unintended anthropogenic pressures on the system. Contemporary upland landscapes result from the interaction of land management and the natural biophysical environment. In this context there are three fundamental reasons why any assessment of these systems should be rooted in the natural ecosystem processes. First, effective management or manipulation of upland landscapes necessarily depends on a clear understanding of the processes of natural change both to ensure the longer-term sustainability of management solutions and to avoid unintended consequences. Second, a clear understanding of rates of natural change is a necessary context for assessment of the significance of anthropogenically forced change. Finally, whilst the uplands represent cultural landscapes, so that the definition of desirable end-points for land management lies in large part within the spheres of politics, economics and public taste, scientific understanding of the 'natural' system can inform the discussion through assessment of local environmental history, and assessment of what landscape states are biophysically achievable through management and

Table 2.1 Classification of the major agents of Holocene change in upland landscapes.

Upland Environmental Change	Type	Timescale
Soil development	Intrinsic	10^2–10^3 years
Evolution of fresh waters	Intrinsic	10^3 years
Vegetation succession		
• Post glacial	Intrinsic	10^3 years
• Post disturbance	Intrinsic	10^1–10^2 years
Climate change	Extrinsic	10^1–10^3 years
Seismic activity	Extrinsic	10^{-3} years
Soil instability	Intrinsic	10^2–10^3 years

conservation. The aim of this chapter is to outline dominant natural trajectories of change in upland systems and, through a case study of eroding peatlands, to demonstrate that an understanding of both the longer-term context of natural change and shorter-term natural responses to disturbance is central to effective management of upland systems.

Definition and classification of natural changes

At Holocene timescales[1] two main modes of landscape change can be identified. Intrinsic changes are a function of the natural evolution of system function with time whilst extrinsic changes result from changing boundary conditions due to environmental change (Table 2.1). Extrinsic change therefore encompasses the response to anthropogenic forcing as well as to natural environmental change. Under the heading of natural change this chapter will therefore consider the natural evolution of biophysical systems, responses to natural climate change, and the natural regeneration of disturbed systems.

Long-term changes in upland landscapes

The notion of a climax vegetation (Clements, 1916) or a soil type (Jenny, 1941) in equilibrium with contemporary environmental conditions is deeply ingrained in the literature of environmental science and has significantly influenced thinking on upland landscape change at longer timescales. The uplands of the UK were either glaciated or subjected to intense periglacial conditions during the last glaciation, so that the development of contemporary soil and vegetation systems has a clearly defined starting point at the end of the last glacial period. The retreat of the ice sheets left large areas of land mantled in barren glacial till and fluvioglacial deposits. Work on contemporary glacier forefields has demonstrated that processes of soil formation and re-vegetation progress rapidly to produce a more stable vegetated landscape (Matthews, 1992). However, the composition of climax vegetation

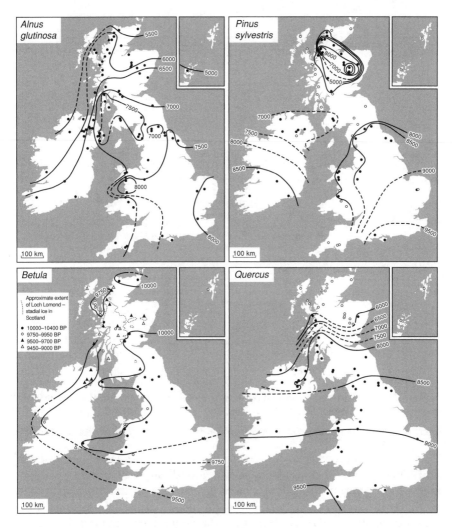

Figure 2.1 The post-glacial spread of key upland tree taxa across Britain (reprinted by permission of Blackwell Publishing from Birks, 1989).

– across most of upland Britain, with the exception of the highest peaks, this means forest cover – evolved over a longer period because of the time required for the migration of tree species from refugia south of the glaciation limit (Birks, 1989) (Figure 2.1).

The idea of a naturally controlled long-term trajectory for the development of upland landscapes is also commonplace in the literature of upland catchments and freshwaters. The classic work by Pearsall (1921) on the development of the lakes of the English Lake District was based on the premise that progressive weathering and soil development in the lake catchments

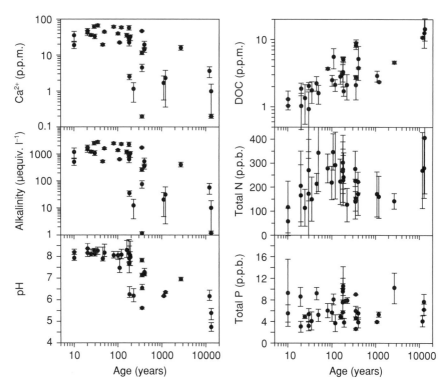

Figure 2.2 Chemical evolution of lake basins in Glacier Bay (reprinted by permission of Macmillan: *Nature* **408**, 162, © 2000, Engstrom *et al.*, 2000).

during the Holocene drove development from 'primitive' lakes with low pH and low base cation concentrations to 'evolved' lakes with higher pH and base cation concentrations and a more diverse and abundant flora. Recent work, however, has cast some doubt on this notion of the unidirectional evolution of upland waters. Engstrom *et al.* (2000) studied a chrono-sequence of lakes exposed by glacial recession in Glacier Bay, Alaska, and demonstrated that over a 10,000-year chrono-sequence older lakes are more acid, more dilute and have higher dissolved organic contents (Figure 2.2). These changes are linked to soil development and terrestrial succession in the lake catchments which promote carbonate leaching, humus accumulation and changes in runoff pathways. Engstrom *et al.* suggest that this pattern may be typical of many lakes in deglaciated areas of the cool temperate zone. The soil development trends they describe, including accumulation of humic material and hard pan development, are common to many areas of upland Britain. In areas of high rainfall, high rates of leaching produce podzolic profiles and often eventually produce iron pans. These layers impede drainage such that the climax soil type is a histosol: either a peaty podzol or blanket peatland. In wetter areas of northern and western Britain, blanket peat development occurred relatively rapidly after deglaciation in favoured locations. Basal dates from below blanket peats of between 9000 and 7000 BP are common (Tallis, 1991; Bennett *et al.*, 1992; Fossit, 1996). In many areas, however, later dates of onset of peat development particularly clustered around *circa* 5000 BP are associated with human intervention in the system (Moore, 1973; 1975). Mesolithic or Neolithic remains are often associated with basal peats (Caulfield, 1978; O'Connell, 1986; Mills *et al.*, 1994), and Moore suggested that the expansion of peatlands across upland Britain was due to waterlogging connected to forest clearance.

The concept of climax soils and indeed climax vegetation cover is reasonable as long as the boundary conditions of the environmental system (e.g. climate, topography, human intervention) remain constant. Indeed, by making this assumption, the degree of soil development can be a useful relative dating tool in landscapes where alternative dating is not available (Birkeland, 1999). However, the processes of soil development and the establishment of climax soil and vegetation cover occur over extended periods whereas, particularly in high-energy upland environments, periods of landscape instability (see Box 2.1) can lead to rapid rejuvenation of land surfaces. Harvey *et al.* (1984) describe soil chrono-sequences from the uplands of the Howgill fells in north-west England where mature podzols are observed on soils inferred to be stable throughout the Holocene but where much more immature soils are typical of valley floors where lateral instability of the river channel causes erosion and deposition and periodic rejuvenation of soils. Such disturbance of land surfaces also has a significant impact on local vegetation cover. In a dynamic landscape the surface vegetation will represent a mosaic of successional stages. Therefore, understanding of vegetation succession in the uplands is important not only to the long-term development of vegetation systems but also to the contemporary patterns and dynamics. Miles *et al.* (2001) emphasised the importance of vegetation recovery from disturbance or 'secondary succession' as a control on the vegetation mosaic of upland Scotland, although they noted that the pattern of the last fifty years in Scotland has been for such change to be a response to changes in land management. Perhaps the most fundamental shift in boundary conditions occurs with climate change. The Holocene has seen significant variations in climate with consequent effects on vegetation cover. The direct control of climate on vegetation patterns and bog ecosystem function is the basis for the numerous palaeo-ecological approaches to reconstructing climate. Some of the most sensitive climate records come from upland peat. Plant macrofossils, peat humification records and testate amoebae from peatlands have all been used to reconstruct Holocene climate (e.g. Barber *et al.*, 1994: Chambers *et al.*, 1997; Woodland *et al.*, 1998; Hughes *et al.*, 2000) and particularly to identify wet and dry shifts in bog surface condition. Chiverell (2001) applied multiple methods to reconstruct hydrological changes from an ombrotrophic bog site in the North York Moors (ombrotrophic peat bogs are defined as entirely dependent on rainwater for their nutrient supply). He identified changes to cooler and wetter climate at 1690–1401 cal. BP, 1400–1300 cal. BP, 1280–970 cal. BP, 600–500 cal. BP, 550–330 cal. BP, and 250–150 cal. BP. Macklin and Lewin (2003) compared wet shifts identified from bog records with radiocarbon-dated alluvial records of major flooding and suggested that wet periods around 8000 BP (Hughes *et al.*, 2000) and since 4000 BP are associated with major flood episodes. They also identified, during the last 4000 years, an increase in the sensitivity of fluvial systems to climate change owing to significant human modification of the land cover. Patterns of upland landscape disturbance are therefore closely associated with climate change through the climatic control of river flooding in addition to the direct control of vegetation by climate.

In the last twenty years the notion of unidirectional 'development' of soils has been increasingly challenged (Johnson *et al.*, 1990; Huggett, 1998). Huggett argues that, in parallel with a shift in emphasis in the vegetation literature away from simplistic applications of succession theory, temporal change in soil properties should be regarded as 'soil evolution' – a term encompassing the possibility of soil development, retrogression, or rejuvenation and the possibility of multiple stable states. Essentially, Huggett argues for a rebalancing of the emphasis on immanent processes of landscape development and configurational changes (*sensu* Simpson, 1963). Some changes in upland systems do occur as a result of the physical, chemical or biological development of stable parts of the landscape driven by natural processes; however, the intensity of the disturbing forces in upland environments, both natural and anthropogenic, and the sensitivity of upland systems mean that much of the form of the contemporary landscape is inherited as an integration of past impacts. It is more appropriate to regard these upland landscapes as being in dynamic equilibrium and resilient to human impacts; given sufficient time and the removal of the stress, they will revert to a 'natural state'. Figure 2.3 is one way to visualise this dynamic equilibrium with natural processes of succession and soil development tending to drive the system to the right of the diagram, and disturbance, anthropogenic or otherwise, driving the system towards the left. The end-points of the spectrum are not fixed but vary according to climatic conditions and the particular history of a given landscape.

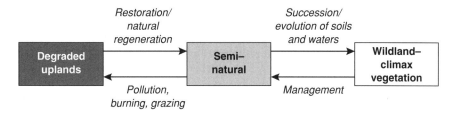

Figure 2.3 Dynamic equilibrium of upland landscapes.

**Box 2.1. Rapid change in upland landscapes:
deep-seated landsliding**

Not all natural change in the uplands is gradual. In numerous locations across the UK, rapid change has occurred as a result of deep-
seated landsliding. Major landslides have occurred across the uplands
of Britain including South Wales (Bentley and Siddle, 1996), North
Yorkshire (Simmons and Cundill, 1974; Waltham and Forster, 1999),
the Lake District (Wilson, 2005) and the South Pennines (Johnson, 1980;
Johnson and Vaughan, 1983:1989). The South Pennines are one of the
largest concentrations of deep-seated landslides, including the largest
inland landslide complex at Alport Castles in the Upper Derwent
Valley in the Peak District. These landslides have been well studied and
provide a good example of highly localised and high-magnitude natural drivers of upland change. Such landslide events are not stochastic
but may be driven by extreme rainfall events, by seismic activity, by
fluvial undercutting, or by long-term weathering-related changes in rock-
mass strength (Johnson, 1965; Skempton *et al.*, 1989; Johnson and
Vaughan, 1989; Wilson, 2005). However, the complexity of interaction
of the potential causes of large-scale landsliding is such that, although
landslide risk can be regionalised on the basis of susceptible litholog-
ies, prediction of landslide occurrence is problematic. The magnitude
of the local effects of deep-seated landsliding on the local environment
is extreme. Remodelling of the slope profile through slope failure can
lead to subsequent instability, so that the initial stochastic impetus for
change drives further slope evolution through retrogressive landsliding. Skempton *et al.* (1998) suggest that the time period required for
stabilisation of deep-seated landsliding in the Peak District is up to
8 ka. During this period secondary landsliding regrades the slope to a
series of successively more stable configurations, with the magnitude
of hydrological forcing required to trigger further movement increasing progressively. More recent work on the Mam Tor landslide
(Arkwright *et al.*, 2003) near Castleton in the UK Peak District has,
however, demonstrated that slip rates in the period 1991–2002 of
15 cm yr^{-1} are three times the long-term average movement rates
reported by Skempton *et al.* (1998). Arkwright *et al.* demonstrated that
movement rates of the landslide correlate with antecedent rainfall and
suggest that groundwater levels are the dominant control on slippage.
They ascribe recent more rapid movement to wetter climates after the
Medieval Warm Period. The implication is that, for the Mam Tor slide
which failed 3200–4000 BP, whilst there may have been change in the
hydrological threshold to movement owing to progressive stabilisation,
the slope system is still highly sensitive to small changes in climate, so
that climate change is the major control on stability. Dixon and Brook

(2007) analysed the probable stability of the Mam Tor slide with respect to predicted climate change, and suggested that increased seasonality and increased winter variability of rainfall will increase instability, but that reduced overall rainfall may to some degree counteract this effect. Land-surface stability in landslip areas is therefore conditioned not only by the initial slippage but also by the ongoing interaction of slope processes with extrinsic change in climate.

Figure 2.4 illustrates the characteristics of a typical landslide complex using LiDAR data (high-resolution topographic data) from a typical South Pennine failure at Cowms Rock, which has been well studied by Johnson and Vaughan (1989). The Cowms Rocks slide at 1.3 km^2 is amongst the largest of the South Pennine landslides. It has not been precisely dated but is suggested to be older than 5000 BP (Johnson and Vaughan, 1989). Johnson and Vaughan suggest that the preconditions for failure were established through rock-mass creep under periglacial conditions during the Devensian Glacial, and they estimate failure to have occurred in the early Holocene triggered by undercutting of the toe slope by the river Ashop. Landsliding on this scale has a dramatic effect on the local landscape. The effects of major failure are likely to include temporary damming of the river and establishment of a new local base-level upstream of the landslide deposit. Local valley constriction and floodplain development upstream of the Cowms Rocks slide are consistent with this pattern (Figure 2.4).

Three phases of landslip impact on the landscape can therefore be identified:

1. initial instantaneous morphological change associated with failure;
2. transient changes as the landscape adjusts to the new form, including vegetation succession and channel adjustments to modified base level (10^1–10^2 years);
3. longer-term effects of ongoing slope instability at timescales of 10^3 years.

Defining the appropriate point on this spectrum for a given upland landscape is the crux of the Lake District foot-and-mouth debate with which this chapter was introduced. Understanding the dynamic processes that control this equilibrium is central to scientifically based upland management.

Natural processes in peatland systems

The themes explored in the first part of this chapter, of intrinsic and extrinsic change, gradual and rapid change, natural responses to disturbance and the dynamic equilibrium of upland landscapes, are well exemplified through

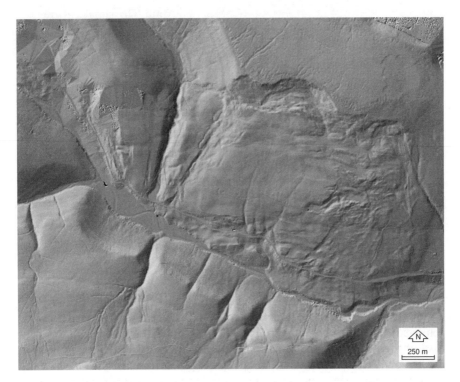

Figure 2.4 LiDAR imagery of the Cowms Rocks Landslide Complex (Alport Valley, Peak District). The extensive main landslide feature is on the north side of the channel in the eastern half of the image. Note secondary toe slope failures and the extensive alluviation of the valley floor upstream of the main slide.

upland peatland systems. Upland peatlands cover 8 per cent of the land area of the UK, 3.3 per cent in England and Wales, and 13 per cent in Scotland (Tallis *et al.*, 1997a; Hamilton *et al.*, 1997; Holden *et al.*, 2006). Most of this area is covered by blanket peatland, and Britain and Ireland support 15 per cent of the total world resource of this land-cover type (Tallis *et al.*, 1997a). The peatlands of the UK, particularly those of England and Wales, have been heavily impacted such that much of the peatland area shows evidence of peat erosion. Depending on the region, 30–74 per cent of peatland is affected by gullying (Tallis, 1997a; Evans and Warburton, 2007).

Peatlands exist because permanently high water tables limit litter decomposition, causing accumulation of partially decomposed organic matter (peat). The local water balance is therefore central to the continued maintenance of peatlands, with the ombrotrophic peatlands, typical of the uplands, confined to areas where there is an excess of precipitation over evapotranspiration. In the case of blanket peatlands, Lindsay (1995) identifies threshold conditions for their existence of greater than 1,000 mm of rainfall,

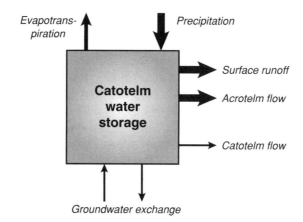

Figure 2.5 Representation of the water budget of ombrotrophic peatlands. The size of the arrows indicates the relative magnitude of the fluxes.

greater than 160 days of rain, and mean July temperature less than 15°C – conditions which describe much of upland Britain. Excess precipitation is removed either as runoff or through evaporation. Figure 2.5 is a representation of the water balance of a typical ombrotrophic mire. It illustrates that the major loss of water from storage in deep peat is evaporation. Rates of lateral drainage are very low owing to the very low hydraulic conductivity of the catotelm, which is typically in the range of 10^{-5}–10^{-8} m s^{-1} (Evans and Warburton, 2007). Reported rates of evaporation from ombrotrophic mires are in the range 1.1–3.8 mm d^{-1} (Evans and Warburton, 2007). Ombrotrophic mires are characterised by perennially high water tables. For example, in blanket peatlands from northern England, Evans *et al.* (1999) report water tables in the upper 5 cm of the peat profile 83 per cent of the time. Even during drought periods, the water table is rarely more than 50 cm below the surface, and the storage capacity of upper peat layers is such that after a drought water tables are often restored to near surface conditions within a single storm (Figure 2.6). The high water tables common to blanket peatlands mean that they are systems highly productive of runoff through the development of saturation overland flow. Runoff is concentrated at the surface or in the upper acrotelm layer of the peat, which has higher hydraulic conductivity. Holden and Burt (2003a, b) demonstrated that, for a North Pennine peatland, overland flow and near-surface stormflow account for 96 per cent of runoff generation under storm conditions (see also Holden, this volume). Low catotelm hydraulic conductivities mean that there is very little lateral drainage from deep peat to maintain streamflow during low flow periods, so that peatland stream systems have characteristically flashy stream hydrographs (e.g. Figure 2.6) with total runoff dominated by stormflow events.

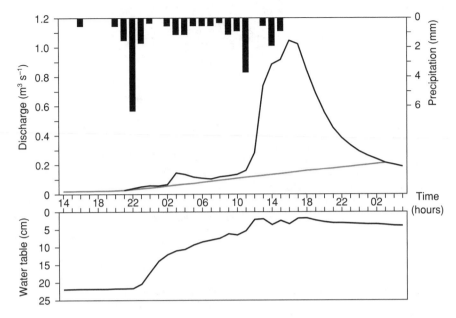

Figure 2.6 Water table and runoff data from the Trout Beck catchment of the Moor House National Nature Reserve in the North Pennines, UK. Data from a storm of 6/7/95. Note that, during the initial rainfall event, water table rises but runoff response is delayed until the second rainfall pulse when water table is close to the surface (after Evans *et al.*, 1999).

The extensive development of overland flow on peatland surfaces generates significant erosive energy at the peatland surface. The peat surface is bound together by the roots of the vegetation cover, which provides resistance to surface erosion. In circumstances in which the vegetation layer is weakened by overgrazing, fire, desiccation, trampling or pollution impacts, physical erosion of the surface may result. The extensive erosion of the peatlands of the UK and Ireland dates largely to the last millennium (Evans and Warburton, 2007) and has been variously ascribed to many of these causes (Shimwell, 1974; Tallis, 1985, 1995, 1997a, b; Anderson, 1986) and also associated with climate changes during the Little Ice Age causing increased runoff and storminess (Rhodes and Stevenson, 1997). Tallis (1987) describes how, for a particular location in the South Pennines at Holme Moss, a history of accumulating stresses on the peatland surface produced the dramatic erosion characteristic of the contemporary system.

Eroding peatlands are amongst the most actively eroding landscapes in the UK. Sediment loads in eroding catchments range up to 265 t km^{-2} a^{-1} (Evans *et al.*, 2006; Evans and Warburton, 2007). The surface impact of these rates is large because of the low density of peat, which means that the volume of material removed is significant. Once bare peat is exposed, rates of

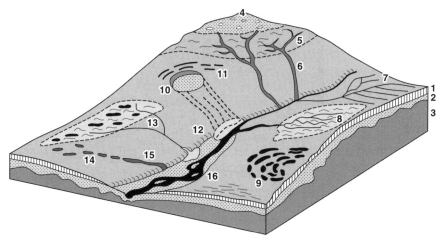

1. Peat deposits
2. Glacial/periglacial deposits (substrate)
3. Bedrock
4. Deflation surface remnant peat hummocks
5. Gully (typeI)
6. Gully (typeII)
7. Artificial channels (grip network)
8. Peat haggs

9. Bog pool complex
10. Peat mass movement
11. Peat tears and tension cracks
12. Valley side peaty debris fan
13. Eroded pool and hummock complex
14. Collapsed pipe system
15. Peat block sedimentation
16. Upland river system (mineral sediment)

Figure 2.7 The peat land-system representing the potential range and connectivity of geomorphological features found on a typical eroding mire (after Evans and Warburton, 2007).

erosion are relatively rapid, with recorded rates of surface recession of up to 74 mm a^{-1} (Phillips *et al.*, 1981). Erosion of the bare peat is facilitated by preparation of the peat surface through processes of frost action and desiccation (Francis, 1990; Labadz *et al.*, 1991) such that the rate of sediment production from eroding peat catchments can be modelled effectively from climate data (Yang, 2005).

The spatial patterning of peat erosion produces the dramatic erosional landscapes of degrading peatlands. Figure 2.7 is a peat land-system model representing the range of characteristic erosional forms and processes found on eroding peatlands.

Catchment vegetation cover is important not only in defining the bare eroded areas but also as a control on delivery of eroded material to the main stream system and its export from the catchment. Evans and Warburton (2005) demonstrated a *circa* 60 per cent reduction in sediment yield from a North Pennine catchment over a forty-year period and argued that the reduction was linked to re-vegetation of the floors of eroding gullies so that eroded material was stored on gully floors and sediment delivery to the main channel was very low. Evans *et al.* (2006) compared severely eroding South Pennine

High sediment yield ⟶ Low sediment yield

Slope sediment sources dominate ⟶ Channel sediment sources dominate

Largely bare gully floors ⟶ Largely vegetated gully floors

High slope–channel linkage ⟶ Low slope–channel linkage

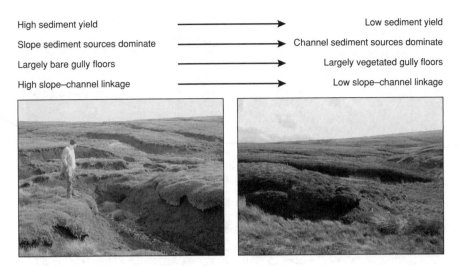

Figure 2.8 A conceptual model of sediment delivery in eroding peatlands (after Evans *et al.*, 2006).

sites with this North Pennine catchment and proposed the conceptual model of peatland sediment flux illustrated in Figure 2.8.

Clearly there is an intimate link between processes of erosion and re-vegetation in degrading peatland systems. Areas such as the North Pennines show evidence of extensive past erosion but also very significant degrees of re-vegetation. In contrast, the South Pennines have larger areas of bare eroding peat, although there is evidence of recent re-vegetation (Figure 2.9, Evans *et al.*, 2005). Traditionally, the extensive bare peat of the South Pennine peatlands has been explained by the heavily impacted nature of the system as documented by Tallis (1995, 1997a). However, the differences in degree of re-vegetation could equally be explained not as variations in the rate of erosion but as variations in the degree of re-vegetation. If the higher rates of pollution in the South Pennines act to suppress re-vegetation, this would cause the accumulation in the landscape of erosion features without any change in the rate of their generation. A complete understanding of landscapes of degraded peatlands is therefore dependent on a clear scientific understanding of the processes of recovery and regeneration as well as of the processes of erosion.

Natural re-vegetation of eroding peatlands is widely reported in the literature (Phillips, 1954; Bowler and Bradshaw, 1985; Large and Hamilton, 1991; Cooper and Loftus, 2001; Evans and Warburton, 2005) but has been relatively little studied. The most comprehensive work on gully re-vegetation has been carried out in the South Pennines (Crowe, 2007). This demonstrates that two cottongrass species, *Eriophorum angustifolium* and *Eriophorum*

Figure 2.9 The blanket peat erosion mosaic. Examples of eroding and re-vegetating
blanket peat found within a 1 km radius in the South Pennines (Bleaklow,
Peak District): (*a*) active gully erosion, (*b*) partial re-vegetation of a broad
mineral gully floor by *Eriophorum vaginatum*, (*c*) recent re-vegetation
of a peat-floored gully by *Eriophorum angustifolium*, (*d*) complete re-
vegetation with a diverse wet bog flora including *Sphagnum.*

vaginatum, are central to the natural re-establishment of vegetation cover in
eroding gullies. Evidence from repeat aerial photography and from macro-
fossil analysis of peat cores from re-vegetated gully floors suggests that the
cottongrass pioneer species are succeeded by a more diverse flora including
mosses and rushes, *Sphagnum, Juncus* and *Polytrichum.* These observations
are consistent with work on the regeneration of peat-cutting sites which suggests that *E. vaginatum* cover provides surface stability and enhanced humid-
ity sufficient to support *Sphagnum* establishment and succession to more diverse
cover (Rochefort, 2000; Lavoie *et al.*, 2003). The timescale for succession from
bare gully floors to a more diverse wet bog flora appears to be of the order
of twenty to forty years, with complete vegetation cover of the gully floors
within five to ten years (Evans *et al.*, 2005; Crowe, 2007). Therefore, where
suitable conditions exist, natural re-vegetation rapidly stabilises eroded systems and significantly reduces the rates of sediment loss from the system.
Further research is required to establish precisely the conditions necessary
for natural re-vegetation to occur. Sufficiently low local slopes to allow deposition of eroded peat as a substrate for cottongrass growth, and a local source
for the vegetative spread of cottongrass appear to be essential (Evans *et al.*,
2005; Crowe, 2007). These conditions can occur through the natural devel-

opment of the gully system, either in locations where gully-bank collapse causes local constriction of the gully, or in the later stages of gully development where gully width has increased to the extent that the channel wanders on the gully floors, promoting lateral deposition (Evans and Warburton, 2007). Crowe (2007) has demonstrated that slightly different successional sequences are associated with particular geomorphic contexts (gully forms). This analysis of the interactions of the erosional system and the natural vegetation succession is a good example of the importance of understanding natural processes as an input to restoration practice. Restoration approaches such as gully-blocking, appropriately applied, have the potential artificially to create conditions suitable for re-vegetation and therefore have the potential to initiate relatively rapid and sustainable re-vegetation of eroded sites. Because upland geomorphic systems are naturally dynamic, it is of particular importance that landscape restoration works with the natural processes of system recovery in order to create restored landscapes which are stable under contemporary conditions. The importance of understanding natural ecosystem recovery as a guide to what a suitable reference point for a restored landscape might be is considered further in the next section.

Natural processes and upland management

Restoration of adverse human impacts on upland systems requires an understanding of natural trajectories of recovery. Restoration efforts that work to promote natural recovery mechanisms are more likely to be sustainable in the long term and more likely to restore ecosystem structure and function.

Fundamental to landscape restoration efforts is a clear understanding of the aims of the restoration project and in particular the desired end-point. Practical restoration of degraded uplands requires a reference condition of the system both as a guide to suitable restoration practice and as a benchmark against which to reference the success of varying restoration approaches (see also Anderson *et al.*, this volume). At its simplest, the desired end-point might be a return of the system to notional 'pristine' conditions that existed prior to significant human impact. Such a notion is incorporated into the recent European Water Framework Directive with the requirement that freshwaters have 'good' ecological status relative to the reference conditions by 2016 (Kallis and Butler, 2001). Palaeo-ecological techniques have been widely applied to define pristine conditions because of the difficulty of identifying sites without land-management impacts in highly modified environments (Bennion *et al.*, 2004). However, in semi-natural environments such as those typical of most of the UK uplands the notion of a pre-impact condition is problematic. Similarly the 'pristine' state of upland landscapes may not be an appropriate end-point for restoration efforts. This is clearly exemplified through consideration of attempts to re-vegetate the eroded peatlands of the South Pennines over the last thirty years (Tallis and Yalden, 1983; Anderson *et al.*, 1997; Evans *et al.*, 2005). Dobson *et al.* (1997) distinguish between restoration and reclamation, where restoration involves a return to a pre-impact landscape condition with both ecosystem structure and function restored, whereas reclamation means an instrumentalist approach to ecosystem manipulation that promotes restoration of ecosystem function. In blanket peat systems restoration to a pristine state is often perceived to require a return to typical peat domes with a diverse sphagnum peat vegetation, perennially high water tables, and active peat growth and carbon fixation. However, other states of the bog ecosystem occur naturally, with phases of sedge domination common, and even tree growth occurring during warm periods (Chambers, 1997). The historical pressures on many British upland mires require that restoration efforts consider alternative stable states of upland mires. In systems where there has been significant erosion, particularly where gullying is extensive and water table is drawn down by gully drainage, it is questionable whether a return to pristine *Sphagnum*-dominated conditions is a feasible medium-term target for restoration. The approach taken to re-vegetation in the UK Peak District (Anderson *et al.*, this volume) has focused on the establishment of an initial grass cover, which stabilises the surface in order to allow colonisation of moorland species. The initial re-vegetation can be regarded as reclamation in that it restores some measure of ecosystem function in terms of limiting erosion and promoting carbon sequestration. The timescale for complete restoration of these systems, particularly where extensive gully erosion has occurred, is close to the time taken for initial peat formation (in excess of 5,000 years) since a return to near-pristine conditions would entail infilling of gullies with new peat growth. Work on natural re-vegetation of eroding systems (e.g. Clement, 2005; Crowe, 2007) suggests a more appropriate medium-term target for restoration is achieving the structure of naturally re-vegetating gully systems that support a diverse wet bog vegetation in gully bottoms. Complete re-vegetation to this condition is achievable on timescales of the order of twenty to forty years (Evans and Warburton, 2005; Clement, 2005; Crowe, 2007).

Conclusions

Upland landscapes of the UK are relatively high-energy systems subject to significant natural disturbance through mass movement, severe temperatures and flashy runoff regimes. They are also semi-natural systems, so that ecosystems are additionally stressed by pollution, grazing, fire (both managed and wildfire), and recreational impacts (Caporn and Emmett; Crowle and McCormack; Gardner *et al.*; McMorrow *et al.*; Yallop *et al.*; all this volume). Upland landscapes are naturally a mosaic of land covers affected by these various impacts at a range of timescales, and the intensity of change in these patches is increased through human impacts. Short-term changes associated with this dynamic mosaic are superimposed on long-term trajectories of change in upland systems driven by processes of plant migration, climate change and soil development.

The primary conservation aim in upland systems should be limiting the stresses on the system. However, in a dynamic semi-natural system, conservation should also focus on managing patch dynamics. Understanding of natural processes is essential to informed management. In addition, the character of natural system recovery should be an important area of study since restoration to conditions akin to natural recovery is an achievable aim within the timescales and budget constraints of practical conservation, whereas a return to pristine conditions may represent only a hypothetical goal. The management of upland landscapes in the twenty-first century during a period of potential climatic instability provides a significant challenge. Natural system responses to change may provide the best guide to what constitutes 'achievable restoration' of degraded systems.

Note

1 The Holocene spans the last 11,500 years or the last 10,000 uncalibrated radio-carbon years. Uncalibrated radiocarbon ages diverge from calendar years before the mid-Holocene, so that early Holocene radiocarbon ages are 1,000–1,500 years younger than the true calendar age. Most dates in this chapter are reported as uncalibrated radiocarbon ages honouring the original sources and are identified as years BP. Where calibrated ages are reported, they are identified as cal. BP.

References

Anderson, P. (1986) *Accidental Moorland Fires in the Peak District.* Bakewell: Peak Park Joint Planning Board.

Anderson, P., Tallis, J. and Yalden, D. (eds) (1997) *Restoring Moorland: Peak District Moorland Management Project phase III Report.* Bakewell: Peak District Moorland Management Project.

Arkwright, J. C., Rutter, E. H. and Holloway, R. F. (2003) The Mam Tor landslip: still moving after all these years. *Geology Today*, **19**, 59–64.

Barber, K. E., Chambers, F. M., Maddy, D., Stoneman, R. and Brew, J. S. (1994) A sensitive high-resolution record of late Holocene climatic change from a raised bog in northern England. *The Holocene*, **4**, 198–205.

BBC News (2001) Lake District faces disease D-day. http://news.bbc.co.uk/1/hi/uk/1243233.stm

Bennett, K. D., Boreham, S., Sharp, M. J. and Switsur, V. R. (1992) Holocene history of environment, vegetation and human settlement on Catta Ness, Lunnasting, Shetland. *Journal of Ecology*, **80**, 241–73.

Bennion, H., Fluin, J. and Simpson, G. L. (2004) Assessing eutrophication and reference conditions for Scottish freshwater lochs using subfossil diatoms. *Journal of Applied Ecology*, **41**, 124–38.

Bentley, S. P. and Siddle, H. J. (1996) Landslide research in the South Wales coalfield. *Engineering Geology*, **43**, 65–80.

Birkeland, P. W. (1999) *Soils and Geomorphology.* New York: Oxford University Press.

Birks, H. J. B. (1989) Holocene isochrone maps and patterns of tree-spreading in the British Isles. *Journal of Biogeography*, **16**, 503–40.

Bowler, M. and Bradshaw, R. H. W. (1985) Recent accumulation and erosion of blanket peat in the Wicklow Mountains, Ireland. *New Phytologist*, **101**, 543–50.

Caulfield, S. (1978) Neolithic fields: the Irish evidence. *Early Land Allotment* (ed. H. C. Bowen and J. C. Fowler), pp. 137–44. Oxford: British Archaeological Reports, British Series.

Chambers, F. M. (1997) Bogs as treeless wastes: the myth and the implications for conservation. *Conserving Peatlands* (ed. L. Parkyn, R. E. Stoneman and H. A. P. Ingram), pp. 168–75. Wallingford: CAB International.

Chambers, F. M., Barber, K. E., Maddy, D. and Brew, J. (1997) A 5500-year proxy-climate and vegetation record from blanket mire at Talla Moss, Borders, Scotland. *The Holocene*, **7**, 391–9.

Chiverell, R. C. (2001) A proxy record of late Holocene climate change from May Moss, northeast England. *Journal of Quaternary Science*, **16**, 9–29.

Clement, S. (2005) The future stability of upland blanket peat following historical erosion and recent re-vegetation. Unpublished PhD thesis, Department of Geography, Durham University.

Clements, F. E. (1916) *Plant Succession: An Analysis of the Development of Vegetation*. Washington, DC: Carnegie Institution of Washington.

Cooper, A. and Loftus, M. (1998) The application of multivariate land classification to vegetation survey in the Wicklow Mountains, Ireland. *Plant Ecology*, **135**, 229–41.

Crowe, S. (2007) Natural revegetation of eroded blanket peat: implications for blanket bog restoration. Unpublished PhD thesis, Geography, School of Environment and Development, University of Manchester.

Dixon, N. and Brook, E. (2007) Impact of predicted climate change on landslide reactivation: case study of Mam Tor, UK. *Landslides*, **4**, 137–47.

Dobson, A. P., Bradshaw, A. D. and Baker, A. J. M. (1997) Hope for the future: restoration ecology and conservation biology. *Science*, **277**, 515–22.

Engstrom, D. R., Fritz, S. C., Almendinger, J. E. and Juggins, S. (2000) Chemical and biological trends during lake evolution in recently deglaciated terrain. *Nature*, **408**, 161–5.

Evans, M. and Warburton, J. (2007) *The Geomorphology of Upland Peat: Erosion, Form and Landscape Change*. Oxford: Blackwell.

Evans, M., Warburton, J. and Yang, J. (2006) Sediment budgets for eroding blanket peat catchments: global and local implications of upland organic sediment budgets. *Geomorphology*, **79**, 45–57.

Evans, M. G., Burt, T. P., Holden, J. and Adamson, J. K. (1999) Runoff generation and water table fluctuations in blanket peat: evidence from UK data spanning the dry summer of 1995. *Journal of Hydrology*, **221**, 141–60.

Evans, M. G. and Warburton, J. (2005) Sediment budget for an eroding peat-moorland catchment in Northern England. *Earth Surface Processes and Landforms*, **30**, 557–77.

Francis, I. S. (1990) Blanket peat erosion in a Mid-Wales catchment during two drought years. *Earth Surface Processes and Landforms*, **15**, 445–56.

Hamilton, A., Legg, C. and Zhaohua, L. (1997) Blanket mire research in north-west Scotland: a view from the front 1997. *Blanket Mire Degradation: Causes, Consequences and Challenges* (ed. J. H. Tallis, R. Meade and P. D. Hulme), pp. 47–54. Aberdeeb: Macaulay Land Use Research Institute.

Harvey, A. M., Alexander, R. W. and James, P. A. (1984) Lichens, soil development and the age of Holocene valley floor landforms: Howgill Fells, Cumbria. *Geografiska Annaler, A*, **66**, 353–66.

Holden, J. and Burt, T. P. (2003a) Hydrological studies on blanket peat: the significance of the acrotelm–catotelm model. *Journal of Ecology*, **91**, 86–102.

Holden, J. and Burt, T. P. (2003b) Runoff production in blanket peat covered catchments. *Water Resources Research*, **39**, 1191.

Holden, J., Chapman, P., Evans, M., Hubacek, K., Kay, P. and Warburton, J. (2006) *Vulnerability of Organic Soils in England and Wales*. Final report Project SP0532. London: Defra.

Holdgate, M. (2001) The ecology of Lakeland, past, present and future. *Cumbrian Wildlife*, **61**, 10–13.

Huggett, R. J. (1998) Soil chronosequences, soil development, and soil evolution: a critical review. *Catena*, **32**, 155–72.

Hughes, P. D. M., Mauquoy, D., Barber, K. E. and Langdon, P. G. (2000) Mire-development pathways and palaeoclimatic records from a full Holocene peat archive at Walton Moss, Cumbria, England. *The Holocene*, **10**, 465–79.

Jenny, H. (1941) *Factors of Soil Formation: A System of Quantitative Pedology*. New York: McGraw-Hill.Johnson, D. L., Keller, E. A. and Rockwell, T. K. (1990) Dynamic pedogenesis: new views on some key concepts, and a model for interpreting Quaternary soils. *Quaternary Research*, **33**, 306–19.

Johnson, R. H. (1965) A study of the Charlesworth landslides near Glossop, North Derbyshire. *Transactions of the Institute of British Geographers*, **37**, 111–26.

Johnson, R. H. (1980) Hillslope stability and landslide hazard – a case study from Longdendale, north Derbyshire, England. *Proceedings of the Geologists' Association*, **91**, 315–25.

Johnson, R. H. and Vaughan, R. D. (1983) The Alport Castles, Derbyshire: a South Pennine slope and its geomorphic history. *East Midland Geographer*, **8**, 79–88.

Johnson, R. H. and Vaughan R. D. (1989) The Cowms Rocks landslide. *Geological Journal*, **24**, 359–70.

Kallis, G. and Butler, D. (2001) The EU water framework directive: measures and implications. *Water Policy*, **3**, 125–42.

Labadz, J. C., Burt, T. P. and Potter, A. W. R. (1991) Sediment yield and delivery in the blanket peat moorlands of the South Pennines. *Earth Surface Processes and Landforms*, **16**, 255–71.

Large, A. R. G. and Hamilton, A. C. (1991) The distribution, extent and causes of peat loss in Central and Northwest Ireland. *Applied Geography*, **11**, 309–26.

Lavoie, C., Grosvernier, P., Girard, M. and Marcoux, K. (2003) Spontaneous re-vegetation of mined peatlands: an useful restoration tool? *Wetlands Ecology and Management*, **11**, 97.

Lindsay, R. (1995) *Bogs: The Ecology, Classification and Conservation of Ombrotrophic Mires*. Edinburgh: Scottish Natural Heritage.

Macklin, M. G. and Lewin, J. (2003) River sediments, great floods and centennial-scale Holocene climate change. *Journal of Quaternary Science*, **18**, 101–5.

Matthews, J. A. (1992) *The Ecology of Recently Deglaciated Terrain*. Cambridge: Cambridge University Press.

Miles, J., Cummins, R. P., French, D. D., Gardner, S., Orrm, J. L. and Shewry, M. C. (2001) Landscape sensitivity: an ecological view. *Catena*, **42**, 125–41.

Mills, C. M., Crone, A., Edwards, K. J. and Whittington, G. (1994) The excavation and environmental investigation of a sub-peat stone bank near Loch Portain, North Uist, Outer Hebrides. *Proceedings of the Society of Antiquaries of Scotland*, **124**, 155–71.

Moore, P. D. (1973) The influence of prehistoric cultures on the initiation and spread of blanket bog in upland Wales. *Nature*, **241**, 350–3.

Moore, P. D. (1975) Origin of blanket mires. *Nature*, **256**, 267–9.

Pearsall, W. H. (1921) The development of vegetation in the English Lakes considered in relation to the general evolution of glacial lakes and rock basins. *Proceedings of the Royal Society of London, B*, **647**, 259–84.

Philips, J., Tallis, J. and Yalden, D. (eds) (1981) *Peak District Moorland Erosion Study: Phase I Report*. Bakewell: Peak Park Joint Planning Board.

Phillips, M. E. (1954) Studies in the quantitative morphology and ecology of *Eriophorum angustifolium* Roth. II. Competition and dispersion. *Journal of Ecology*, **42**, 187–210.

Rhodes, N. and Stevenson, A. C. (1997) Palaeoenvironmental evidence for the importance of fire as a cause of erosion of British and Irish blanket peats. *Blanket Mire Degradation: Causes, Consequences and Challenges* (ed. J. Tallis, R. Meade and P. Hulme), pp. 64–78. Aberdeen: British Ecological Society.

Rochefort, L. (2000) *Sphagnum* – a keystone genus in habitat restoration. *The Bryologist*, **103**, 503–8.

Shimwell, D. W. (1974) Sheep grazing intensity in Edale, Derbyshire, 1692–1747, and its effect on blanket peat erosion. *Derbyshire Archaeological Journal*, **94**, 35–40.

Simmons, I. G. and Cundill, P. R. (1974) Late Quaternary vegetational history of the North York Moors. I. Pollen analyses of blanket peats. *Journal of Biogeography*, **1**, 159–69.

Simpson, G. G. (1963) Historical science. *The Fabric of Geology* (ed. C. C. Albritton, Jr.), pp. 24–48. Stanford, Calif.: Freeman Cooper.

Skempton, A. W., Leadbeater, A. D. and Chandler, R. J. (1989) The Mam Tor landslide, North Derbyshire. *Philosophical Transactions of the Royal Society of London, A*, **329**, 503–47.

Tallis, J. H. (1985) Mass movement and erosion of a South Pennine blanket peat. *Journal of Ecology*, **73**, 283–315.

Tallis, J. H. (1987) Fire and flood at Holme Moss: erosion processes in an upland blanket mire. *Journal of Ecology*, **75**, 1099–129.

Tallis, J. H. (1991) Forest and moorland in the South Pennine uplands in the mid-Flandrian period. III. The spread of moorland local regional and national. *Journal of Ecology*, **79**, 401–15.

Tallis, J. H. (1995) Climate and erosion signals in British blanket peats: the significance of *Racomitrium lanuginosum* remains. *Journal of Ecology*, **83**, 1021–30.

Tallis, J. H. (1997a) The South Pennine experience: an overview of blanket mire degradation. *Blanket Mire Degradation: Causes, Consequences and Challenges* (ed. J. H. Tallis, R. Meade and P. D. Hulme, pp. 7–16. Aberdeen: Macaulay Land Use Research Institute.

Tallis, J. H. (1997b) The pollen record of *Empetrum nigrum* in South Pennine peats: implications for erosion and climate change. *Journal of Ecology*, **85**, 455–65.

Tallis, J. H., Meade, R. and Hulme, P. D. (eds) (1997) *Blanket Mire Degradation: Causes, Consequences and Challenges*. Aberdeen: Macaulay Land Use Research Institute.

Tallis, J. H. and Yalden, D. (1983) *Peak District Moorland Restoration Project Phase II Report: Re-vegetation Trials*. Bakewell: Peak Park Joint Planning Board.

Waltham, T. and Forster, A. (1999) Man as a geological agent. *Geology Today*, **15**, 217.

Wilson, P. (2005) Paraglacial rock-slope failures in Wasdale, western Lake District, England: morphology, styles and significance. *Proceedings of the Geologists' Association*, **116**, 349–61.

Woodland, W. A., Charman, D. J. and Sims, P. C. (1998) Quantitative estimates of water tables and soil moisture in Holocene peatlands from testate amoebae. *The Holocene*, **8**, 261–73.

Yang, J. (2005) Monitoring and modelling sediment flux from a blanket peat catchment in the South Pennines. Unpublished PhD thesis, Geography, School of Environment and Development, University of Manchester.

3 Threats from air pollution and climate change to upland systems

Past, present and future

Simon J. M. Caporn and Bridget A. Emmett

Introduction

The impacts of air pollution on ecosystems were probably most widespread in the nineteenth and early twentieth centuries in newly industrialising countries where coal-burning, smelting and other activities released large amounts of pollutants, including sulphur and various metals (e.g. lead, copper, zinc, iron), into their local environments. Problems caused by large emissions of pollutants of heavy industry have diminished in recent decades in much of Western Europe and North America where sulphur emissions have declined and been dispersed over a wider area away from point sources. The drop in emissions in regions such as Western Europe contrasts with the steep rise now seen in many developing countries. While pollutants of traditional heavy industry are now more important in rapidly developing nations, but less so in developed countries, the pollutants created largely by motor vehicles and intensive use of fertilisers in farming (nitrogen, ozone and hydrocarbons) are increasing or remain high in practically all populated world regions (Bell and Treshow, 2002).

The consequences for global ecosystems are highly complex. While some areas of the northern temperate ecosystems may have seen the worst of the impacts of widespread sulphur-based air pollution, typically known as 'acid rain', in some tropical and arid parts of developing regions the problems are growing. At the same time, all biomes of the world are experiencing continuing nitrogen-related eutrophication, ozone and rising concentrations of atmospheric CO_2 due to human activity. Owing to the steady increase in greenhouse gases, we are now facing significant global warming and other changes in climate (Houghton, 2004).

Air pollutants have had large effects on the ecology of some natural ecosystems (Lee, 1998); and, in many world regions, upland and mountainous areas are particularly vulnerable. These landscapes contain species and habitats of high conservation status, and provide vital ecosystem services such as carbon storage and water purification, often being located in remote areas away from high population densities. Yet frequently the uplands are the areas most affected by air pollution and climate change. For example, exposure of the UK uplands to acid rain pollution is often considerable because of the high

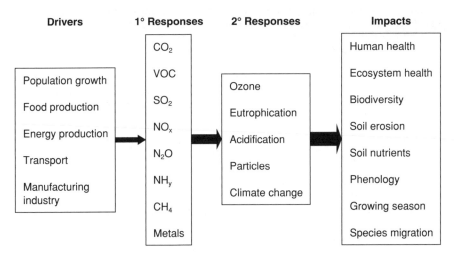

Figure 3.1 Drivers, responses and effects of air pollution in ecosystems.

rainfall, while at the same time the underlying geology of many upland soils makes them poorly buffered and therefore vulnerable to the changes caused by deposited acidity. Another defining feature of upland areas is a cooler climate in comparison to surrounding lowlands; and, since organisms of the uplands have adapted to this regime, they are likely to be especially sensitive to warming. In recent years the rapid change in climate, probably resulting from air pollution, has brought new threats to the uplands, which now face relatively sudden physical and biological transition.

This chapter investigates the nature of air pollution and climate change – the background drivers, the chemicals responsible, their sources, emissions and impacts (Figure 3.1) – particularly in semi-natural upland ecosystems, with a focus on Britain as an example. Attention is centred on pollutants of industry, transport and farming, particularly sulphur, nitrogen, ozone, metals and long-lived greenhouse gases affecting the global atmosphere.

Sources and fate of emissions contributing to acidification, eutrophication and photochemical air pollution

The major cause of global air pollution is alteration of natural biogeochemical cycles through human activities increasing the availability of biologically reactive forms of natural elements (e.g. carbon, sulphur, nitrogen and metals). The natural cycling of sulphur has been perturbed greatly by human action; mining and fuel combustion convert mineral sulphur (e.g. as iron sulphide) into the reactive and phyto-toxic oxidised forms including sulphur dioxide, which are released into the environment. Similarly, humans have significantly disrupted the nitrogen cycle, increasing the conversion of inert N_2 from the atmosphere into reactive oxidised and reduced chemical forms (NO_x and NH_y).

Table 3.1 The main primary and secondary pollutants emitted to the atmosphere that have a role in environmental toxicology and climate change.

	Primary or Secondary Pollutant	Main Sources
Primary	CO_2	Fuel combustion, deforestation, land management (e.g. drainage)
	SO_2	Fuel combustion
	NO	Fuel combustion
	NH_3	Farm animals, (coal burnt cool)
	Particles	Fuel combustion, soot, soil, quarry dust etc.
	Volatile organic compounds (VOCs)	Incomplete fuel combustion; industrial processes
	Metals	Mining; Waste from industrial processes
	CH_4	Wetland soils, fuel combustion, agriculture
	N_2O	Wetland soils, agriculture
	Halocarbons (e.g. CFCs)	Industry
Secondary	NO_2 ($NO_x = NO + NO_2$)	Product of oxidation of NO
	Ozone	Product of photochemical reactions between NO_x and VOCs
	Acid rain	Complex mix of compounds, including sulphuric (H_2SO_4) and nitric acids (HNO_3), derived from SO_2, NO_2 and NH_3 and other reactive compounds in the atmosphere
	Particles & Aerosols	Aerosols comprising various secondary pollutants formed from sulphur dioxide, nitrogen oxides, volatile organic compounds, ammonia

The natural cycling of carbon has been changed through the increased emission of CO_2 due to human activities (fuel combustion and land-use change). Pollution also arises from the release of synthetic industrial compounds such as organo-halogen compounds (e.g. chloro-fluoro-carbons [CFCs]) and by-products of industrial or combustion processes (e.g. volatile organic compounds [VOCs]). Air pollution is released from these various sources into the atmosphere as primary pollutants which can subsequently undergo complex reactions to generate secondary pollutants (Table 3.1).

Emission trends of pollutants

Since the industrial revolution, SO_2 pollution from coal-burning has probably had the greatest wide-scale impact on the natural environment because

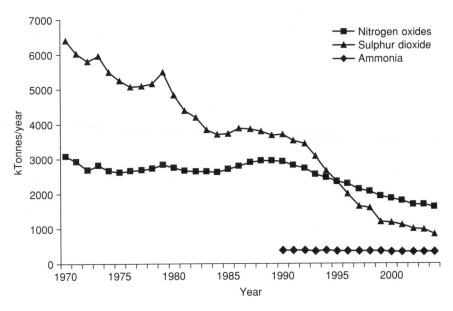

Figure 3.2 UK total emissions of NO_x, SO_2 and NH_3. Over the same period (1970–2004) CO_2 emissions fell from 187,000 to 154,000 kT per year (NAEI, 2006).

of its toxicity and the scale of emissions. Across Europe, anthropogenic SO_2 emissions increased tenfold between the 1880s and the 1970s and then declined during the 1980s (Mylona, 1996). In the UK the emissions of SO_2 dropped by 87 per cent between 1970 and 2004 (Figure 3.2) owing to reduced industrial activity, clean air legislation, alternative fuel sources, and clean fuel technology. Sulphur emissions nowadays are also dispersed from tall stacks over larger areas with greater potential to deposit on remote upland and montane regions compared with earlier times of domestic coal-burning in homes and industry where the local impact was greater. In the UK, the steep decline in sulphur emission contrasts with the trends in nitrogen pollution. Oxidised forms of nitrogen (NO_x) emissions, from transport and other energy-generating sources, peaked as recently as the late 1980s and have fallen slower than sulphur (47 per cent reduction from 1970 to 2004) but are expected to continue slowly downwards. The emissions of reduced forms of nitrogen (NH_y), presently the main atmospheric pollutants causing eutrophication, have increased substantially over the past century, initially owing to domestic coal-burning but more recently because of agricultural sources (Fowler *et al.*, 2004). Between 1990 and 2004 there was an estimated emissions decline of 12 per cent, and future releases of NH_y are likely to continue to show a modest fall in the next few decades, owing to management of farm ammonia losses and agricultural policy, but the actual improvement is highly uncertain (NEGTAP, 2001).

Transport and transformation of air pollutants

The chemical transformation and dispersion of pollution by prevailing air masses results in upland and remote landscapes being exposed to a pollution climate dominated by secondary pollutants, whereas closer to the sources the primary pollutants are typically more important. The primary pollutant SO_2 reacts with oxidants (e.g. OH^- radical) in the atmosphere to generate sulphuric acid H_2SO_4, while NO oxidises quickly to NO_2 and then further to nitric acid HNO_3. Ammonia gas (NH_3) in the atmosphere reacts quickly with oxidised nitrogen to form ammonium nitrate or with oxidised sulphur to form ammonium sulphate. The majority of these reaction products form aerosols (fine particles e.g. 0.1 μm) which, if not scavenged by rain, have relatively long lifetimes of up to several days and can be transported over potentially long distances (Fowler, 2002). The pollutant ozone (O_3), which is of increasing importance – especially in the uplands (NEGTAP, 2001) – is a photochemical product of reaction between NO_x and VOCs. Chemical transformations of atmospheric pollutants are highly complex and not fully understood. Cuts in the amount of pollutant emissions have not necessarily resulted in the expected benefits in atmospheric concentrations (Fowler *et al.*, 2005).

Exposure to dry deposited air pollution

Upland ecosystems are exposed to air pollution in the form of dry and wet deposition – processes discussed in greater depth elsewhere by Fowler (2002). Dry deposition is the direct input to the landscape of gases, aerosols and particles, and is a product of the concentration in air and the deposition velocity (related to reactivity or affinity with surfaces). The dry deposition of primary pollutant particles and gases, such as SO_2 and NO_2, occurs closest to their sources and for remote upland regions is generally less important than the secondary pollutants of sulphate, nitrate and acidity that constitute long-range transported acid rain.

A key group of air pollutants currently causing concern in the UK uplands are nitrogen compounds. The most important is gaseous ammonia, which quickly forms secondary compounds or rapidly deposits to plant and soil surfaces owing to its reactivity and high deposition velocity. The problems of ammonia pollution have come to light only in recent decades, partly owing to difficulties in monitoring the low concentrations found in rural air (often <1 μg m^{-3}, an order of magnitude less than NO_2). The wet and dry deposition of ammonia and reaction products (NH_y) contribute about 70 per cent to the total nitrogen loading to upland forest and moorland in the UK, the other 30 per cent being from deposition of NO_x (Fowler, 2002), and these forms of nitrogen affect landscapes both through their role as a plant nutrient and in soil and water acidification (see Allott, this volume).

The uplands of the more populated regions are threatened with dry deposited air pollution from the growing road traffic network. The majority of the gaseous emissions from cars disperse quickly over a wider area than the immediate roadside, contributing to the regional pollutant input. Although the concentrations of gaseous NO_x decrease quickly with distance from the road, the growing use of catalytic converters in vehicles converts some of the NO_x to ammonia, and the latter is more rapidly deposited, so that the sum of nitrogen pollutants at the roadside is probably important for nearby habitats (Truscott *et al.*, 2005). The NO_x and VOCs from vehicles react in sunlight, generating ozone and related photo-oxidants which form the characteristic photochemical smogs seen in the valleys of many mountain regions (e.g. European Alps, San Bernadino Mountains, California). Ozone is an important phyto-toxic gaseous pollutant which, unlike SO_2 and NO_x, is an increasing threat (Ashmore, 2005), with global concentrations in the lower atmosphere rising at approximately 0.1 ppb per year. As a secondary pollutant, its concentrations are normally higher in rural than in nearby urban areas, and in spring and summer the night-time concentrations in the uplands can often remain elevated, in contrast to the stronger cyclical pattern seen in the lowlands (Figure 3.3). This phenomenon, observed widely across mountain and upland areas of the world (NEGTAP, 2001), may result in continuous exposure to elevated concentrations for several days.

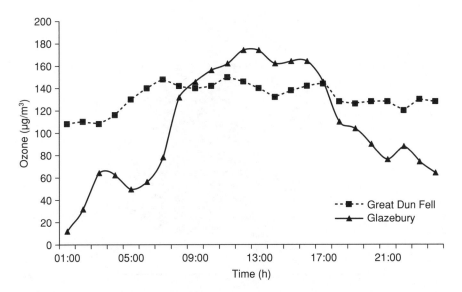

Figure 3.3 Diurnal pattern in ozone concentrations on 2 July 2006 during a hot summer at an upland (Great Dun Fell, altitude 848 m asl) and a lowland (Glazebury, 23 m asl) site in northern England (source data: UK Air Quality Archive http://www.airquality.co.uk).

Exposure to wet deposited air pollution

Owing to the high rainfall, exposure to air pollution in most upland regions is commonly dominated by wet deposition, and the maps of total deposition of several pollutants (e.g. sulphate, nitrate and acidity) reflect the combined influence of distance from the source and the geographical distribution of rainfall (Figure 3.4) despite the low concentrations of pollutant

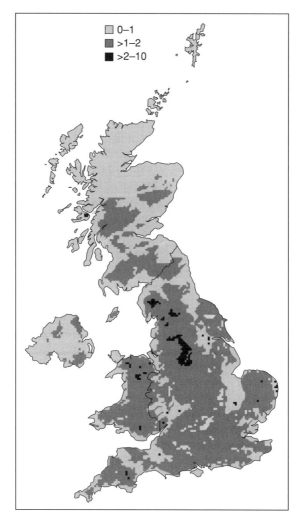

Figure 3.4 Measured total deposition of nitrogen compounds (kequivalents N ha^{-1} y^{-1} where 1 kequivalent equals 14 kg) to the UK in 2002–4, showing the importance of inputs to high ground in northern England and Wales (source data: National Focal Centre for Critical Loads Modelling and Mapping, CEH, Bangor).

ions measured in remote upland rain. Montane north Wales is typical of a rural area where the rainwater is relatively clean but the heavy rainfall results in high total pollutant deposition.

The uplands are exposed to frequent cloud cover – for example, almost a quarter of the year in the English North Pennines (Fowler, 2002) – and this is of great significance for upland wet deposition. Orographic hill cloudwater droplets, derived from the long-range transported pollutant aerosols, move up from the lowland source regions; the aerosols form condensation nuclei, and resulting cloudwater drops contain much higher concentrations of solutes (e.g. H^+, NH_4^+, NO_3^-, SO_4^-) than rain at the same locations (Dore *et al.*, 2001). Orographic cloud droplets are much larger than aerosols and as a result deposit easily to the aerodynamically rough surfaces of upland vegetation. Part of the additional wet deposition of pollution into the uplands occurs by the process of 'seeder–feeder scavenging' whereby less-polluted raindrops from the higher (seeder) clouds scavenge the polluted hillcap orographic (feeder) clouds. Pollutant exposure in cloudwater is particularly important for tree bryophytes and lichens since upland forests may receive the majority of atmospheric sulphur and nitrogen inputs from cloudwater deposition. Snowfall pollution is another feature of deposition in montane zones since snow is an efficient scavenger of atmospheric pollution and at snowmelt can release relatively large amounts in 'acid flushes' potentially affecting bryophytes and other sensitive organisms as found in the Cairngorm mountains of Scotland (Woolgrove and Woodin, 1996).

Rural upland landscapes are therefore exposed to a pollution climate characterised mainly by high wet deposition of secondary nitrogen pollutants and acidity in rain but also in the very significant cloudwater inputs. They are also exposed to increasing background concentrations of gaseous ozone and, depending on proximity to farm sources, ammonia. Transfer of these pollutants to land is typically rapid in the uplands owing to factors that increase the deposition velocities of pollutants – the high wind-speeds and aerodynamically rough canopies of forests and moorlands.

Anthropogenic emissions of greenhouse gases and their effect on climate change

Greenhouse gases

Numerous gases found in trace concentrations in air absorb and release infrared radiation emitted by the earth's surface, the atmosphere and clouds, and this radiation increases the temperature of the earth giving rise to the greenhouse effect (Houghton, 2004). The increases in atmospheric concentrations of the principal greenhouse gases (GHG) (Table 3.2) are attributed to two types of human activity: first, the growth of fossil fuel burning and industry and, second, alteration in land use such as increases in agriculture and reductions in forest cover. Both of these activities raise the net transfer of

Table 3.2 Radiative forcing (global warming potential), average concentrations and trends of anthropogenic greenhouse gases and other components in 2005 (IPCC, 2007).

Component	Radiative Forcing (Wm^{-2})	Concentration (ppm)	Rise since pre-industrial times	Global trends
CO_2	+1.66	379	+36%	+
CH_4	+0.48	1.8	+148%	+
N_2O	+0.16	0.32	+18%	+
Halocarbons	+0.34	0.001	(b)	0
Ozone (Tropospheric)	+0.35	0.030	(c)	+
Aerosols	−1.2	(a)	(c)	(a)
Net anthropogenic factors	+1.6			

Additional factors: stratospheric ozone, stratospheric water vapour, Albedo, linear contrails, solar irradiance. Notes: (a): Aerosols are highly variable in composition and concentration in space and time; (b) halocarbons were invented recently; (c) ozone and aerosols changes highly uncertain (see IPCC, 2007).

GHG between the earth's surface and atmosphere, but the balance between sources and sinks of GHG and the relative contribution of natural and anthropogenic processes are not fully understood. These gaps in knowledge add to uncertainties regarding the growth in GHG and thus the predicted climate change.

A molecule of CO_2 has much less global warming potential than a molecule of most other greenhouse gases, such as CH_4 (eight times as effective as CO_2) or halocarbons (many thousand times more effective), but the much greater atmospheric concentration of CO_2, its steady rate of increase and long lifetime make it the most important GHG (Table 3.2). Global emissions of fossil fuel CO_2 rose from around 0.5 Gt C per year in 1900 to 6.5 Gt C per year in 2000, by which time they far exceeded the net releases of carbon due to land-use change, including deforestation, which in the 1990s were around 1.6 Gt C per year. Present levels of CO_2 exceed the estimated range (180–300 ppm) over the entire past 650,000 years, and in the last 160,000 years there has been a strong correlation between ice cores estimates of atmospheric CO_2 and temperature (Intergovernmental Panel on Climate Change [IPCC], 2007).

Global warming

The view that increases in CO_2 and other GHG are the main causes of recent rapid climate change is not only founded on the observed correlations between these gases and temperature, but is also based on theory developed by physical scientists since the early nineteenth century (Houghton, 2004). Physical and mathematical models enable prediction of both positive and

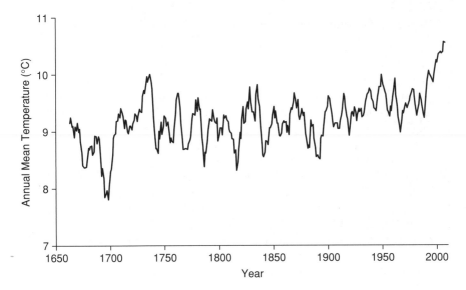

Figure 3.5 Central England temperatures from 1659 to 2007 shown as a five-year running average (source data: UK Met Office, 2008 http://www.metoffice. gov.uk/research/hadleycentre/obsdata/cet.html).

negative radiative forcing by different atmospheric components (Table 3.2). The world's longest thermometer record, started in 1659 in central England, illustrates warming over the twentieth century with a steady, steep rise in annual mean temperatures since the late 1980s (Figure 3.5), up to around 1°C higher in the past few years (up to 2007) than for most of the past century. Globally, a similar picture emerges from analysis of average land and sea surface air temperature from 1850 to 2006, showing that the 1990s were the warmest decade and that eleven of the warmest twelve years have occurred since 1995. According to the IPCC, the rise in global mean surface temperature over the hundred years up to 2005 was 0.07°C per decade. However, the change in recent decades has been much faster; and, furthermore, the land surface temperatures have increased at 0.27°C per decade since 1979, about twice the rate of temperatures over the oceans (IPCC, 2007).

Mountain regions have fewer long-term temperature records than lowlands, but data from the British uplands indicate warming in the past two decades that is similar to that seen in the lowlands. In the English North Pennines, most of the recent warming occurred in the winter months with associated reductions in lapse rates (drop in temperature with rising altitude) and a fall in the number of cold days (Holden and Adamson, 2002) (see Box 3.1). In the European Alps warming has increased twice as fast as the global average over the last century (Pauli *et al.*, 2007), and minimum temperatures have risen more than the mean (Korner, 2003). Warming correlates with changes

---

Box 3.1. Is climate changing in the British uplands?

Until recently it was not clear if the uplands of Britain were seeing the warming trends apparent in the long-term monitoring in the English lowlands and elsewhere in the world. Garnett *et al.* (1997) analysed temperature records from Moor House in the North Pennines from 1931 to 1995 and found no overall warming, and it was felt that upland areas might respond differently from the lowlands. However, the late 1990s were particularly warm, and re-appraisal of the records collected up to 2000 by Holden and Adamson (2002) found a significant increase in temperature and changes in related climate indicators (Table 3.3). Holden and Adamson (2002) contrasted the climate from the 1990s (1991–2000, when the station became part of the Natural Environment Research Council's Environmental Change Network) with the period 1953–79. Recent data up to 2006 illustrate that the warming trend at Moor House has continued (Figure 3.7), and a similar trend is evident at Holme Moss, a warmer site further south in the Pennine hills.

Table 3.3 Comparison of climatic variables averaged over two time periods at Moor House (556 m asl) in the English North Pennines (after Holden and Adamson, 2002).

Climate variable	1991/1992–2000, compared with 1953–1979
Temperature Annual	Warmer by 0.7 °C
Temperature January-February	Warmer by 1.4–2.0 °C
Temperature March-December	No significant increase
Days with Frost	Fewer (101 compared to 133)
Days with Snow on ground	Fewer (50 compared to 69)
Precipitation	Winter increase, Summer decrease

---

in other critical components of climate in the mountain areas. Snow cover for a wide range of northern hemisphere locations dropped slowly from the early 1920s; this decline has accelerated since the 1970s and at many sites is related to earlier spring melt (IPCC, 2007). In Britain, similar trends are apparent in records from the North Pennines and Snowdonia where, in the latter, snow cover in the early 1980s was about twice that seen in recent years, since 2000 (Figure 3.6). In high-altitude montane zones of the world, glaciers and ice caps have receded, adding about 0.8 mm per year to global sea-level rise, and the thickness of the permafrost layer and the amount of seasonally frozen

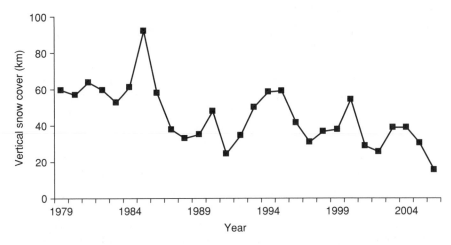

Figure 3.6 Accumulative snow cover in Snowdonia, north Wales, 1979–2006. The vertical distance (m) from summit to snow line each day is summed over each
year starting at the end of the year shown. Data recorded by: Mr C. Aron,
Pentraeth (1979–94); Dr J. Williams, Envirodata-Eryi (1994–2007).

ground at medium altitudes have also declined, again usually linked to
spring warming (IPCC, 2007).

Warming of the earth's surface inevitably leads to greater evaporation, and
in many parts of the world this links to observations of increasing rainfall
over the twentieth century (IPCC, 2007). Data from England and Wales from
1766 to the present (Met Office, 2007) show no clear trend in total annual
rainfall, although in the upper catchment of the river Wye in mid-Wales a
trend of increasing total annual rainfall since the early 1970s was observed
(Marc and Robinson, 2007). However, a steady rise in winter rain and a decline
in summer rain is apparent in the UK. Osborn and Hulme (2002) analysed
the period 1961–95 and revealed that the largest increases in winter rainfall
occurred in Scotland and north-western England, areas dominated by
uplands, owing mainly to increased amounts of rain on wet days (more than
just an increase in the number of wet days).

The contrasting trends in rainfall between the summer and the winter over
the last 240 years can be seen as part of an emerging wider pattern of increased
variability in the weather with a greater frequency of extreme events. More
extreme weather in the uplands associated with overall warming will lead to
longer periods of drying and heat stress in summer and more frequent heavy
rainfall events, with wide-ranging implications for wildfires, soil erosion and
biological populations. The widespread increase in extreme weather is believed to have resulted from anthropogenic activity and will probably continue
(IPCC, 2007).

Predictions of future climate

Climate predictions are derived using complex numerical models based on the fundamental mathematical equations that describe the physics and dynamics of the movements and processes taking place in the atmosphere, in the ocean, in the ice and on the land (Houghton, 2004). The warming trends of the past few decades are likely to continue into the next, even if GHG emissions were to be stopped, owing not only to the long life of most greenhouse gases but also to the heat already absorbed by the earth's surface, particularly the oceans, that will be released to the atmosphere to gain equilibrium. The latest IPCC report, based on a large number of simulations run on a broad range of climate models, predicts that by the end of the present century the rise in atmospheric GHG concentrations will result in an increase in global mean surface temperatures of between 1.8 and 4.0°C compared with the period 1980–99, but a worst-case scenario is a 6.4°C rise (IPCC, 2007). The varying predictions are based on widely differing scenarios, assuming from the least likely to the worst changes in GHG emissions, related to our methods of energy generation, and our use of energy and materials linked to consumer demands, economic and population growth.

In the UK, the government Climate Impacts Programme (Hulme *et al.*, 2002; http://www.UKCIP.org.uk) predicts climate change in line with recent IPCC forecasts (Table 3.4). The mean annual temperatures are expected to increase by 1–5°C by 2100, with warming greater in summer and more in the south-east than in the north-west of the country. Rainfall is expected to increase in winter and decline in summer, and these changes may be greater in the south than in the north. Confidence in the forecasts is high for overall climatic change but lower for more episodic weather patterns. Most of these predictions mirror trends observed over the past two or three decades. However, in parts of the British uplands warming has been greater in winter than in summer (Table 3.3). An expected future rise of, for example, 3°C

Table 3.4 Summary of selected UK climate change scenarios (after UK Climate Impacts Programme; Hulme *et al.*, 2002).

Climate variable	Changes by 2100 in relation to 1961–1990	Confidence
Annual temperature	Warming by 1–5 deg C	High
	Summer warming > winter	Medium
	South & east warming > north & west	High
Very hot summer days	increase	Medium
Very cold winter days	decrease	Medium
Winter Rainfall	Increase (+ 30%) & heavier events	High
Summer rainfall	Decrease (−50%)	Medium
Snowfall	decrease	High
Winter storms; mild wet, windy winters	increase	Low

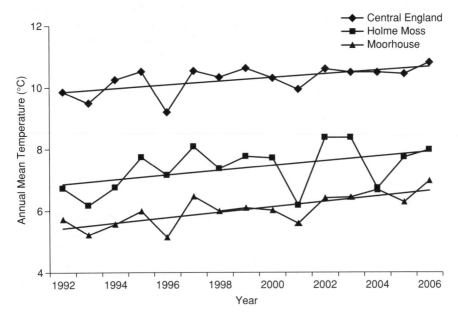

Figure 3.7 Annual average temperatures from the central England Temperature data set (CET), a South Pennine site at Holme Moss (520 m asl) and Moor House (556 m asl) in the North Pennines from 1992 to 2006. Linear trends are also shown. CET data from the UK Met Office; Moor House from the Natural Environment Research Council Environmental Change Network; Holme Moss data from the Met Office (1992–4) and J. White-head, UMIST/University Manchester (1995–2006).

by 2100 appears small compared with our own daily and seasonal experience of temperature change, but 3°C is all that separates the annual average temperature of northern Scotland (7.9°C) and southern England (11.0°C; data for 2006; Met Office, 2007), while around 1.5°C is the difference between the North and South Pennines (Figure 3.7). The influence of elevation on annual mean temperature is more marked, with typical changes of around 0.75°C per 100 m in northern England (Holden and Adamson, 2002), suggesting that a rise of 3°C would be equivalent to a substantial drop in altitude of around 400 m.

Impacts of air quality and climate change on upland ecosystems

The effects of air pollution and climate change on biological and physical components of the natural environment are widespread, and include likely alterations in ecological and agricultural resources and other ecosystem properties (Figure 3.1). The impacts, particularly of climate change, spread far beyond ecological systems, and potentially have a variety of far-reaching social and economic consequences. These are considered in more detail later in this book and elsewhere (e.g. IPCC, 2007) but potentially are of great significance for the uplands. Lifestyle and demographic changes – for example, increased leisure activity in the mountains or migration of human populations northwards and upwards in Britain and Europe – could quickly feed back to affect upland landscapes through increased pressures on habitats already disrupted by changing climate and pollution stress.

Ecological responses are strongly influenced by the underlying sensitivity of ecosystems. The major factors governing vulnerability to air pollution are geology, soils and the type of vegetation. Many upland regions are built on slowly weathering rocks and covered with peat or other organic soils that are leached of their base cations and other nutrients by heavy rainfall and provide only weak buffering of pH changes caused by acidification. The same acidic soils, low in available nitrogen and supporting ecological communities adapted to nutrient-poor conditions, are prone to the effects of eutrophication caused by nitrogen deposition. In Europe the sensitivity of the landscape and its vegetation to acid rain and eutrophication is nowadays expressed by the critical loads approach (NEGTAP, 2001), and these illustrate in the UK the particular sensitivity of the uplands to pollution inputs (Figure 3.8; Hall *et al.*, 2004).

With increasing altitude the form, life cycles and survival chances of organisms are increasingly defined by their responses and adaptations to cold, snow and ice; and therefore upland life, especially the cold-niche specialist organisms of mountain summits, are likely to be especially threatened by global warming as their habitats change dramatically. All species occupy habitat niches including requirements for climate, food, breeding sites and other factors. When the environment changes, some generalist species may adapt or modify their requirements, others may migrate, but specialists may die out locally (and, in extreme cases, globally) if they can neither adapt nor successfully migrate. This will lead to species invasions, local species losses and perhaps species extinctions. New species may alter existing communities, ecosystems and the physical environment in ways that are difficult to predict.

Evidence of responses to climate change and air pollution in the uplands

Evidence that air pollution and climate change affect upland ecosystems comes from monitoring programmes, one-off spatial surveys where a space-for-time substitution is accepted, and manipulation experiments. In the UK, vegetation-monitoring schemes (e.g. Smart *et al.*, 2003) and surveys across deposition gradients (e.g. Stevens *et al.*, 2006), supported by experiments (see Emmett, 2007), indicate that long-range nitrogen and sulphur pollution is responsible for community changes and significant losses of plant diversity across large areas of the uplands. Trends in soil and water chemistry also

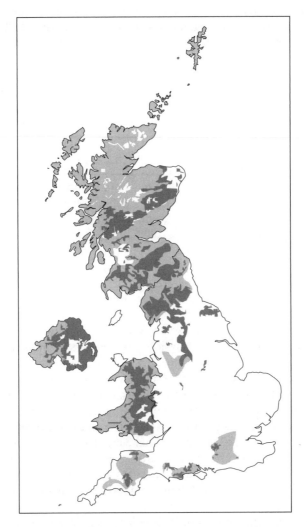

Figure 3.8 Exceedance of nutrient nitrogen critical loads for dwarf shrub heath by total N (NO_x + NH_y) deposition for 2001–3. The map shows that the critical load is exceeded for most of the UK dwarf shrub communities (white areas: no data, i.e. no mapped habitat; grey: critical loads not exceeded; black: critical loads exceeded; source data: National Focal Centre for Critical Loads Modelling and Mapping, CEH, Bangor).

indicate that acidification, eutrophication and contamination with heavy metals has occurred in many sensitive areas of upland UK, although some regions are now recovering (e.g. NEGTAP, 2001). The extent and timescale of any recovery in both chemical signals and ecological communities, as nitrogen and sulphur pollution gradually improves, are unknown, although information derived from a few deposition reduction experiments (see Emmett, 2007) and trends detected from continuing monitoring programmes such as the UK Acid Waters Monitoring Network (see Allott, this volume) provide valuable information.

Recent global warming has already caused movement upwards and northwards in distribution of many species of plants and animals (Hickling *et al.*, 2006; Pauli *et al.*, 2007). For example, the mountain ringlet butterfly *Erebia epiphron* in northern Britain moved its range boundary upwards in elevation by 130–150 m over a recent nineteen-year study period (Franco *et al.*, 2006). Changes in phenology – earlier timing of development stages – has been widely documented in a wide range of organisms (Sparks *et al.*, 2006). In montane regions the tree line has been observed to respond to climate change – both recent and historical – but whether this will widely happen may depend on other potentially limiting factors such as soil nutrients and grazing pressure (Grace *et al.*, 2002). Importantly, our understanding of the long-term impact on communities and ecosystems of climate change in combination with air pollution – for example elevated CO_2, ozone and nitrogen deposition – is still in its infancy.

Current knowledge of the impacts of environmental change may be exemplified within three categories: direct effects, indirect effects and interactions.

Direct effects of a driver such as temperature or elevated CO_2 often stimulate an immediate response in physiological processes such as an increase in photosynthesis. For example, warming will speed up biophysical and biochemical processes, leading to rapid responses in cellular growth causing faster and earlier development of leaves, insects and other biota, and quicker metabolism including rates of mitochondrial respiration and associated CO_2 release. Mild temperatures in early winter may also cause problems since cold tolerance develops in response to seasonal cues of shortening day-length and falling temperature. Plants failing to experience sufficient cold during early winter may not acquire adequate hardiness to tolerate the sudden frosts and, in some locations, waterlogging conditions of mid- and late winter (Crawford, 2002).

Alterations in phenology are particularly significant in upland areas where development is typically regulated by accumulated warmth (thermal time, in degree-days) and governs, for example, flowering and seed set in heath rush *Juncus squarrosus* growing at its upland limit. Since warming may affect development to differing extents within the upland ecological community, and not all species will share the capacity to migrate upwards, many essential interactions between organisms, such as pollination and herbivory, could become spatially and temporally separated and fail. The specialists of the upland and mountain summits will be faced with a diminishing habitat space and invaders from lower elevations, causing major shifts in biodiversity (Pauli *et al.*, 2007). Experimental warming of dwarf-shrub heathland in Wales led to increased cover of *Calluna vulgaris* and a decline in the more northern species *Empetrum nigrum* (Penuelas *et al.*, 2007).

Box 3.2. Recent air pollution trends in the South Pennines

Air pollution has been blamed for the poor condition of habitats in the South Pennines for generations. Grindon (1859) attributed the decline of lichen species around Manchester to coal-smoke pollution, and Smith (1872) concluded from chemical analysis of polluted rain that it must be having serious effects on vegetation. A century later, Tallis (1987) found that the appearance of a layer of soot in the profile of peat cores coincided with the demise of *Sphagnum* moss from the peat layer. Evidence that sulphur pollution was the most likely culprit was provided by exposing *Sphagnum* to controlled levels of SO_2 (Ferguson *et al.*, 1978). But has air quality improved following introduction of the 1950s clean air legislation, improved practices in energy production and the demise of heavy industry? The concentrations of SO_2 in the moorland areas have fallen dramatically from around 50 to a few $\mu g\ m^{-3}$ in the past three decades, but these hills lie sandwiched between major agricultural sources of NH_3 and industrial and traffic sources of NO_x. Despite the local fall in NO_2, the rainfall ammonium and nitrate (Figure 3.9) and total nitrogen deposition to the region have declined much less in the past twenty years. Atmospheric nitrogen pollution is now a greater source of deposited acidity than sulphur, and the South Pennines remain probably the upland region most affected by acid rain in the UK (Evans and Jenkins, 2000).

Twenty years of monitoring ground-level ozone pollution in the South Pennines illustrates the global trend of increasing average concentrations (NEGTAP, 2001). The potential problems due to increased ozone exposure at altitude exist in the South Pennines as well as at other upland sites, but whether upland vegetation is any more sensitive than other plants to this gas remains uncertain. Recent heavy metal monitoring shows that the deposition of metals is higher to the South Pennines than to most other UK regions, but this is still much less than in the industrial past. The legacy of historical metal deposition, however, poses a continuing problem as inspection of the profile below intact peat vegetation reveals very high concentrations of lead and other metals, and where surfaces erode this metal store is remobilized into aquatic systems (Rothwell *et al.*, 2007).

Although the South Pennines is probably the worst-affected upland region in the country, the sorts of air pollution problems are similar to those of other UK upland regions. Some features of air quality are still improving (SO_2, NO_2), others are getting worse (ozone), some are changing less (total nitrogen deposition), while the legacy of stored pollution (metals, sulphur and nitrogen) will long remain. However, recent observations of increased diversity of *Sphagnum* species and other bryophytes since 1983–4 suggest that the biology is benefiting from the overall improvement in air quality (Figure 3.10).

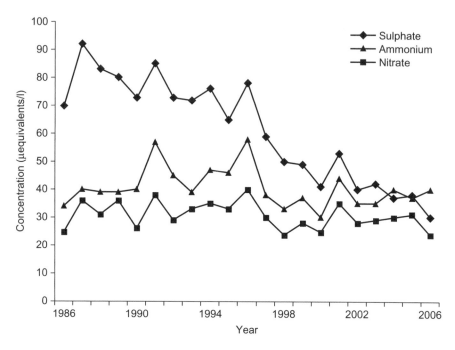

Figure 3.9 Pollutant concentrations in rainwater at Wardlow Hay Cop, 1988–2000 (in the South Pennines). Sulphate is estimated non-marine sulphate (source data: UK Air Quality Archive http://www.airquality.co.uk).

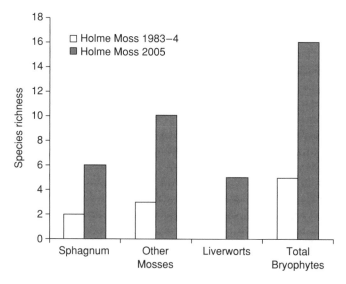

Figure 3.10 Increase in the number of species of *Sphagnum*, other mosses and liverworts in open plots at Holme Moss in the South Pennines between 1983–5 and 2005–6 (Caporn *et al.*, 2006).

The clearest direct effects of phytotoxic air pollutants, like SO_2 and acid rain, are apparent in lichens and bryophytes, which, unlike higher plants, lack the protection of an outer cuticle. Aerial nitrogen deposition can cause an immediate increase in nutrient nitrogen supply, usually prompting a positive growth response in higher plants, but in lower plants nitrogen accumulates (Mitchell *et al.*, 2004) and results, in some species, in damage such as in the montane bryophyte *Racomitrium lanuginosum* (Pearce *et al.*, 2003).

Indirect effects of pollution or climate change are seen when a primary factor, such as drought, results in a secondary response, such as the wildfires regularly experienced in the South Pennine moorlands of northern England (McMorrow *et al.*, this volume) and on a larger scale in the boreal peatlands of Canada, causing ecological damage and release to the atmosphere of long-term soil-stored carbon.

Indirect effects of environmental change are not always predictable and may lead to complex chains of responses, particularly where different trophic levels and soil processes are involved. Prolonged exposure of plants to elevated CO_2 (e.g. double the ambient level – as might occur later this century) tends to lower the nitrogen concentration of foliage, increasing herbivore consumption of plant tissue to gain the equivalent amount of food nitrogen (Stiling and Cornelissen, 2007). Thus, the extent of plant growth response to CO_2 is often limited by nitrogen supply (Reich *et al.*, 2006). Warming inevitably leads to increased microbial activity, accelerated decomposition and nutrient cycling, which may increase nutrient availability and the potential for growth in upland systems normally constrained by low temperature and both low and saturated water conditions (Emmett *et al.*, 2004).

Food chain studies found that soil acidification resulted in increased leaching and lowering of calcium in forest soil and vegetation and knock-on reductions in populations of snails and their bird predators (Graveland *et al.*, 1994). Similarly, acidification of upland streams in Wales reduced invertebrates, fish and a bird species – the European dipper *Cinclus cinclus* – populations through the combined effect of low pH, low calcium and high aluminium in stream waters (Kowalik *et al.*, 2007).

Many factors indirectly affect the species composition of ecological communities through changing the balance between stronger and weaker competitors. For example, while elevated nitrogen promotes growth in many higher plants (in the absence of other limiting factors), the competitive species typically respond more than others, such as the slow-growing stress-tolerating plants (Grime, 2002), resulting in shifts in the structure of the vegetation community in favour of nitrogen-loving plants (Smart *et al.*, 2003) which may ultimately cause a loss in species diversity (Stevens *et al.*, 2006). A drop in grassland species diversity could significantly reduce total community biomass (Reich *et al.*, 2001), which is likely to lead to a fall in net carbon accumulation within the soil system and ultimately feed back to increase atmospheric GHG accumulation.

Interactive effects of environmental change occur when the impact of one factor is altered by the effect of one or more others. For example, in normal air, plants are commonly exposed to mixtures of air pollutants (e.g. gases SO_2, NO_2 and ozone), and their combined impact is often greater than the sum of their individual effects (Fangmeier *et al.*, 2002). Rising levels of ozone are a particular concern for the uplands (Hayes *et al.*, 2006), but a contrasting interaction occurs between ozone and CO_2 since an increase in the latter reduces the stomatal pore size and the uptake of potentially damaging ozone (Harmens *et al.*, 2007). For the same reason, higher CO_2 may lower foliar transpiration and thereby increase drought tolerance. If CO_2 reduces canopy foliar water loss, this could increase soil water and flow through river catchments (Gedney *et al.*, 2006).

Pollutants frequently influence the response of vegetation to other 'natural' stress factors. In mountains and uplands the cold, often combined with wind exposure, is a major influence on development and survival. In winter, evergreens normally develop cold tolerance; but several pollutants, such as nitrogen, acid mist and ozone, can weaken cell membranes, change cell composition or alter the timing of hardening, leaving them more prone to freezing stress (Davison and Barnes, 2002). A further natural threat to vegetation is either increased risk of disease (Nordin *et al.*, 2006) or damage caused by herbivorous pests due to changes in plant chemistry and palatability (Fluckiger *et al.*, 2002). Grazing has major impacts on upland plant production, species composition and in some places soil erosion. Several experiments found important interactions with air pollution, with increased sensitivity to nitrogen observed under elevated grazing (van der Wal *et al.*, 2003). It has also been proposed that heavy grazing pressure may increase sensitivity to climate extremes.

Finally, interactive effects of environmental change may take effect after a delay. For example, dry summers bring desiccation of upland peats, oxidation of stored sulphur, and generation of sulphuric acid, causing increased mobility and elevated concentrations of streamwater aluminium and other metals, which may have been stored for decades (Tipping *et al.*, 2003).

Conclusions

Our understanding of the role of air pollution as a driver of change in the uplands has greatly changed over the past half century. Atmospheric sulphur dioxide and sulphur-driven acidification are still important but have declined dramatically, and some related ecological improvements have been recorded. Nitrogen deposition is now more important and presents a continuing threat to ecosystems. Background levels of ozone, a product of nitrogen pollution, are increasing, and their impacts on ecology are very uncertain. Rising CO_2 will have direct but as yet uncertain impacts on ecosystems; but its contribution, along with other greenhouse gases, to changing climate, particularly the increased intensity of the water cycle (drier summers, wetter winters), presents major new threats to the uplands. The ecology of temperature-sensitive organisms is already changing and will face further upheaval if even the 'best-case' climate change predictions are realised.

What of the future? Ecological responses both to single or combinations of factors are species-dependent, and understanding the outcome of complex interactions between genotype or soil type, climate and pollution over generations is difficult to achieve solely from experiments, since the number of treatment combinations and the lengthy duration required for realistic trials may not be feasible. Computer models – for example, GBMOVE (Smart *et al.*, 2007) which describes plant species behaviour in response to gradients such as soil pH, fertility, moisture and disturbance – offer a possible way forward to predict the likely impacts of such complex interactions when linked to dynamic biogeochemical soil models and plant succession models. However, models are only as good as the basic observations on which they are built, and more experiments investigating interactions between changing variables are particularly required to improve our fundamental understanding of the structure and function of upland ecosystems and how they may respond to environmental change.

Nevertheless, it is already evident that environmental change will cause uneven changes in ecosystems as some types of organisms or species respond more than others, altering the geography and structure of ecological communities. Given the speed of environmental change predicted for the future, we are faced with crucial questions over the capacity for natural adaptation within upland ecosystems and over our abilities to mitigate change by management.

References

Ashmore, M. R. (2005) Assessing the future global impacts of ozone on vegetation. *Plant Cell and Environment*, **28**, 949–64.

Bell, J. N. B. and Treshow, M. (2002) *Air Pollution and Plant Life*. London: John Wiley.

Caporn, S. J. M., Carroll, J. A., Studholme, C. and Lee, J. A. (2006) *Recovery of Ombrotrophic Sphagnum Mosses in Relation to Air Pollution in the South Pennines.* Report to Moors for the Future, Edale, Derbyshire.

Crawford, R. M. M. (2002) Ecological hazards of oceanic environments. *New Phytologist*, **147**, 257–81.

Davison, A. W. and Barnes, J. D. (2002) Air pollutant–abiotic stress interactions. *Air Pollution and Plant Life* (ed. J. M. Bell and M. Treshow), pp. 359–77. London: John Wiley.

Dore, A. J., Choularton, T. W. and Inglis, D. W. F. (2001) Monitoring studies of precipitation and cap cloud chemistry at Holme Moss in the South Pennines. *Water, Air and Soil Pollution: Focus*, **1**, 381–90.

Emmett, B. A. (2007) Nitrogen saturation of terrestrial ecosystems: some recent findings and their implications for our conceptual framework. *Water Air and Soil Pollution: Focus*, **7**, 99–109.

Emmett, B. A., Beier, B., Estiarte, M., Tietema, A., Kristensen, H. L., Williams, D., Penuelas, J., Schmidt, I. and Sowerby, A. (2004) The response of soil processes to climate change: results from manipulation studies of shrublands across an environmental gradient. *Ecosystems*, **7**, 625–37.

Evans, C. D. and Jenkins, A. (2000) Surface water acidification in the South Pennines. II. Temporal trends. *Environmental Pollution*, **109**, 21–34.

Fangmeier, A., Bender, J., Weigel, H.-J. and Jager, H.-J. (2002) Effect of pollutant mixtures. *Air Pollution and Plant Life* (ed. J. M. Bell and M. Treshow), pp. 251–72. London: John Wiley.

Ferguson, P., Lee, J. A. and Bell, J. N. B. (1978) Effects of sulphur pollution on the growth of *Sphagnum* species. *Environmental Pollution*, **16**, 151–62.

Fluckiger, W., Braun, S. and Hiltbrunner, E. (2002) Effects of air pollutants on biotic stress. *Air Pollution and Plant Life* (ed. J. M. Bell and M. Treshow), pp. 379–406. London: John Wiley.

Fowler, D. (2002) Pollutant deposition and uptake by vegetation. *Air Pollution and Plant Life* (ed. J. M. Bell and M. Treshow), pp. 43–67. London: John Wiley.

Fowler, D., O'Donoghue, M., Muller, J. B. A., Smith, R. J., Dragosits, U., Skiba, U., Sutton, M. A. and Brimblecombe, P. (2004) A chronology of nitrogen deposition in the UK between 1900 and 2000. *Water, Air and Soil Pollution Focus*, **4**, 9–23.

Fowler, D., Smith, R. I., Muller, J. B. A., Hayman, G. and Vincent, K. J. (2005) Changes in the atmospheric deposition of acidifying compounds in the UK between 1986 and 2001. *Environmental Pollution*, **137**, 15–25.

Franco, A. M. A., Hill, J. K., Kitschke, C., Collingham, Y. C., Roy, D. B., Fox, R., Huntley, B. and Thomas, C. D. (2006) Impacts of climate warming and habitat loss on extinctions at species' low-latitude range boundaries. *Global Change Biology*, **12**, 1545–53.

Garnett, M. H., Ineson, P. and Adamson, J. K. (1997) A long-term upland temperature record: no evidence for recent warming. *Weather*, **52**, 342–51.

Gedney, N., Cox, P. M., Betts, R. A., Boucher, O., Huntingford, C. and Stott, P. A. (2006) Detection of a direct carbon dioxide effect in continental river runoff records. *Nature*, **439**, 835–8.

Grace, J., Berninger, F. and Nagy, L. (2002) Impacts of climate change on the tree line. *Annals of Botany*, **90**, 537–44.

Graveland, J., Van Der Wal, R., Van Balen, J. H. and Van Noordwijk, A. J. (1994) Poor reproduction in forest passerines from decline of snail abundance on acidified soils. *Nature*, **368**, 446–8.

Grime, J. P. (2002) *Plant Strategies, Vegetation Processes, and Ecosystem Properties.* Chichester: John Wiley.

Grindon, L. H. (1859) *The Manchester Flora.* London: W. White.

Hall, J., Ullyett, J., Heywood, L., Broughton, R. and 12 UK experts (2004) *Status of UK Critical Loads: Critical Loads Methods, Data and Maps.* February 2004. Report to Defra. http://critloads.ceh.ac.uk/status_reports.htm

Harmens, H., Mills, G., Emberson, L. D. and Ashmore, M. R. (2007) Implications of climate change for the stomatal flux of ozone: a case study for winter wheat. *Environmental Pollution*, **46**, 763–70.

Hayes, F., Mills, G., Williams, P., Harmens, H. and Büker, P. (2006) Impacts of summer ozone exposure on the growth and overwintering of UK upland vegetation. *Atmospheric Environment*, **40**, 4088–97.

Hickling, R., Roy, D. B., Hill, J. K., Fox, R. and Thomas, C. D. (2006) The distributions of a wide range of taxonomic groups are expanding polewards. *Global Change Biology*, **12**, 450–5.

Holden, J. and Adamson, J. K. (2002) The Moor House long term upland temperature record: new evidence of recent warming. *Weather*, **57**, 119–27.

Houghton, J. (2004) *Global Warming. The Complete Briefing.* 3rd edn. Cambridge: Cambridge University Press.

Hulme, M., Jenkins, G. J., Lu, X., Turnpenny, J. R., Mitchell, T. D., Jones, R. G., Lowe, J., Murphy, J. M., Hassell, D., Boorman, P., McDonald, R. and Hill, S. (2002) *Climate Change Scenarios for the United Kingdom: The UKCIP02 Scientific Report.* Tyndall Centre, School of Environmental Sciences, University of East Anglia, Norwich. http://www.ukcip.org.uk/images/stories/Pub_pdfs/UKCIP02_tech.pdf

IPCC (2007) *Fourth Assessment Report.* Intergovernmental Panel on Climate Change. http://www.ipcc.ch/

Körner, C. (2003) *Alpine Plant Life.* Berlin: Springer.

Kowalik, R. A., Cooper, D. M., Evans, C. D. and Ormerod, S. J. (2007) Acidic episodes retard the biological recovery of upland British streams from chronic acidification. *Global Change Biology*, **13**, 2439–52.

Lee, J. A. (1998) Unintentional experiments with terrestrial ecosystems: ecological effects of sulphur and nitrogen pollutants. *Journal of Ecology*, **86**, 1–12.

Marc, V. and Robinson, M. (2007) The long term water balance (1972–2004) of upland forestry and grassland at Plynlimon, mid-Wales. *Hydrology and Earth System Sciences*, **11**, 44–60.

Met Office (2007) UK Met Office. http://www.metoffice.gov.uk/climate/uk/index.html

Mitchell, R. J., Sutton, M. A., Truscott, A.-M., Leith, I. D., Cape, J. N., Pitcairn, C. E. R. and van Dijk, N. (2004) Growth and tissue nitrogen of epiphytic Atlantic bryophytes: effects of increased and decreased atmospheric N deposition. *Functional Ecology*, **18**, 322–9.

Mylona, S. (1996) Sulphur dioxide emissions in Europe 1880–1991 and their effect on sulphur concentrations and depositions. *Tellus*, B, 48, 662–89.

NAEI (2006) *UK Emissions of Air Pollutants 1970 to 2004.* Report of the UK National Atmospheric Emissions Inventory. Netcen, AEA Technology, Harwell, Oxfordshire. http://www.airquality.co.uk/archive/reports/cat07/0701221151_Full_Report_NAEI_2004.pdf

NEGTAP (2001) *Transboundary Air Pollution: Acidification, Eutrophication and Ground Level Ozone in the UK.* Prepared on behalf of Defra and devolved administrations, London. http://www.maposda.net/negtap/finalreport.htm

Nordin, A., Strengbom, J. and Ericson, L. (2006) Responses to ammonium and nitrate additions by boreal plants and their natural enemies. *Environmental Pollution*, **141**, 167–74.

Osborn, T. J. and Hulme, M. (2002) Evidence for trends in heavy rainfall events over the United Kingdom. *Philosophical Transactions of the Royal Society London, Series A*, **360**, 1313–25.

Pauli, H., Gottfried, M., Reiter, K., Klettner, C. and Grabherr, G. (2007) Signals of range expansions and contractions of vascular plants in the high Alps: observations (1994–2004) at the GLORIA master site Schrankogel, Tyrol, Austria. *Global Change Biology*, **13**, 147–56.

Pearce, I. S. K., Woodin, S. J. and Van der Wal, R. (2003) Physiological and growth responses of the montane bryophyte *Racomitrium lanuginosum* to atmospheric nitrogen deposition. *New Phytologist*, **160**, 145–55.

Penuelas, J., Prieto, P., Beier, C., Cesaraccioz, C., De Angelis, P., DeDatos, G., Emmett, B. A., Estiarte, M., Garadnai, J., Gorissen, A., Kovacs-Lang, E., Kroel-Dulay, G., Llorens, L., Pellizzaro, G., Riis-Nielsen, T., Schmidt, I. K., Sirca, C., Sowerby, A., Spano, D. and Tietema, A. (2007) Response of plant species richness and primary productivity in shrublands along a north–south gradient in

Europe to seven years of experimental warming and drought: reductions in primary productivity in the heat and drought year of 2003. *Global Change Biology*, **13**, 2563–81.

Reich, P. B., Hobbie, S. E., Lee, T., Ellsworth, D. S., West, J. B., Tilman, D., Knops, J. M. H., Naeem, S. and Trost, J. (2006) Nitrogen limitation constrains sustainability of ecosystem response to CO_2. *Nature*, **440**, 922–5.

Reich, P. B., Knops, J., Tilman, D., Craine, J., Ellsworth, D., Tjoelker, M., Lee, T., Wedin, D., Naeem, S., Bahauddin, D., Hendrey, G., Jose, S., Wrage, K., Goth, J. and Bengston, W. (2001) Plant diversity enhances ecosystem responses to elevated CO_2 and nitrogen deposition. *Nature*, **410**, 809–12.

Rothwell, J. J., Robinson, S. G., Evans, M. G., Yang, J. and Allott, T. E. H. (2005) Heavy metal release by peat erosion in the Peak District, South Pennines, UK. *Hydrological Processes*, **19**, 2973–89.

Smart, S., Rowe, E., Evans, C. D., Roy, D., Moy, I., Bullock, J. and Emmett, B. A. (2007) Vegetation module for dynamic modelling. *Final Report: Terrestrial Umbrella – Effects of Eutrophication and Acidification on Terrestrial Ecosystems, July 2007* (ed. B. A. Emmett and 57 UK experts), pp. 197–216. London: Defra.

Smart, S. M., Robertson, J. C., Shield, E. J. and van de Poll, H. M. (2003) Locating eutrophication effects across British vegetation between 1990 and 1998. *Global Change Biology*, **9**, 1763–74.

Smith, R. A. (1872) *Air and Rain*. London: Longmans.

Sparks, T. H., Collinson, N., Crick, H., Croxton, P., Edwards, M., Huber, K., Jenkins, D., Johns, D., Last, F., Maberly, S., Marquiss, M., Pickup, J., Roy, D., Sims, D., Shaw, D., Turner, A., Watson, A., Woiwod, I. and Woodbridge, K. (2006) *Natural Heritage Trends of Scotland: Phenological Indicators of Climate Change*. Scottish Natural Heritage Commissioned Report No. 167 (ROAME No. F01NB01). http://www.snh.org.uk/pdfs/publications/commissioned_reports/F01NB01.pdf

Stevens, C. J., Dise, N. B., Gowing, D. J. and Mountford, J. O. (2006) Loss of forb diversity in relation to nitrogen deposition in the UK: regional trends and potential controls. *Global Change Biology*, **12**, 1–11.

Stiling, P. and Cornelissen, T. (2007) How does elevated carbon dioxide (CO_2) affect plant–herbivore interactions? A field experiment and meta-analysis of CO_2-mediated changes on plant chemistry and herbivore performance. *Global Change Biology*, **13**, 1–20.

Tallis, J. H. (1987) Fire and flood at Holme Moss: erosion processes in an upland blanket mire. *Journal of Ecology*, **75**, 1099–129.

Tipping, E., Smith, E. J., Lawlor, A. J., Hughes, S. and Stevens, P. A. (2003) Predicting the release of metals from ombrotrophic peat due to drought-induced acidification. *Environmental Pollution*, **123**, 239–53.

Truscott, A. M., Palmer, S. C. F., McGowan, G. M., Cape, J. N. and Smart, S. (2005) Vegetation composition of roadside verges in Scotland: the effects of nitrogen deposition, disturbance and management. *Environmental Pollution*, **136**, 109–18.

van der Wal, R., Pearce, I., Brooker, R., Scott, D., Welch, D. and Woodin, S. (2003) Interplay between nitrogen deposition and grazing causes habitat degradation. *Ecology Letters*, **6**, 141–6.

Woolgrove, C. E. and Woodin, S. J. (1996) Current and historical relationships between the tissue nitrogen content of snowbed bryophyte and nitrogenous air pollution. *Environmental Pollution*, **3**, 283–8.

4 Policy change in the uplands

Ian Condliffe

Introduction

This chapter traces the development of agricultural and environmental policies in England that have helped to shape the uplands since a government department of agriculture first came into existence. Agricultural policy was fairly single-mindedly focused on production from the Second World War up to the 1980s. Around that time it became more widely realised that some policies were having a seriously detrimental effect on the rural environment. From then on, agricultural and environmental policy took a new direction, and the pace of change quickened. Some policies were at odds with each other, and most were directed at farmers, who became increasingly confused at what the government, 'the public' or the European Commission (EC) wanted from them. Most policies were not aimed directly at the uplands but at the countryside in general. More recently, as the environmental and ecosystems services value of the uplands has been more greatly appreciated, some policies have become more upland specific.

The last twenty years in particular tell a complicated story, with new policies and changes to existing policies happening almost simultaneously or in quick succession. For this reason, after 1980, the changes are recorded roughly by decade and in two areas – agricultural and environmental. In fact, until the turn of the century, there was little consultation between the two departments. Only with the union of the Ministry of Agriculture, Fisheries and Food (MAFF) and parts of the Department of Environment, Transport and the Regions (DETR) into the Department for the Environment, Food and Rural Affairs (Defra) in 2001 did agricultural and environmental policies really start to come together. It was also recognised that sustainable rural development and nature conservation are intricately linked, and that a more integrated approach was needed for the management of natural resources and public access and enjoyment of the countryside. In 2006, this led to the three organisations responsible for implementing wildlife and countryside policies – English Nature, the Countryside Agency, and Defra's Rural Development Service – merged into a new agency, Natural England.

Context

Upland landscapes are a function of climate, topography, geology, soils and, most importantly, human activity. In the UK, it is human activity that has given upland areas the landscape fabric and biodiversity that are valued today, particularly the management of herbivores which denuded areas of their wood-land cover and led to the grassland, heathland, mire and enclosure that we now associate with the uplands. Livestock production remains the main direct land management use in the uplands (see also Burton *et al.*; Gardner *et al.*, both this volume). In some areas, grouse moor management is also a strong driver of landscape and habitat (Sotherton *et al.*, this volume).

In terms of agricultural policy, the uplands are recognised as areas of moun-tain, moor and heath and the enclosed grasslands associated with them. These are mapped as Less Favoured Areas (LFA), a European Union designation, although a similar area was recognised and mapped by the UK government in the early 1960s. LFAs need not be upland; but, in the UK, the natural and socio-economic disadvantages they represent correspond with upland farming systems.

The English LFAs contain many of the country's areas of high landscape and nature conservation value. Often not having been intensively cultivated, they also contain a wealth of historical landscapes and artefacts. All this is reflected in the national land designations that lie within them. Covering 17 per cent of the land area, they encompass 7 National Parks, 9 Areas of Outstanding Natural Beauty (AONB), 9 Environmentally Sensitive Areas (ESA), 46 National Nature Reserves (NNR), 815 Sites of Special Scientific Interest (SSSI), 54 Special Areas of Conservation (SAC) and 8 Special Protection Areas (SPA).

The past fifty years have seen significant changes in agriculture. In one way, these tell a story of success, with upland farmers moving the country closer to self-sufficiency in meat products. In another, they tell of failure, in particular for the conservation of landscapes and habitats, many of which are now realised to be of international importance. Table 4.1 summarises some of the milestones in UK and EU agricultural policy development.

1915–80: the drive for self-sufficiency and growing environmental awareness and action

Agriculture

The first examples of government intervention in agricultural production were during the First World War. At its outbreak, only 30 per cent of the UK's food needs were home grown. County War Agricultural Committees were established to encourage and advise on cereal production, and the area of arable cropping rose from 4 to 5.3 million hectares from 1915 to 1918 (Adams, 1986).

In 1919, the Ministry of Agriculture and Fisheries was established. During the early interwar years, agricultural production stagnated. Guaranteed cereal prices were reduced, and the area under production fell. By the late 1930s, however, with the possibility of a second war in Europe, the government once again started to increase its level of intervention. In 1937, UK self-sufficiency in agricultural produce was around 40 per cent. The Ministry of Food became the sole buyer of food products, and guaranteed commodity prices and markets for farmers. For the first time, subsidies were made available for sheep production and the spreading of lime and basic slag to build up soil fertility. Ploughing grassland over seven years old for arable production attracted a subsidy of £2/acre (£5/ha), and a target was set to bring an additional 600,000 ha under the plough in 1939–40. This led to a rise in food production to around 60 per cent self-sufficiency by the end of the war (Adams, 1986; Foreman, 1989).

Postwar agricultural policy was set out in a statement to Parliament in November 1940. It stated that the government recognised the importance of maintaining a healthy and well-balanced agriculture as an essential and permanent feature of national policy. The guarantee was given to secure and maintain production stability, not only during hostilities but also for a sufficient length of time thereafter to put into action a permanent postwar policy for home agriculture (Hansard, 26 November 1940).

This led to a forty-year policy of significant financial incentive and support for agricultural production. Self-sufficiency in indigenous food production rose from its postwar level to a high of around 87 per cent in 1991, since when it has fallen to around 72 per cent (Bowers, 1985; Spedding, 2007; Defra, 2007a). Most of today's farmers have grown up on farms and managed the land in accordance with what was seen as a highly successful and culturally embedded policy.

Agriculture in the uplands was far more suited to livestock production than to arable. This potential was recognised and led to the 1946 Hill Farming Act. The Act made provision for grants at a rate of 50 per cent for the rehabilitation and improvement of 'hill farming land' (including common land), defined as 'Mountain, hill and heath land which is suitable for use for the maintenance of sheep of a hardy kind'. These improvements included applications of lime, basic slag and fertilisers, and land drainage. On open moorland this involved the digging of open channels, known as grips, to increase the area and condition of heather for the benefit of both sheep and red grouse. The Act also made provision for subsidies for hill sheep and hill cattle, and for the regulation of heather and grass burning in England and Wales.

This was the first time that upland agriculture had been singled out for specific policies. It allowed for production incentives to be higher than elsewhere. Upland farmers also benefited from the 1947 Agriculture Act. This maintained the price guarantees established during the war and made provision for their annual review. Both these Acts and all subsequent farming Acts also required that eligibility for support depended upon farmers

Table 4.1 Milestones in UK and European policy affecting upland agriculture. Milestones for conservation in italics; more and more integrated policies for environment and agriculture in the twenty-first century.

Year	Milestone	Objectives for UK uplands
1919	Ministry of Agriculture and Fisheries (MAF) established	Farming recognised as an industry. Guaranteed prices for some agricultural commodities.
1940	Parliamentary statement on future Government support for farming	Long term security and agricultural production stability. Subsidies for agricultural land improvement and intensification.
1946	Hill Farming Act	Grants for rehabilitation and improvement of 'hill farming land' and subsidy payments on livestock.
		National Agricultural Advisory Service established.
1947	Agriculture Act	Provision of guaranteed prices and assured markets. Grants for improvement of land and infrastructure.
1949	*National Parks and Access to the Countryside Act*	*Opens way for designation of National Parks, National Nature Reserves, Areas of Outstanding Natural Beauty and Sites of Special Scientific Interest (SSSI). Nature Conservancy Council (NCC) formed.*
1951	*First National Park designated*	*Peak District becomes first of 10 National Parks, all in the uplands, designated in the coming decade.*
1951	*Forestry Act*	*Forestry Commission empowered to provide amenity.*
1968	*Countryside Act*	*Countryside Commission (CC) established to encourage access and recreation in the countryside as a whole. MAFF required to advise farmers on conservation and enhancement of the natural beauty and amenity of countryside. Management agreements between NCC and SSSI owners/tenants possible.*
1972	UK joins European Economic Community (EEC)	Intervention purchasing under the CAP. EEC livestock headage payments.

Year	Scheme / Legislation	Description
1975	EC Directive 75/268 (LFA)	Introduction of Less Favoured Areas (LFA) and UK Hill Livestock Compensatory Allowance scheme (HLCA) to support the continuation of (hill) farming, maintain minimum populations and to conserve the countryside.
	White Paper, *Food from our own resources*	Continued expansion of agricultural production by an annual target of 2.5%.
1981	Wildlife and Countryside Act	*Increased legal protection of SSSIs including owners required to notify NCC of potential damaging operations.*
1985	Agricultural Improvement scheme	Continued support for agricultural land improvement and farm infrastructure. Higher grants paid in the LFA.
1986	Agriculture Act	*MAFF required to balance efficient food production with socio-economic, environmental and public enjoyment of the countryside. Enables the introduction of ESAs.*
1987	Agri-environment schemes	*First pilot Environmentally Sensitive Area schemes launched.*
1990	LFA expansion	UK LFA expanded and divided into Severely Disadvantaged (SDA) and Disadvantaged land (DA).
	Environment Protection Act	NCC and CC nationally regionalised. In England NCC becomes English Nature. Joint Nature Conservation Committee becomes UK nature conservation coordinating body.
1991	Pilot Countryside Stewardship scheme	*Agri-environment scheme available throughout England.*
1992	EEC signs the Convention on Biological Diversity. EC Habitats Directive	*Protection for threatened habitats and species of European importance leading to designation of Natura 2000 (SPA & SAC) sites.*
	Environmental cross compliance	*Prevention of environmental damage from UK-funded livestock subsidies.*
	McSharry CAP reform	Introduction of obligatory agri-environment schemes for EU member state and CAP moves away from output-based subsidies.

Table 4.1 (cont'd)

Year	Milestone	Objectives for UK uplands
1993	Wildlife Enhancement Scheme launched (WES)	Enhancement of SSSIs where agri-environment schemes unavailable or unsuitable.
1994	EC Environmental cross compliance	Applied to EU livestock headage payments. 1993/94 Major expansion of ESAs.
	Signing of the GATT Uruguay Round	Reduction in agricultural production subsidies.
1996	Moorland scheme	Reduction of sheep numbers on heather moorland.
		Countryside Stewardship scheme expanded.
1997	Cork Declaration	Start of EU integrated, sustainable rural development policy funded from the CAP.
1999	Countryside Agency (CA)	CA formed from the CC and Rural Development Commission to improve the quality of the rural environment and the lives of those living in it.
2000	Agenda 2000 CAP reform	Creation of a second support pillar of the CAP designed to fund non-market objectives such as rural, social and environmental support for sustainable development.
	Countryside and Rights of Way Act (CROW)	Open access to mountain, moor, heathland and common land.
	Water Framework Directive	Requirement for all inland and coastal waters to reach 'good status' by 2015.
	Task Force for the Hills	Development of sustainable upland farming.
2001	Hill Farm Allowance	First decoupled subsidy payment, replacing HLCA.
	Foot and Mouth Disease outbreak	Most upland areas loose a high proportion of livestock. Leads to fundamental review of agricultural and countryside policies.
	Department for the Environment, Food and Rural Affairs	Emphasis switched from food production to food safety and protection of the environment.

	Rural Task Force	Farmers recognised as managers of the rural landscape and all that it provides for the public, not only in food but also amenity.
	Policy commission on the future of farming and food	An end to government policy of subsidising food production. Instead, farmers to be rewarded for good environmental management.
	UK introduces voluntary modulation	*2.5% of EU subsidy payments used to fund Rural Development Programme including a new suite of rural development schemes.*
2002	*National sheep envelopes*	*Proportion of livestock subsidy payments used for encouraging sustainable grazing.*
2003	*CAP reform*	*Decoupling of EU subsidy payments. EU livestock headage payments to cease.*
	Pilot ELS launched	*Broad and shallow agri-environment scheme accessible to all farmers.*
2005	*Decoupled subsidy payments commence*	*Removal of incentives for high livestock numbers in the Single Payment Scheme, including Good Environmental and Agricultural Condition (GAEC) cross compliance. Compulsory and voluntary modulation to fund rural development, principally agri-environment.*
	New agri-environment schemes	*Entry and Higher level Environmental Stewardship Scheme launched with specific upland objectives and options.*
	Millennium Ecosystem Assessment	
2006	Commons Act	Enables establishment of commons councils with statutory powers.
	Natural Environment and Rural Communities Act	*English agencies for conservation, access and recreation and rural development, join into one integrated agency, Natural England.*
2007	*Rural development programme for England (RDPE)*	*84% of RDPE funds for environmental outcomes using up to 14% voluntary modulation. HFA to be replaced by a new Upland ELS by 2010.*
	Natural Environment Public Service Agreement (PSA)	*Defra adopts Ecosystems services approach as framework for decision making to secure a healthy natural environment now and for future generations.*

maintaining 'good levels of estate management and husbandry'. The concept of cross-compliance is not new. Only, then the emphasis was on good agricultural stewardship.

The uplands were also targeted for a massive expansion in woodland production started in 1919 with the creation of the Forestry Commission. Its principal objective was to create a strategic reserve of timber as a matter of national security to replace timber stocks that were heavily depleted after the First World War. In this, it was highly successful, and in the following eighty years over 1.5 million hectares of new planted forests had been created – the biggest single change in land use in the United Kingdom in modern times (Rollinson, 2003).

The period between the early 1940s and the 1980s was one of government supported agricultural improvement of upland grasslands and moorlands. Successive Hill Farming and Agriculture Acts renewed and expanded various grant schemes and livestock subsidies to hill farmers.

Financial incentives for farm production were boosted by the UK's entry into the European Economic Community (EEC) in 1972. The method of commodity support changed from guaranteed prices to intervention purchasing under the Common Agricultural policy (CAP). Additionally, the UK maintained many of its own production incentives, coupled with grants for land and infrastructure improvements. The government White Paper *Food from Our Own Resources*, published in 1975, confirmed government policy of expanding agricultural production by an annual target of 2.5 per cent (MAFF, 1975).

Grants, subsidies and government-funded agricultural research, development and extension services had the desired effect on production. For the uplands, this meant large increases in livestock numbers, particularly sheep, and improvements in animal breeds, health, birth rates and meat quality. It is difficult to extract early agricultural census data solely for upland areas, but county data between 1950 and 2005 for Derbyshire and Devon illustrate changes in the livestock population, and show similar trends (Figure 4.1a, b). The boundaries of both counties have changed little since the nineteenth century, and both have significant areas of upland (Defra, 2007b).

Sheep numbers rose steadily (Anderson and Yalden, 1981) and then dramatically from 1980 with the launch of the EEC's sheepmeat regime aimed at addressing a shortfall in mainland Europe. The moorland areas of the UK, and of England and Wales in particular, saw the highest rise in numbers as in-bye was improved and cross-bred ewes were produced for sale to lowland farms.

Less Favoured Area (LFA) support

When the UK joined the EEC it wanted to maintain its special support systems for hill farming. However, farms in upland areas did not always fulfil the eligibility criteria for existing EEC schemes aimed at improving

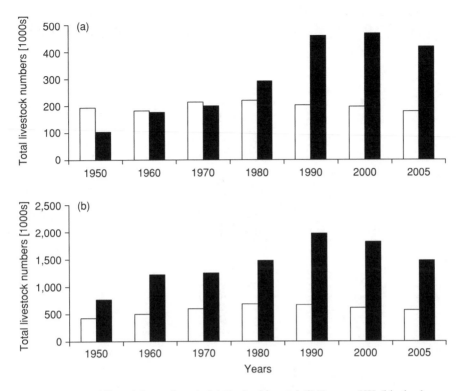

Figure 4.1 Total livestock numbers in (*a*) Derbyshire and (*b*) Devon, UK (black: sheep; white: cattle; source data: Defra, June Agricultural Census).

agricultural structures. As part of the accession process, the UK pressed for an additional support mechanism for hill farming systems. This concept was accepted and led, in 1975, to Directive 75/268 establishing a framework for support of 'mountain and hill farming in certain less favoured areas'. The aim was 'to support the continuation of farming to maintain a minimum popu-lation and to conserve the countryside' (EEC, 1975).

This was welcomed, and in 1984 work started on designating the LFA. Essentially, this involved expanding the upland area delineated in the mid-1960s that was used to define eligibility for hill farm grants and subsidies. For the UK, this resulted in 8.4 million ha of land being designated – about 45 per cent of the utilisable agricultural area (UAA). The majority of this is in Scotland and Wales. England has 2 million ha – just over 17 per cent of the UAA. The LFA was divided into two areas: Disadvantaged Area (DA) and Severely Disadvantaged Area (SDA), the latter corresponding to the exist-ing hill farming area (Figure 4.2). Higher rates of support were given to the farms in the SDA, which comprises 74 per cent of the LFA.

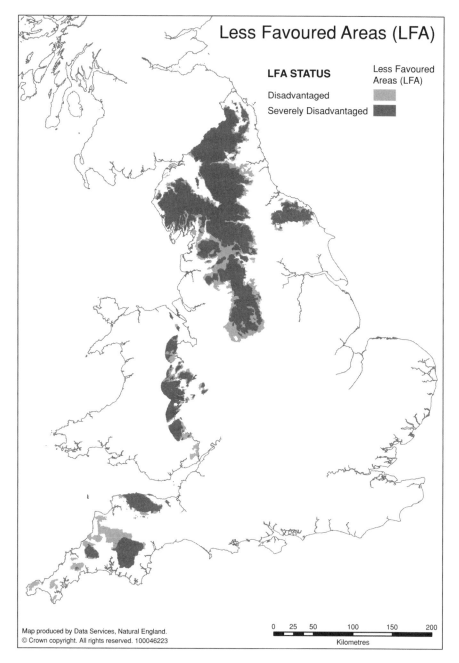

Figure 4.2 Spatial coverage of Less Favoured Areas (LFA) in England. © Crown copyright. All rights reserved Defra. Licence number 100018880 [2007].

Environment

It was not only agriculture that was changing in the countryside after the Second World War. There was recognition that areas of the countryside should be protected and made more accessible to the general public, and urban development controlled. Limited progress was made up to the outbreak of war owing to the strong landowning interests in and around government.

The end of the Second World War and the demand for a 'better Britain' made the development of national parks and open-access arrangements politically possible. The National Parks and Access to the Countryside Act was passed in 1947. This provided the framework for the creation of National Parks and Areas of Outstanding Natural Beauty in England and Wales, and formalised Public Rights of Way (PROW) and some access to open countryside. It also enabled the establishment of the Nature Conservancy, the role of which was to establish National Nature Reserves (NNR) for the protection and management of the most important habitats. The Conservancy was also charged with establishing a network of Sites of Special Scientific Interest (SSSI) on areas of significant interest for their flora, fauna, physiographical or geological features.

Over the next forty years policies for protecting the countryside, its wildlife, landscape, historical and cultural value continued to develop. The 1968 Countryside Act changed the National Parks Commission (set up to designate national parks) to the Countryside Commission with a wider remit, including encouraging recreation in the countryside as a whole. It also gave powers for the Nature Conservancy to enter into management agreements with owners or occupiers of SSSIs. By 1980, there were around 3,000 SSSIs in Great Britain, and the Nature Conservancy had changed to the Nature Conservancy Council (NCC). The Act also required MAFF to give advice to agricultural businesses on the conservation and enhancement of the 'natural beauty and amenity of the countryside'. It should be noted that this responsibility was given neither to the Countryside Commission nor to the NCC. For the next thirty-three years (1968–2001), responsibility for nature and landscape conservation would rest with the then Department of the Environment (DoE) and its agencies, whilst the land on which delivery of these responsibilities depended was firmly under the agricultural policies of MAFF. This gave rise to long-running tensions between the two departments, with the DoE having all the environmental responsibilities whilst MAFF had almost exclusive access to the money, tools and farmers on whose land the environmental interests and concerns lay.

1980–90

Agriculture

By the end of the 1980s agricultural production in the LFAs was at its peak. European and UK agricultural policies were achieving their objectives.

Food was plentiful and, in real terms, falling in price. There was a thriving agricultural industry making a significant contribution to rural economies. However, the 1980s proved to be the turning point in UK upland agricultural and environmental policy. They saw the start of a slow but steady U-turn in the way that farmers received support from public money. In 2008 this turn-around is probably still not complete, but farmers are now being asked and encouraged with incentives to do almost the opposite to what they were asked from the mid-1940s to the 1990s.

Environment

By the early 1980s, it was evident that the intensification of agriculture was having a significant and detrimental effect on the wildlife and landscape of the countryside, although in the uplands the changes were slower and not as readily evident.

The Wildlife and Countryside Act of 1981 was designed to help address these issues. It increased the legal protection of SSSIs, requiring owners or occupiers to notify the NCC of any intended actions that were likely to damage the site. Such actions could include operations to intensify agricultural production such as land drainage or applications of inorganic fertiliser. The Act also required National Park authorities to map all areas of mountain, moor and heath. Woodland and coastal features were added in 1985. These areas then became ineligible for agricultural improvement grants.

The CAP was now the significant driver for agricultural production, providing guaranteed prices and funding for infrastructure. This could not be changed easily. What could be changed were the UK-funded support mechanisms. One way to do this was to provide payments to compensate farmers willing to forgo production support payments and farm in a less intensive manner – a system that was tested in a pilot scheme jointly funded by MAFF and the Countryside Commission in Norfolk in 1985. This approach was embedded in the 1986 Agriculture Act by enabling the introduction of the Environmentally Sensitive Area agri-environment scheme. The Act also required efficient food production to be balanced with the socio-economic, environmental and public enjoyment interests of the countryside.

Environmentally Sensitive Areas (ESA)

The designation criteria for ESAs are set out in section 18 of the 1986 Agriculture Act. They could be designated where it was particularly desirable

a)   to conserve and enhance the natural beauty of an area;
b)   flora or fauna, or geological or physiographical features of an area; or
c)   to protect buildings and other objects of archaeological, architectural or historic interest, where the maintenance or adoption of particular agricultural methods was likely to facilitate such conservation.

The logic for MAFF to run this scheme rather than the DoE was the fact that its success relied on adopting particular agricultural methods thought to be best-understood by the Ministry. It would be true to say that not all in the DoE, the NCC and the Countryside Commission agreed with this decision.

MAFF launched five pilot ESAs in 1987. In consultation with the NCC and the Countryside Commission, these areas were designated because their environmental interest was particularly under threat from intensification of agriculture. Two of these ESAs were in the uplands.

At first, farmer interest in the ESA schemes was limited. The concept was so different from other MAFF grant schemes. It was only with individual farm visits by MAFF advisory staff that farmers started to understand what was being asked of them. Uptake of the schemes grew, and by the end of the third year averaged around 60 per cent of the eligible areas. Greater uptake was recorded in the LFAs than on the lowland arable schemes. In 1988 a further five ESA pilots were launched, one of which was in the uplands. This was the North Peak in the Peak District designated primarily to halt the loss of heather moorland.

In a further reflection of the impact of increased environmental awareness, MAFF replaced the Agricultural Improvement Scheme with the Farm and Conservation Grant scheme (F&CGS). This switched capital payments towards conservation works such as hedgerow-planting, reinstatement of traditional farm buildings, and farm waste storage and disposal facilities. Free advice on agricultural production was stopped, but was still available for conservation and pollution control.

1990–2000: the pendulum swings

In 1990 the responsibilities of the Countryside Commission and the NCC were split into the three territories of Great Britain. In England the Rural Development and Countryside Commissions combined to form the Countryside Agency, and English Nature became the country's nature conservation agency.

The message that some farmers were damaging parts of the countryside was growing. The decade saw the turnaround in rural policy from an emphasis on agricultural production to environmental protection and enhancement.

It was a decade of confusion. Upland farmers were now being accused of destroying the countryside, even though the production subsidies on which most upland farmers were becoming more and more reliant continued. Unsurprisingly, most upland farmers argued to the contrary: that it was they who valued and understood the countryside the most. They became deeply suspicious of English Nature and the Countryside Agency. MAFF, still very defensive of the farming industry, was beginning to understand that further changes had to be made and policy drivers changed. It also understood that, contrary to the views of some of the conservation bodies, these could not happen overnight without significant damage to rural livelihoods. Also, because of the influence of the CAP, national changes would have limited impact. However, MAFF started setting down markers, and the UK's example and influence on changing the direction of the CAP would be significant.

Hill Livestock Compensatory Allowance (HLCA) greening

In 1990 the NCC reported that, of the estimated 4,571 km^2 of heather moorland recorded in 1940, 812 km^2 had changed to upland grasses, 50 km^2 to improved grassland and crops, and 180 km^2 to forest plantation. There was concern that increased sheep numbers were grazing out the heather, aided in places by government grants for liming and fertilising. It was also assumed that the introduction of the EEC sheepmeat regime was accelerating the loss of heather as sheep numbers continued to rise, primarily in the uplands (Felton and Marsden, 1990).

Mindful of this report, MAFF explored ways of discouraging high sheep and cattle numbers by manipulating the government-funded Hill Livestock Compensatory Allowance scheme. This was the Ministry's first attempt at directly manipulating support systems to minimise environmental impact. Unfortunately, agreement could not be reached with other UK agricultural departments, so no scheme was launched. However, agreement was reached to introduce environmental cross-compliance on the scheme.

Overgrazing cross-compliance

Introduced in 1992, overgrazing cross-compliance on the HCLA is believed to be the first example in the EEC of manipulating a subsidy payment system to address its potential negative environmental effects. It was deeply unpopular with the upland farming community, and led to confusion and uncertainty about MAFF policy. The Ministry was now threatening to reduce subsidy if animals were destroying the semi-natural vegetation, particularly on moorland where, five years previously, financial incentives where available to convert it to grassland.

One problem was that the HLCA payments were not high enough in comparison with the EEC headage payments. In one case, a large cattle enterprise that was causing overgrazing simply ceased claiming HLCA payments. It was more economic for the business to forgo the payments than to reduce cattle numbers and income from the main ECC subsidy schemes. This ploy was short-lived as, in 1994, the European Commission (EC) applied environmental cross-compliance to its headage-based payments. Farmers began to realise that public money to support agriculture would not be given if it resulted in damage to the environment.

Pressure from cross-compliance proved to be a valuable incentive for entering moorland into ESA agreements. Over the next fifteen years, over 175,000 ha of moorland entered into ESA agreement (Condliffe, 2006).

McSharry CAP reforms

Agricultural overproduction in Europe, and its environmental, economic and social unsustainability, was recognised in the 1992 CAP reforms. Known as the McSharry reforms, after the EU Agricultural Commissioner at the time, they marked the start of the greening of the CAP. Support was moved from output-based subsidies, such as guaranteed prices, to direct payments. The problem of past increases in sheep numbers was recognised, and a quota was imposed on the number of ewes eligible for subsidy. This quota was ring-fenced by UK regions, with the LFA as one of these. The very fact that the quota was a tradable item showed that farmers were still trying to increase sheep numbers. Income from livestock subsidy payments in some years accounted for the only profit made by hill farmers. For many, the number of sheep eligible for subsidy was more important than the quality of the product.

The McSharry reforms also saw the introduction of obligatory agri-environment schemes for EU member states. This was the first time that CAP payments were specifically directed at the environment. UK agri-environmental policy had a significant influence on EU policy where the main driver for these types of payment was, and still is, considered to be environmental. The McSharry reforms were in no small measure based on the lead of the UK with its ESA experiment. The development of UK agri-environment policy was driven originally by internal environmental pressures rather than by external environmental or trade interests. However, in making the schemes compulsory under the McSharry reforms, the attraction of using them as a mechanism for supporting farmers was not overlooked (P. Murphy, Under-secretary, MAFF, 1986–96; J. Robbs, Director, Wildlife and Countryside Directorate, Defra, personal communication, 2008).

EC regulations, governed by 'Green Box' rules, limit agri-environment schemes payments to the equivalent of the income forgone in complying with the agreement and for capital grants solely for environmental benefit. No incentive payments are allowed.

General Agreement on Tariffs and Trade (GATT)

A seven-and-a-half-year negotiation on the GATT commenced in 1986. Known as the Uruguay round, it covered many aspects of world trade, particularly agriculture, banking, insurance, and intellectual property rights. It also led to the establishment of the World Trade Organisation (WTO). The round ended with the signing of a new agreement in 1994, leading to a reduction in agricultural production subsidies. Agriculture payments not linked to production such as agri-environment schemes were, and still are, exempted. They are part of what is known as the 'Green Box' payments. Such schemes pre-date the signing of the Uruguay round by ten years, as outlined in the previous paragraphs.

The growth of agri-environment schemes: launch of the Countryside Stewardship scheme and development of ESAs

The success of ESA schemes led to the demand for a similar scheme to be available across the country, not just in designated areas. In 1991 the Countryside Commission launched the pilot Countryside Stewardship Scheme (CS). Unlike the ESA scheme, it was open to all landowners and managers, not just farmers, and there was no automatic right of entry. The emphasis was on environmental enhancement, not maintenance, with the additional objective of providing public access to land. The application process was competitive and judged on the amount of environment benefit being offered. There was a wide range of management options; and, unlike most ESA schemes, it did not take a whole farm approach. Land managers could choose what land to put into agreement. The scheme proved to be very popular and, in 1996, was revised and moved to MAFF's administration as a fully approved agri-environment scheme eligible for partial EU funding reimbursement. The scheme, however, met with limited success on upland moorlands owing to a narrow range of options. This problem was rectified by further revision in 1999, which gave a wider range of options and a welcome opportunity for farmers who were faced with overgrazing cross-compliance prescriptions on land outside ESAs. They now had the opportunity to enter their land into an agri-environment scheme. By 2005, over 314,000 ha of moorland were under agreement. Over half of this (166,800 ha) was on 288 upland commons (Condliffe, 2006).

Also during this decade, the ESA schemes expanded in number and scope. Whilst the pilots had concentrated on maintaining environmental features, the revised schemes offered an enhancement tier in which, for additional payment, management prescriptions were aimed at trying to increase environmental interest, especially in terms of biodiversity. In addition, the scheme allowed for Conservation Plans. These were capital grants at percentage rates higher than available under the F&CGS scheme for the enhancement of specific features of conservation interest such as traditional barns, derelict walls and new ponds.

The years 1993–4 saw a major expansion of ESAs with an additional twelve schemes, five in upland areas, including the South West Peak. The principal driver for their designation was to arrest the loss of heather moorland, much of it on common land.

International environmental obligations

In 1992 the Convention on Biodiversity (CBD) was signed, with significant impact on farming and the uplands (see Bonn, Rebane and Reid, this volume). Its objective is to develop national strategies for the conservation and sustainable use of biological diversity. This led to the Habitats Directive of the same year (EEC, 1992). The provisions of the Directive required member states to introduce a range of measures including the protection of named species and habitats of European importance, largely by means of a network of designated sites called Special Areas of Conservation (SACs). Along with Special Protection Areas (SPAs), classified under the earlier EC Birds Directive (79/409/EEC), they form a network of protected areas known as Natura 2000. In the UK, terrestrial Natura 2000 sites have been designated with large spatial overlap with suitable SSSIs, also to enhance their protection under Natura 2000 legislation. Ten years later, almost 17 per cent of the LFA was designated as SAC and 12.4 per cent as Special Protection Areas (SPA), almost all on moorland areas.

Wildlife Enhancement Scheme (WES)

Options and prescriptions in ESA and CS schemes were sometimes not entirely suited to the positive and sometimes specialist management required to enhance some SSSIs. English Nature therefore developed its own environmental scheme, the Wildlife Enhancement Scheme, launched in 1993. This was fully UK-funded and, not being bound by EU payment regulations, proved to be a very flexible tool.

The Moorland scheme

In an effort to reduce livestock numbers on moorland further, Defra launched the Moorland scheme in 1996. Unlike agri-environment schemes, which paid by area, the Moorland scheme was an extensification scheme that paid on a headage basis for each breeding ewe removed not only from the moor but also from the farm enterprise. This was different from the ESA and CS schemes where, although moorland payments were based on removing livestock from the moorland, the farmer did not have to part with the animal, which could be grazed elsewhere as long as it caused no environmental damage. The subsidy payment was therefore retained, making these schemes financially very attractive. With the Moorland scheme, this was not possible, and uptake was very low, with only fifteen agreements nationally compared to the hundreds under the ESA and CS. The failure of the scheme emphasised the fact that most farmers join such schemes mainly for financial advantage.

The Cork Declaration

In 1996 the European Commission had started to consider an integrated rural policy for Europe, using funds saved from changes to support payments in the McSharry reforms. This idea was politicised at a European Rural Development conference in Ireland in the same year. A ten-point rural development programme for Europe to be funded through the CAP was set out and became known as the Cork Declaration. It placed integrated sustainable rural development at the top of the European agenda (EU, 1997).

End of a confusing decade

From a farmer's viewpoint, some of the irony of 1990s agricultural policies can be appreciated. One hand of MAFF was offering payments for encouraging agricultural production, whilst the other was doing the opposite. At the same time, some conservation charities and government agencies were advocating an end to all subsidies and wanting to bring farmers to account on the 'polluter pays' principle. Some sections of government considered that, in times of food surplus, MAFF was being overprotective to the farming industry. MAFF, in its turn, acknowledged this but sought change through incentives and allowing time for the industry to adapt to the changes that were becoming inevitable. It was argued that too strong a regulatory approach could become counterproductive, difficult and expensive to enforce.

2000–7

Agriculture

Agenda 2000

The proposals in the Cork Declaration were to form the basis of the 2000 review of the CAP. Known as Agenda 2000, this review marked a radical shift in European agricultural policy, which was welcomed by the UK government. The review created a second support pillar of the CAP designed to fund non-market objectives such as rural, social and environmental support for sustainable development. Although very modest in comparison to the support for markets and direct payments, known as Pillar 1, this second pillar marked the beginning of increased emphasis on sustainability, putting more funds into agri-environment and encouraging land-based rural business enterprises.

Additionally, member states were allowed to modulate payments. That is, transfer up to 20 per cent of their Pillar 1 payments across to Pillar 2 on condition that the modulated funds were 'match funded' by the member state. The UK was the only country that chose to do this and instigated a modulation rate of 2.5 per cent in 2001–2 rising to 4.6 per cent by 2006. These additional funds were used specifically for the agri-environment schemes, which, with a number of other schemes, were encompassed in the EU Rural Development Regulation (EU, 1999).

Rural Development Regulation (RDR)

This regulation required each member state to draw up a seven-year Rural Development Programme (RDP). This outlined the types of measure to be used, their expected impact, financial plans, and how they would be implemented. Only agri-environment was compulsory. Other schemes included supporting rural enterprises, vocational training and woodland planting. Anyone joining a land-based scheme also had to comply with standards of Good Farming Practice. These were basic verifiable standards of environmental care that should be expected from a 'reasonable' standard of farm management. Welcome as these reforms were, the UK government considered that they had not gone far enough in redirecting Pillar 1 payments and moving support into rural development.

There was disquiet from the farming community that part of their production subsidy payments were moved to the RDP with no guarantee of access to the money in the RDR schemes. They were thus receiving lower Pillar 1 payments than their contemporaries in mainland Europe.

The Hill Farm Allowance (HFA)

Agenda 2000 saw the LFA objectives reframed. These were 'to ensure continued agricultural land use and, thereby, to contribute to the maintenance of the countryside, and maintenance of a viable rural community and promotion of environmentally sustainable farming systems' (Articles 18, 19, 20 EC 1257/1999). LFA payments were no longer considered a production subsidy, and the scheme was moved into the RDR.

Consequently, in 2001, the HLCA was replaced with an area-based payment scheme called the Hill Farm Allowance (HFA). The scheme included supplementary payments for more environmentally based practices, such as lower stocking densities and organic certification. Although the majority of financial support still came from the direct EU headage payments, MAFF was sending a clear message to the farming community that it wished to see a de-coupling of support from production.

Task Force for the Hills

By the late 1990s, hill farming production systems were in financial crisis, with many farms unable to survive without significant support payments. Recognising this, in late 2000, MAFF commissioned a Task Force for the Hills to look at ways that government could help English hill farmers develop sustainable business enterprises that could contribute to the rural economy and environment. The Task Force reported in March 2001, soon after the outbreak of foot-and-mouth disease. This rather overshadowed the report's findings, but its recommendations proved valuable to the Rural Task Force and the Policy Commission on the Future of Farming and Food that were to be commissioned as a result of the foot-and-mouth disease outbreak.

The Task Force's report made sixty-three recommendations. The thrust of these was centred on helping to ease and increase farmer access to rural development funds and to promote access to integrated business and environmental advice (MAFF, 2001).

Foot-and-mouth disease

The outbreak of foot-and-mouth disease had a devastating effect on upland livestock farming and the rural economy. The disease was first reported in February 2001, and the last case reported seven months later. During this period, 9,515 farms in Britain had their livestock compulsorily slaughtered, including 2,026 where the disease had been diagnosed. This resulted in the loss of over half a million cattle, 3.4 million sheep and 145,000 pigs. The majority of cases lay within the LFA of England, Wales and southern Scotland. Livestock movement restrictions meant that a further 170,000 cattle, 1.5 million sheep and 290,000 pigs were also slaughtered for welfare reasons (Defra/DCMS, 2002).

Large areas of the uplands were closed to public access for up to seven months. This had a severe effect on the rural economy, especially on the tourist industry. It was estimated that 40 per cent of businesses were adversely affected in Cumbria, Devon and Cornwall, and that between March and October 2001 the revenue loss to the English tourist industry exceeded £3 billion (Defra, 2001; Curry, this volume).

Rural Task Force

During the disease outbreak, MAFF set up a Rural Task Force, led by Lord Haskins, to advise on how to tackle the impact of foot-and-mouth disease on the rural economy (Defra, 2001). One of the key findings was that;

> Farming and tourism are interdependent and intertwined with the wider rural economy. Farmers have a vital role in the life of the nation as providers of food and managers of the rural landscape. Future policies for farming must take into account the links with the wider rural economy in a way they have not done in the past.

Up until then, the role of farmers as managers of the rural landscape had not been widely appreciated. This is no more evident than in the LFAs, which attract the majority of visitors to the inshore countryside. In 2002 the estimated income from tourism in the Lake District National Park was £528 million (Cartwright, 2003). The estimated annual public spend to farmers in subsidy and agri-environment payments was £70 million (M. E. Edwards, Natural England, personal communication). Farmers argue that public money given to support them shows a high return for both public enjoyment and other rural businesses.

Defra

The re-election of the New Labour government in May 2001 heralded a new era in the governance of agriculture and rural policy. The Department for

the Environment, Food and Rural Affairs (Defra) was created by amalgam-
ating MAFF with parts of the DETR. This new department had, at its core,
food safety, environmental management and public well-being. Support
for agricultural production was a lower priority – a fact reflected in the
absence of agriculture in the department's title.

The Curry Commission

The Rural Task Force concluded that agriculture and food production needed
a thorough review. This was started in August 2001 with the launch of the
Policy Commission on the Future of Farming and Food led by Sir Don Curry.

The Commission report (Cabinet Office, 2002) acknowledged the work of
the Task Force for the Hills and, in principle, supported the main thrust behind
the long-term policy measures with 105 recommendations, ranging widely
over the farming and food production sectors. Concerning agriculture and
the environment, it recommended that farmers should be rewarded for
looking after their land and for providing an attractive countryside. This should
be achieved by increasing funds for agri-environment schemes through further modulation of Pillar 1 payments. Existing agri-environment schemes
should be merged to become the upper tiers of a new single stewardship scheme;
and a new, broad and shallow 'entry level' stewardship tier should be introduced, open to as many farms as possible.

Defra published its response to the Commission's report and launched
its strategy for the future of agriculture and food production later in the
year (Defra/DCMS, 2002; Defra, 2002a, b) in broad agreement with the
Commission recommendations. The government policy of subsidising food
production was officially brought to an end. The strategy seeks to 'recon-
nect the food chain to its customers'. It recognises that farming has a unique
part to play in preserving and enhancing the countryside, whilst acknowledging the evidence of environmental damage from past agricultural practices. It seeks to reward farmers for good environmental management and
encourage market-led, good quality assured food production.

One of the first initiatives was the development of a pilot Entry Level
Stewardship scheme (ELS). Soon after, work started on the development of
a Higher Level Stewardship scheme (HLS) that would eventually replace the
ESA and CS schemes. Also, for the first time, a small policy unit was created in Defra to address upland issues. Its remit was to review the HFA scheme
and the implementation of the overgrazing cross-compliance policy.

Environment

Common land reform

Over 55 per cent of common land is SSSI, the majority of which (304,000 ha,
83 per cent) lies within the LFA. The government had given a commitment

in the 2000 Rural White Paper to provide for the protection of commons, to increase its ability to tackle overgrazing and to provide fairer and more effective systems of registration and management (MAFF, 2000; Defra, 2002c). This was followed in 2002 by a Common Land Policy Statement, which included proposals on how the above commitment could be implemented (Defra, 2002c).

One of the main problems regarding agricultural management was that remedial measures to address overgrazing and applications to join agri-environment schemes were sometimes being blocked by a minority of commoners against the wishes of the majority. One of the government's proposals was to allow the voluntary establishment of commons councils with statutory powers. If the majority of rights holders wanted to change the grazing management on the common, all rights holders would have to comply. Any who refused could be subject to legally binding penalties imposed by the commons council. This and other reforms, such as prohibiting the severance of common rights, streamlining consents and updating commons registers, were subject to public consultation. After a positive response, proposed reforms were included in the Commons Act, which received Royal Assent in 2006.

Public Service Agreement targets

Another factor for Defra in encouraging improved environmental management in the uplands was one of its ten Public Service Agreement (PSA) targets to:

> Care for our natural heritage, make the countryside attractive and enjoyable for all, and preserve biological diversity by . . . bringing into favourable condition for 2010, 95% of all nationally important wildlife sites.
>
> (Defra, 2004)

All government departments have PSA targets set at major spending reviews and for which they can be held to account by Parliament. The biodiversity element of this became, and still is, a very significant driver in agri-environmental policy, especially for SSSIs. English Nature bore the main responsibility for delivering this target, although most of the tools available rested within the agri-environment schemes administered by Defra.

Following the foresight of the UN Millennium Ecosystem Assessment (MA, 2005), which recognises the wider importance of resilient ecosystems in providing vital ecosystem services for society, the UK government has adopted the Ecosystem Approach (see Bonn, Rebane and Reid, this volume). Its importance is reflected in the new cross-government PSA target announced in 2007 to 'secure a healthy natural environment for today and the future' (Defra, 2007c). This integrative framework will hopefully further stimulate sustainable management within acceptable environmental limits.

*Sheep National Envelope, Quota Purchase and Sheep Wildlife
Enhancement Scheme*

In 2002, Defra implemented the 'national envelope' provision in the EU
Sheepmeat Regulation (2529/2001). National sheep and beef envelopes were
a form of voluntary modulation of headage payments. Funds released had
to be used to provide extra support to producers, improve the marketing and
production of sheepmeat/beef or encourage more environmentally friendly
farming practices.

In the first year, the money was used to fund a sheep quota purchase scheme
designed to reduce sheep numbers on areas that had been historically over-
grazed. For the following two years, some of the money was used to promote the marketing of sheep meat, but £2–3 million annually was allocated
to English Nature for a Sheep Wildlife Enhancement Scheme. The five-year
agreements usually involved significant reduction of sheep numbers on SSSI
moorland and support for shepherding flocks to encourage even grazing across
a moorland.

2003 CAP reform

In June 2003 the CAP underwent one of its regular reviews. The outcome
was unexpected and dramatic. Farm ministers agreed that, from 2005, the
majority of farm subsidies should be 'de-coupled' from production. That is,
they would be paid partially or wholly independently of the volume or area
of production. In return, farmers would have to follow a set of environmental,
food safety and animal welfare cross-compliance standards. Additionally, there
would be compulsory modulation (5 per cent) of Pillar 1 payments into Pillar
2, with the option for voluntary modulation if member states wished. The
future emphasis of the CAP would be on strengthening rural development
policies and funding measures to promote environmental protection, food
quality and animal welfare (EU, 2003; USDA, 2004).

The UK implemented these changes in 2005. England implemented a flat
rate payment system (Single Payment Scheme, SPS). To limit the potentially
large redistribution of payments, generally from intensive to extensive farm
enterprises, payments vary according to the land's agricultural production
potential. Moorland receives the lowest payment, and non-LFA the most
per hectare. To give farmers time to adjust, the payment is being switched
from historic to flat rate over an eight-year period. Scotland, Wales and
Northern Ireland opted for a system based on the historic payments to individual farms.

Switching to the SPS is likely to have a significant effect on English agriculture, farm incomes and the environment. Agricultural production is not
compulsory. Claimants need only follow cross-compliance, including maintaining the land in 'good agricultural and environmental condition' (GEAC)
and ensuring that it is available for agriculture.

Agri-environment strategy

The de-coupling of support payments enabled the government, for the first time, to develop a rural environmental strategy that did not clash directly with parts of its agricultural production strategy. For the past eighteen years, environmental payments to farmers had largely been based on discouraging farming practices encouraged by production subsidies. The new strategy, developed in 2004–5, confirmed that payments to farmers should only be made in return for the supply of ecosystems services (see introductory chapter Bonn *et al.*, this volume). These can be defined as the environmental assets for which there is public demand. They range from clean air and water to food and fibre, countryside access, and landscapes that evoke a sense of well-being.

The strategy can be summarised in what has become known as the 'Defra pyramid' (Figure 4.3).

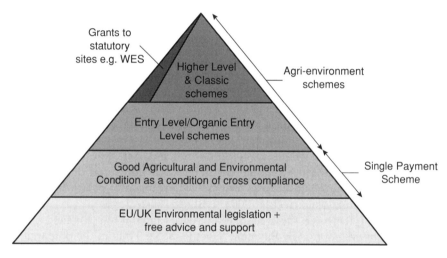

Figure 4.3 Diagram of Defra's agri-environment strategy. At its widest, statutory legislation on environmental protection applies to all, there is no payment, but some free advice. Above this is the Single Payment Scheme (SPS), available to most land managers, the receipt of which is dependent on adherence to cross-compliance 'good agricultural and environmental condition' (GEAC) standards. Additional payments are available for Entry Level Scheme (ELS) designed to deliver ecosystem services at a maintenance and low-enhancement level. At the highest level is the carefully targeted Higher Level Scheme (HLS) and remaining Classic schemes (CSS, ESA) designed to deliver 'quality' ecosystem services. These often demand very specific land management practices for which payments can be high. Alongside these are carefully targeted non-agri-environment schemes such as the Wildlife Enhancement Scheme (WES).

Environmental Stewardship

Defra's flagship Environmental Stewardship Scheme (ESS) was launched in January 2005. There are two broad and shallow schemes, the Entry Level scheme (ELS) and Organic Entry Level scheme (OELS). The OELS has additional management prescriptions to ELS, and payments are double in recognition of the additional environmental benefits of organic production. The aim of both is to encourage a large number of farmers across a wide area of farmland to deliver simple yet effective environmental management. The narrower and deeper Higher Level Scheme (HLS) focuses on achieving significant environmental enhancement in targeted high-priority situations and areas. As well as options that are applicable everywhere, there are options specifically for the upland environment.

The scheme is intended to build on the recognised success of the Environmental Sensitive Areas scheme and the Countryside Stewardship scheme. An additional primary objective of natural resource protection has been added together with two secondary objectives of genetic conservation and flood protection.

Agri-environment uptake

In the LFA, uptake of agri-environment schemes remains high. Table 4.2 compares agri-environment scheme uptake on LFA and non-LFA land.

Emerging policy

2007–13 Rural Development Regulation

The Rural Development Regulation of the reformed CAP introduces three priority axes:

(1) improving the competitiveness of the agricultural and forestry sector;
(2) land management (including animal welfare);
(3) diversification of the rural economy and improving the quality of life in rural areas.

Defra has made axis 2, land management through agri-environment schemes, its priority.

The 2007–13 Rural Development Programme for England (RDPE) is ambitious. Total funding over the life of the programme is £3.9 billion, which is more than double that of the previous programme. This is only possible by continuing and increasing the rate of voluntary modulation, which will rise to 14 per cent by 2009.

The ESS will receive 80 per cent of the voluntary modulation funding, which will also benefit from 40 per cent national match funding. In total, 84 per

Table 4.2 Comparison of recent uptake of agri-environment schemes in Less Favoured Areas (LFA) and non-LFA in England. Uptake of the Classic schemes (ESA, CSS) is significantly higher in the LFA, although those with agreements usually cannot enter Environmental Stewardship schemes (ESS: ELS, HLS) at present. As uptake figures for Classic schemes are a year older than for ESS, some Classic scheme agreements will have ended and may have gone into either ELS or HLS. It is recognised that a significant proportion of farmland in the Classic schemes has not been entered, or accepted into the HLS (Natural England, personal communication) WES uptake is shown separately. It is not strictly an agri-environment scheme; but, more importantly, agreements often occur on the same land as Classic scheme agreements, so there is a significant element of double counting.

Scheme		LFA (UAA = 1.8 million ha)			Non-LFA (UAA = 7.8 million ha)		
		No. agrmts	Uptake ha	area uptake	No. agrmts	Uptake ha	% area uptake
Classic	ESA*	5,112	417,500	23%	5,019	210,453	3%
	CSS*	2,871	235,678	13%	11,461	286,767	4%
ESS	ELS**	8,130	562,100	31%	44,491	4,982,532	64%
	HLS**	1,252	15,540	1%	3,384	440,122	6%
Total		**17,365**	**1,230,818**	**68%**	**64,355**	**5,919,874**	**75%**
	WES	837	403,900	22%	1,173	51,762	1%

(* Uptake, May 2006 ** Uptake, May 2007, source: Natural England, pers. comm.)

cent of programme funds are allocated to axis 2 for achieving environmental outcomes. The other axes receive £277 million each. Spread over six years, these budgets are comparatively low and reflect the government's environmental priorities (Defra, 2007d).

Water Framework Directive

Allied to agri-environment policy is the requirement to comply with the EU Water Framework Directive (EU, 2000). Adopted in 2000, this is the most substantial piece of water legislation to date. It requires all inland and coastal waters to reach 'good status' by 2015. Most member states are starting to implement this far-reaching directive. England has started with a Catchment Sensitive Farming pilot programme. This is aimed at improving surface-water quality in targeted, mainly lowland priority catchments by improving agricultural practices and land management. The main mechanism for achieving this is through the ESS, coupled with some modest capital grants. The Water Framework Directive (WFD) is now one of the biggest drivers for proactive upland catchment management and restoration projects, and acts as an important lever for channelling funding towards upland projects by agencies and water companies.

Replacement for the HFA scheme

The HFA scheme is presently under review. It is Defra's intention that the scheme should deliver more tangible environmental benefits. The current proposal is to develop a specific Upland Entry Level Stewardship scheme (UELS). The HFA budget will be combined with the ELS budget for a scheme better-targeted to the upland environment. The socio-economic element recommended by the Task Force for the Hills is not included.

Changing role of the farmer and farming in the uplands: where next?

The last seven years have seen the most significant changes in agricultural policies since the Second World War. Although this started in the mid-1980s, it was not until the 2003 CAP reforms, partly driven by WTO pressures, that EU and UK public spending on agriculture could be set in the direction envisaged by the UK government around ten years previously. Farmers are now recognised as managers for environmental change, but the extent to which they have taken on or wish to take on this mantle is not yet clear. UK policy now dictates that financial support from the public purse will be primarily for ecosystem services. Present levels of CAP funding are unlikely to be maintained beyond 2012, and direct farm payments will continue to fall. It is, however, probable that the balance of payments will continue to swing towards rural development, including the mitigation of the effects of climate change.

The results of the 2005 Farm Business Survey showed that the average LFA farm business would run at a loss without subsidy payments (Figure 4.4).

There is a general acceptance that under the present agricultural and rural development policies the number of upland farmers will continue to decline. There is concern about abandonment of farm land, but little evidence other than for moorland. In the North York Moors National Park, the number of moorland flocks has fallen from 125 in 1998 to 101 in 2005. In a questionnaire survey carried out in 2005, 32 per cent of respondents indicated that they planned to stop keeping moorland flocks within the next five years and 75 per cent in the next ten (R. Pickering, North York Moors National Park Authority, personal communication).

Research carried out by the National Trust points to a 'bleak future' for tenanted upland farms with, in many cases, subsidy payments halved by 2012 and negative net farm incomes (National Trust, 2005). This outlook is not accepted by all (Defra Upland Land Management Advisory Panel meeting, June 2005, personal communication).

Most studies predict significant reductions in cattle numbers in the SDA. Unless prices increase, they are not an economically viable option except for niche markets. What these analyses have difficulty costing, however, is the advantages of a mixed livestock grazing system such as summer/winter

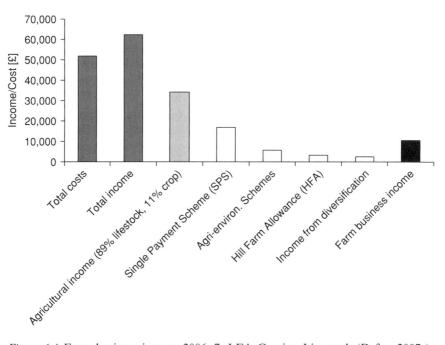

Figure 4.4 Farm business income 2006–7, LFA Grazing Livestock (Defra, 2007e). Livestock production, the main component of agricultural income, accounts for around 49 per cent of total farm income, and farms would make a loss when fixed and variable costs are deducted. Only through additional 'non-producer' sources of income, such as Single Payment Scheme (SPS), agri-environment schemes, Hill Farm Allowance (HFA) and diversification, does the farmer make a profit which averaged £10,545.

labour distribution, parasite disease control and habitat diversity. These may not outweigh the economic disadvantage, and cattle numbers may well fall. This is likely to have a detrimental effect on grassland biodiversity and landscape infrastructure as fewer field boundaries and barns will be required. It is also predicted that sheep numbers will continue to fall to more to manageable levels, with a predicted increase in quality (Defra, 2003; Silcock *et al.*, 2005; ADAS, 2006).

Studies carried out for the North York Moors National Park Authority and English Nature indicate that agri-environment schemes are going to be critical in maintaining farm viability; and, once moorland flocks disappear, they are unlikely to return (Lewis and Beetham, 2005). This would bring about new upland landscapes and habitats.

The recognition of the present and future potential for carbon sequestration and storage in the organic soils of the uplands is rising rapidly up the political agenda (Worrall and Evans, this volume). This may become a future driver equal to, or more important than, the present main drivers of biodiversity targets and meeting the demands of the water framework directive. Delivery of present and future environmental targets relies principally on agri-environment schemes. As income from subsidies falls, and if livestock farming remains unprofitable, it is questionable whether scheme payments based on income forgone can provide sufficient financial incentive or income to support farming enterprises. Little attention is being given to the wider aspects of upland environments in terms of tradition, culture and cultural landscapes.

For many upland farmers, it would make economic sense not to farm actively but solely to draw the SPS and comply with cross-compliance standards (Gardner *et al.*, this volume). This may also be an attractive prospect to help reduce peat loss, aid peat restoration and flood control, although it may not be always desirable for the conservation and enhancement of landscape and biodiversity. Agri-environment schemes offer an additional income source to farmers. However, as long as payments are based on the income forgone principle, they cannot compete with the present level of subsidy payments nor, in the present economic circumstances, are they sufficient to support farm enterprises if subsidies were to be removed.

Whatever future changes may be, the uplands of England and the UK are likely to remain the principal areas of high nature conservation, carbon, thus providing many of the ecosystem services now being recognised. In securing these values, there is strong evidence that policies are becoming more joined up, so making more sense. In a country the size of England it is difficult to envisage these areas delivering the desired ecosystems services without the land management and livestock husbandry skills of farmers and the culture of their communities.

Acknowledgements

The author would like to acknowledge the assistance of Natural England Data Services and Graphics Unit for the production of maps and diagrams.

References

Adams, W. M. (1986) *Nature's Place: Conservation Sites and Countryside Change.* London: Allen & Unwin.

ADAS (2006) *Farmers' Intentions in the Context of CAP Reform: Analysis of ADAS Farmers' Voice 2006 Survey of England and Wales.* Report for Defra, London. http://statistics.defra.gov.uk/esg/ace/research/pdf/farmersvoice2006.pdf

Anderson, P. and Yalden, D. W. (1981) Increased sheep numbers and the loss of heather moorland in the Peak District, England. *Biological Conservation*, **20**, 195–213.

Bowers, J. K. (1985) British agricultural policy since the Second World War. *Agricultural History Review*, **33**, 66–76.

Cabinet Office (2002) *Farming and Food: A Sustainable Future.* Report of the Policy Commission on the Future of Farming and Food, London. http://image. guardian.co.uk/sys-files/Guardian/documents/2002/01/29/foodreport.pdf

Cartwright, B. (2003) The importance of the economic value of tourism and recreation in the Lake District National Park. *Proceedings of the 18th IEEM Conference* (ed. P. Anderson), pp. 141–7. Buxton.

Condliffe, I. (2006) Agri-environment schemes in the uplands: past and present. *The International Journal of Biodiversity Science and Management*, **2**, 200–4.

Defra (2001) *Report of the Rural Task Force: Tackling the Impact of Foot-and-Mouth Disease on the Rural Economy.* Defra, London. http://www.defra.gov.uk/rural/ pdfs/rural_task_force.pdf

Defra (2002a) *Response to the Report of the Policy Commission on the Future of Farming and Food by HM Government.* Defra, London. http://www.Defra.gov.uk/farm/ policy/sustain/pdf/policycom-response.pdf

Defra (2002b) *The Strategy for Sustainable Farming and Food: Facing the Future.* Defra, London. http://www.defra.gov.uk/farm/policy/sustain/strategy.htm

Defra (2002c) *Common Land Policy Statement.* Defra, London. http://www.defra. gov.uk/wildlife-countryside/issues/common/pdf/clps.pdf

Defra (2003) *Impact of Decoupling on UK Agricultural Production.* Defra, London. http://statistics.defra.gov.uk/esg/reports/decoupling/default.asp

Defra (2004) *Public Service Agreements, 2005–2008.* Defra, London. http://www. defra.gov.uk/corporate/busplan/spending-review/psa2004.htm

Defra (2007a) *Food Self Sufficiency.* Defra, London. http://statistics.defra.gov.uk/ esg/datasets/selfsuff.xls

Defra (2007b) *June Agricultural Census.* Defra, London. http://farmstats.defra. gov.uk/cs/farmstats_data/DATA/historical_data/hist_pub_search.asp

Defra (2007c) *Securing a Healthy Natural Environment: An Action Plan for Embedding an Ecosystems Approach.* Defra, London. www.defra.gov.uk/wildlife-countryside/natres/pdf/eco_actionplan.pdf

Defra (2007d) *Voluntary Modulation and the New Rural Development Programme for England.* Defra, London. http://www.defra.gov.uk/corporate/ministers/statements/ dm070329.htm

Defra (2007e) *Farm Business Survey Data.* Defra, London. http://statistics.defra. gov.uk/esg/publications/fab/2007/excel.asp

Defra/DCMS (2002) *Economic Cost of Foot-and-Mouth Disease in the UK: A Joint Working Paper.* Defra/DCMS, London. http://archive.cabinetoffice.gov.uk/fmd/ fmd_report/documents/d-govtpublications/DEFRA_DCMS.pdf

EEC (1975) *Council Directive 75/268/EEC of 28 April 1975 on Mountain and Hill Farming and Farming in Certain Less-Favoured Areas.* http://www.legaltext.ee/ text/en/U70631.htm

EEC (1992) *Council Directive 92/43/EEC of 21 May 1992 on the Conservation of Natural Habitats and of Wild Fauna and Flora.* http://www.internationalwildlifelaw.org/ EUCouncilDirective92.html

EU (1997) *The Cork Declaration.* http://ec.europa.eu/agriculture/rur/cork_en.htm

EU (1999) *Council Regulation 1257/1999 on Support for Rural Development from the European Agricultural Guidance and Guarantee Fund (EAGGF) and Amending and Repealing Certain Regulations.* http://ec.europa.eu/agriculture/rur/leg/index_en.htm

EU (2000) *The EU Water Framework Directive: Integrated River Basin Management for Europe.* http://ec.europa.eu/environment/water/water-framework/index_en.html

EU (2003) *CAP Reform: A Long-Term Perspective for Sustainable Agriculture.* http://ec.europa.eu/agriculture/capreform/index_en.htm

Felton, M. and Marsden, J. H. (1990) *Heather Regeneration in England and Wales.* Peterborough: Nature Conservancy Council.

Foreman, S. (1989) *Loaves and Fishes: An Illustrated History of the Ministry of Agriculture, Fisheries and Food, 1889–1989.* London: MAFF.

Lewis, M. and Beetham, M. (2006) *North York Moors Sheep Economic Study 2005.* York: Askham Bryan College.

MA (2005) *Millennium Ecosystem Assessment. Ecosystems and Human Well-being: Synthesis.* Washington, DC: Island Press. www.millenniumassessment.org

MAFF (1975) *Food from Our Own Resources.* Government White Paper, London.

MAFF (2000) *Our Countryside: The Future – a Fair Deal for Rural England.* Government White Paper, London. http://www.Defra.gov.uk/rural/ruralwp/default.htm

MAFF (2001) *Task Force for the Hills.* MAFF, London. http://www.hillfarming.org.uk/

National Trust (2005) *English Uplands Facing Bleak Future.* http://www.nationaltrust.org.uk/webpack/bin/webpack.exe/livebase?object=LiveBase1&itemurn=1747&mode=wbFullItem

Rollinson, T. (2003) *Changing Needs – Changing Forests: The UK Experience.* http://www.maf.govt.nz/mafnet/unff-planted-forestry-meeting/conference-papers/changing-needs-changing-forests.htm

Silcock, P., Swales, V. and Dwyer, J. (2005) *Assessment of the Impact of CAP Reform and Other Key Policies on Upland Farms and Land Use Implications in Both Severely Disadvantaged & Disadvantaged Areas of England.* Report for Defra, London. http://statistics.Defra.gov.uk/esg/reports/cap%20uplandfarms%20report.pdf

Spedding, A. (2007) *Food Security and the UK.* RuSource briefing 445, Arthur Rank Centre. http://www.arthurrankcentre.org.uk/projects/rusource_briefings/rus07/445.pdf

USDA (2004) *EU-25 Trade Policy Monitoring. CAP Reform 2003 – Deconstructing Decoupling 2004.* http://www.fas.usda.gov/gainfiles/200408/146107107.pdf

Part II

Ecosystem services and drivers of change

5   The carbon budget of upland peat soils

Fred Worrall and Martin G. Evans

Introduction

Within the terrestrial biosphere the northern peatlands are the most important carbon store. Gorham (1991) has estimated that 20–30 per cent of the
global terrestrial carbon is held in 3 per cent of its land area, i.e. in northern peatlands, storing 450 Gtonnes Carbon (C). Over the Holocene these
peatlands have accumulated carbon at an average rate of 0.96 Mtonnes C/yr,
making this ecosystem not only a substantial store but also a large potential sink of atmospheric carbon. However, with climate warming, increase
drought frequency, and changes in rainfall there is the risk that this important store could be transformed from a net sink to a net source of atmospheric carbon. Climatically driven causes of enhanced carbon loss could be
extenuated by other factors, including changes in atmospheric deposition and
land management.

There are up to 29,209 km^2 peatlands in the UK (12 per cent of UK land
area: Milne and Brown, 1997); and, unlike most peatlands in the northern
hemisphere, UK peatlands are extensively managed and under intense pressure within this densely populated island. This chapter will consider the complete carbon cycle in peatlands, the drivers upon each component of the cycle,
and the prognosis for these components given the continuing pressures
upon upland peats in the UK.

Carbon budgets of upland peat soils

Carbon budgets of peatlands have in general been estimated by two types
of method: dating of peat accumulation, and measuring carbon fluxes from
peat. Rates of carbon accumulation (RCA) have been reported from across
the northern hemisphere peatlands. Reported rates of accumulation have varied between as high as 88.6 gC/m^2/yr (Tolonen and Turunen, 1996) and as
low as 0.2 gC/m^2/yr on Baffin Island (Schlesinger, 1990). There are recognised problems with the technique, and in order to address some of these
issues the short-lived radioisotope ^{210}Pb has been used (e.g. Turetsky *et al.*,

Box 5.1. Carbon cycle in upland peats

The principal fluxes involved in peatland carbon cycling include different components and pathways (Figure 5.1).

Net ecosystem exchange of CO_2 (NEE)

The net ecosystem exchange of CO_2 (NEE) from a peatland is defined as the combination of the release of CO_2, largely by soil respiration and the extraction of CO_2 from the atmosphere by primary productivity. In general, for UK peats, the primary productivity is larger than the soil respiration and one of the major reasons why in a pristine peat that carbon would accumulate. Ranges for the UK are given in Table 5.1.

Methane (CH_4)

Methane production in upland peatlands is often low in comparison to other carbon release pathways. However, its importance is out of proportion because it is a more powerful greenhouse gas than CO_2 – a factor of twenty-one times stronger is often quoted (Table 5.1).

Dissolved organic carbon (DOC)

Dissolved organic carbon (DOC) includes both the colloidal fraction and organic carbon in true solution in waters leaving the peat profile.

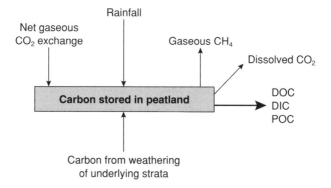

Figure 5.1 Schematic diagram of the carbon uptake and release pathways that control the carbon budget of an upland peat soil.

Table 5.1 Summary of carbon exports and inputs for the Trout Beck catchment at Moor House. Areal input/export rate is quoted as the preferred value, where a positive value represents an input to the catchment. The range refers to possible range of values for the Trout Beck site and the total based upon literature values.

Input/Output route	Areal input/export rate (tones $C/km^2/yr$)	Range (Literature range)
Rainfall inputs	4.1	4.1
Net ecosystem exchange	55	40–70
CH_4	−7.1	−1.5--−11.3
DOC	−9.4	−7--−24
POC	−19.9	−0.12--−38.8
Dissolved CO_2	−3.8	−0.26--−3.8
DIC	−4.1	0--−5.9
Total	14.9	13.9 ± 14.6

It is normally separated from particulate matter on the basis that it does not settle out without chemical coagulant; in practice this is operationally defined by the size of the filter paper used, typically between 0.2 μm and 1 μm. Ranges are given in Table 5.1.

Particulate organic carbon (POC)

Particulate organic carbon (POC) losses from peatlands have been less studied than dissolved and gaseous losses. In part this is because POC losses from intact peatlands are relatively low (Table 5.1). Eroding peatlands are dynamic, so that POC flux from these systems can be temporally variable over time. POC production is primarily controlled by vegetation cover; re-vegetation of eroding systems initially reduces connectivity between bare peat slopes and channels, and eventually limits sediment production as the degree of bare peat exposure is reduced (see Evans, this volume, Figure 2.8).

Dissolved inorganic carbon (DIC)

The dissolved CO_2 values measured for a North Pennines catchment vary between 8.4 and 25.6 tonnes $C/km^2/yr$ (Worrall *et al.*, 2005). However, it should be noted that DIC coming in from the weathering of underlying strata (Figure 5.1) does not contribute to the peatland carbon store but has to be accounted for if fluvial fluxes are to be measured and appropriately assigned to changes in the peat carbon store (Table 5.1).

Rainfall inputs

Willey *et al.* (2000) estimated that global precipitation input of DOC was 0.4×10^9 tonnes C/yr, of which 70 per cent fell on land, which is an average 1.88 tonnes $C/km^2/yr$ (Table 5.1). The scale of this input is almost negligible in relation to the other flux pathways. The best estimate of the influx of DOC from rainfall on to an upland peat soil is 1.29 tonnes C/km^2 in 2003 and 1.65 tonnes C/km^2 in 2004. Reported ranges of DOC concentration in rainwater vary from 0.82 to 2 mg C/l.

Minor components

There are no reported values for dissolved CH_4 export in the literature, although some evasion of dissolved CH_4 from peatland streams and ponds is reported. Hope *et al.* (2001) found maximum evasion rates as high as 345 mg $C/m^2/d$ – at least an order of magnitude less than measured evasion rates of dissolved CO_2. Similarly, particulate inorganic carbon can be considered negligible as no precipitation of carbonates would be expected at the low pH, low alkalinity and low base cation concentrations typical of peat-hosted streams.

2004), but resolution is no greater than ten years. Innate markers on the stems of mosses have also been used (Tolonen *et al.*, 1988). Relative age dating has been used based upon a well-dated synchronous base of the peat (Zoltai, 1991); similarly Garnett *et al.* (2001) have used spherical carbon particles to data peat cores based on the assumption of a peak production of soot particles with changes in industrialisation in the region. However, such rates of accumulation measures are only capable of measuring accumulation of peat and not losses. Estimation of recent carbon balance based on long-term accumulation rates can therefore be unrepresentative.

The second method of carbon balance estimation is to calculate present-day carbon budgets based upon estimating fluxes of carbon exchanges at the surface of the peatland. It has been recognised that results from long-term peat accumulation (Trumbore *et al.*, 1999) and empirical studies from Finland suggest that present rates of accumulation are on average two-thirds of the long-term accumulation rate (Tolonen and Turunen, 1996). Worrall *et al.* (2003) produced the first peatland carbon budget to consider both fluvial and gaseous exchanges. Fluvial carbon release includes: DOC, particulate organic carbon (POC), dissolved inorganic carbon (DIC) and dissolved CO_2. Frolking *et al.* (2002) in their peatland carbon simulator model do include DOC as well as CO_2 and CH_4 but no other release pathway. The limited focus on fluvial carbon flux has stemmed from an assumption that only direct atmospheric exchange of carbon is important, and so loss of carbon via fluvial pathways need not be considered. Proper consideration of fluvial fluxes is, however, vital for two reasons; first, the fate of peatlands is a distinct issue from the storage of atmospheric carbon and, second, fluvial fluxes do contribute to atmospheric carbon.

Box 5.2. Carbon budget for Moor House NNR

The first complete carbon budget of peat-covered catchment published is by Worrall *et al.* (2003). Moor House is England's highest and largest National Nature Reserve (NNR), situated in the North Pennines uplands (National grid reference NY 756326, Figure 5.2). The Trout Beck catchment is one of the Environmental Change Network Freshwater sites, and details of the site and carbon budget calculation can be found in Worrall *et al.* (2003). The results show that, of all the carbon uptake and release pathways (Table 5.1), the net exchange remains by far the largest; however, the combination of the fluvial release pathways (DOC, POC, dissolved CO_2, DIC), often ignored in carbon budgets studies, does amount to −37.2 tonnes C/km²/yr in comparison to 55 tonnes C/km2/yr for NEE. If the largest percentage variation is found for the route with the most information, it might be safe to assume that the percentage variation is in fact the same for the other routes, i.e. 80 per cent variation in CH_4 (Table 5.2). Given such ranges, the peat would be a sink of 13.6 ± 28.7 tonnesC/km²/yr. Given the literature ranges reported

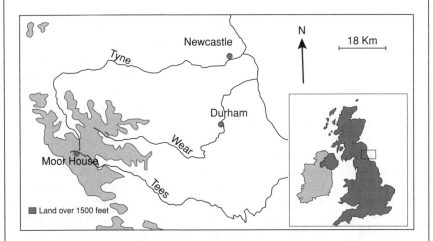

Figure 5.2 Location of the Moor House study site.

Table 5.2 Summary of carbon export and input ranges (all values in tonnes C/km^2/yr) used for calculation of carbon budget of British peats, based on a 80 per cent variation or the largest range reported for Britain. Error is quoted the standard deviation after stochastic combination.

Input/Output route	Range (+ 80% variation)
Rainfall inputs	0.8–7.6
Net ecosystem exchange	11–99
CH$_4$	−1.5−−11.3
DOC	−2.4−−22.0
POC	−4.1−−37.2
Dissolved CO$_2$	−0.6−−5.2
DIC	0−−9.0
Total	13.6 ± 28.7

for UK peats, as opposed to those known for Moor House, the peat would be a sink of 13.9 ± 14.6 tonnes C/km^2/yr.

Various estimates of the area of peat in the UK have been made. Milne and Brown (1997) estimate the area of blanket peat in Scotland to be 25,641 km^2 and the area of raw peat soils in England and Wales as 3,568 km^2–29,209 km^2 in total. The lowest estimate of area of blanket mire is 14,790 km^2 (Tallis and Meade, 1997). Given the assumption that the range of variability is equivalent to that of the largest reported variability, and including the variability in the estimate of the area of peat within the stochastic approach, the overall size of the peatland sink in Britain would be 0.26 ± 0.64 Gg C/yr. Given the ranges reported for the UK, the overall size of the sink is 0.30 + 0.35 Gg C/yr, and a 19 per cent chance that British peats are a net source.

However, the estimated carbon budget proposed by Worrall *et al.* (2003) had a number of flaws. It is possible to correct some of these errors. First, the dissolved inorganic carbon component can simply be corrected by removing the weathering and DIC components. This makes a difference of 4.1 tonnes C/km^2/yr. However, more importantly, the dissolved CO$_2$ needs to be corrected for in-stream processes. The correction for in-stream processes meant that the excess dissolved CO$_2$ concentration of water at emergence from the peat profile was between 9.6 and 25.6 tonnes C/km^2/yr and that DOC losses were equivalent to extra loss of carbon of between 4.0 and 7.4 tonnes C/km^2/yr. Given these amendments, the catchment would now be a small net source of carbon of 4 tonnes C/km^2/yr. However, one further source of underestimation is the potential in-stream processing of the POC. Finally, it should be noted that Moor House may be unusual in the context of UK peatlands as it is a national nature reserve (NNR) and has not been under active management since 1954.

Potential drivers of change

Climate change

Temperature

In general most reactions in nature increase their rate within an increase in temperature. Considering the individual carbon uptake release pathways, both soil respiration of CO_2 and DOC show increases with increasing temperature (e.g. Lloyd and Taylor, 1994). In the case of dissolved CO_2, competing reactions in the peat profile would mean that there would be very little increase in the overall production of dissolved CO_2; that is, as soil respiration increases the concentration of CO_2 in soil, water temperature increases also increase the consumption of dissolved CO_2 by weathering reactions. Likewise the picture would be more confused for methane. Although the production reaction of methane would increase with increasing temperature, it is most likely that methane flux from the surface of peat bog would decrease with increasing temperature for two reasons: first, the rate of methane oxidation would also increase and, second, increasing temperature would increase evapotranspiration and so increase the size of the aerobic zone, i.e. increasing the volume within which methane oxidation could occur. This latter effect would also help to increase the production of DOC and the soil respiration of CO_2. Worrall *et al.* (2004) show that temperature increase over a period of thirty years would lead to a 17 per cent increase in DOC loss from a peat-covered catchment. In contrast, Clark *et al.* (2005) only ascribe a 5 per cent increase in DOC losses to changes in the production rate. The difference between these two rates can be ascribed to the change in the water table increasing the aerobic zone in the peat profile. The two pathways that cannot be directly linked to temperature increases are POC and primary productivity. The former is generally accepted as being produced by physical rather than biogeochemical processes. As for primary productivity, the major driver is light and not temperature. However, changes in temperature may alter the species composition.

Elevated atmospheric CO_2

The underlying cause of climate change is increased concentrations of certain gases in the atmosphere, especially CO_2. Elevated CO_2 has been shown to increase primary production (e.g. Gill *et al.*, 2002), and greater carbon input is expected to increase carbon sequestration in soil by increased biomass (Berendse *et al.*, 2001). However, elevated CO_2 may also change the plant community composition, which may favour vascular plants over mosses and so decrease carbon sequestration (e.g. Freeman *et al.*, 2004). Further, Freeman *et al.* (2004) have observed an increase in DOC from peat soils under elevated CO_2, which they attributed to elevated net primary productivity (NPP), and increased root exudation of DOC. They suggest that the labile carbon released by roots stimulates microbial activity, leading to enhanced degradation of soil organic matter; this process is known as the 'priming mechanism'. Hence Freeman *et al.* (2004) suggest that the increase in CO_2 is responsible for the increase in concentration of DOC observed in freshwaters.

Rainfall

Changes in water balance do control through a number of mechanisms. First, changes in the position of the water table – discussed above. However, second, changes in rainfall could result in changes to runoff. Tranvik and Jansson (2002) have suggested that the DOC concentration increases observed by Freeman *et al.* (2001) could be hydrological changes in discharge being associated with changes in concentrations. Worrall and Burt (2007) have shown that the pattern of DOC flux from the UK, which is dominated by flux from peatlands, can be explained by an underlying increase in air temperature and by changes in river flow. Rainfall is a key driver of POC flux, and runoff is the primary agent of peatland erosion; and increases in runoff have the potential to trigger fresh erosion through increasing the erosive force on stressed vegetation surfaces and also to exacerbate the rate of POC flux from eroding systems. The former poses much the greater risk as the shift from vegetated to eroded status entails at least an order-of-magnitude increase in POC flux. Changes of rate of erosion at bare sites will be of a lower order and will be significantly affected by changes in the frequency of high-intensity storms which carry a large proportion of total sediment load (Evans and Warburton, 2007).

Drought

There are several lines of evidence to support drought as a distinct driver of change, and drought frequency is increasing in the peatlands of the UK (Worrall *et al.*, 2006). Two biogeochemical mechanisms have been proposed that link drought to carbon uptake and release pathways. Freeman *et al.* (2001) have suggested an 'enzymic latch' mechanism, and Clark *et al.* (2005) a DOC solubility suppression mechanism. There are several lines of evidence to support these proposed mechanisms, including: observed change in the relationship between flow and DOC after a severe drought (Worrall and Burt, 2004); and decoupled soil respiration and DOC production (Worrall *et al.*, 2005).

Alternatively, drought may alter the physical structure of peat and influence carbon release either by change of flowpath or by changing access to parts of the peat profile or by returning to parts of the peat profile not accessible during the drought, parts of the profile with increased DOC concentration.

Increasing drought frequency is potentially significant for POC flux. Francis (1990) showed that desiccation during drought periods was an important process driving sediment production from bare gully walls; increases in summer drought coupled with enhanced autumn rainfalls are therefore likely to enhance POC flux. Drought conditions have also been implicated in the initiation of peat erosion in the South Pennines (Tallis, 1998). Moisture stress on the surface vegetation and cracking due to desiccation have the potential to destabilise peat masses and produce a step change in POC flux from the system. A second POC-related risk of drought periods relates to the risk of wildfire. Wildfires destroy vegetation, creating large areas of bare peat; and deep-burning fires destroy roots, inhibiting regeneration.

Land management

Drainage

A common land management technique in UK peatlands is the use of open drainage channels. Peat drainage has been common in many European countries. In the UK it has been estimated that 1.5 million ha of the country's 2.9 million ha of peat has been drained (Milne and Brown, 1987). In UK upland peat these drains are referred to as grips. The reasons for draining are commonly stated as being for the lowering of water tables in order to improve grazing or hunting, or to develop forestry (Ratcliffe and Oswald, 1988). However, Stewart and Lance (1991) have shown that there is no evidence for any of the claims made for it. The consequences of peat drainage for the environment have been recently reviewed by Holden *et al.* (2004). The drains may lower water tables and cause additional carbon production by increasing the depth to the water table. Increased soil CO_2 respiration has been observed upon drainage of peatlands. Komulainen *et al.* (1999) have shown that soil respiration of CO_2 decreased upon restoration of the water table in a peatland in Finland. Hargreaves *et al.* (2003) show that, while an undisturbed peat had a NEE of 25 tonnes $C/km^2/yr$, a newly drained peat had a NEE that was a source of between 200–400 tonnes $C/km^2/yr$, though this massive source reverted to a sink within four to eight years. The solar radiation cannot be lessened by the presence of drainage ditches, but the vegetation may have been affected by the presence of drainage, causing less productive plants or species to become dominant. Mitchell and McDonald (1995) have shown that at a catchment scale the areas of the highest drainage density are the largest sources of DOC. Hughes *et al.* (1999) artificially lowered the water table of wetland in Wales and found decreased DOC in summer, but increases in concentration in winter. Conversely, the blocking of drains has been considered a simple method for mitigating the widespread increases in DOC observed across upland UK. However, evidence from several studies is equivocal. Wallage *et al.* (2006) observed decreased concentrations of DOC in blocked drains compared to open drains, but did not compare the same drains before and after blocking. Alternatively, Worrall *et al.* (2007) showed that statistically significant increases in DOC concentrations occurred within drains in comparison to both pre-blocking concentrations and concentrations in unblocked drains; however, despite increases in DOC concentration in blocked drains the actual flux of DOC would decrease.

It should also be noted that many of the effects of lowered water table are also associated with natural drainage owing to the development of extensive gully erosion. Daniels (2006) has demonstrated lowered water table associated with gullying and increasing importance of sub-surface flow paths similar to that noted by Holden *et al.* (2006) for drained systems.

While it would be expected that aerobic processes would increase upon the draining of peats and decrease again upon restoration, methane production is an anaerobic process and so would be expected to decrease with drainage and increase upon restoration. Tuittila *et al.* (2000) have shown that upon restoring a cut-away peatland there was a statistically significant increase in CH_4 flux.

Afforestation

Afforestation has been the main cause of the net loss of moorland habitat over the past century. Nine per cent of upland UK peatland has been afforested (Cannell *et al.*, 1993); and, in Scotland, 25 per cent of Caithness and Sutherland peatlands have been affected by afforestation (Ratcliffe and Oswald, 1988). Narrowly spaced drainage ditches (ribbon plough furrows) are commonly dug across moorland areas before forests are planted. Fertiliser is also often applied. The drains lower the water table and result in associated subsidence of the peat surface due to compression and shrinkage (Anderson *et al.*, 2000). The peat tends to dry out further after canopy closure, and increased interception and transpiration cause a much greater lowering in the water table than drainage alone, further encouraging surface subsidence (Shotbolt *et al.*, 1998) and increasing hydraulic conductivity in the upper layers, often with large-scale cracking of the peat. Felling of the trees causes the water table to rise, but the water table tends to fluctuate much more than in intact moorlands because of changes to soil structure and enhanced hydraulic conductivity. The impact of afforestation of moorlands is not restricted to the planted area alone. Drying and shrinkage of the organic soils can occur at some distance away from the forest depending on local topography and drainage. Runoff, too, is affected by afforestation. Streamflow tends to increase both in total and in peakedness with increased low flows in the first years following drainage (perhaps twenty years), followed by decreases in water yield as the forest matures. Water quality may also change downstream as afforested moorland streams often become more acidic with higher concentrations of aluminium. While carbon is taken up by tree biomass as the forest grows, there may be severe depletion of the soil carbon store through enhanced decomposition of the organic soil

(Cannell *et al.*, 1993). Studies have reported contrasting results regarding the effect of drainage upon decomposition rates. For example, Laiho (2006) summarises Finnish studies of decomposition of organic matter in peats drained for forestry, which show initial losses of carbon, as measured by decomposition, but longer-term changes which are more variable and dependent upon the climate setting and extent of drainage: this coincides with studies in British peats drained for forestry (Cannell *et al.*, 1993). However, in such settings the number of measured carbon pathways is limited, and the long-term balance is maintained by leaf-litter inputs and above-ground biomass that would not be present in peat not drained for forestry. There are fewer data on the effect of rewetting of peatlands. Drainage associated with forestry has been shown to have significant effects on suspended sediment production from afforested areas and hence on POC flux (Francis and Taylor, 1989).

Managed burning

In England, it has been estimated that 40 per cent of moorland has received some burn management (Thomas *et al.*, 2004, quoted in Glaves *et al.*, 2005; Yallop *et al.*, this volume).

There have been very few direct studies of the fate of carbon under managed burns. Garnett *et al.* (2000) examined peat accumulation of carbon under three treatments (grazed/unburnt, grazed/burnt, and ungrazed/unburnt). Recalculating the data of Garnett *et al.* (2000) shows that the mean difference between burnt and unburnt treatments is 2.48 kg/m^2 (not 2.3 as reported). This gives a mean effect of burning of 55 tonnes C/km^2/yr (not 73 tonnes C/km^2/yr as reported). Garnett *et al.* (2000) do not scale their estimate of the loss of carbon accumulation; but, given that there is between 14,900 and 29,000 km^2 of peat in the UK (Milne and Brown, 1997), and given that it is estimated that 40 per cent of peat has experienced rotational burn management, this means that between 0.34 and 0.63 Gg C/yr are lost across the UK owing to managed burning of heather and grass upon peat. One further caveat is that the loss of carbon due to managed burning will probably be dependent upon the frequency of burning. The data supplied by Garnett *et al.* (2000) are for burning every ten years.

In a recent review of the consequences of heather and grassland burning, including that on peat, Glaves *et al.* (2005) were not able to report any studies upon individual components of the carbon cycle and found very few studies which examined the consequences of burning for hydrology or water quality. With regard to primary productivity, we must assume that it follows the changes in vegetation with managed burning. Rotational burning of the heather tends to shift plant communities from heather dominated towards domination by grasses and sedges, and this shift is stronger with increased frequency of burning (Forrest, 1971). Worrall and Adamson (2007) have shown that there are significant differences in the depth to the water table between different burn frequencies, with the lowest water tables on sites where there has been no burning for forty years and the heather is mature. It could therefore be expected that, with increasing burn frequency, soil respiration of CO_2 would decrease, CH_4 flux would increase and DOC fluxes would decrease. However, Worrall *et al.* (2007) have shown significantly lower DOC concentrations in soil water beneath more frequently burnt sites.

Intentional and catastrophic burns have been linked to increased peat erosion (Tallis, 1998). However, Kinako and Gimmingham (1980) showed that erosion only increased for the first two years after burning, i.e. the period before vegetation was clearly established. This would imply that POC losses increase with increased burn frequency or severity.

Grazing

Grazing on uplands in the UK can be by cattle or by deer but is predominantly by sheep. At eleven sites in the Scottish Highlands, where sheep had been excluded for up to twenty-five years, dwarf shrubs (*Calluna vulgaris, Erica* spp. and *Vaccinium myrillus*) came to dominate over grasses, with one site showing the invasion of birch woodland (Hope *et al.*, 1998). Depending upon its intensity, grazing can reduce competitive vigour, or even kill plants through defoliation and direct damage. Overgrazing is thought to be a major cause of loss of heather moorland (Shaw *et al.*, 1996).

Increased grazing has been associated with soil erosion in uplands (Evans, 1996). Grazing is one of the potential triggers for widespread peat erosion and consequent step changes in the POC flux. Shimwell (1974) used parish records to demonstrate a temporal correlation between rapid increases in stocking densities and the period of onset of peat erosion in the South Pennines. A range of studies have associated increased sheep numbers with changes in runoff which may change fluvial carbon losses (e.g. Langlands and Bennett, 1973). As with the effects of burning, the number of studies into the effects on soil and water quality are limited. The effect of grazing on other carbon uptake and release pathways is little reported. Garnett *et al.* (2000) showed no significant difference in the peat accumulation beneath grazed and ungrazed plots. In contrast Worrall *et al.* (2007) have reported significant changes. Very few studies have considered the interaction of grazing and burning; the authors could only find one study which investigated such interactions.

Atmospheric deposition

Sulphur deposition

Sulphur deposition has declined rapidly in the UK in the last twenty years (Fowler *et al.*, 2005), but this is after decades of severe and damaging deposition. *Sphagnum* spp. are highly susceptible to sulphur deposition, and in many UK peatlands atmospheric deposition of sulphur has led to the virtual elimination of these mosses, slowing the accumulation of peat. However, the acidification of peat soils also decreases the natural processes of soil break-down, so that litter turnover decreases, causing an increase in carbon accu-mulation but not in humified carbon. The recovery from acidification has been observed in upland streams across the country (Evans *et al.*, 2005), and the recovery from acidification has been correlated with the widespread observed increases in DOC concentrations in upland streams (Evans *et al.*, 2006). However, DOC increases are observed in catchments which never expe-rienced acidification, and are observed to decrease in catchments which have experienced acidification and are now recovering. Similarly, increases in DOC were observed before decreases in acid deposition occurred. Therefore, declines in sulphur deposition can only be a contributing factor.

Nitrogen deposition

Increased N deposition would lead to increased litter production (Aerts *et al.*, 1992) and could accelerate organic matter decomposition by lowering the C/N ratio; it enhances the release of carbon from roots to the soil and may inhibit CH_4 oxidation (Steudler *et al.*, 1989). Nitrogen deposition has been observed to increase through the 1980s and into the 1990s for many industrialised countries (Wright *et al.*, 2001). Evans and Monteith (2001) have examined twenty-two stream and lake sites across upland UK; the sites have shown no significant declines over a twelve-year period from 1988 during a period when twenty of the sites showed significant increases in DOC con-centration. The amount of stream nitrate in upland, non-forested catchments is not closely related to N-deposition, and there is evidence of extensive N-saturation in upland environments (Harriman *et al.*, 1998). Significant correlations have been found between DOC concentration and nitrate con-centrations in upland streams (Harriman *et al.*, 1998), but increases in nitrate concentration were the result of increasing DOC concentrations and not vice versa.

There are other carbon release pathways from a peatland, and there have been several studies of the effect of nutrient input on carbon dioxide and methane release. Aerts and Ludwig (1997) found that increased N supply decreased CO_2 efflux from a peat; this had been previously ascribed to a pH effect (Bridgham and Richardson, 1992). The same study shows a short-lived effect of N addition on CH_4 efflux that has been ascribed to negative effects on methane oxidation rather than upon methane production (Crill *et al.*, 1994). Silvola *et al.* (2003) found that only one out of five sites where they arti-ficially enhanced N additions showed a significant increase in CH_4 efflux. Saarnio *et al.* (2003) found only a small increase in CO_2 and CH_4 exchange following N addition on a peat bog over a three-year period. Saarnio *et al.* (2000) found a negligible effect on CH_4 efflux upon N fertilisation, as any effect of N addition was short-lived if present at all.

The prognosis for peatland carbon stores

Given the changes observed in the climatic drivers, the fate of carbon storage in peatlands would appear bleak (Jenkins *et al.*, 2007). Air temperature in the UK is likely to increase over the next fifty years. Rainfall patterns across the UK are diverging to give wetter winters and drier summers, which in turn leads to both greater runoff and greater probability of severe drought (see Caporn and Emmett, this volume). The change in air temperature also means a change in precipitation pattern, with fewer days with snow. If we consider each possible pathway in turn, we expect the following changes.

- *Soil respiration of CO_2* would increase, with increasing depth to water table and increasing temperature. Data from the Moor House catchment show a 9 per cent increase in soil respiration flux over thirteen years from 1993 to 2005, equivalent to 0.7 per cent per year.
- *Uptake of CO_2 by primary productivity* would not change in the short term as it is controlled by radiation conditions, which are not affected by air temperature. With increasing atmospheric CO_2, however, uptake might increase in the longer term as warmer temperatures enable lower-altitude species to encroach upon the wetland. The encroachment of shrubby vegetation and grasses would have a detrimental effect upon water tables, leading to increased decomposition rates. At Moor House there is no evidence of a significant increase or decrease in primary productivity over thirteen years.
- *Methane (CH_4).* Warming of the soil would increase rates of both CH_4 production and oxidation; but increasing temperatures result in increases in the aerobic zone, thus leading to an overall decrease in CH_4 production.
- *Dissolved organic carbon (DOC)* fluxes would be expected to increase for a number of possible reasons: increasing air temperatures, increasing atmospheric CO_2, decreasing atmospheric deposition, and so on. Worrall and Burt (2004) have examined the long-term trend in the DOC flux from the Moor House catchment, which shows a significant increase of 17 per cent over the years 1970–2000, i.e. an annual increase of 0.6 per cent.
- *Particulate organic carbon (POC).* The loss of POC is not directly linked to biogeochemical processes and is therefore more difficult to predict in response to climate change and other drivers. Increased runoff would suggest increases in POC; but the important part of the runoff is the very large storms, and increases in storminess are proposed as part of climate change. However, increases in shrubby vegetation cover would limit the erosive power of runoff. The potential for enhanced instability of peatlands under conditions of climate change is the main risk. The most dramatic increases in carbon loss come from new or renewed erosion in currently stable areas rather than from changes of rate in eroding areas. The conservation challenge is therefore to reduce erosion extent.

Moore *et al.* (1998) tabulated their predictions for the trend in individual carbon uptake and release pathways, and predicted declines in DOC with climate change but did not comment upon POC. This study would agree with Moore *et al.* (1998) that the size of the carbon sink in peatlands will decrease. However, we would also envisage that many peatlands, especially those at lower altitudes, would become net sources of carbon and may already be sources.

Mitigation of change and remediation of damage

Considering the drivers upon each of the carbon uptake and release pathways, there are several potential changes in land management to limit the loss of carbon.

Managed burning

As discussed above, frequent intense burns have tended to cause loss of carbon (see also Yallop *et al.*, this volume), therefore cessation of managed burning should preserve carbon. However, there are caveats to this. First, there is some evidence that DOC may increase under unburnt sites in comparison to frequently burnt sites (Worrall *et al.*, 2007). Second, the generation of large areas of mature heather that would result in large areas prone to severe wildfire (see McMorrow *et al.*, this volume) could have led to greater carbon losses than infrequent managed burn. Third, mature heather as opposed to young heather may add little to carbon fixation from primary productivity. In general, it would seem that some degree of managed burning amongst heather could be desirable but to scale and at a frequency required to maximise carbon storage.

Drainage

Drain-blocking has been regarded as a universal good, especially by water companies who see it as one easy method of reversing the upward trends in DOC. However, field results for drain-blocking are equivocal, with both positive and negative consequences for DOC being reported (Worrall *et al.* 2007; Wallage *et al.*, 2006). As for other pathways, drain-blocking could minimise carbon export. For POC export, it removes a potential point of erosion and a pathway for sediment transport. Raising the water table by drain-blocking would limit the aerobic zone and so limit the losses via soil respiration of CO_2. It may also limit the production of DOC but may increase CH_4 fluxes. Any success of drain-blocking in limiting fluvial fluxes of carbon could simply be due to limiting water flux rather than to limiting DOC production. However, the drain represents a volume of missing peat, and so blocking that leads to infilling of these drains does represent a carbon benefit.

Other restoration techniques

There are approaches to peat restoration other than controlling the burn management or water table. The approaches can generally be classified as attempts at re-vegetation, but include the use of fertiliser, liming, mulches, re-seeding, nurse crops, and so on (see Anderson *et al.*, this volume). In general, re-vegetation is positive with regard to improving carbon storage as it means that primary productivity returns to the ecosystem and the potential for erosion, and hence loss of POC, is diminished.

Conclusions

The eventual future for upland peats in the UK is uncertain. Upland peats are a phenomenon of cold-wet climates, and we in the UK are moving towards a warmer-drier scenario. At present we can assume that large areas of upland peats are net sinks of atmospheric carbon, but we can only assume that the balance of carbon uptake and release will shift with more peatlands becoming net sources of carbon and thus providing a positive feedback accelerating further climate change. However, these are long-term processes, the carbon store is very large, and climate futures are uncertain. Therefore, in the short to medium term there are appropriate strategies to support the increasingly stressed peatland system. In order to prevent the loss of this habitat and the release of stored carbon, urgent action is required to restore and mitigate and prevent carbon losses in whatever form is possible.

References

Aerts, R. and Ludwig, F. (1997) Water-table changes and nutritional status affect trace gas emissions from laboratory columns of peatland soils. *Soil Biology and Biochemistry*, **29**, 1691–8.

Aerts, R., Wallen, B. and Malmer, N. (1992) Growth limiting nutrients in sphagnum-dominated bogs subject to low and high atmospheric nitrogen supply. *Journal of Ecology*, **80**, 131–40.

Anderson, A. R., Ray, D. and Pyatt, D. G. (2000) Physical and hydrological impacts of blanket bog afforestation at Bad a' Cheo, Caithness: the first 5 years. *Forestry*, **73**, 467–78.

Berendse, F., Van Breemen, N., Rydin, H., Buttler, A., Heijmans, M., Hoosbeek, M. R., Lee, J. A., Mitchell, E., Saarinen, T., Vasander, H. and Wallen, B. (2001) Raised atmospheric CO_2 levels and increased N deposition cause shifts in plant species composition and production in Sphagnum bogs. *Global Change Biology*, **7**, 591–8.

Bridgham, S. D. and Richardson, C. J. (1992) Mechanisms controlling soil respiration (CO_2 and CH_4) in southern peatlands. *Soil Biology and Biochemistry*, **24**, 1089–99.

Cannell, M. G. R., Dewar, R. C. and Pyatt, D. G. (1993) Conifer plantations on drained peatlands in Britain: a net gain or loss of carbon? *Forestry*, **66**, 353–69.

Clark, J. M., Chapman, P. J., Adamson, J. K. and Lane, S. J. (2005) Influence of drought-induced acidification on the mobility of dissolved organic carbon in peat soils. *Global Change Biology*, **11**, 791–809.

Crill, P. M., Martikanen, P. J., Nykanen, H. and Silvola, J. (1994) Temperature and N fertilisation effects on methane oxidation in drained peatland soils. *Soil Biology and Biochemistry*, **26**, 1331–994.

Daniels, S. (2006) Controls on streamwater acidity in a South Pennine headwater catchment. PhD thesis, School of Geography, University of Manchester.

Evans, C. D., Chapman, P. J., Clark, J. M., Monteith, D. T. and Cresser, M. S. (2006) Alternative explanations for rising dissolved organic carbon export from organic soils. *Global Change Biology*, **12**, 2044–53.

Evans, C. D. and Monteith, D. T. (2001) Chemical trends at lakes and streams in the UK acid waters monitoring network, 1988–2000. Evidence of recovery at the national scale. *Hydrology and Earth Systems Sciences*, **5**, 351–66.

Evans, C. D., Monteith, D. T. and Cooper, D. M. (2005) Long-term increases in surface water dissolved organic carbon: observations, possible causes and environmental impacts. *Environmental Pollution*, **137**, 55–71.

Evans, M. G. and Warburton, J. (2007) *The Geomorphology of Upland Peat: Erosion, Form, and Landscape Change.* Oxford: Blackwell.

Evans, R. (1996) *Soil Erosion and Its Impacts in England and Wales.* London: Friends of the Earth Trust.

Forrest, G. I. (1971) Structure and production of North Pennine blanket bog vegetation. *Journal of Ecology*, **59**, 453–79.

Fowler, D., Smith, R. I., Muller, J. B. A., Hayman, G. and Vincent, K. J. (2005) Changes in the atmospheric deposition of acidifying compounds in the UK between 1986 and 2001. *Environmental Pollution*, **137**, 15–25.

Francis, I. S. (1990) Blanket peat erosion in a Mid-Wales catchment during 2 drought years. *Earth Surface Processes and Landforms*, **15**, 445–56.

Francis, I. S. and Taylor, J. A. (1989) The effect of forestry drainage operations on upland sediment yields – a study of two peat covered catchments. *Earth Surface Processes and Landform*, **14**, 73–83.

Freeman, C., Fenner, N., Ostle, N. J., Kang, H., Dowrick, D. J., Reynolds, B., Lock, M. A., Sleep, D., Hughes, S. and Hudson, J. (2004) Export of dissolved organic carbon from peatlands under elevated carbon dioxide levels. *Nature*, **430**, 195–8.

Freeman, C., Ostle, N. and Kang, H. (2001) An enzymic 'latch' on a global carbon store – a shortage of oxygen locks up carbon in peatlands by restraining a single enzyme. *Nature*, **409**, 149.

Frolking, S., Roulet, N. T., Moore, T. R., Lafleur, P. M., Bubier, J. L. and Crill, P. M. (2002) Modeling seasonal to annual carbon balance of Mer Bleue Bog, Ontario, Canada. *Global Biogeochemical Cycles*, **16**, Art. No. 1030.

Garnett, M. H., Ineson, P. and Stevenson, A. C. (2000) Effects of burning and grazing on carbon sequestration in a Pennine blanket bog, UK. *The Holocene*, **10**, 729–36.

Garnett, M. H., Ineson, P., Stevenson, A. C. and Howard, D. C. (2001) Terrestrial organic carbon storage in a British moorland. *Global Change Biology*, **7**, 375–88.

Gill, R. A., Polley, H. W., Johnson, H. B., Anderson, L. J., Maherali, H. and Jackson, R. B. (2002) Nonlinear grassland responses to past and future atmospheric CO_2. *Nature*, **417**, 279–82.

Glaves, D. J., Haycock, N. E., Costigan, P., Coulson, J. C., Marrs, R. H., Robertson, P. A. and Younger, J. (2005) *Defra Review of the Heather and Grass Burning Regulations and Code: Science Panel Assessment of the Effects of Burning on Biodiversity, Soils and Hydrology.* Defra, London. http://www.defra.gov.uk/rural/pdfs/uplands/science-panel-full-report.pdf

Gorham, E. (1991) Northern peatlands: role in the carbon cycle and probable responses to climate warming. *Ecological Applications*, **1**, 182–95.

Hargreaves, K. J., Milne, R. and Cannell, M. G. R. (2003) Carbon balance of afforested peatland in Scotland. *Forestry*, **76**, 299–317.

Harriman, R., Curtis, C. and Edwards, A. C. (1998) An empirical approach for assessing the relationship between nitrogen deposition and nitrate leaching from upland catchments in the United Kingdom using runoff chemistry. *Water Air & Soil Pollution*, **105**, 193–203.

Holden, J., Burt, T. P., Evans, M. G. and Horton, M. (2006) Impact of land drainage on peatland hydrology. *Journal of Environmental Quality*, **35**, 1764–78.

Holden, J., Chapman, P. J. and Labadz, J. C. (2004) Artificial drainage of peatlands: hydrological and hydrochemical process and wetland restoration. *Progress in Physical Geography*, **28**, 95–123.

Hope, D., Palmer, S. M., Billet, M. F. and Dawson, J. J. C. (2001) Carbon dioxide and methane oxidation evasion from a temperate peatland stream. *Limnology & Oceanography*, **46**, 847–57.

Hope, D., Picozzi, N., Catt, D. C. and Moss, R. (1998) Effects of reducing sheep grazing in the Scottish Highlands. *Journal of Range Management*, **49**, 301–10.

Hughes, S., Dowrick, D. J., Freeman, C., Hudson, J. A. and Reynolds, B. (1999) Methane emissions from a gully mire in mid-Wales, UK under consecutive summer water table drawdown. *Environmental Science & Technology*, **33**, 362–5.

Jenkins, G. J., Perry, M. C. and Prior, M. J. O. (2007) *The Climate of the United Kingdom and Recent Trends.* Met Office Hadley Centre, Exeter. http://www.ukcip.org.uk/images/stories/08_pdfs/Trends.pdf

Kinako, P. D. S. and Gimmingham, C. H. (1980) Heather burning and soil erosion on upland heaths in Scotland. *Journal of Environmental Management*, **10**, 277–84.

Laiho, R. (2006) Decomposition in peatlands: reconciling seemingly contrasting results on the impacts of lowered water levels. *Soil Biology and Biochemistry*, **38**, 2011–24.

Langlands, J. P. and Bennett, I. L. (1973) Stocking intensity and pastoral production. I. Changes in the soil and vegetation of a sown pasture grazed by sheep at different stocking rates. *Journal of Agricultural Sciences*, **81**, 193–4.

Lloyd, J. and Taylor, J. A. (1994) On the temperature dependence of soil respiration. *Functional Ecology*, **8**, 315–23.

Milne, R. and Brown, T. A. (1997) Carbon in the vegetation and soils of Great Britain. *Journal of Environmental Management*, **49**, 413–33.

Mitchell, G. and McDonald, A. T. (1995) Catchment characterisation as a tool for upland water management. *Journal of Environmental Management*, **44**, 83–95.

Moore, T. R., Roulet, N. T. and Waddington, J. M. (1998) Uncertainty in predicting the effect of climatic change on the carbon cycling of Canadian peatlands. *Climatic Change*, **40**, 229–45.

Ratcliffe, D. A. and Oswald, P. H. (1988) *The Flow Country.* Peterborough: Nature Conservancy Council.

Saarnio, S., Jarvio, S., Saarinen, T., Vasander, H. and Silvola, J. (2003) Minor changes in vegetation and carbon gas balance in a boreal mire under a raised CO_2 or NH_4NO_3 supply. *Ecosystems*, **6**, 46–60.

Saarnio, S., Saarinen, T., Vasander, H. and Silvola, J. (2000) A moderate increase in the annual CH_4 efflux by raised CO_2 or NH_4NO_3 supply in a boreal oligotrophic mire. *Global Change Biology*, **6**, 137–44.

Schlesinger, W. H. (1990) Evidence from chronosequence studies for a low carbon storage potential of soils, *Nature*, **348**, 232–4.

Shaw, S. C., Wheeler, B. D., Kirby, P., Phillipson, P. and Edmunds, R. (1996) *Literature Review of the Historical Effects of Burning and Grazing of Blanket Bog and Upland Wet Heath.* English Nature Research Report No172, English Nature, Peterborough. http://naturalengland.communisis.com/NaturalEnglandShop/default.aspx

Shimwell, D. W. (1974) Sheep grazing intensity in Edale, Derbyshire, 1692–1747, and its effect on blanket peat erosion. *Derbyshire Archaeological Journal*, **94**, 35–40.

Shotbolt, L., Anderson, A. R. and Townend, J. (1998) Changes in blanket bog adjoining forest plots at Bad a' Cheo, Rumster Forest, Caithness. *Forestry*, **71**, 311–24.

Silvola, J., Saarnio, S., Foot, J., Sundh, I., Greenup, A., Heijmans, M., Ekberg, A., Mitchell, E. and van Breemen, N. (2003), Effects of elevated CO_2 and N deposition on CH_4 emissions from European mires. *Global Biogeochemical Cycles*, **12**, 1068.

Steudler, P. A., Bowden, R. D., Melillo, J. M. and Aber, J. D. (1989) Influence of nitrogen fertilization on methane uptake in temperate forest soils. *Nature*, **341**, 314–16.

Stewart, A. J. A. and Lance, A. N. (1991) Effects of moor-draining on the hydrology and vegetation of North Pennine blanket bog. *Journal of Applied Ecology*, **28**, 1105–17.

Tallis, J. H. (1998) Growth and degradation of British and Irish blanket mires. *Environmental Review*, **6**, 81–122.

Tallis, J. H. and Meade, R. (1997) Blanket mire degradation and management. *Blanket Mire Degradation: Causes, Challenges and Consequences* (ed. J. H. Tallis, R. Meade and P. D. Hulme), pp. 212–16. Aberdeen: Macaulay Land Use Research Institute.

Thomas, G., Yallop, A. R., Thacker, J., Brewer, T. and Sannier, C. (2004) A history of burning as a management tool in the English uplands. Draft report to English Nature, Cranfield University, Silsoe.

Tolonen, K., Davis, R. B. and Widoff, L. (1988) Peat accumulation rates in selected Maine peat deposits. *Department of Conservation Bulletin*, **33**, 1–99.

Tolonen, K. and Turunen, J. (1996) Accumulation rates of carbon in mires in Finland and implications for climate change, *The Holocene*, **6**, 171–8.

Tranvik, L. J. and Jansson, M. (2002) Terrestrial export of organic carbon. *Nature*, **415**, 861–2.

Trumbore, S. E., Bubier, J. L., Harden, J. W. and Crill, P. M. (1999) Carbon cycling in boreal wetlands: a comparison of three approaches. *Journal of Geophysical Research*, **104**, 27673–82.

Tuittila, E.-S., Komulainen, V.-M., Vasander, H., Nykanen, H. and Martikainen, P. J. (2000) Methane dynamics of a restored cut-away peatland. *Global Change Biology*, **6**, 569–81.

Turetsky, M. R., Manning, S. W. and Wieder, R. K. (2004) Dating recent peat deposits. *Wetlands*, **24**, 324–56.

Wallage, Z. E., Holden, J. and McDonald, A. T. (2006) Drain blocking: an effective treatment for reducing dissolved organic carbon loss and water discolouration in a drained peatland. *Science of the Total Environment*, **367**, 811–21.

Willey, J. D., Kieber, R. J., Eyman, M. S. and Yavitt, J. B. (2000) Rainwater dissolved organic carbon: concentrations and global flux. *Global Biogeochemical Cycles*, **14**, 139–48.

Worrall, F. and Adamson, J. K. (2007) Change in runoff initiation probability over a severe drought – implications for peat stability. *Journal of Hydrology*, **345**, 16–26.

Worrall, F., Armstrong, A. and Adamson, J. K. (2007) The effect of burning and sheepgrazing on water table depth and soil water quality in a blanket bog. *Journal of Hydrology*, **339**, 1–14.

Worrall, F., Armstrong, A. and Holden, J. (2007) Short-term impact of peat drain-blocking on water colour, dissolved organic carbon concentration, and water table depth. *Journal of Hydrology*, **337**, 315–25.

Worrall, F. and Burt, T. P. (2004) Time series analysis of long term river DOC records. *Hydrological Processes*, **18**, 893–911.

Worrall, F. and Burt, T. P. (2007) The flux of dissolved organic carbon from UK rivers. *Global Biogeochemical Cycles*, **21**, art. no GB1013.

Worrall, F., Burt, T. P. and Adamson, J. (2004) Can climate change explain increases in DOC flux from upland peat catchments? *Science of the Total Environment*, 326, 95–112.

Worrall, F., Burt, T. P. and Adamson, J. K. (2005) Fluxes of dissolved carbon dioxide and inorganic carbon from an upland peat catchment: implications for soil respiration. *Biogeochemistry*, **73**, 515–39.

Worrall, F., Burt, T. P. and Adamson, J. K. (2006) Trends in drought frequency – the fate of northern peatlands. *Climatic Change*, **76**, 339–59.

Worrall, F., Reed, M., Warburton, J. and Burt, T. P. (2003) Carbon budget for British upland peat catchment. *Science of the Total Environment*, **312**, 133–46.

Wright, R. F., Alewell, C., Cullen, J. M., Evans, C. D., Marchetto, A., Moldan, F., Prechtel, A. and Rogora, M. (2001) Trends in nitrogen deposition and leaching in acid-sensitive streams in Europe. *Hydrology and Earth System Science*, **5**, 299–310.

Zoltai, S. C. (1991) Estimating the age of peat samples from their weight: a study from west-central Canada. *The Holocene*, **1**, 68–73.

6 Upland hydrology

Joseph Holden

Introduction

The uplands of the oceanic temperate-humid zone, on which this book is focused, are dominated either by thin soils on steep slopes or, where slopes are more gentle, by thicker organic soils which range from raw peats and earthy peats to organo-mineral soils. Where slopes are gentle and soils in the uplands are deep, they tend to be dominated by organic matter (e.g. Paramo ecosystem of the Andes; Buytaert *et al.*, 2006). Organic soils of the uplands tend to have a large water content and are quickly saturated during rainfall thereby generating fast-moving surface or near-surface hillslope runoff. This is characteristic both for gentle upland slopes with deep organic soils and steeper slopes with thin soil layers, and creates a system allowing water to be rapidly shed from headwater catchments. This means that, even without management intervention or future climate change, such systems remain source areas for flooding. The impact of management practice on flood risk depends on a number of factors including drainage network structure, local topography and location of a given management practice with respect to these landscape features.

Over the last century there have been changes in upland management, with increased drainage, grazing, liming and coniferous afforestation, which has led to changes in the vegetation cover, structure and hydrology of these soils in many parts of the world (Buytaert *et al.*, 2006; Holden *et al.*, 2007b). The hydrology of organic soils is not only fundamental for their development and decay, as it is the semi-waterlogged nature of the soils that helps them remain in place; the hydrology is also important for their function as a carbon store (see also Worrall and Evans, this volume) and as a source area for river and drinking water downstream. Changes in the hydrology of the uplands may drive changes in the hydrological, ecological and hydrochemical functions in other parts of the upland and lowland system. Therefore, in order to predict the consequences of environmental change on the uplands and the connected downstream impacts, an understanding of the temporal and spatial variability of hydrological processes is required. While this chapter will reference material from a range of international sources, it will focus on material from the UK uplands to illustrate the discussion. In particular it will examine the nature of research into impacts of management and climate change on hydrological processes in UK uplands.

River flow

There has been some debate about whether upland soils such as peat act to increase or decrease flood risk downstream. The extent of downstream inundation depends on both the discharge peak and the total volume of water moving downstream. These both depend on the nature of the precipitation event and the function of the landscape to mediate water movement before it reaches the river channel network. Bullock and Acreman (2003) produced a database of research on the role of wetland soils in the hydrological cycle and found only very limited support for the idea that they acted to buffer floods. This is because peats and many organo-mineral soils store large quantities of water, leaving little room for storage of fresh rainfall. Saturated peat tends to be 90–8 per cent water by mass. Even above the water table (maximum height of the saturated zone), peat can still hold large volumes of water (approximately 90–5 per cent water by mass). In many peatlands the water table is within just 40 cm of the surface for 80 per cent of the year at least.

Ombrotrophic (rain-fed) peatland catchments tend to have very flashy hydrological regimes (e.g. Evans *et al.*, 1999). Studies of various peatlands show that streamflows are dominated by high peak flows and discontinuous summer flow (Holden & Burt, 2003c). Response to rainfall has been shown to be rapid, and peat streams tend to have hydrographs with steep recessional curves and minimal baseflow (e.g. Figure 6.1). Thus, in contradiction to an

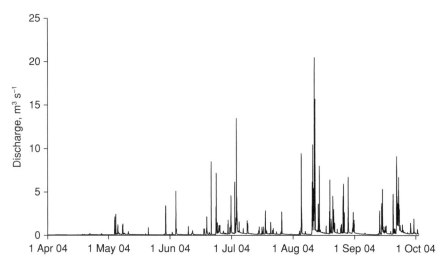

Figure 6.1 Discharge from Oughtershaw Moss, a peatland catchment in the Yorkshire Dales, over a six-month period.

often expressed view (first put forward by Turner, 1757), peatlands do not always behave like a 'sponge'. Rather, water is released rapidly following rainfall or snowmelt, and baseflows are often poorly maintained as many small tributaries dry up completely after only a week without rain. This poor maintenance of baseflow is a problem for water companies reliant on streamflow to supply their intakes despite high water tables for most of the year. Conversely, many upland areas with wet organic soils tend to be source areas for flooding. Activities such as grazing or drainage can increase the flood risk even further so that intact (i.e. not degraded) upland soils are preferred where possible (Holden *et al.*, 2007a). Some uplands do contribute to baseflow but these tend to be ones where the soils and the underlying geology are both more permeable and thick enough to prevent saturation-excess overland flow from developing (e.g. chalk-based uplands).

Hillslope hydrology

The movement of water across and through any landscape occurs in a number of ways (Figure 6.2). These include infiltration-excess overland flow (where inputs of water are in excess of the rate at which water can infiltrate into the surface), saturation-excess overland flow (where the soil is saturated, and water ponds up and flows back out on to the surface), and throughflow (where water flows through the soil or rock substrate). Throughflow can occur through

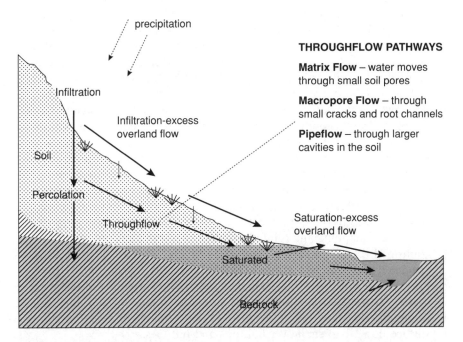

Figure 6.2 Main hillslope runoff pathways.

the tiny pores of soils or rocks (matrix flow), or through larger cavities and pores (macropore flow or pipeflow). All of these processes operate in uplands and lead to the generation of riverflow, although the relative importance of each process varies with the type of upland soil, the type of management and the state of soil degradation.

Many intact organic soils, especially peats, appear to be dominated by saturation-excess overland flow or throughflow in the upper peat layers (Box 6.1). Table 6.1 provides data from an undisturbed blanket peatland hill-slope in Upper Wharfedale, UK (54° 13′ 51″ N, 2° 13′ 38″ W). The dominant vegetation is *Eriophorum* spp. with some *Sphagnum* cover. The peats here are from 0.5 m to 2.5 m deep, and formed during the Holocene, and are underlain by glacial boulder clay. The climate is oceanic, with 1,800 mm of precipitation per year (Environment Agency gauge on site recording

---

Box 6.1. Acrotelm–catotelm model

Although peat soils have large water content and high porosity, they have very low saturated hydraulic conductivities (rate at which water moves through the saturated soil), and so tend to retain large amounts of water, which help them maintain their saturated status. Since the mid-twentieth century Russian scientists have adopted a two-layered system for understanding peats, and this is now widely adopted to describe hydro-ecological processes (Bragg and Tallis, 2001; Holden and Burt, 2003a, 2003b, 2003c). The layering system comprises an upper 'active' peat layer with a high hydraulic conductivity and fluctuating water table (the 'acrotelm'), and a more 'inert' lower layer which corresponds to the permanently saturated main body of peat (the 'catotelm'). According to Ingram (1983), the acrotelm is affected by a fluctuating water table (the lowest water-table depth is therefore the base of the acrotelm), has a high hydraulic conductivity and a variable water content, is rich in peat-forming aerobic bacteria and other micro-organisms, and has a live matrix of growing plant material. The catotelm has an invariable water content, a small hydraulic conductivity, is not subject to air entry, and is devoid of peat-forming aerobic micro-organisms. The acrotelm–catotelm model implies that most runoff production and nutrient transfer will occur within the upper peat layer, close to or at the peat surface. While field mapping and rainfall simulation experiments on peats have confirmed the dominance of saturation-excess overland flow on both vegetated and bare peat surfaces (Holden and Burt, 2002a, 2003b), they have also demonstrated the spatial and temporal variability of the processes. Steeper midslope sections of slopes produce overland flow less frequently on many upland soils (with concomitant increases in sub-surface flow) than shallower hill tops and hill toes.

Table 6.1 Percentage runoff collected in automated throughflow troughs from peat layers on hillslopes in Upper Wharfedale, December 2002–December 2004.

Peat layer (depth, cm)	Percent runoff from hillslope layers
0–1	74
1–8	21
8–20	5
>20	<0.01

between 1999 and 2006) and a mean annual temperature of 6.3°C (based on Hobo temperature logger on site from January 2003 to December 2006). The water table at one location within the catchment is shown in Figure 6.3 for January to June 2004. For 74 per cent of the time the water table is within 10 cm of the surface (Figure 6.3). Only for short periods during the summer does the water table decline to levels below this. Even then, the maximum water-table depth recorded from the site between December 2002 and December 2006 was 27 cm, which is very shallow when compared to other soil types. Most runoff (74 per cent) measured from runoff troughs was produced from the surface of the peat, and most of the rest from the upper 20 cm of the peat profile. However, such measurements rarely include components of flow through macropores and soil pipes (Box 6.2); and so, while peats may appear to be surface-flow dominated, the lack of other measurements may mask the full range of processes.

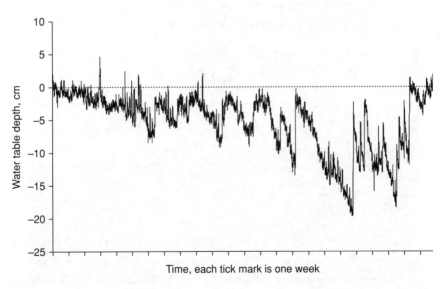

Figure 6.3 Water table depth for an undisturbed peat soil, Upper Wharfedale, UK, January–June 2004.

Box 6.2. Soil pipes in upland soils

The traditional acrotelm–catotelm model described in Box 1 ignores the important role of turbulent flow in macropores (here defined as pores greater than 1 mm in diameter) and pipes (>10 mm). Baird (1997) and Holden *et al.* (2001) have shown that over 30 per cent of runoff in fens and blanket peats moves through macropores, which results in water and nutrients being transferred between deep and shallow layers of the peat profile. Soil pipes (e.g. Figure 6.4) can be several metres in diameter and are present in most upland soil types in the British Isles. In fact cavers in the English Peak District often explore these pipes where they are known as 'slutch caves' (Chapman, 1993). Pipes have been well researched on the stagnopodzols and shallow peats of the Maesnant catchment of mid-Wales by Tony Jones and colleagues (e.g. Jones, 1997, 2004; Jones and Crane, 1984). Here, pipeflows contribute 50 per cent to streamflow, and the areas of the catchment with more piping yield more sediment to the stream system than other parts of the catchment. Most of the pipes occur at the interface between the organic horizon and the underlying mineral substrate. The hydrological importance of soil pipes has also been reported in many other upland environments including in New Zealand, Indonesia, China, Japan and South

Figure 6.4 Submerged soil pipe surrounded by cracked peat.

America (e.g. Carey and Woo, 2000; Roberge and Plamondon, 1987; Terajima *et al.*, 2000; Uchida *et al.*, 2005).

The study by Holden and Burt (2002c) is the only detailed study of pipeflow in a deep peat soil anywhere in the world, and they identified 10 per cent of streamflow moving through the pipe network. Pipes may produce dissolved and particulate organic carbon, but there are very few data available. Very little is understood about the role of pipes in peat hydrology, erosion or carbon cycling. Often, sediment is deposited on the peat and vegetation surface, where a pipe has overflowed during a storm event. This sediment can contain a large proportion of mineral material from the underlying substrate, as pipe networks undulate throughout the soil profile (unlike in the stagno-podzols investigated in mid-Wales). The existence of pipes and macro-pores therefore opens the way for the fluxes of water, sediment and nutrient contributions from deep within and below the organic soil rather than simply by rapid transfer through the upper organic soil layers. This is important, particularly in ombrotrophic peats, because, even if some pipe networks are actually 'dead-ends' and have little effect on water delivery to streams, they will still act to provide vertical coupling of sediments and solutes, and provide additional sub-surface connect-ivity across peatlands.

It is now possible, for the first time, systematically to examine pip-ing and macroporosity in peatlands in order to determine what con-trols their location and frequency. Macropores can be measured through tension devices and dye staining, and recently it has been shown that pipes can be detected using ground-penetrating radar (Holden, 2004; Holden *et al.*, 2002). Holden (2005a) performed a ground-penetrating radar survey of 160 peatlands in the UK and detected piping (when greater than 100 mm) in all catchments surveyed. Results showed that land management can dramatically increase piping. A mean density of piping equivalent to 69 pipes per km of radar transect was deter-mined. Topographic position (but not slope angle) was found to be a significant control both on soil pipe frequency and on macroporosity ($p < 0.001$). Topslopes and toeslopes were found to have significantly higher densities of soil pipes and macropores than midslopes. Gully ero-sion (sometimes a product of pipe collapse) occurs in some peatlands, and this appears to have the same topographic pattern. This suggests that there are links between small-scale sub-surface erosion and water transfer processes (<1 mm matrix pores, 1–10 mm macropores, 100–3,000 mm pipes) and hillslope-scale surface geomorphology and parti-culate carbon loss.

Hydrological impacts of upland drainage

Many upland soils around the world have been drained, principally to aid agricultural expansion. In Britain, land drainage commenced before Roman times. However, expansion in upland drainage is relatively recent: and, in the 1960s and 1970s, 100,000 hectares of blanket peat per year in Britain were drained by digging open ditches (Robinson and Armstrong, 1988). Often, drains were contoured or shaped like a 'herring bone', with short lateral feeder ditches collecting into a central ditch. The drainage aimed to improve the quality of soils for sheep- and grouse-rearing. However, Stewart and Lance (1983) demonstrated that there was no evidence that drainage fulfilled the claims made for it. Grouse populations did not seem to increase (in fact many grouse-moor managers reported that grouse chicks and lambs became stranded in the drains and died), and upland organic soils cannot sustain large stocking densities anyway.

Upland drainage has been associated with environmental degradation. Drainage has resulted in changes in water flow paths through and over organic soils (Holden *et al.*, 2006b) and has been reported both to increase and to decrease flood peaks (Holden *et al.*, 2004). Given that both increases and decreases in flood risk have been reported as a potential result of drainage, it is important to be able to understand the conditions under which such effects occur and the magnitude of such effects. While lowering the water table buffers (slightly) the impacts of a rainfall event by providing extra soil storage capacity for rainwater and reducing saturation-excess overland flow, the ditches themselves speed up the removal of water from the land into streams. Therefore, the local impacts on flooding might depend on factors such as ditch network design, slope and local vegetation (e.g. Gilman, 2002, at Cors y Llyn). Moreover, the position of the drainage within the catchment as a whole is important because, even if drainage slowed and decreased the flood peak from a tributary, it may cause this peak to be delayed, to the extent that it occurs at the same time as the main channel flood peak (Holden *et al.*, 2004). This could therefore cause flood peaks to increase overall. Therefore, unless the large majority of the catchment is covered by one type of land management, a spatial approach which takes account of the nature of the drainage network and the timing of flows from each part of the drainage network and how they are influenced by specific management practices in their area is essential to understanding the impacts of management activity on environmental processes.

Many drained peatland catchments exhibit increases in low flows (Baden and Eggelsmann, 1970). This has often been attributed to catchment 'de-watering' following drainage (Burke, 1975) and changes to soil structure (Holden, 2005a), and is often only a temporary response. Organic soils shrink, crack (Holden and Burt, 2002a, b) and decompose when dried. This change in soil structure is important for hydrology, water quality and ecology. Holden (2005a) found that peats that had been drained had significantly higher amounts of soil piping than other undrained peats. In blanket peats, Holden (2006) has shown across England, Wales and Scotland that, as the drain networks get older, the density of piping increases. This long-term pipeflow response to drainage (which can continue even eighty years after drainage) can result in long-term changes to river regime (Holden *et al.*, 2006b). Because the pipes also get larger, this means that there can be an exponential increase in sediment (or particulate carbon) release from soil pipes as the drains get older (Holden, 2006). This suggests that drain-blocking should occur where drains are oldest, if sediment and carbon release is considered to be a problem worth tackling. In addition to sediment release from soil piping, the ditches themselves can be subject to severe scouring, widening and deepening, often by several metres. Site characteristics (e.g. steep slopes) often mean that even recently drained catchments may be significant sources of sediment and carbon. Holden *et al.* (2007c) showed that, for an upland catchment, peat drains were major sources of suspended sediment with 18.3 per cent of the sediment originating from drains which drained 7.3 per cent of the area.

The creation of drain channels interferes with the natural pattern of water flow across hillslopes. Figure 6.5 shows the mean water-table depth and occurrence of overland flow between bi-weekly visits over a two-year period for two similar plots. For the intact plot, overland flow and high water tables are to be expected. However, for the plot with drains crossing it, the downslope area below each drain tends to be driest. This is simply because that part of the slope no longer receives water from upslope. Effectively, the drains have shortened the slope length. This means that anywhere downslope of a land drain will be drier than it would otherwise have been and will have less overland flow. It is possible to predict which drains will have the biggest impact on downslope saturation and therefore on peatland ecology or carbon cycling, simply by mapping the topography of the landscape and the location of the drains. In other words, Figure 6.5 is based on real data, but we have simple tools that can predict these maps for large areas without having to go through the time-consuming and laborious process of collecting new water-table data for each area we are interested in restoring. Such information can be useful to land managers who are considering blocking land drains because it can guide them to target particular drains and use their resources more effectively (Holden *et al.*, 2006a).

Hydrological impacts of upland burning

Many uplands have been burned to manage the landscape for grazing and to enhance game-bird populations. There have been a number of recent and comprehensive reviews of the impacts of upland burning of heather and grass (both prescribed and wildfire) on environmental processes (e.g. Glaves *et al.*, 2005; Shaw *et al.*, 1996). A key element to note from these reviews is that virtually nothing is known about whether burning influences soil hydrology,

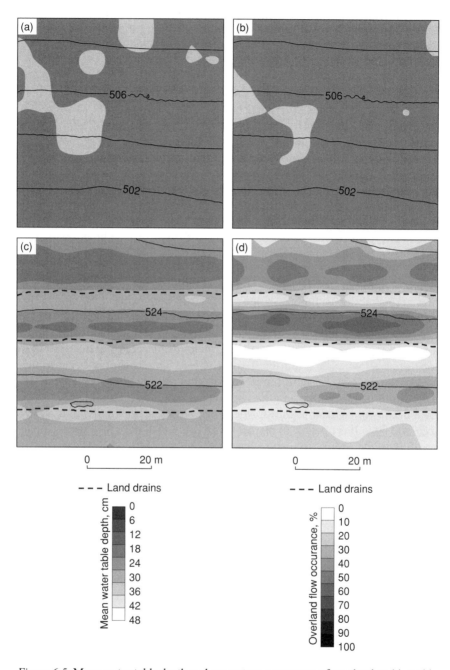

Figure 6.5 Mean water-table depth and percentage occurrence of overland on bi-weekly
monitored plots October 2002 to October 2004 for an intact slope (a, b)
and a drained slope (c, d). Contour lines are heights at 2 m intervals, right-
hand diagrams are overland flow and left-hand diagrams are water-table.

sediment release and water quality. These are all experimentally determinate factors that require scientific funding. Of the little research that has been done, the work by Holden (2005b) is notable because it has shown that heather is associated with more soil piping in upland soils and this may lead to changes in hydrological flowpaths and changes in water quality and carbon fluxes. In terms of more direct influences of burning on soils, wildfire (which often burns for longer and to hotter temperatures than managed burns) has been shown to result in the development of water-repellent compounds (Clymo, 1983). The removal of vegetation can make the soil surface susceptible to wind and fluvial erosion as well as to increased freeze–thaw action. In many studies of upland organic soil fire erosion there has been a lack of careful experimental design, so that results cannot be interpreted more widely. Some authors have attributed the onset of major erosion episodes to historic wildfire (Dunn and Mackay, 1996) or historic human-induced fire (Tallis, 1987). There is a dearth of data on infiltration following fire on upland soils, but increases and decreases have been reported.

Hydrological impacts of upland grazing

There have been very few studies of the influence of grazing on upland soil hydrology, and particularly on organic upland soils, but Carroll *et al.* (2004) demonstrated an increased bulk density (weight of material per unit volume) with stocking density in Snowdonia, while the reverse was the case at ADAS Pwllpeiran plots in the Cambrian Mountains. However, bulk density was not related to infiltration in a simple manner, and the Carroll *et al.* (2004) study had a very limited number of samples. Sheep tracks are important hydrological agents, providing direct connectivity across slopes for water, sediment and pollutants. This is because sheep tracks are compacted and infiltration capacities reduced, so that infiltration-excess overland flow becomes more common. Some summary data on steady-state infiltration rates, hydraulic conductivity, bulk density and proportion of flow moving through macropores are presented in Table 6.2 for two blanket peatland sites with and without grazing (Holden and Burt, 2003a; 2003c; Holden *et al.*, 2001). Where grazing occurs, the hydraulic conductivity and infiltration rate is much lower across the hillslope than where grazing has been restricted. Five years without grazing can be enough to allow the system to recover towards conditions similar to no grazing for over forty years. These changes in hillslope hydrology could result in changes in river flow and indicate that cessation of grazing may reduce flood risk. Meyles *et al.* (2006) have suggested that grazing on stagnohumic gleys on Dartmoor caused more rapid connectivity of hillslope water with streams and therefore contributes to enhanced flood peaks. This occurs even before vegetation has been removed as a result of soil structural changes, particularly in the topsoil. Hence, even where animal pressures are not immediately obvious in the landscape (i.e. through visible erosion or stripping of vegetation), there can still be marked effects

Table 6.2 Mean summary hydrological characteristics for two sites with and without grazing during 2005 (unpublished data from Y. Zhao and J. Holden).

Grazing condition	Wharfedale				Teesdale			
	None since 1960	None since 2000	2 ewes ha^{-1}	Sheep track	None since 1954	None since 1997	0.5 ewes ha^{-1}	Sheep track
Mean infiltration rate, mm hr^{-1} (n = 50)	22.7	20.3	16.3	9.6	22.0	16.3	10.2	5.9
Soil bulk density in upper 5 cm, g cm^{-3} (n = 50)	0.033	0.037	0.040	0.088	0.030	0.031	0.037	0.012
Surface saturated hydraulic conductivity × 10^{-8} cm s^{-1} (n = 25)	2753	1388	376	7	8937	4741	931	23
Saturated hydraulic conductivity at 10 cm depth × 10^{-8} cm s^{-1} (n = 25)	11	13	3	1	44	56	13	2
% macropore flow at surface (n = 25)	33	35	29	18	36	37	35	21
% macropore flow at 10 cm depth (n = 25)	24	32	23	21	29	33	26	21
% occasions overland flow had occurred at 50 locations between bi-weekly visits during 2005	73.3	73.1	80.9	84.1	90.7	89.9	90.5	91.1

n is the number of samples per category.

of livestock on organic soil and catchment processes. Sansom (1999) noted that in the north Derwent catchment sheep numbers had doubled between 1944 and 1975 to 24,000, and in that time annual water yield had increased by 25 per cent. It is not known whether other factors contributed to this change, but such an increase in grazing is likely to have had some hydrological impact. Therefore, there may be sensitive parts of the catchment where grazing will have a much greater impact on stream flow (e.g. by compacting valley bottoms) than in other parts of the catchment. The role of sheep tracks also reminds us that, if we are to understand the environmental impacts (and make reliable predictions) of reductions in grazing, we need to use spatial modelling techniques that incorporate topographical processes rather than simply rely on statistical models that just assume that a proportion of the catchment is managed in a certain way. This means moving away from the idea that if we change a catchment from being 20 per cent grazed to 30 per cent grazed we simply change the runoff delivery prediction by 10 per cent.

Hydrological impacts of vegetation cover and severe degradation

Different vegetation covers are likely to be associated with different rates of evapotranspiration. This is an important mechanism of water loss from upland soils. In fact, even different *Sphagnum* moss species have been found to have different capabilities to hold and transport water, and so the surface wetness and the cover of vascular plants tends to vary among the micro-relief (Kellner, 2001). Where there is a relatively large quantity of non-transpiring biomass (brown leaves, *Ericaceae* stems, dead grass) sheltering the ground, there can be a large surface resistance to evapotranspiration.

In some uplands, such as the Peak District, UK, there has been severe soil degradation and there are large areas of bare peat dissected by gullies (e.g. Figure 6.6). Such gully networks are likely to operate in the same way as drains by increasing drainage density and increasing the velocity of flow from hillslopes to streams. Evans and Warburton (2005) evaluated the effect of gully-blocking on total flow through the gullies (see also Anderson *et al.*, this volume). Using high-resolution topographic data (LiDAR), model estimations showed that blocking some gullies might exacerbate flow through other nearby gullies, making the problem worse, and it was possible to predict where blocking would be most and least effective.

Figure 6.6 Gully erosion in the Peak District.

It would be expected that bare surfaces would enhance the velocity of overland flow thereby leading to shorter lag times and higher flood peaks. An experiment using tracers to measure the velocity of overland flow (Holden *et al.*, 2008) found that overland flow on bare peat typically occurred at twice the velocity of that on vegetated surfaces. In addition, *Sphagnum* provided a significantly greater effective hydraulic roughness than peatland grasses (*Eriophorum* or *Eriophorum–Sphagnum* mixes) thereby slowing flow more effectively. Re-establishment of vegetation and especially of *Sphagnum* on degraded peatlands may therefore be important for increasing water-storage potential and reducing the potential for sheet erosion (Evans and Warburton, 2005; Holden and Burt, 2002a). However, data on such mechanisms are required to understand how re-vegetation of damaged upland soils might affect water-flow velocity across peats and therefore streamflow hydrographs and sedimentological processes.

Hydrological impacts of afforestation

One of the major changes in upland cover is mass deforestation leading to destabilised slopes and a faster response to rainfall. This is because without tree cover the water table is raised and hence saturation is more rapid under rainfall conditions. In the Paramo of Ecuador and in the British Isles, however, there has been an expansion of coniferous plantations in the uplands. Forest drains lower the water table and result in associated subsidence of the soil surface owing to compression and shrinkage (Anderson *et al.*, 2000). The organic soil tends to dry out after canopy closure, but the furrows often continue to provide wetter hollows. Increased interception and transpiration causes a much greater lowering in the water table than drainage alone and enhanced surface subsidence. Hydrological studies in the 1970s showed that afforestation increased evaporative losses, leading to a reduction in runoff (e.g. Calder and Newson, 1979) and concerns about the sustainability of water supplies. This is a particular problem for mature forests during low flow periods. However, in the early stage of plantations, land preparation techniques for forestry in the uplands, such as ploughing and drainage practices, have been shown to increase peak flows (Robinson, 1986). There is often large-scale cracking in afforested peat soils, and the hydraulic conductivity tends to increase in the upper soil layers. When the conifers are harvested there can be a sudden increase in discharge peaks as the drains are reactivated and evapotranspiration suddenly declines, meaning that there is no longer such a great soil moisture deficit that would have buffered rainfall.

While there are currently pressures to reduce coniferous afforestation in many areas, there are growing demands for upland soils to be planted with native tree species (Gimmingham, 1995). Some woodland planting is seen as a 're-wilding' of the landscape, while there is also a view that woodland planting might reduce flood risk. However, in many upland areas with organic soils there is limited evidence that this is the case except where the plantations cover very large proportions of the catchment. It is possible that flood-plain trees provide a hydraulic roughness that slows flow in the uplands, which then lowers the flood peak downstream. However, much more research is needed to determine optimal locations for such plantations and to determine whether there would be a measurable impact.

Hydrological impacts of construction

Upland soils are often under threat from development pressures such as new roads, new building developments and infrastructure (pipelines). Recently wind farms have come under scrutiny for potential damage to organic soil function and landscape character. While construction and foundation of the turbine masts themselves has a direct influence on the hydrology of the surrounding peat, the largest impacts of wind farms on organic soil processes probably relate to the access tracks that are installed on site. While 'floating tracks' are advocated, there is evidence to suggest that the peat can subside around tracks, and the tracks and drainage systems installed interfere with natural runoff processes in their vicinity. There have been a limited number of studies into wind farm impacts on upland soil processes and function, but most of these remain confidential to wind farm developers and agencies (e.g. Gunn *et al.*, 2002), and there is thus a need for more open research into wind farm impacts on soil and ecosystem processes.

Hydrological impacts of climate change

Climate change has always played an important role in upland ecosystems. The most dramatic impacts have occurred when ice sheets and glaciers covered upland zones and the advance and retreat of such features impacts the landscapes and ecosystems we see today. In terms of contemporary climate change, such impacts are of great importance to large parts of the world's population. In some parts of the world glacier meltwater in the summer supplies water resources to vast populations (e.g. Hindu-Kush region). Climate change here might shrink glaciers to the extent that these water resources become more scarce over time.

The current rate of anthropogenic climate-forcing is a particular cause for concern for upland regions, too. Temperatures across the UK uplands, for example, are likely to increase by 0.8 to 2°C by 2050 (Hulme *et al.*, 2002), although most of the recent upland warming has been confined to the winter months with associated decreases in lapse rates (rate at which temperature declines with altitude) (Holden and Adamson, 2002; see also Caporn and Emmett, this volume). Smaller winter snowpacks will have beneficial flood risk impacts downstream as historically many large floods have occurred when a warm front has quickly melted an upland snowpack releasing large volumes of water. Precipitation totals are predicted to vary across upland regions. In the British Isles precipitation has been predicted to increase in the north and west, with a stronger winter–summer contrast (Burt *et al.*, 1998), but to decrease in the south and east, enhancing existing environmental gradients and placing the most southerly and easterly UK uplands under more extreme pressure of degradation due to drying out, while other uplands will produce more runoff (Werrity, 2002). Furthermore, changes in seasonality of rainfall and temperature may lead to increased frequency and/or severity of summer drought.

Changes in hydrological processes due to climate are likely to drive changes in other processes, too. The change in air temperature and precipitation regimes with climate change will mean increased depths to water table in some upland soils. Upland peatlands represent the most significant terrestrial carbon pool in the UK (Cannell *et al.*, 1999; Hope *et al.*, 1997). However, such peats can become large sources of carbon to the atmosphere and water courses if they degrade. Many organic soils, such as peats, convert some sequestered carbon anaerobically into CH_4 which is much more potent as a greenhouse gas than CO_2. If the water table is lowered, the carbon sink–source relationship is likely to be disturbed because a greater percentage of the peat is available for oxidation in biochemical reactions. In addition, the rate of peat decomposition will increase with lowered water tables, and effectively more CO_2 and dissolved organic carbon will be available for release. However, as a potential counterbalance, reduced water tables would result in a reduction in the concentration of CH_4 released because the increase in aerobic conditions will suppress the activity of the anaerobic methanogenic bacteria and increase the volume of peat in which CH_4 oxidation may occur. However, Hughes *et al.* (1999) artificially drained a moorland soil to simulate climatically driven changes in water table and found that CH_4 emissions demonstrated a three-year cycle (large increased emissions, then very low emissions and then recovery back to pre-drainage state).

Climate change in uplands will also alter the water balance and hence change the amount and/or the nature of runoff. Tranvik and Jansson (2002) and Worrall *et al.* (2007) have both ascribed much of the observed variation in dissolved organic carbon to changes in the amount of runoff from upland catchments (see also Worrall and Evans, this volume). However, for other types of carbon release, runoff changes may alter the release rates and pathways (e.g. Billett *et al.*, 2006). The evidence described above suggests that enhanced peat piping due to summer drought or vegetation change (more woody *Calluna* cover) might lead to more deep carbon loss in eroded, dissolved and gaseous form. An increased frequency of winter storms could have severe short-term erosion impacts on upland soils. Greater peak flows in streams and gullies can strip the soil resulting in erosion at the margins of flood plains and in gully systems often yielding large soil blocks. Mass failures of the hillslopes (see Evans, this volume) may leave bare surfaces, which are susceptible to secondary erosion processes and gullying of the mineral substrate.

Conclusions

The uplands of the oceanic temperate-humid zone receive more precipitation than the lowlands. Therefore, land management change in the uplands has the potential to have a greater impact on river flow than the same management change in the lowlands. Where the uplands are dominated by organo-mineral or organic soils they are likely to be dominated by high water tables and saturation-excess overland flow, which can be rapidly transmitted to the river channel network. Drainage, grazing, forestry and burning can all influence the propensity for the soils to saturate and can influence how water is partitioned between overland flow and sub-surface flow. However, the impacts of many management activities on upland hydrological processes remain poorly understood (e.g. impact of burning), and the combining of impacts of multiple management interventions makes teasing apart individual impacts difficult. Uplands tend to remain source areas for flooding; and it should be remembered that, no matter what management activity takes place, this will remain the case unless the system is underlain by very permeable bedrock such as chalk and the soils allow water to percolate through them to the bedrock. Therefore, in general terms, uplands do not mitigate against flooding. Their management is unlikely to have much of an impact during very extreme rainfall events because the propensity for quick saturation is high. It may be, however, that for smaller magnitude-duration flood events upland management could make an impact, although this is likely to be a function of the shape of the landscape and the timing of how water is delivered from different parts of the drainage network.

The location of a particular management activity within the catchment is important for determining its wider downstream impact. This is because local changes in the amount and timing of runoff will have different downstream effects depending on the relative phasing with other runoff sources within the catchment. Therefore, generalised statements on the impact of a particular local management activity on downstream flood risk are not possible unless that management activity covers a large proportion of the catchment or you have an understanding of whole catchment hydrological behaviour. We have a good understanding at the local scale (~10 km^2) of management impacts on hydrological processes (and therefore riverflow at this scale) because that is closer to the scale over which upland management practices occur. Indeed there are simple topographically based tools for predicting effects of management such as drainage or gully erosion on both the local soil saturation and the timing and magnitude of local downstream runoff. Given that many upland managers are aiming to restore hydrological function to fulfil a number of objectives (e.g. water quality, habitat improvement, reduced flood risk, decreased sediment/carbon losses), these tools can be useful guides to the most effective locations to target resources (e.g. where drains or gullies should be blocked).

However, despite the importance of local upland management and impacts on downstream flood risk, we still do not have adequate approaches for measuring or predicting the impacts of past or future change at the larger scale (e.g. 1,000 km^2) without very large uncertainty. We need new physically based, spatially distributed modelling approaches to understand how local management propagates the impact of frequent and rare (extreme) events downstream at the larger scale.

Despite the known upland hydrological impacts caused by management change described in this chapter, it remains the case in the temperate oceanic zone that climate variability is the dominant factor influencing flood or water-shortage magnitude and frequency in temperate-humid upland catchments. This is because, even if a management practice like drainage or coniferous plantation lowers the water tables, the soil responds to this change by quickly allowing the release of any new water added to the soil surface. It does not require much rainfall to raise the water table to the surface even in a degraded organic soil, and furthermore degraded organic soils tend to have more throughflow pathways such as soil pipes or faster matrix flow which allows water to escape quickly from the system.

Notwithstanding the flooding issue, upland management certainly impacts soil hydrological processes which then drive other important processes (e.g. water quality and carbon fluxes). While the integrated downstream impacts are important to consider, including provision of clean drinking water, the local impacts on carbon flux and ecosystem function are crucial. One particular area of remaining uncertainty, however, is whether or not some long-term changes in upland soil hydrology resulting from past management are reversible, such as soil pipe development and enhanced sub-surface carbon release. It may well be that upland restoration practices fulfil some hydrological objectives, but it is unlikely that they will fulfil all of them, at least in the short-term.

References

Anderson, A. R., Ray, D. and Pyatt, D. G. (2000) Physical and hydrological impacts of blanket bog afforestation at Bad a' Cheo, Caithness: the first 5 years. *Forestry*, **73**, 467–78.

Baden, W. and Eggelsmann, R. (1970) Hydrological budget of high peat bogs in the Atlantic region. *Proceedings of the Third International Peat Congress, 1968*, pp. 260–311. Ottawa: Department of Energy, Mines and Resources.

Baird, A. J. (1997) Field estimation of macropore functioning and surface hydraulic conductivity in a fen peat. *Hydrological Processes*, **11**, 287–95.

Billett, M. F., Deacon, C. M., Palmer, S. M., Dawson, J. J. C. and Hope, D. (2006) Connecting organic carbon in stream water and soils in a peatland catchment. *Journal of Geophysical Research*, **111**, G02010, doi:10.1029/2005JG000065.

Bragg, O. M. and Tallis, J. H. (2001) The sensitivity of peat-covered upland landscapes. *Catena*, **42**, 345–60.

Bullock, A. and Acreman, M. (2003) The role of wetlands in the hydrological cycle. *Hydrology and Earth System Sciences*, **7**, 358–89.

Burke, W. (1975) Effect of drainage on hydrology of blanket bog. *Irish Journal of Agricultural Research*, **14**, 145–62.

Burt, T. P., Adamson, J. K. and Lane, A. M. J. (1998) Long-term rainfall and streamflow records for north central England: putting the Environmental Change Network site at Moor House, Upper Teesdale, in context. *Hydrological Sciences Journal–Journal des sciences hydrologiques*, **43**, 775–87.

Buytaert, W., Celleri, R., De Bievre, B., Cisneros, F., Wyseure, G., Deckers, J. and Hofstead, R. (2006) Human impact on the hydrology of the Paramo ecosystem, a review. *Earth-Science Reviews*, **79**, 53–72.

Calder, I. R. and Newson, M. D. (1979) Land use and upland water resources – a strategic look. *Water Resources Bulletin*, **16**, 1628–39.

Cannell, M. G. R., Milne, R., Hargreaves, K. J., Brown, T. A. W., Cruickshank, M. M., Bradley, R. I., Spencer, T., Hope, D., Billett, M. F., Adger, W. N. and Subak, S. (1999) National inventories of terrestrial carbon sources and sinks: the UK experience. *Climatic Change*, **42**, 505–30.

Carey, S. K. and Woo, M. K. (2000) The role of soil pipes as a slope runoff mechanism, subarctic Yukon, Canada. *Journal of Hydrology*, **233**, 206–22.

Carroll, Z. L., Reynolds, B., Emmett, B. A., Sinclair, F. L. and Ruiz de Ona, C. (2004) *The Effect of Stocking Density on Soil in Upland Wales.* CCW Science Report No 630, Countryside Council for Wales, Bangor.

Chapman, P. (1993) *Caves and Cave Life.* London: HarperCollins.

Clymo, R. S. (1983) Peat. *Ecosystems of the World 4A, Mires: Swamp, Bog, Fen and Moor* (ed. A. J. P. Gore), pp. 159–224. Oxford: Elsevier.

Dunn, S. M. and Mackay, R. (1996) Modelling the hydrological impacts of open ditch drainage. *Journal of Hydrology*, **179**, 37–66.

Evans, M. and Warburton, J. (2005) Sediment budget for an eroding peat-moorland catchment in northern England. *Earth Surface Processes and Landforms*, **30**, 557–77.

Evans, M. G., Allott, T., Holden, J., Flitcroft, C. and Bonn, A. (2005) *Understanding Gully Blocking in Deep Peat.* Moors for the Future Report No 4, Moors for the Future Partnership, Castleton.

Evans, M. G., Burt, T. P., Holden, J. and Adamson, J. K. (1999) Runoff generation and water table fluctuations in blanket peat: evidence from UK data spanning the dry summer of 1995. *Journal of Hydrology*, **221**, 141–60.

Gilman, K. (2002) *A Review of Evapotranspiration Rates from Wetland and Wetland Catchment Plant Communities, with Particular Reference to Cors y Llyn NNR, Powys, Wales.* CCW Science Report, 504, Countryside Council for Wales, Bangor.

Gimmingham, C. H. (1995) Heaths and moorland: an overview of ecological change. *Heaths and Moorland: Cultural Landscapes* (ed. D. B. A. Thompson, A. J. Hester and M. B. Usher), pp. 9–19. Edinburgh: HMSO.

Glaves, D. J., Haycock, N. E., Costigan, P., Coulson, J. C., Marrs, R. H., Robertson, P. A. and Younger, J. (2005) *Defra Review of the Heather and Grass Burning Regulations and Code: Science Panel Assessment of the Effects of Burning on Biodiversity, Soils and Hydrology.* Defra, London. http://www.defra.gov.uk/rural/pdfs/uplands/science-panel-full-report.pdf

Gunn, J., Labadz, J. C., Dykes, A. P., Kirk, K. J., Poulson, S. J. and Matthews, C. (2002) Blanket bog hydrology at Mynydd Hiraethog SSSI: an investigation of peat properties and hydrology and assessment of effects of proposed wind farm construction. *CCW Science Report*, 501, Countryside Council for Wales, Bangor.

Holden, J. (2004) Hydrological connectivity of soil pipes determined by ground-penetrating radar tracer detection. *Earth Surface Processes and Landforms*, **29**, 437–42.

Holden, J. (2005a) Controls of soil pipe frequency in upland blanket peat. *Journal of Geophysical Research*, **110**, F01002, doi:10.1029/2004JF000143.

Holden, J. (2005b) Piping and woody plants in peatlands: cause or effect? *Water Resources Research*, **41**, W06009.

Holden, J. (2006) Sediment and particulate carbon removal by pipe erosion increase over time in blanket peatlands as a consequence of land drainage. *Journal of Geophysical Research*, **111**, F02010.

Holden, J. and Adamson, J. K. (2002) The Moor House long-term upland temperature record – new evidence of recent warming. *Weather*, **57**, 119–26.

Holden, J. and Burt, T. P. (2002a) Infiltration, runoff and sediment production in blanket peat catchments: implications of field rainfall simulation experiments. *Hydrological Processes*, **16**, 2537–57.

Holden, J. and Burt, T. P. (2002b) Laboratory experiments on drought and runoff in blanket peat. *European Journal of Soil Science*, **53**, 675–89.

Holden, J. and Burt, T. P. (2002c) Piping and pipeflow in a deep peat catchment. *Catena*, **48**, 163–99.

Holden, J. and Burt, T. P. (2003a) Hydraulic conductivity in upland blanket peat: measurement and variability. *Hydrological Processes*, **17**, 1227–37.

Holden, J. and Burt, T. P. (2003b) Hydrological studies on blanket peat: the significance of the acrotelm–catotelm model. *Journal of Ecology*, **91**, 86–102.

Holden, J. and Burt, T. P. (2003c) Runoff production in blanket peat covered catchments. *Water Resources Research*, **39**, 1191, doi:10.029/2003WR002067.

Holden, J., Burt, T. P. and Cox, N. J. (2001) Macroporosity and infiltration in blanket peat: the implications of tension disc infiltrometer measurements. *Hydrological Processes*, **15**, 289–303.

Holden, J., Burt, T. P. and Vilas, M. (2002) Application of ground-penetrating radar to the identification of subsurface piping in blanket peat. *Earth Surface Processes and Landforms*, **27**, 235–49.

Holden, J., Chapman, P. J., Evans, M. G., Hubacek, K., Kay, P. and Warburton, J. (2007a) Vulnerability of organic soils in England and Wales. *Final Technical Report to Defra, Project SP0532*, London. http://randd.defra.gov.uk/Document.aspx?Document=SP0532_5213_TRP.pdf

Holden, J., Chapman, P. J. and Labadz, J. C. (2004) Artificial drainage of peatlands: hydrological and hydrochemical process and wetland restoration. *Progress in Physical Geography*, **28**, 95–123.

Holden, J., Chapman, P. J., Lane, S. N. and Brookes, C. J. (2006a) Impacts of artificial drainage of peatlands on runoff production and water quality. *Peatlands: Evolution and Records of Environmental and Climate Changes* (ed. I. P. Martini, A. M. Cortizas and W. Chesworth), pp. 501–28. Amsterdam: Elsevier.

Holden, J., Evans, M. G., Burt, T. P. and Horton, M. (2006b) Impact of land drainage on peatland hydrology. *Journal of Environmental Quality*, **35**, 1764–78, doi:10.2134/jeq005.0477.

Holden, J., Gascoigne, M. and Bosanko, N. (2007c) Erosion and natural revegetation associated with surface land drains in upland peatlands. *Earth Surface Processes and Landforms*, **32**, 1547–57.

Holden, J., Kirkby, M. J., Lane, S. N., Milledge, D. G., Brookes, C. J., Holden, V. and McDonald, A. T. (2008) Factors affecting overland flow and drain flow velocity in peatlands. *Water Resources Research*, **44**, WO6415, doi:10.1029/2007WR006052.

Holden, J., Shotbolt, L., Bonn, A., Burt, T. P., Chapman, P. J., Dougill, A. J., Fraser, E. D. G., Hubacek, K., Irvine, B., Kirkby, M. J., Reed, M. S., Prell, C., Stagl, S., Stringer, L. C., Turner, A. and Worrall, F. (2007b) Environmental change in moorland landscapes. *Earth-Science Reviews*, **82**, 75–100.

Hope, D., Billett, M. F., Milne, R. and Brown, T. A. W. (1997) Exports of organic carbon in British rivers. *Hydrological Processes*, **11**, 325–44.

Hughes, S., Dowrick, D. J., Freeman, C., Hudson, J. A. and Reynolds, B. (1999) Methane emissions from a gully mire in mid-Wales, UK under consecutive summer water table drawdown. *Environmental Science and Technology*, **33**, 362–5.

Hulme, M., Jenkins, G. J., Lu, X., Turnpenny, J. R., Mitchell, T. D., Jones, R. G., Lowe, J., Murphy, J. M., Hassell, D., Boorman, P., McDonald, R. and Hill, S. (2002) *Climate Change Scenarios for the United Kingdom: The UKCIP02 Scientific Report.* Tyndall Centre, School of Environmental Sciences, University of East Anglia, Norwich. http://www.ukcip.org.uk/images/stories/Pub_pdfs/UKCIP02_tech.pdf

Ingram, H. A. P. (1983) Hydrology. *Ecosystems of the World 4A, Mires: Swamp, Bog, Fen and Moor* (ed. A. J. P. Gore), pp. 67–158. Oxford: Elsevier.

Jones, J. A. A. (1997) Pipeflow contributing areas and runoff response. *Hydrological Processes*, **11**, 35–41.

Jones, J. A. A. (2004) Implications of natural soil piping for basin management in upland Britain. *Land Degradation & Development*, **15**, 325–49.

Jones, J. A. A. and Crane, F. G. (1984) Pipeflow and pipe erosion in the Maesnant experimental catchment. *Catchment Experiments in Fluvial Geomorphology* (ed. T. P. Burt and D. E. Walling), pp. 55–72. Norwich: Geo Books.

Kellner, E. (2001) Surface energy fluxes and control of evapotranspiration from a Swedish *Sphagnum* mire. *Agricultural and Forest Meteorology*, **110**, 101–23.

Meyles, E. W., Williams, A. G., Ternan, J. L., Anderson, J. M. and Dowd, J. F. (2006) The influence of grazing on vegetation, soil properties and stream discharge in a small Dartmoor catchment, southwest England, UK. *Earth Surface Processes and Landforms*, **31**, 622–31.

Roberge, J. and Plamondon, A. P. (1987) Snowmelt runoff pathways in a boreal forest hillslope, the role of pipe throughflow. *Journal of Hydrology*, **95**, 39–54.

Robinson, M. (1986) Changes in catchment runoff following drainage and afforestation. *Journal of Hydrology*, **86**, 71–84.

Robinson, M. and Armstrong, A. C. (1988) The extent of agricultural field drainage in England and Wales, 1971–1980. *Transactions of the Institute of British Geographers*, **13**, 19–28.

Sansom, A. (1999) Upland vegetation management: the impacts of overstocking. *Water Science and Technology*, **39**, 85–92.

Shaw, S. C., Wheeler, B. D., Kirby, P., Phillipson, P. and Edmunds, R. (1996) *Literature Review of the Historical Effects of Burning and Grazing of Blanket Bog and Upland Wet Heath.* English Nature Research Report No 172, English Nature, Peterborough. http://naturalengland.communisis.com/NaturalEnglandShop/default.aspx

Stewart, A. J. A. and Lance, A. N. (1983) Moor-draining – a review of impacts on land-use. *Journal of Environmental Management*, **17**, 81–99.

Tallis, J. H. (1987) Fire and flood at Holme Moss: erosion processes in an upland blanket mire. *Journal of Ecology*, **75**, 1099–129.

Terajima, T., Sakamoto, T. and Shirai, T. (2000) Morphology, structure and flow phases in soil pipes developing in forested hillslopes underlain by a Quaternary sand–gravel formation, Hokkaido, northern main island in Japan. *Hydrological Processes*, **14**, 713–26.

Tranvik, L. J. and Jansson, M. (2002) Climate change – terrestrial export of organic carbon. *Nature*, **415**, 861–2.

Turner, N. (1757) *An Essay on Draining and Improving Peat Bogs; in which Their Nature and Properties Are Fully Considered.* London: Baldwin & Pew.

Uchida, T., Tromp-van Meerveld, I. and McDonnell, J. J. (2005) The role of lateral pipe flow in hillslope runoff response: an intercomparison of non-linear hillslope response. *Journal of Hydrology*, **311**, 117–33.

Werrity, A. (2002) Living with uncertainty: climate change, river flows and water resource management in Scotland. *Science of the Total Environment*, **294**, 29–40.

Worrall, F., Burt, T. P., Adamson, J. K., Reed, M. S., Warburton, J., Armstrong, A. and Evans, M. G. (2007) Predicting the future carbon budget of an upland peat catchment. *Climatic Change*, **85**, 139–58.

7 The state of upland freshwater ecosystems

Tim Allott

Introduction

Freshwaters in the form of headwater stream systems and lakes are an intrinsic part of the upland landscape. These waters are characterised by generally dilute, nutrient-poor, well-oxygenated chemical conditions with high biodiversity values including species and communities distinct from those found in lowland systems. They also contribute a range of important ecosystems services including recreation and water supply, with some 60 per cent of UK water supply sourced from the uplands. Surface waters in upland environments are often assumed to be pristine and minimally impacted by anthropogenic pressures or pollution, and this can indeed be the case in remote regions. Nevertheless, upland waters are highly sensitive to environmental change in general, and atmospheric processes in particular, and in many regions have experienced significant levels of environmental degradation.

This chapter introduces key factors affecting the state of upland freshwaters. Although there is some focus on surface-water acidification, the most persistent status problem for upland waters, it also reviews other important status issues including heavy metal pollution, nutrient enrichment, problems associated with catchment land-use, and recent concerns over water colour. Upland waters are generally under-represented in national freshwater monitoring schemes. The data available for evaluating their status primarily come from more restricted, specialised monitoring networks (e.g. the UK Acid Waters Monitoring Network [AWMN] www.ukawmn.ucl.ac.uk) or from one-off surveys of spatial patterns in water chemistry or biology (e.g. Curtis and Simpson, 2004). This chapter draws on recent studies of this type to evaluate the state of upland waters, and illustrates some of the key status issues using a case study of freshwaters draining the uplands of the Peak District National Park in the UK.

Surface-water acidification: cause and effect

Despite more than thirty years of research activity, and widespread national and international measures to reduce levels of atmospheric deposition, surface-water acidification remains the single most significant influence on the ecological health of upland surface waters. The effects of freshwater acidification have been particularly well documented across Europe and North America, but the issue is of global scale with acidification increasingly recognised in regions such as Nepal, China and SE Asia more generally.

Freshwater acidification first came to prominence in the 1970s through observations of acid waters and declining salmonid fisheries across the uplands of southern Scandinavia. The link was made to acid deposition associated with emissions of sulphur dioxide and nitrous oxide gases from power plants and heavy industry (see Caporn and Emmett, this volume), resulting in elevated levels of sulphate and nitrate and associated acidity in upland surface waters. The cause–effect relationship between acid deposition and acidification was demonstrated through the development of palaeo-limnological techniques for the reconstruction of lake-water acidity, in particular the use of diatom analysis of lake sediments and associated pH transfer functions (Battarbee *et al.*, 1990). These approaches allowed the chemical histories of lakes to be evaluated for a large number of sites in Britain, Scandinavia, the north-east USA, and Canada (see Battarbee *et al.*, 1990; Battarbee and Charles, 1994). A clear pattern emerged. Lakes in upland regions with base-poor geology, e.g. slow-weathering granitic rocks, where levels of acid deposition were high, had experienced significant acidification. This acidification occurred after AD *c.*1850, post-dating contamination by atmospheric deposition as evidenced by increases in metal and spherical carbonaceous particle concentrations in the recent lake sediments. Acidification can be predicted on the basis of two primary factors: acid loading and site sensitivity as determined by base cation status (Battarbee *et al.*, 1996).

Simultaneous to the palaeo-limnological studies, significant research efforts were made to understand the ecological effects of acidification and acid waters (see Schindler, 1988; Steinberg and Wright, 1994). Acidification has a profound influence on the ecological health of lakes and streams, resulting in changes to biological communities, reductions in species richness and the loss of acid-sensitive taxa. Although the most well publicised effects are on fish, extensive field and laboratory studies have demonstrated significant effects at all trophic levels within aquatic ecosystems, including on microbes, algae, aquatic macrophytes, invertebrates, fish, amphibians, riparian birds and other vertebrates. The effects of acidification on aquatic biota can be direct (e.g. toxicity associated with changing water chemistry) or indirect (e.g. changes in habitat or food availability). In low-alkalinity waters with low calcium concentrations (typically associated with slow-weathering base-poor bedrock), pH and aluminium (Al) are the key chemical variables associated with toxicity. In acid conditions Al is released from soil in an inorganic form (typically as Al^{3+}) toxic to a variety of aquatic organisms including salmonid fish, e.g. salmon *Salmo salar* and brown trout *Salmo trutta*. Salmonids and invertebrates seem to be affected by similar physiological processes, in particular associated with the disruption of gill functioning (Stenberg and Wright, 1994).

Salmonid fish are also particularly sensitive to high Al levels during acid episodes in springtime (e.g. snowmelt), with the failure of successful hatching in such conditions leading to missing year classes within the population. An example of an indirect effect of acidification on aquatic biota is provided by the dipper *Cinclus cinclus*, a riparian bird which experienced significant declines in abundance in regions of pronounced stream acidification (Tyler and Ormerod, 1992). This decline has been linked to changes in the abundance of calcium-rich prey (invertebrates) within acidified streams influencing the thickness and size of eggs and impairing reproduction.

Evaluating the acidification status of upland freshwaters: the critical loads approach

Over the last fifteen years, research has focused on (1) establishing the extent and severity of acidification, (2) evaluating the emissions reductions required to protect freshwater ecosystems, and (3) assessing the processes and likely timescales of recovery. A major component of this research has been the development of the critical loads approach to evaluate the acidification status of surface waters at both national and international scales.

A critical load can be defined as 'a quantitative estimate of an exposure to one or more pollutants below which significant harmful effects to the environment do not occur according to present knowledge' (see http://critloads.ceh.ac.uk/). The critical load of acidity for a freshwater is exceeded when the total amount of acid deposition is greater than the ability of the systems to neutralise the deposited acidity (see Figure 7.1). A variety of approaches and models are available for calculating critical loads for surface waters, including the steady-state water chemistry (SSWC) model (Henriksen *et al.*, 1992) and the first-order acidity balance (FAB) model (Posch *et al.*, 1997). In all cases, water chemistry data are required to calculate the critical load for a lake or stream, and an estimate of acid deposition at the site is then required to calculate critical load exceedance (effectively a prediction of acidification). The SSWC and FAB models provide an estimate of the level of acid deposition below which acid-neutralising capacity (ANC) will remain above a pre-determined level. In UK critical loads modelling, an ANC limit of zero was initially used, representing the ANC at which there is a 50 per cent probability of damage to brown trout populations (see Battarbee *et al.*, 2005). Current UK and European critical load applications use the FAB model and an ANC limit of 20 μeq l^{-1}, representing a more precautionary approach and a higher level of protection for aquatic ecosystems.

Critical loads have been used to map patterns of acidification at UK and European scales, in conjunction with large-scale surveys of freshwater chemistry and data on sulphur and nitrogen deposition (e.g. Posch *et al.*, 1997; NEGTAP, 2001; Curtis and Simpson, 2004). Exceedance data for the UK show that freshwater acidification is overwhelmingly an upland problem, although also occurring at some lowland sites with poorly buffered geologies

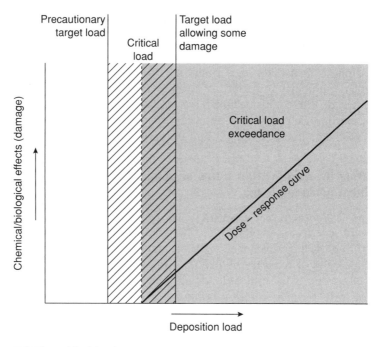

Figure 7.1 The critical loads concept.

(e.g. greensands) (see Figure 7.2). The data largely confirm the findings of palaeo-limnological research (cf. Battarbee *et al.*, 1990), with surface-water acidification a particular problem in Wales, the Lake District, the Pennines, south-west Scotland and central Scotland. Although less severe, critical loads exceedance is also predicted for the remote areas of north-west Scotland. Although these areas have historically received relatively low levels of acid deposition, many lakes and streams in this area are highly sensitive with naturally low acid-neutralising capacities, and some acidification has occurred (Allott, Golding and Harriman, 1995).

In addition to allowing the assessment of acidification status, the critical loads approach has been used extensively as a policy tool to predict future acidification status under scenarios representing reduced sulphur and nitrogen deposition. Figure 7.2 indicates the difference in UK freshwater critical load status between 1995–7 and 2010, taking into account the commitments to emissions reductions over this period. Even though substantial improvements will result from reductions in acid deposition associated with international agreements such as the UN-ECE Gothenburg Protocol, the most sensitive freshwater sites will still not be protected from acid deposition in 2010, with approximately 30 per cent of the survey sites still exceeding their critical load (Curtis and Simpson, 2004).

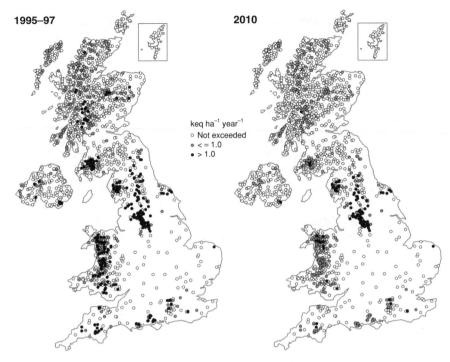

Figure 7.2 Critical loads exceedance maps for UK freshwaters in 1995–7 and 2010 calculated using the first-order acidity balance (FAB) model (see Curtis and Simpson, 2004). Data supplied courtesy of Chris Curtis, Environmental Change Research Centre, University College London.

Recovery from surface-water acidification

Over the last few decades there have been substantial changes in atmospheric deposition across Europe and North America as a result of industrial restructuring and recent clean air legislation such as the UNECE Convention on the Long Range Transport of Air Pollution (NEGTAP, 2001; Caporn and Emmett, this volume). The current focus of freshwater acidification research is therefore on the potential recovery of acidified systems. Critical load exceedance models based on future emission scenarios have been important for developing national and international policies on emissions reductions. However, these models assume steady-state conditions, i.e. that freshwater chemistry and biology will respond immediately to emission and deposition reductions. This is not realistic, and several important processes can affect the rates and timescales of recovery from acidification. Robust evaluation and prediction of chemical and biological recovery relies on two types of research: first, long-term monitoring of the chemical and biological status

Box 7.1. The acidification status of the Peak District moorland stream network

The Peak District National Park is located in the South Pennines of northern England and is surrounded by the conurbations of Manchester, Sheffield and Leeds (Figure 7.3). It has experienced high levels of atmospheric pollution and acid deposition for over 150 years (see Caporn and Emmett, this volume). Perhaps surprisingly, there has been limited systematic study of the extent and severity of surface-water acidification in the Peak District uplands, although Evans *et al.* (2000) evaluated acidification in South Pennine reservoirs. Consequently, in 2004 a team from the University of Manchester carried out the Peak District Moorland Stream Survey (PD-MSS), a systematic survey of water chemistry, diatoms and macro-invertebrate assemblages. The PD-MSS was carried out in summer baseflow conditions, and included thirty-seven stream systems (50 per cent of the total number of third-order systems draining moorland areas).

Concentrations of sulphate and nitrate in these streams are extremely high relative to freshwaters in other upland regions (see Figure 7.3; Helliwell *et al.*, 2007), reflecting the historically very high atmospheric sulphur and nitrogen loadings to these uplands. However, the acid-base status of the streams is highly variable, with pH showing a pronounced bimodal distribution. The Peak District moorlands are located on millstone grit bedrock, which is generally base-poor but geochemically highly variable, with some deposits containing relatively high concentrations of calcium and magnesium. Groundwaters draining such deposits are well buffered from acidification, whereas other catchments are extremely acid (pH < 5.0) even under baseflow conditions. The bimodal distribution in water chemistry is reflected in critical load data (Figure 7.3), which indicate that eleven (30 per cent) of the catchments have exceeded their critical load and can therefore be considered acidified. There is a strong relationship between critical load exceedance and biological status, with invertebrate species richness significantly lower at exceeded sites, indicating potential biological damage associated with acidification (Figure 7.4). The PD-MSS provides a conservative evaluation of the acidification status of these stream systems, as the critical load data represent baseflow conditions and take no account of the potential importance of acid episodes (cf. Kowalik and Ormerod, 2006; see Box 7.2).

of upland streams and lakes and, second, the development of dynamic models of acidification which realistically represent the processes of acidification and de-acidification, incorporating nitrogen dynamics and biological responses to changing water chemistry.

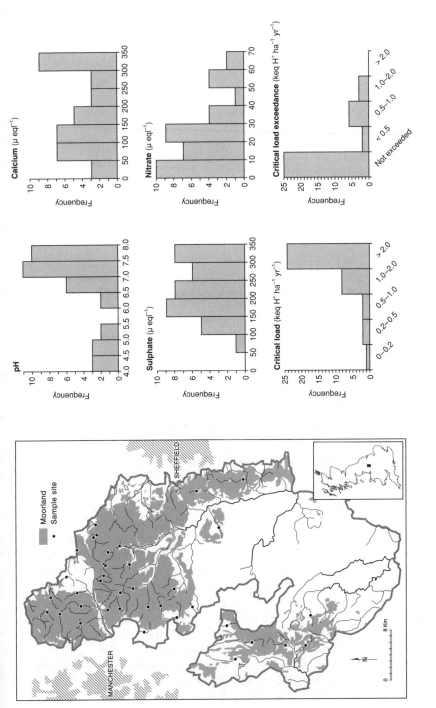

Figure 7.3 The 2004 Peak District Moorland Stream Survey (PD-MSS) sampling points, distributions of key chemical variables, critical loads and exceedances. Critical loads calculated using the Steady State Water Chemistry (SSWC) model (Henriksen *et al.*, 1992). Critical load exceedance data calculated using 1995–7 UK deposition data supplied by Jane Hall (CEH-Bangor) courtesy of CEH-Edinburgh.

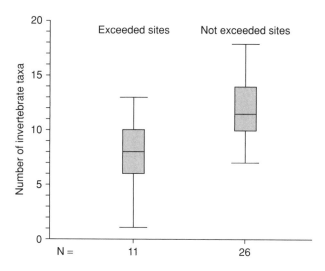

Figure 7.4 Differences in macro-invertebrate species richness between sites exceeding and not exceeding their critical acidity load in the 2004 Peak District
Moorland Stream Survey (PD-MSS).

A key concern is the increasing importance of nitrate to surface-water
acidification. The dominant acidifying anion in upland surface waters has
typically been sulphate associated with sulphur deposition. Unlike sulphur,
however, nitrogen deposition has not significantly declined over the past twenty
years and has even increased slightly in some upland areas (Fowler *et al.*,
2005). Nitrogen deposition is therefore becoming proportionally more
important within the total acid loading to upland areas. Understanding the
role of nitrogen deposition and nitrate leaching to acidification is complex,
as most N deposition to upland catchments occurs directly on to terrestrial
ecosystems and biological controls on nitrogen uptake and cycling therefore
control nitrate leaching into surface waters. Nitrogen is normally tightly cycled
within terrestrial ecosystems, but elevated levels of nitrate in the waters of
many upland regions (e.g. Allott, Curtis *et al.*, 1995) suggest that levels
of N deposition are exceeding the ability of upland catchments to retain N,
resulting in N 'saturation' and associated leaching into surface waters
(Curtis *et al.*, 2005; Helliwell *et al.*, 2007). If terrestrial systems start to leach
significant quantities of nitrate into surface waters ('N breakthrough'), this
could result in enhanced acidification (Curtis *et al.*, 1998), potentially off-
setting recovery associated with S deposition reductions.

High-quality monitored data of water chemistry and biology in uplands
regions is only generally available for the last twenty years or so, represented
by networks such as the UK AWMN and the United Nations ICP Waters
Programme. In the UK the substantial declines in sulphur deposition since
the mid-1980s (Fowler *et al.*, 2005; Caporn and Emmett, this volume) have

been reflected in significant declines in the sulphate concentrations of upland waters, with the majority of AWMN sites showing corresponding increases in pH, alkalinity and ANC (Monteith and Evans, 2005; see Box 7.2). Skjelkavåle *et al.* (2005) report ICP Waters data from twelve upland regions of Europe and North America, revealing similar widespread declines in sulphate, mostly static nitrate concentrations and a general overall tendency of increasing ANC. Additionally, the UK AWMN data reveal clear evidence for biological recovery associated with the chemical trends, although this is more restricted and shows significant differences between sites and between different groups of organisms (Monteith *et al.*, 2005). It is clear that the processes of biological recovery are complex. Despite general improvements in chemical conditions, continuing sporadic acid episodes can restrict species recovery (Kowalik and Ormerod, 2006). There may also be restraints on the effective dispersal of some groups of organisms and non-linear responses of biology to chemical change because of 'threshold' effects (Monteith *et al.*, 2005). Changes to some biological communities associated with the acidification process could also potentially result in resistance to re-invasion ('community closure') (Ledger and Hildrew, 2005) and delays in biological response.

The potential timescales of chemical recovery from acidification have been evaluated using dynamic hydrochemical models which simulate soil solution and surface-water chemistry changes, calibrated using site-specific or regional soil and water chemistry data and driven by assumptions of future trends in acid deposition. The most widely applied is MAGIC (Model of Acidification of Groundwaters in Catchments, e.g. Cosby *et al.*, 2001), although a variety of alternative models have also been developed including the CHemistry of the Uplands Model (CHUM) (Tipping *et al.*, 2006a). These models provide predictions of major ion and acid-base status of streams and lakes on monthly or annual timescales. The model simulations generally emphasise the long-term nature of chemical recovery, with ANC values for severely acidified systems only returning to near pre-acidification levels on timescales of decades to centuries (see Box 7.2). In the UK, MAGIC predictions of acidification status in 2020 indicate that negative ANC values will persist in some regions, including the Mourne Mountains (Northern Ireland), the South Pennines and the Lake District (Curtis and Simpson, 2004). In an application of the CHUM model to catchments in the UK Lake District, Tipping *et al.* (2006a) emphasise the important role of nitrogen deposition to future acidification status. Although these systems have already shown significant chemical recovery as a result of reduced sulphur deposition, the model predicts that continued deposition of nitrogen at current rates will lead to terrestrial nitrogen saturation and re-acidification of surface waters. These modelling exercises demonstrate the likely persistence of surface-water acidification problems in upland regions. Together with monitoring and field data, they suggest that full ecological recovery of the many acidified waters in Europe and North America will be a slow and sporadic process, contingent on the complexities of biological recovery and further reductions in acid deposition (particularly nitrogen).

Box 7.2. Current and future trends in the status of freshwaters in the South Pennines, UK

The uplands of the South Pennines have been subjected to historically high levels of atmospheric deposition with significant declines in sulphur deposition since the 1980s (Fowler *et al.*, 1995; Caporn and Emmett, this volume). Consequently, there is significant interest in current and future trends in the state of freshwaters in the region, with emphasis on monitoring and evaluating recovery from acidification. Although water chemistry data are routinely collected from many of the drinking-water supply reservoirs in the region, the most detailed data on recent chemical and biological trends come from the UK Acid Waters Monitoring Network (AWMN) site at the River Etherow, operational since 1988 (UK national grid reference SK 116996; see Monteith and Evans, 2005). This site has experienced changes in water chemistry consistent with recovery (Figure 7.5), including a decline in non-marine sulphate, increases in ANC and pH, and a decline in labile aluminium concentrations. Nitrate concentrations show no significant decline between 1988 and 2006, and are increasingly important relative to sulphate. There is also evidence that biological recovery is underway, with changes to macro-invertebrate species assemblages consistent with the recent chemical trends, and more restricted responses in some macrophyte taxa (Monteith *et al.*, 2005). In common with many acidified upland stream systems the site is affected by acid episodes (Figure 7.5), with pH < 5.0 during high flow conditions possibly limiting the rates of biological recovery. Perhaps the most striking chemical trend at the river Etherow since 1988 has been the very significant increase in dissolved organic carbon (DOC) concentrations, characterised by an increased frequency of high (>10 mg l^{-1}) DOC conditions in the post-1996 period (see discussion in main text).

Evans *et al.* (2007) applied the MAGIC model to a dataset of sixty-two reservoirs in the South Pennines in order to predict future trends in water chemistry under current legislated emissions reductions (see Figure 7.6). The application also provides hindcasts of water chemistry conditions for AD 1850 (pre-acidification) and AD 1970 (maximum levels of acid deposition). The model indicates significant increases in the ANC of these systems between 1970 and 2010, a trend consistent with monitored data from the region (e.g. Figure 7.5). However, it predicts that chemical recovery will be more restricted over the next century. By 2100, ANC values will still be well below those of the pre-acidification period, with approximately 30 per cent of the reservoir sites still failing to meet the target chemical status of ANC > 20 μ eq l^{-1}.

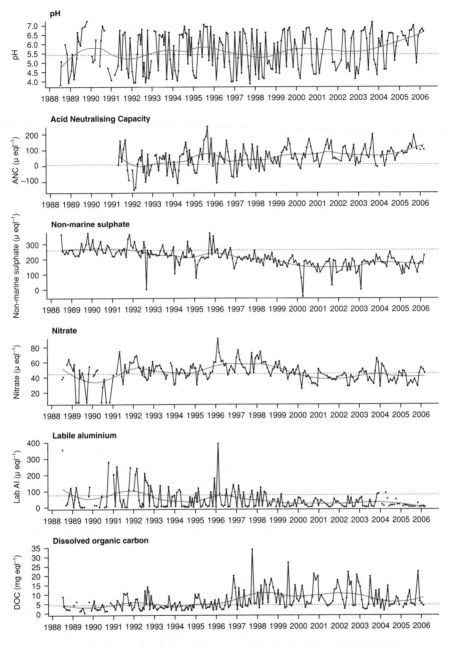

Figure 7.5 Streamwater chemistry trends for the River Etherow 1988–2006. Dotted lines represent the 1988–93 mean. Solid lines represent LOWESS regression. Data from the UK Acid Waters Monitoring Network (AWMN) courtesy of Don Monteith (Environmental Change Research Centre, UCL).

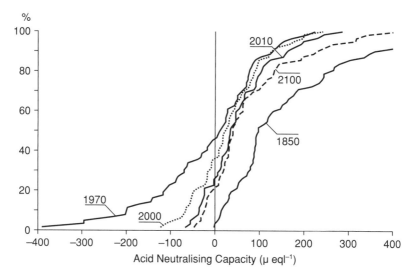

Figure 7.6 MAGIC model hindcasts and forecasts of the distribution of acid-neutralising capacity (ANC) in South Pennine reservoirs for the years 1850, 1970, 2000, 2010 and 2100. Data courtesy of Chris Evans, CEH-Bangor. See also Evans *et al.* (2007).

Heavy metal pollution

In addition to the effects of acidification, biological communities in upland waters can be subject to toxicity from heavy metal pollution (Mance, 1987). In some upland regions metals in aquatic systems are found at higher concentrations than background (geological) levels as a result of past excavations of metal ores or runoff from spoil heaps associated with mining activities. This can lead to substantial ecological effects such as reductions in species abundance and richness, and the loss of sensitive taxa or groups of organisms. For example, in upland Wales and south-west England discharges from abandoned metal mines result in locally elevated streamwater metal concentrations and significant impacts on stream fauna and flora (Hirst *et al.*, 2002). Such effects are often spatially restricted but can represent the dominant control on the ecological health of affected systems.

A more widespread problem comes from metal pollution from atmospheric sources. Over the past few centuries potentially toxic metals, for example lead (Pb), copper (Cu), nickel (Ni), cadmium (Cd), zinc (Zn), mercury (Hg) and arsenic (As), have been released into the environment by industrial processes and the burning of fossil fuels. Although critical load approaches have been used to evaluate current levels of heavy metal deposition (Tipping *et al.*, 2005), the legacy of accumulated metal pollution presents a particular issue. After deposition on to upland catchments, the affinity of many metals to organic matter has resulted in their storage in organic soils and peats. Upland envir-

Box 7.3. Metal concentrations and drinking-water guidelines in Peak District streams

Rothwell *et al.* (2007) present data on dissolved metal concentrations from a stream network in the Peak District National Park draining into water-supply reservoirs. These peatlands are highly atmospherically contaminated, and concentrations of lead (Pb) in near-surface peats can exceed 1500 mg kg^{-1}. Dissolved metal concentrations were evaluated during a range of flow conditions and were elevated under stormflow conditions. Concentrations of dissolved Cu, Ni and Zn did not approach World Health Organisation (WHO) drinking-water guidelines. Pb concentrations exceeded the WHO guideline of 10 μg l^{-1} for approximately 10 per cent of the stormflow period, but flow-weighted mean Pb concentrations were well below the guideline values. Despite high levels of terrestrial metal contamination in the Peak District, streamwater concentrations are currently below levels which would cause concern for drinking-water supply. Nevertheless there are potential ecosystem effects from elevated stormflow metal concentrations (cf. Tipping *et al.*, 2005) and additional concerns over the impact of climate change on future metal release (Rothwell *et al.*, 2008).

onments therefore typically represent sinks for atmospherically derived metals, and in regions of historically high atmospheric deposition near-surface peat deposits can be heavily contaminated with metal pollution (e.g. Rothwell *et al.*, 2008). A key issue is the extent to which this stored metal pollution is being released from catchment soils into freshwater systems, particularly as free-ions in the dissolved phase, which are most strongly associated with toxicity to aquatic biota. In particularly contaminated systems the concentrations of some heavy metals can approach World Health Organisation (WHO) drinking-water guideline limits during high flow conditions (see Box 7.3). Tipping *et al.* (2005) summarise total dissolved metal concentration data for a series of British upland surface waters against critical limit values representing the maximum metal concentrations that can be tolerated without causing significant ecosystem damage. Although they stress the complexity of the data and associated uncertainties, they conclude that ecosystem damage is likely to be occurring in these upland waters owing to metal release. The CHUM model has also been used to model future trends in aquatic heavy metal concentrations for upland waters in Cumbria (Tipping *et al.*, 2006b), predicting slow responses (centuries to millennia) of strongly sorbing metal such as Pb and Cu to changes in atmospheric deposition. It is clear that the legacy of atmospheric metal pollution will be a long-term problem for many upland catchments. Greater understanding is needed of both the short- and the long-term ecological significance of elevated concentrations of metals in upland surface waters, as well as more specific work on poorly studied metals of particular concern (e.g. Hs and As).

Nutrient enrichment

Upland waters are characterised by relatively low concentrations of inorganic plant nutrients (e.g. phosphorus and nitrogen), and are generally classified as oligotrophic with low primary productivity. The problems associated with nutrient enrichment and eutrophication so prevalent in lowland waters are therefore more restricted in upland systems, in terms of both spatial extent and severity. Nevertheless, the nutrient-poor status of upland lakes results in high sensitivity to increased nutrient fluxes and enrichment, and the associated effects of eutrophication have been reported from some upland systems. Lakes located on the upland fringes are particularly vulnerable as their catchments often incorporate areas of improved agriculture or settlement representing potentially significant sources of nutrients. Upland freshwaters are generally phosphorus-limited, and consequently this is the nutrient of primary concern. For example, in the uplands of the English Lake District several lakes have been affected by eutrophication associated with increased phosphorus inputs from sewage works (Bennion *et al.*, 2000; Barker *et al.*, 2005) leading to impacts on biological communities and threats to populations of rare fish species. Eutrophication has also been reported from remote high alpine lakes owing to inappropriate sewage systems of alpine huts within the lake catchments (e.g. Vreca and Muri, 2006).

Increased phosphorus loadings from site-specific catchment sources can therefore result in important conservation issues for upland waters. However, a potentially more widespread status issue is enrichment associated with atmospheric deposition, in particular with the elevated concentrations of nitrate in the waters of many upland regions resulting from continued high levels of nitrogen deposition. As well as causing enhanced acidification, there is concern that nitrate leaching may result in nutrient enrichment and aquatic eutrophication, with associated impacts on biodiversity (see Milne and Hartley, 2001; Curtis *et al.*, 2005). Conclusive evidence for this effect is currently limited, except for in the mountain systems of western North America where clear ecological changes associated with aquatic nitrogen enrichment have been demonstrated (e.g. Wolfe *et al.*, 2001). Further work is needed in other upland regions to evaluate fully the impact of deposited nitrogen on freshwater nutrient status.

Catchment change and habitat disturbance

As outlined above in relation to nutrient enrichment, upland waters can be highly sensitive to catchment processes and changes in land use and cover. This volume defines the uplands in accordance with the concept of Less

Favoured Areas (see introductory chapter, Bonn *et al.*, this volume), and upland catchments can therefore include significant areas of improved agriculture. There have been significant concerns over the potential aquatic impacts of diffuse pollutants from agricultural sources, including pathogens, nutrients, sheep dips and other pesticides. In many regions, upland catchments are subject to pastoral agriculture and are grazed by stock including cattle, sheep and goats. In the UK there has been a huge increase in animal grazing in the uplands over the last fifty year or so, largely driven by subsidy systems for hill farmers (see Condliffe, this volume). There has been relatively little research focus on the effects of this major land-use change on freshwater systems (cf. Holden, this volume). One key concern relating to high stock levels in the uplands centres on the possible faecal contamination of drinking-water supplies, and in particular on the risk of contamination of water supplies by the protozoan parasite *Cryptosporidium* (Sturdee *et al.*, 2007). This is associated with the faecal matter of both wild and farmed animals, and is a major concern because of its association with the diarrhoeal disease crypto-sporidiosis and its resistance to standard water-treatment procedures. In an extensive study of an upland catchment in Cumbria, Sturdee *et al.* (2007) demonstrate the occurrence of *Cryptosporidium* oocysts above recommended levels in almost a third of water samples taken. This emphasises the importance of adequate water-treatment procedures for water supply from upland regions and the need for more comprehensive study of catchment grazing and faecal indicator organisms and pathogens in freshwaters.

A key land-use change over the last century in the UK uplands has been the expansion of plantation forestry. This has been widely implicated in the enhancement of acid deposition through scavenging processes, but has also led to a number of other concerns for freshwater ecosystems draining areas of upland forestry. These include increases in turbidity and sedimentation due to soil disturbance during planting, eutrophication associated with phosphorus fertilization of young forestry, and loss of habitat heterogeneity along forest streams (Nisbet, 2001; Neal *et al.*, 2004). Harvesting of plantation forestry can also disrupt terrestrial nutrient cycles, resulting in elevated leaching of nitrate into surface waters. This can potentially result in ecosystem changes through increased acidity or metal concentrations, but in practice such effects tend to be localised owing to current UK policy of phased felling of catchment areas (Neal *et al.*, 2004). Indeed, Nisbet (2001) argues that the use of current best management practices within forest systems can effectively limit the impact of forestry on freshwater systems.

The disturbance of aquatic habitats through the sedimentation of eroded sediments has also been observed in relation to the severe peat erosion affecting many upland areas of the UK (see Evans, this volume). Increased organic sediment fluxes associated with peat erosion can lead to decreased light transparency, sedimentation on aquatic habitats and subsequent impacts on aquatic communities. For example, Jones *et al.* (1989) present palaeo-limnological data from an upland lake in Scotland, demonstrating that significant increases in organic sediment deposition associated with peat erosion led to significant impacts on aquatic macrophyte assemblages, including the loss of quillwort *Isoetes lacustris*.

Trends in dissolved organic carbon and water colour

A major change in the state of upland surface waters over the past twenty years has been the widespread increase in water colour, as represented by dissolved organic carbon (DOC) concentrations. This has occurred across a very wide geographical area, including Europe, the north-east United States and eastern Canada. In the UK AWMN, for example, DOC concentrations have increased at sites across the network with an average near-doubling between 1988 and 2003 (Monteith and Evans, 2005; Evans *et al.*, 2006). At stream sites the trend of DOC increase is most pronounced during high flow conditions (see Figure 7.5). This rising trend of water colour is a particular issue for water supply companies as it significantly increases the cost of water treatment. It also has important implications for upland carbon balances (see Worrall and Evans, this volume).

A number of hypotheses have been proposed to explain the trends, in particular relating to changes in either land management, climate or atmospheric pollution (see Evans *et al.*, 2006). Yallop *et al.* (this volume) show a compelling correlation between stream water colour and catchment burning for reservoir systems in Yorkshire. However, the observations of increasing DOC concentrations at so many sites across such a wide geographical distribution, including AWMN sites, where no significant land-use changes have occurred over the last few decades, suggests that land management is not the primary cause of the general trend.

Climate hypotheses have centred on recent trends in temperature and atmospheric CO_2 and on potential hydrological changes associated with increased drought or storm frequency. Seasonal variations in DOC are known to be closely coupled to temperature variation, and so early interpretations of the DOC increases focused on a possible link with recent temperature changes associated with global warming (Freeman *et al.*, 2001). Similarly, Freeman *et al.* (2004) demonstrate that increasing atmospheric CO_2 can lead to increased DOC production. Hydrological processes associated with more frequent drought occurrence may also affect decomposition rates in catchment peats through the 'enzymatic latch' mechanism, elevating DOC release after periods of unusually low water table (Freeman *et al.*, 2001; Worrall *et al.*, 2004). However, questions remain over the extent to which recent climate change and associated effects can account for the observed near-doubling of surface-water DOC concentrations. Evans *et al.* (2006) propose that the DOC trends result from recent changes in acid deposition. DOC solubility is suppressed by high soil-water acidity and ionic strength; and, based on both laboratory experiments and field monitoring, Evans *et al.* argue that reductions in sulphur deposition since the 1980s can account for increased

DOC production in upland peat soils. In a comprehensive time-series study of 522 lake and stream sites across Europe and North America, Monteith *et al.* (2007) demonstrate that spatial variation in DOC trends can be concisely explained by a simple model based on changes in deposition chemistry and catchment acid sensitivity. This study provides very significant support for the hypothesis that reductions in sulphur emissions during the last twenty years are the primary cause of the trends of rising DOC in upland waters.

In contrast to the concerns over water supply problems, it is interesting to note that, although the biological effects of the DOC increases are uncertain, they have potential ecological benefits. In particular, high DOC concentrations can complex metals such as Al and Pb, reducing their toxicity to aquatic biota. There have also been recent concerns over the impact of ultraviolet (UV) light penetration on the ecology of clear-water upland lake systems (e.g. Pienitz and Vincent, 2000), and increased DOC concentrations can act as a screen for ultraviolet radiation. If the acid deposition hypothesis is correct, this implies that the DOC increases represent the recovery of upland waters rather than destabilisation associated with land use or climate change (Evans *et al.*, 2006). Nevertheless, it is clear that a range of processes can affect DOC production, including climate change, and further research and modelling studies are needed to enable reliable predictions of future trends in DOC and water colour.

The future for upland freshwater ecosystems

Despite their location in relatively remote landscapes with low intensities of development, upland surface waters have been subject to a range of environmental pressures with subsequent impacts on their ecological health and on ecosystem services such as water supply. Their future status will therefore be controlled by the drivers of these pressures, in particular by trends in atmospheric deposition as well as land management and local land-use change. An important challenge is to assess the likely effects of current and future trends in upland climates. These effects are likely to be complex, including interactions with other drivers of change such as air pollution, and could potentially exacerbate or even offset trends associated with acidification and other status issues. Climate change can have direct effects on stream biology, for example through changes in thermal regimes and associated effects on phenology and species distributions. Data are already emerging which demonstrate the sensitivity of upland aquatic communities to both decadal climatic oscillations (e.g. the North Atlantic Oscillation) and directional climate change (e.g. Durance and Ormerod, 2007). Changes in temperature, precipitation and storminess also have the potential to affect surface-water chemistry, with a range of associated impacts on freshwater ecosystems. For example, climate change could alter terrestrial nitrogen cycles with associated implications for nitrogen saturation, acidification and nutrient enrichment. Potential relationships between climate factors and surface-water

DOC have been outlined above, and climate change could also accelerate the rates of mobilization of legacy metal pollution stored in upland catchments (Rothwell *et al.*, 2008). There is therefore an imperative to develop clearer understanding of the mechanisms linking climate change to water chemical and biological change, as well as potential interactions with other key processes such as acidification, nitrate leaching and metal release (e.g. Wright and Dillon, 2008).

In the European context, the EU Water Framework Directive (WFD) requires the achievement of 'good ecological status' in inland waters by 2015. This presents a major challenge for upland surface waters. Catchment-specific processes such as nutrient enrichment and land-use change can often be managed on a local scale, and there is the potential to provide protection to aquatic ecosystems through approaches such as WFD River Basin Management Plans and the Defra Catchment Sensitive Farming Programme for managing agricultural pollutants. However, the most widespread and severe impacts on upland waters result from diffuse pressures, in particular from the current and legacy effects of atmospheric deposition. In regions with historically high levels of atmospheric deposition, acidification and metal contamination remain persistent problems and freshwater status significantly degraded in comparison to background (pre-industrial) conditions. The management of these problems relies on national and international policy rather than on catchment-specific intervention. Nevertheless, significant progress has been made. Reductions in sulphur emissions and deposition have resulted in some recovery of acidified surface waters and ecological improvements at many sites. Recovery to 'good ecological status' at severely impacted sites will be slow and possibly contingent on further emissions reductions and the impacts of climate change. However, it is important to remember that these systems have been degraded over decadal to centennial timescales, and consequently the 2015 WFD target needs to be considered against these longer timescales of system response.

References

Allott, T. E. H., Curtis, C. J., Hall, J., Harriman, R. and Battarbee, R. W. (1995) The impact of nitrogen deposition on upland freshwaters in Great Britain: a regional assessment of nitrate leaching. *Water Air and Soil Pollution*, **85**, 297–302.

Allott, T. E. H., Golding, P. N. E. and Harriman, R. (1995) A palaeolimnological assessment of the impact of acid deposition on surface waters in north-west Scotland, an area of high sea-salt inputs. *Water Air and Soil Pollution*, **85**, 2425–30.

Barker, P. A., Pates, J. M., Payne, R. J. and Healey, R. M. (2005) Changing nutrient levels in Grasmere, English Lake District, during recent centuries. *Freshwater Biology*, **50**, 1971–81.

Battarbee, R. W., Allott, T. E. H., Juggins, S., Kreiser, A. M., Curtis, C. and Harriman, R. (1996) An empirical critical loads model for surface water acidification, using palaeolimnological data. *Ambio*, **25**, 366–9.

Battarbee, R. W. and Charles, D. F. (1994) Lake acidification and the role of pale-olimnology. *Acidification of Freshwater Ecosystems: Implications for the Future* (ed. C. E. W. Steinberg and R. F. Wright), pp. 51–65.

Battarbee, R. W., Curtis, C. J. and Binney, H. A. (eds) (2005) *The Future of Britain's Upland Waters.* London: ENSIS Publishing.

Battarbee, R. W., Mason, J., Renberg, I. and Talling, J. F. (1990) *Palaeolimnology and Lake Acidification.* London: The Royal Society.

Bennion, H., Monteith, D. and Appleby, P. (2000) Temporal and geographical variation in lake trophic status in the English Lake District: evidence from (sub)fossil diatoms and aquatic macrophytes. *Freshwater Biology*, **45**, 394–412.

Cosby, B. J., Ferrier, R. C., Jenkins, A. and Wright, R. F. (2001) Modelling the effects of acid deposition: refinements, adjustments and inclusion of nitrogen dynamics in the MAGIC model. *Hydrology and Earth System Science*, **5**, 499–517.

Curtis, C. and Simpson, G. (eds) (2004) *Summary of Research under the DEFRA Contract 'Recovery of Acidified Freshwaters in the UK', EPG/1/3/183.* ECRC Research Report No. 98, Environmental Change Research Centre, University College London. http://www.freshwaters.org.uk/resources/documents/raw-uk_final_report.php

Curtis, C. J., Allott, T. E. H., Reynolds, B. and Harriman, R. (1998) The prediction of nitrate leaching with the first-order acidity balance (FAB) model for upland catchments in Great Britain. *Water, Air and Soil Pollution* **105**, 205–15.

Curtis, C. J., Monteith, D., Evans, C. and Helliwell, R. (2005) Nitrate and future achievement of 'good ecological status' in upland waters. *The Future of Britain's Upland Waters* (ed. R. W. Battarbee, C. J. Curtis and H. A. Binney), pp. 31–5. London: ENSIS Publishing.

Durance, I. and Ormerod, S. J. (2007) Climate change effects on upland stream macro-invertebrates over a 25-year period. *Global Change Biology*, **13**, 942–57.

Evans, C., Hall, J., Rowe, E., Aherne, J., Helliwell, R., Jenkins, A., Cosby, J., Smart, S., Howard, D., Norris, D., Coull, M., Bonjean, M., Broughton, R., O'Hanlon, S., Heywood, E. and Ullyett, J. (2007) *Critical Loads and Dynamic Modelling.* Final report to Defra under Contract No. CPEA 19. http://critloads.ceh.ac.uk/

Evans, C. D., Chapman, P. J., Clark, J. M., Monteith, D. T. and Cresser, M. S. (2006) Alternative explanations for rising dissolved organic carbon export from organic soils. *Global Change Biology*, **12**, 2044–53.

Evans, C. D., Jenkins, A. and Wright, R. F. (2000) Surface water acidification in the South Pennines. 1. Current status and spatial variability. *Environmental Pollution*, **109**, 11–20.

Fowler, D., Smith, R. I., Muller, J. B. A., Hayman, G. and Vincent, K. J. (2005) Changes in the atmospheric deposition of acidifying compounds in the UK between 1986 and 2001. *Environmental Pollution*, **137**, 15–25.

Freeman, C., Evans, C. D., Monteith, D. T., Reynolds, B. and Fenner, N. (2001) Export of organic carbon from peat soils. *Nature*, **412**, 785.

Freeman, C., Fenner, N., Ostle, N. J., Kang, H., Dowrick, D. J., Reynolds, B., Lock, M. A., Sleep, D., Hughes, S. and Hudson, J. (2004) Export of dissolved organic carbon from peatlands under elevated carbon dioxide. *Nature*, **430**, 195–8.

Helliwell, R. C., Coull, M. C., Davies, J. J. L., Evans, C. D., Norris, C., Ferrier, R. C., Jenkins, A. and Reynolds, B. (2007) The role of catchment characteristics in determining surface water nitrogen in four upland regions in the UK. *Hydrology and Earth System Science*, **11**, 356–71.

Henriksen, A., Kämäri, J., Posch, M. and Wilander, A. (1992) Critical loads of acidity: Nordic surface waters. *Ambio* **26**, 304–11.

Hirst, H., Jüttner, I. and Ormerod, S. J. (2002) Comparing the responses of diatoms and macro-invertebrates to metals in upland streams of Wales and Cornwall. *Freshwater Biology*, **47**, 1752–65.

Jones, V. J., Stevenson, A. C. and Battarbee, R. W. (1989) Acidification of lochs in Galloway, Southwest Scotland: a diatom and pollen study of the post-glacial history of the Round Loch of Glenhead. *Journal of Ecology*, **77**, 1–23.

Kowalik, R. A. and Ormerod, S. J. (2006) Intensive sampling and transplantation experiments reveal continued effects of episodic acidification on sensitive stream invertebrates. *Freshwater Biology*, **51**, 180–91.

Ledger, M. E. and Hildrew, A. G. (2005) The ecology of acidification and recovery: changes in herbivore–algal food web linkages across a stream pH gradient. *Environmental Pollution*, **137**, 103–18.

Mance, G. (1987) *Pollution Threat of Heavy Metals in Aquatic Environments.* London: Elsevier.

Milne, J. A. and Hartley, S. E. (2001) Upland plant communities – sensitivity to change. *Catena*, **42**, 333–43.

Monteith, D. T. and Evans, C. D. (2005) The United Kingdom Acid Waters Monitoring Network: a review of the first 15 years and introduction to the special issue. *Environmental Pollution*, **137**, 3–13.

Monteith, D. T., Hildrew, A. G., Flower, R. J., Raven, P. J., Beaumont, W. R. B., Collen, P., Kreiser, A., Shilland, E. M. and Winterbottom, J. H. (2005) Biological responses to the chemical recovery of acidified fresh waters in the UK. *Environmental Pollution*, **137**, 83–101.

Monteith, D. T., Stoddard, J. L., Evans, C. D., de Wit, H. A., Forsius, M., Høgåsen, T., Wilander, A., Skjelvåle, B. L., Jeffries, D. S., Vuorenmaa, J., Keller, B., Kopácek, J. and Vesely, J. (2007) Dissolved organic carbon trends resulting from changes in atmospheric deposition chemistry. *Nature*, **450**, 537–41.

Neal, C., Ormerod, S. J., Langan, S. J., Nisbet, T. R. and Roberts, J. (2004) Sustainability of UK forestry: contemporary issues for the protection of freshwaters, a conclusion. *Hydrology and Earth System Science*, **8**, 589–95.

NEGTAP (2001) *Transboundary Air Pollution: Acidification, Eutrophication and Ground Level Ozone in the UK.* Prepared on behalf of Defra and devolved administrations, London. http://www.maposda.net/negtap/finalreport.htm

Nisbet, T. R. (2001) The role of forest management in controlling diffuse pollution in UK forestry. *Forest Ecology and Management*, **143**, 215–26.

Pienitz, R. and Vincent, W. F. (2000) Effect of climate change relative to ozone depletion on UV exposure in subarctic lakes. *Nature*, **404**, 484–7.

Posch, M., Kämäri, J., Forsius, M., Henriksen, A. and Wilander, A. (1997) Exceedance of critical loads for lakes in Finland, Norway and Sweden: reduction requirements for acidifying nitrogen and sulphur deposition. *Environmental Management*, **21**, 291–304.

Rothwell, J. J., Evans, M. G., Daniels, S. M. and Allott, T. E. H. (2007) Baseflow and stormflow metal concentrations in streams draining contaminated peat moorlands in the Peak District National Park. *Journal of Hydrology*, **341**, 90–104.

Rothwell, J. J., Evans, M. G., Daniels, S. M. and Allott, T. E. H. (2008) Peat soils as a source of lead contamination to upland fluvial systems. *Environmental Pollution*, **153**, 582–9.

Schindler, D. W. (1988) Effects of acid rain on freshwater ecosystems. *Science*, **239**, 149–57.

Skjelkvåle, B. L., Stoddard, J. L., Jeffries, D. S., Tørseth, K., Høgåsen, T., Bowman, J., Mannio, J., Monteith, D. T., Mosello, R., Rogora, M., Rzychon, D., Vesely, J., Wieting, J., Wilander, A. and Worsztynowicz, A. (2005) Regional scale evidence for improvement in surface water chemistry 1990–2001. *Environmental Pollution*, **137**, 165–76.

Steinberg, C. E. W. and Wright, R. F. (eds) (1994) *Acidification of Freshwater Ecosystems: Implications for the Future.* Chichester: John Wiley.

Sturdee, A., Foster, I., Bodley-Tickell, A. T. and Archer, A. (2007) Water quality and *Cryptosporidium* distribution in an upland water supply catchment, Cumbria, UK. *Hydrological Processes*, **21**, 873–85.

Tipping, E., Lawlor, A. J. and Lofts, S. (2006a) Simulating the long-term chemistry of an upland UK catchment: major solutes and acidification. *Environmental Pollution*, **141**, 151–66.

Tipping, E., Lawlor, A. J., Lofts, S. and Shotbolt, L. (2006b) Simulating the long-term chemistry of an upland UK catchment: Heavy metals. *Environmental Pollution*, **141**, 139–50.

Tipping, E., Lofts, S., Lawlor, A., Ashmore, M., Shotbolt, L. and Rose, N. (2005) Heavy metals in British upland waters. *The Future of Britain's Upland Waters* (ed. R. W. Battarbee, C. J. Curtis and H. A. Binney), pp. 36–9. London: ENSIS Publishing.

Tyler, S. J. and Ormerod, S. J. (1992) A review of the likely causal pathways relating the reduced density of breeding dippers *Cinclus cinclus* to the acidification of upland streams. *Environmental Pollution*, **78**, 49–56.

Vreca, P. and Muri, G. (2006) Changes in the accumulation of organic matter and stable nitrogen isotopes in sediments of two Slovenian mountain lakes (Lake Ledvica and Lake Planina) induced by eutrophication changes. *Limnology and Oceanography*, **51**, 781–90.

Wolfe, A. P., Baron, J. S. and Cornett, J. R. (2001) Anthropogenic nitrogen deposition induces rapid ecological change in alpine lakes of the Colorado Front Range (USA). *Journal of Paleolimnology*, **25**, 1–7.

Worrall, F., Burt, T. and Adamson, J. (2004) Can climate change explain the increases in DOC flux from upland peat catchments? *Science of the Total Environment*, **326**, 95–112.

Wright, R. F. and Dillon, P. J. (2008) Role of climate change in recovery of acidified surface waters. *Hydrology and Earth System Science*, **12**, 333–5.

8 Condition of upland terrestrial habitats

Alistair Crowle and Fay McCormack

Introduction

Variations in climate, geology, topography and management have led to the development of a range of upland habitats that are both nationally and internationally important within the UK uplands (Ratcliffe and Thompson, 1988). The EU Habitats and Species Directive (Council Directive 92/43/EEC, 1992) identifies habitats that are of international importance, and member states are obliged to identify those which occur within their own country and take steps to designate a range of examples that are found. These are known as Special Areas of Conservation (SACs). Sites of Special Scientific Interest (SSSIs) recognise species, habitats, or geological features that are of country importance and are notified under domestic legislation (Nature Conservancy Council, 1989).

Legislation enacted in 1949 (Minister of Town and Country Planning, 1947) created the Nature Conservancy, the first science-based government-funded nature conservation organisation in the world (Sheail, 1998). Work by the Conservancy and its successors meant that the majority of important wildlife sites in the UK had been recognised and most notified as SSSIs by the time the UK began the process of identifying sites in response to both the Birds Directive (Council Directive 79/409/EEC, 1979) and the Habitats and Species Directive (1992).

The designation of an area of land as an SSSI does not automatically prevent damaging activities, sometimes funded through public subsidy, from taking place. The obvious example is the overgrazing of large areas of the uplands as a result of agricultural policy and payments (Condliffe; Gardner *et al.*, both this volume). Concern over the condition of SSSIs led to the setting of challenging targets by government that need to be achieved by 2010 (England and Scotland) and 2015 (Wales and Northern Ireland). It should be noted that, at the time of writing, the Department for the Environment, Food and Rural Affairs (Defra) has announced that the target for England will be revised to take account of wider objectives (e.g. social) for the countryside. A priority will be to establish robust baselines to measure the new targets and build upon what has already been achieved.

In addition to the safeguarding of international habitats of wildlife import-ance, the UK government also has a duty to report to Europe on the Favour-able Conservation Status of Priority Habitats. The assessment will need to include the non-designated elements of these habitats, which will have suf-fered all of the problems that occur on designated sites but without some of the mechanisms that allow management to be altered through negotiation.

The United Kingdom uplands

The UK uplands can be divided into two zones (Thompson *et al.*, 1995). The montane zone starts at approximately 600–700 metres above sea level, and the sub-montane zone stretches down to the edge of enclosed agricul-tural land, around 300 metres above sea level. Both zones can extend to lower altitudes in some areas, especially in the north and west of Britain. Regardless of the altitude or geographical location, the areas that fall within these two zones share many common features. They have high rainfall, the soils are often peat soils, and the management is principally for sheep, deer or red grouse. In Britain, there are also strong geographical gradients of these features, with, for example, higher rainfall in the west than in the east and subsequently increased vegetation growth rates in the east compared to the west (Thompson *et al.*, 1995).

Interest features and Condition Monitoring

The reasons for notification/designation of a protected site (in this case habitats) are known as 'interest features', and Condition Monitoring is the process by which an assessment is made of the status of an interest feature on any given site. The measures by which upland habitats are assessed in the process of Condition Monitoring are the same across the UK, hence the term 'Common Standards'.

The interest features for upland habitats in the UK identified within the Habitats and Species Directive along with the National Vegetation Clas-sification (NVC) code (Rodwell, 1991a, b; 1992) that represent or most closely equates to the feature name are listed in Table 8.1. The Common Standards Monitoring (CSM) interest feature name attempts to identify more clearly the precise habitat(s) to be monitored. There are twenty-eight CSM interest features within the UK uplands including twenty-two features of inter-national importance.

Common Standards Monitoring in the United Kingdom

There are 2,431,000 ha of SSSI/ASSI in the United Kingdom, which repre-sent 10 per cent of the land area of the UK. The Joint Nature Conservation Committee (JNCC) is required by statute to develop CSM throughout the United Kingdom for the monitoring of nature conservation activity and for the analysis of the resulting information.

Table 8.1 European interest features in the UK uplands (NVC – British National Vegetation Classification Community, see Rodwell 1991, 1992).

European Habitat Feature Name	NVC# community where assigned	Area of habitat where known (hectares)	Common Standards Monitoring Interest Feature Name	Additional wholepart NVC communities included in CSM Feature
Grassland communities				
Calaminarian grasslands of the Violetalia calaminariae	0V37	Unknown	Calaminarian grassland and serpentine heath (upland)	
Siliceous alpine and boreal grasslands	U7, U8, U9, U10	150,000	Alpine summit communities of moss, sedge and three-leaved rush	U11 (See also Moss, dwarf-herb, and grass-dominated snow-bed), U12, U14
Alpine and subalpine calcareous grasslands	CG12, CG13, CG14	500–1,000	Calcareous grassland (upland)	CG10, CG11, U4 (species rich types), U5c
Semi-natural dry grasslands & scrubland facies: on calcareous substrates (Festuco – Brometalia)	CG1, CG2, CG3, CG4, CG5, CG6, CG7, CG8, CG9	<530,000	Calcareous grassland (upland)	
Species-rich Nardus grassland on siliceous substrates in mountain areas*	CG10 & CG11 on siliceous substrates, U4, U5 species-rich sub-types	Unknown	Calcareous grassland (upland)	
Hydrophilous tall herb fringe communities of plains and of the mountain to alpine levels	U17	100–300	Tall herbs (upland)	U4, CG10, U16, U19
Mountain hay meadows	MG3	<1,000		
Woodland or Scrub communities				
Tilio-Acerion forests of slopes, screes and ravines*	W8, W9	8,000–15,000	Broadleaved, mixed and yew woodland, Upland	

Annex I habitat type	NVC types	Area (ha)	Broad habitat (BAP)	Other associated NVC types
Old sessile oak woods with *Ilex* and *Blechnum* in the British Isles	W10e, W11a–b, W16b, W17a–d	91,900	Broadleaved, mixed and yew woodland, Upland	
Juniperus communis formations on heaths and calcareous grasslands	W19	1,000–3,000	Juniper heath and scrub (upland)	
Alluvial forests with *Alnus glutinosa* and *Fraxinus excelsior**	W2a, W5, W6, W7	4,500–8,000	Broadleaved, mixed and yew woodland	
Bog Woodland*	W4, W18, (M18, M19)	<1,200	Bog woodland	
Sub-Arctic *Salix* spp. scrub	W20	<10	Montane willow scrub	
Heathland communities				
Northern Atlantic wet heaths with *Erica tetralix*	M14, M15, M16, H5	432,000–492,000	Wet heath (upland)	
European dry heaths	H4, H8a,b,c,e, H9, H10, H12, H16,H18, H21	988,000–1,138,000	Subalpine dry dwarf-shrub heath	H7, H8, H22
Alpine and Boreal heaths	H12, H13, H14, H15, H16, H17, H18, H19, H20, H21, H22	91,000	Alpine dwarf-shrub heath	H10b, H13
Mire communities				
Blanket bog*	M1, M17, M18, M19, M20	1,913,000–2,665,000	Blanket bog and valley bog (upland)	M2, M3, M21. On deep peat: H9, H12, M15, M16, M25, U6
Transition mires and quaking bogs	M4, M5, M8, M9, S27	Unknown	Transition mire, ladder fen and quaking bog (upland)	
Depressions of peat substrates of the *Rhynchosporion*		Unknown	Blanket bog and valley bog (upland)	
Petrifying springs with tufa formation (*Cratoneurion*)*	M37, M38	<100	Spring-head, rill and flush (upland)	M7 (See also transition mires), M31, M33, M34, M35

Table 8.1 (cont'd)

European Habitat Feature Name	NVC# community where assigned	Area of habitat where known (hectares)	Common Standards Monitoring Interest Feature Name	Additional whole/part NVC communities included in CSM Feature
Alkaline Fens	M9, M10, M13	Unknown	Alkaline Fen	M11 (but see also below), M13
Alpine Pioneer formations of the *Caricion bicoloris-atrofuscae**	M11, M12	250	Alpine flush	M10 (high altitude only), M34
Rocky Habitats				
Siliceous scree of the montane to snow levels (*Androsacetalia alpinae and Galeopsietalia*)	U18, U21	50,000–80,000	Fellfield Fern-dominated snowbed Siliceous scree	
Calcareous and calshist screes of the montane to alpine levels (*Thlaspietea rotundifolii*)		500–800	Calcareous scree	OV38, OV39, OV40, CG14
Calcareous rocky slopes with chasmophytic vegetation		300–900	Calcareous rocky slope	OV39, OV40
Siliceous rocky slopes with chasmophytic vegetation		37,000–43,000	Siliceous rocky slopes	U21
Limestone pavements*		2967	Limestone pavement	
Nationally important Common Standards Monitoring Features				
—	U2, U3, U4, U5, U6	Unknown	Acid grassland (upland)	
—	U7, U8, U11, U12, U13, U14	Unknown	Moss, dwarf-herb and grass-dominated snowbed	
—	M4, M5, M6	Unknown	Short-sedge acidic fen (upland)	
—	M29	Unknown	Soakway and sump (upland)	
—		Unknown	Upland assemblage (Scotland only)	
—	U15	Unknown	Yellow *Saxifrage* bank	

The purpose of CSM is primarily threefold:

- At the site level, it indicates the degree to which current conservation measures are proving effective in achieving the objectives of the designation, and identifies any need for further measures.
- At the country level, it indicates the effectiveness of current conservation action and investment, and identifies priorities for future action.
- At the United Kingdom level, it enables government to undertake its national and international reporting commitments in relation to designated sites and more widely, and helps identify any areas of shortfall in implementation.

The monitoring can be split into the following activities:

- Identification of the interest features for the site: reason(s) for the notification of the site.
- Setting of conservation objectives for the site: management objectives for the interest features.
- Monitoring of the interest features to determine whether the management objectives are being met.

Once assessed, the condition of the feature(s) is assigned one of the following categories:

- *Favourable condition*: objectives for that feature are being met;
- *Unfavourable condition*: state of the feature is currently unsatisfactory;
- *Destroyed* (partially or completely): feature is no longer present, and there is no prospect of being able to restore it.

Where the feature is *Favourable*, it is classed as:

- *Maintained*: feature has remained favourable since the previous assessment;
- *Recovered*: feature has changed from unfavourable since the last assessment;

Where the feature is *Unfavourable*, a further assessment is made as to whether the state of the feature is:

- *Recovering*: feature is moving towards the desired state;
- *Declining*: feature is moving away from the desired state;
- *No change*: feature is neither improving nor declining.

The Condition Monitoring criteria for habitats have been developed so that monitoring can be carried out by fieldworkers who have a basic understanding of upland management and ecological processes, although some specialist input may on occasion be required. The monitoring cycle is spread over a period of six years with all SSSIs being visited at least once. Sites that are perceived to be vulnerable to damage for whatever reason may be visited several times within this time period.

Many upland sites have multiple designations at both domestic and international level. The interest features may not just be restricted to habitats but also include birds, invertebrates, individual plants, geology and geomorphology. All these different interest features will have their own monitoring protocols, and it is the role of the local Natural England staff supported by national specialists to balance the varying requirements of these features so that they are all being managed appropriately on any given site. Data collected as part of Condition Monitoring are also used to develop management and restoration plans, and play an important role in the targeting of resource allocation.

The condition of upland habitats in England

In England, 419,000 ha of upland are designated as SSSIs. These sites are split into units, which are usually based upon management but may also be based upon features that can be easily mapped. Upland unitisation has predominantly been based upon management units, some of which can be very large, with the average size of 103 ha (the largest is 2,555 ha). The drive to improve the condition of SSSIs from 2003 when only 35 per cent of upland units were in favourable or recovering condition has resulted in an increase to 71.7 per cent (December 2007) of units reaching favourable or recovering condition (Figure 8.1). Results of SSSI condition assessments carried out

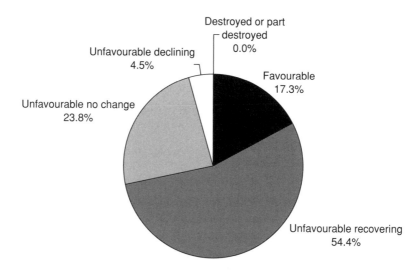

Figure 8.1 Condition of upland SSSIs in England, December 2007.

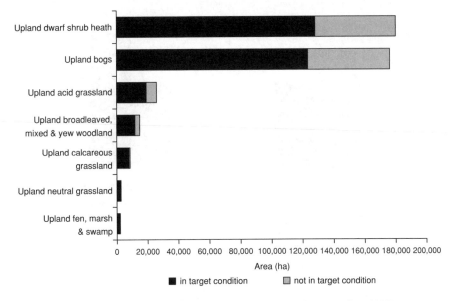

Figure 8.2 Condition of upland SSSI habitat in England, December 2007.

in England are recorded on ENSIS, Natural England's information system. The information held includes the interest feature(s) of any given site along with ownership, the condition of individual units and, in the case of unfavourable units, the reason for the adverse condition category and the required remedial action to achieve favourable or recovering condition.

Overall, two habitats – upland dwarf shrub heath and upland bogs – account for the majority of the area in unfavourable condition (Figure 8.2), with the largest causes of unfavourable condition being burning, over-grazing and drainage (Figure 8.3). The relative impacts of the causes of unfavourable condition on the two dominant upland habitats are illustrated in Figure 8.4. These impacts are discussed further in the sections that follow. Air pollution figures relate to the historical erosion and damage to blanket peat resulting from the loss of *Sphagnum* mosses following sulphur deposition post-industrialisation (Caporn and Emmett, this volume). Whilst sulphur emissions have declined, the levels of nitrogen are increasing, and it is uncertain how this will affect vegetation composition in future.

It is interesting to note that 'Wildfires' (see McMorrow *et al.*, this volume) and 'Public Access/Disturbance' (see Pearce-Higgins *et al.*, this volume), the two factors that are often cited as a major problem by moorland managers, actually only account for relatively small areas of problem zones recorded within SSSIs (Figure 8.3). This suggests that, although these may be a significant issue in some areas, such as the Peak District National Park, it is not the case in the wider context.

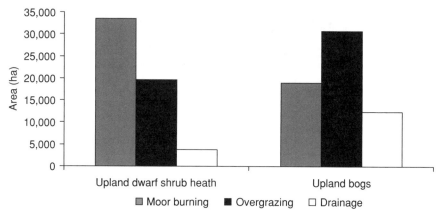

Figure 8.3 Moor burning, overgrazing and drainage on upland heath and bogs in England, December 2007.

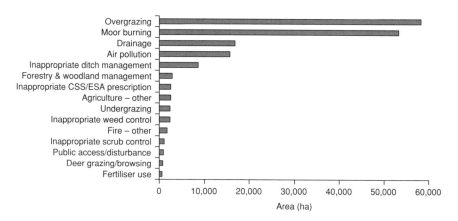

Figure 8.4 Top fifteen reasons for adverse condition on upland SSSIs in England, December 2007.

Burning and site condition

Burning has been used as a management tool in the uplands from the time of the first forest clearances (Mellars, 1976; Simmons and Innes, 1981), but the intensity of the past 150 years has been unprecedented (Yallop *et al.*, this volume). There are three types of burning that take place within upland areas: controlled burning for grouse management, controlled burning for agricultural management, and uncontrolled wildfires. The objective of controlled burning is to provide a fresh flush of growth for grazing by livestock and grouse (Sotherton *et al.*, this volume). In addition, where grouse management is practised the aim is also to provide a range of heather covers for sheltering and nesting by grouse.

There is an assumption by many land managers that, because a certain practice has taken place for many years, it must be acceptable. However, concerns relating to burning practices go back fifty years or more (Pearsall, 1950; McVean, 1959), although these have not always been articulated clearly until recently. Fortunately, one of the worst practices, that of generating 'hot' burns, is now widely recognised as bad practice. In these cases, hot and intense fires remove all vegetation, thereby exposing the soil to the elements, which could result in significant erosion (Imeson, 1971; Kinako and Gimmingham, 1980). Since the release of the draft guidance on CSM there has been greater awareness of the need to carry out 'cool' burning, which removes the vegetation but leaves plenty of 'stick' as well as the moss layer.

Reasons for an individual moor being in unfavourable condition as a result of burning range from too short a rotation through to burning into 'sensitive areas'. The Heather and Grass Burning Code (new revised code: Defra, 2007) has attempted to provide guidance on some of the situations in which burning should not take place, but historically this guidance does not appear to have been very effective in controlling many practices. Work by Chambers *et al.* (2006) has shown that, despite many claims to the contrary, the *Calluna vulgaris* (heather) monocultures found on many upland areas have only developed from the time of industrialisation, that is to say within the last 150–200 years. Before that, pollen analysis shows that the vegetation community was made up of a wider range of species than is presently found in many upland areas. This supports the conclusions by Rodwell (1991b) that many of the vegetation communities have been derived from a combination of burning, grazing and drainage. In addition, Gimmingham (1972) reported that burning reduces the diversity of plant species. Increasingly, moorland estates in England are attempting to burn on 7–8-year rotations rather than the 10–15-year or more rotations that have developed historically. This leads to further dominance by *Calluna* at the cost of other dwarf-shrub species. This loss of diversity is a common cause of a moor being classified as unfavourable.

Large areas of the uplands are covered in blanket bog (also known as blanket peat), and the combination of burning, grazing and drainage has in some areas seen the replacement of typical bog species such as bog mosses *Sphagnum* spp. and cotton grasses *Eriophorum* spp. with heather *Calluna vulgaris*. These sites are treated as degraded blanket bog rather than as 'true' dry heath, which occur on thinner, usually mineral, soils. When Condition Monitoring is carried out on these sites they usually fail the assessment criteria through the absence of blanket bog plants. A priority for these sites is to return them to a condition that allows them to become functioning as blanket bog once more. This becomes even more important when considered in the light of the research that suggests that many blanket bog sites may become net sources of carbon in coming years unless managed sensitively (see Worrall and Evans, this volume).

Table 8.2 Areas on Sites of Special Scientific Interest (SSSIs) where burning can result in the land being recorded as in unfavourable condition.

- Sensitive areas (e.g. bryophyte rich areas, fire sensitive species).
- Shallow soil and areas where soils are less than 5 cm deep or ground made up of scree or talus and where there is high incidence of exposed rock.
- Haggs, erosion gullies and areas of bare peat.
- Land above 600 metres, where burning is likely to damage slow-growing (montane) vegetation and vulnerable habitats.
- Areas with native trees or shrubs or immediately adjacent to planting enclosures.
- Areas with a noticeably uneven structure most commonly found in very old heather stands, and in blanket bog and wet heath characterised by *sphagnum* hummocks, lawns and hollows or mixtures of well-developed cotton-grass tussocks and spreading bushes of dwarf shrubs.
- Within 5–10 m of watercourses (including grips) where the watercourse has a well developed bankside vegetation structure and cover; or where bankside erosion is an issue; or where the watercourse performs an important hydrological function in taking water off a site.
- Steep slopes and gullies greater than 1 in 3 on blanket bog or other peat soils and 1 in 2 on dry heath.
- Areas not obviously recently burnt, so as to protect vegetation composition and structure and fire-sensitive species that might be lost by a resumption of burning.

Additional causes of Unfavourable Condition in relation to burning management are:

- 'Hot burns' which remove all vegetation and expose peat.
- Too short a return time for re-burning.

There are many areas on a moor where burning should not take place either because of the steepness of slope, the proximity of watercourses or vegetation that is susceptible to damage by burning (Table 8.2).

Many land managers burn intensively as a means of controlling the damage that can be caused by wildfires. Research has shown that wildfires are associated with hot periods and access routes (McMorrow *et al.*, this volume). It seems clear that the most appropriate way to deal with wildfires is to prevent them rather than try to repair the damage once a fire has taken place.

Grazing and vegetation condition

Sansom (1999) charted the rise in the number of sheep in Great Britain from around 8 million in the 1860s to 44 million in 1993. The majority of this expansion in numbers took place after the Second World War, but by 2002 the overall sheep numbers in Britain had dropped to 35.8 million (Defra, 2008). The increase in numbers of sheep was accompanied by changes in farming practice that saw animals being overwintered in large numbers that often required additional feeding. These changes had a profound effect upon the UK uplands.

Historically, high year-round stocking levels have been responsible for the large losses in heather cover (Anderson and Yalden, 1981; Bardgett *et al.*, 1995) with the main damage taking place over winter when the vegetation is being grazed at a time when growth is not taking place. The high numbers of stock also caused physical damage to the soil (Van der Post *et al.*, 1997; Evans, 1997). Some habitats, such as flushes, are relatively small, and a few animals can still have a negative impact upon the vegetation through either trampling or grazing.

Whilst overgrazing has consistently been the largest cause of unfavourable condition, the targeted use of management and agri-environment agreements since 2003 has seen a reduction in the area suffering damage by 135,000 ha (ENSIS).

Drainage and site condition

Government grants in the 1950s turned what had been relatively small-scale attempts at draining blanket peat into a widespread intensive management practice (Hudson, 1984; Condliffe, this volume). Land managers believed that, if they dried out the peat enough through creating drainage channels, also known as 'grips', heather *Calluna vulgaris* would dominate the vegetation with benefits for sheep and red grouse. Using aerial photographs, Coulson *et al.* (1990) estimated that in some areas over 50 per cent of the land in upland England and Wales had been drained, and Hudson (1984) reported that 55 per cent of grouse-moor owners in northern England had drained parts of their moorland estates.

Historically, conservationists have been mainly concerned about the negative impact of gripping upon the hydrology of the blanket peat, which in turn may reduce the range of specialised plants that are associated with the habitat. One of the earliest studies, by Conway and Miller (1960), discovered that drainage channels increased the sensitivity of blanket peat to rainfall with earlier and higher peak flow rates per unit area. They also noted large quantities of silt associated with the drained catchment. The erosion associated with drainage channels has been observed by most people who have visited upland areas where this activity has taken place, but it was not until the study by Newborn and Booth (1991) that the scale of erosion became apparent. Comparing two different drainage systems, they found that over the course of the three-year study 369 tonnes and 714 tonnes of soil was lost. Using this data, Hudson (1992) estimated that a kilometre of moorland with a normal drainage system of drains at 22-metre intervals would carry in the region of 45.5 km of drains that would produce a minimum of 319 tonnes and up to 13,650 tonnes of material per square kilometre over the first three years.

Attention is now increasingly focused upon climate change and the role of blanket peat as a carbon store (Worrall and Evans, this volume). Drainage channels in particular have been associated with carbon loss in one form or another. Equally alarming has been the discovery by Holden (2006) and Holden *et al.* (2006) that drainage channels are associated with sub-surface soil pipes, with numbers increasing with the age of the drain. Holden calculated that at sites that had been drained for forty years particulate carbon loss from sub-surface piping was likely to be in the region of $5.8\ 10^3$ kg C km^{-2} yr^{-1} over the period compared to that from an undrained slope, and this would be in addition to any surface erosion related to ditch channel incision or other surface processes (see also Holden, this volume).

Conclusions

The development of CSM Guidance (JNCC, 2006) has been an important step in the process of evaluating the effectiveness of site protection in the UK. The value of CSM goes far beyond fulfilling a reporting requirement. Primarily, it is directed at informing site management by defining the state of the site that is required and identifying the need for any further conservation management action (Williams, 2006). The UK was one of the first countries to attempt a monitoring programme at a site network level, and other countries such as Norway, Sweden and Ireland are applying many of the lessons from the UK experiences in the development of their own guidance (J. Williams, personal communication). These lessons include, for instance, ensuring that methodologies are consistent. In the UK, country agencies have applied different methodologies, largely as a result of the differences in resources available to carry out the assessments. Another lesson is that the data collected can only be analysed in relation to the current thresholds. If these change, the data cannot be re-analysed. However, as more and more Condition Monitoring is completed, this data set becomes more valuable in its own right. The development of electronic recording devices offers a potential way of gathering data that can be analysed in a variety of ways. This avenue requires further exploration as it also offers the opportunity to reduce the time and costs associated with existing approaches.

One of the current difficulties for the conservation agencies in the UK is the government's desire to reduce public spending. It is clear that a big driver for the future is the requirement to report to Europe on the Favourable Conservation Status of international sites, and to do this will require continued funding for survey, monitoring and, in many cases, restoration for the foreseeable future.

Acknowledgements

The authors would like to thank James Williams and Dave Chambers of JNCC for providing useful information and discussion during the writing of this chapter. The reviewers provided valuable input at the draft stage.

References

Anderson, P. and Yalden, D. W. (1981) Increased sheep numbers and the loss of heather moorland in the Peak District, England. *Biological Conservation*, **20**, 195–213.

Bardgett, R. D., Marsden, J. H. and Howard, D. C. (1995) The extent and condition of heather on moorland in the uplands of England and Wales. *Biological Conservation*, **71**, 155–61.

Chambers, F. M., Daniell, J. R. G., Mauquoy, D., Newberry, J. and Toms, P. S. (2006) *A Preliminary Examination of the Vegetation History of Moorland in Northern England.* Report to English Nature, Peterborough.

Conway, V. M. and Millar, A. (1960) The hydrology of some small peat-covered catchments in the North Pennines. *Journal of the Institute of Water Engineers*, **14**, 415–24.

Coulson, J. C., Butterfield, J. E. L. and Henderson, N. (1990) The effect of open drainage ditches on the plant and invertebrate communities of moorland and on the decomposition of peat. *Journal of Applied Ecology*, **27**, 549–61.

Council Directive 79/409/EEC (1979) On the conservation of wild birds. http://www.jncc.gov.uk/page-1373

Council Directive 92/43/EEC (1992) On the conservation of natural habitats and of wild fauna and flora. http://www.jncc.gov.uk/page-1374

Defra (2007) *The Heather and Grass Burning Code.* Defra, London. http://www.Defra.gov.uk/rural/pdfs/uplands/hg-burn2007.pdf

Defra (2008) *Historical Time Series for 1983–2005.* Defra, London. http://www.Defra.gov.uk/esg/work_htm/publications/cs/farmstats_web/2_SURVEY_DATA_SEARCH/HISTORICAL_DATASETS/HISTORICAL_DATASETS/historical_datasets.htm

Evans, R. (1997) Soil erosion in the UK initiated by grazing animals: a need for a national survey. *Applied Geography*, **17**, 127–41.

Gimmingham, C. H. (1972) *Ecology of Heathlands.* London: Chapman & Hall.

Holden, J. (2006) Sediment and particulate carbon removal by pipe erosion increase over time in blanket peatlands as a consequence of land drainage. *Journal of Geophysical Research,* 111, F02010.

Holden, J., Evans, M. G., Burt, T. P. and Horton, M. (2006) Impact of land drainage on peatland hydrology. *Journal of Environmental Quality*, **35**, 1764–78.

Hudson, P. J. (1984) Some effects of sheep management on heather moorlands in Northern England. *Agriculture and the Environment* (ed. D. Jenkins), pp. 143–9. Proceedings of the ITE Symposium No. 13. Natural Environment Research Council, Lavenham Press, Suffolk.

Hudson, P. J. (1992) *Grouse in Space and Time: The Population Biology of a Managed Gamebird.* Fordingbridge: Game Conservancy Ltd.

Imeson, A. C. (1971) Heather burning and soil erosion on the North Yorkshire Moors. *Journal of Applied Ecology*, **8**, 537–42.

JNCC (2006) *Common Standards Monitoring Guidance for Upland Habitats.* Joint Nature Conservancy Council, Peterborough. www.jncc.gov.uk/page-2217

Kinako, P. D. S. and Gimmingham, C. H. (1980) Heather burning and soil erosion on upland heaths in Scotland. *Journal of Environmental Management*, **10**, 277–84.

McVean, D. N. (1959) Moor burning and conservation. *Scottish Agriculture*, **39**, 79–82.

Mellars, P. A. (1976) Fire, ecology, animal populations and man: a study of some ecological relationships in prehistory. *Proceedings of the Prehistoric Society*, **42**, 15–45.

Minister of Town and Country Planning (1947) *Conservation of Nature in England and Wales: Report of the Wild Life Conservation Special Committee.* London: HMSO. Cmd 7122.

Nature Conservancy Council (1989) *Guidelines for Selection of Biological SSSIs.* Nature Conservancy Council, Peterborough. http://www.jncc.gov.uk/page-2303

Newborn, D. and Booth, F. (1991) The ecological impact of moorland drainage. *Game Conservancy Review*, **23**, 106–9.

Pearsall, W. H. (1950) Mountains and moorlands. *The New Naturalist*, No. 11. London: Collins.

Ratcliffe, D. A. and Thompson, D. B. A. (1988) The British uplands: their ecological character and international significance. *Ecological Change in the Uplands* (ed. M. B. Usher and D. B. A. Thompson), pp. 9–36. Oxford: Blackwell Scientific Publishing.

Rodwell, J. S. (ed.) (1991a) *British Plant Communities*, Vol. 1, *Woodland and Scrub.* Cambridge: Cambridge University Press.

Rodwell, J. S. (ed.) (1991b) *British Plant Communities*, Vol. 2, *Mires and Heaths.* Cambridge: Cambridge University Press.

Rodwell, J. S. (ed.) (1992) *British Plant Communities*, Vol. 3, *Grassland and Montane Communities.* Cambridge: Cambridge University Press.

Sansom, A. L. (1999) Upland vegetation management: the impacts of overstocking. *Water Science and Technology*, **39**, 85–92.

Sheail, J. (1998) *Nature Conservation in Britain – the Formative Years.* London: The Stationery Office.

Simmons, I. G. and Innes, J. B. (1981) Tree remains in a North York Moors peat profile. *Nature*, **294**, 76–8.

Thompson, D. B. A., MacDonald, A. J., Marsden, J. H. and Galbraith, C. A. (1995) Upland heather moorland in Great Britain: a review of international importance, vegetation change and some objectives for nature conservation. *Biological Conservation*, **71**, 163–78.

Van der Post, K. D., Oldfield, F., Haworth, E. Y., Crooks, P. R. and Appleby, P. G. A. (1997) A record of accelerated erosion in the recent sediments of Blelham Tarn in the English Lake District. *Journal of Paleolimnology*, **18**, 103–20.

Williams, J. M. (ed.) (2006) *Common Standards Monitoring for Designated Sites: First Six Year Report 2006.* Joint Nature Conservation Committee, Peterborough. http://www.jncc.gov.uk/page-3520

9 Burning issues

The history and ecology of managed fires in the uplands

Adrian R. Yallop, Ben Clutterbuck and Jonathan I. Thacker

Introduction

Fire was undoubtedly the first tool widely used by mankind to alter the natural environment. Its use is still commonplace today, and it is essential for the maintenance of many ecological communities worldwide, primarily to prevent scrub and woodland development in open ecosystems such as grasslands. In the upland regions of England, fire is used to maintain dwarf-shrub habitats primarily for grouse-shooting interests and to a lesser extent to improve grazing. The rich biodiversity of the resultant heaths is due to the mosaic of different-aged stands of heather they contain. However, excessive and inappropriate burning is now cited as the second most important reason for the poor condition of nature conservation sites in these areas (English Nature, 2003). In this chapter we review the history of managed burning in the British uplands and draw on both recent studies and our own research to raise concerns over current burn practices, particularly as these relate to burning on upland bog. We argue that the long-term ecological integrity of the uplands may be dependent on reconsidering some widespread and firmly held, but historically short-term, views on appropriate management strategies for these areas.

The prehistory of upland burning

Following the last significant glacial retreat at *c.*12,500 years BP (before present) woodland colonisation across the British Isles proceeded rapidly (Birks, 1989). Although forest cover temporarily declined during the Upper Dryas, by around 9,000 years BP it was essentially complete (Goodwin, 1975; Birks, 1988) including the Pennine summits (Turner and Hodgson, 1979). The extent of early anthropogenic clearances using fire and stone tools following this forest maxima are not fully documented, although there is evidence of temporary woodland clearances from *c.*6000 BC (Caseldine, 1999; Edwards *et al.*, 2007). Later Neolithic peoples may have used fire to improve browse to attract red deer for hunting, and later for cattle (Simmons and Innes, 1996; Fyfe *et al.*, 2003). Later a shifting pattern of farming developed in which small areas of woodland were burnt and crops grown for a few years, creating an upland mosaic of woods, dwarf-shrub heath and scrub (Simmons and Innes, 1996; Dark, 2005).

Concurrent with these clearances, a series of climatic changes (e.g. Steig, 1999) altered local environments over most of the UK (e.g. Tipping *et al.*, 2006), and in the uplands wetter conditions were an important factor in longer-term transition from woodland to extensive peat bog both in Scotland (Gear and Huntley, 1991) and the South Pennines (Tallis, 1991). As a consequence, much of the uplands of the UK are now covered in deep blanket peats created over thousands of years by the failure of senescing vegetation to decompose in anaerobic soil environments (see discussion in Evans, this volume).

Recent history of upland burning

Sporadic moor burning appears to have been a common practice during the late Middle Ages, and Rackham (1986) notes that by the 1300s burning of large areas of grassland and heath was practised to improve pasture on Exmoor and Dartmoor ('swaling' or 'swiddening'), an activity that continued there until recently (e.g. Ward *et al.*, 1972; Miller *et al.*, 1984). Scottish parliament archives and barony court records also provide documented evidence of the use of fire to manage moorland from at least 1410 (Dodgshon and Olsson, 2006). At some later point, however, probably during the mid-1800s, the purpose of fire in the uplands changed from being used primarily to improve grazing to include the specific goal of managing habitat for red grouse *Lagopus lagopus scoticus* (Simmons, 2003) for game-shooting. The degree to which this occurred varied across the UK and was less extensive in areas where grouse were less numerous, e.g. South West England (Miller *et al.*, 1984). Although the use of fire for game management has varied in intensity and extent since this time, over the past thirty years there appears to have been a marked increase in its use in parts of England (Yallop *et al.*, 2006b; Box 9.1).

Use of fire for grouse management

Management for red grouse primarily aims to increase the dominance and structure of heather *Calluna vulgaris* in upland communities, by the combined use of drainage and fire to remove competitor species. Cyclical burning is used to create a mosaic of new growth for forage amongst stands of older heather for cover (Miller, 1980). It therefore breaks the natural phasal development of *Calluna* (Watt, 1947; Figure 9.2) and prevents a stand from entering the degenerate phase (Hobbs and Gimmingham, 1987). This practice spread rapidly in the 1860s (Simmons, 2003) following observations of higher grouse densities on patches of burnt heather (see also Miller *et al.*, 1966; Picozzi, 1968). Following an inquiry into moorland practices in the UK, Lovat (1911) promoted the burning of heather in small patches or

Box 9.1. The scale of burning in the English uplands

Despite the importance of management burning, there is no formal national monitoring of its use and thus few data on burn frequency. To address this, Yallop *et al.* (2006b) undertook a national assessment of management burns within a random 2 per cent sample (equivalent to 208 km^2) of the English uplands. Aerial photographic interpretation (API) of images from the year 2000 was used to record main vegetation types and burn signatures, with the latter being assigned to four classes representing time since last burn (Figure 9.1). Changes over the past forty years were assessed by comparing a sub-set of this area for which matching images were available from the 1970s, mostly from upland areas of the English national parks.

In 2000, just over 17 per cent of the total area of heather-dominated upland habitat had been burnt within the previous four years, with over 30 per cent being burnt within the previous eight years, equivalent to an average of 114 km^2 being burnt annually in the English uplands. Within the matching sub-set of the imagery, there had been a highly significant increase in the extent of new burns (from 15.1 per cent to 29.7 per cent) between 1970 and 2000. Although this latter figure does not represent a national estimate, it does show substantial intensification of burning regimes in some areas – a trend in fire regime that in places is conspicuous (Figure 9.1). These data represent something of a 'snapshot', and need interpretation within the context of changing patterns of management, but serve to highlight how extensive fire use is and in particular the need for a more extensive monitoring programme to inform debate.

narrow strips (0.12–0.5 acres or 500–2000 m^2) with – to account for the variation in regeneration – a return burn period of eight to twenty-five years. Guidance was also given on how to 'treat' specific areas (Table 9.1).

How these practices were initially adopted is unclear as quantitative information on burning in England is lacking prior to the 1970s. Since then the return period seems to be about twenty years (Yallop *et al.*, 2006b). The more recent Heather and Grass Burning Code for England (Defra, 2007) recommends a similar practice with small fires in long narrow strips of up to 30 m in width. However, this guidance also differentiates upland habitat types, and makes a presumption against burning 'sensitive areas' such as peat bog or wet heathland.

Much research on the effects of burning on heathland vegetation was conducted in the 1980s (e.g. Hobbs and Gimmingham, 1980, 1984, 1987). The intensity and heat generated by fires was found to increase with stand ages up to twenty-six years (mature phase) but decrease as plants became

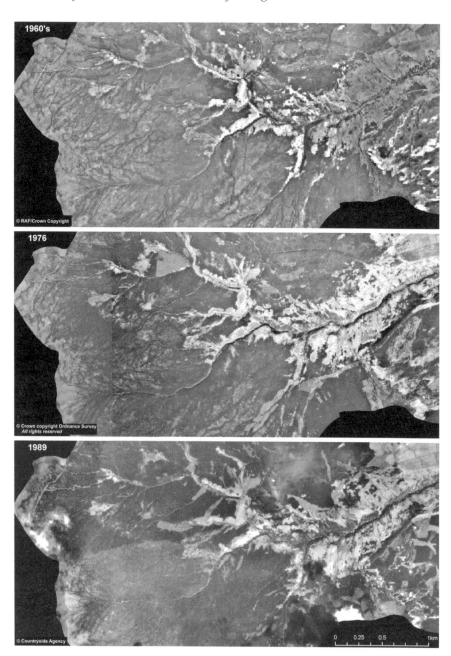

Figure 9.1 An example of rapid increase in extent of management burning over the
previous fifty years from aerial photography for an upland catchment in
the South Pennines, UK (see Yallop *et al.*, 2006b). The lightest burn patches
are typically around <4 years old. The bright areas alongside the main
drainage channels are Bracken stands.

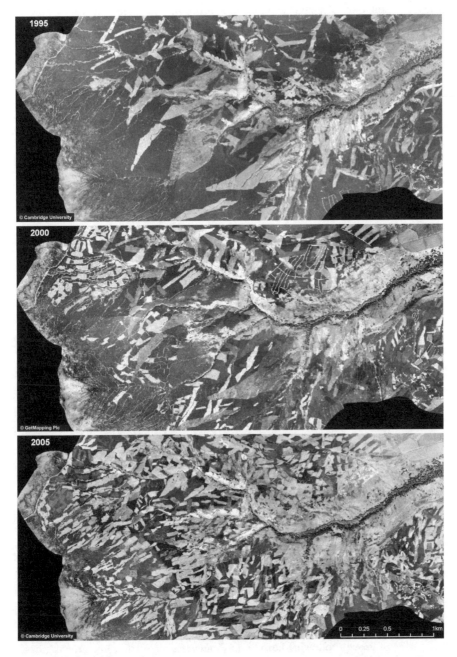

Figure 9.1 (cont'd)

Table 9.1 Summary of guidance on burning for grouse management from Lovat (1911).

- Burn old heather in strips 50 yards wide and let the strip run as far as the fire will take it.
- Burn average 1.5 ft heather in strips and patches of 0.25–0.5 acres.
- Burn patches and strips on the steep faces of the wintering grounds in small blocks of not more than 0.10–0.25 acres each.
- Burn the burnsides, knolls and nesting grounds of grouse in even smaller plots.
- Burn the wet flow ground in big patches of one to ten acres.
- Burn the high ground with northern exposure in large three-acre blocks.
- Burn good broad strips round each of the boundaries.
- Treat specifically those portions of the moor, which have a tendency to revert to grass.

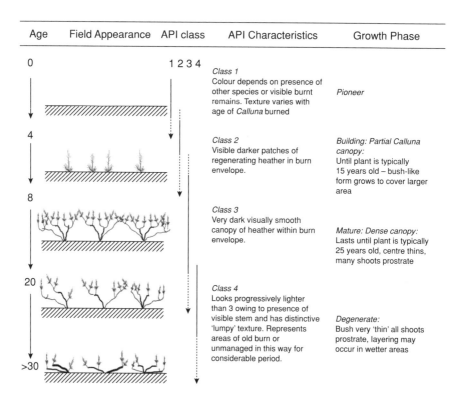

Figure 9.2 Illustrative relationship between aerial photograph interpretation (API) of growth following burning in *Calluna vulgaris* within the growth phase of Gimmingham (1959). Note there is not a perfect correspondence between growth phases and API interpretable classes. It should also be noted that on wetter areas of bog this simple interpretation will be modified as *Calluna* may not achieve dominance or progress to a dense late mature/degenerate phase (Yallop *et al.*, 2006b).

degenerate (Hobbs and Gimmingham, 1984). Differences in the type of burn were also noted to affect the speed of spread and intensity of the fire. In most instances controlled fires are burnt with the wind to facilitate propagation; but, when burnt against the wind, 'back-firing', the rate of spread is much slower and a more intense fire is produced (Hobbs and Gimmingham, 1987). Such fires are used on old woody heather, on wet ground, or to produce a clean fire-break, although anecdotal records also indicate the deliberate use of intense fires during drier conditions, often called 'hot-burning', to produce near-monoculture stands of *Calluna*.

One difference between Lovat's (1911) observations and those of the current authors lies in his description of the progress of recovery following burning of mature heather. He notes that on 'badly burned moor . . . covered by partly withered heather of an average height of two feet' burns will remain 'black' for two years, covered with grass and cross-leaved heath for the next three to five years and will require a further six years before a full yield of edible heather develops. Although this description is perhaps typical of burns on shallow peat or mineral soils where recovery can be quick and complete, the current authors have observed numerous instances where, following the burning of woody degenerate heather on deep peat, *Calluna* is the only plant to recover. This observation is supported by Stewart *et al.* (2004), who identify a decline in diversity with age of heather burnt. Not only does recovery from such fire appear species poor; it may also be slow, leaving an essentially bare peat surface for up to seven years before something approaching a full canopy regenerates (Yallop *et al.*, 2006b, see Figure 9.3). During this long recovery period the peat surface is exposed and at risk of decomposition and erosion (see, for example, Imeson, 1971) (Figure 9.3). Hobbs and Gimmingham (1984) were also prompted to suggest that burning may be unsuitable management for old stands, and as early as the 1920s Woodhead (1929) was hypothesising the importance of burning and draining for peat erosion on the South Pennines. By the Second World War, Pearsall (1941) described how these two processes combine to convert *Sphagnum*-rich bog on Stainmore to grouse moor, ascribing the loss of *Sphagnum* to drying out following burning.

Ecological effects of managed burning for grouse

Well-managed burns on upland heath produce a mosaic of different ages of heather, which benefit other wildlife, and these areas host important bird populations including curlew *Numenius arquata* and golden plover *Pluvialis apricaria* (Whittingham *et al.*, 2000; Tharme *et al.*, 2001). Heather maintained by rotational burning is also the main breeding site for hen harriers *Circus cyaneus* and merlin *Falco columbarius* (Thompson *et al.*, 1995) and is responsible for the high diversity of invertebrates of upland heaths: e.g. the North York Moors support 15 per cent of British carabid species and 20 per cent of spider species (Usher and Thompson, 1993).

Figure 9.3 Burn exhibiting poor recovery on a blanket bog SSSI in the Peak District National Park. Heather, visible as shrubby clumps, is the only vascular plant present around four to six years after the fire and covers only *c.*40 per cent of the burnt surface. Most of the rest of the peat surface remains exposed.

If burning is too frequent, it may convert upland heath into acid grassland (Hobbs, 1984; Hobbs and Gimmingham, 1984; Miles, 1988; Shaw *et al.*, 1996; Marrs *et al.*, 2004) although too-infrequent burning is also cited as leading to a decline in heather cover (Miles, 1988). In general terms, many more invertebrate species are associated with the woody plants of moorland and bog than with the grasses, sedges and rushes of acid grassland, and this shift from shrubs to monocots inevitably leads to a loss of invertebrate diversity, although this may be taxonomically patchy (Littlewood *et al.*, 2006).

Such changes are also detrimental to grouse-rearing interests, since grouse chicks depend on invertebrates as food (Park *et al.*, 2001). It can be argued fairly therefore that moderate burning for grouse on upland heaths, generally indicated by thin peat overlying mineral soils, brings biodiversity benefits – at least compared to most acid grassland growing in the same circumstances.

However, burning of blanket bog communities that have created deep peat over thousands of years is both contentious and under-researched (Glaves and Haycock, 2005). In pristine condition, blanket bogs are dominated by continuously accumulating layers of bog-mosses, *Sphagnum* spp., penetrated by cottongrass, *Eriophorum* spp., and through which dwarf shrubs such as *Calluna* grow by layering. Bogs are considered to be extremely sensitive to external factors (e.g. Bragg and Tallis, 2001), and the radical effects on *Sphagnum* growth that arise through burning have been noted previously (see Pearsall, 1941). Although reconstruction of wildfire history provides evidence that *Sphagnum* spp. can re-establish after burning in the absence of other impacts (e.g. Forrest and Smith, 1975; Kuhry, 1994), this only occurs with repeat times exceeding hundreds of years, and higher frequencies may reduce or stop peat formation completely (e.g. Garnett *et al.*, 2000). It is therefore probable that the development of the bog communities, and the accumulation of deep peat, only occurred under low-intensity grazing with very infrequent burning. Today the present balance of evidence indicates that burning of these habitats leads to reduction in *Sphagnum* spp. and increasing dominance of graminoids (Thompson *et al.*, 1995; Stewart *et al.*, 2004) and is therefore highly detrimental for conservation interests (Shaw *et al.*, 1996; Tucker, 2003; Stewart *et al.*, 2004). It is therefore debatable whether bog should be burnt at any time – and, indeed, such management is proscribed by the Heather and Grass Burning Code (Defra, 2007).

However, the effects of moorland burning, whether for grouse or for agricultural grazing, have not occurred in isolation from those arising from grazing, drainage, and nitrogen deposition. While there is a paucity of data with which to unravel this intimate history, the combination of these effects is probably synergistically destructive. For example, drainage may lower water tables (Holden *et al.*, 2004); and, where this occurs on bog, it may serve to increase both the depth and the duration of periods of aeration in the upper layers of peat. This will lead to increased aerobic decomposition and render the surface more susceptible to damage by fire. The amount of dissolved organic carbon (DOC) in waters draining some upland catchments – a measure of this peat decomposition – has more than doubled in the past few decades (Freeman *et al.*, 2001; see Box 9.2). The exposed peat surface following fire is also particularly prone to erosion (Imeson, 1971).

British blanket bog represents around 10–15 per cent of the world's blanket peat resource (Tallis, 1998); it is a priority habitat within the UK obligations to the Convention on Biological Diversity (Rio Earth Summit, 1992) and is protected under the EC Habitat and Species Directive. The need to

---

Box 9.2. Fire, peat condition and DOC concentrations in Pennine catchments

The presence of deep peat deposits shows that large areas of upland ecosystems have functioned as net carbon sinks for thousands of years. However, there is now increasing evidence of large-scale losses of carbon from such soils (Bellamy *et al.*, 2005), and concentrations of dissolved organic carbon (DOC) in rivers draining upland zones have also increased markedly (Freeman *et al.*, 2001). Suggestions of drivers to explain these phenomena include drainage (Worrall *et al.*, 2003), reduction in acid deposition (Evans *et al.*, 2005) and increasing temperatures (Freeman *et al.*, 2001). DOC production is greatly influenced by drought–rewetting cycles (McDonald *et al.*, 1991). See Allott (this volume) for a fuller discussion of carbon dynamics in the uplands.

In 2003 we conducted an investigation into reports of elevated concentrations of water 'colour' (DOC) in three drinking-supply reservoirs in the Pennines, UK. We measured winter (January) DOC concentrations in thirteen sub-catchments, and mapped the main vegetation, land use and management (including burn signature, see Box 9.1) for these sub-catchments. These were combined in a GIS with soil data to provide estimates for the proportions and combinations of each factor present. Multiple regression was used to evaluate the predictive power of each factor for measured water colour. The single strongest predictor for water colour was the proportion of exposed peat surface on deep peat soils arising from recent burning (Figure 9.4).

These results represent a temporally and spatially restricted study, which needs further validation over a wider area, and it is therefore premature to speculate on exactly how fire management and enhanced peat decomposition may be linked without further research. Nevertheless, the strength of the correlation indicates a systematic relationship between burning and DOC release in these systems, suggesting that burning practice may influence water colour.

---

manage bog appropriately is unquestionable. However, despite increasing evidence of damage, the clear and categorical presumption against burning on bog within the MAFF (now Defra) code, and the legal powers of statutory bodies responsible for most of our uplands that are protected as Sites of Special Scientific Interest (SSSIs) and National Parks, burning on blanket bog appears widespread. For example, Yallop *et al.* (2006a) found that 19 per cent of bog within the North Pennines Area of Outstanding Natural Beauty (AONB) had been burnt within the last six or seven years. For SSSIs in the AONB, the figure was even higher with *c.*22 per cent of bog being so managed.

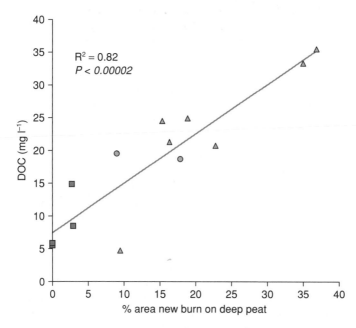

Figure 9.4 Relationship between area of new *Calluna* burn on deep peat soils and winter dissolved organic carbon (DOC) concentrations from thirteen sub-catchments within three Pennine drinking-water supply catchments. Sample point shapes indicate the three primary catchments in which sampling took place. This relationship was identified as the most significant factor from an examination of all land use and soil factors present in the sample areas.

Conclusions and outlook: reconciling conservation and gamekeeping interests

Fire, first as wildfire (see McMorrow *et al.*, this volume) and latterly also as a controlled management tool, has a long history in the uplands. It would be fair to say, however, that the continuing use of fire as a management tool has become something of a contentious issue between practitioners and conservation agencies. Few would dispute that controlled burning for grouse management, when appropriately executed, brings biodiversity, cultural and aesthetic benefits in many upland areas, and this clearly has an important and continuing role in the upland landscape. Problems arise because this frequently appears to be taken as evidence that burning regimes are appropriate for all upland areas – a claim that on conservation grounds is simply not sustainable, as is evidenced by the high level of poor condition assessments within upland conservation areas (English Nature, 2003). Poor management can of course result in the creation of species-poorer acid grassland communities, so in that sense well-managed grouse moors are of biodiversity benefit. However, we argue that many areas currently used as grouse moors have been derived by inappropriate management of what are, or were, blanket bogs. In these situations *Calluna* dominance and continued burning reduces biodiversity from what it 'should be' if assessed as the bog communities they were for thousands of years. The Joint Nature Conservation Committee's (JNCC) Common Standards for Monitoring of Upland Habitats (JNCC, 2006) recognises this, stating that where restoration of a degraded bog is 'considered feasible' the habitat should be assessed as blanket bog, not the heath or acid grassland it may have become. Thus, fire regimes in these habitats will lead to assessment of poor condition, effectively defining burning as an inappropriate management strategy or aspiration for these habitats.

This debate will only progress through dialogue, something possibly not assisted by a lack of clear terms and definitions of habitat type. If we choose to define habitat by the extant flora, large tracts of the uplands that are now covered in virtual monocultures of *Calluna* as a result of human activity would be defined as some sort of upland heath for which burning would be a suitable regime. However, the presence of thick peat deposits under much of this habitat indicates the presence of active bog for many thousands of years. It is against these millennia of ecological history that the 'traditional' practices of fire management undertaken for perhaps 100–200 years should be considered. Although it is true that the extent to which restoration of blanket bog is possible is currently unclear, there appears to be ample justification for suggesting that all deep-peat areas of the uplands, irrespective of whether they are currently described as upland heath, moor, bog, or the rather quaintly oxymoronic term 'dry bog' used by the former UK Agricultural Development and Advisory Service (ADAS, 1997), should be treated as recoverable bog (in concordance with Glaves and Haycock, 2005) and should not be burnt regardless of the present plant community. Fire management should of course continue, but there are good reasons why it should be restricted to those areas where it can be shown to be sustainable.

References

ADAS (1997) *Environmental Monitoring in the North Peak ESA 1988–1996.* ADAS report to the Ministry of Agriculture, Fisheries and Food, London.

Bellamy, P. H., Loveland, P. J., Bradley, R. I., Lark, R. M. and Kirk, G. J. D. (2005) Carbon losses from all soils across England and Wales 1978–2003. *Nature,* **437**, 245–8.

Birks, H. J. B. (1988) Long-term ecological change in the British uplands. *Ecological Change in the Pplands* (ed. M. B. Usher and D. B. A. Thompson), pp. 37–56. Oxford: Blackwell Scientific Publications.

Birks, H. J. B. (1989) Holocene isochrone maps and patterns of tree-spreading in the British Isles. *Journal of Biogeography,* **16**, 503–40.

Bragg, O. M. and Tallis, J. H. (2001) The sensitivity of peat-covered upland landscapes. *Catena,* **42**, 345–60.

Caseldine, C. J. (1999) Archaeological and environmental change on prehistoric Dartmoor – current understanding and future directions. *Quaternary Proceedings*, 7, 575–83.

Dark, P. (2005) Mid- to late-Holocene vegetational and land-use change in the Hadrian's Wall region: a radiocarbon-dated pollen sequence from Crag Lough, Northumberland, England. *Journal of Archaeological Science*, 32, 601–18.

Defra (2007) *The Heather and Grass Burning Code. 2007 Version.* Defra, London. http://www.naturalengland.org.uk/planning/farming-wildlife/burning/docs/HeatherGrassBurningCode.pdf

Dodgshon, R. A. and Olsson, G. A. (2006) Heather moorland in the Scottish Highlands: the history of a cultural landscape, 1600–1880. *Journal of Historical Geography*, 32, 21–37.

Edwards, K. J., Langdon, P. G. and Sugden, H. (2007) Separating climatic and possible human impacts in the early Holocene: biotic response around the time of the 8200 cal. yr BP event. *Journal of Quaternary Science*, 22, 77–84.

English Nature (2003) *England's Best Wildlife and Geological Sites: The Condition of Sites of Specific Scientific Interest in England in 2003.* Peterborough: English Nature.

Evans, C. D., Monteith, D. T. and Cooper, D. M. (2005) Long-term increases in surface water dissolved organic carbon: observations, possible causes and environmental impacts. *Environmental Pollution*, 137, 55–71.

Forrest, G. I. and Smith, R. A. H. (1975) The productivity of a range of blanket bog vegetation types in the North Pennines. *Journal of Ecology*, 63, 173–202.

Freeman, C., Evans, C. D., Monteith, D. T., Reynolds, B. and Fenner, N. (2001) Export of organic carbon from peat soils. *Nature*, 412, 785.

Fyfe, R. M., Brown, A. G. and Rippon, S. J. (2003) Mid- to late-Holocene vegetation history of Greater Exmoor, UK: estimating the spatial extent of human-induced vegetation change. *Vegetation History and Archaeobotany*, 12, 215–32.

Garnett, M. H., Ineson, P. and Stevenson, A. C. (2000) Effects of burning and grazing on carbon sequestration in a Pennine blanket bog, UK. *The Holocene*, 10, 729–36.

Gear, A. J. and Huntley, B. (1991) Rapid changes in the range limits of Scots pine 4000 years ago. *Science*, 251, 544–7.

Gimmingham, C. H. (1959) *The Maintenance of Good Heather: Enquiry into the Decline of Red Grouse.* Scottish Landowners Federation 5th Progress Report, 24–8.

Glaves, D. J. and Haycock, N. E. (2005) *Science Panel Assessment of the Effects of Burning on Biodiversity, Soils and Hydrology.* Report to Defra Conservation, Uplands and Rural Europe Division, Upland Management Branch.

Goodwin, H. (1975) *The History of the British Flora.* 2nd edn. Cambridge: Cambridge University Press.

Hobbs, R. J. (1984) Length of burning rotation and community composition in high-level *Calluna–Eriophorum* bog in N England. *Vegetatio*, 57, 129–36.

Hobbs, R. J. and Gimmingham, C. H. (1980) Some effects of fire and grazing on heath vegetation. *Bulletin d' écologie*, 11, 709–15.

Hobbs, R. J. and Gimmingham, C. H. (1984) Studies on fire in Scottish heathland communities. II. Post fire vegetation development. *Journal of Ecology*, 72, 585–610.

Hobbs, R. J. and Gimmingham, C. H. (1987) Vegetation, fire and herbivore interactions in heathland. *Advances in Ecological Research*, 16, 87–193.

Holden, J., Chapman, P. J. and Labadz, J. C. (2004) Artificial drainage of peatlands: hydrological and hydrochemical process and wetland restoration. *Progress in Physical Geography*, 28, 95–123.

Imeson, A. C. (1971) Heather burning and soil erosion on the North Yorkshire moors. *Journal of Applied Ecology*, **8**, 537–42.

JNCC (2006) *Commons Standards Monitoring Guidance for Upland Habitats.* Joint Nature Conservation Committee, Peterborough. http://www.jncc.gov.uk/page-2237

Kuhry, P. (1994) The role of fire in the development of *Sphagnum*-dominated peatlands in western boreal Canada. *Journal of Ecology*, **82**, 899–910.

Littlewood, N. A., Pakeman, R. J. and Woodin, S. J. (2006) The response of plant and insect assemblages to the loss of *Calluna vulgaris* from upland vegetation. *Biological Conservation*, **128**, 335–45.

Lovat, L. (1911) Heather burning. *The Grouse in Health and Disease* (ed. A. S. Leslie), pp. 392–412. London: Smith, Elder.

McDonald, A. T., Mitchell, G. N., Naden, P. S. and Martin, D. S. J. (1991) *Discoloured Water Investigations.* Final report to Yorkshire Water plc. Unpublished report, Yorkshire Water plc and University of Leeds.

Marrs, R. H., Phillips, J. D. P., Todd, P. A., Ghorbani, J. and Le Duc, M. G. (2004) Control of *Molinia caerulea* on upland moors. *Journal of Applied Ecology*, **41**, 398–411.

Miles, J. (1988) Vegetation and soil change in the uplands. *Ecological Change in the Uplands*, (ed. M. B. Usher and D. B. A. Thompson), pp. 57–70. Oxford: Blackwell Scientific Publications.

Miller, G. R. (1980) The burning of heather moorland for red grouse. *Bulletin d'écologie*, **11**, 725–33.

Miller, G. R., Jenkins, D. and Watson, A. (1966) Heather performance and red grouse populations. 1. Visual estimates of heather performance. *Journal of Applied Ecology*, **3**, 313–26.

Miller, G. R., Miles, J. and Heal, O. W. (1984) Moorland management: a study of Exmoor. Institute of Terrestrial Ecology, Cambridge.

Park, K. J., Robertson, P. A., Campbell, S. T., Foster, R., Russell, Z. M., Newborn, D. and Hudson, P. J. (2001) The role of invertebrates in the diet, growth and survival of red grouse (*Lagopus lagopus scoticus*) chicks. *Journal of Zoology*, **254**, 137–45.

Pearsall, W. H. (1941) The 'Mosses' of the Stainmore District. *Journal of Ecology*, **29**, 161–75.

Picozzi, N. (1968) Grouse bags in relation to the management and geology of heather moors. *Journal of Applied Ecology*, **5**, 483–8.

Rackham, O. (1986) *The History of the Countryside.* London: Phoenix.

Shaw, S. C., Wheeler, B. D., Kirby, P., Phillipson, P. and Edmunds, R. (1996) *Literature Review of the Historical Effects of Burning and Grazing of Blanket Bog and Upland Wet Heath.* English Nature Research Report No 172, English Nature, Peterborough. http://naturalengland.communisis.com/NaturalEnglandShop/default.aspx

Simmons, I. G. (2003) *The Moorlands of England and Wales: An Environmental History 8000 BC–AD 2000.* Edinburgh: Edinburgh University Press.

Simmons, I. G. and Innes, J. B. (1996) The ecology of an episode of prehistoric cereal cultivation on the North York Moors, England. *Journal of Archaeological Science*, **23**, 613–18.

Steig, E. J. (1999) Mid-Holocene Climate Change. *Science*, **286**, 1485–7.

Stewart, G. B., Coles, C. F. and Pullin, A. S. (2004) *Does Burning Degrade Blanket Bog?* Systematic Review No 1. Centre for Evidence-Based Conservation, Birmingham, UK. http://www.cebc.bangor.ac.uk/

Tallis, J. H. (1991) Forest and moorland in the South Pennine uplands in the Mid-Flandrian period. III. The Spread of Moorland – Local, Regional and National. *Journal of Ecology*, **79**, 401–15.

Tallis, J. H. (1998) The South Pennine experience: an overview of blanket mire degradation. *Blanket Mire Degradation* (ed. J. H. Tallis, R. Meade and P. D. Hulme), pp. 5–15. Aberdeen: Proceedings British Ecological Society.

Tharme, A. P., Green, R. E., Baines, D., Bainbridge, I. P. and O'Brien, M. (2001) The effect of management for red grouse shooting on the population density of breeding birds on heather-dominated moorland. *Journal of Applied Ecology*, **38**, 439–57.

Thompson, D. B. A., MacDonald, A. J., Marsden, J. H. and Galbraith, C. H. (1995) Upland heather moorland in Great Britain: a review of international importance, vegetation change and some objectives for nature conservation. *Biological Conservation*, **71**, 163–78.

Tipping, R., Davies, A. and Tisdall, E. (2006) Long-term woodland dynamics in West Glen Affric, northern Scotland. *Forestry*, **79**, 351–9.

Tucker, G. (2003) *Review of the Impacts of Heather and Grassland Burning in the Uplands on Soils, Hydrology and Biodiversity.* English Nature Research Report No. 550, English Nature, Peterborough. http://naturalengland.communisis.com/Natural EnglandShop/default.aspx

Turner, J. and Hodgson, J. (1979) Studies on the vegetational history of the North Pennines. 1. Variations in the composition of Early Flandrian forests. *Journal of Ecology*, **67**, 629–46.

Usher, M. B. and Thompson, D. B. A. (1993) Variation in the upland heathlands of Great Britain: conservation importance. *Biological Conservation*, **66**, 69–81.

Ward, S. D., Jones, A. D. and Manton, M. (1972) The vegetation of Dartmoor. *Field Studies*, **4**, 505–33.

Watt, A. S. (1947) Pattern and process in the plant community. *Journal of Ecology*, **35**, 1–22.

Whittingham, M. J., Percival, S. M. and Brown, A. F. (2000) Time budgets and foraging of breeding golden plover *Pluvialis apricaria*. *Journal of Applied Ecology*, **37**, 632–46.

Woodhead, T. W. (1929) History of the vegetation of the South Pennines. *Journal of Ecology*, **17**, 1–34.

Worrall, F., Burt, T. and Shedden, R. (2003) Long term records of riverine dissolved organic matter. *Biogeochemistry*, **64**, 165–78.

Yallop, A. R., Thacker, J. I. and Clutterbuck, B. (2006a) *Mapping Extent of Burn Management in the North Pennines: Review of Extent Year 2001–2003.* English Nature Research Report No. 698, English Nature, Peterborough. http://naturalengland. communisis.com/NaturalEnglandShop/default.aspx

Yallop, A. R., Thacker, J. I., Thomas, G., Stephens, M., Clutterbuck, B., Brewer, T. and Sannier, C. A. D. (2006b) The extent and intensity of management burning in the English uplands. *Journal of Applied Ecology*, **43**, 1138–48.

10 Moorland management with livestock

The effect of policy change on upland grazing, vegetation and farm economics

Sarah M. Gardner, Tony Waterhouse and C. Nigel R. Critchley

Introduction

British moorlands are a semi-natural habitat, created and maintained for millennia by land management activities through grazing, burning and peat-cutting to produce a mosaic of plant communities of varying composition and structure (Backshall *et al.*, 2001). This mosaic is associated with a diverse suite of animal species (Usher and Thompson, 1993; Thompson *et al.*, 1995) – particularly birds (Pearce-Higgins *et al.*, this volume) – and is valued as a resource for livestock, game, recreation and tourism (Condliffe; Curry; Sotherton *et al.*, all this volume).

Livestock affect vegetation by their selective foraging behaviour and off-take requirements, which alter the competitive dynamics, extent, condition and spatial distribution of moorland plant species (Gardner, 2002; Palmer *et al.*, 2004; Hartley and Mitchell, 2005). Thus, land management plays a key role in determining the composition and character of the moorland landscape and its suitability for farming, wildlife and other public goods (Burton *et al.*; Hanley and Colombo; Swanwick, all this volume).

Moorlands are associated with low-input, extensive agricultural production and poor economic viability, and within the UK have attracted considerable amounts of government support initially to boost production but more recently to deliver specific environmental benefits (Condliffe, this volume).

This chapter considers how changes in UK agricultural support policy have influenced and continue to influence upland farming, in particular grazing, and their environmental impact (Bardgett and Marsden, 1995; English Nature, 2001). Specifically, we consider how policy changes may influence the future choices made by upland graziers and the economics of upland grazing. In addition, we review the potential effect of grazier choices on vegetation change and on the maintenance of a sustainable mosaic of moorland vegetation. Finally, we examine the match between likely choices and environmental outcomes, and discuss what is needed to secure the match. We draw on the findings from two ADAS study sites. The background to these sites is described in Box 10.1.

Box 10.1. ADAS study sites: Redesdale and Pwllpeiran

The study site at ADAS Redesdale within the Northumberland National Park comprises 103 ha of degraded wet heath, predominantly *Scirpus cespitosus–Erica tetralix* (M15) vegetation (Rodwell, 1991). The heath is a heterogeneous mix of heather *Calluna vulgaris*, purple moor grass *Molinia caerulea*, mat grass *Nardus stricta*, sedge *Carex* spp and rush *Juncus* spp. dominated and *Calluna–Molinia* co-dominant communities. ADAS Pwllpeiran within the Cambrian Mountains Environmentally Sensitive Area (CMESA) is a discrete 300 ha site of exposed mountain land. For this study, a 72 ha area of mat grass heath (similar to *Nardus stricta–Galium saxatile* [U5] grassland: Rodwell, 1992), formerly dwarf shrub heath but degraded by past heavy grazing, was used. Within this heath, three communities dominated by cotton grasses *Eriophorum* spp, mat grass or sedges were present.

The original management objective for both sites was to enhance the cover and condition of dwarf shrubs present by reducing sheep numbers. At Redesdale, the site was divided into two paddocks and sheep stocking rates were reduced from 2.1 ewes ha^{-1} to rates corresponding to North Peak ESA prescriptions of 1.5 ewes ha^{-1} (Tier 1, 1990–2002) and 0.66 ewes ha^{-1} (Tier 2, 1995–2002). Pwllpeiran remained ungrazed from 1990 to 1994. In 1995 it was split into two paddocks and grazed at 1.5 and 1.0 ewe ha^{-1} (CMESA Tier 1 and Tier 2 prescriptions). From 2003 to 2006, management focused on reducing the abundance of purple moor grass (Redesdale) or mat grass (Pwllpeiran) in order to facilitate the restoration of a mosaic of dwarf shrub and wet heath plant communities. To achieve this, the paddocks at Redesdale were divided, and summer cattle were introduced into one half of each of the existing ESA sheep grazing regimes to give: sheep, low sheep, mixed and low mixed grazing with cattle (regimes 1b, 1c, 5a, 5c, Table 10.1). The site at Pwllpeiran was divided into a series of replicated plots and grazed under the following treatments: low sheep (1.0 sheep ha^{-1}), sheep (1.5 sheep ha^{-1}), mixed (1.0 sheep + 0.5 summer cattle ha^{-1}) and cattle grazing (0.5 summer cattle ha^{-1}) (Critchley *et al.*, 2007). The breeds used were Scottish Blackface sheep (Redesdale) and Welsh Mountain ewes (Pwllpeiran) grazing throughout the year except at lambing (April), mating (November) and during December–March, when 25 per cent of the ewes were removed. The cattle were non-lactating, autumn-calving Simmental X Holstein and Belgium Blue X Holstein mature cows (mid-June to mid-August only, Redesdale) or yearling Welsh Black heifers (July to August only, Pwllpeiran) (Critchley *et al.*, 2007).

Table 10.1 Grazing regimes used in the economics and vegetation change modelling studies (Boxes 10.2 and 10.3).

Regime	Period (months)	Annual frequency	Ewes/ha	Cattle/ha	Other
1. All Year Sheep					
a) High stocking	12	annual	2.1	0	25% of ewes removed in winter
b) ESA stocking	12	annual	1.5	0	25% of ewes removed in winter
c) Low stocking	12	annual	0.66	0	25% of ewes removed in winter
2. No grazing (B)	12	annual	0	0	
3. Summer sheep only					
a) High stocking	4	annual	2.1	0	May–August inclusive
b) Low stocking	4	annual	0.66	0	May–August inclusive
4. Summer cattle only					
a) High stocking	2	annual	0	0.75	July–August inclusive
b) Low stocking	2	annual	0	0.225	July–August inclusive
5. Mixed grazing					
a) all year low sheep & summer only high cattle	12 & 2 mths	annual	0.66	0.75	Cattle in July & August only
b) all year low sheep & summer only low cattle	12 & 2 mths	annual	0.66	0.225	Cattle in July & August only
c) all year ESA sheep & summer only high cattle	12 & 2 mths	annual	1.5	0.75	Cattle in July & August only
6. Rotational Grazing					
a) short rotation – all year high sheep stocking	12	2 years on, 3 years off	2.1		25% of ewes removed in winter when grazed
b) short rotation – summer only high cattle	2	2 years on, 3 years off	0.75		Cattle in July & August only
c) long rotation – all year high sheep stocking	12	1 year on, 4 years off	2.1		25% of ewes removed in winter when grazed
d) long rotation – summer only high cattle	2	1 year on, 4 years off	0.75		Cattle in July & August only

The influence of policy on the selection and economics of moorland grazing regimes

The 1975 Less Favoured Areas (LFA) Directive and European Union Common Agricultural Policy (CAP) subsidies favouring livestock production triggered major increases in sheep numbers in many upland areas during the 1980s (Fuller and Gough, 1999). Cattle numbers did not increase, and in many areas declined, shifting hill farming increasingly towards sheep-only grazing (English Nature, 2001; Condliffe, this volume). Intensification of sheep-grazing practices was followed by a loss of dwarf shrub species (particularly heather *Calluna vulgaris*), increases in competitive and/or unpalatable species (e.g. purple moor grass *Molinia caerulea* and mat grass *Nardus stricta*) and significant soil/peat erosion (Anderson and Yalden, 1981).

Concern over vegetation and environmental changes on moorland led to the inclusion of significant areas of the uplands in the Environmentally Sensitive Areas (ESAs) schemes and other stewardship schemes (Condliffe, this volume). The focus of all these 'old' voluntary schemes was a reduction in sheep stocking rates with the aim of halting the decline of dwarf shrub heath and enhancing its condition and cover.

The effect of reducing sheep stocking rates on moorland vegetation change has been very variable (e.g. Hope *et al.*, 1996). On many sites, the reduction has maintained the existing moorland vegetation, but has often been insufficient to increase the cover of dwarf shrubs (Hulme *et al.*, 1999; Gardner *et al.*, 2001) or to enhance the balance of grass, heath and mire communities or overall biodiversity (Gordon *et al.*, 2004). Moreover, significant increases in the extent and vigour of problem species such as purple moor grass have given additional concern (Hulme *et al.*, 1999; Gardner *et al.*, 2001; Milligan *et al.*, 2004).

In England, such results have prompted a re-appraisal of the implementation of agri-environment schemes to focus site aims and objectives on the achievement of specific environmental outcomes rather than on the implementation of fixed management prescriptions. As a result, the plans and management protocols within the new English Environmental Stewardship (ESS) Higher Level Scheme (HLS) (Condliffe, this volume) are more flexible and objective-driven (Rural Development Service, 2005a). New and modified environmental stewardship schemes (ESSs) have also been introduced in Wales (Tir Cynnal and Tir Gofal) and Scotland (Land Management Contracts and Rural Stewardship Schemes), both widening the range of options, rules and payment levels for moorland management.

The introduction of the Single Payment Scheme (SPS) in 2005 as part of CAP reform marked a profound change in government support for upland farming. In particular, for livestock, it shifted support from headage- to area-based payments, reducing any incentive to stock land above its carrying capacity. As a de-coupled payment, replacing direct subsidies, it has widened the range of livestock management systems and financial support mechanisms open to upland livestock farmers, and together with the new ESSs offers greater flexibility for the development of publicly supported grazing regimes.

The attractiveness of different grazing regimes to hill farmers

Reductions in sheep and suckler cow numbers in the uplands have been evident in the UK for some time. Fuller and Gough (1999) noted the flattening of sheep numbers in the 1990s, the foot-and-mouth outbreak in 2001 led to significant local drops, and numbers have continued to fall both in advance of the introduction of SPS in January 2005 and since. Overall, breeding ewes declined in England by 6 per cent and suckler cows by 3 per cent over the period 12/2004–12/2006 (Defra, 2006).

These data are not specific to the English uplands, and information for upland farming suggests that numbers are declining more rapidly here, possibly shifting towards intensification of the lower fields and extensification of the upper moorland parts of farms (Cumulus, 2005; Eftec, 2006). The Farmers' Voice postal survey work undertaken in England (ADAS, 2006) compared farmers' intentions on lowland versus LFA farms. Proposed reductions for cows and sheep were greater on LFA farms, at 17 per cent and 8 per cent respectively, than on lowland farms – 13 per cent and 2 per cent respectively. Indeed, a significant number of lowland farms appeared to be planning to increase or start sheep flocks.

A study targeting hill farmers in mid-Wales, the Lake District, Speyside/ Wester Ross in Scotland and the Peak District found that changes in stock numbers (notably reducing sheep) and management since 2001 had occurred on many hill farms (Waterhouse and Morgan-Davies, 2008). Table 10.2 shows the main responses. Some farmers had already made changes, whilst others had done little yet and would do more in the future. Of all farmers, 45 per cent thought their neighbours would further reduce their sheep numbers, suggesting future reductions on local hill farms. Many factors interacted to influence these farmers' plans, such as farm size, tenure, farmer age and geographic location, but the underlying trend was for stock, particularly cattle, to be reduced on livestock-grazing farms.

In the same study, hill farmers were also offered a choice of four future strategic directions for their farming system (Waterhouse and Morgan-Davies, 2008) and showed a preference for managing their farms according to ESSs (Table 10.3). Almost identical results emerged from a Scottish workshop focused on upland conservation workers, who were asked how they thought farmers would plan for the future (Table 10.3). The majority of the focus-group farmers were involved in one or more ESSs. They saw these as a means of obtaining guaranteed financial benefit, in the face of poor possibilities for direct incomes from livestock-based farming. Reducing or diversifying labour or freeing up time were seen as positive potential features of farming systems supported by ESSs. Potential benefits to wildlife were of lower importance, and farmers did not believe that ESSs might benefit the

Table 10.2 Responses to questions about changes in farm policy, past and future from hill sheep farmers in mid-Wales, the Scottish Highlands, the Lake District and the Peak District in 2006 (percentages in columns from a total of seventy-five responses).

Change options	Proportion changed since 2001	Proportion changed since 2005	Proportion planning change in next 5 years	How will other local farmers respond?
No change	41	44	43	0
Reduce sheep numbers	24	22	16	54
Reduce cattle numbers	5	11	0	0
Increase sheep numbers	2	0	3	4
Increase cattle numbers	0	0	3	0
Change livestock management	22	16	8	21
Diversify/off farm income	0	2	0	14
Reduce labour	0	0	5	0
Retire	0	0	3	7
Other options	5	4	19	0

Table 10.3 Preferred strategies for future hill farming. Proportion of responses for farmers from four focus group meetings held in mid-Wales, the Scottish Highlands, the Lake District and the Peak District in 2006 (n = 75). Results for conservationists from a workshop held at National Trust for Scotland, Glencoe, on CAP reform for upland land use in 2007 (n = 34).

Four strategies for future of hill farming	Farmers	Conservationists
Intensify (more livestock)	9%	5%
Extensify (fewer livestock)	29%	29%
Change breed or output type	9%	16%
Target agri-environmental schemes	53%	50%

land or infrastructure of the farm. High levels of bureaucracy and farming according to other people's rules were issues of concern against the establishment of ESSs, and undergrazing and irreversible land degradation were seen as possible negative consequences of adoption (Waterhouse and Morgan-Davies, 2008).

Boatman *et al.* (2007), reporting on recent experience with the English Entry Level Scheme (ELS) and HLS, found similar results to those of Waterhouse and Morgan-Davies (2008). Finances were important, but other factors, including an interest in wildlife per se, were important to farmers joining HLS. However, the application process was seen by many farmers, applicants and non-applicants, as a barrier to uptake, and rather low levels of uptake were reported. For example, by November 2006, in the second year of these new schemes, only 1.2 per cent of upland livestock farmers had successful applications for HLS options, and moorland management, and restoration options were a low proportion of these.

Using information from recent surveys of livestock trends on hill farms, we explore the potential variation in economic returns associated with different moorland grazing regimes operating within the context of current English upland policy instruments (Box 10.2). This study, which uses economic data from the two ADAS upland farm study sites in Redesdale, Northumberland, and Pwllpeiran, mid-Wales (Box 10.1), highlights the importance of public payments for delivering economically viable grazing in the uplands. Thus, hill grazing regimes that operate outside SPS and the ESSs appear unlikely to be economically viable (Figure 10.1a); and, even with SPS included in the farm account, only those regimes that adopt very low levels of stock, labour and fixed costs may be viable (Box 10.2). By comparison, the inclusion of an HLS agreement has the potential to render almost all regimes profitable with the exception of the more intensive all-year sheep-grazing regimes (Figure 10.1b). The profitability of regimes involving cattle may be further enhanced by the use of breeds at risk (for genetic diversity), which would attract the higher HLS cattle payment. Thus, it is evident that the scale of income from livestock production (lambs, ewes and wool) is low compared

---

Box 10.2. The economic potential of different moorland grazing regimes

The economics of fifteen different moorland grazing regimes (Box 10.1, Table 10.1) were explored using a bio-economic model (Conington *et al.*, 2004), using data from the two farming systems at ADAS Redesdale and ADAS Pwllpeiran (Box 10.1). The modelling process featured two core elements: first, an energy-based model focusing on hill pasture systems working at flock/herd level; and, second, a farm-scale model which calculated financial margins based on assumptions used for each scenario. Data on livestock numbers, performance, management and economics from experimental farm systems studies described in Box 10.1 were scaled up to 200 ha of moor. Standardised figures for inputs and outputs (based on SAC, 2006) were used to produce Gross and Net Margin data, and published English HLS payment levels (Rural Development Service, 2005b, 2006) were used as the potential ESS payments at both sites.

For both sheep and cattle, a whole year's productive farming cycle was modelled. Farm income and costs were split between the moorland area and the remainder of the notional overall farm to cover the different time periods when sheep and cattle were on the moorland (Box 10.1). This enabled financial figures for the different grazing regimes to be estimated for the moorland part only of a larger whole farm system. Very broad assumptions were made about the level of support to which the modelled regimes were eligible. For example, regimes involving cattle were presumed to be eligible for HLS cattle payment, and also for the higher-level payment if appropriate breeds were used. Throughout the modelling study, the application of different HLS options and payments was illustrative only. The same standard figures were used for each regime for SPS and LFA payments. Pwllpeiran is in Wales; but, for modelling purposes and to enable comparison with ADAS Redesdale, the English ESS (Higher Level Scheme: HLS) and LFA (Hill Farm Allowance: HFA) payments were used. A further assumption was that SPS and HFA payments could be obtained for the No Grazing scenario (Table 10.1), although current cross-compliance guidelines state the need to graze or mow the whole area at least every five years (Rural Payments Agency and Defra, 2005). This illustrative approach was undertaken to enable the financial issues associated with the introduction of SPS and the new ESSs to be highlighted without becoming immersed in the detail of scheme options and eligibility.

Net margins for different grazing regimes

The economic models predicted negative net margins for all grazing regimes without de-coupled subsidies (Figure 10.1a). With SPS included, no grazing (regime 2, Table 10.1) was predicted to be the most profitable regime followed by rotational sheep grazing, low summer cattle and summer-only or all-year low sheep grazing (regimes 6a, 6b, 4b, 3a, 3b, 1c). Mixed grazing, all-year sheep and high-summer cattle (regimes 5a–c, 4a, 1a, 1b) were still predicted to yield a negative return. These results reflect the standard situation for upland farms, with negative margins for the livestock enterprise, even when SPS is re-coupled within the farm account, as is typical of the way many farmers treat the SPS. The dependence of farms upon outside income and undercosted family labour is widely accepted (Hill Task Force, 2001).

With the addition of an HLS agreement (assuming that both land and grazing regimes proposed were eligible), almost all grazing regimes were predicted to become profitable (Figure 10.1b) and, for the most part, more profitable than no grazing, which could not justifiably obtain HLS payments. The more intensive all-year sheep regimes (1a and 1b in Table 10.1) without HLS payments remained unprofitable, but even mixed grazing (regime 5a) with HLS payments remained loss-making owing to high fixed costs. For regimes involving cattle, the addition of the higher HLS cattle payment to support the use of breeds at risk (Rural Development Service, 2006) could enhance the margins depicted in Figure 10.1b. Figure 10.2 shows the different income sources for each regime and highlights the disparity between income from production and that from public payments.

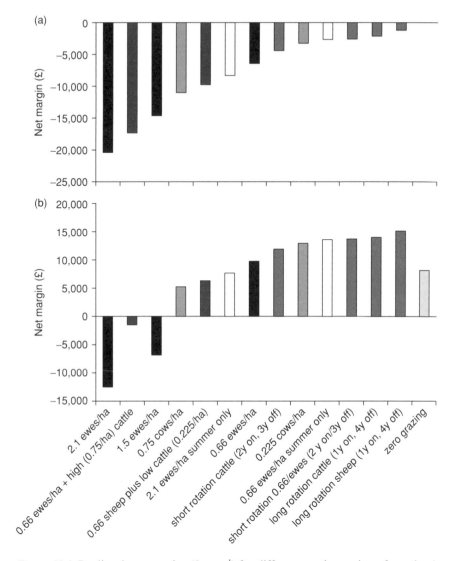

Figure 10.1 Predicted net margins (£ year^{-1}) for different grazing regimes for upland moor at ADAS Redesdale with (*a*) no Single Payment Scheme (SPS) or Higher Level Stewardship (HLS) payments, ranked right to left in order of net margins, and (*b*) with SPS and basic HLS payments included (i.e. no added cattle breed HLS payment).

to public payments per hectare; and, where livestock numbers are low, the ratio of public payments (SPS, HFA and HLS combined) to farmed income is potentially very high (Figure 10.2).

Results from the economics models (Box 10.2) support the preferred strategy of actual hill farmers, highlighted by Waterhouse and Morgan-Davies

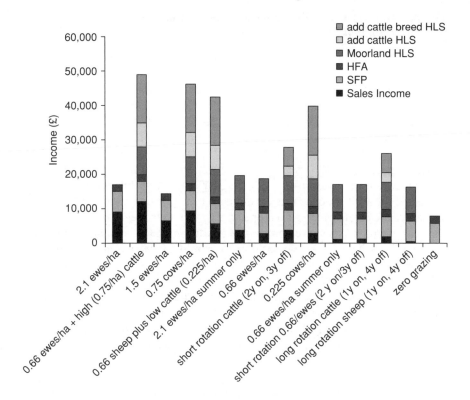

Figure 10.2 Income sources for the different grazing regimes listed in Table 10.1.

(2008), to reduce moorland stock and to manage their moorland according to ESS schemes. Specifically, both modelling and experimental studies suggest that it is the number of animals and especially the eligibility of a site for SPS, LFA and ESS payments that are important to the financial viability of a farm. The recent focus-group work has shown that hill farmers remain receptive to ESSs, but the latter need to be compatible with the main farming activities. Specifically, they need to be financially sensible, offer opportunities for reducing labour and not be too constraining in terms of rules or paperwork if they are to be adopted. Whilst the models have not dwelt on the details of the schemes and their impact, they highlight clearly that, without a grazing management plan linked to a financially rewarding ESS, livestock systems (with either or both sheep and cattle) will struggle to be economically viable. The scale of ESS payments illustrated by the current English HLS has the potential to lift moorland grazing into viability. Whilst the performance of the animals may not be as important financially (Critchley *et al.*, 2007), schemes need to meet the aspirations of land managers, be practical and meet other public-good needs, such as animal welfare.

The potential impact of grazing choices on moorland vegetation change

Whilst economic drivers may no longer be actively promoting degradation of moorland through intensive land use, and farmers are perhaps more receptive to stewardship schemes, there remain significant challenges in implementing land management regimes that will restore moorland. In particular, a policy of reducing sheep numbers using prescribed and predetermined stocking rates within agri-environment schemes (most notably ESAs and Countryside Stewardship) has had variable success in reversing vegetation loss and constraining the vigour of problem species such as purple moor grass.

A consistent outcome of the reduction or removal of hill sheep on former intensively grazed moorland is an increase in vegetation biomass and a halt in the decline of dwarf shrubs (Hope *et al.*, 1996; Gardner *et al.*, 2001, 2002). This can signal an improvement in the condition of the vegetation and may in some cases lead to an increase in the extent of dwarf shrubs and other moorland species (e.g. Welch, 1998; Pakeman *et al.*, 2003). More frequently, enhancement of dwarf shrub extent is very slow and tends to arise from the expansion of remnant plants rather than from the establishment of new ones (Marrs *et al.*, 2004). There are a number of reasons for this. First, a reduction in grazing pressure benefits both desirable and problem species, with the latter often responding faster than slower-growing dwarf shrubs (Hulme *et al.*, 1999, 2002; Milligan, 2004). This differential response rate provides one reason why variation in the starting composition of the vegetation has a strong influence on the rate and direction of moorland vegetation change (Hulme *et al.*, 1999; Marrs *et al.*, 2004; Vandvik *et al.*, 2005). Second, following a period of heavy sheep grazing, the spatial distribution of heather and other grazed species tends to become more aggregated within and between different moorland communities (Gardner *et al.*, 2001). This aggregation limits the ability of these species to expand into neighbouring areas when grazers are removed and significantly reduces the rate and size of increase in dwarf shrub extent (Gardner, 2002). Moreover, if the dwarf shrub is positioned close to palatable species such as bent-fescue *Agrostis–Festuca* grassland, its expansion may still be constrained by selective grazing by sheep even when stocking rates are low (Clarke *et al.*, 1995; Palmer *et al.*, 2003, 2004).

The slow expansion of dwarf shrubs, combined with the persistent and increasing presence of problem species and significant increases in plant biomass in some areas, has highlighted the need for greater flexibility in the application of grazing prescriptions and livestock species within agri-environment schemes. In addition, concern has been expressed over the decline in hill cattle which (with their greater energy requirement and heavier weight) play an important role in reducing plant biomass, increasing structural diversity and creating gaps in the sward for seedling establishment (Anderson *et al.*, this volume).

The new suite of ESSs includes some incentives for grazing with cattle and, together with the implementation of SPS, provides an opportunity for hill farmers to diversify their grazing regimes and to tailor them to both environmental and economic objectives for their land. In Box 10.3 we explore the effectiveness of different moorland grazing regimes (Table 10.1) for delivering vegetation management objectives within degraded wet heath and mat-grass-dominated vegetation. Whilst these case studies represent just two sites, the results illustrate some of the issues that need to be considered by land managers and policy-makers in identifying sustainable grazing options for managing moorland.

First, the case studies demonstrate that the effectiveness of different livestock species and grazing regimes in enhancing moorland vegetation varies with vegetation type. Thus, while summer cattle (grazing alone or with a low stocking rate of sheep) were effective for managing purple moor grass within the degraded wet heath vegetation at Redesdale, in mat-grass-dominated vegetation at Pwllpeiran low seasonal sheep or no grazing regimes were the most effective in reducing the extent of mat grass. This latter effect was not due to direct grazing by sheep (Critchley *et al.*, 2007). Instead it appears that under low or no sheep grazing an accumulation of bent grasses that can outcompete *Nardus* (Grime *et al.*, 1988) was the main driver of mat grass loss. Similar effects of grazing mediating the competitive interactions between mat grass and heather have been reported by Hartley and Mitchell (2005).

Second, the rate of vegetation change at both sites was predicted to be slow (Box 10.3). Within the degraded wet heath, this was due to the variable distribution of purple moor grass across the different plant communities present, which resulted in uneven grazing of purple moor grass by cattle. However, on similar sites where purple moor grass was distributed more evenly across the different plant communities, a rapid rate of change was predicted under summer cattle grazing (Critchley *et al.*, 2007). Thus, the spatial distribution of a species across a site can strongly influence the rate of vegetation change and the effectiveness of a specific grazing regime.

For the mat-grass-dominated site, the slow recovery of dwarf shrub vegetation was due to a lack of heather seed. Thus, although cattle grazing may have been effective in opening up the sward, the lack of viable heather seed and continued grazing of bilberry led to little change in dwarf shrub extent (Critchley *et al.*, 2007).

At both sites, the accumulation of grasses (purple moor grass on the wet heath and bents on the mat grass heath) under low sheep or no grazing regimes would in time reduce the structural diversity of the vegetation – valued by birds and invertebrates (Hartley *et al.*, 2003; Pearce-Higgins and Grant, 2006; Gardner *et al.*, 1997) – and also the quality of the grazing forage; the latter having an adverse effect on the welfare of and financial return from each animal (Merrell *et al.*, 2001). By comparison, cattle by their grazing pattern, greater offtake and ability to open up the sward may deliver greater benefits for biodiversity through the creation of a more heterogeneous sward.

This single example highlights the complex nature of the interaction of grazing and moorland vegetation change, even before the requirements of

Box 10.3. Modelling the effect of grazing regimes on the delivery of preferred moorland vegetation and sustainable land management

The potential of fifteen grazing regimes (Table 10.1) for maintaining and enhancing moorland vegetation and managing problem species at two contrasting upland sites (Box 10.1) was explored using a spatially explicit vegetation model (Gardner *et al.*, 2001; Gardner, 2002). The model was defined by a gridded lattice (Wissel, 2000), which was divided into units of different size. Within the lattice, the smallest units, the cells, were occupied by single plant species of known age or by bare ground. Cells were grouped into tile types – each tile type representing a different plant community. Field data on plant community composition for each site were used to create the tile types. These were then distributed across the lattice in a manner mimicking the mosaic of plant communities mapped in the field. Species change across the lattice was driven by plant competition, which in turn was influenced by grazing animals and by the age, condition, starting abundance and spatial distribution of the plant species present. The abundance of each species present in the lattice was quantified as the percentage of the total cells available that were occupied by a particular species. This value was expressed as species percentage occupancy. Species abundance was measured at two scales, as percentage occupancy of the whole lattice and of each set of tile types (equivalent to species abundance in different plant communities).

Sixteen vegetation categories were available in the model: *Calluna vulgaris*, *Carex* sp., *Deschampsia flexuosa*, *Empetrum nigrum*, *Erica tetralix*, *Eriophorum* sp., *Juncus squarrosus*, *Molinia caerulea*, *Nardus stricta*, *Scirpus cespitosus*, *Vaccinium myrtillus*, Broad-leaved grasses, Fine-leaved grasses, Mosses, Rushes and Bare ground. The lattice created for a site was used as the starting template for simulating each grazing regime. Livestock nutritional requirements, grazing preferences, numbers and season of grazing were adjusted for each regime, using information from the bio-economics model (Box 10.2), and for the species and breed of stock used at the site. Simulations of each site-regime combination were run for twenty cycles (equivalent to twenty years), and the potential effect of each regime on vegetation change at each site was assessed from predictions of species percentage occupancy.

Vegetation change under different grazing regimes

For the wet heath vegetation at Redesdale, summer cattle and mixed grazing (regimes 4a, 5a and 5c: Table 10.1) were predicted to be the most effective in limiting *Molinia* and enhancing heather extent. When averaged across the six communities present on the site (Box 10.1), these regimes were predicted to result in a slow convergence in the extent of *Molinia* and heather over a twenty-year period (Figure 10.3). For individual plant communities, the effect of cattle grazing on *Molinia* was predicted to be very variable, with *Molinia* declining in communities where it was dominant, and increasing in communities where it was sub-dominant (Figure 10.4). These predictions were supported by data from field experiments (Critchley *et al.*, 2007).

By contrast, under sheep-only grazing (regimes 1a–c, 3a and 3b) *Molinia* was predicted to increase markedly across the field and within all communities present (Figures 10.3 and 10.4). Heather was predicted to show little overall change in extent (Figure 10.3), increasing in communities where it was rare and decreasing where it was dominant (Figure 10.4). Field data from a ten-year study of the effect of ESA sheep stocking rates on vegetation change at the site supported these predictions (Gardner *et al.*, 2002; Figure 10.5).

For the mat-grass-dominated heath at Pwllpeiran, rotational or summer-only sheep (regimes 6a, 6c, 3a, 3b: Table 10.1) were predicted to be the most effective in reducing the extent of mat grass across the whole site and within the three different plant communities. Under these regimes, bent grasses *Agrostis* sp. and bilberry were predicted to increase (Table 10.4). Under summer cattle and mixed grazing, mat grass was also predicted to decrease (regimes 4a, 5a, 5c: Table 10.1) and bilberry to increase, but by a smaller extent than under rotational or summer sheep, and broad-leaved grasses to decrease (Table 10.4). Field data assessing the effects of CMESA stocking prescriptions on this site (applied from 1995 to 2002, Box 10.1) supported model predictions by indicating an increase in the biomass and extent of bent grasses under low sheep grazing (regime 1b, Table 10.1; Hetherington *et al.*, 2002). Experimental studies (2003–6, Box 10.1) of sheep and cattle grazing detected no significant differences in the vegetation response to the different grazing regimes (Critchley *et al.*, 2007), although mat grass declined on both sheep-only, mixed and cattle-only grazing treatments as predicted (Table 10.4). This latter study was relatively short at four years compared to the model simulation of twenty years (Critchley *et al.*, 2007).

economic sustainability and delivery of public-service goods are considered. In the following section we see that, without a clear alignment of environmental and economic benefits, the aspirations of graziers and conservationists may continue to be thwarted.

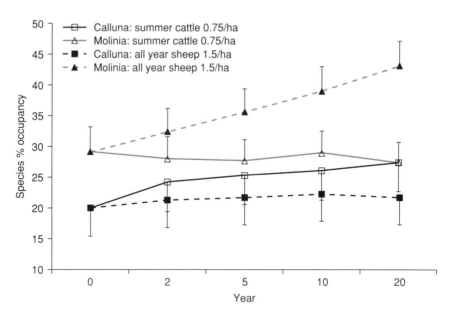

Figure 10.3 Effect of summer cattle and reduced all-year sheep (regimes 4a and 1b,
Table 10.1) on the predicted abundance of heather and purple moor grass
(mean ± S.E. percentage species occupancy) at ADAS Redesdale.

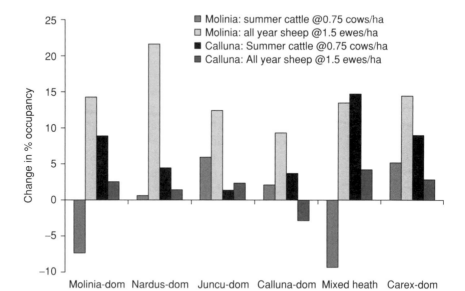

Figure 10.4 Variation between the six plant communities at ADAS Redesdale in the
predicted change in abundance of heather and purple moor grass (per
cent species occupancy) after twenty years of summer cattle or all-year
sheep grazing (regimes 4b and 1b, Table 10.1).

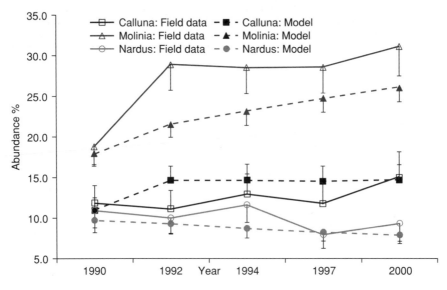

Figure 10.5 Comparison of field and model estimates of abundance (mean ± S.E.) for heather, purple moor grass and mat grass under reduced sheep stocking (regime 1b, Table 10.1) at ADAS Redesdale 1990–2000. Abundance measured in the field as species percentage top cover and in the model as species percentage occupancy of the whole lattice.

Table 10.4 Model predictions for abundance (mean ± S.E. of species percentage occupancy) of three key species in mat grass heath at ADAS Pwllpeiran under Best and Worst (for vegetation management) grazing regimes over twenty years. See Table 10.1 for grazing regime codes and details.

Grazing regime code	Bent grasses Agrostis spp.	Mat grass Nardus stricta	Bilberry V. myrtillus
Starting abundance	13.9 ± 0.7	22.3(±0.5)	8.8(±0.4)
BEST regimes			
6a) Short rotation sheep	23.2 ± 1.2	14.7(±0.7)	17.9(±1.1)
6c) Long rotation sheep	22.5 ± 1.4	13.3(±0.6)	16.7(±0.9)
6d) Long rotation cattle	19.8 ± 1.0	15.1(±0.6)	17.9(±0.9)
WORST regimes			
4a) Summer cattle	12.1(±0.8)	19.0(±0.9)	13.5(±0.7)
5a) Mixed grazing	10.8(±1.0)	19.5(±0.8)	13.6(±0.7)

The potential match between economics and management regimes delivering desired vegetation change

A simple ranking of the different grazing regimes suggests that at Redesdale the best regimes for vegetation change would have low economic viability

Table 10.5 Comparison of ranks of Best (1) and Worst (14) grazing regimes for vegetation management and economic viability for the sites at ADAS Redesdale and ADAS Pwllpeiran.

Grazing regime codes	Ranking for vegetation	Ranking for economics
BEST at Redesdale		
4a) Summer cattle	1	11
5a) Mixed grazing	2	12
WORST at Redesdale		
6a) Short rotation sheep	12	3
3b) Low summer sheep	13	4
1b) All year sheep	14	14
BEST at Pwllpeiran		
6a) Short rotation sheep	1	3
6c) Long rotation sheep	2	1
6d) Long rotation cattle	3	2
WORST at Pwllpeiran		
4a) Summer cattle	13	11
5a) Mixed grazing	14	12

under SPS and HLS, whilst those worse for vegetation change, for example low summer and short rotational sheep, would be considerably more financially attractive (Table 10.5). Inclusion of higher supplementary cattle payments under the HLS scheme may enhance the profitability of the best vegetation management regimes, but to obtain the higher level of incentive payment would require the grazier to use specific cattle breeds defined as being at risk. This is an option that could be impractical and expensive for graziers with existing cattle stock.

For Pwllpeiran, there was a better match between rankings for predicted vegetation change and economics performance. Rotational sheep or cattle grazing, the regimes predicted as best for reducing mat grass, gave the best financial return under SPS and HLS. Inclusion of HLS cattle payments would appear to skew business profitability towards mixed or summer cattle grazing regimes, which might be less beneficial for the vegetation at the Pwllpeiran site.

Thus, the choice of grazing regime might be expected to differ between the two sites with a more difficult choice at Redesdale, in terms of the optimal balance for economics and vegetation management, than at Pwllpeiran.

Conclusions

The introduction of the Single Payment Scheme has enabled the economic losses of grazing livestock on moorlands without subsidy to be apparent to both farmers and policy-makers. Results from the case studies suggest that many moorland grazing situations would not be economically viable without support. Payments to undertake environmental stewardship management are therefore potentially highly attractive, although the adoption of such management will depend upon its availability and practicality, the marginal economics, transaction costs and risks of the modified grazing system, personal motivation and a farmer's circumstances. The English HLS scheme, used in the economics modelling exercise, is actually targeted at particular aspects of moorland, for example specific landscape or heritage features, habitats and species, and is thus not available to all applicants. We have deliberately not discussed issues of site eligibility in our modelling, but the targeted approach used for HLS will limit its availability and its contribution to the hill farm budget.

Alongside the economics is the question of what type of management is appropriate for delivering the ecosystem services (landscape, wildlife, heritage protection, game stock, water, carbon storage) required by other end-users. The effect of grazers on landscape, wildlife and game has been well researched but its impact on water management, carbon storage and heritage is less clearly understood. Grazing has delivered significant change in the past (Anderson and Yalden, 1981; Bardgett and Marsden, 1995), but it is clear from these case studies that a policy of just reducing sheep numbers is insufficient to reverse the damaging effects to moorland of high stocking rates.

The choice of grazing regime needs to reflect the management task required and the ecological dynamics of the vegetation present. Results from the case studies have emphasized the variable effectiveness of different grazing regimes operating on different types of moorland vegetation. This is due to differences in the life-history strategies, spatial distribution and competitive vigour of the plant species present, which, together with variation in livestock foraging preferences and energy requirements, interact to influence which species will dominate a site. In focusing policy on reducing sheep numbers, the role of these ecological processes in constraining (or enhancing) vegetation change has often been overlooked. For example, the aggregation of plant species under intensive grazing, which can severely constrain the rate of species increase, cannot be readily reversed by reducing sheep numbers (Gardner, 2002). In this case, additional management approaches such as controlled burning, seeding or a change of livestock species may be required to alter the topology of the vegetation and stimulate the expansion of desired species. Similarly, it is increasingly recognized that summer grazing by cattle is required to limit the accumulation of vegetation biomass particularly of problem species such as purple moor grass.

It is to be hoped that the introduction of SPS and the new ESSs will enable greater flexibility in grazing and other management options to improve the match between economic viability and environmental gain to be obtained from moorland grazing. However, a number of practical difficulties still remain. This study has highlighted the potential benefits of summer-only or rotational grazing on moors. This raises questions about where sheep and cattle go for the remainder of the year. For small numbers, this issue may not be too challenging as it is already common for farmers to send livestock to the moor for part of the year only, whilst for rotational scenarios it should be feasible to graze one part of a hill one year and a different part the following year. In addition, forecast reductions in livestock numbers throughout the UK suggest that more land may become available for grazing or supporting livestock. The economics of these transactions is likely to be similar to existing transhumance and agistment (seasonal movement of stock) systems, although the issues surrounding bio-security may make the large-scale movement of stock more difficult.

Scenarios requiring high stocking densities of cattle for short periods may be more challenging to implement, and payments would need to be sufficient to offset the predicted reductions in cows for other economic reasons. The availability of appropriate cattle is also an issue. Many herds are spring/ summer calving, and moorland vegetation may be considered insufficient to meet production requirements. Support for grazing moorland with cattle is available in the English HLS, but results from this study suggest that payments may not be sufficient to meet the total costs unless the additional supplementary payment for using breeds under threat is also awarded.

Even with sufficient finances, there is still a question of whether there will be sufficient people with the appropriate skills remaining in the uplands to manage the stock (see Burton *et al.*, this volume). Skill shortages in shepherding and gathering of extensive sheep flocks have been widely reported (Hill Task Force, 2001), and a similar argument must hold true for cattle. As stock numbers continue to fall and grazing regimes extensify, these skills become increasingly rare but remain essential both to animal welfare requirements and to protecting plant communities of high nature conservation value.

It is clear from this study that, to be profitable, grazing management is dependent on agri-environment schemes. Such dependence maintains an inherent instability in the future of upland management as a significant portion of the farm business income remains in the hands of national government and ultimately with the European Commission. The appropriateness of this situation and the level of sustainability it offers to the maintenance of upland land management and ecosystem services is open to debate.

To help ensure continued government support, it is important that land management activities become recognised and valued not just for the production of saleable goods such as meat, wool, animals and handicrafts, but also for the delivery of public goods and ecosystem services such as provision of wildlife habitat management, landscape and heritage protection, water resource and carbon management, public rights of way and access management. Awareness and appreciation of these skills need to be fostered and encouraged among politicians and the public such that stewardship of the countryside is seen as a skill to be valued and paid for if they are to be retained for future generations. The value that the public and politicians place on upland resources will define their future as much as any land management activity.

Acknowledgements

The authors would like to acknowledge the financial support for this work provided by Defra (contracts BD1211, BD1218, BD1228 and LS1509), Natural England (BD1228) and Countryside Council for Wales (BD1228). We also acknowledge the hard work and dedication given by the scientific, support and farm staff at ADAS Pwllpeiran and ADAS Redesdale, without whom completion of this work would not have been possible. Our particular thanks, too, to Francis Kirkham, Aletta Bonn, Jon Stewart and two anonymous referees whose comments and editing input have enhanced the digestibility of this chapter.

References

ADAS (2006) *Farmer's Intentions in the Context of CAP Reform – Analysis of ADAS Farmers' Voice 2006 Survey of England and Wales.* Report to Defra, London. http://statistics.defra.gov.uk/esg/ace/research/pdf/farmersvoice2006.pdf

Anderson, P. and Yalden, D. W. (1981) Increased sheep numbers and the loss of heather moorland in the Peak District, England. *Biological Conservation,* 20, 195–213.

Backshall, J., Manley, J. and Rebane, M. E. (2001) *The Upland Management Handbook.* English Nature, Peterborough. http://www.english-nature.org.uk/pubs/handbooks/upland.asp?id=1

Bardgett, R. D. and Marsden, J. H. (1995) The extent and condition of heather on moorland in the uplands of England and Wales. *Biological Conservation,* 71, 155–61.

Boatman, N., Jones, N., Garthwaite, D., Bishop, J., Pietraville, S., Harrington, P. and Parry, H. (2007) *Evaluation of the Operation of Environmental Stewardship.* Defra Project MA1028 Final Report, Defra, London. http://randd.defra.gov.uk/Document.aspx?Document=MA01028_6197_FRP.pdf

Clarke, J. L., Welch, D. and Gordon, I. J. (1995) The influence of vegetation pattern on the grazing of heather moorland by red deer and sheep. II. The impact on heather. *Journal of Applied Ecology,* 32, 177–86.

Conington, J., Bishop, S. C., Waterhouse, A. and Simm, G. (2004) A bio-economic approach to derive economic values for pasture-based sheep genetic improvement programmes. *Journal of Animal Science,* 82, 1290–304.

Critchley, C. N. R., Davies, O. D., Adamson, H. F., Anderson, P. A., Buchanan, G. M., Fraser, M. D., Gardner, S. M., Grant, M. C., McLean, B. M. L., Mitchell, R. J., Pearce-Higgins, J. W., Rose, R. J., Sanderson, R. A. and Waterhouse, A. (2007) *Determining Environmentally Sustainable and Economically Viable Grazing Systems for the Restoration and Maintenance of Heather Moorland in England and Wales.* ADAS/CEH/IGER/Newcastle University/PAA/SAC/RSPB Defra project BD1228 Final Report, Defra, London. http://randd.defra.gov.uk/Default.aspx?Menu=MenuandModule=MoreandLocation=NoneandCompleted=0andProjectID=10072

Cumulus (2005) *Assessment of the Impact of CAP Reform and Other Key Policies on Upland Farms and Land Use Implications in Both Severely Disadvantaged and Disadvantaged Areas of England.* Report to Defra, London. http://statistics.defra.gov.uk/esg/reports/cap%20uplandfarms%20report.pdf

Defra (2006) *Farm Accounts in England 2005/6*. London: Defra.

Eftec (2006) *Economic Valuation of Environmental Impacts in the Severely Disadvant-aged Areas*. Report to Defra, London. http://statistics.defra.gov.uk/esg/reports/disareas/SDA%20FINAL%20Report%20030106.pdf

English Nature (2001) *State of Nature: The Upland Challenge*. English Nature, Peterborough. http://www.english-nature.org.uk/pubs/publication/pdf/wildnat.pdf

Fuller, R. J. and Gough, S. J. (1999) Changes in sheep numbers in Britain: implications for bird populations – cultural landscapes. *Biological Conservation*, **91**, 73–89.

Gardner, S. M. (2002) Managing upland vegetation for sheep and conservation. *Conservation Pays? Reconciling Environmental Benefits with Profitable Grassland Systems* (ed. J. Frame), BGS Occasional Symposium No. **36**, 115–18, British Grassland Society.

Gardner, S. M., Hartley, S. E., Davies, A. and Palmer, S. C. F (1997) Carabid com-munities on heather moorlands in North East Scotland: the consequences of graz-ing pressure for community diversity. *Biological Conservation*, **81**, 275–86.

Gardner, S. M., Hetherington, S. L. and Allen, D. (2002) *Assessment of Vegetation Change and* Calluna/Nardus *Interactions in Relation to Spatial Variation in Grazing Pressure on Upland Moor*. Defra contract BD1211 Final Report, Defra, London. http://www.defra.gov.uk/science/publications/default.htm

Gardner, S. M., Ross, S. Y. and Adamson, H. F. (2001) *Assessment of the Effect of Spatial Variation in Sheep Grazing on* Calluna vulgaris–Molinia caerulea *Interac-tions*. Defra contract BD1218 Final Report, Defra, London.

Gordon, I. J., Hester, A. J. and Festa-Bianchet, M. (2004) The management of wild large herbivores to meet economic, conservation and environmental objectives. *Journal of Applied Ecology*, **41**, 1020–31.

Grime, J. P., Hodgson, J. G. and Hunt, R. (1988) *Comparative Plant Ecology: A Functional Approach to Common British Species*. London: Unwin Hyman.

Hartley, S. E., Gardner, S. M. and Mitchell, R. J. (2003) Indirect effects of grazing and nutrient addition on the hemipteran community of heather moorlands: the role of soil type, vegetation structure and plant species richness. *Journal of Applied Ecology*, **40**, 793–803.

Hartley, S. E. and Mitchell, R. J. (2005) Manipulation of nutrients and grazing levels on heather moorland: changes in *Calluna* dominance and consequences for com-munity composition. *Journal of Ecology*, **93**, 990–1004.

Hetherington, S. L., McLean, B. M. L., Gardner, S. M., Wildig, J. and Griffiths, J. B. (2002) The impact of Environmentally Sensitive Areas policy in relation to con-servation and farming objectives. *Conservation Pays? Reconciling Environmental Benefits with Profitable Grassland Systems* (ed. J. Frame), BGS Occasional Symposium No. **36**, 85–8, British Grassland Society.

Hill Task Force (2001) *Task Force for the Hills*. http://www.hillfarming.org.uk/

Hope, D., Picozzi, N., Catt, D. C. and Moss, R. (1996) Effects of reducing sheep grazing in the Scottish Highlands. *Journal of Range Management*, **49**, 301–10.

Hulme, P. D., Merrell, B. G., Torvell, L., Fisher, J. M., Small, J. L. and Pakeman, R. J. (2002) Rehabilitation of degraded *Calluna vulgaris* (L.) Hull-dominated wet heath by controlled sheep grazing. *Biological Conservation*, **107**, 351–63.

Hulme, P. D., Pakeman, R. J., Torvell, L., Fisher, J. M. and Gordon, I. J. (1999) The effects of controlled sheep grazing on the dynamics of upland *Agrostis–Festuca* grassland. *Journal of Applied Ecology*, **36**, 886–900.

Marrs, R. H., Phillips, J. D. P., Todd, P. A., Ghorbani, M. and LeDuc, M. G. (2004) Control of *Molinia caerulea* on upland moors. *Journal of Applied Ecology*, **41**, 398–411.

Merrell, B., Wildig, J. and Davies, O. (2001) Moorland conservation and hill sheep. *Integrated Upland Management for Wildlife, Field Sports, Agriculture and Public Enjoyment* (ed. J. D. P. Philips, D. B. A. Thompson and W. E. Gruellich), pp. 75–93. Battleby: Scottish Natural Heritage.

Milligan, A. L., Putwain, P. D., Cox, E. S., Ghorbani, J., LeDuc, M. G. and Marrs, R. H. (2004) Developing an integrated land management strategy for the restoration of moorland vegetation on *Molinia caerulea*-dominated vegetation for conservation purposes. *Biological Conservation*, **119**, 371–85.

Pakeman, R. J., Hulme, P. D., Torvell, L. and Fisher, J. M. (2003) Rehabilitation of degraded fry heather (*Calluna vulgaris* (L.) Hull) moorland by controlled sheep grazing. *Biological Conservation*, **114**, 389–400.

Palmer, S. C. F., Gordon, I. J., Hester, A. J. and Pakeman, R. J. (2004) Introducing spatial grazing impacts into the prediction of moorland vegetation dynamics. *Landscape Ecology*, **19**, 817–27.

Palmer, S. C. F., Hester, A. J., Elston, D. A., Gordon, I. J. and Hartley, S. E. (2003) The perils of having tasty neighbours: grazing impacts of large herbivores at vegetation boundaries. *Ecology*, **84**, 2877–90.

Pearce-Higgins, J. W. and Grant, M. C. (2006) Relationships between bird abundance and the composition and structure of moorland vegetation. *Bird Study*, **53**, 112–25.

Rodwell, J. S. (1991) *British Plant Communities*. Vol. 2. *Mires and Heaths*. Cambridge: Cambridge University Press.

Rodwell, J. S. (1992) *British Plant Communities*. Vol. 3. *Grasslands and Montane Communities*. Cambridge: Cambridge University Press.

Rural Development Service (2005a) *Higher Level Stewardship Handbook – Terms and How to Apply*. Defra, London. http://www.defra.gov.uk/erdp/pdfs/es/hls-handbook.pdf

Rural Development Service (2005b) *Higher Level Stewardship – Payment for Land Management Options, Supplements and Capital Items*. Defra, London. http://www.defra.gov.uk/erdp/pdfs/es/hls-payment-booklet.pdf

Rural Development Service (2006) *Addendum: New Options for Environmental Stewardship*. Defra, London http://www.defra.gov.uk/erdp/pdfs/es/HLS-Handbook-addendum.pdf

Rural Payments Agency and Defra (2005) *Single Payment Scheme: Cross Compliance Handbook for England*. Defra, London. http://www.defra.gov.uk/farm/capreform/pubs/pdf/XCHandbook2006.pdf

SAC (2006) *Farm Management Handbook 2006/7*. Edinburgh: SAC.

Thompson, D. B. A., Macdonald, A. J., Marsden, J. H. and Galbraith, C. A. (1995) Upland heather moorland in Great Britain: a review of international importance, vegetation change and some objectives for nature conservation. *Biological Conservation*, **71**, 163–78.

Usher, M. B. and Thompson, D. B. A. (1993) Variation in upland heathlands of Great Britain: conservation importance. *Biological Conservation*, **66**, 69–81.

Vandvik, V., Heegaard, E., Maren, I. E. and Aarrestad, P. A. (2005) Managing heterogeneity: the importance of grazing and environmental variation on post-fire succession in heathlands. *Journal of Applied Ecology*, **42**, 139–49.

Waterhouse, A. and Morgan-Davies, C. (2008) CAP Reform and new agri-environment schemes – impacts on welfare. *Proceedings of a Workshop Held at Macaulay Institute* (ed. P. Goddard). Aberdeen.

Welch, D. (1998) Response of bilberry *Vaccinium myrtillus* L. stands in the Derbyshire Peak District to sheep grazing, and the implications for moorland conservation. *Biological Conservation*, **83**, 155–64.

Wissel, C. (2000) Grid-based models as tools for ecological research. *The Geometry of Ecological Interactions: Simplifying Spatial Complexity* (ed. U. Dieckmann, R. Law and J. A. J. Metz), pp. 94–115. Cambridge: Cambridge University Press.

11 International importance and drivers of change of upland bird populations

James W. Pearce-Higgins, Murray C. Grant, Colin M. Beale, Graeme M. Buchanan and Innes M. W. Sim

Introduction

The UK holds an internationally important assemblage of upland birds, comprising a unique mix of oceanic, boreal and northern species, with many at the edge of their breeding ranges and some with exceptional breeding densities (Thompson *et al.*, 1995). As well as the intrinsic conservation value of this assemblage, its role in contributing to the tourism potential and the economy of such areas is increasingly recognised, whilst further economic benefits arise from the sport shooting of red grouse *Lagopus lagopus scoticus* (Price *et al.*, 2005; Sotherton *et al.*, this volume). Thus, upland birds provide a valued cultural and recreational ecosystem service. The assemblage includes top-level predators, as well as a wide range of invertebrate feeders and a few species that are largely herbivorous. The maintenance of viable upland bird populations from across a range of trophic levels may therefore provide a useful indicator of environmental change in upland areas at a range of scales, from local management-driven alteration to large-scale climatic changes.

Upland bird populations

The focus of this chapter is upland bird species that breed on unenclosed ground above the more intensively managed enclosed land and in-bye grasslands, excluding species requiring open water, riparian species, gulls and seabirds, and rare (<10 breeding pairs) species. Whilst recognising that many of these are important components of the upland bird fauna, here we focus on those species for which the main drivers of population change are likely to relate to moorland management. We consider twenty-four species for which montane, moorland and blanket bog provide important breeding habitat (Table 11.1), of which fourteen have breeding populations occurring almost exclusively within these habitats (red grouse, ptarmigan *Lagopus mutus*, black grouse *Tetrao tetrix*, golden plover *Pluvialis apricaria*, dunlin *Calidris alpina*, greenshank *Tringa nebularia*, dotterel *Charadrius morinellus*, whimbrel

Table 11.1 The latest UK population estimates of upland bird populations, and assessments of conservation importance. Varied information is used to summarise UK population trends for each species, which are presented alongside the current conservation listing from Birds of Conservation Concern (Gregory *et al.*, 2002). Unless specified, UK population estimates are from Baker *et al.* (2006). European importance is the UK estimate divided by the European estimates (Birdlife International, 2004; Thorup, 2006).

	UK population (95% confidence interval)	European importance	Summary trend	Conservation listing	Reference
Red Grouse	155,000	6.00%[a]	Long term decline	amber	Sim *et al.*, in press
Ptarmigan	10,000	1.50%	Unknown	green	Sim *et al.*, 2007b
Black grouse	5,082 (3,920–6,156)	<1%	Decline	red	Eaton *et al.*, 2007
Hen Harrier	806 (732–889)	1.40%	Increase following historical decline	amber	
Golden Eagle	435	4.40%	Stable following historical decline	amber	
Merlin	1,330 (1,130–1,530)	3.50%	Increase following historical decline	amber	
Peregrine	1,400	7.90%	Increase following historical decline	amber	Banks *et al.*, 2003
Dotterel	630 (510–750)	2.90%	Unknown	amber	
Golden Plover	38,400–59,400	7.50%	Declines in some areas	green	Thorup, 2006
Dunlin	18,300–33,500	5.80%	Decline	amber	Thorup, 2006
Snipe	59,300 (52,600–69,000)	4.40%	Increase in uplands	amber	
Curlew	107,000 (99,500–125,000)	39.30%	Decline	amber	
Whimbrel	500	<1%	Unknown	amber	
Greenshank	1,080	<1%	Unknown	green	
Short-eared Owl	1,000–3,500	2.60%	Unknown	amber	
Skylark	1,785,000	3.30%	Slight decline in some upland areas	red	
Meadow Pipit	1,680,000	17.30%	Contrasting trends in different upland areas	amber	
Whinchat	11,000–22,100	<1%	Increase in uplands	green	
Stonechat	19,300–49,400	1.20%	Increase	amber	
Wheatear	56,000	<1%	Decline	green	
Ring Ouzel	6,157–7,549	1.60%	Decline	red	
Raven	12,900	2.10%	Increase following historical decline	green	
Twite	10,000 (7,600–16,700)	3.60%	Decline	red	
Snow Bunting	70–100	<1%	Unknown	amber	

[a] Compared against the willow grouse population estimate for Europe, of which red grouse is a UK endemic subspecies.

Numenius phaeopus, merlin *Falco columbarius*, hen harrier *Circus cyaneus*, golden eagle *Aquila chrysaetos*, ring ouzel *Turdus torquatus*, twite *Carduelis flavirostris*, snow bunting *Plectrophenax nivalis*). For many of the remaining species, the uplands represent a refuge from agricultural intensification and consequent habitat loss in the lowlands (Shrubb, 2003; see also Yalden, this volume), where species such as snipe *Gallinago gallinago*, meadow pipit *Anthus pratensis*, skylark *Alauda arvensis* and whinchat *Saxicola rubetra* have declined (Gibbons *et al.*, 1993; Baillie *et al.*, 2006).

The national population estimates presented for each species vary in their accuracy and dates. Comparisons with European population estimates (also subject to variation in quality and accuracy between countries) indicate that curlew and meadow pipit are the two species for which the UK is particularly important (Table 11.1).

Population trends of upland bird species are often poorly known. Extensive monitoring schemes, such as the Common Bird Census (CBC), and more recently the Breeding Bird Survey (BBS), have relied mainly upon volunteer effort, always lowest in the remote uplands. For some species (e.g. skylark and snipe), national declines are related mainly to that part of the population breeding in lowland habitats (Baillie *et al.*, 2006; Sim *et al.*, 2005). For black grouse and ring ouzel, recent national surveys provide evidence of marked population declines. When considered with the known severe range contractions, these surveys suggest that these species may be some of the UK's most rapidly declining birds (Wotton *et al.*, 2002; Gibbons *et al.*, 1993; Sim *et al.*, in press). Populations of upland raptors have historically been limited by persecution and organo-chloride poisoning (Newton, 1979). Although some have shown recovery from these pressures (e.g. peregrine *Falco peregrinus*), others (e.g. hen harrier and golden eagle) are still restricted in range and abundance.

Findings from recent re-surveys of an extensive range of upland sites, first surveyed ten to twenty years previously, suggest widespread declines in some wader (notably dunlin and curlew) and passerine (for example wheatear *Oenanthe oenanthe* and twite) populations, but recorded widespread increases in upland populations of whinchat, stonechat *Saxicola torquata* and raven *Corvus corax* (Sim *et al.*, 2005). There was significant regional variation in population change, with, for example, wader populations generally faring poorly in North Wales, North Staffordshire, the Lake District, southern Scotland and the eastern Flow Country, but tending to increase on Lewis and Harris and the western Flow Country.

Drivers of population change

Four main land uses have predominated on open upland habitats over the last fifty years; sheep grazing, sport shooting of grouse or of deer, and conifer afforestation. Postwar increases in deer and sheep numbers, sometimes combined with liming and re-seeding with grasses, have caused significant losses of heather *Calluna vulgaris* moorland – for example in Scotland, 7 per cent of heather moorland was converted to grassland from the 1940s to the 1980s (Grant, 1992; Mackey *et al.*, 1998; Fuller and Gough, 1999). During the same period, the area of moorland managed intensively for grouse shooting has declined, with potential for concomitant declines in rotational heather burning (muirburn) and predator control (Hudson, 1992). However, levels of muirburn have not declined in all regions (Hester and Sydes, 1992), and have even increased recently in some parts of England (Yallop *et al.*, 2006; this volume). In addition to these changes to open habitats, moorland and blanket bog have been afforested, causing habitat loss and fragmentation. In Scotland, 14 per cent of open upland habitats were afforested between the 1940s and the 1980s (Mackey *et al.*, 1998). These land-use changes have often occurred in tandem, with areas retaining grouse moor management losing less heather and suffering less afforestation than other areas (Robertson *et al.*, 2001), whilst there has been much regional variation in the extent and nature of change (for example no afforestation on Orkney and Shetland).

Furthermore, recreational use of the uplands has increased, with tourism now making an important contribution to rural economies, for example contributing 30 per cent of the GDP to the Highlands region of Scotland (Price *et al.*, 2005). This increase, promoted by recent changes in access legislation, may impose additional pressures on upland bird populations in certain areas. However, the evidence to date suggests that in most circumstances, and for most species, the resulting disturbance has little population-level effect, with possible exceptions along extremely heavily visited footpaths and access points (Finney *et al.*, 2005; Pearce-Higgins *et al.*, 2007a; Baines and Richardson, 2007). Therefore, the potential effects of recreational disturbance are not considered in detail in this review, although there are other issues associated with increasing visitor pressure, such as heightened fire risk and the associated impacts on habitat, that should also be considered (McMorrow *et al.*, this volume).

Below, we review the evidence that the land-use changes described above have contributed to changes in the population sizes of upland birds. Tables summarise the results from studies within the UK, whilst reference is made to specific examples in the text, including studies from overseas, where appropriate.

Increases in sheep and deer: effects of grazing pressure

Because the focus of this chapter is on unenclosed upland habitats, we do not consider the impacts of increases in stocking levels and intensification on the management of enclosed grassland. Although some species which breed on moorland and blanket bog also regularly commute to feed on these areas (e.g. Whittingham *et al.*, 2000; Robson *et al.*, 2002; Pearce-Higgins and Yalden, 2003; Rayne, 2006), there is little evidence that changes in enclosed grasslands have driven changes in upland wader populations (e.g. Pearce-Higgins and Yalden, 2003), although the conversion of enclosed herb-rich hay meadows to silage has contributed to twite declines (Reed, 1995; Rayne, 2006).

On unenclosed upland habitats, increased grazing by sheep and deer has caused the conversion of heather-dominated areas to grass-, sedge- or rush-dominated swards. In some areas, grazing pressure fragmented previously continuous heather-dominated vegetation (Clarke *et al.*, 1995), whilst in the most extreme situations heather has been eliminated (Thompson *et al.*, 1995). Few studies have considered how grazing management affects the demography and size of bird populations, and much of the evidence for assessing the management impacts derives from correlative studies of bird abundance in relation to vegetation characteristics, particularly dwarf shrub (largely heather) cover and vegetation structure (Table 11.2).

Red grouse are the species most strongly associated with heather, being dependent upon it as their main food plant (Jenkins *et al.*, 1963). Heather loss is a likely cause of the long-term population decline (Hudson, 1992; Thirgood *et al.*, 2000), although the highest densities occur on moorland where some graminoid vegetation is interspersed amongst the heather, rather than on an extensive heather monoculture (Pearce-Higgins and Grant, 2006). Merlin, hen harrier and short-eared owl *Asio flammeus* each nest in tall, dense vegetation, particularly heather, but forage in grass or grass–heather mixes for their meadow pipit or vole prey (Bibby, 1986; Redpath and Thirgood, 1997; Redpath *et al.*, 1998; Smith *et al.*, 2001; Pearce-Higgins and Grant, 2006). Heterogeneity in heather and grass cover will therefore benefit these predators also. Similarly, heather is an important nesting habitat for ring ouzel, twite and black grouse (Picozzi, 1986; Brown *et al.*, 1995; Burfield, 2002), with territory abandonment by both ring ouzel and twite linked to losses of nesting habitat (Rayne, 2006; Sim *et al.*, 2007a), although declines in foraging habitat may be the proximate cause of the latter's decline. Ring ouzels feed on earthworms in short grass (Burfield, 2002), whilst grass-, rush- and sedge-dominated areas are important foraging areas for black grouse chicks (Picozzi, 1986; Baines, 1994; Starling-Westerberg, 2001), so both species require mosaics of heather and grass habitats (Buchanan *et al.*, 2003; Pearce-Higgins *et al.*, 2007b).

None of the waders shows consistent strong associations with heather, although dotterel favour *Racomitrium* heaths, the extent of which may have declined because of nitrogen deposition and high grazing levels (van der Wal *et al.*, 2003). Some studies link golden plover with dwarf shrub habitats (Table 11.2), but short, open structure is the main determinant of their abundance (Pearce-Higgins and Grant, 2006; Buchanan *et al.*, unpubl.). For both snipe and curlew there is little evidence for strong associations with heather; both species being associated with vegetation typical of flush or other wetland habitats – for example sedges and rushes (Pearce-Higgins and Grant, 2006). Similarly, whinchat abundance is largely unrelated to dwarf shrub cover, but instead is related strongly to bracken *Pteridium aquilinum* cover (Allen, 1995,

Table 11.2 Variation in the distribution, abundance, survival, productivity or population trends of upland bird species as a function of dwarf shrub cover and vegetation density. Symbols describe the shape of the relationships as follows: ↑ – positive correlation; ↓ – negative correlation; ∩ – maximised at intermediate levels; 0 – no significant effect. Studies which were not specifically aimed at understanding the relationships between moorland bird distribution and vegetation condition, and are therefore likely to be less rigorous, are in parentheses. Habitat selection studies have been excluded because results do not necessarily relate to variation at the population level.

	Dwarf shrub cover	*Vegetation density*	*References*
Red Grouse	↑↑↑0(↑↑↑↑↑0)	↑↑∩0(000)	1, 2, 3, 4, 6, 7, 8, 9, 10, 27
Ptarmigan			
Black grouse	∩(↓)	∩(↑∩)	6, 15, 16, 60
Hen Harrier	↓↓(↑)	↑↓	17, 18, 19
Golden Eagle	↑↑↓		21, 22, 23
Merlin	↑∩(↑↑)	(↑)	25, 26, 27, 28
Peregrine	(0)	(0)	27
Dotterel	↑(↑)	(↓)	29, 30
Golden Plover	000(↑↑↑∩0)	↓↓↓↓(↓↓)	1, 6, 7, 8, 9, 10, 25, 27
Dunlin	0(↓00)	0(0)	1, 9, 25, 27
Snipe	↓00(↓00)	↑∩↓(00)	6, 7, 8, 9, 10, 27
Curlew	∩00(↑∩↓↓0)	∩∩∩(↑↑∩)	1, 6, 7, 8, 9, 10, 25, 27
Whimbrel			
Greenshank			
Short-eared Owl	(↑↓)		25, 27
Skylark	↓↓↓0(↓↓)	↓↓0(↓)	6, 7, 8, 9, 10, 34
Meadow Pipit	∩∩∩↓0(∩0)	∩00(0)	4, 6, 7, 8, 9, 10, 35, 36
Whinchat	∩∩∩0(00)	↑∩∩(0)	6, 7, 8, 9, 10, 27
Stonechat	↑↑∩	↑↑0	8, 9, 10
Wheatear	∩↓0(↓↓↓)	∩0(↓0)	6, 7, 8, 9, 10, 27
Ring Ouzel	↑∩∩∩(↑↓)	0	9, 25, 27, 37, 38, 39
Raven			
Twite	↑(↑↓)	(0)	25, 27, 40
Snow Bunting			

Pearce-Higgins and Grant, 2006). Both skylark and wheatear tend to be least abundant in areas of extensive heather and dwarf shrub cover, but associate with grass moorland (Pearce-Higgins and Grant, 2006; Pearce-Higgins *et al.*, 2006; Buchanan *et al.*, unpublished).

Fewer studies have examined the influence of vegetation structure on upland birds (Table 11.2). However, changes in grazing levels produce much quicker responses in vegetation structure than in plant species composition. Most species show an association either for short, open vegetation (e.g. skylark and golden plover), for intermediate vegetation heights, or for heterogeneous swards of tall and short vegetation. For many, such as snipe, curlew, stonechat and whinchat, tall vegetation probably provides either nesting habitats and cover or sources of high invertebrate abundance, whilst short, open swards increase access to surface and sub-surface invertebrate prey, and enhance mobility of chicks of precocial species. For example, tall swards support higher invertebrate abundance for black grouse broods (Baines *et al.*, 1996); but, where they become too extensive, breeding success declines (Calladine *et al.*, 2002). Similarly, meadow pipit densities increased under an experimental treatment of cattle and sheep at intermediate stocking rates, relative to alternative treatments with higher or lower stocking (Evans *et al.*, 2006b).

Moorland berry crops such as bilberry *Vaccinium myrtillus* and crowberry *Empetrum nigrum* are an important component of the diet in late summer and autumn of a number of birds, such as grouse and ring ouzel (Picozzi and Hepburn, 1986; Appleyard, 1994). Although there is no evidence linking population changes to berry availability, it is possible that high levels of grazing, which can reduce berry abundance (Welch, 1988; Hegland *et al.*, 2005), may restrict the ability of birds to gain condition in preparation for migration or severe winter weather.

For golden eagle and raven, high grazing levels by large herbivores may affect populations more directly through carrion availability (Newton *et al.*, 1982; Dare, 1986; Watson *et al.*, 1992; Ratcliffe, 1997). However, grazing levels that cause heather loss can reduce densities of live prey (notably red grouse and mountain hares *Lepus timidus*) and hence golden eagle breeding success (Watson *et al.*, 1992).

Declines in grouse moor management

Two of the main management techniques associated with grouse moors are the rotational burning of heather, and legal predator control (primarily foxes *Vulpes vulpes*, mustelids and corvids). Grouse moors may also be associated with the illegal persecution of raptors. Additional managements, such as the provision of medicated grit to control parasites (Hudson, 1992), also occur but are unlikely to affect other species significantly.

Likely effects of rotational heather burning can, in part, be assessed from the previous section on grazing. Thus, species requiring some short, open vegetation will probably benefit from rotational muirburn; and, indeed, both curlew and golden plover nesting on grouse moors often select recently burnt areas for nesting, and for the broods to forage (Robson, 1998; Whittingham *et al.*, 2000, 2001). Furthermore, the association of grouse moors with heather vegetation (Robertson, 2001) means that species associated with some heather in the landscape, such as black grouse, merlin, hen harrier, short-eared owl and ring ouzel, tend to be more abundant on grouse moors (Thompson *et al.*, 1997).

The other potential effect of grouse moor management on upland bird populations is through predator control. Whilst this produces obvious benefits for red grouse (Jenkins *et al.*, 1964; Hudson, 1992; Dobson and Hudson, 1995), the evidence for effects on non-target species, is currently limited to autecological and correlative studies (Table 11.3). Densities of both curlew and

Table 11.3 Summary of the likely impacts of grouse moor management on upland bird density, breeding success or population change. Symbols describe the shape of the relationships as follows: ↑ – positive correlation; ↓ – negative correlation; 0 – no significant effect. Studies which were not specifically aimed at understanding the effects of grouse moor management on birds, and are therefore likely to be less rigorous, are in parentheses.

	Density	Breeding success	Change	References
Red Grouse	↑(↑↑)		↑	6, 8, 10, 41
Ptarmigan		↑0	0	42, 43, 44
Black grouse	00	↑↑0	0	12, 16, 45, 46
Hen Harrier	↑(↓)	↓↓	↑↓	6, 17, 47, 48, 49, 50
Golden Eagle	↓	↓	↓	52, 53
Merlin	(↑↓)			6, 25
Peregrine	↓(0)	↓		6, 54
Dotterel				
Golden Plover	↑(↑↑↑0)	(↑)	(0)	6, 8, 9, 10, 25, 55
Dunlin	(00)		(0)	9, 25
Snipe	0(000)		(0)	6, 8, 9, 10
Curlew	↑(↑↑00)	↑	(0)	6, 8, 9, 10, 25, 56
Whimbrel				
Greenshank				
Short-eared Owl	(↑)			25
Skylark	0(↓↓0)			6, 8, 9, 10
Meadow Pipit	↓(000)			6, 8, 9, 10
Whinchat	0(↑00)		(0)	6, 8, 9, 10
Stonechat	(↑00)		(0)	8, 9, 10
Wheatear	0(↓↓0)		(0)	6, 8, 9, 10
Ring Ouzel	0(↑0)		0(0)	9, 25, 38
Raven	(↓0)			6, 57
Twite	(0)			25
Snow Bunting				

golden plover are greater on grouse moors than on non-grouse moors, probably resulting at least in part from predator control (Tharme *et al.*, 2001) as the nests, in particular, of these species are vulnerable to predation by corvids, foxes and mustelids (Parr, 1992; Grant *et al.*, 1999). Available evidence therefore points to likely population-level benefits of grouse moor management on some ground-nesting waders, although a comparison of recent changes in moorland bird populations on grouse moors and non-grouse moors failed to detect significant differences (Pearce-Higgins *et al.*, 2006).

Several studies demonstrate likely reductions in black grouse breeding success and density as a result of predation, particularly by foxes in Scandinavia (Marcstrom *et al.*, 1988; Lindstrom *et al.*, 1994; Smedshaug *et al.*, 1999) or crows *Corvux corone* in Scottish pinewoods (Summers *et al.*, 2004). However, correlative studies have so far failed to reveal significant effects of either gamekeeper density or grouse moor management on black grouse breeding success and density in Britain (Baines, 1996; Tharme *et al.*, 2001).

There is little evidence for benefits of grouse moor management to moorland passerines, with meadow pipit densities reduced on grouse moors, possibly linked to detrimental effects of muirburn (Smith *et al.*, 2001; Tharme *et al.*, 2001). Putative relationships from other studies of passerine density and grouse moors (Table 11.3) probably result from associations with either heather (stonechat and ring ouzel) or grass cover (skylark and wheatear).

Owing to their predation of red grouse, some raptors are persecuted on grouse moors. Thus, golden eagles are largely absent from some areas of intensive grouse moor management in the eastern Highlands of Scotland, despite the availability of suitable habitat (Whitfield *et al.*, 2004a, b). Similarly, hen harriers have declined recently in regions of Scotland where grouse moor management is most intensive, and remain absent from much of the English uplands where grouse moors prevail (Sim *et al.*, 2001, 2007b). Effects of persecution in reducing hen harrier productivity are sufficient to limit population size (Etheridge *et al.*, 1997). In the absence of persecution, grouse moor management could potentially benefit harriers, through reduced nest predation by foxes, although evidence for this is currently lacking (Green and Etheridge, 1999). Peregrine productivity may also be limited on some grouse moors (Hardey *et al.*, 2003) but does not appear to be restricting range expansion to the same extent for this species.

Afforestation

The most obvious impact of the extensive postwar afforestation of the uplands has been direct habitat loss; most open-country species abandon afforested areas after the first few years. Although precise estimates of the likely number of breeding pairs lost as a result do not exist, afforestation during the 1980s was estimated to have reduced numbers of breeding golden plover, dunlin and greenshank in the Flow Country by 17–19 per cent (Stroud *et al.*, 1987; Avery and Haines-Young, 1990), whilst Ratcliffe (2007) crudely estimated that 5,000 pairs of curlew and 300 pairs of golden plover may have disappeared across the Southern Uplands.

The process of afforestation may provide short-term benefit for some species, though, with the exclusion of grazing livestock and deer producing a flush in field-layer growth resulting in higher densities of invertebrates, passerines and voles (Avery and Leslie, 1991; Evans *et al.*, 2006a). Pre-thicket forests can therefore provide an important foraging area for raptors, such as hen harrier, merlin, short-eared owls (Avery and Leslie, 1991; Madders, 2000, 2003) and black grouse (Cayford, 1993). Once the forest canopy closes, the field layer is lost and these moorland birds tend to be excluded (Cayford, 1993; Madders, 2000, 2003; Rebecca, 2006) – a process that appears to have caused the decline in black grouse during the 1990s in Perthshire (Pearce-Higgins *et al.*, 2007b).

Considerable uncertainty exists over the magnitude and extent of any negative effects of afforestation on the bird populations of the surrounding

Table 11.4 Summary of the likely impacts of afforestation on the density, breeding success or population changes of upland birds on adjacent moorland. Symbols describe the shape of the relationships as follows: ↑ – positive correlation; ↓ – negative correlation; 0 – no significant effect. Studies that were not specifically aimed at understanding the effects of afforestation on birds, and are therefore likely to be less rigorous, are in parentheses.

	Density	*Breeding success*	*Change*	*References*
Red Grouse	↓(00)			1, 8, 10
Ptarmigan				
Black grouse	↑↑ pre-thicket ↓↓ closed canopy		↑ pre-thicket ↓ closed canopy	16, 58
Hen Harrier	↑↑ pre-thicket ↓↓ closed canopy		↑ pre-thicket ↓ closed canopy	17, 59
Golden Eagle	0	↓↓	↓↓	23, 32, 61
Merlin	↓0	↓↓	↓↓↓	5, 24, 28, 62
Peregrine	↓	↓		54
Dotterel				
Golden Plover	↓↓↓0(↓↓0)	(↓)	(↓)	1, 8, 10, 11, 13, 14, 20
Dunlin	↓(↓)			1, 13
Snipe	(000)			8, 10, 13
Curlew	00(↓↓0)			1, 8, 10, 13
Whimbrel				
Greenshank				
Short-eared Owl				
Skylark	(00)			8, 10
Meadow Pipit	(00)			8, 10
Whinchat	(⌒0)			8, 10
Stonechat	(00)			8, 10
Wheatear	(00)			8, 10
Ring Ouzel	0		↓0(0)	38, 39, 51
Raven	↓0	↓0	↓0	24, 31
Twite				
Snow Bunting				

moorland (Table 11.4). Declines in the productivity and occupancy of golden eagle, merlin and raven territories have been documented following the afforestation of foraging habitat (Marquiss *et al.*, 1978; Whitfield *et al.*, 2001, 2007; Rebecca, 2006). Significant effects of afforestation on the densities of waders breeding on adjacent open habitats have been detected, but such effects are often small in magnitude and are not detected consistently (Avery, 1989; Stroud *et al.*, 1990). Between 1988 and 2000, the abundance of red grouse, dunlin and golden plover declined close to forestry plantations in the Flow Country, although the effects of forest proximity on the two waders were not significant once other habitat effects were accounted for (Hancock *et al.*, in press). In Scotland, ring ouzel declines were found

2

to be greater on moorland surrounded by extensive forest cover (Buchanan *et al.*, 2003), although this effect was not detected in England and Wales (Sim *et al.*, unpublished data).

Future drivers of change

Drivers of upland land use are changing (Price *et al.*, 2005). Recent years have seen considerable declines in livestock densities on hill farms (Defra, 2008; SEERAD, 2007; Welsh Assembly, 2007), which may cause land abandonment if continued. Rates of conifer planting have also declined (Ratcliffe, 2007). New land-use pressures may become increasingly important. Given the large carbon stores in our peatlands, and the potential for land management to influence carbon balance on peatlands, there will be an increasing requirement for upland management to minimise carbon losses (Worrall and Evans, this volume). Furthermore, pressure from water companies to improve water quality at source may also drive changes to upland management (Holden; Allott, both this volume), whilst upland habitats may become important sources of renewable energy, particularly wind.

There is an urgent need to understand the impacts that these changes will have on upland birds. For example, if management of blanket bog to improve carbon storage, water quality and retention (e.g. re-wetting by drain-blocking) increases habitat quality and invertebrate abundance, it may benefit upland birds. However, if there are associated reductions in grazing and rotational heather burning, this is likely to be detrimental to those species dependent on short, open swards, although other bird species are likely to benefit from such change in the longer term as scrub and woodland may develop through vegetation succession. Therefore, the land-use changes that are likely to occur will represent opportunities for bird populations in the uplands as well as threats. Future conservation strategies will need to recognise this, and reconcile these opportunities and threats (for example by considering the value of spatial planning between and within different UK upland regions) to achieve the greatest overall benefits. However, a greatly improved understanding of the impacts of these changes on both bird populations and their habitats is required to inform such strategies.

Superimposed on these past and potential future land-use changes are the effects of climate change. IPCC predictions for the UK are for hotter, drier summers and milder, wetter winters, with a general increase in storminess (Hulme *et al.*, 2002). The recent trend for warmer springs appears to be advancing the laying dates of a wide range of upland species (Moss *et al.*, 2005). Over time, this may result in a phenological mismatch between timing of breeding and availability of food, especially invertebrates with narrow periods of synchronised emergence, reducing breeding success, as predicted for golden plovers (Pearce-Higgins *et al.*, 2005). The recent trend for milder winters in the UK has probably improved the over-winter survival of upland species that remain in temperate regions, such as golden plover and skylark (Yalden and Pearce-Higgins, 1997; Wolfenden and Peach, 2001), and probably contributed to the widespread increases in small passerine populations (e.g. wren *Troglodytes troglodytes* and stonechat) in upland areas (Sim *et al.*, 2005; Pearce-Higgins *et al.*, 2006). Weather effects on migrants may be more complex (Newton, 2004). For example, fluctuations in ring ouzel population correlate with climate on both the Moroccan wintering grounds and UK breeding grounds, with declines in the Moorfoot Hills, Scotland, being linked to warmer summers (Beale *et al.*, 2006). Future climate change is predicted to result in shifts in the distribution of many species northwards and upwards (Walmsley *et al.*, 2007; Huntley *et al.*, 2007), potentially threatening populations of many upland birds, particularly those at the southern range margins. As many upland species are on the periphery of their arctic or subarctic ranges in the UK, it is essential that research be undertaken to monitor these populations adequately and understand the potential for adaptive management (e.g. drain-blocking) to maximise the resilience of vulnerable populations to these effects.

Conclusions and outlook

This chapter summarises evidence concerning the effects of grazing pressure, grouse moor management and afforestation in particular on upland bird populations. Changes to each land use have the potential to limit bird abundance, but it seems unlikely that any single driver is responsible for the major population changes that have occurred in some upland regions. Postwar increases in grazing may have caused declines in red grouse, black grouse, dotterel, ring ouzel and golden eagle in some areas. The control of generalist predators appears to benefit ground-nesting waders and grouse; and, logically, some declines in these species may have resulted from reductions in grouse moor management. However, illegal persecution associated with grouse moors continues to limit populations of some raptor species. Aside from the direct loss of moorland habitat, afforestation has caused declines in some raptors, black grouse and certain raven populations. The magnitude of edge effects on other open-country species remains equivocal. In some areas, these land-use changes have operated in tandem, and further research is required to disentangle their relative importance fully.

Future land-use and management priorities in the uplands are likely to change, and will be an important determinant of the long-term viability of the UK's important and unique upland bird assemblage. Results from the studies summarised in this chapter provide a valuable source of information for managers and policy-makers to promote effective conservation management for upland birds, and maximise the benefit associated with future management changes for carbon and water. With upland birds predicted to be some of the most vulnerable to future climate change (Huntley *et al.*, 2007), it is vital to use such information to maximise the resilience of populations to the likely future changes to which they will be subject.

Acknowledgements

We are grateful to Aletta Bonn, Andy Brown, Nick Sotherton and Jerry Wilson for commenting on earlier drafts of this chapter.

References

Allen, D. S. (1995) Habitat selection by whinchats: a case for bracken in the uplands? *Heaths and Moorland: Cultural Landscapes* (ed. D. B. A. Thompson, A. J. Hester and M. B. Usher), pp. 200–5. Edinburgh: HMSO.

Appleyard, I. (1994) *Ring Ouzels of the Yorkshire Dales.* Leeds: W. S. Maney.

Avery, M. I. (1989) Effects of upland afforestation on some birds of the adjacent moorlands. *Journal of Applied Ecology*, **26**, 957–66.

Avery, M. I. and Haines-Young, R. H. (1990) Population estimates for the dunlin *Calidris alpina* derived from remotely sensed satellite imagery of the Flow Country of northern Scotland. *Nature*, **344**, 860–2.

Avery, M. and Leslie, R. (1991) *Birds and Forestry.* London: Poyser.

Baillie, S. R., Marchant, J. H., Crick, H. Q. P., Noble, D. G., Balmer, D. E., Coombes, R. H., Downie, I. S., Freeman, S. N., Joys, A. C., Leech, D. I., Raven, M. J., Robinson, R. A. and Thewlis, R. M. (2006) *Breeding Birds in the Wider Country-side: Their Conservation Status 2005.* BTO Research Report No. 435. BTO, Thetford. http://www.bto.org/birdtrends

Baines, D. (1994) Seasonal differences in habitat selection by black grouse *Tetrao tetrix* in the North Pennines, England. *Ibis*, **136**, 39–43.

Baines, D. (1996) The implications of grazing and predator management on the habitats and breeding success of black grouse *Tetrao tetrix. Journal of Applied Ecology*, **33**, 54–62.

Baines, D. and Richardson, M. (2007) An experimental assessment of the potential effects of human disturbance on black grouse in the North Pennines, England. *Ibis*, **149 suppl. 1**, 56–64.

Baines, D., Wilson, I. A. and Beeley, G. (1996) Timing of breeding in black grouse *Tetrao tetrix* and capercaillie *Tetrao urogallus* and distribution of insect food for the chicks. *Ibis*, **138**, 181–7.

Banks, A. N., Coombes, R. H. and Crick, H. Q. P. (2003) *The Peregrine Falcon Breeding Population of the UK and Isle of Man in 2002.* BTO Research Report No. 330. BTO, Thetford.

Beale, C. M., Burfield, I. J., Sim, I. M. W., Rebecca, G. W., Pearce-Higgins, J. W. and Grant, M. C. (2006) Climate change may account for the decline in British ring ouzels *Turdus torquatus. Journal of Animal Ecology*, **75**, 826–35.

Bibby, C. J. (1986) Merlins in Wales: site occupancy and breeding in relation to vegetation. *Journal of Applied Ecology*, **23**, 1–12.

Brown, A. F., Crick, H. Q. P. and Stillman, R. A. (1995) The distribution, numbers and breeding ecology of twite *Anthus flavirostris* in the South Pennines of England. *Bird Study*, **42**, 107–21.

Buchanan, G. M., Pearce-Higgins, J. W., Wotton, S. R., Grant, M. C. and Whitfield, D. P. (2003) Correlates of the change in ring ouzel *Turdus torquatus* abundance in Scotland from 1988–91 to 1999. *Bird Study*, **50**, 97–105.

Burfield, I. J. (2002) The breeding ecology and conservation of the ring ouzel *Turdus torquatus* in Britain. PhD thesis, University of Cambridge.

Calladine, J., Baines, D. and Warren, P. (2002) Effects of reduced grazing on population density and breeding success of black grouse in northern England. *Journal of Applied Ecology*, **39**, 772–80.

Cayford, J. T. (1993) *Black Grouse and Forestry: Habitat Requirements and Management.* Forestry Commission Technical Paper 1, Edinburgh.

Clarke, J. L., Welch, D. and Gordon, I. J. (1995) The influence of vegetation pattern on the grazing of heather moorland by red deer and sheep. II. The impact on heather. *Journal of Applied Ecology*, **32**, 177–86.

Dare, P. J. (1986) Raven *Corvus corax* populations in two upland regions of North Wales. *Bird Study*, **33**, 179–89.

Defra (2008) *Historical Time Series for 1983–2005.* Defra, London. http://www.defra. gov.uk/esg/work_htm/publications/cs/farmstats_web/2_SURVEY_DATA_SEARCH/ HISTORICAL_DATASETS/HISTORICAL_DATASETS/historical_datasets.htm

Dobson, A. and Hudson, P. (1995) The interaction between the parasites and predators of red grouse *Lagopus lagopus scoticus. Ibis*, **137**, S87–S96.

Eaton, M. A., Dillon, I. A., Stirling-Aird, P. K. and Whitfield, P. (2007) The status of the golden eagle A*quila chrysaetos* in Britain in 2003. *Bird Study*, **54**, 212–20.

Etheridge, B., Summers, R. W. and Green, R. E. (1997) The effects of illegal killing and destruction of nests by humans on the population dynamics of the hen harrier *Circus cyaneus* in Scotland. *Journal of Applied Ecology*, **34**, 1081–105.

Evans, D. M., Redpath, S. M., Elston, D. A., Evans, S. A. J., Mitchell, R. J. and Dennis, P. (2006a) To graze or not to graze? Sheep, voles, forestry and nature conservation in the British uplands. *Journal of Applied Ecology*, **43**, 499–505.

Evans, D. M., Redpath, S. M., Evans, S. A., Elston, D. A., Gardner, C. J., Dennis, P. and Pakeman, R. J. (2006b) Low intensity, mixed livestock grazing improves the breeding abundance of a common insectivorous passerine. *Biology Letters*, **2**, 636–8.

Finney, S. K., Pearce-Higgins, J. W. and Yalden, D. W. (2005) The effect of recreational disturbance on an upland breeding bird, the golden plover *Pluvialis apricaria. Biological Conservation*, **121**, 53–63.

Fuller, R. J. and Gough, S. J. (1999) Changes in sheep numbers in Britain: implications for bird populations. *Biological Conservation*, **91**, 73–89.

Gibbons, D. W., Reid, J. B. and Chapman, R. A. (1993) *The New Atlas of Breeding Birds in Britain and Ireland (1988–1991).* London: Poyser.

Grant, M. C. (1992) The effects of re-seeding heathland on breeding whimbrel *Numenius phaeopus* in Shetland. I. Nest distributions. *Journal of Applied Ecology*, **29**, 501–8.

Grant, M. C., Orsman, C., Easton, J., Lodge, C., Smith, M., Thompson, G., Rodwell, S. and Moore, N. (1999) Breeding success and causes of breeding failure of curlew *Numenius arquata* in Northern Ireland. *Journal of Applied Ecology*, **36**, 59–74.

Green, R. E. and Etheridge, B. (1999) Breeding success of the hen harrier *Circus cyaneus* in relation to the distribution of grouse moors and the red fox *Vulpes vulpes. Journal of Applied Ecology*, **36**, 472–83.

Hancock, M., Baines, D., Gibbons, D., Etheridge, B. and Shepherd, M. (1999) Status of male black grouse *Tetrao tetrix* in Britain in 1995–96. *Bird Study*, **46**, 1–15.

Hancock, M. H., Grant, M. C. and Wilson, J. D. (in press) Associations between distance to forest and spatial and temporal variation in abundance of key peatland breeding bird species. *Bird Study*.

Hardey, J., Rollie, C. J. and Stirling Aird, P. K. (2003) Variation in breeding success of inland peregrine falcon (*Falco peregrinus*) in three regions of Scotland 1991–2000. *Birds of Prey in a Changing Environment* (ed. D. B. A. Thompson, S. M. Redpath, A. H. Fielding, M. Marquiss and C. A. Galbraith), pp. 99–109. Edinburgh: Scottish Natural Heritage.

Hegland, S. J., Rydgren, K. and Seldal, T. (2005) The response of *Vaccinium myrtillus* to variations in grazing intensity in a Scandinavian pine forest on the island of Svanøy. *Canadian Journal of Botany*, **83**, 1638–44.

Hester, A. J. and Sydes, C. (1992) Changes in the burning of Scottish heather moorland since the 1940s from aerial photographs. *Biological Conservation*, **60**, 25–30.

Hudson, P. J. (1992) Grouse in space and time: the population biology of a managed gamebird. *Game Conservancy Trust, Fordinbridge*.

Hulme, M., Jenkins, G. J., Lu, X., Turnpenny, J. R., Mitchell, T. D., Jones, R. G., Lowe, J., Murphy, J. M., Hassell, D., Boorman, P., McDonald, R. and Hill, S. (2002) *Climate Change Scenarios for the United Kingdom: The UKCIP02 Scientific Report*. http://www.ukcip.org.uk/resources/publications/pub_dets.asp?ID=14

Huntley, B., Green, R. E., Collingham, Y. C. and Willis, S. G. (2007) *A Climatic Atlas of European Breeding Birds*. Barcelona: Lynx Edicions.

Jenkins, D., Watson, A. and Miller, G. R. (1963) Population studies of red grouse in north-east Scotland. *Journal of Animal Ecology*, **1**, 183–95.

Jenkins, D., Watson, W. and Miller, G. R. (1964) Predation and red grouse populations. *Journal of Applied Ecology*, **1**, 183–95.

Lindström, E. R., Andrén, H., Angelstam, P., Cederlund, G., Hörnfeldt, B., Jäderberg, L., Lemnel, P., Martinsson, B., Sköld, K. and Swenson, J. E. (1994) Disease reveals the predator: sarcoptic mange, red fox predation, and prey populations. *Ecology*, **75**, 1042–9.

Mackey, E. C., Shewry, M. C. and Tudor, G. J. (1998) *Land Cover Change: Scotland from the 1940s to the 1980s*. Edinburgh: The Stationery Office.

Madders, M. (2000) Habitat selection and foraging success of hen harriers *Circus cyaneus* in west Scotland. *Bird Study*, **47**, 32–40.

Madders, M. (2003) Hen harrier *Circus cyaneus* foraging activity in relation to habitat and prey. *Bird Study*, **50**, 55–60.

Marcström, V., Kenward, R. E. and Engren, E. (1988) The impact of predation on boreal tetraonids during vole cycles: an experimental study. *Journal of Animal Ecology*, **57**, 859–72.

Marquiss, M., Newton, I. and Ratcliffe, D. A. (1978) The decline of the raven *Corvus corax* in relation to afforestation in southern Scotland and northern England. *Journal of Applied Ecology*, **15**, 129–44.

Moss, D., Joys, A. C., Clark, J. A., Kirby, A., Smith, A., Baines, D. and Crick, H. Q. P. (2005) *Timing of Breeding of Moorland Birds*. BTO Research Report No. 362, BTO, Thetford.

Newton, I. (1979) *Population Ecology of Raptors*. Berkhamsted: Poyser.

Newton, I. (2004) Population limitation in migrants. *Ibis*, **146**, 197–226.

Newton, I., Davis, P. E. and Davis, J. E. (1982) Ravens and buzzards in relation to sheep-farming and forestry in Wales. *Journal of Applied Ecology*, **16**, 681–706.

Parr, R. (1992) The decline to extinction of a population of golden plover in north east Scotland. *Ornis Scandinavica*, **23**, 152–8.

Pearce-Higgins, J. W., Breale, C. M., Wilson, J. and Bonn, A. (2006) *Analysis of Moorland Breeding Bird Distribution and Change in the Peak District.* Moors for the Future Report No. 11. Moors for the Future Partnership, Edale.

Pearce-Higgins, J. W., Finney, S. K., Yalden, D. W. and Langston, R. H. W. (2007a) Testing the effects of recreational disturbance on two upland breeding waders. *Ibis*, **149 suppl. 1**, 45–55.

Pearce-Higgins, J. W. and Grant, M. C. (2006) Relationships between bird abundance and the composition and structure of moorland vegetation. *Bird Study*, **53**, 112–25.

Pearce-Higgins, J. W., Grant, M. C., Robinson, M. C., and Haysom, S. L. (2007b) The role of forest maturation in causing the decline of black grouse *Tetrao tetrix. Ibis*, **149**, 143–55.

Pearce-Higgins, J. W. and Yalden, D. W. (2003) Variation in the use of pasture by breeding European golden plover *Pluvialis apricaria* in relation to prey availability. *Ibis*, **145**, 365–81.

Pearce-Higgins, J. W., Yalden, D. W. and Whittingham, M. J. (2005) Warmer springs advance the breeding phenology of golden plovers *Pluvialis apricaria* and their prey (*Tipulidae*). *Oecologia*, **143**, 470–6.

Picozzi, N. (1986) Black grouse research in North East Scotland. Unpublished report to the World Pheasant Association. ITE, Banchory.

Picozzi, N. and Hepburn, L. V. (1986) A study of black grouse in north-east Scotland. *Proceedings of the International Grouse Symposium*, **3**, 462–81.

Price, M. F., Dixon, B. J., Warren, C. R. and Macpherson, A. R. (2005) *Scotland's Mountains: Key Issues for Their Future Management.* Battleby: Scottish Natural Heritage.

Ratcliffe, D. A. (1997) *The Raven.* London: Poyser.

Ratcliffe, D. A. (2007) *Galloway and The Borders.* London: HarperCollins.

Rayne, A. F. (2006) The breeding ecology of twite *Cardules flavirostris* and the effects of upland agricultural intensification. PhD Thesis, University of East Anglia.

Rebecca, G. W. (2006) The breeding ecology of the merlin (*Falco columbarius aesalon*) with particular reference to north-east Scotland and land use change. PhD thesis, Open University.

Redpath, S., Madders, M., Donnelly, E., Anderson, B., Thirgood, S., Martin, A. and McLeod, D. (1998) Nest site selection by hen harriers in Scotland. *Bird Study*, **45**, 51–61.

Redpath, S. M. and Thirgood, S. J. (1997) *Birds of Prey and Red Grouse.* London: The Stationery Office.

Reed, S. (1995) Factors limiting the distribution and population size of twite in the Pennines. *Naturalist*, **120**, 93–102.

Robertson, P. A., Park, K. J. and Barton, A. F. (2001) Loss of heather *Calluna vulgaris* moorland in the Scottish uplands: the role of red grouse *Lagopus lagopus scoticus* management. *Wildlife Biology*, **7**, 11–16.

Robson, G. (1998) The breeding ecology of curlew *Numenius arquata* on North Pennine Moorland. PhD thesis, University of Sunderland.

Robson, G., Percival, S. M. and Brown, A. F. (2002) The use of marginal farmland by curlew *Numenius arquata* breeding on upland moors. *Aspects of Applied Biology*, **67**, 75–84.

SEERAD (2007) *Abstract of Scottish Agricultural Statistics 1982 to 2005.* http://www.scotland.gov.uk/Publications/2006/02/13092129/0

Shrubb, M. (2003) *Birds, Scythes and Combines: A History of Birds and Agricultural Change*. Cambridge: Cambridge University Press.

Sim, I. M. W., Burfield, I. J., Grant, M. C., Pearce-Higgins, J. W. and Brooke, M. de L. (2007a) The role of habitat composition in determining breeding site occupancy in a declining ring ouzel *Turdus torquatus* population. *Ibis*, **149**, 378–85.

Sim, I. M. W., Dillon, I. A., Eaton, M. A., Etheridge, B., Lindley, P., Riley, H., Saunders, R., Sharpe, C. and Tickner, M. (2007b) Status of the hen harrier *Circus cyaneus* in the UK and the Isle of Man in 2004, and a comparison with the 1988/89 and 1998 surveys. *Bird Study*, **54**, 256–67.

Sim, I. M. W., Eaton, M. A., Setchfield, R. P., Warren, P. and Lindley, P. (in press) Abundance of male black grouse *Tetrao tetrix* in Britain in 2005, and change since 1995–96. *Bird Study*.

Sim, I. M. W., Gibbons, D. W., Bainbridge, I. P. and Mattingley, W. A. (2001) Status of hen harrier *Circus cyaneus* in the UK and the Isle of Man in 1998. *Bird Study*, **48**, 341–53.

Sim, I. M. W., Gregory, R. D., Hancock, M. H. and Brown, A. F. (2005) Recent changes in the abundance of British upland breeding birds. *Bird Study*, **52**, 261–75.

Smedshaug, C. A., Selås, V., Lund, S. E. and Sonerud, G. A. (1999) The effect of a natural reduction of red fox *Vulpes vulpes* on small game hunting bags in Norway. *Wildlife Biology*, **5**, 157–66.

Smith, A. A., Redpath, S. M., Campbell, S. T. and Thirgood, S. J. (2001) Meadow pipits, red grouse and the habitat characteristics of managed grouse moors. *Journal of Applied Ecology*, **38**, 390–400.

Starling-Westerberg, A. (2001) The habitat use and diet of black grouse *Tetrao tetrix* in the Pennine Hills of northern England. *Bird Study*, **48**, 76–89.

Stroud, D. A., Reed, T. M. and Harding, N. J. (1990) Do moorland breeding waders avoid plantation edges? *Bird Study*, **37**, 177–86.

Stroud, D. A., Reed, T. M., Pienkowski, M. W. and Lindsay, R. A. (1987) *Birds, Bogs and Forestry*. Peterborough: Nature Conservancy Council.

Summers, R. W., Green, R. E., Proctor, R., Dugan, D., Lambie, D., Moncrieff, R., Moss, R. and Baines, D. (2004) An experimental study of the effects of predation on the breeding productivity of capercaillie and black grouse. *Journal of Applied Ecology*, **41**, 513–25.

Tharme, A. P., Green, R. E., Baines, D., Bainbridge, I. P. and O'Brien, M. (2001) The effect of management for red grouse shooting on the population density of breeding birds on heather dominated moorland. *Journal of Applied Ecology*, **38**, 439–57.

Thirgood, S. J., Redpath, S., Rothery, P., Newton, I. and Hudson, P. (2000) Habitat loss and raptor predation: disentangling long and short term causes of red grouse declines. *Proceedings of the Royal Society, B*, **267**, 651–6.

Thompson, D. B. A., Gillings, S. D., Galbraith, C. A., Redpath, S. M. and Drewitt, J. (1997) The contribution of game management to biodiversity: a review of the importance of grouse moors for upland birds. *Biodiversity in Scotland: Status Trends and Initiatives* (ed. L. V. Fleming, A. C. Newton, J. A. Vickery and M. B. Usher), pp. 198–212. Edinburgh: The Stationery Office.

Thompson, D. B. A., MacDonald, A. J., Marsden, J. H. and Galbraith, C. A. (1995) Upland heather moorland in Great Britain: a review of international importance, vegetation change and some objectives for nature conservation. *Biological Conservation*, **71**, 163–78.

Thorup, O. (comp.) (2006) Breeding waders in Europe 2000. *International Wader Studies 14.* International Wader Study Group, UK.

van der Wal, R., Pearce, I., Brooker, R., Scott, D., Welch, D. and Woodin, S. (2003) Interplay between nitrogen deposition and grazing causes habitat degradation. *Ecology Letters*, **6**, 141–6.

Walmsley, C. A., Smithers, R. J., Berry, P. M., Harley, M., Stevenson, M. J. and Catchpole, R. (eds) (2007) *MONARCH: Modelling Natural Resource Responses to Climate Change – a Synthesis for Biodiversity Conservation.* UKCIP, Oxford. http://www.eci.ox.ac.uk/research/biodiversity/monarch.php

Watson, J., Rae, S. R. and Stillman, R. (1992) Nesting density and breeding success of golden eagles in relation to food supply in Scotland. *Journal of Animal Ecology*, **61**, 543–50.

Welch, D. (1998) Response of bilberry *Vaccinium myrtillus* L. stands in the Derbyshire Peak District to sheep grazing, and implications for moorland conservation. *Biological Conservation*, **83**, 155–64.

Welsh Assembly (2007) StatsWales IoP/IoC datasets: Sheep on agricultural holdings (Thousands) http://www.statswales.wales.gov.uk/TableViewer/tableView.aspx?ReportId=2869

Whitfield, D. P., Fielding, A. H., Gregory, M. J. P., Gordon, A. G., McLeod, D. R. A. and Haworth, P. F. (2007) Complex effects of habitat loss on golden eagles *Aquila chrysaetos. Ibis*, **149**, 26–36.

Whitfield, D. P., Fielding, A. H., McLeod, D. R. A. and Haworth, P. F. (2004a) The effects of persecution on age of breeding and territory occupation in golden eagles in Scotland. *Biological Conservation*, **118**, 249–59.

Whitfield, D. P., Fielding, A. H. S., McLeod, D. R. A. and Haworth, P. F. (2004b) Modelling the effects of persecution on the population dynamics of golden eagles in Scotland. *Biological Conservation*, **119**, 319–33.

Whitfield, D. P., McLeod, D. R. A., Fielding, A. H., Broad, R. A., Evans, R. J. and Haworth, P. F. (2001) The effects of forestry on golden eagles on the island of Mull, western Scotland. *Journal of Applied Ecology*, **38**, 1208–20.

Whittingham, M. J., Percival, S. M. and Brown, A. F. (2000) Time budgets and foraging of breeding golden plover *Pluvialis apricaria. Journal of Applied Ecology*, **37**, 632–46.

Whittingham, M. J., Percival, S. M. and Brown, A. F. (2001). Habitat selection by golden plover *Pluvialis apricaria* chicks. *Basic and Applied Ecology*, **2**, 177–91.

Wolfenden, I. H. and Peach, W. J. (2001) Temporal changes in the survival rates of skylarks *Alauda arvensis* breeding in duneland in northwest England. *The Ecology and Conservation of Skylarks* Alauda arvensis (ed. P. F. Donald and J. A. Vickery), pp. 79–89. Sandy: RSPB.

Wotton, S. R., Langston, R. H. W. and Gregory, R. D. (2002) The breeding status of ring ouzel in the UK in 1999. *Bird Study*, **49**, 26–34.

Yalden, D. and Pearce-Higgins, J. W. (1997) Density dependence and winter weather as factors affecting the size of a population of golden plover. *Bird Study*, **44**, 227–34.

Yallop, A., Thacker, J. I., Thomas, G., Stephens, M., Clutterbuck, B., Brewer, T. and Sannier, C. A. D. (2006) The extent and intensity of management burning in the English uplands. *Journal of Applied Ecology*, **43**, 1138–48.

Reference list for Tables 11.2–11.4

[1] Avery (1989) *Journal of Applied Ecology*, 26, 957–66; [2] Thirgood *et al.* (2000) *Proceedings of the Royal Society B*, 267, 651–6; [3] Smith *et al.* (2000) *The influence of moorland management on grouse and their predators.* ETR HMSO, Norwich; [4] Smith *et al.* (2001) *Journal of Applied Ecology*, 38, 390–400; [5] Newton (1986) *British Birds*, 79, 155–70; [6] Tharme *et al.* (2001) *Journal of Applied Ecology*, 38, 439–57; [7] Brown & Stillman (1993) *Journal of Applied Ecology*, 33, 413–24; [8] Pearce-Higgins & Grant (2006) *Bird Study*, 53, 112–25; [9] Pearce-Higgins *et al.* (2006) *Analysis of moorland breeding bird distribution and change in the Peak District. Moors for the Future Report No. 11.* Moors for the Future Partnership, Edale; [10] Buchanan *et al.* (unpubl.); [11] Parr (1992) *Ornis Scandinavica*, 23, 152–8; [12] Baines (1996) *Journal of Applied Ecology*, 33, 54–62; [13] Stroud *et al.* (1990) *Bird Study*, 37, 177–86; [14] Buchanan & Pearce-Higgins (2002) IALE(UK) 118–25; [15] Calledine *et al.* (2002) *Journal of Applied Ecology*, 39, 772–80; [16] Pearce-Higgins *et al.* (2007) *Ibis*, 149, 143–55; [17] Sim *et al.* (2007) *Bird Study*, 54, 256–67; [18] Amar & Redpath (2005) *Ibis*, 147, 37–47; [19] Amar *et al.* (2008) *Ibis*, 150, 400–4; [20] Finney *et al.* (2005) *Biological Conservation*, 121, 53–63; [21] Watson *et al.* (1992) *Journal of Animal Ecology*, 61, 543–50; [22] Whitfield *et al.* (2006) *Biological Conservation*, 130, 465–80; [23] Whitfield *et al.* (2007) *Ibis*, 149, 26–36; [24] Marquiss *et al.* (1978) *Journal of Applied Ecology*, 15, 129–44; [25] Haworth & Thompson (1990) *Journal of Applied Ecology*, 27, 562–77; [26] Haworth & Fielding (1988) *Biological Conservation*, 46, 247–60; [27] Stillman & Brown (1994) *Biological Conservation*, 69, 307–14; [28] Rebecca (2006) PhD thesis Open University; [29] Watson & Rae (1987) *Journal of Animal Ecology*, 61, 543–50; [30] Galbraith *et al.* (1993) *Bird Study*, 40, 161–9; [31] Newton *et al.* (1982) *Journal of Applied Ecology*, 16, 681–706; [32] Whitfield (2001) *Journal of Applied Ecology*, 38, 1208–20; [33] Hudson (1992) *Grouse in Space and Time: The Population Biology of a Managed Gamebird.* Game Conservancy Trust, Fordinbridge; [34] Chamberlain (2001) *The ecology and conservation of skylarks* Alauda arvensis, RSPB, Sandy, 25–39; [35] Vanhinsberg & Chamberlain (2001) *Bird Study*, 48, 159–72; [36] Redpath & Thirgood (1997) *Birds of Prey and Red Grouse*, The Stationery Office, London; [37] Burfield (2001) PhD thesis, University of Cambridge; [38] Buchanan *et al.* (2003) *Bird Study*, 50, 97–105; [39] Sim *et al.* (2007) *Ibis*, 149, 378–85; [40] Brown *et al.* (1995) *Bird Study*, 42, 107–21; [41] Dobson & Hudson (1994) *Ibis*, 137, S87–S96; [42] Watson (1965) *Journal of Animal Ecology*, 34, 135–72; [43] Watson *et al.* (1998) *Ecology*, 79, 1174–92; [44] Watson & Moss (2004) *Biological Conservation*, 116, 267–75; [45] Baines (1991) *Ornis Scandinavica*, 22, 264–9; [46] Summers *et al.* (2004) *Journal of Applied Ecology*, 41, 513–25; [47] Etheridge *et al.* (1997) *Journal of Applied Ecology*, 34, 1081–105; [48] Green & Etheridge (1999) *Journal of Applied Ecology*, 36, 472–83; [49] Summers *et al.* (2003) *Birds of Prey in a Changing Environment* SNH, Edinburgh 487–97; [50] Redpath *et al.* (2002) *Animal Conservation*, 5, 113–18; [51] Sim *et al.* (unpubl); [52] Whitfield *et al.* (2004) *Biological Conservation*, 118, 249–59; [53] Whitfield *et al.* (2004) *Biological Conservation*, 119, 319–33; [54] Hardey *et al.* (2003) *Birds of prey in a changing environment. SNH, Edinburgh* 99–109; [55] Pearce-Higgins & Yalden (2003) *Bird Study*, 50, 170–7; [56] Grant *et al.* (1999) *Journal of Applied Ecology*, 36, 59–74; [57] Gibbons *et al.* (1994) *Ibis*, 137, S75–S84; [58] Cayford (1993) *Journal of Applied Ecology*, 39, 772–80; [59] Bibby & Etheridge (1993) *Bird Study*, 40, 1–11; [60] Baines (1996) *Journal of Applied Ecology*, 33, 54–62; [61] Marquiss *et al.* (1985) *Biological Conservation*, 34, 121–40; [62] Orchel (1992) *Forest Merlins in Scotland: Their requirements and management.* London: Hawk and Owl Trust.

12 Mammals in the uplands

Derek W. Yalden

Introduction

Internationally, uplands hold special mammal communities, especially those found in open landscapes above the tree-line. These ecosystems are discontinuously distributed, patchy, and vulnerable to human land-management pressures (overgrazing, burning, deforestation) as well as climate change. While many upland species are seriously endangered, uplands generally retain more complete mammal assemblages than lowlands, because variously of their remoteness, lower human population density or better protection status (e.g. as national parks and wilderness areas). Historically, they have often served as refuges for lowland species (e.g. in Britain). This has led to ideas that, in future, they may be appropriate places to consider 're-wilding' – the reintroduction of extinct, often larger and charismatic, mammals with a view to re-creating something resembling the mammal community of pre-agricultural times.

The international context

Worldwide, there is a charismatic and characteristic fauna associated with the highest mountain chains. It frequents the open habitats that occur largely above the tree-line. Although montane forests may also have characteristic mammals, it is very hard to discern a separate montane forest fauna in any continent, simply because it merges imperceptibly into the local lowland forest fauna. For mammals, such open highland areas provide 'island' habitats, isolated by surrounding lowlands from neighbouring 'islands'. The most spectacular and diverse highland mammal fauna occurs in the most extensive and highest mountain chain, stretching from the Hindu Kush and Pamirs through the Himalayas to the Tibetan Plateau; it includes such distinctive and iconic species as snow leopard *Panthera uncia*, yak *Bos mutus* and chiru (Tibetan antelope) *Panthalops hodgsonii*. Marmots *Marmota himalayana*, zokors *Myospalax fontanierii*, hares *Lepus oiostolus* and pikas *Ochotona cansus, O. dauurica* are also typical members of this montane fauna. So is a spectacular diversity of related bovids, including bharal *Pseudois nayaur*, serow *Capricornis sumatraensis*, goral *Nemorhaedus goral* and tahr *Hemitragus jemlahicus*, as well as markhor *Capra falconeri* and argali *Ovis ammon*, suggesting that it is the evolutionary centre from which this group of montane ungulates spread (Schaller, 1977, 1998; Fernandez and Vrba, 2005). A zoogeographically filtered remnant of this Asian fauna extends westwards through western Asia into Europe, where it is represented only by ibex *Capra ibex*, chamois *Rupicapra rupicapra/R. pyrenaica* and alpine marmot *M. marmota*, together with a few endemic voles such as *Chionomys nivalis* and *Dinaromys bogdanovi*. A similar thin representation crossed the Bering Strait perhaps 4–5 million years ago to penetrate the Rocky Mountains of North America, where sheep *Ovis dalli, O. canadensis*, mountain goat *Oreamnos americanus* and pikas *Ochotona princeps, O. collaris* are among the most distinctive species. Various marmots (e.g. *M. flaviventris*), voles (*Microtus montanus, Phenacomys intermedius*) and cotton-tails (*Sylvilagus nuttalli*) also frequent the high grasslands there.

The southern continents evolved their own distinctive montane faunas. Ethiopia provides over 50 per cent of the land above 2,000 m in Africa (and 80 per cent of that above 3,000 m: Yalden, 1981); this montane area is clearly demarcated and isolated by surrounding drier lowlands. Its small specialised high-altitude fauna includes gelada *Theropithecus gelada*, mountain nyala *Tragelaphus buxtoni* and Ethiopian wolf *Canis simensis*, while the less familiar small mammals, about 10 per cent of the country's fauna (around twenty-nine species out of 277), are high-altitude endemics (Yalden *et al.*, 1996). The Ethiopian wolf is the extreme example of a threatened upland mammal; no more than 500 individuals, spread between seven isolated fragments of suitable habitat above about 3,200 m, are threatened by overgrazing (which removes the cover and food for their small-mammal prey) and rabies caught from village dogs (Marino, 2003). In South America, the Andes are better-known for their bird faunas than for their mammals, but the guinea-pig *Cavia tschudii* and camelids *Lama guanocoe* and *L. vicugna* provided the Incas with their meat, skins, wool and beasts of burden. As elsewhere, rodents provide a selection of smaller montane species, with the mountain viscacha *Lagidium peruanum* a good ecological surrogate for northern marmots. It is harder to detect an obvious montane mammal fauna in Australasia, where the mountain chains only support high-altitude grasslands in New Zealand, and birds, rather than mammals, fill the equivalent niches (e.g. takahe *Notornis mantelli*, kea *Nestor notabilis* and extinct moas Dinornithidae). In Australia, only the scree-inhabiting mountain possum *Burramys parva* is regarded as a specialist montane mammal (Menkhorst and Knight, 2001).

The nature of upland mammal communities

The habitats for these upland faunas, extensive grasslands (alpine steppe and meadow, puna, afromontane heathlands), occur only in the more extensive highlands. Grasslands have a higher productivity within easy reach of (grazing) mammals than the woodlands that usually occupy the lower slopes of mountain ranges, and the biomass of rodents living on such grasslands can be very high. In Ethiopia, the afroalpine moorlands in the Bale Mountains support up to 25 kg/ha of diurnal rodents, representing some 125 individuals/ha (murids *Lophuromys melanonyx* and *Arvicanthis blicki* plus giant mole-rats *Tachyoryctes macrocephalus*); as a result the ground is often spongy through their burrowing (Sillero-Zubiri *et al.*, 1995). A similar description is made of the Tibetan plateau, as a result of zokor and pika activity (Zhang *et al.*, 2003). These rodents in turn support a range of predators, including such specialists as Ethiopian wolf and Tibetan fox *Vulpes ferrilata*. Rocky slopes, as refuges for larger herbivores, or scree similarly for some of the smaller species such as pikas, are an important component of the habitat. Sheep and especially goats are well adapted to a precarious existence on steep slopes, and when threatened by wolves retreat uphill to the steepest-possible cliffs (Mech *et al.*, 1998). The narrow hoofs of artiodactyls may be considered a pre-adaptation for this (the unrelated klipspringer *Oreotragus oreotragus* and beira *Dorcotragus megalotis* of eastern Africa present the most extreme manifestations of this adaptation). Other small herbivores, such as mole-rats, marmots, zokors and guinea-pigs, seek sanctuary in burrows they dig themselves, but these in turn require an adequate depth of soil. Given their diversity in montane habitats, it seems likely that the sub-family Caprinae of the Bovidae evolved as a response to the emergence of the Himalayas and related mountains. If so, their adaptation to montane habitats was an essential part of their evolutionary heritage, and the diversity of these mountains a mainspring for their radiation. The smaller montane mammals do not seem to be similarly members of specialist montane mammal groups, but represent locally adapted species, evolved from local relatives, that have individually and idiosyncratically adapted themselves to montane life. For example, the alpine marmot *Marmota marmota* is a member of a worldwide group of burrowing squirrels, with about fourteen species; some live in lowland habitats (e.g. *M. monax* in America, *M. bobak* in Eurasia) whereas others, such as the Himalayan *M. himalayana* and the American *M. flaviventris*, are montane species. Phylogenetic analysis (Steppan *et al.*, 1999) confirms that *Marmota* constitutes a monophyletic group, and that the Palaearctic species derive probably from a single crossing of the Bering land-bridge; they must then have crossed on low ground, and re-invaded montane areas several times. An adaptation to open ground, the ability to hibernate and to withstand severe winters, and to dig burrows, perhaps also their large size (Bergman's rule?) compared with their relatives in *Spermophilus*, must have served the genus well in its dispersal, and in its exploitation of montane habitats, but it is difficult to categorise these as specifically montane adaptations. One can see similar evolutionary opportunism in, for instance, montane hares such as the Tibetan *Lepus oiostolus*, pikas such as *Ochotona collaris* and *O. curzoniae*, or the giant mole-rat *Tachyoryctes macrocephalus* of Ethiopia. The basic ecology of these genera is such that little specific adaptation was necessary to suit them to high-altitude life, beyond perhaps larger size, thicker coat, or behavioural sensitivity to alpine conditions.

Threats

Because most upland species rely on grasslands for their food, and these are usually also exploited by itinerant or transhumant pastoralists (seasonal or migrant graziers), all these high-altitude communities are vulnerable to overgrazing by herds of domestic livestock. In most of the world, these are sheep and goats, which are in any case the descendants of upland species; on the Tibetan plateau, the domesticated yak is a similar threat (Schaller, 1998), and domesticated lamas and alpacas likewise threaten upland habitats in the Andes. Generally, upland grasslands are too high for arable exploitation, although in Ethiopia cultivation of the native grass *Eragrostis tef* is an additional threat to the grasslands in the Simien National Park.

The British perspective

Britain does not have a specialised upland mammal fauna. The land is not high enough, and 8,000 years ago it was nearly all wooded. There are a few specialist upland birds – dotterel *Charadrius morinella*, ptarmigan *Lagopus muta*, red grouse *L. lagopus scotica*, snow bunting *Plectrophenax nivalis* (see Pearce-Higgins *et al.*, this volume) – but the only mammalian species restricted to the uplands of Great Britain is the mountain hare *Lepus timidus*. Elsewhere in Europe, even indeed in Ireland, this is by no means a specialist upland species, though it is a northern one. During the last glaciation, about 20,000 years ago, it occurred extensively across the lowlands of western Europe, as far south as the Pyrenees, and it survives, as a relict subspecies *L. t. varronis*, above about 1,500 m in the Alps. About 15,000 years ago, it was the principal target of human hunters living in Robin Hood Cave, Creswell Crags (Charles and Jacobi, 1994), but the spread of woodland in post-glacial times seems to have restricted its British range to Highland Scotland (and Ireland). With clearance of woodland by humans since Neolithic times, and the more recent creation of moorlands, open upland habitats appropriate for it have been re-created. It was re-introduced to both the Southern Uplands of Scotland and the Peak District by sporting interests about 150 years ago: owners of grouse moors who had seen mountain hares in Scotland felt that the fauna would be more complete with their presence elsewhere (Box 12.1). Re-introductions made to several other British uplands (Snowdonia, the moors of Denbighshire, the Lake District, the Cheviots), at about the same time, have not survived. Overgrazing by sheep within the last thirty years seems to have eliminated them. By contrast, management of moors for grouse-shooting in the Peak District and the South Pennines has been maintained, continuing to provide their favoured habitat – a mixture of short, recently burnt and regenerating heather *Calluna vulgaris* for

---

Box 12.1. The mountain hare Lepus timidus in the Peak District

The mountain hare was native locally from 15,000 to about 5,000 years ago. It was re-introduced to the Peak District from Scotland at four sites in the north in 1860–90, and probably to one in the south-west in 1894. By 1926, it had spread throughout the High Peak, occurred 6 km beyond the Peak District to the north at Blackstone Edge, and to the south on Eyam Moor, Comb's Moss and Danebower Moss. A cumulative re-survey during 1969–84 confirmed its presence throughout the High Peak, in 246 monads (one-kilometre squares), but it has gone from the southern moors and is no longer present further north. A collaborative survey during winter 2000–1, involving 113 recorders, covered its whole range within one winter; the hare was present in 332 monads, in essentially the same range, though extending marginally outside the north of the Peak Park. Summing numbers seen in each monad suggested populations of only 1,000–2,000, but DISTANCE sampling (Buckland *et al.*, 1993) from line transects in 2001–2 suggested a total population of 12,000, though with wide 95 per cent confidence limits of 7,000–20,000 (Wheeler, 2002). Regular counts undertaken annually on the Derwent Edges since 1973 suggest that the population is currently strong: annual counts have exceeded 150 since 2000 (Figure 12.1).

The current high numbers are thought to result from a combination of better moorland management (better burning and fox-culling) and a sequence of mild snowless winters. Environmentally Sensitive Areas (ESA) management over the past fifteen years has paid for extra gamekeepers, fewer sheep on the hills in winter and some moorland restoration work, all of which have helped. Moorland restoration work undertaken by Moors for the Future and small exclosures to encourage vegetation recovery on damaged areas have been popular with the hares. Back in 1986, after a severe late-winter snowfall, only eight were counted. If numbers were to fall that low again (to under 5 per cent, implying only 600 hares in the Peak District), its future would be more problematic, given that the population is fragmented and suffers appreciable road mortality.

Historical information and the 2000–1 survey are well summarised by Mallon (2001). A popular account including details of the recent population estimate is given by Mallon *et al.* (2003).

---

food, and taller vegetation of older heather, cotton-grass *Eriophorum* spp. and *Molinia* providing cover. However, heather only provides some of their food, especially in winter; particularly in summer, grasses are preferred (Flux, 1970). It may be that direct competition with sheep for food in summer, when

Figure 12.1 Mountain hare distribution in the Peak District National Park (counts per km² grid cells across all moorland habitat within the Dark Peak area, shaded in grey; see also Mallon, 2000).

the females are lactating and have highest energy needs, has been the most acute cause of their loss elsewhere, but this has not been directly studied.

Uplands as refugia

The British uplands are noted as the places to see several other mammals, including pine marten *Martes martes*, polecat *Mustela putorius*, wildcat *Felis silvestris*, roe deer *Capreolus capreolus* and red deer *Cervus elaphus*. None of these are specialised upland mammals, but the uplands are the places where, because of much lower human presence and lower agricultural and game-keeping pressures, they were able to survive historically through periods of intense pressure. Roe deer and red deer were exterminated from England and Wales by the end of the eighteenth century (except that red deer possibly survived in the Lake District) and only survived in about six Scottish 'deer forests' (open moorland – forests were originally places for deer, not trees). Elsewhere, they were displaced by the pressure to expand sheep-rearing. However, the realisation that sporting interests would pay better rents for shooting red deer than could be gleaned from farming upland sheep led to a substantial increase in deer forests during the first half of the nineteenth century, such that there were at least forty-five deer forests by 1845, and their extent continued to increase throughout that century (Clutton-Brock and Albon, 1989).

Red deer as threat to upland biodiversity

Now red deer number about 360,000 in the Highlands, and their concentration in large herds on lower ground in winter threatens the survival of some of the last remnants of the Caledonian pine woodlands. Although heather and grasses are their main food, seedlings and saplings of pine *Pinus sylvestris*, birch *Betula* spp. and rowan *Sorbus aucuparia* also get eaten, so that woodland does not regenerate. The natural tree-line, where birch, pine and willow *Salix* spp. scrub straggle uphill on to moorland, is barely evident anywhere in Scotland. Consequently, in some woodland nature reserves and estates, strenuous efforts have been made to restore the balance between trees and deer, by variously fencing and heavy culling (e.g. at Creag Meagaidh National Nature Reserve [NNR] and in the Royal Society for Protection of Birds's [RSPB's] Abernethy Forest) or otherwise disturbing deer to give semi-natural regeneration a chance.

Predatory mammals in the uplands

When land was privatised and enparked, landowners were able to protect it and the game species that lived on it; this led to the profession of game-keeping (see Sotherton *et al.*, this volume). Gamekeepers protect and manage the habitat, and persecute the predators of the favoured game species (primarily pheasants *Phasianus colchicus*, partridge *Perdix perdix* and grouse

L. lagopus, Tetrao tetrix). The profession reached its maximum, of about 23,000 gamekeepers, in the 1911 census, when there was roughly one per 10 km^2 (1,000 ha) across the whole of Great Britain. In the most densely keepered lowland county there were only 444 ha per keeper (Tapper, 1992). Since a keeper could effectively manage about 400 ha, virtually all the land was keepered. The only counties with more than 2,500 ha per keeper were Caithness and Sutherland in northern Scotland and Cardiganshire and Carmarthenshire in western Wales. By 1915, it was only in these thinly keepered counties and their immediate neighbours that pine marten *Martes martes*, wildcat *Felis sylvestris* and polecat *Mustela putorius* survived (Langley and Yalden, 1977). Polecats are not upland animals at all; even in Wales, where they survived, they are largely mammals of river valleys and farmland. Wildcats and pine martens do occur at higher altitudes, but are primarily species of woodland, a habitat not especially associated with uplands in Britain. Scree certainly gives pine martens alternative harbourage to tree dens; the ability to avoid foxes is thought to be critical for them. With the substantial decline in numbers of gamekeepers after the First World War, the persecution of these carnivores diminished, and within a decade they had begun their spread back into areas where they had been lost (Langley and Yalden, 1977; Tapper, 1992). More recently, legal protection has been extended to these rarer species (under the Wildlife and Countryside Act, 1981), and they continue to spread.

An equivalent modern example of this upland refuge effect is evidenced by the water vole *Arvicola terrestris*. As recently as the 1970s, this was a widespread, essentially lowland, species, present on most rivers, lakes and canals, especially those with deeper, slow-flowing water and good marginal vegetation. During the 1980s and especially the 1990s, a dramatic decline was evident, prompting national surveys to determine its current status and distribution (Strachan and Jefferies, 1993). It became evident, from a combination of correlative evidence and direct observation, that two rates of decline had acted: a slow long-term decline due to loss of habitat, which has lasted at least a century (perhaps 4,000 years or more: Jefferies, 2003), and a more recent, sharper decline associated with the spread of the American mink *Mustela vison*. The latter has been most dramatically documented for the Thames catchment, where water voles declined from being present at 130 (out of 161) survey sites in 1975, still present at 100 in 1990, to only 31 in 1995; mink were only present at 9 sites in 1975, but had increased to 32 in 1990, and to 59 in 1995; water voles were no longer present at any site that had mink, and the direct impact of the arrival of mink on study populations of water voles was also documented (Macdonald and Strachan, 1999).

Mink depend on medium-sized mammals for most of their diet; water voles are vulnerable because both are amphibious and about the same diameter, so mink can enter their burrows, but rabbits, essentially a lowland species, are the major prey in Britain. In the uplands, where rabbits are largely absent so unavailable to support mink, water voles have frequently managed to survive in small isolated refugial populations. This was first documented for the Dee catchment in Scotland (Aars *et al.*, 2001), but it also describes the situation in the Peak District. Water voles used to be a common, readily visible presence on limestone rivers such as the Dove and the Wye; now they are scarce or absent on those rivers, but a dedicated survey (Perkins and Mallon, 1999) has located small isolated colonies on many of the upland rivers where there are dense beds of rushes *Juncus effusus* – not good water vole food but good cover. In both Deeside and the Peak District, this is a dynamic system; mink sometimes locate and eliminate these small colonies but, in the absence of a rabbit population to sustain them, must then move on to find more food. In a thinly spread network of water vole colonies, a few usually survive to repopulate other refuges.

Two other British mammals have important moorland populations: the pigmy shrew *Sorex minutus* and the field vole *Microtus agrestis*. Neither is an upland species (both occur very widely in the lowlands), but the moorlands do host perhaps 50 per cent of their national populations. Unlike other shrews, pygmy shrews do not burrow or eat earthworms but they eat a wide range of smaller invertebrates that live in taller vegetation, both suitable habits for life on moorland. On blanket bog, it is probably the most common small mammal. Field voles prefer the denser purple moor-grass *Molinia* communities, and populations are greatly reduced by sheep-grazing, which removes both their food and their cover. In the Peak District, comparison of grazed areas with ungrazed exclosures suggests that the moorland population might double, from 411,000 to 800,000, if all grazing ceased. This would benefit vole predators such as short-eared owls *Asio flammeus*, whose distribution reflects vole availability (Wheeler, 2002).

The future for upland mammals

At present, the uplands of Great Britain are dominated by domestic grazing mammals, mostly sheep but also beef cattle. About 20 million breeding sheep and about 1.4 million beef cattle, mostly in the uplands, greatly outnumber the 360,000 red deer, though the latter are more important in the Scottish Highlands. The future of this agricultural system is currently dubious. Sheep-farming, in particular, has relied on agricultural subsidies for up to 65 per cent of its income (Condliffe, this volume), and under EU agricultural reform this will cease over the next few years. The intention is to pay instead comparable amounts of subsidy for positive management of the landscape, to improve its scenic and biodiversity value. The future of Environmentally Sensitive Area (ESA) payments, which have supported moorland management over the last decade or more, is also uncertain.

What might take the place of these payments, and these agricultural systems? Recreational management (e.g. for grouse-shooting and deer-stalking) may continue, though concerns about the impact of increasing deer numbers on landscape, biodiversity and forestry are already manifested in attempts to limit their numbers and impact. A very different scenario is offered by discussion of re-wilding. It was argued over twenty years ago that re-introducing large mammals to the Highlands, such as wolves *Canis lupus*, lynx *Lynx lynx*, bear *Ursus arctos* and beaver *Castor fiber*, would provide a tourist attraction comparable to that now offered in the Yellowstone National Park by the re-introduced wolves. Specifically, it was suggested that Rum, a National Nature Reserve (NNR), would be a suitable place for a re-wilding experiment (Nevard and Penfold, 1978; Yalden, 1986). Since then, white-tailed eagles *Haliaeetus albicilla* have been re-introduced to the Inner Hebrides and are already a major tourist attraction, for example to Mull. The consensus is that the British Isles are too crowded for such large mammals, and, more specifically, that Rum is too small to host a wolf population (though it has three times more potential prey than the famous Isle Royale wolves). In a critical review, Wilson (2003) argued that there was enough prey in the Highlands to support the three top predators, but that public concern would prevent wolf or bear being realistically considered, and that lynx should be considered more thoroughly. These suggestions have been developed further by Hetherington (2006) and Nilson *et al.* (2007). Beavers, subject to a formal proposal, have been thought too threatening to salmon fisheries and forestry, and so far have not been released. In Europe, wolves have already returned, naturally, to France (Mercantour National Park), while beaver and lynx have been re-introduced to many European countries (Yalden, 1999). In the Netherlands, a more densely populated country than Great Britain, a major experiment in re-wilding, in the Oostvaardersplassen, has seen red deer, ponies and Heck cattle (as a surrogate for the extinct aurochsen) allowed to increase and regulate the grazing succession with little human interference (Kampf, 2000). They have created areas of open water for wildfowl, altered the dynamics of grassland–scrub–woodland succession, and generated critical thinking about the management of such systems. Should corpses be left for scavengers? When is veterinary intervention justified? So far, carnivores have not been added to that ecosystem.

Thought has been given to such experiments in Great Britain, both by government agencies (e.g. Kirby, 2003) and by private estates. Formal re-introductions of large mammals have not yet happened, though wild boar *Sus scrofa* may have re-introduced themselves by escaping from specialist farms. Currently, whether to tolerate, manage or eradicate these is under discussion (Wilson, 2004, 2005; Moore and Wilson, 2005). It is perhaps unfortunate that they escaped in lowland England (Wilson, 2003). Arguably, they would be more tolerable in the uplands (Leaper *et al.*, 1999).

If agricultural change will have the most immediate future impact on upland mammals, the most insidious and unpredictable threat is posed by climate change. If warming proceeds as predicted, moorlands may be turned to grasslands as soils dry, and heather and cotton-grass suffer from summer drought. Wildfires would become more frequent (McMorrow *et al.*, this volume), and loss of peat more complete (Worrall and Evans, this volume). Grouse-shooting, which currently maintains the moorlands, would die out, no longer economically worthwhile (public or political antipathy to blood sports could produce a similar result). Mountain hares and other moorland specialists may then be lost, to be replaced by more southern species.

Conclusions

It is impossible to predict the future scene in the uplands. Biological speculation is likely to be overtaken by political action. Nevertheless, biologists can dream. As a mammalogist, I have dreamt of large extinct species being returned to Great Britain for twenty years or more. I have documented the overwhelming domination of the current landscape by ourselves and our domestic supporters (Yalden, 1999, 2003). It is inconceivable that this will change in the lowlands. It could change in the uplands, if we wish it to. The current agricultural and forestry systems have been largely supported by taxpayers. Taxpayers could instead opt to spend their money on re-wilding, on landscape conservation, on the re-introduction of large mammals (and birds), and on creating real national parks resembling those of North America or East Africa in combining truly wild scenery with truly wild ecosystems. Dangerous? Of course. Why else do tourists visit Serengeti or Amboseli? Certainly not to see the Maasai cattle. If carbon taxes rule out package tours to East Africa in the near future, British tourists will want something else to watch. Wolves in our own uplands would be an appropriate substitute. It is at least arguable that a tourist-based economy may result in a more sustainable use of the uplands.

References

Aars, J., Lambin, X., Denny, R. and Griffin, A. (2001) Water vole in the Scottish uplands: distribution patterns of disturbed and pristine populations ahead and behind the American mink invasion front. *Animal Conservation*, 4, 187–94.

Buckland, S. T., Anderson, D. R., Burnham, K. P. and Laake, J. L. (1993) *DISTANCE Sampling: Estimating the Abundance of Biological Populations.* London: Chapman & Hall.

Charles, R. and Jacobi, R. M. (1994) A Lateglacial fauna from Robin Hood Cave, Creswell: a reassessment. *Oxford Journal of Archaeology*, 13, 1–32.

Clutton-Brock, T. H. and Albon, S. D. (1989) *Red Deer in the Highlands.* Oxford: Blackwell.

Fernandez, M. H. and Vrba, E. S. (2005) A complete estimate of the phylogenetic relationships in Ruminantia: a dated species-level supertree of the extant ruminants. *Biological Reviews*, 80, 269–302.

Flux, J. E. C. (1970) Life history of the mountain hare (*Lepus timidus scoticus*) in north-east Scotland. *Journal of Zoology*, 161, 75–123.

Hetherington, D. A. (2006) The lynx in Britain's past, present and future. *ECOS*, 27, 66–74.

Jefferies, D. J. (2003) *The Water Vole and Mink Survey of Britain 1996–1998 with a History of the Long-Term Changes in the Status of Both Species and Their Causes.* London: Vincent Wildlife Trust.

Kampf, H. (2000) The role of large grazing mammals in nature conservation – a Dutch perspective. *British Wildlife*, **12**, 37–46.

Kirby, K. J. (2003) What might a British forest landscape driven by large herbivores look like? *English Nature Research Report* 530. Peterborough: English Nature.

Langley, P. J. W. and Yalden, D. W. (1977) The decline of the rarer carnivores in Great Britain during the nineteenth century. *Mammal Review*, **7**, 95–116.

Leaper, R., Massei, G., Gorman, M. L. and Aspinall, R. (1999) The feasibility of reintroducing wild boar *Sus scrofa* to Scotland. *Mammal Review*, **29**, 239–59.

Macdonald, D. and Strachan, R. (1999) *The Mink and the Water Vole: Analyses for Conservation.* Oxford: Wildlife Conservation Research Unit and Environment Agency.

Mallon, D. (2001) *The Mountain Hare in the Peak District.* Belper: Derbyshire Wildlife Trust.

Mallon, D., Wheeler, P., Whitely, D. and Yalden, D. W. (2003) Mountain hares in the Peak District. *British Wildlife*, **15**, 110–16.

Marino, J. (2003) Threatened Ethiopian wolves persist in small isolated Afroalpine enclaves. *Oryx*, **37**, 62–71.

Mech, L. D., Adams, L. G., Meier, T. J., Burch, J. W. and Dale, B. W. (1998) *The Wolves of Denali.* Minneapolis, Minn.: University of Minnesota Press.

Menkhorst, P. and Knight, F. (2001) *A Field Guide to the Mammals of Australia.* Oxford: Oxford University Press.

Moore, N. P. and Wilson, C. (2005) *Feral Wild Boar in England. Implications of Future Management Options.* London: Defra.

Nevard, T. D. and Penfold, J. B. (1978) Wildlife conservation in Britain: the unsatisfied demand. *Biological Conservation*, **14**, 25–44.

Nilson, E. B., Milner-Gulland, E. J., Schofield, L., Mysterud, A., Stenseth, N. C. and Coulson, T. (2007) Wolf reintroduction to Scotland: public attitudes and consequences for red deer management. *Proceedings of the Royal Society*, *B*, **274**, 995–1002.

Perkins, H. M. and Mallon, D. P. (1999) *The Water Vole in Derbyshire.* Elvaston Castle, Derby: Derbyshire Wildlife Trust.

Schaller, G. B. (1977) *Mountain Monarchs.* Chicago, Ill.: University of Chicago Press.

Schaller, G. B. (1998) *Wildlife of the Tibetan Steppe.* Chicago, Ill.: University of Chicago Press.

Sillero-Zuberi, C., Tattershall, F. H. and Macdonald, D. W. (1995) Bale Mountains rodent communities and their relevance to the Ethiopian wolf (*Canis simensis*). *African Journal of Ecology*, **33**, 301–20.

Steppan, S. J., Akhverdyan, M. R., Lyanpunova, E. A., Fraser, D. G., Vorontsov, N. N., Hoffman, R. S. and Braun, M. J. (1999) Molecular phylogeny of the marmots (*Rodentia, Sciuridae*): tests of evolutionary and biogeographic hypotheses. *Systematic Biology*, **48**, 715–34.

Strachan, R. and Jefferies, D. J. (1993) *The Water Vole* Arvicola terrestris *in Britain 1989–1990: Its Distribution and Changing Status.* London: Vincent Wildlife Trust.

Tapper, S. (1992) *Game Heritage.* Fordingbridge: Game Conservancy.

Wheeler, P. M. S. (2002) The distribution of mammals across the upland landscape. PhD thesis, University of Manchester.

Wilson, C. (2003) Distribution and status of feral wild boar *Sus scrofa* in Dorset, southern England. *Mammal Review*, **33**, 302–7.

Wilson, C. (2004) Could we live with reintroduced large carnivores in the UK? *Mammal Review*, **34**, 211–32.

Wilson, C. (2005) *Feral Wild Boar in England: Status, Impact and Management*. London: Defra.

Yalden, D. W. (1981) The extent of high ground in Ethiopia compared to the rest of Africa. *Sinet: Ethiopian Journal of Science*, **6**, 35–9.

Yalden, D. W. (1986) Opportunities for reintroducing British mammals. *Mammal Review*, **16**, 53–63.

Yalden, D. W. (1999) *The History of British Mammals*. London: Poyser.

Yalden, D. W. (2003) Mammals in Britain – a historical perspective. *British Wildlife*, **14**, 243–51.

Yalden, D. W., Largen, M. J., Kock, D. and Hillman, J. C. (1996) Catalogue of the mammals of Ethiopia and Eritrea. 7. Revised checklist, zoogeography and conservation. *Tropical Zoology*, **9**, 73–164.

Zhang, Y., Zhang, Z. and Liu, J. (2003) Burrowing rodents as ecosystem engineers: the ecology and management of plateau zokors *Myospalax fontanierii* in alpine meadow ecosystems on the Tibetan Plateau. *Mammal Review*, **33**, 284–94.

13 Managing uplands for game and sporting interests

An industry perspective

Nick Sotherton, Richard May,
Julie Ewald, Kathy Fletcher and
David Newborn

Introduction

For at least 150 years, the British uplands have been dominated by the three main land-use practices of sheep farming, forestry and game management that have led to the characteristic landscapes we treasure today (Tapper, 2005). These land uses have always been the only means of producing any revenue; and, in the absence of government subsidy, maximising productivity from any area of land is the only means of sustaining that land's future and maintaining employment. In recent years other management objectives have emerged, which include tourism and conservation, provision of drinking water, alleviation of downstream flooding, as well as carbon management. These objectives reflect the recognition both nationally and internationally of uplands as cultural landscapes with multiple functions and benefits to our wider society.

Over 70 per cent of the Peak District's moorland is privately owned, and so maintaining moorland is likely to remain dependent upon the ability and motivation of landowners and the financial returns they generate. Historically, grazing and tree-planting have received fiscal subsidies, but these have been reduced or reviewed as their impacts on landscape and wildlife have become apparent (Condliffe, this volume). Also, public funding for environmental improvements is reducing, and it must be questionable whether, with the need for increased public investment in health and education, funding for Britain's uplands will ever be a priority.

Game management has a long history going back to the early/mid-nineteenth century (Tapper, 1992) and has only recently received agri-environment subsidies. Game management in the uplands is based on the maintenance of moorland for red grouse *Lagopus lagopus scoticus*. Red grouse only survive on heather *Calluna vulgaris* and numbers cannot be artificially buffered by introducing reared birds, unlike lowland species such as pheasant *Phasianus colchicus* (Hudson and Rands, 1988). In this chapter we seek to explain the workings of a grouse moor, and to document the contribution of grouse management to conserving and maintaining the unique character, landscape and wildlife of the uplands. However, the opportunities provided by grouse management must also be balanced against several conflicts, both actual and perceived; and these, too, will be discussed.

The extent of moorland managed for red grouse

Uplands in England cover 7,958 km^2 (land above the designated moorland line defined by the Department for Environment, Food and Rural Affairs [Defra]). Of this area, 4,428 km^2, is managed as grouse moors – 56 per cent of the total. The estimated extent of grouse moor management recorded in the early 1990s was 191 grouse moors in the highlands of Scotland (average size 52 km^2), 105 moors in the southern uplands of Scotland (average size 38 km^2), 153 moors in northern England (18 km^2) and 10 in Wales (8 km^2) (Hudson, 1992). Since 1992, the scale of grouse management will have decreased, with losses in Wales, Bowland and Cumbria, the southern uplands and the highlands of Scotland. Between 1990 and 2002, 495 upland estates returned data to the Game and Wildlife Conservation Trust's National Gamebag Census Scheme. Annual bags showed strong annual fluctuations. Bags were high until the outbreak of the Second World War, followed by a collapse during the war years. Numbers slowly recovered until the early 1970s, when a further 40 per cent decline was recorded over the next thirty years (Aebischer, 2005).

Much of the English uplands have been given special protection status under European Union designations because of their biodiversity values. In England, 74 per cent of upland Special Protection Areas (SPAs) are managed as grouse moors (Tapper, 2005). In the Peak District National Park (PDNP), 35,000 hectares of moorland are within the boundaries of estates managed for red grouse shooting – or 65 per cent of the PDNP upland area. Grouse moors also cover 70 per cent of the Peak District Special Area of Conservation (SAC) set up to protect and enhance specific habitats of international importance and 76 per cent of the Peak District SPA designations set up to protect areas which support internationally important populations of birds (Daplyn and Ewald, 2006). In the North York Moors National Park, 95 per cent of the SPA area is grouse moor (Tapper, 2005). Equivalent data are not available for Wales and Scotland, but grouse moors form a much smaller proportion of the total uplands in these countries.

Management for grouse

Grouse moor managers aim to produce a grouse surplus for shooting. Grouse numbers must be high enough in the late summer to provide a sufficiently large bag for sporting purposes, so that shooting income can cover the management costs. We present figures for a typical moor in the Peak District in Box 13.2. The *national* financial breakeven point for one gamekeeper covering 10 km² (2,500 acres) is 550 brace (pairs) of birds shot on this area. To do this, 3,300 birds need to be present if the harvest is to be sustainable. At densities less than 60 grouse per km², the employment of a gamekeeper is no longer financially viable; and, with the loss of the gamekeeper, it is argued that the associated management and benefits to biodiversity go too (Hudson, 1992).

Grouse moors are managed by gamekeepers and funded by private landowners or shoot tenants. They achieve harvestable levels of grouse by managing habitats and predators. When grouse densities begin to build, a nematode gut parasite *Trichostrongylus tenuis* can cause grouse densities to crash, and so disease control becomes a third management issue on some moors (Hudson, 1992, 1995; Hudson and Newborn, 1995).

Predator control

Gamekeepers seek to remove the predators of red grouse particularly in the early spring when red grouse begin to nest (Watson and Miller, 1976). Protecting the sitting hen as she incubates her eggs is especially important in determining grouse densities later in the season. The main predators of red grouse are foxes, carrion crows and stoats. Protected species, particularly the hen harrier *Circus cyaneus*, have also been shown to contribute to the reduction of a shootable surplus (Thirgood, Redpath, Haydon et al., 2000; Thirgood, Redpath, Rothery and Aebischer, 2000). This issue remains the biggest conflict surrounding grouse moor management (Etheridge et al., 1997).

Heather-burning

Red grouse use heather for nesting cover, shelter and food. Grouse prefer to feed on young heather growing on plants 2–6 years old (about 15–50 mm high). They need older heather for shelter and they nest in above average height heather (about 300 mm) (Campbell et al., 2002). Moulting grouse spend time under very tall heather to avoid predators. Grouse will also move to escape cover to avoid predation. Gamekeepers seek to provide heather of different heights in each grouse's territory (about 2 ha) by rotational burning (Watson and Miller, 1976).

Gamekeepers aim to burn heather once it gets too tall for grouse to feed on (above 300 mm high: Watson and Miller, 1976). Heather will regenerate from the root stock of burnt plants or from seed provided the plant is not too old or the fire not too hot. Root stock regeneration is best before the heather has become too mature and woody when stems are numerous, when stems are less than 10 mm thick at the base and the heather plant is between 10 and 20 years old (300–80 mm high). The ideal size of burn is 0.4 ha and is best-achieved in long narrow strips rather than in rectangular or circular patches. Strips should be no more than 30 m wide but can be any length – the longer the better, as grouse are reluctant to stray more than 15 m from tall cover to avoid predation. Strips are created so that tall heather remains down one long side to provide cover. Burning is carried out in England and Wales between 1 October and 15 April, and in Scotland between 1 October and 15 April but may be extended to 30 April. Exceptions are granted for wet springs and ground above 450 m, so that the date extends to 15 May (Defra, 2007). A typical burning rotation might last twelve to fifteen years (Watson and Miller, 1976).

Moorland management also requires grazing of the heather and invasive grasses to be controlled. Unrestricted grazing can cause harm to heather and has been responsible for the loss of large tracts in many areas. The concentration of sheep flocks through the winter by providing additional food has a detrimental impact on the heather by concentrating sheep in specific areas often on the moorland edge (Hudson, 1992; Lovegrove *et al.*, 1995). High sheep densities are not compatible with grouse management, so moor owners seek to control stocking rates on their tenanted land or take the grazing rights in hand so that damage can be minimised. One ewe to the hectare is considered a maximum to allow heather maintenance but can vary from 0.5 to 2.0 sheep per hectare according to the type of ground and the availability of other food (Hudson, 1992).

Conservation of biodiversity in the uplands

Moorland plant communities and their associated fauna are regarded as having great value because of their high conservation interest both nationally and internationally (Usher and Thompson, 1993; Thompson *et al.*, 1995). In the European drive for agricultural intensification, moorlands have been poorly regarded. Their conservation importance was greatly undervalued and suffered from agricultural intensification, afforestation and development (Condliffe; Crowle and McCormack, both this volume). The lowland heathland of Dorset has been all but destroyed or fragmented (Gimmingham, 1981). Elsewhere, Sweden and Denmark have lost between 60 per cent and 70 per cent of their moorland, and the Netherlands have lost 95 per cent of the heather present in 1835 (Gimmingham, 1981).

Only Britain has retained a substantial proportion of its heather moorland, and it is suggested that this is largely due to the presence of grouse-shooting. Shooting remained the only viable alternative to forestry, even when successive UK governments provided financial incentives to encourage tree-planting as an alternative to sheep and grouse. Between the 1940s and the 1980s heather declined by 25 per cent in Scotland and by 20 per cent in England and Wales, and the cause was attributed to the expansion of grassland and forestry (Mackey *et al.*, 1998). In Wales, where grouse management has been replaced by sheep-farming, reversion from heather to species-poor grassland followed. The Berwyn Mountains have lost 46 per cent of their heather moorland since 1946 (Lovegrove *et al.*, 1995). By the 1970s, Scotland had

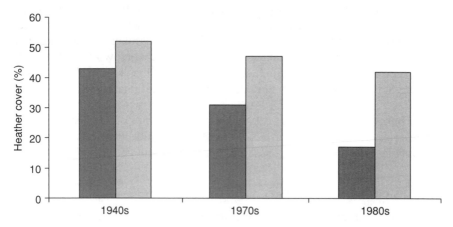

Figure 13.1 Percentage heather cover on moorland in Scotland where grouse moor management has either been retained or abandoned in the 1940s, 1970s and 1980s (dark grey: grouse moor abandoned; light grey: grouse moor retained; reproduced by kind permission by the Wildlife Biology Editorial Office from Robertson *et al.*, 2001).

lost 18 per cent of its heathland and 8 per cent of its blanket mire – some 62 per cent of this to subsidised forestry (Tudor and Mackay, 1995).

Evidence for the value of grouse management in retaining heather moorland comes from a study in Scotland in which Robertson *et al.* (2001) analysed historical aerial photographs. A random sample of sites photographed in the 1940s showed that 49 per cent were being managed as grouse moors. By the 1980s, fifty-seven sites remained as active grouse moors, and forty-six had given up. Over the forty-year period the grouse moors lost 24 per cent of their heather cover. Where the grouse-shooting was lost, the heather cover declined by 41 per cent (Figure 13.1).

Concerns over the loss of heather stimulated the production of a Biodiversity Action Plan for upland heathland, which set out targets for the retention of the nation's coverage of heather and other sensitive upland plants (Anon., 1995). The Action Plan identified overgrazing and poor burning practices as the cause of the deterioration and ultimate loss of shrub heath (see also Crowle and McCormack, this volume). Overgrazing results in a shift from heathland to unpalatable grasses and bracken encroachment. Grouse management seeks to implement grazing regimes that do not damage heather (Hudson and Newborn 1995).

Inappropriate burning has been implicated in the loss of heather (Tucker, 2004), damage to mosses (Vanduick *et al.*, 2005) and lichens (Coppins and Shimwell, 1971), and an increase in peat erosion following large, hot fires removing vegetation from the peatlands (Crowle and McCormack, this volume). However, Cornelissen *et al.* (2001) and Davies and Legg (2008) suggest that the diversity of some lichen communities declines as the biomass of vascular species and some bryophytes increases, and that disturbance is needed to maintain diversity. The most damaging larger fires are caused by graziers, by accident and by arson (McMorrow *et al.*, this volume), especially in areas of high fuel loads such as tall grasses or older, woody heather. Subsequent fires burn hot and damage the peat. Stands of long heather therefore represent a fire hazard, which could be mitigated by the rotational cooler burns set by gamekeepers. Large, even-aged stands of heather are potential fire risks, too, because the lack of fire-breaks makes their control almost impossible. However, even grouse moor fires can still get out of control!

Impacts on wider biodiversity

Many conservationists agree that grouse management retains heather moorland (Gimmingham, 1981; Magnusson, 1995; Brown and Bainbridge, 1995), but they have not agreed that such management helps support upland biodiversity. None the less, most of the English grouse moors are selected as designated sites under European law because of their high-density bird assemblages (Figure 13.2).

In 1995 and 1996, over 120 properties, covering 320 km^2 of upland habitat, were surveyed both on and off grouse moors for breeding birds (Tharme *et al.*, 2001). Red grouse were more numerous on grouse moors while carrion crow *Corvus corone*, hen harrier, meadow pipit *Anthus pratensis* and skylark *Alauda arvensis* were less abundant on grouse moors. Golden plover *Pluvialis apricaria*, curlew *Numenius arquata* and lapwing *Vanellus vanellus* were all much more abundant on grouse moors (Figure 13.3). Although these wader species are still relatively common, they are currently undergoing significant national population declines (Gibbons *et al.*, 1993). Individually positive correlations have been found between the abundance of golden plover and grouse bags and gamekeeper density (Hudson, 1992). Golden plover, curlew and redshank *Tringa tetanus* were found more frequently on upland managed by gamekeepers (Haworth and Thompson, 1990).

At a more localised level, the distribution of upland birds in relation to grouse management was determined using two repeat bird surveys in the Peak District National Park (Brown and Shepherd, 1991; Carr and Middleton, 2004). Some analyses of these surveys are published elsewhere (Pearce-Higgins *et al.*, 2006), where the amount of muirburn within land management units was taken as a measure of grouse moor management intensity; this is also included in a review of management effects on moorland birds (Pearce-Higgins *et al.*, this volume). Daplyn and Ewald (2006) examined the impact of the two separate aspects of grouse moor management (muirburn density and presence of a keeper) on this bird distribution data using information on levels of gamekeepering provided by the Game and Wildlife Conservation Trust, with habitat data provided by Defra and data on muirburn locations digitised by Moors for the Future from aerial photography

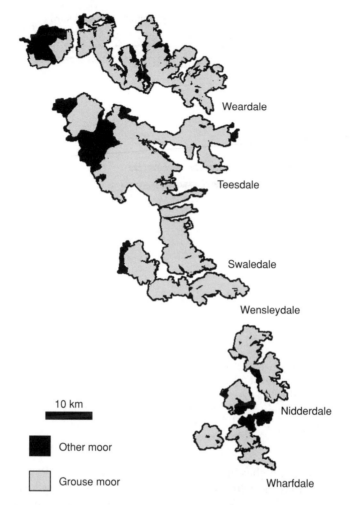

Figure 13.2 Map of the North Pennines Special Protection Area (SPA) showing the extent of moorland managed and not managed for red grouse. The North Pennines SPA was set up for curlew (3,390 breeding pairs listed as present in the designation), golden plover (1,400 pairs), dunlin (330 pairs), merlin (136 pairs), peregrine (15 pairs) and hen harrier (11 pairs).

(Getmapping). Separating muirburn from grouse keeper presence lets the effect of a management undertaken by a grouse keeper other than muirburn, including but not limited to predation control, be compared to the effect of muirburn. This analysis used statistical modelling of survey data to examine these effects and was not the result of an experimental investigation.

Differences were found between the habitat compositions of areas managed and not managed for grouse ($F_{4,31} = 4.70$, P = 0.004). A higher proportion of heath and mire cover were found on the areas managed for grouse

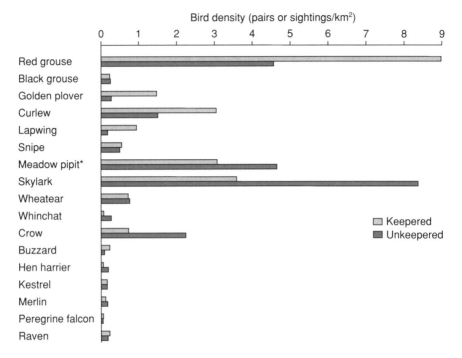

Figure 13.3 Breeding pairs of birds (per 100 ha) observed on 320 upland kilometer squares with similar vegetation types but separated into those managed for red grouse or those that were not managed. *Meadow pipits were very numerous and have been divided by ten on this graph (reproduced by permission of Blackwell Publishing from Tharme *et al.*, 2001).

(Figure 13.4) and a higher incidence of muirburn ($t_{32} = 2.43$, P = 0.020). Bird data sets (densities in 1990 and 2004, and change in density from 1990 to 2004) were analysed at the estate level using generalised linear modelling and at the local (1 km²) scale using generalised linear mixed models. This permitted testing for differences between areas managed and not managed for grouse, while controlling for habitat and the proportion of each estate/area that was burnt. The analysis at the local scale corrected for spatial autocorrelation, as well as for habitat and muirburn. Habitats were classed into four groups with (1) grasses: grassland, marsh, tall herb and fern communities, (2) heath and mire: cotton grass moorlands, dwarf shrub heath, eroding moorland and blanket bog, (3) woodland: woodland and shrub communities, and (4) other (see Figure 13.4).

After controlling for burning and habitat composition, three moorland birds of conservation concern were found at higher densities in 1990 and 2004 on grouse estates and at a local level (the 1 km² scale) where grouse keepers were present (controlling for burning, habitat and spatial autocorrelation);

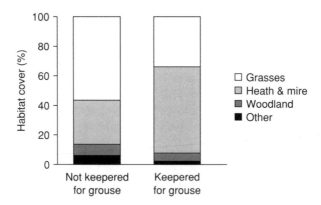

Figure 13.4 Percentage habitat composition of four vegetation types on moorland in the Peak District National Park on estates managed or not managed for red grouse (compositional analysis: $F_{12,87} = 5.76$, $P < 0.001$).

these were dunlin *Calidris alpina*, golden plover and red grouse (Table 13.1). Reed bunting *Emberiza schoeniclus* density was lower on grouse estates and grouse-managed areas (local scale) in both years. In 1990 curlew and snipe *Gallinago gallinago* density were lower on estates managed as grouse moors. In 1990 the density of ring ouzel *Turdus torquatus* was positively related to the presence of a grouse keeper at both the estate and the local level, with twite *Carduelis flavirostris* density higher on areas with a grouse keeper at only the local scale in 1990. At the local scale the density of wheatear *Oenanthe oenanthe* on areas with a grouse keeper was lower in both 1990 and 2004, while the density of whinchat *Saxicola rubetra* was lower in 1990.

The analysis of the changes in bird density at the estate level (again controlling for habitat and muirburn) revealed that only for dunlin was there a positive effect of the presence of a grouse keeper; the relative decrease in dunlin density between 1990 and 2004 was less on gamekeepered areas than on non-gamekeepered areas. Changes in ring ouzel density were positively related to the presence of muirburn, while changes in twite density were negatively related to muirburn. At the local scale (again controlling for habitat, muirburn and spatial autocorrelation), positive relationships were found between the presence of a grouse keeper and changes in the density of four birds species, namely dunlin, golden plover, red grouse and whinchat. A negative relationship was found between changes in the density of ring ouzel, at the local scale and the presence of a grouse keeper.

Daplyn and Ewald (2006) found that the highest number of changes in the density of birds of conservation concern between 1990 and 2004 were associated with habitat (Table 13.1) – a similar finding to Pearce-Higgins *et al.* (2006). The two approaches differed particularly in their measures of grouse moor management. Pearce-Higgins *et al.* (2006) used density of

Table 13.1 Comparisons in the density of moorland birds of conservation concern on areas managed for grouse shooting within the Peak District National Park in 1990 and 2004, and relationships between habitat, density of muirburn and presence of a grouse gamekeeper with changes in the density of these birds from 1990 to 2004. Analysis was undertaken at both the estate and the local (1 km²) level. The analysis at the estate level compared the effect of habitat, muirburn and keeper presence simultaneously, whilst the analysis at the local level controlled for spatial location and habitat through the use of generalised linear mixed models. Minus symbols indicate a negative relationship, plus symbols indicate a positive one. Details of analysis in Daplyn and Ewald (2006).

| Bird species | Density on keepered moorlands | | | | Change in bird density from 1990 to 2004 | | | | |
| | 1990 | | 2004 | | Estate level analysis | | | Local level analysis | |
	Estate	Local	Estate	Local	Habitat	Muirburn	Keeper	Muirburn	Keeper
Curlew	-*				**			+**	
Dunlin	+*	+***	+**	+***	***		+*		+***
Golden plover	+***	+***	+***	+***	***				+***
Lapwing					***			+**	
Meadow pipit					**			-*	
Red grouse	+*	+***	+**	+**	***				+***
Reed bunting	-**	-*	-***	-***	***			-**	
Ring ouzel	+*	+*			**	+*		+**	
Skylark					***			-*	
Snipe	-***				***			-*	
Twite		+**			***	-***			-**
Wheatear		-***		-*	**			-***	
Whinchat		-***		-*	***			-***	+**

* P < 0.05 ** P < 0.01 *** P ≤ 0.001.

Table 13.2 Percentage losses in breeding range of three moorland birds in different regions where grouse shooting has been retained (N England) compared with areas where it has been lost (Wales and SW England). Data from BTO Bird Atlases for 1970s and 1990 (Gibbons *et al.*, 1993; Sharrock, 1976).

	N England	Wales	SW England
Red grouse	−13%	−36%	−66%
Dunlin	−7%	−25%	−75%
Golden plover	−8%	−32%	−50%

muirburn; whilst Daplyn and Ewald (2006) included two measures of grouse moor management: muirburn and the presence of a gamekeeper employed to produce a shootable surplus of red grouse and whose duties include the legal control of predators in order to do this. Pearce-Higgins *et al.* (2006), who analysed in great detail the habitat associations of different bird species, also used different measures of habitat composition, differentiating between heather, cotton grass and non-heather dwarf shrub communities as well as accounting for vegetation structure and topography. This may account for some of the differences in results. Daplyn and Ewald (2006) found more effects of management, muirburn and gamekeepering than did Pearce-Higgins *et al.* (2006), but the difference in the measures between the two studies should be borne in mind. Daplyn and Ewald (2006) found that increasing amounts of muirburn were associated with one positive and one negative relationship with changes in bird density between 1990 and 2004 at the estate level and three positive and six negative relationships at the more localised level, in addition to the results above for the presence of a grouse keeper. Comparing the analysis of change in bird density between the two approaches, Daplyn and Ewald (2006) found more positive relationships with the two aspects of keepering they examined than did Pearce-Higgins *et al.* (2006) with their one measurement of the effect of grouse moor management. Both of the analyses suffer from the fact that the surveys are two snapshots in time, making comparisons between them difficult, and with difficulties regarding measures of habitat and muirburn.

The analyses of the Peak District data rely on surveys of existing land use and so therefore lack the rigour of an experimental investigation. This is needed, if we are to find out what caused the differences between species on moors managed and not managed for grouse. At present it cannot be said with complete certainty if differences were caused by predator control or habitat management (specifically muirburn). Such an experiment began in 2000 in Northumberland and is scheduled to finish in 2008. Although the final conclusions are yet to be reached, this is one of the largest and longest experiments of its kind (Box 13.1).

Neither the Peak District surveys nor our experiment address how well waders are doing at the much wider scale at which grouse management is

---

Box 13.1. The Uplands Predation Experiment

The Uplands Predation Experiment investigates whether predator removal by moorland gamekeepers improves numbers and breeding success of moorland birds. The project takes place on four plots, each about 12 km² (1,200 hectares), on which bird numbers and breeding success have been monitored since 2000. There are two long-term plots with fixed treatments, with predator control (Ray Demesne) and without (Emblehope). For the other two plots, treatment was switched over in autumn 2004 with predator control at Otterburn between 2001 and 2004 and at Bellshiel between 2004 and 2008. The switch-over allows us to study breeding success and abundance on the same plot with and without predator removal. Predator control began in 2001; but, because data collection faltered owing to the outbreak of foot-and-mouth disease, 2002 is regarded as the first post-treatment year on the long-term plots.

On the long-term plots, predator indices on the keepered plots indicated low numbers of all the main predators compared to the unkeepered plot. In the second spring since keepering commenced on the switch plot, Bellshiel, the indices for foxes and crows were 70 per cent and 90 per cent lower respectively, compared with the average during unkeepered years. The stopping of predator control on the other switch plot, Otterburn, was linked to an increase in foxes, from 0.24 scats/km on average in the keepered years to 0.34 scats/km in 2006, and an increase in crows from 0.03 crows/km on average in keepered years to 0.9 crows/km in 2006.

In the years with predator control on the long-term keepered Ray Demesne plot, 120 of the 211 nesting attempts by curlew, golden plover and lapwing fledged chicks (57 per cent) (Figure 13.5). On the long-term unkeepered Emblehope plot, 11 out of 51 nesting attempts by waders fledged chicks over the same period (22 per cent) (Figure 13.5). In 2006, 3 out of 30 nesting attempts by waders fledged chicks (10 per cent) on the unkeepered Otterburn plot, compared to 60 out of 86 attempts (71 per cent) in the years when the plot was keepered (Figure 13.5). The opposite trend occurred on keepered Bellshiel with 5 out of the 8 wader nesting attempts fledging chicks (63 per cent) in 2006 compared to 4 out of the 51 attempts (8 per cent) during the unkeepered phase (Fletcher, 2006).

---

undertaken. If the breeding ranges of upland bird species and how they have changed between successive breeding atlases (Sharrock, 1976; Gibbons *et al.*, 1993) are analysed, we can detect large area differences (Table 13.2). The declines in range of three species of upland ground-nesting birds were lowest in areas of northern England where a high proportion of the land is

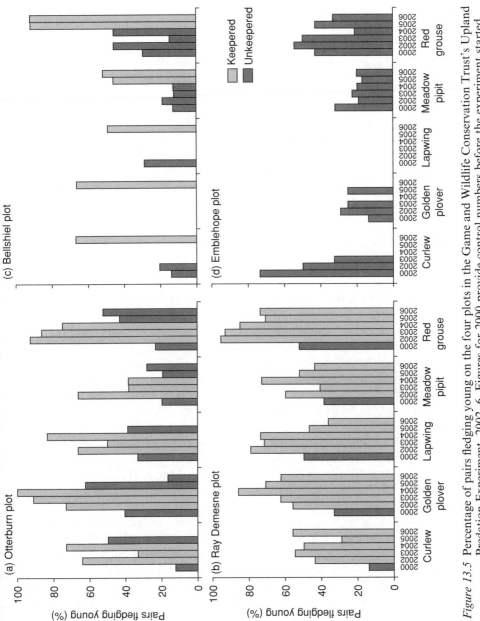

Figure 13.5 Percentage of pairs fledging young on the four plots in the Game and Wildlife Conservation Trust's Upland Predation Experiment, 2002–6. Figures for 2000 provide control numbers before the experiment started.

managed for red grouse compared to two areas where red grouse management is absent and where large range contractions were evident (Table 13.2, Tapper 2005). For lapwing, Wilson *et al.* (2001) found that range declines were 77 per cent in Wales and 64 per cent in south-west England. In Yorkshire/Humberside (a region which included the heavily managed North York Moors and North Pennines) range declines were only 28 per cent. However, the presence of grouse moors is not the only determinant of wader numbers in the UK, nor is the lack of grouse management the only factor causing the decline of waders throughout the UK (Pearce-Higgins *et al.*, this volume). There is evidence for wader decline in the North Pennines where grouse moors predominate and for wader increase in areas such as the Outer Hebrides where grouse management is absent (Sim *et al.*, 2005). However, the impact of grouse moor management can only be addressed when accurate maps of grouse moors are available or detailed management of wader survey squares has been quantified. Such data rarely exist, and so such detailed analyses are rare.

Challenges to grouse moor management

Birds of prey

Many species of raptor feed on grouse; and, despite the recent resurgence of several raptors from very low densities, most species can be tolerated on grouse moors as long as numbers do not rise too far. The one exception to this rule is the hen harrier, which represents a serious impediment to grouse-shooting and therefore the economic driver that provides the management of so much of the British uplands. Hen harrier populations have been recovering since the 1970s, although the current increase does not include English grouse moors, where they are mostly absent or fall below their predicted density (Potts, 1998).

The lack of scientific quantification of the effect of hen harriers on red grouse prompted an investigation on Langholm Moor in south-west Scotland between 1992 and 1997. The Joint Raptor Study (JRS) (Redpath and Thirgood, 1997) was able to assess the extent of predation by raptors on red grouse. For 1995 and 1996, it was calculated that half the autumn stock of grouse was killed by birds of prey, and these losses were compounded in successive years (Thirgood, Redpath, Haydon *et al.*, 2000). During the JRS, the hen harrier population increased from two to twenty nesting pairs on the moor. At the same time, the grouse cycle, driven by parasites, was going through a low. The grouse population at Langholm, in the presence of this number of hen harriers, was unable to withstand the losses and continued to decline instead of recovering as expected. On adjacent moors with many fewer hen harriers, populations of grouse in the same phase of their parasite cycle recovered, and shooting was resumed. Not so at Langholm; grouse-shooting was stopped and the gamekeepers redeployed (Thirgood, Redpath, Rothery and Aebischer, 2000). Grouse numbers in the absence of game-keepering have remained low. Nesting pairs of hen harriers decreased to two pairs. In 2006, four pairs nested, but three failed to rear any chicks. Field signs suggested that the cause of mortality was fox predation. Also, since game-keepering ceased, the numbers of waders have fallen to very low densities (Baines *et al.*, 2008).

If hen harriers were responsible for the decrease in grouse numbers of Langholm Moor, how many other grouse moors might suffer the same fate? Smith *et al.* (2001) calculated that about half the current grouse moors would experience similar outcomes to Langholm, described as being very typical of many moors, if hen harriers were allowed to build up in the same way. Here is a conflict in need of resolution. National populations of hen harriers need to be safeguarded but not at the expense of good management that safeguards a unique habitat and its accompanying wildlife. Grouse moors need to support some hen harriers but possibly not more than unkeepered ground.

Other ecosystem services

Other chapters of this book describe in greater detail the impacts of heather management on issues such as water quality (colour) and carbon sequestra-tion. There is still considerable concern expressed over the impact of heather-burning on the environment (Tucker, 2004). However, in recent sub-missions to an independent Defra expert panel charged with reviewing sci-entific evidence with the purpose of making changes to the current Burning Regulations and Codes of Practice for England, the panel concluded that there was not sufficient scientifically robust evidence produced to justify any changes regarding burning dates (Glaves and Haycock, 2005). Much uncer-tainty existed as to the causes of observed problems, and many conflicting opinions as to likely mechanisms were put forward. However, because the evidence produced was not good enough to prove a problem, that does not mean that problems do not exist. Research is needed to address the impact of heather-burning on biodiversity, carbon flux, wildlife prevention and other ecosystem services, and some important studies are currently under-way in the Peak District National Park to help resolve these conflicts.

The economic driver

Much upland habitat is in private ownership. Hudson (1992) estimated that there were 459 grouse moors in the UK, employing 480 grouse keepers in Scotland and 223 in England. A recent study calculated that these moors employed the equivalent of 120 full-time jobs managing heather and pro-viding 5,700 shooting days per year (PACEC, 2006).

On each shoot day, upwards of thirty people will be employed as beaters, flankers or with trained dogs to retrieve the game. In the winter months, grouse-shooting provides rural employment in these Less Favoured Areas (LFAs). This was calculated to be worth £14.7 million in staff wages in Scotland in the early 1990s and to have supported 904 full-time jobs in hotels and pubs (McGilvray, 1995). Grouse-shooting represents 12 per cent of the total UK shooting provision, calculated as being worth £1.6 billion to the UK economy. In other words, £120 million was spent in the UK uplands from grouse-shooting in the good grouse years (PACEC, 2006). In years when the grouse crash, these funds are sorely missed in the rural communities. Running costs for a typical grouse moor in the Peak District National Park are outlined in Box 13.2.

Box 13.2. Economics of a grouse moor estate in the Peak District National Park

In the Peak District National Park, an average annual density of 350 pairs each spring on a 1,000 hectare moor would be a realistic objective (although that density is well below the national financial breakeven level of 550 brace). If one aims to achieve four chicks per pair on average, experience dictates that an annual shootable surplus of 700 birds can be taken. This takes into account losses to disease, predation, accident and emigration off the moor, and it allows for the stock of 350 pairs to be maintained.

The opportunity to shoot 350 brace of red grouse can produce revenue of around £50,000 (£140 per brace). The costs of producing those grouse are outlined in Table 13.3.

Even in a reasonable year, outgoings exceed income. Most grouse moor owners do not seek to make a profit, in the same way that no one expects to make a profit from joining a golf club. However, in poor breeding years, because of parasite-driven crashes or bad weather in late May reducing chick survival, the losses increase, even to the point at which no shooting takes place and all the costs must be borne without an income.

Similarly, the sheep enterprise on the 1,000 hectares only generates an income of about £12,000 (600 lambs @ £20). Prices vary from £15 to £25 each. The costs to be covered as well as the shepherd's wages may well include grazing during the winter months (50p per ewe per week), and extra food adds another £6,000 with shearing, vets' bills, fuel and equipment (fencing, and so on) also to be added, leaving a total cost of about £29,000. So the moorland estate's sheep run at an annual loss of £17,000, only possible historically because headage payments at £13 per ewe produced £13,000, topped up by the Hill Farm Allowance at £19 per hectare providing another £19,000.

Table 13.3 The costs of a grouse moor in the Peak District.

Item	Annual costs (£)
Keeper costs	20,500
Insurance	6,000
Housing costs	9,250
Operating costs	15,000
Beater's wages	4,000
Heather burning	2,000
TOTAL	**56,750**

The only way sheep-farming can break even financially without subsidy is to cut out extra feeding and to keep them on the moor throughout the year. However, this is detrimental to the habitat, and on many uplands sheep numbers are reduced to protect moorland biodiversity. Therefore, moorland sheep farming is currently not economically sustainable (for national statistics, see Condliffe, this volume).

At present, predators, disease and weather take their share of the annual grouse surplus. If this level of loss due to predation were to increase, as happened at Langholm (Thirgood, Redpath, Rothery and Aebischer, 2000) and throughout almost all of the Welsh uplands (Lovegrove *et al.*, 1995), driven grouse would cease to be of value. When that happens, the gamekeepers would be redeployed and the last remaining privately funded revenue source from the estate's heather moorland would disappear.

Conclusion and outlook

Management of the uplands by private landowners motivated by red grouse shooting is a powerful force in the uplands. Moorland management for red grouse serves three important purposes.

- It maintains a multiple land-use system. It provides the labour and management skills to maintain heather habitats; usually it is only the shooting estates that care for heather moorland and, in doing so, maintain a multiple system. Without grouse the heather would probably be replaced by a single land-use practice such as sheep-grazing or commercial afforestation, and both may conflict with the conservation objectives in the uplands. Conversely, if made the responsibility of the public sector, the protection of heather without grouse management would require huge additional amounts of public funding.
- It indirectly supports conservation objectives. Heather moorland is a habitat of international importance for rare plants and animals, and management for grouse helps support them.

- It provides important income and community support in these Less Favoured Areas. Shooting provides employment, attracts income into upland areas, and helps support ancillary activities (hotels, B&Bs, restaurants and catering) during off-peak seasons.

Grouse moor management plays an important role in conservation and local economics. Heather has been lost at nearly twice the rate where grouse-shooting has been abandoned compared to where it has been retained. Grouse moor management has retained and is currently providing important habitats for some upland birds. However, one of the stumbling-blocks to the acceptance of such virtues is the low densities and poor breeding success of hen harriers on grouse moors in England. Site designation is not enough. Real compromise and conflict resolution are needed urgently to improve the conservation status of raptors in the uplands and retain economically viable management for red grouse. Burning heather for grouse also has its critics, and sound research is urgently needed to identify problems and their solutions with respect to the impacts of burning on carbon sequestration and water quality.

However, before we abandon grouse moor management, it is important to be aware of what it is capable of delivering for our wildlife, rural economies and social cohesion in our upland habitats.

References

Aebischer, N. J. (2005) Long-term bag trends of three gamebirds, *Game and Wildlife Conservation Trust Annual Review for 2004*. Fordingbridge, 78–9.

Anon. (1995) *Biodiversity: The UK Steering Group Report – Meeting the Rio Challenge*. HMSO, London. http://www.ukbap.org.uk/Library/Tranche1.pdf

Baines, D., Redpath, S., Richardson, M. and Thirgood, S. (2008) The direct and indirect effects of predation by hen harriers on some moorland birds. *Ibis.* (Suppl. 1), **150**, 27–36.

Brown, A. F. and Bainbridge, I. P. (1995) Grouse moors and upland breeding birds. *Heaths and Moorlands: Cultural Landscapes* (ed. D. B. A. Thompson, A. J. Hester and M. B. Usher), pp. 51–66. Edinburgh: HMSO.

Brown, A. F. and Shepherd, K. B. (1991) *Breeding Birds of the South Pennine Moors*. Joint Nature Conservation Committee Report No. 7, Peterborough.

Campbell, S., Smith, A., Redpath, S. and Thirgood, S. (2002) Nest site characteristics and nest success in red grouse *Lagopus lagopus scoticus*. *Wildlife Biology*, **8**, 169–74.

Carr, G. and Middleton, P. (2004) *Breeding Bird Survey of the Peak District Moorlands*. Moors for the Future Report No. 1, Moors for the Future Partnership, Edale.

Coppins, B. and Shimwell, D. (1971) Cryptogam complement and biomass in dry *Calluna* heath of different ages. *Oikos*, **22**, 204–9.

Cornelissen, J., Callaghan, T. and Alatalo, J. (2001) Global change and arctic ecosystems: is lichen decline a function of increases in vascular plant biomass? *Journal of Ecology*, **89**, 984–94.

Daplyn, J. and Ewald, J. A. (2006) *Birds, Burning and Grouse Moor Management.* Small grant project report prepared for Moors for the Future Partnership, Edale.

Davies, G. and Legg, C. (2008) The effect of traditional management burning on lichen diversity. *Applied Vegetation Science* doi:10.3170/2008-7-18566.

Defra (2007) *The Heather and Grass Burning Code.* Defra, London. http://www. defra.gov.uk/rural/pdfs/uplands/hg-burn2007.pdf

Ethridge, B., Summers, R. W. and Green, R. E. (1997) The effects of illegal killing and destruction of nests by humans on the population dynamics of the hen harrier *Circus cyaneus* in Scotland. *Journal of Applied Ecology*, **34**, 1081–105.

Fletcher, K. (2006) Predator control and ground nesting waders. *Game and Wildlife Conservation Trust Annual Review for 2005.* Fordingbridge, 80–3.

Gibbons, D. W., Reid, J. B. and Chapman, R. A. (1993) *The New Atlas of Breeding Birds of Britain and Ireland 1998–1991.* Berkhamsted: Poyser.

Gimmingham, C. H. (1981) Conservation: European heathlands. *Heathland and Related Shrublands of the World. B. Analytical studies* (ed. R. L. Specht), pp. 249–59. Amsterdam: Elsevier Scientific Publishing.

Glaves, D. and Haycock, N. (2005) *Defra Review of the Heather and Grass Burning Regulations and Code: Science Panel Assessment of the Effects of Burning on Biodiversity, Soils and Hydrology.* http://www.defra.gov.uk/rural/pdfs/uplands/science-panel-full-report.pdf.

Haworth, P. F. and D. B. A. Thompson (1990) Factors associated with the breeding distribution of upland birds in the South Pennines, England. *Journal of Applied Ecology*, **27**, 562–77.

Hudson, P. J. (1992) *Grouse in Space and Time: The Population Biology of a Managed Gamebird.* Fordingbridge: Game Conservancy.

Hudson, P. J. (1995) Ecological trends and grouse management in upland Britain. *Heaths and Moorlands: Cultural Landscapes* (ed. D. B. A. Thompson, A. J. Hester and M. B. Usher), pp. 282–93. Edinburgh: HMSO.

Hudson, P. J. and Newborn, D. (1995) *Red Grouse and Moorland Management.* Fordingbridge: Game Conservancy.

Hudson, P. J. and Rands, M. R. W. (1988) *Ecology and Management of Gamebirds.* Oxford: BSP Professional Books.

Lovegrove, R., Shrubb, M. and Williams, I. (1995) *Silent Fields: The Current Status of Farmland Birds in Wales.* Newtown: Royal Society for the Protection of Birds.

McGilvray, J. (1995) *An Economic Study of Grouse Moors.* Fordingbridge: Game Conservancy.

Mackay, E., Shewry, M. and Tudor, G. (1998) *Landcover Change: Scotland from the 1940s to the 1980s.* Edinburgh: The Stationery Office.

Magnusson, M. (1995) Foreword. *Heaths and Moorlands: Cultural Landscapes* (ed. D. B. A. Thompson, A. J. Hester and M. B. Usher), pp. xii–xvi. Edinburgh: The Stationery Office.

PACEC (2006) *The Economic and Environmental Impact of Sporting Shooting.* A report prepared by Public and Corporate Economic Consultants (PACEC) on behalf of BASC, CA, and CLA and in association with GCT, Cambridge. http://www.shootingfacts.co.uk/

Pearce-Higgins, J., Breale, C., Wilson, J. and Bonn, A. (2006) *Analysis of Moorland Breeding Bird Distribution and Change in the Peak District.* Moors for the Future Report No. 11. Moors for the Future Partnership, Edale.

Potts, G. R. (1998) Global dispersion of nesting hen harriers (*Circus cyaneus*): implications for grouse moors in the UK. *Ibis*, **140**, 76–88.

Redpath, S. M. and Thirgood, S. J. (1997) *Birds of Prey and Red Grouse.* London: The Stationery Office.

Robertson, P. A., Park, K. J. and Barton, A. F. (2001) Loss of heather *Calluna vulgaris* moorland in the Scottish uplands: the role of red grouse *Lagopus lagopus scoticus* management. *Wildlife Biology*, **7**, 11–16.

Sharrock, J. T. R. (1976) *The Atlas of Breeding Birds in Britain and Ireland.* Tring: BTO.

Sim, I., Gregory, R., Hancock, M. and Brown, A. (2005) Recent changes in the abundance of British upland breeding birds. *Bird Study*, **52**, 261–75.

Smith, A. A., Redpath, S. M., Campbell, S. T. and Thirgood, S. J. (2001) Meadow pipits, red grouse and habitat characteristics of managed grouse moors. *Journal of Applied Ecology*, **38**, 390–400.

Tapper, S. (1992) *Game Heritage: An Ecological Review from Shooting and Gamekeeping Records.* Fordingbridge: Game Conservancy.

Tapper, S. (2005) *Nature's Gain: How Gamebird Management Has Influenced Wildlife Conservation.* Fordingbridge: Game Conservancy.

Tharme, A. P., Green, R. E., Baines, D., Bainbridge, I. P. and O'Brien, M. (2001) The effect of management for red grouse shooting on the population density of breeding birds on heather-dominated moorland. *Journal of Applied Ecology*, **38**, 439–57.

Thirgood, S. J., Redpath, S. M., Haydon, T. J., Rothery, P., Newton, I. and Hudson, P. J. (2000) Habitat loss and raptor predation: disentangling long and short-term causes of red grouse declines. *Proceedings of the Royal Society of London*, B, **267**, 651–6.

Thirgood, S. J., Redpath, S. M., Rothery, P. and Aebischer, N. J. (2000) Raptor predation and population limitation in red grouse. *Journal of Animal Ecology*, **69**, 504–16.

Thompson, D., MacDonald, A., Marsden, A. and Galbraith, C. (1995) Upland heather moorland in Great Britain: a review of international importance, regulation change and some objectives for nature conservation. *Biological Conservation*, **71**, 163–78.

Tucker, D. (2004) *Review of the Impacts of Heather and Grassland Burning in the Uplands on Soils, Hydrology and Biodiversity.* Report to English Nature No. 550, Peterborough. http://www.english-nature.org.uk/pubs/publication/PDF/550.pdf

Tudor, G. J. and Mackay, E. C. (1995) Upland land cover change in post-war Scotland. *Heaths and Moorlands: Cultural Landscapes* (ed. D. B. A. Thompson, A. J. Hester and M. B. Usher), pp. 28–42. Edinburgh: The Stationery Office.

Usher, M. and Thompson, D. (1993) Variation in the upland heathlands of Great Britain: conservation importance. *Biological Conservation*, **66**, 69–81.

Vanduik, V., Heegaerd, E., Maren, I. E. and Aarrestad, P. A. (2005) Managing heterogeneity: the importance of grazing and environmental variations on post-fire succession in heathlands. *Journal of Applied Ecology*, **42**, 139–49.

Watson, A. and Miller, G. R. (1976) *Grouse Management.* Fordingbridge: Game Conservancy.

Wilson, A. M., Vickery, J. A. and Browne, S. J. (2001) Numbers and distribution of northern lapwings *Vanellus vanellus* breeding in England and Wales in 1998. *Bird Study*, **48**, 2–17.

14 Moors from the past

Bill Bevan

Introduction

Britain's uplands have an important place in landscape history. While they have often been perceived as marginal to lowland settlement, they have been subject to changing land use and subsequently land cover, leading to today's rich socio-cultural landscapes. Uplands are not untouched wildernesses, but cultural creations shaped by millennia of past human activity.

The uplands have been a rich source of natural resources since the first human settlements following the end of the last Ice Age, providing fuel (peat, wood), building materials (timber, stone), water, minerals (metal ores), and productive land for raising livestock (pastures and meadows) (Simmons, 2003). During the last thousand years – approximately a tenth of the history of moorlands following the retreat of the glaciers approximately 8000 BP – strong drivers of change in the uplands have been social organisation, agricultural policy, industrialisation and urbanisation to meet the continuing demand for the provision of ecosystem goods and services. This chapter will focus on important aspects of upland land use and change during this period, and demonstrate the importance of the study of archaeological sites and historical documents in understanding environmental and social change.

As most of the British uplands are covered by moorlands, the good levels of preservation afforded by peatlands make the uplands a rich source of palaeo-environmental evidence that provides data from which past land uses and settlement patterns can be interpreted dating back to the last Ice Age. Well-preserved material remains, artefacts and environmental deposits can be interpreted alongside historical maps and documents to study how past individual experience actively inter-related with wider social structures across space and time. In more intensively managed lowland landscapes these have often been destroyed. Therefore, in many instances, the history of moorlands can inform wider social trends that help us to understand national histories during the last thousand years.

Here, I present a historical biography that will chart the life of moorlands from the early medieval period onwards, starting with the time of the Domesday Book, 'published' in 1086, to the modern day, with particular reference to case studies from the Peak District. These case studies are based on fieldwork and research in the Burbage valley for the Moors for the Future partnership and in the Upper Derwent valley for the Upper Derwent Officers' Working Group with the Peak District National Park Authority (Bevan, 2003, 2004, 2006; see also Barnatt and Smith, 2004).

Medieval wastes

The biography begins when the moorlands have already been long established following extensive woodland clearance and the dominance of livestock grazing originating in the Neolithic. The sub-montane uplands of medieval Britain can generally be characterised as a mix of dispersed farmstead settlement associated with small irregular fields in the valleys, woodlands and moorlands. Moors were the open marginal unimproved lands beyond the enclosed and cultivated land, often referred to as forest or waste in landowning documents and under the direct control of the lords of the manors they were within, as recorded in the Domesday Book. Most of these moorlands were commons, and they formed an important component of land use during the medieval period (Rackham, 1986). Tenants had various rights over moorland common such as pasturing livestock, cutting peat (turbary), quarrying stone and collecting plants such as bracken, berries and brushwood. Long-distance routeways crossed moorlands and can often be seen to fan out from the tight confines of walled lanes when they reach the moorland. In some remote areas the moorlands were visited by sheep farming families, who moved livestock seasonally and lived in temporary dwellings known as shielings. Vast tracts of moorland in England and Wales were also incorporated into the royal and baronial hunting forests that the Normans created out of Anglo-Viking estates (Aston, 1985).

However, the boundary between field and moor was never stationary, though in some places, such as the central Lakeland fells, they were separated by a continuous boundary known variously as a ring garth or head dike that became enshrined in legal documents and tradition as a significant local landmark. These ring garths can still often be traced on the ground or on maps long after further moorland has been enclosed beyond them. That there are fields beyond them shows that the edges of moorlands were continually being taken into enclosure, an activity that has left a rich vein of field names called 'intake' in northern England. It could be impossible to say when this practice started, but it is probably as old as moorland commons and the setting of boundaries between tenanted farmland and moorland are themselves. In the Lake District there are often small irregular walled fields tacked on to the outside of ring garths, and these are generally thought to be sixteenth-century in date (Winchester, 1987). It is thought that increased demand for produce as a result of growing towns promoted this enclosure into less productive land. In actual fact, trying to enclose and farm moorland pre-dates the Norman Conquest. Small early medieval enclosures, known as assarts, can be found throughout the uplands, some of which may have first been settled as shielings. The medieval settlement history of the Lake District is a continual story of permanently settling further and further into the central fells by converting shielings to farmsteads (Winchester, 1987). Lawrence Field near Burbage Moor in the Peak District is a good example of a 'failed' assart. As large as four football pitches, and enclosed within a low earth-and-stone bank, it occupies a low-lying shelf above the Derwent valley and probably dates to the eleventh or twelfth century. Many other similar locations are now occupied by farms and have probably been continually worked for a thousand years or more. Surviving thirteenth-century records for the Royal Forest of the Peak list twenty-two cases of illegally creating enclosed cultivated land and 131 cases of illegal building (Cox, 1905). In both types of case, the enclosures and the buildings were usually allowed to remain, with the people concerned being fined, having to pay annual fees per acre and their heirs double rent for the first year after inheriting the land. The boundary of the moorland continued to be pushed further out by families trying to create new farms out of the moorland and by farmers enclosing fields next to their existing farms.

Monasteries also played an important part in the medieval history of moorland land use. Landowners had granted moorland to monasteries since the seventh century, and after the Norman Conquest there was a large expansion in such grants by the new ruling classes (Aston, 2000). These patrons were motivated by the desire to have prayers said in ecclesiastic foundations for their souls and their families, which would hopefully ensure their passage to heaven, and advance their social status through the amount of money granted and the order chosen to receive it. By the twelfth century, the Benedictine and Cluniac orders were well established in England, and a rash of new orders were being formed by those who felt that the existing orders had strayed from the monastic ideal by indulging in too many home comforts (Aston, 2000). Many of these new orders were founded in the twelfth century: Cistercian, Carthusian and Grandmontine monks, Knights Templars and Hospitallers, and the canonical orders of the Augustinians, Gilbertines and – of direct relevance to the Upper Derwent – Premonstratensians. The new orders looked to establish their monasteries in remote locations, idealising the concept of the biblical wilderness within the context of European landscapes. The Cistercians actually developed wilderness foundation myths to construct a moral, or spiritual, landscape rather than to adhere to a strict representation of reality (Menuge, 2000).

Much of the High Peak moorland was part of the Royal Forest of the Peak, which was administered from Castleton and Peak Forest (Kerry, 1893). Rights to cut peat and to pasture livestock on commons within the Royal Forest date to at least the thirteenth century (Cox, 1905). At least three monasteries were granted estates in the High Peak: the Premonstratensian Welbeck Abbey in the Upper Derwent, Basingwerk in Longdendale and Merivale in Glossop.

Mapping the moorlands

From the sixteenth century onwards, changing landowning patterns brought major changes to the use and perception of the moorlands. The dissolution of the monasteries and the disafforestation of many forests brought more moorland commons under secular, non-royal ownership throughout Britain. The new owners were local gentry – a class that rose to greater influence and prominence during the seventeenth and eighteenth centuries, largely through the exploitation of property, which came to define their class (Daniels, 1990). A land-based social hierarchy was established comprising landlord, small freeholder, tenant farmer and landless agricultural labourer (Bunce, 1994). Fluid property markets and upward mobility in society led to increasing investment in land and the acquisition of greater swathes of the rural landscape by the aristocracy and yeoman farmers (Butlin, 1982). Property came to define the ruling classes; and as land became the basis of economic wealth, social status and political authority, so the influence of the landed gentry increased (Daniels, 1990). The management of estates was bound up with the creation of the landowners' identity as part of the elite classes, the methods of overseeing estates providing a metaphor for the nation state and its governance. As landowners, the gentry were considered natural statesmen with a leading role to play in the nation as a whole. In their desire to catalogue their estates, landowners produced increasingly detailed estate records, which included the first maps of many moorland areas. There is a series of beautifully drawn seventeenth-century maps of the Duke of Devonshire's estates which are some of the earliest maps of the Peak District's moorlands. It is during this period that the moorlands come out of the shadows to be defined and depicted by pen and ink.

These transformations are evident in many upland landscapes. The changing structure of landowning slowly brought major changes to the moorlands. Developing trends in estate organisation set the conditions within which tenant farmers worked their landholdings (including the adjacent moorlands). Agricultural production was extended through clearing and enclosing more land. By doing so, farmers structured their landscapes by wall-building to enclose land. The use of the moorlands was also well organised and demarcated (see Box 14.1).

Enclosing the moorlands

During the later eighteenth and the nineteenth centuries, radical changes were wrought across much of the landscape of Britain as industrialisation, urbanisation, agricultural improvement and the commodification of objects which had begun in the sixteenth and seventeenth centuries increased at a scale and pace previously unknown. These intertwined social and economic trends had major impacts on rural landscapes, and their reach would not only take in moorlands but also lead to early-twentieth-century conflicts over access that

Box 14.1. Ownership and land use in the Upper Derwent

The Upper Derwent in the Peak District is a good case study for how moorlands could be utilised and 'owned' in different ways (Figures 14.1, 14.2). In Hope Woodlands township, to the west of the River Derwent, and in Howden, the only part of Bradfield parish within the area, each farmstead had a well-defined area of common reserved solely for its use (Harrison, 1637; Senior, 1627). Each farm had a block of enclosed moorland known as a moor, hassock or hey above its farmland, and beyond the hey was a strip of open moorland known as an outpasture or sheepwalk. Heys were divided from the outpastures, by banks and ditches, dikes or walls. These were pasture and turbary grounds, which were technically part of the common, but were strongly linked with specific farmsteads through their enclosure and by access along trackways. They are part of the systematic division of the moorland characteristic of Hope Woodlands and Howden. The right to cut peat was restricted by the landowner to these heys, though there is surviving evidence for peat extraction in similar topographical locations that were not technically heys. Outpastures were reserved in tenancy documents solely for livestock grazing (Harrison, 1637; Senior, 1627). The outpastures of Hope Woodlands were carefully demarcated, both on maps from the early seventeenth century onwards and physically on the ground. There is no evidence that numbers of sheep were regulated within tenancy agreements. It is actually the older farmsteads in Hope Woodlands that had this sole access to a moorland strip. Later additions to the settlement pattern had to make do with shared pastures on the more distant moorlands around the head of the Snake Pass.

Across the river in Derwent township any occupant of the township had the right to access any part of the common, which was used by up to nine farms and a number of households in the hamlet. This was not always the case in practice, as shown by the locations of routeways and moorland boundaries. Each farm cut peat on the most proximate area of moorland above the valley side – except, that is, for the occupants of Derwent village. They had to take their peat from a shared area below Derwent Edge, but each household defined their area by leaving baulks in the peat between them and their neighbours. This is a good example of how individuals living within the same township, and technically working the moorland in common, set boundaries between each other. Derwent tenants had also been using commons in Bradfield since before 1574, for which they paid an annual sum of 16 pence (Anon., 1724). This practice of the tenants of one township grazing their livestock on the moorland common of a neighbouring township is found throughout the uplands where the commons abutted each other across large areas of relatively featureless moorland.

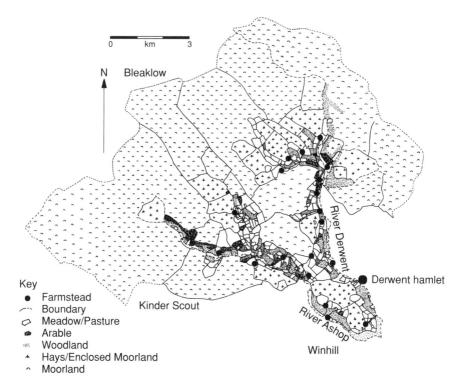

Figure 14.1 Hope woodlands township and Howden farmholding (Derbyshire) in the early seventeenth century, reconstructed from estate surveys (reproduced by kind permission of The History Press from Bevan, 2004).

would eventually lead to the foundation of the National Parks of England and Wales. The market economy and rational method came to dominate social relations within the traditional institutions of the local manors (Johnson, 1996; Wrigley, 1990). By the 1750s, Britain was predominantly a market economy and the world's leading trading nation (Bunce, 1994). Production became increasingly standardised, and the amount of material culture available expanded phenomenally as a wider section of society was able to own a greater range and number of personal and household objects (Howard-Davis, 2001).

An aspect of rationality of particular relevance to moorlands was the widespread acceptance by the British landowning classes of the ideal of agricultural improvement and its application on their rural estates. The belief in the need for good, rational agricultural practices, and that land held privately could be more effectively and efficiently productive than land farmed in common, began in the sixteenth century, but really flourished from the mid-eighteenth century onwards (Johnson, 1996; Newman, 2001). Improvement was seen as progressive, rational and scientifically testable, and therefore 'good', by landowners who saw land increasingly as a commodity. Use of land by

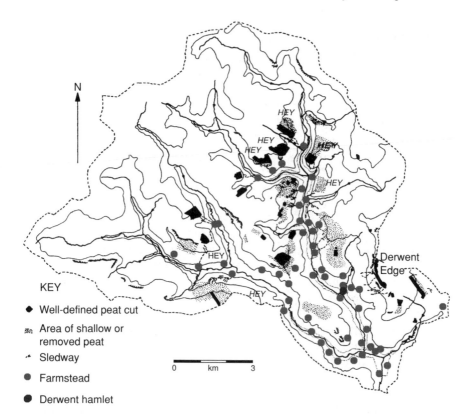

N

KEY

◆ Well-defined peat cut

Area of shallow or
removed peat

Sledway

● Farmstead

● Derwent hamlet

0   km   3

Figure 14.2 Post-medieval farmsteads, peat cuts and trackways (reproduced by kind
permission of The History Press from Bevan, 2004).

common rights was perceived as backward, inefficient and a block to progress. Handbooks to land management, instructions on using drains and
fertilisers, and estate maps recording land use and value were produced increasingly. Improvement was undertaken through a combination of drainage, par-
ing back turfs, and the application of vast quantities of lime. In some cases
landowners had little knowledge of agriculture, and sometimes fashionable
ideas were tried in inappropriate areas with little hope of success (Williamson,
2002). Experiments with fast-maturing breeds of livestock and strains of cereal
were designed to maximise output, which relied on high inputs of raw materials manufactured from outside the farm, such as fertilisers (Williamson, 2002).
New farm buildings were constructed and laid out in relation to each other
on the basis of ideas about how to increase efficiency in use and movement.
Local histories of enclosure of common land, reorientation of building and
farmstead layouts, and land improvement occurred throughout Britain as
landowners increasingly influenced the lives of their tenants in order to improve
agricultural production rationally and systematically.

Box 14.2. Peat-cutting

Deep deposits of peat have been accumulating in the British uplands since the last Ice Age (Evans, this volume). The clearance of forests and changing climate during the Atlantic period (*c.*5500 BC) has contributed to the expansion of blanket peat and the development of the moorlands we recognise today.

Peat has a variety of historical uses: as a fuel for domestic and industrial purposes, as litter for stalled animals, and – in the form of ashes – as an agricultural soil improver (Ardron, 1999). Peat cuts can be readily recognised in many Pennine areas and are an important part of the archaeological evidence that indicates how practice often differed from legal regulations. Cuts are often well-defined areas, identified by vertical edges and as regular depressions cut into the peat or by differences in vegetation type covering areas thin in peat. Most of these latter areas are extensions to recognisable peat cuts. The cuts are usually linked to farmsteads in the valley bottoms by hollowed sledways and in some regions, such as the Lake District, accompanied by stone-built peat-drying huts.

Industrial peat use appears limited in the Peak District compared to the North Pennines, where it was important in iron, steel and lead smelting (Ardron, 1999). In the Upper Derwent peat was the only domestic fuel source from the sixteenth century, when woodlands were successfully reserved for the landowner, until the nineteenth century when railways and better road routes allowed the transport of cheap coal. Turf, the surface sod of earth and vegetation, was also used as a building material.

Almost all moorland commons were subject to enclosure as part of the ideology of agricultural improvement, and as a physical expression of the landowning classes' willingness to improve land and output, so legitimising landowners' rights of inclusion within the ruling classes (Williamson, 2000). Enclosure was sometimes conducted by application to Parliament for an Act by the landowners of a given parish. In other cases landowners of large estates undertook private enclosure or agreed amongst themselves to enclose common land across a parish without recourse to Parliament. Enclosure removed common rights, apportioned the land amongst a select number of landowners, and facilitated the activities and movements of some people while restraining others (Rotman and Nassaney, 1997). Enclosure was often, but largely unsuccessfully, resisted by tenants who saw their traditional rights of access to resources eroded (Johnson, 1996). Methods of resistance are evident in the late-seventeenth-century private enclosure of Castleton commons, where the larger landowners agreed to divide the moorland between them, while providing strip-like enclosures for smallholders (Frazer, 1999). These enclosures were never built, as smallholders continued to pasture their live-stock in accordance with customary rights (Frazer, 1999). But in many places, and with the ruling of Parliament, enclosure caused commoners to lose their rights to pasture livestock on moorlands, so removing the ability of many families to sustain their own livelihood. It was from this rural disenfranchised that many of the labourers essential to Britain's industrialisation came as the rural poor migrated *en masse* to swell the growing industrial cities.

Thousands of miles of enclosure-movement boundaries were built to divide and protect the newly created plots of land across the moorlands. These are usually distinctively straight, dividing the land into regular blocks, as a result of being laid out by surveyors on a map rather than constructed in relation to local topography. Such boundaries can be seen on many of the lower moor-land shelves and valley sides of the Peak District, the Pennines, the Lake District and elsewhere, but they are rarer on the higher moorlands. On lower land where improvement was successful there are now established farms and fields that are no longer considered moorland. But in many other locations the ordered skeletons of ruined walls, silted open drains and, occasionally, the turfed-over mound of abandoned lime are a testament to the folly of try-ing to turn such high-altitude land into improved grassland pasture.

In some cases enclosure was undertaken not for agricultural purposes but to enhance the recreational opportunities of the landowner, who desired to reserve the land to this sole use as vast shooting estates. It was during the eighteenth century that many moorlands were turned over to grouse shooting. Grouse shooting had grown in popularity across Britain during the eighteenth century, as the landed classes became increasingly enthusiastic for wild upland scenery (Williamson, 2002). The consumption and hunting of game was one of the main ways in which the elite defined themselves in the eighteenth and nineteenth centuries (Newman, 2001). Better transport, first provided by turnpikes and then by railways, improved gun technology, and a repeal of game laws in 1831 increased its popularity further in the mid-nineteenth century by widening the geographic distances people could comfortably travel to the moorlands and broadening the social classes who could participate to include the wealthier middle classes of the north-ern industrial areas (Muir, 2001). Grouse shooting became perceived as an important act of manly identity, and codes of conduct enshrined the ideal of the noble sportsman (Muir, 2001). Beating of grouse over prepared posi-tions was introduced during the mid-nineteenth century leading to the con-struction of lines of grouse shooting butts (Byford, 1981; see also Sotherton *et al.*, this volume). Shooting cabins and graded access tracks also survive across Britain's moors as part of the archaeology of landed recreation. This may have been related to the building of parliamentary enclosure walls across moorlands. These blocked stalking routes and provided shooting lines into which butts were often built (Williamson, 2002). During the nineteenth cen-tury, grouse shooting came to be seen by many landowners in Derbyshire as a more important and profitable use of the moors than livestock-pasturing, and was one of the motivations behind many parliamentary enclosure Acts (Ward, 1931).

In the lowlands, the cities grew and caused change to uplands in various ways. Mixed farming gave way during the nineteenth century to mono-agriculture concentrating on faster-maturing breeds of sheep, beef and dairy to supply the nearby urban populations. While small local water mills had existed since the time of Domesday Book, from the late eighteenth century industrial mills were built for the textile industry with large cotton-spinning mills and some wool, flax and silk mills characteristic for many upland towns in Britain (Barnatt and Smith, 2004). Industrialisation led to the extension of quarries for providing stone for buildings and transport routes as well as lime-mortar and lime for the steel industry.

The need for water in growing cities and towns led to Acts of Parliament being passed in the late nineteenth and early twentieth centuries which enabled upland valleys to be flooded to create reservoirs to improve water supplies to growing towns and cities. Town planners in northern England looked to the valleys of the Pennines and other uplands as potential reservoirs. This flooding of the valleys necessitated the removal of much of the existing dispersed farming population and associated patterns of land use while leaving the grouse moors largely undisturbed. The creation of reservoirs has involved decades of major construction work and led to the transformation of valley landscapes in many upland valleys in northern England.

Box 14.3. Privatising Burbage

A good example of the impact of both enclosure and recreational grouse-shooting on moorlands can be seen on the moors of Burbage, Houndkirk and Hathersage. Common since the medieval period, they were owned by the respective lords of the manors of Dore in Yorkshire and Hathersage in Derbyshire. Tenants of these lords had rights to pasture their livestock. The moorland commons were enclosed by two parliamentary Acts. The Derbyshire side was enclosed under the Hathersage, Derwent and Outseats Act of 1808, with the Award following in 1830 (Anon, 1830). The Dore Act was passed in 1809, and the Award drawn up in 1822, so enclosing the Yorkshire part of the moorlands (Fairbank, 1822). In both cases, the Duke of Devonshire had acquired the manors in the eighteenth century. Both Awards resulted in the physical enclosure of small areas of the moorland common, with ruler-straight boundaries subdividing the land into regular fields. In Hathersage, this resulted in a series of new fields on gently sloping ground below, and to the west of Millstone Edge, that were probably farmed from Hathersage Booths. Three distinct areas were physically enclosed in Dore and farmed from newly built model farms. Sheephill was parcelled up into small fields, improved and farmed from a new farmstead – Sheephill Farm, built between 1822 and 1840 (Fairbank, 1822; Ordnance Survey, 1840). Ox Stones was divided into two large rectangular areas by a drystone wall and a ditch and bank, and farmed from Oxdale Lodge, located along an ambitious turnpike now known as Houndkirk Road. The area of moorland to the west of Fox House, running along the north side of the current A6187, was divided into a series of regular fields that were farmed from three newly built farms: Parson House, Stone House and Piper House.

Nineteenth-century enclosure therefore resulted in two new physical manifestations to the Burbage landscape – farmsteads and field walls enclosing improved grass pasture. These all appeared within a 58-year time period, between 1822 and 1880.

At the same time as this enclosure was beginning, the 5th Duke of Rutland acquired a large estate that incorporated a block of moorland on the Peak District's Eastern Moors from Burbage and Houndkirk moors in the north to Gardom's and Birchen Edges in the south. He was not primarily interested in experimenting with the agricultural potential of the moorlands, though he did employ shepherds. He was the first of a succession of five dukes to use the estate as a recreational retreat and built Longshaw Lodge as a 'shooting box' during the 1820s. This was actually a few years before the details of the Enclosure Act were finalised by the Award, suggesting that the Duke was confident enough in his social position to divide his estate before the Award. His mark is left not only in the architectural grandeur of Longshaw Lodge. To facilitate his enjoyment of his grouse-shooting estate, he had a number of terraced and graded drives built leading out across the estate from the Lodge, so that he could access different moorland areas by horse or by carriage for shooting and the display of his estate to guests. He had lines of grouse-shooting butts and shooting lodges for refreshments constructed. Gamekeepers were employed to manage the moorlands for grouse-breeding and they were housed in cottages.

The large-scale development of forestry occurred alongside the development of reservoirs with widespread tree-planting by water boards in reservoir catchments to stabilise ground and provide a supplementary income to water supply. Timber supplies hit an all-time low following the industrial revolution and then the First World War. This led to the establishment of the Forestry Commission in 1919 (see Condliffe, this volume). Large tracts of the uplands were afforested by the Forestry Commission to secure timber supplies for the nation, mainly after the Second World War, coinciding with the development of new machinery enabling extraction from remote upland areas.

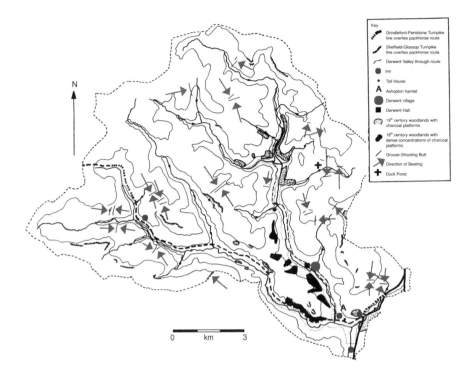

Figure 14.3 Post-medieval features in the Upper Derwent (reproduced by kind permission of The History Press from Bevan, 2004).

Cities themselves sprawled on to the moorland fringes, taking in farm and
open land for residential development. Sheffield is just one example where
the city boundaries extended outwards and upwards to include upland
areas, such as parts of the Peak District National Park.

Recreation: rambling moors

Within a few decades of moorland enclosure, a new social trend appeared
that, in effect, brought the descendants of some of the disenfranchised rural
poor who had migrated to neighbouring industrial cities back into conflict with moorland landowners. In 1826 the Manchester Society for the
Preservation of Ancient Footpaths was formed, and in 1831 a petition was
raised in Manchester against the stopping of footpaths. By the end of the
nineteenth century, walking clubs were being founded to promote rambling
throughout Britain. The first working class rambling organisation in
England was the Sheffield Clarion Ramblers founded in 1900. Their first
ramble was in the Peak District and took place on Sunday, 2 September 1900,
with fourteen people who travelled by train from Sheffield to Edale (Sissons,

2002). The Clarion Ramblers was founded specifically to enable urban labourers to organise themselves to escape the drudgery and pollution of the cities (Sissons, 2002). As such, it was as much a self-improvement organisation as it was recreational, for people to develop mentally and physically through experiencing the open spaces and beauty of the countryside.

The walk around Kinder Scout was pioneering at the time, though fifty years later it had become known as the 'usual round' (Sissons, 2002). The railway line had only opened to passengers between Sheffield and Edale in 1894, and the Hayfield to Snake Inn section of footpath had only been opened in 1897 after twenty-one years of campaigning. On reaching the Snake Inn, tea for fourteen people was not readily available, and the proprietor baked cakes. They decided that the day should be just the start of organised rambles and undertook to organise more trips in 1901. Until its demise in 1964, the Sheffield Clarion Ramblers was one of the most prolific publicists, campaigners and organisers of walks in and public access to the Dark Peak (Sissons, 2002).

The Sheffield Clarion Ramblers was started by Bert Ward, an activist for access rights and a Labour politician. Born in Sheffield in 1876, he worked as a fitter and turner in a steel works. As an active trade unionist, he became the first secretary of the Sheffield branch of the Labour Representation Party, a precursor of the Labour Party. He was a founder member of numerous walking, conservation and heritage societies, and believed that there was no better way to build character and self-improvement than to battle with the elements on the hills. Ward often quoted from Walt Whitman, William Wordsworth, John Ruskin, William Morris and any other author who wrote on the spiritual pleasure of walking, looking at scenic landscape and breathing fresh air. He used, in print, such slogans as 'A Rambler Man is a Man Improved' and 'The Man who never was Lost never went very Far'. Ward campaigned against the loss of public access to the moors through parliamentary enclosure and for the formation of national parks by writing in the Sheffield Clarion Ramblers handbook. He researched the history of areas, including archival documents, archaeological sites and place names, with the aim of educating handbook readers about the moorlands and establishing historical rights of access.

Improved transport and roads in the 1930s drew more people out of the cities to explore the moorlands. At the same time, the campaign for freedom to roam on moorland and calls for national parks to help preserve countryside were intensified and drew people from all parts of the political spectrum, including socialists, anarchists and conservatives. Campaigning included well-organised mass trespasses that brought the urban working classes into direct conflict with the landowners' gamekeepers over moorland access. The Kinder Mass Trespass of 1932 is the most famous (Figure 14.4) and was followed the same year by a trespass on to Abbey Brook by a group of Sheffield clubs. Battle lines were drawn. The trespasses led to the long walk to freedom to roam that began with the Access to Mountains Bill being

Figure 14.4 The Mass Trespassers on their way to Kinder Scout in 1932. Many ramblers were members of sports clubs, which promoted access to the countryside as an antidote to city life and industrial labouring (source: Peak District National Park Authority).

presented to Parliament in 1939, led to the formation of the National Parks in the 1950s and has culminated with the Countryside and Rights of Way (CROW) Act of 2000. In the UK, the access movement was a key driver for the creation of national parks and conservation in the uplands (see also Curry, this volume).

Conclusion

Upland land use today, in the early twenty-first century, can be characterised by four major trends: recreation, conservation, production (sheep-farming, forestry) and water provision. These are quite different modes of land use, and there are both connections and tensions between them. In many ways, they are the latest development in the long history of the uplands as marginal yet integral landscapes fundamentally related to the surrounding lowlands. The ecological and cultural history of the uplands since AD 1000 has been created in a tangible relationship with wider socio-political trends at national and international scales. Upland heritage is as much the product of the European monastic system, aristocratic nation building and industrial urbanisation as it is about sheep grazing, peat cutting and grouse shooting.

Moorland heritage in the UK has always involved widely different social and economic perceptions, and has left a rich legacy of archaeological features and folklore. Shielings, boundaries, packhorse routes, peat cuts, shepherd huts and grouse shooting butts are the tangible clues to how moorlands have been used and perceived since the medieval period onwards. Going back to prehistory, when the moorland landscape was created out of the post-glacial forest – a subject beyond the scope of this chapter – it should be remembered that human activity for almost 10,000 years has shaped the moorlands as we know them today (see Simmons, 2003). They are not a wilderness but a complex cultural artefact. The centuries of continued management for sheep grazing, and more recently for grouse shooting, have led to the characteristic habitats and open vistas which now define the moorlands. It is sobering to think that the space provided by these open moorlands, and the thought that they were Britain's last wildernesses, attracted the pioneering ramblers out of the cities and ultimately led to the creation of our National Parks. Recreation, conservation and production are now the three threads that will bind our moors for the future.

Acknowledgements

Special thanks to Ros Tratt and two anonymous reviewers for comments and suggestions that improved the chapter.

References

Anon (1724) *Papers Relating to William Jessop's Award as to Moscar Common.* Sheffield Archives, ACM S60.

Anon (1830) *Enclosure Award for Hathersage, Outseats and Derwent.* Derbyshire Record Office, Q/R1 5/105.

Ardron, P. (1999) Peat cutting in upland Britain with special reference to the Peak District: its impact on landscape, archaeology and ecology. PhD Thesis, Department of Landscape, University of Sheffield.

Aston, M. (1985) *Interpreting the Landscape: Landscape Archaeology in Local Studies.* London: Batsford.

Aston, M. (2000) *Monasteries in the Landscape.* Stroud: Tempus.

Barnatt, J. and Smith, K. (2004) *The Peak District: Landscapes through Time.* Bollington: Windgather Press.

Bevan, B. (2003) The Upper Derwent: long-term landscape archaeology in the Peak District. PhD thesis, Department of Landscape, University of Sheffield.

Bevan, B. (2004) *The Upper Derwent: 10,000 Years in the Peak District Valley.* Stroud: Tempus.

Bevan, B. (2006) *From Cairns to Craters: Conservation Heritage Assessment of Burbage.* Moors for the Future report No. 8, Edale.

Bunce, M. (1994) *The Countryside Ideal: Anglo-American Images of Landscape.* London: Routledge.

Butlin, R. (1982) *The Transformation of Rural England c. 1580–1880.* London: Oxford University Press.

Byford, J. S. (1981) *Moorland Heritage.* Wood Cottage, Snake Pass Road, Bamford: James S. Byford.

Cox, Rev. J. C. (1905) Forestry. *The Victoria History of the Counties of England* (ed. W. Page), pp. 397–426. Folkestone/London: Dawsons.

Daniels, S. (1990) Goodly prospects: English estate portraiture 1670–1730. *Mapping the Landscape: Essays on Art and Cartography* (ed. S. Daniels and N. Alfrey), pp. 9–12. Nottingham: University of Nottingham.

Fairbank, B. and Fairbank, J. (1822) *A Map of That Part of Dore Referred to by the Commissioners Award*. DRO Q/RI 35.

Frazer, B. (1999) Common recollections: resisting enclosure 'by agreement' in seventeenth-century England. *International Journal of Historical Archaeology*, **3** (2), 75–100.

Harrison, J. (1637) *Exact and Perfect Survey of the Manor of Sheffield with the Manors of Cowley and Ecclesfield*. Sheffield Archives, S75/76.

Howard-Davies, C. (2001) Artefacts. *The Historical Archaeology of Britain, c. 1540–1900* (ed. R. Newman), pp. 211–24. Stroud: Sutton.

Johnson, M. (1996) *The Archaeology of Capitalism*. London: Blackwell.

Kerry, Rev. C. (1893) A history of Peak Forest. *Derbyshire Archaeological Journal*, **15**, 67–98.

Menuge, N. J. (2000) The foundation myth: Yorkshire monasteries and the landscape agenda. *Landscapes*, **1**, 22–37.

Muir, R. (2001) The landscape history of grouse shooting in the Yorkshire Dales. *Rural History*, **12**, 195–210.

Newman, R. (ed.) (2001) *The Historical Archaeology of Britain, c. 1540–1900*. Stroud: Sutton.

Ordnance Survey (1840) *One Inch to a Mile Map, Derbyshire*. First edition.

Rackham, O. (1986) *The History of the Countryside*. London: Dent.

Rotman, D. L. and Nassaney, M. S. (1997) Class, gender and the built environment: deriving social relations from cultural landscapes in southwest Michigan. *Historical Archaeology*, **31**, 42–62.

Senior, W. (1627) *Duke of Devonshire's Woodlands Estates*. Chatsworth Archives.

Simmons, I. G. (2003) *The Moorlands of England and Wales: An Environmental History 8000 BC to AD 2000*. Edinburgh: Edinburgh University Press.

Sissons, D. (2002) *The Best of the Sheffield Clarion Ramblers' Handbooks*. Halsgrove, Devon.

Ward, G. H. B. (1931) Derbyshire moorlands and production of food. *Sheffield Clarion Ramblers*, **30**, 109–17.

Williamson, T. (2000) Understanding enclosure. *Landscapes*, **1**, 56–79.

Williamson, T. (2002) *The Transformation of Rural England: Farming and the Landscape 1700–1870*. Exeter: University of Exeter Press.

Winchester, A. J. L. (1987) *Landscape and Society in Medieval Cumbria*. Edinburgh: John Donald.

Wrigley, A. E. (1990) Urban growth and agricultural change: England and the Continent in the early modern period. *The Eighteenth Century Town* (ed. P. Borsay), pp. 39–82. London: Longman.

15 Leisure in the landscape

Rural incomes and public benefits

Nigel Curry

The uplands are a popular destination the world over for those seeking to enjoy outdoor recreation. In the Asian massif they have been places of pilgrimage, of human endeavour (particularly mountain-climbing) and of adventure tourism. In the New World they have been places of wildness, engendering a national sense of belonging where access to them has often been based on traditions of the 'old country'. In Europe, walking in the uplands had a certain social cachet. When the train brought transport and mobility to the masses, a stroll in the Alps had an exclusivity about it. In England, the uplands were the theatre where access battles were determined. The mass trespass of Kinder Scout in the Peak District was to have a significant influence over postwar access legislation and the introduction of national parks.

Whilst focusing on England and Wales, this chapter illustrates much that is of wider relevance to upland access. The mechanisms of access (section 2) have many parallels with land rights issues in different countries, and the nature of leisure patterns (section 3) has similarities with most developed countries. A number of values derive from this rural leisure participation that are also internationally relevant. For many rural areas, income from tourism can provide a mainstay to the rural economy, but this is not a panacea. There are costs associated with seeking to make tourism sustainable, and with its small scale (section 4). But not all values from rural leisure consumption are market ones. There can be benefits from the environment of upland areas (in all parts of the world) through maintaining its quality in order to attract the visitor (section 5). For consumers, too, much consumption of countryside recreation is free at the point of access and can provide health benefits – a focus for the final section of this chapter.

The nature of the access resource

The mechanisms through which we use upland areas for outdoor recreation vary the world over, and have been determined by a long history of cultural traditions, and land-use practices, laws and institutions (Williams, 2001). In some countries, such as England and Scotland, public rights of access to the upland resource are being extended; whilst in others, such as New Zealand

and America, there are moves towards 'privatisation'. Whatever access mechanisms are adopted, the need to understand access rights is critical to the confident use of the uplands.

Certainly, the available access resource is growing in England and Wales. Between 1990 and the introduction of the Countryside and Rights of Way Act, 2000 (the CROW Act), it has been estimated that the *net* growth in the access resource was at least 450,000 hectares of land and some 20,000 kilometres of linear access, an increase of about 20 per cent (Curry, 2001). The CROW Act 2000 changed the available resource in England and Wales[1] considerably. Its main provisions for rights of way and open country are in Box 15.1 below.

The passing of the CROW Act 2000 was, however, controversial. Even though the Act provided a somewhat limited 'right to roam' (Parker and Ravenscroft, 2001), it was seen by many as one element of a larger 'urban attack' (including the ban on fox hunting) on the rural way of life (Parker, 2007). In reviewing the implementation of the CROW Act, the National Audit Office (NAO) (2006) and the Welsh Audit Office (WAO) (2006) suggest that it was managed successfully, but both raise questions about the levels and types of use that these new acts have brought about. Against a budget of £28 million, implementing the provisions of the Act had cost £69 million by March 2006. The NAO (2006) concludes (p. 2): '. . . it is difficult to establish to what extent the outcome justified the costs incurred.'

Community involvement

In addition to provisions for open country and the rights-of-way system as access resources, part V of the CROW Act also introduced Local Access Forums (LAFs) to reinforce a community involvement ethos in provision –

Box 15.1. Main provisions of the CROW Act 2000

Part I provides access to open country (defined as mountain, moorland, downland and heathland) and to common land. Increase of access land by 6.5 per cent in England and 21 per cent in Wales. Available for public use by 31 October 2005. Provision is allowed only on foot except on certain rights of way, and certain closures, restrictions and exceptions are allowed.

Section 16 allows landowners to dedicate *any* land for access purposes.

Part II modernises the public rights of way system with nearly fifty separate sections and clauses covering maintenance and obstruction, definition and re-definition, restrictions and changes, including 'finishing' the definitive map.

an ethos that has grown in most Western economies in the last twenty years, consistent with the 'citizenship' agenda. These LAFs are now established in England and Wales for most local highways authorities to provide independent advice on public access to land, for open-air recreation and for other purposes. An early review of their operation suggested that, whilst some were operating effectively, others had found it difficult to recruit members and clarify their objectives (Short *et al.*, 2005).

This community involvement in access had had earlier successes. The Parish Paths Partnership had been designed in the mid-1990s to address the increasingly visible problems with the maintenance of, legal definition of, and publicity for the Statutory Rights of Way system. Other community schemes had been running at a county level, and community-based 'greenways' were introduced in the mid-1990s (Land Use Consultants, 1997); but the flagship initiative has been the development of Millennium Greens. These were introduced as areas of open space, developed, implemented and managed into the longer term by communities themselves. The scheme opened in October 1996, and by the time it closed to new proposals at the end of July 1998 some seventy-six MG agreements had been secured and nearly 800 further proposals were being actively assessed (Millennium Greens Newsletter, 1998). Such initiatives have ensured that community involvement has remained an important part of the national access portfolio.

Future developments in provision

For England and Wales, the WAO's (2006) suggestion that the lessons from the CROW Act 2000 might usefully be applied to access to the coast chimed in England with Department for the Environment, Food and Rural Affairs (Defra) 2004 strategy to improve coastal access and with the Labour Party's rural manifesto of 2005. In July of that year, ministers proposed that action to improve coastal access should be an early 'flagship' initiative for Natural England, and by 2007 the intention to secure access along the length of the English coastline, make it more accessible and balance the needs of wildlife, landscape and enjoyment was announced (Natural England, 2007a).

With the restructuring of the recreation portfolio in government in 2006 from the Countryside Agency to Natural England, the production of a national outdoor recreation strategy was underway by the beginning of 2007. This is to have a strong orientation towards healthy lifestyles, and promoting and marketing outdoor recreation, particularly to the young and the disabled. But does this reflect what people want?

Shifts in rural leisure patterns

National leisure patterns

One of the principal concerns of the NAO (2006) and the WAO (2006) in monitoring the implementation of the CROW Act 2000 was the extent to which this net new access provision was likely to be used. Their concerns are well founded. Any use of open country is simply likely to be a diversion from elsewhere because overall the consumption of outdoor recreation in Britain has been falling since about 1977.

Using the National Surveys of Countryside Recreation, the House of Commons Environment Committee (1995) noted 'with some surprise' that there had been no growth in countryside recreation trips at all since the surveys began in 1977. The successor UK Day Visits Survey showed a decline in countryside visits from 1994 to 1998 (Curry and Ravenscroft, 2001), and the 2002–3 Great Britain Survey noted that 'between 1998 and 2002/03, all day trips to the countryside declined by 12%' (Great Britain Day Visits Survey, 2004). Fewer than 25 per cent of all day visits were to the countryside.

Whilst some of this decline, particularly more recently, could have been influenced by foot-and-mouth disease (which is considered in the following section), the 2005 England Leisure Visits Survey suggests not. All leisure visits in this year were down 33 per cent on 2002–3, and visits to the countryside were down by a huge 45 per cent[2] (Natural England, 2006). Over 40 per cent of the adult population never visited the countryside at all during the year. The structural decline in rural leisure consumption, according to the government's own surveys, continues apace. And, as for the effects of the CROW Act 2000, only 0.05 per cent of leisure visits was to open country; but, even then, only 34 per cent of the people who made these visits were aware that they were on open country (Natural England, 2006). All this has led Dr Helen Phillips, chief executive of Natural England, to note that 'People are missing out on the wide range of benefits that the natural environment offers, particularly to their health and wellbeing' (Natural England, 2007c).

The reasons for this lack of consumption are consistent over time and they are largely to do with people's preferences rather than with constraints. The UK Day Visit Surveys for both 1996 and 1998 (Social and Community Planning Research, 1999) indicate that around 20 per cent of non-visitors have no particular reason for non-participation; they simply have not gone. About 18 per cent are too busy to go, and 18 per cent simply have no interest. These patterns are consistent with the reasons for non-consumption in 2005, shown in full in Table 15.1. Here the first four categories (73 per cent of respondents) show that non-visits are due to a lack of interest or of time (although this does include an undefined 'other' category).

Reasons for current patterns

Why are these consumption patterns as they are? First, a range of 'intervening home-based leisure opportunities' (the widescreen television, digital satellite and DVD, the CD player, the computer and the Internet) have created a huge increase in leisure choices. Increasing proportions of leisure time are spent at home in a sedentary way. This lies behind the more recent policy impetus to use outdoor recreation to make the nation healthier – an issue considered further in the final part of this chapter. Second, as working lives

Table 15.1 Main reasons for not visiting the countryside in England in 2005 (source: data analysed from Natural England, 2006).

	Number	%
No particular reason	4,554	29
Always too busy/lack of time	3,213	20
Other	2,413	16
Not interested	1,229	8
Physical disability	717	5
Other health reason	696	4
Not enough money/can't afford	585	4
Lack of suitable means of transport	552	4
Prefer to go to other places outside of England	466	3
No-one to go with	223	1
Too difficult with elderly	157	1
Don't know	154	1
Preferred to spend money on something else	125	1
Too difficult with children	98	1
Dislike traveling	95	1
Lack of information on possible destinations	90	1
Prefer to save my money	50	0
No-one to look after matters AT HOME while I am away	44	0
Access to countryside prevented or discouraged by land owners/managers	21	0
Feel nervous or uneasy about what might happen including personal safety, getting lost	21	0
Lack of information on where access is permitted to countryside visits	16	0
No-one to look after matters AT WORK while I am away	13	0
	15,532	100

have become increasingly busy, leisure-time budgets have been divided into smaller 'bites'. Outdoor leisure consumption has become shorter, more intensive, more specialised and, inevitably, more local (Lowe *et al.*, 1995).

Third, Clark *et al.* (1994) suggest that the increases in *personal choice* noted in the UK Day Visits Survey result from an information-based society and fuel a market orientation in leisure consumption. Thus, people are attracted to private market goods such as golf courses, sports facilities and holiday village resorts because of their status as well as their enjoyment. They provide *exclusivity*. This is exacerbated as different social groups express their identity through leisure activity differently, as is explored in the Suckall *et al.* chapter in this volume. In these contexts, commoditised outdoor recreation becomes less space extensive. The 'outdoor' significance becomes incidental in the process of enjoyment. Activity becomes devoid of its social, cultural and landscape context, being replaced by its consumptive context.

The decline in outdoor leisure consumption over the past thirty years is therefore overwhelmingly caused by consumer preferences and leisure lifestyle changes, rather than by any particularly strong constraints on participation. Because of this, significantly, outdoor leisure consumption will not be changed through tinkering with the supply side. Most worryingly, perhaps, is that, in the face of this long-term structural decline in consumption, public provision continues to increase apace and is set to do so into the future, as has been noted in the first part of this chapter.

Rural tourism

Arguments about whether or not rural tourism (and rural recreation) is of any significant economic value to individual localities the world over are evenly balanced. It has been widely promoted as a way of addressing the social and economic challenges of rural areas, particularly peripheral ones (Hegarty and Przezborska, 2005). It offers the potential of being small scale, thus allowing easy entry into the sector, and it can also exploit the environmental, cultural and historic capital of rural areas (Wilson *et al.*, 2001). It is labour intensive (and therefore job-creating) and does not require particularly high skills levels (and is therefore accessible to many).

One of the important economic effects of rural tourism is that it is effectively 'exporting' local goods, services and environments, bringing income from outside the region (Silva *et al.*, 2007). This in turn has indirect or multiplier effects through which it helps to maintain the other businesses in rural areas: shops, garages and transport. In this way tourism, particularly in remoter regions, transfers wealth from the richer urbanised areas to the poorer peripheral regions (Telfer, 2002). From this, rural tourism benefits accrue. Some salient characteristics of these benefits in relation to Britain are presented in Box 15.2.

Box 15.2. Some economic benefits from rural tourism in Britain (Internet sources)

1999   Britain, recreation and tourism rural spend, *circa* £14 billion
2000   Britain, recreation and tourism rural spend, *circa* £12 billion
2005   England-only (after foot-and-mouth) recreation and tourism rural spend, *circa* £9.4 billion
1998   North East of England, recreation and tourism rural spend, *circa* £226 million
2000   South East Region, recreation and tourism rural spend, *circa* £1 billion

Other examples:

1999   Whale tourism, Scotland, value to economy £7.8 million
2000   Walkers and cyclists in Scotland, value to economy £438 million
2005   Walkers in Wales, value to economy £550 million

Economic limitations

But what these figures mean in the context of the economic potential of rural areas more generally is not clear. Some argue that rural tourism as an economic engine has its limitations. Getz and Carlsen (2005), for example, note the small size of rural tourism businesses and limits to the incomes that can be derived from them. In most areas, too, there is little potential for growth. Wages are inherently low, and there is little career structure. In some areas, too, labour has to be imported. The drive to earn revenue can also often conflict with principles of sustainable tourism (Sharpley, 2007). As businesses, rural tourism enterprises often find it difficult to secure finance, recruit appropriate staff, access training and be competitive. The sector is fragmented, with few large organisations, and so it has a dissipated political voice (Morison and Thomas, 2004). Despite the multiplier effects noted above, the income 'leakage' from rural areas is high (because there are limited services that support rural tourism in these areas), there is market volatility, a limited number of entrepreneurs and an inherent conservatism amongst investors in this area (Getz and Carlsen, 2005).

These factors have led Roberts and Hall (2001) to suggest that tourism is not appropriate for all rural areas. In some, opportunity costs and comparative advantages make it an unrealistic proposition. It offers, perhaps, the most potential in remote areas where there are few alternatives (Skuras *et al.*, 2006). But, even in these areas, rural tourism is vulnerable to economic cycles, the weather and, notoriously in Britain at the turn of the millennium, disease.

Foot-and-mouth disease

Rural tourism in many parts of upland Britain was devastated by foot-and-mouth disease in 2001. This is a highly infectious disease of cloven-hoofed animals but carries no public health risks, and 95 per cent of infected animals would recover within two weeks without treatment (Scottish Parliament, 2002). Despite this, it is European Union (EU) policy to keep member states infection-free, through slaughter (European Commission, 1985).

The disease was first confirmed on 20 February in Northumberland, and spread into the Scottish Borders, Dumfries and Galloway and as far south as Devon and Cornwall by March. For purposes of containment, footpaths were closed in all infected areas until the end of June. Exclusion zones (restricted-area designations) of a minimum of 10 km around infected premises also were introduced. Many tourist attractions were closed as a result, and events were cancelled. But the method of slaughter also created a ubiquitous picture of burning pyres of animals and mass burial grounds, which was a disastrous image for rural tourism, particularly since it attracted global publicity. In the first half of 2001, nearly 6.5 million animals were slaughtered. The economic consequences were considerable, and tourism rather than agriculture bore the brunt of the disease (Donaldson *et al.*, 2006), as Box 15.3 indicates.

> **Box 15.3. Foot-and-mouth: some economic consequences in Britain**
>
> Compensation to farmers for livestock loss: £1.34 billion
> Compensation to all other businesses affected: £39 million
> Losses to the tourism sector in 2001: up to £3.2 billion
> Overall losses to the rural economy: up to £8 billion

Ecosystem goods and services and sustainable tourism

As outdoor recreation consumption and rural tourism incomes in Britain both face an uncertain future, increasing attention is being given to the non-market values of rural leisure, as Hanley and Colombo's chapter in this volume illustrates. Globally, there is particular interest in what the ecosystem values and costs associated with rural leisure consumption might be. Whilst recreation, access and tourism provide market values and monetary flows into rural areas, their overall worth is much greater than this. There is a wide range of benefits that arise from these activities that are not paid for through the market. Such benefits include use values, option values and bequest values (Edwards and Abivardi, 1998). Use values include the use of the countryside that is not paid for at the point of consumption (walking on the rights-of-way system, for example) and also values that arise from things such as flood control, which can make recreation consumption easier and also can protect ecological value.

Option values lie in the value to people of knowing that a certain tract of countryside exists should they wish to use it at some time in the future (this is sometimes termed non-use value). However, option values can also lie in the possible future medical values of species diversity – a diversity that might have been maintained as a result of recreational use. Bequest values are the values of the recreational resource, if maintained, to future generations.

The Economics for the Environment Consultancy (2005) report on ecosystem goods and services defines six types of ecosystem services. Of particular interest for non-market recreation and tourism values are those they term information and life-fulfilling ecosystem services – those that provide aesthetic, cultural, educational and spiritual values. These enhance well-being in a variety of ways through recreation. They provide opportunities for exercise, the subject of the final section of this chapter, offer a backcloth for artistic and scientific endeavour, and provide one of the justifications for the role of recreation in the development of national parks (Donelley, 1986).

For developing countries in particular, the appropriate husbandry of ecosystem goods and services can create wealth through tourism, although the distribution of this wealth has to be carefully managed. Studies have enumerated the ecosystem values for tourism of wetlands (WWF, 2004), forests (Vedeld *et al.*, 2004) and conservation (Salafsky and Wollenberg, 2000).

Walking and health

Many consider that health benefits are the most important non-market bene-fits from outdoor recreation. Alongside the need to increase rural tourism incomes, health provides a principal justification of state outdoor recreation policy (Parker, 2007). The health benefits of walking are beyond dispute. What is less clear, however, is whether access to the countryside is the most appropriate peg upon which to hang such a health policy.

Public recreation and access policies have had a series of successive justifications since the National Parks and Access to the Countryside Act, 1949, of which health is just the most recent. The fear of a 'recreation explo-sion' so handsomely articulated by Michael Dower (1965) justified recreation policy at all levels for nearly twenty-five years as being one of containment, necessary to 'control' the 'urban hordes' in the countryside lest they de-stroyed the very thing they had come to see (Curry, 1994). This justifica-tion began to ebb only in the 1990s when it became accepted in policy circles that the recreation explosion never actually happened, as has been noted in the second part of this chapter.

By the early 1990s, the justification for recreation and access provision was shifting more towards the economic value of countryside recreation, driven by agricultural policies seeking to sustain income for farmers. A host of new agri-environment income supplements were paid for access to farm land, inher-itance tax exemptions were exploited, and focus was given at the local level to the economic potential of rural tourism, as has been noted in the third section of this chapter.

Public countryside recreation policies have been increasingly justified on the grounds that they promote healthy lifestyles since the late 1990s. Cer-tainly they do, but are they the most effective means of targeting the health message at those who need it most? The evidence in the second part of this chapter suggests that countryside recreation participation stubbornly re-mains dominated by the more educated higher-income sectors of the popu-lation. Principal health problems, particularly relating to a lack of exercise, however, predominate amongst lower-income groups, the less well educated and the more vulnerable members of society (World Health Organisation [WHO], 2003) – precisely those who indulge in countryside recreation least. Targeting the exercise interests of these more vulnerable groups might be more effective at securing health benefits than investing in the dominantly middle class pursuits of 'quiet enjoyment' in the countryside. The equity effects of such a policy justification are negative.

The Millennium Greens initiative illustrates how countryside recrea-tion policy can actually limit health benefit potential (Goodenough, 2007). Under this initiative, communities were invited to apply for funding to set up local 'leisure spaces' by the then Countryside Agency, but the Greens had to conform to a set of qualifying criteria reflecting all of the 'tranquillity' notions of countryside recreation enshrined in the 1949 Act – quiet places, wild-flower meadows, and a place to sit and relax. More affluent rural areas did well under this scheme: what was required was what they wanted, and they had the knowledge, skills and cultural understanding to make successful funding applications.

The larger, more run-down, former council estate areas of the metropolitan fringe did rather less well. Aspirations for space for more 'rough and tumble' activity – mountain-biking, skateboarding and the like – were not really part of this tranquillity ethos. It was wild flowers or nothing. An opportunity to provide exercise opportunities for the disaffected youth of these areas in particular was largely passed up.

Health benefits

With this cautionary note on the importance of equity considerations in recreation and access policy, what are the health benefits of walking in the countryside? Longitudinal epidemiological studies have demonstrated a clear link between physical inactivity and higher levels of chronic diseases and premature mortality. Relatively small amounts of physical activity, equivalent to walking briskly for thirty minutes each day, can offer protection against cardiovascular disease, obesity, type 2 diabetes, musculoskeletal conditions and cancer (Department of Health, 2004).

More specific benefits in relation to green environmental spaces have been identified in relation to mental health. Exercising in green spaces was found by Pretty *et al.* (2005) to improve self-esteem, although this was not influenced by the intensity of exercise. Moods also became more positive with exercise, and generally the natural environment was found to have a positive effect on mental health both therapeutically and recuperatively. The WHO (2003) estimates that depression and related illnesses will become the largest source of ill health by 2020. Coping mechanisms in relation to stress (smoking, over-eating, excess alcohol, drugs) have their own health-related consequences. The benefits of green exercise therefore are likely to be highly significant.

Policy

In terms of policy, the Walking the Way to Health Initiative (WHI) was introduced, along with a number of other referral schemes, during the late 1990s (Natural England, 2007b). It was to promote local exercise, particularly amongst the more sedentary. The British Heart Foundation and Natural England still work together (with Big Lottery funding) under this scheme to offer information and support, and have helped to create a network of over 350 local 'health walk' schemes. The British Trust for Conservation Volunteers has developed the 'Green Gym' (environmental volunteerism plus workouts); and a number of drug rehabilitation schemes, too, have used active countryside recreation instrumentally (Curry *et al.*, 2001).

A number of individual, particularly metropolitan, areas have developed 'health walk' schemes. Several cities have produced CDs with health walk maps as well as the designation of particular routes on the ground. Other 'supply side' initiatives such as green lanes and community forest walks have provided encouragement to healthy walking.

Building on these schemes, Natural England has more recently introduced a 'Green Exercise' programme to encourage physical activity and improve mental health. Importantly, this represents moves away from the 'quiet enjoyment of the countryside' as a backcloth to exercise, explicitly focusing on local and urban areas to target hard-to-reach groups and deprived areas. Green Exercise includes walking, cycling and conservation activities, but also extends to any activity that takes place in the natural environment and is designed to increase the amount of physical activity undertaken by individuals.

Natural England and the Department of Health are also working together on the National Step-O-Meter Programme (NSP), which is a 'Choosing Health' White Paper project. It aims to make pedometer use accessible, affordable and effective in clinical practice, particularly to sedentary, 'at risk' or 'hard to reach' groups (Jarrett *et al.*, 2004).

However, the extent to which supply-side policies (making available the physical space for exercise and the physical technology to monitor it) will influence people's exercise patterns, relative to explicitly addressing the causes of inactivity (which are unlikely to be primarily driven by lack of available space or technology), still remains to be seen. These causes are likely to be both material (barriers to participation) and attitudinal. Supply-side policies for health are probably best-viewed as an adjunct to changing lifestyles more generally.

Notes

1 Other arrangements have subsequently been made for Scotland through part 1 of the 2003 Land Reform (Scotland) Act (see Sellar, 2006).
2 Natural England (2006) suggests that caution must be expressed in these figures as the methods of data collection between the two surveys differed slightly.

References

Clark, G., Darrell, J., Grove-White, R., Macnaghten, P. and Urry, J. (1994) *Leisure Landscapes*. London: Council for the Protection of Rural England.

Curry, N. R. (1994) *Countryside Recreation, Access and Land Use Planning*. London: Spon.

Curry, N. R. (2001) Access for outdoor recreation in England and Wales: production, consumption and markets. *Journal of Sustainable Tourism*, **9**, 400–16.

Curry, N. R., Joseph, D. and Slee, R. W. (2001) To climb a mountain? Social inclusion and outdoor recreation in Britain. *World Leisure*, **3**, 3–15.

Curry, N. R. and Ravenscroft, N. (2001) Countryside recreation provision in England: exploring a demand-led approach. *Land Use Policy*, **18**, 281–91.

Department of Health (2004) *At Least Five a Week: Evidence on the Impact of Physical Activity and Its Relationship to Health*. http://www.dh.gov.uk/assetRoot/04/08/09/83/04080983.pdf

Donaldson, A., Lee, R., Ward, N. and Wilkinson, K. (2006) *Foot and Mouth – Five Years On: The Legacy of the 2001 Foot and Mouth Disease Crisis for Farming and the British Countryside*. Centre for Rural Economy, University of Newcastle upon Tyne. http://rogue.ncl.ac.uk/file_store/nclep_231204294788.pdf

Donnelley, P. (1986) The paradox of parks: politics of recreational land use before and after the mass trespass. *Leisure Studies*, **52**, 231–48.

Dower, M. (1965) The fourth wave: the challenge of leisure. A Civic Trust survey. *Architects' Journal* (special issue).

Economics for the Environment Consultancy (2005) *The Economic, Social and Ecological Value of Ecosystem Services: A Literature Review*. Report to Defra, London. http://statistics.defra.gov.uk/esg/reports/ecosystem/default.asp

Edwards, P. J. and Abivardi, C. (1998) The value of biodiversity: where ecology and economy blend. *Biological Conservation*, **83**, 239–48.

European Commission (1985) Directive 85/511/EEC. http://ec.europa.eu/food/fs/ah_pcad/ah_pcad_05_en.pdf

Getz, D. and Carlsen, J. (2005) Family businesses in tourism: state of the art. *Annals of Tourism Research*, **32**, 237–58.

Goodenough, A. (2007) Children's voices in the development of Millennium Greens. PhD thesis, University of Gloucestershire.

Great Britain Day Visits Survey (2004) *Survey for 2002–03*. TNS Travel and Tourism, Edinburgh. www.countryside.gov.uk/LAR/Recreation/visits/dayvisits02-03.asp

Hegarty, C. and Przezborska, L. (2005) Rural and agri-tourism as a tool for reorganising rural areas in old and new member states – a comparison. Study of Ireland and Poland. *International Journal of Tourism Research*, **7**, 63–77.

House of Commons Environment Committee (1995) *The Impact of Leisure Activities on the Environment*. HC 246–I. London: The Stationery Office.

Jarrett, H., Peters, D. and Robinson, P. (2004) *Evaluating the 2003 Step-o-meter Loan Pack Trial*. Report to the British Heart Foundation and the Countryside Agency.

Land Use Consultants (1997) *Greenways: Consensus Building and Conflict Resolution*. Cheltenham: Countryside Commission.

Lowe, P., Ward, N., Ward, S. and Murdoch, J. (1995) *Countryside Prospects, 1995–2010: Some Future Trends*. Centre for Rural Economy, University of Newcastle upon Tyne, Research Report.

Millennium Greens Newsletter (1998) *It's Official, Millennium Greens Are a Success*. Issue 4, p. 5. The Commission, Birmingham.

Morison, A. and Thomas, R. (eds) (2004) *SMEs in Tourism and International Perspective*. ALTALS, Holland.

National Audit Office (2006) *Department for Environment, Food and Rural Affairs and the Countryside Agency, the Right of Access to Open Country*. Report by the Comptroller and Auditor General, HC 1046 Session, 2005–06 June 10th. London. http://www.nao.org.uk/publications/nao_reports/05-06/05061046.pdf

Natural England (2006) *England Leisure Visits: Report of the 2005 Survey*. Cheltenham: Natural England. http://www.naturalengland.org.uk/leisure/recreation/dayvisits05.pdf

Natural England (2007a) *Improving Coastal Access.* Natural England Board, Meeting 3, 21 February Paper No: NEB P07 03. http://www.naturalengland.org.uk/about/board/feb07/210207_coastal_access_NEB_P07_03.pdf

Natural England (2007b) Walking the way to health initiative. http://www.countryside.gov.uk/LAR/Recreation/WHI/index.asp

Natural England (2007c) *Too Busy to Go Out?* Press release. http://www.naturalengland.org.uk/press/news2007/090107.htm

Parker, G. (2007) Countryside access and the 'right to roam' under New Labour: nothing to CROW about? *New Labour's Countryside: Rural Policy in Britain since 1997* (ed. M. Woods).

Parker, G. and Ravenscroft, N. (2001) Land, rights and the gift: CROW 2000 and the negotiation of citizenship, *Sociologia Ruralis*, **41**, 381–98.

Pretty, J., Griffin, M., Peacock, J., Hine, R., Sellens, M. and South, N. (2005) *A Countryside for Health and Well Being: The Physical and Mental Health Benefits of Green Exercise.* Report to the Countryside Recreation Network, Sheffield.

Roberts, L. and Hall, D. (2001) *Rural Tourism and Recreation: Principles to Practice.* CABI Publishing, Oxfordshire.

Salafsky, N. and Wollenberg, E. (2000) Linking livelihoods and conservation: a conceptual framework and scale for assessing the integration of human needs and biodiversity. *World Development*, **28**, 1421–38.

Scottish Parliament (2002) *Rural Tourism.* SPICe Briefing. Produced for the Enterprise and Lifelong Learning Committee, 02/92, 21 August. Edinburgh.

Sellar, W. (2006) The great land debate and the Land Reform (Scotland) Act 2003. *Norsk Geografisk Tidsskrift*, **60**, 100–9.

Sharpley, R. (2007) Flagship attractions and sustainable rural tourism development: the case of the Alnwick Garden, England. *Journal of Sustainable Tourism*, **15**, 125–43.

Short, C., Curry, N. and Taylor, K. (2005) *An Evaluation of Local Access Forums.* Final report to the Countryside Agency, Countryside and Community Research Unit, University of Gloucestershire.

Silva, G., Edwards, J. and Vaughan, R. (2007) Entrepreneurship in rural areas: the case of tourism-related businesses. Paper to the 5th Rural Entrepreneurship Conference, Riseholme Campus, University of Lincoln, 23/24 February.

Skuras, D., Petrou, A. and Clark, G. (2006) Demand for rural tourism: the effects of quality and information. *Agricultural Economics*, **35**, 183–92.

Social and Community Planning Research (1999) *United Kingdom Leisure Day Visits Survey 1998.* London: Social and Community Planning Research.

Telfer, D. J. (2002) Tourism and regional development issues. *Tourism and Development: Concepts and Issues* (ed. R. Shapley and D. J. Telfer), pp. 112–48. Clevedon: Channel View Publications.

Vedeld, P., Angelsen, A., Sjaasrad, E. and Berg, G. K. (2004) *Counting on the Environment: Forest Incomes and the Rural Poor.* Environmental Economics Series No. 98, The World Bank Environmental Department, The World Bank, Washington DC.

Welsh Audit Office (2006) *Public Access to the Countryside.* The Auditor General for Wales, Cardiff. http://www.wao.gov.uk/assets/englishdocuments/WAO_Public_Acc_Eng_web.pdf

Williams, D. R. (2001) Sustainability and public access to nature: contesting the right to roam. *Journal of Sustainable Tourism*, **9**, 361–71.

Wilson, S., Fesenmaier, J. and van Es, J. (2001) Factors for success in rural tourism development. *Journal of Travel Research*, **40**, 132–8.

World Health Organisation (2003) *Social Determinants of Health: The Solid Facts*. 2nd edn (ed. R. Wilkinson and M. Marmot). Copenhagen: WHO Europe. http://www.euro.who.int/document/e81384.pdf

Worldwide Fund for Nature (WWF) (2004) *The Economic Values of the World's Wetlands*. Report prepared with support from the Swiss Agency for the Environment, Forests and Landscape (SAEFL), Gland/Amsterdam. Summary in http://assets.panda.org/downloads/wetlandsbrochurefinal.pdf

Part III

Social change, land management and conservation

Driving change

16 Description of the upland economy

Areas of outstanding beauty and marginal economic performance

Klaus Hubacek, Katharina Dehnen-Schmutz, Muhammad Qasim and Mette Termansen

Introduction

Long-term sustainable management of UK uplands as socio-ecological systems is critical for maintaining their value as areas of natural beauty and for the continued provision of important ecosystem services. Over centuries, human–environment interactions have evolved, resulting in a multitude of often competing land uses. Recognising changing socio-economic patterns is important for understanding the pressures on current management of the uplands. Especially over the last few decades, a number of social, economic and institutional forces have significantly influenced the pressures on the uplands.

In this chapter we explore such interactions by characterising the upland economy and discussing the impacts on the management of UK uplands of various changing socio-economic forces. The discussion throughout the chapter will refer to UK upland areas in general and be illustrated, where data are available, with reference to the Peak District National Park (PDNP). The Peak District is typical of upland regions around the UK and Europe, which are often plagued by very similar issues. Most are economically marginal and tend to be environmentally sensitive, and generally they face rapid socio-economic changes that are often driven by national and international policies which are themselves responses to a range of pressures that include demographic shifts (Lobley and Potter, 2004), economic development (Gray, 2000) and environmental changes such as climate change, pollution and the loss of biodiversity (Fraser *et al.*, 2006).

Characteristics and trends of UK upland economies

There are a number of apparent commonalities, with regard to the socio-economic makeup, that can be used to characterise upland areas. There are also similarities in driving forces that provide challenges and opportunities for these areas. In the following section we shall describe some of these characteristics and trends.

Low population density

Frequently, rural areas are simply defined as less populated areas. More specifically, in the UK, there are three measurement criteria that are used to distinguish urban and rural areas: (1) settlement form distinguishing between dispersed dwellings, hamlet, village, small town, urban fringe and urban (with populations larger than 10 k); (2) sparsity or remoteness – based on the number of households in a specified area; and (3) function, classified by the number and type of commercial addresses within a given area (Countryside Agency, 2004).

Closely related to remoteness and sparse populations, the 'rural' has often been associated with backward or lagging economies, an ageing population and migration into cities. These are subject to change, and the direction of change is less clear than one might expect. In the UK, migration from rural areas into cities is a persistent force especially amongst the younger (Buller *et al.*, 2003), resulting in an ageing rural population. This trend is highlighted by the fact that, in rural areas, the population in age bands under 40 has decreased at a greater rate than in urban areas, and the reverse is true in age bands over 40 (Defra, 2002). In the PDNP, there is a higher proportion of 50–65-year-olds than in England, with otherwise constant population numbers in the time period 1991–2001, and overall much lower population density (26 people/km^2) than the East Midlands (267 people/km^2) or England (377 people/km^2) in 2001 (PDNPA, undated).

At the same time, we can observe a strong migration into many rural areas in what has been referred to as 'counter-urbanisation'. There are a wide variety of reasons discussed in the literature, such as 'rural industrialisation' – following cheap labour, de-industrialisation and decentralisation, together with improved infrastructure and employment opportunities (Brown *et al.*, 1997; Buller *et al.*, 2003).

In addition to structural and spatial changes within the economy, there are other important reasons why an increasing number of people are 'buying into the rural idyll' (Buller *et al.*, 2003). Many are attracted by social amenity factors such as the perceived 'rural way of living', slower pace and lower crime rates, and physical amenity factors such as open spaces, attractive scenery and other natural amenities attracting well-off retirees or skilled specialists able to work over the Internet or other infrastructures (Lowe and Ward, 2007). Powers (1996b) referred to this phenomenon as 'footloose income', which is income that arrives no matter where its intended recipient goes. It is not tied directly to available jobs or resource extraction activities. Johnson and Beale (1999) showed that, for the US, those counties attractive for retired people and tourists showed greater influx of population than counties based on traditional rural economies based on extractive industries. Some of the demographic characteristics of the PDNP seem also to point in this direction. The proportion of individuals in professional or managerial occupations is 33 per cent in the PDNP in 2001, whereas in the East Midlands region and England as a whole this proportion is only 24 per cent and 26 per cent respectively. In the UK over the last thirty years or so, the movement of people from the towns into the countryside has been the dominant migratory trend (e.g. Murdoch, 1997). In fact, the population in rural areas has risen almost eight times as fast as the population in urban areas, by 5.5 per cent and 0.7 per cent respectively (Defra, 2002).

Similarly, an increasing number of businesses are choosing rural locations owing to perceived advantages for their market position, including a better living environment for management and workers, improved personal contact with customers, access to principal suppliers, and lower costs (Raley and Moxey, 2000). This migration into rural areas has helped transform the rural economy. Findlay *et al.* (1999) found that these new rural enterprises created by 'rural loving' in-migrants have a strong job-generating potential of 1.7 million rural jobs. On the down side of this movement are the pressures on the rural housing market out-pricing the young rural population, which in turn has effects on the social fabric leading to a social restructuring of rural areas (Newby, 1986; Murdoch and Marsden, 1994; Buller *et al.*, 2003). The trend of rural in-migration is often perceived by the existing rural population as a 'threat to a cherished, and largely mythical, rural way of life, to the landscapes and the communities of the countryside' (Buller *et al.*, 2003, p. 5).

Social relationships

Rural life is often characterised as being based on strong social relationships. Such strong social networks, also referred to as social capital, can facilitate collective action and thus potentially improve economic performance of a region and its environmental sustainability (Pretty and Ward, 2001; Putnam, 2001). As Maskell *et al.* (1998) observed, 'some geographical environments are endowed with a structure as well as a culture which seem to be well suited for dynamic and economically sound development of knowledge, while other environments can function as a barrier to entrepreneurship and change' (quoted after Winter and Rushbrook, 2003). A study focusing on the PDNP found that the success of an integrated rural development scheme was partly due to existing social networks and its role in the development and implementation of rural development proposals (Blackburn *et al.*, 2000). This might be partly due to the area's farming history (Sobels *et al.*, 2001). A number of studies show a strong connection between social capital and effective environmental management, especially in the case of common resources but also where individual resource management is traditionally done in cooperation (Pretty and Ward, 2001). Upland farming often involves

farmers sharing grazing rights on communally owned land. The resulting cooperation in grazing arrangements on the common land, which extended to other
aspects of village life, often become part of the culture of upland regions
(Burton *et al.*, 2005). Owing to the changes in a multi-functional agricultural
sector, new forms of cooperative activity such as direct marketing of farm
produce are increasing while others are declining. Overall, the traditionally
cohesive network of farmers seems to break up (see Burton *et al.*, this volume). This trend is amplified by a decline in the number of farmers, which
makes environmental and land management increasingly difficult: '. . . the
traditional management systems (co-operative fell management) may not be
effective anymore' (Burton *et al.*, 2005). Thus, the loss of social capital in
farming communities through the above-described social restructuring, loss
of farmers, immigration, and so on, and thus potentially weakened social
links could have major impacts on the supply of public goods provided from
upland regions (Burton *et al.*, 2005).

Composition of the upland economy

Until recently, the rural economy was seen as more or less synonymous with
the agricultural sectors, with a large portion of the rural population engaged
in agricultural activities. Traditionally the rural economy consisted of black-
smiths, carpenters, millers, bakers, and so on, providing services for agriculture,
rural industries and the local population of the region (Brassley, 2005). On a
national level, agriculture's share has now dropped to about 0.8 per cent of GDP
and 1.8 per cent of the labour force (Office for National Statistics, undated).

Today, the composition as well as the focus of the rural economy has
changed, now catering not only to a regional but also to national and international markets (DETR/MAFF, 2000). The structure of the regional economy is radically different from a few decades ago. Today's rural economies
largely display employment and business profiles similar to those of urban
areas (Lowe and Ward, 2007). Similarly, the economy in the PDNP is fairly
similar to the ones in the East Midlands and England in terms of major employ-
ers. The industries that in 2001 employed the largest proportions of Peak
District residents were manufacturing (15 per cent), followed by wholesale
and retail trade, repair of motor vehicles (13 per cent), real estate, renting
and business activities (12 per cent), health and social work (11 per cent),
education (10 per cent), and hotels and catering (7.5 per cent). The most pronounced differences to the East Midlands and England were with regard to
lower shares for manufacturing, and higher shares for the agriculture and
tourism sectors. For example, in terms of hotels and catering, the share in
the PDNP is roughly 70 per cent higher than in the East Midlands and England
(PDNPA, undated). With regard to the employment structure, we can
observe that in rural areas there are a higher number of businesses per head
of population (the majority of them are micro-businesses); there are higher
rates of self-employment – over a third of the economically active residents

are self-employed – three times the level in urban areas; and a higher level of those in employment work from home (Commission for Rural Communities, 2006; Lowe and Ward, 2007).

On average, the incomes in rural areas are higher than in urban areas. For example, the Peak District National Park population ranks amongst the 30 per cent least-deprived areas in England and is generally less deprived than populations immediately surrounding it (PDNPA, 2005a). However, there is evidence of declining availability of certain services in rural areas such as local schools, health services, small village shops, local retailers and post offices (Lowe *et al.*, 1986; Roberts, 2002; Winter and Rushbrook, 2003). Furthermore, there are pockets of deprivation and lower incomes in certain areas (Roberts, 2002). More specifically, the hill farming community itself is faced with falling incomes and reduction in the agricultural labour force, an ageing demographic structure and farmland abandonment (Burton *et al.*, 2005). This mirrors wider structural problems of the agricultural sector struggling with fluctuating and gradually declining prices (Brassley and Lobley, 2005). Farm incomes in the Peak District National Park have fallen by 75 per cent over the last ten years (PDRDF, 2004). Without subsidies in the Peak District, only dairy farms would generate profit, earning an average income of just £4,622 per annum, without considering farmer wages; small beef and sheep farm incomes would be –£2,320, and larger farms would be –£3,380 per annum (PDRDF, 2004; see also Condliffe, this volume).

A number of specific policies were designed to address the structural disadvantages of upland farming due to factors such as climate, topography, altitude and remoteness. This is based on the assumption that if farming ceased in these areas there would be further out-migration and land abandonment. To counter the disadvantage of upland farming compared to other farming areas, the Less Favoured Areas (LFA) designation was created. Under this designation, European Union member states were required to identify both Severely Disadvantaged Areas (SDA) and Disadvantaged Areas (DA), and allowed to provide payments in compensation for the handicaps faced by farmers, contributing significantly to the income of upland farmers in those designated areas. All UK uplands are classified as LFA. There is government commitment to continue the support for upland communities owing to their perceived contribution to (1) the environment (wildlife and landscapes), (2) the social fabric in relatively remote rural areas, and (3) the economy through livestock production and maintaining the assets on which other economic activities such as tourism depend (Defra, 2003; Burton *et al.*, 2005).

Land-based sectors

It is important to emphasise that the upland economy does go beyond farming and tourism, relying on a wide network of other important sectors (see e.g. Winter, 1996). But, at the same time, land-based sectors with their distinctive characteristics directly and indirectly provide important functions for the wider economy, and have considerable influence on the appearance of the landscape and functioning of ecosystems. These land-based sectors will be the focus of this section.

Farming

Under the current Rural Development Regulation within England some 2.2 million hectares of land is classified as LFA, the majority of which is upland. A total of 1.8 million hectares of the LFA is in agricultural production, which is approximately 19 per cent of the total agricultural land in England (Cumulus, 2005). Eighty per cent of the LFA is classified as SDA, with the remainder as DA. In terms of ownership structure in SDAs, we can observe that larger farms (100 ha and over) account for 76 per cent of the agricultural area, whereas the smallest farms (less than 20 ha) account for just 4 per cent, although they comprise 54 per cent of the number of holdings (Cumulus, 2005). The predominant land use in the LFAs is grassland and rough grazing, representing around 90 per cent of agricultural land (Cumulus, 2005), and accordingly most holdings are either sheep or cattle farms or a mixture of both types. Forty per cent of beef cows and 45 per cent of breeding sheep are in the English LFAs (ADAS, 2003). Another important aspect is that the average age of cattle and sheep farm holders in the LFA has increased slightly over the last fifteen years, with the largest proportion of holders (29 per cent) now aged 65 and over.

Farming in the uplands from the sale of products alone is economically unsustainable and is thus depending heavily on subsidies, in particular the agri-environmental scheme and the hill farm allowance (HFA) (see also Condliffe, this volume). This dependence on subsidies also means that land use and density of livestock are influenced by the economic incentives central to these policies. Changes in the EU Common Agricultural Policy (CAP), in particular the Agenda 2000 reform and the change from the headage-based Hill Livestock Compensatory Allowances scheme to the area-based HFA scheme in 2001, have already resulted in a decline in livestock numbers in the uplands (Cumulus, 2005). A further decline in stocking density may have resulted from the 2004 CAP reform, although it is expected that cattle will be more affected than sheep (Dwyer, 2005). In general, there is a shift in policies from subsidising farm products to paying farmers for the environmental benefits of sustainable farming in the uplands.

For the uplands in the Peak District, little separate data exist that would allow a comparison with the situation of upland farming in Britain in general. There are 1,800 farms in the PDNP, most of them small, with less than 40 hectares (PDNPA, undated); some of them are farmed by tenants of large landowners. Agricultural census data by the Department of Environment, Food and Rural Affairs (Defra) evidence large changes in composition of the livestock in the PDNP over the period 1990–2005. Sheep-grazing and beef-rearing now dominate the area, whereas dairy farming and breeding ewes and beef herds have been declining. The number of cattle has increased by 28 per cent whereas the number of lambs has declined by 9 per cent. These changes have occurred alongside changes to the composition of farmers. Between 2000 and 2005 the number of farmers in the area has declined by 5 per cent, while the number of part-time farmers has increased by 18 per cent. This trend is also evident in the changes of farm sizes, where an increase in smallholdings has been observed. This is partly due to non-farmers acquiring farms to use the building but not the land, which is then rented or sold to other farms. Analysis of the changes in land use between 1990 and 2005 shows a 12 per cent increase in permanent grassland and a 5 per cent decline in rough grazing.

With regard to landscape effects, hill farming is important in contributing to habitat and landscape maintenance (including maintaining traditional landscape features such as hedges and drystone walls and traditional farm buildings). On the other hand, hill farming can also have negative effects through creation of farm tracks, habitat deterioration and soil erosion arising from heavy grazing pressure (see Gardner *et al.*, this volume). On a wider scale, grazing and burning can have major effects on the species composition of moorland communities (English Nature, 2001; Crowle and McCormack, this volume).

Forestry and energy crops

Apart from mainly semi-natural woodlands not actively managed for wood products, the main types of woodland that can be found in the uplands are large-scale conifer plantations and to a lesser extent broad-leaved woodland, both actively managed for timber or wood products (English Nature, 2001). It is estimated that about 40 per cent of the total wooded area in England is in the uplands (Cumulus, 2005).

Since the 1990s there have been several funding schemes to increase the area of woodland (Cumulus, 2005). Economic interests in benefits resulting from forestry have shifted from focusing on timber production to a wide range of environmental and social benefits, for example for recreational use or carbon dioxide reduction (Price, 1997). Upland areas are not regarded as highly favourable for many renewable energy crops; however, a study in the uplands in Wales found that short-rotation coppice with willow *Salix* species on peaty soils produced reasonable yields, although at a lower level than on highly fertile lowland soils. While short-rotation coppice is harvested every three years, another possibility is short-rotation forestry, using fast-growing trees that reach their economically optimum size between eight and twenty years. Broad-leaved species are preferred over conifers in these schemes, as conifers are less suitable for energy combustion, the uplands seem to be less favourable for these crops (LTS International, 2006). In addition, long distances to the market are seen as another reason why many upland areas are not suitable for energy crops, as these would have a negative impact on the overall energy balance and costs. From a conservation point of view, the establishment of energy crop plantations on land previously unmanaged or under a low management regime is also regarded as negative (e.g. LTS International, 2006), thus ruling out most of the upland areas.

An economic analysis over a period of twenty-five years compared sheep production in the Welsh uplands with short-rotation coppice and found that sheep production was only the better economic choice if the high level of subsidies was maintained (Heaton *et al.*, 1999). A more recent and up-to-date study by the Scottish Agricultural College and the University of Cambridge (2005) found that energy crops produce a negative net margin on average, which suggests that they are unlikely to be widely grown without more long-term support commitments. However, the UK government has set itself the target of 20 per cent of electricity produced from renewable sources by 2020 and has therefore introduced different schemes to encourage the growth of energy crops, for example by providing grants for setting up the infrastructure as well as annual subsidies based on areas under cultivation (BERR, 2007).

Grouse and deer management

Large areas of the uplands, in particular heather moorland, are managed by landowners for red grouse *Lagopus lagopus scoticus*. The vegetation of about 25 per cent (15,000 km^2) of the British uplands is estimated to be heather moorland, with about half of this area managed for grouse (Bunce and Barr, 1988; Bardgett *et al.*, 1995). In the PDNP about 65 per cent of the park's upland area is within the boundaries of estates managed for red grouse shooting (Sotherton *et al.*, this volume). Moorland management for grouse plays an important role in maintaining the extent of open heath and some of its wildlife. In many areas, heather moorland has survived where the shooting interest has provided the incentive and the funding to retain it (English Nature, 2001; Sotherton *et al.*, this volume).

In Scotland, it has been estimated that grouse-shooting contributes £5 million to the Scottish economy, contributing to 1,240 jobs either directly or through the associated industry (McGilvray, 1995). Thirgood *et al.* (2000) estimate that, if similar economic conditions held in England, the annual contribution to the English economy would be £10 million, contributing to about 2,500 jobs. They conclude that, although this may seem small in relation to other industries, its importance can be high for remote rural communities where other employment opportunities may be scarce. Furthermore, moorland owners are keen to emphasize that, compared to other moorland management options, the management for grouse does not rely on any subsidies (Sotherton *et al.*, this volume).

Deer populations in the uplands are seen as far more controversial owing to the considerable vegetation damage that can be caused if population levels are too high. Conflicts surrounding increasing deer populations, conservation interests and economic interests of hunting estates have been studied particularly in Scotland where deer populations have doubled over the last thirty years (MacMillan, 2004). Damage caused by deer arises mainly from overgrazing of open vegetation as well as in forestry, where in particular natural tree species regeneration is affected, but also from road traffic accidents involving deer. Economic benefits are generated by the provision of jobs related to deer management and hunting activities, and the related increase in tourism revenues. In Scotland, around a thousand staff were estimated to work in a variety of jobs related to red deer in 1990, although the majority of these jobs were part-time (Hunt, 2003).

Tourism

Upland areas have long provided important recreational activities for urban-dominated societies. In addition, outdoor activities provide an important potential for raising visitor awareness and support for nature conservation (English Nature, 2001).

One of the most cited facts about the Peak District is the high number of visitors the National Park attracts, which reportedly makes it one of the most visited national parks worldwide. This is no surprise given that about a third of the English population live within sixty miles of the PDNP (PDNPA, 2005b). These numbers are in contrast to other rural areas in Britain with declining visitor numbers (Curry, this volume), but there are no reports on such trends for the PDNP, except for the year affected by foot-and-mouth disease.

Income from visitors is an important contributor to the local upland economy operating in several business sectors such as accommodation, hospitality, retail trade, transportation, travel services, events and attractions, outdoor recreation, and business and conferences (Godde *et al.*, 2000; Saxena, 2006). Within the Peak District National Park most businesses in the tourism sector operate either in accommodation (36 per cent) or catering (24 per cent), and overall this is estimated to be one of the biggest industrial sectors (15 per cent of all businesses) in the area (Derbyshire Chamber of Commerce, 2005). Other businesses within this sector are less easily categorised as they mainly operate outside tourism, as for example in retail or farming. In fact, more than a third of the responding businesses in a survey of the Derbyshire Chamber of Commerce (2005) regarded themselves as tourist-related. Based on a regional economic model, we found that tourism has very strong backward linkages to other economic sectors within the upland economy; that is, it buys a significant amount of its inputs from local sources, thus contributing to the growth of other local industries along its supply chain.

In 2000, the Peak District Rural Development Partnership developed the *Peak District Sustainable Tourism Strategy* (Peak District Tourism Forum, 2000), acknowledging the industry's strong dependence on the conservation of the environmental quality of the area as its unique selling point. The strategy therefore aims to increase visitors' spending and encourage longer stays but also to provide conditions for a more sustainable use of the area by, for example, improved public transport or use of local products (see, for example, the Peak District Environmental Quality Mark for local food produced following environmental standards).

When compared to other types of land use – for example, grazing and burning management – recreational impacts are usually considered as having little long-term detrimental conservation impacts, depending on the type of outdoor activity. For example, hill walking, four-wheel-drive vehicles, motorcycles, horse riding can lead to a loss of vegetation and erosion, and can have a long-term effect of disturbance on birds, mammals and invertebrates, but usually on a rather localised basis (English Nature, 2001).

Ecosystem services: potential economic sectors of the future?

The uplands comprise extensive ecosystems that provide important services of public benefit (see Bonn, Rebane and Reid; Hanley and Colombo, both this volume). The role of biodiversity and wildlife for recreation, tourism and the local economy has long been recognised (e.g. Crabtree *et al.*, 1994; MacLellan, 1999).

Only very recently, attention has been drawn to the uplands potential for carbon storage, which may become economically significant owing to carbon pricing policies aimed at climate change mitigation. Upland areas contain the single largest carbon reserve in the UK. The UK's peat stores more carbon than the forests of Britain and France combined. Within the UK carbon inventory, peatlands are considered a net sink (Worrall *et al.*, 2003; Worrall *et al.*, in press). Thus, peat areas are actively sequestering carbon. However, Bellamy *et al.* (2005) found alarming evidence that 80 per cent of UK soils carbon losses might be from upland peat soils. Similarly, Worrall *et al.* (2003) estimate that all of the peatlands in England and Wales combined could absorb around 400,000 tonnes of carbon a year if in pristine condition; these same areas could emit up to 381,000 tonnes of carbon a year if they were damaged by practices such as overgrazing, excessive burning or drainage (see Worrall and Evans, this volume). Thus, to take full advantage of this carbon sequestration potential, changes in land-use practice and further peatland restoration as well as changes in the institutional framework are required. For example, large-scale restoration could be financed as Certified Emission Reductions on the carbon offset market, which is currently dominated by forestry, renewable energy and energy-efficiency projects. The voluntary UK carbon offset industry could help to pay land managers who incur the costs of changes in their land management regime, for the services they provide through carbon sequestration.

Similarly, degradation of upland peat areas has been blamed for other significant environmental impacts such as ecological degradation, increased accidental fire risk, downstream flash flooding, and water colouration and sedimentation. Therefore, there is also a close link between land management activities in the upland areas and the interests of water utilities. Water companies spend large amounts of money removing colour from water coming from upland water catchments. Thus, the water quality benefits could provide an additional incentive for water utilities to promote conservation activities in the uplands.

In principle, a wide variety of ecosystem services could be sold. For example, in Costa Rica forested conservation areas are credited with income for the services that they provide both as watersheds and as carbon sinks (Chomitz *et al.*, 1999). Similarly, New York City, amongst a number of other cities in the US, reduced its costs for drinking-water provision by investing in the restoration of the integrity of the ecosystem of the upland watershed (Chichilnisky and Heal, 1998). This additional income to land owners or land managers could tip the balance in favour of conserving marginal agricultural land.

Conclusions

The reality of the rural economy has moved from being mainly a producer of food, fibres and minerals to providing a multitude of consumption and production activities. This is accompanied by a better understanding and appreciation of environmental values attracting inflow of capital and skills (Power, 1996a; Courtney *et al.*, 2006). This changing perception is mirrored in the literature by the shift from the economic base model to increasing recognition of ecosystems services and their contribution to the local economy. The economic base theory builds on the idea that exports based on extraction of resources or manufacturing are driving the growth of a regional economy. Income earned in export-related activities circulates through the local economy and thus creates jobs and contributes to the health of the economy (Power, 1996a, b). This view ignores the structure and character of a local economy, which influence what happens with money injected or created within an economy. The more quickly income leaks out of the local economy, the smaller the effect on jobs and economic well-being via the multiplier effect. Thus, the focus should be on the diversity and interconnectedness of local economic activities rather than on the unconditional promotion of extraction and production for exports (Power, 1996b; Sacks, 2002). Examples for increasing the interconnectedness of the local economy are sourcing inputs from within the region, as shown by the new Environmental Quality Mark within the PDNP and many other similar initiatives across the UK and internationally (Ward and Lewis, 2002).

There is little disagreement that land-based extractive sectors are decreasing in importance in the UK uplands. Numerous reports and national statistics have come to this conclusion, and our analysis for the PDNP *vis-à-vis* other upland areas supports this trend. However, sectors based on the provision of ecosystem services and amenity values are becoming increasingly significant. The longer-term economic prosperity of the upland regions will depend on the extent to which these economic values are captured and re-invested in the development of the region. This chapter points to several mechanisms by which this might be achieved. First, the concept of a foot-loose economy highlights the impact of generating attractive local communities in locations rich in natural capital. Second, the presence of second-home owners, retired people looking for a more tranquil environment, or specialised professionals working from home or a small office, who have chosen to live in a rural area because of its natural and socio-economic attributes, and the income of such people leads through multiplier effects to further jobs in the area, mainly for provision of local services. Third, provision of ecosystem services and policy reforms allows upland regions to reap the benefits of investing in a productive ecosystem. Ecosystem services such as carbon sequestration and provision of high water quality seem to be promising economic sectors for the UK uplands.

Upland areas are often recognised for their outstanding beauty and for their provision of ecosystems services. This includes beneficiaries outside the park boundaries. This can lead to a mismatch of costs incurred by those who provide for ecosystems services and those who enjoy their benefits. Policies directed to sustaining the long-term functioning of ecosystems services and at the same time providing for a vibrant rural community therefore need fully to recognize and appreciate the inseparable interaction between the biophysical environment and economic activities taking place in the area. Failure to address the socio-economic characteristics of the uplands and the driving forces influencing the behaviour of land managers would likely jeopardise future environmental management, with conservation initiatives potentially suffering the greatest consequences.

Acknowledgements

We thank Fred Worrall and Mark Reed for providing inputs on the carbon section, and Jeremy Phillipson and Mark Reed for providing feedback to earlier drafts. Mette Termansen and Klaus Hubacek are co-funded through the Rural Economy and Land Use (RELU) programme, co-sponsored by Defra and SEERAD (project RES-224-25-0088).

References

ADAS (2003) *The Mid-term Evaluation of the England Rural Development Programme, Hill Farm Allowance*. Wolverhampton: ADAS Consulting.

Bardgett, R. D., Marsden, J. H. and Howard, D. C. (1995) The extent and condition of heather on moorland in the uplands of England and Wales. *Biological Conservation*, **71**, 155–61.

Bellamy, P. H., Loveland, P. J., Bradley, R. I., Lark, M. R., Guy, J. D. and Kirk, G. J. D. (2005) Carbon losses from all soils across England and Wales 1978–2003. *Nature*, **437**, 245–8.

BERR (2007) *Energy White Paper: Meeting the Energy Challenge.* Department for Business, Enterprise and Regulatory Reform, London. http://www.dti.gov.uk/energy/whitepaper/page39534.html

Blackburn, S., Errington, A. and Lobley, M. (2000) *Review of the Peak District IRD, 11 Years On: Final Report to Countryside Agency.* London: Countryside Agency.

Brassley, P. (2005) One thousand years of rural life. *The Countryside Notebook* (ed. R. Soffe), pp. 3–12. Oxford: Blackwell.

Brassley, P. and Lobley, M. (2005) The common agricultural policy of the European Union. *The Countryside Notebook* (ed. R. Soffe), pp. 103–19. Oxford: Blackwell.

Brown, D. L., Fuguitt, G. V., Heaton, T. and Waseem, S. (1997) Continuities in size of place preferences in the United States, 1972–1992. *Rural Sociology,* **62**, 408–28.

Buller, H., Morris, C. and Wright, E. (2003) The demography of rural areas: a literature review. Research report to Defra. Countryside and Community Research Unit, University of Gloucestershire. http://www.defra.gov.uk/rural/pdfs/research/demography.pdf

Bunce, R. G. H. and Barr, C. J. (1988) The extent of land under different management regimes in the uplands and the potential for change. *Ecological Change in the Uplands* (ed. M. B. Usher and D. B. A. Thompson), pp. 415–26. Oxford: Blackwell.

Burton, R., Mansfield, L., Schwarz, G., Brown, K. and Convery, I. (2005). *Social Capital in Hill Farming: Report for the Upland Centre.* Penrith: International Centre for the Uplands.

Chichilnisky, G. and Heal, G. (1998) Economic returns from the biosphere. *Nature,* **391**, pp. 629–30.

Chomitz, K. M., Brenes, E. and Constantino, L. (1999) Financing environmental services: the Costa Rican experience and its implications. *The Science of the Total Environment,* **240**, 157–69.

Commission for Rural Communities (2006) *State of the Countryside Report.* Commission for Rural Communities, London. http://www.ruralcommunities.gov.uk/publications/crc22stateofthecountryside2006

Countryside Agency (2004) *The State of the Countryside 2004: Annex and Reference Information.* Cheltenham: Countryside Agency.

Courtney, P., Hill, G. and Roberts, D. (2006) The role of natural heritage in rural development: an analysis of economic linkages in Scotland. *Journal of Rural Studies,* **22**, 469–84.

Crabtree, J. R., Leat, P. M. K., Santarossa, J. and Thomson, K. J. (1994) The economic impact of wildlife sites in Scotland. *Journal of Rural Studies,* **10**, 61–72.

Cumulus (2005) *Assessment of CAP Reform and Other Key Policies on Upland Farms and Land Use Implications in SDAS and DAS in England.* Final report for Defra. Gloucestershire, Cumulus Countryside and Rural Consultants.

Defra (2002) *Population Trends in Rural Areas of England: 1991–2001.* Rural Statistics Unit. Statistics (Census and Surveys) Division. Defra, London.

Defra (2003) *Review of the Hill Farm Allowance in England: Consultation Document,* Defra, London. http://www.defra.gov.uk/erdp/reviews/default.htm

Derbyshire Chamber of Commerce (2005) *Survey of Businesses in the Peak District and Rural Action Zone.* Report for the Peak District National Park. Derbyshire Chamber of Commerce, Chesterfield. http://peakresources.gemini.titaninternet.co.uk/pubs/research/businesssurvey.pdf

DETR/MAFF (2000) *Our Countryside: The Future. Government's Rural White Paper*. DETR, London. http://www.defra.gov.uk/rural/ruralwp/whitepaper/default. htm

Dwyer, J. (2005) *The Economics of Extensive Livestock Grazing after CAP Reform.* Overview report to English Nature. Countryside and Community Research Unit, University of Gloucestershire. http://www.english-nature.org.uk/pubs/publication/ PDF/SummaryLivestockReport.pdf

English Nature (2001) *The Upland Management Handbook*. http://www.english-nature.org.uk/pubs/handbooks/upland.asp?id=1

Findlay, A., Short, D. and Stockdale, A. (1999) *Migration Impacts in Rural England: Report to the Countryside Agency*. Cheltenham: The Countryside Agency.

Fraser, E., Dougill, A. J., Mabee, W., Reed, M. and McApline, P. (2006) Bottom up and top down: analysis of participatory processes for sustainability indicator identification as a pathway to community empowerment and sustainable environmental management. *Journal of Environmental Management*, **78**, 114–27.

Godde, P. M., Price, M. F. and Zimmerman, F. M. (eds) (2000) *Tourism and Development in Mountain Regions*. Wallingford: CABI Publishing.

Gray, J. (2000) The common agricultural policy and the re-invention of the rural in the European community. *Sociologia Ruralis*, **40**, 30–52.

Heaton, R. J., Randerson, P. F. and Slater, F. M. (1999) The economics of growing short rotation coppice in the uplands of mid-Wales and an economic comparison with sheep production. *Biomass and Bioenergy*, **17**, 59–71.

Hunt, J. F. (2003) *Impacts of Wild Deer in Scotland – How Fares the Public Interest?* http://wwf.org.uk/filelibrary/pdf/deerreport.pdf

Johnson, K. M. and Beale, C. L. (1999) The continuing population rebound in nonmetro America. *Rural Development Perspectives*, **13**, 2–10.

Lobley, M. and Potter, C. (2004) Agricultural change and restructuring: recent evidence from a survey of agricultural households in England. *Journal of Rural Studies*, **20**, 499–510.

Lowe, P., Bradley, T. and Wright, S. (eds) (1986) *Deprivation and Welfare in Rural Areas*. Norwich: Geobooks.

Lowe, P. and Ward, N. (2007) Sustainable rural economies: some lessons from the English experience. *Sustainable Development*, **15**, 307–17.

LTS International (2006) *A Review of the Potential Impacts of Short Rotation Forestry: Final Report*. http://www.forestry.gov.uk/pdf/SRFFinalreport27Feb.pdf/ $FILE/SRFFinalreport27Feb.pdf

McGilvray, J. (1995) *An Economic Study of Grouse Moors*. Fordingbridge: The Game Conservancy.

MacLellan, L. R. (1999) An examination of wildlife tourism as a sustainable form of tourism development in north west Scotland. *International Journal of Tourism Research*, **1**, 375–87.

MacMillan, D. (2004) Tradeable hunting obligations – a new approach to regulating red deer numbers in the Scottish highlands. *Journal of Environmental Management*, **71**, 261–70.

Murdoch, J. (1997) *Why Do People Move into the Countryside? Report for the Countryside Commission*. Cheltenham: Countryside Commission.

Murdoch, J. and Marsden, T. (1994) *Reconstituting Rurality*. London: UCL Press.

Newby, H. E. (1986) Locality and rurality: the restructuring of rural social relations. *Regional Studies*, **20**, 209–15.

Office for National Statistics (undated) *Agriculture and Food in the National Economy 1973–2003: Agriculture in the United Kingdom.* http://www.statistics.gov.uk/statbase/ssdataset.asp?vlnk=3734andMore=Y.

PDNPA (2001) *State of the Park Report 2000.* Peak District National Park Authority, Bakewell. http://www.peakdistrict.gov.uk/index/pubs/sopr.htm

PDNPA (2005a) *The Index of Multiple Deprivation 2004 in the Peak District National Park.* Peak District National Park Authority, Bakewell. http://peakresources.gemini.titaninternet.co.uk/pubs/research/IMD2004.pdf

PDNPA (2005b) *Visitor Survey 2005.* Peak District National Park Authority, Bakewell. http://www.peakdistrict.gov.uk/visitorsurvey.pdf

PDNPA (undated) *Living and working in the Peak District National Park: 2001 Census of Population Results.* Peak District National Park Authority, Bakewell. http://www.peakdistrict.org/census2001.pdf

PDRDF (2004) *Hard Times: A Research Report into Hill Farming and Farming Families in the Peak District.* Peak District Rural Deprivation Forum, Hope. http://pdrdf.org/publications.htm

Peak District Tourism Forum (2000) *Peak District Sustainable Tourism Strategy.* http://www.highpeak.gov.uk/culture/tourismpolicy.pdf

Power, T. M. (1996a) *Environmental Protection and Economic Well-being: The Economic Pursuit of Quality.* Armonk, NY: M. E. Sharpe.

Power, T. M. (1996b) *Lost Landscapes and Failed Economies: The Search for the Value of Place.* Washington, DC: Island Press.

Pretty, J. and Ward, H. (2001) Social capital and the environment. *World Development,* **29,** 209–27.

Price, C. (1997) Twenty-five years of forestry cost–benefit analysis in Britain. *Forestry,* **70,** 171–89.

Putnam, R. D. (2001) Social capital: measurements and consequences. *Isuma,* **2,** 41–51.

Raley, M. and Moxey, A. (2000) *Rural Microbusinesses in North East England: Final Survey Results.* Centre for Rural Economy, University of Newcastle upon Tyne.

Roberts, S. (2002) *Key Drivers of Economic Development and Inclusion in Rural Areas.* Defra, London. http://statistics.defra.gov.uk/esg/temp_rural/sion.pdf

Sacks, J. (2002) *The money Trail: Measuring Your Impact on the Local Economy Using LM3.* London: New Economics Foundation/The Countryside Agency.

Saxena, G. (2006) Beyond mistrust and competition – the role of social and personal bonding processes in sustaining livelihoods of rural tourism businesses: a case of the Peak District National Park. *International Journal of Tourism Research,* **8,** 263–77.

Scottish Agricultural College and University of Cambridge (2005) *Farm Level Economic Impacts of Energy Crop Production.* Defra, London. randd.defra.gov.uk/Document.aspx?Document=NF0431_4015_FRA.doc

Sobels, J., Curtis, A. and Lockie, S. (2001) The role of landcare group networks in rural Australia: exploring the contribution of social capital. *Journal of Rural Studies,* **17,** 265–76.

Thirgood, S., Redpath, S., Newton, I. and Hudson, P. (2000) Raptors and red grouse: conservation conflicts and management solutions. *Conservation Biology,* **14,** 95–104.

Ward, B. and Lewis, J. (2002) *Plugging the Leaks: Making the Most of Every Pound That Enters Your Local Economy.* London: New Economics Foundation.

Winter, M. (1996) The rural economy. *Our countryside* (ed. B. White-Spunner), pp. 89–101. Cambridge: Baily's.

Winter, M. and Rushbrook, L. (2003) *Literature Review of the English Rural Economy.* Final report to Defra. Defra, London. http://www.defra.gov.uk/rural/pdfs/research/lit_rev_rural_econ.pdf

Worrall, F., Burt, T. P., Adamson, J. K., Reed, M., Warburton, J., Armstrong, A. and Evans, M. (in press) Predicting the future carbon budget of an upland peat catchment. *Climatic Change.*

Worrall, F., Reed, M. S., Warburton, J. and Burt, T. (2003) Carbon budget for a British peat catchment. *Science of the Total Environment,* **312**, 133–46.

17 The future of public goods provision in upland regions

Learning from hefted commons in the Lake District, UK

Rob J. F. Burton, Gerald Schwarz,
Katrina M. Brown, Ian T. Convery and
Lois Mansfield

Introduction: the uplands and public goods provision

The nature of agriculture in Europe is changing. Problems with overproduction and environmental damage in the 1980s led to the adoption of the 'public goods model', by which farmers and landowners are encouraged to provide agri-environmental goods voluntarily in return for payments for income forgone (Falconer and Ward, 2000). For upland communities, this change could be particularly important. In terms of agricultural production, upland areas are often very poor (Caskie *et al.*, 2001), as is evidenced from the high level of support through special compensatory payments such as the Hill Farm Allowance available in Less Favoured Areas. However, upland areas in the UK and across Europe are major suppliers of scenic and environmental public goods, with regions such as Dartmoor (Devon) and the Lake District (Cumbria) acting as 'honey-pots' for recreational and leisure tourism. Thus, the provision of public goods is currently the main economic rationale for supporting upland farmers.

Hodge (2000, p. 264) observes that the public goods debate 'is premised on agricultural systems that have often co-evolved with the environment over substantial periods of time to the extent that there is a close relationship between the valued characteristics of the environment and certain attributes of agricultural systems'. Upland regions are particularly important in this regard. Whereas many landscapes across Europe are now characterised by industrial-scale agriculture, the rugged nature of much of the uplands combined with their relative isolation and poor agricultural productivity (making mechanisation and intensification difficult) has preserved much of the established character (Gueydon and Hoffmann, 2006). Areas such as the Lake District have maintained the traditional core of both their livestock systems and their farming cultures for centuries, leaving the relationship between the system of farming and the environment relatively unchanged and, arguably as a consequence, highly valuable as a conservation and landscape resource (Short, 2000).

One particular characteristic of upland regions in the UK is that many are managed as *common grazings*, where right to pasture is shared by a number of 'commoners'. Common grazings are not unique to the UK. Throughout the world, many countries have at least some remnant common grazing systems operating in upland areas, for example Mongolia (Mearns, 1996), Germany (Gueydon and Hoffmann, 2006) and Poland (Niemeyer and Riseth, 2004), where the communal management systems rely on voluntary compliance with local rules and arrangements (Thomas, 1999) and therefore high levels of social capital. The communality and complexity of social arrangements within commons adds an extra challenge for management. However, Short and Winter (1999) suggest that it is precisely this characteristic – coupled with, and compelled by, harsh biophysical environments – that has enabled the production of high levels of environmental public goods through the impediment of more intensive management.

What is unusual about the UK situation is the extent to which the practice of hefting continues to be used as a management tool. Hefts are 'unfenced named areas of hill whose natural topography provides ewes with both adequate grazing and shelter' (Gray, 1998, p. 350) generally managed as part of a single fell farm. Sheep are territorial and will remain within their hefts provided that shepherding and pressure from neighbouring hefts prevents excessive straying (Short, 2000). As knowledge of the heft boundaries is transferred from mother to lamb, once a heft has been established it can be maintained without substantial effort by the farmer. However, the restocking of hefts can be a laborious task, as it requires a long period of intensive shepherding. The advantage of the hefting system is that, while the spatial distribution of grazing pressure can be closely managed to avoid areas of under- and over-grazing (Short, 2000), the fell nevertheless remains unfenced – thus providing potential scenic, recreational and environmental benefits.

Where common grazing systems provide these benefits, it could be argued that policy should aim to ensure their continuation to secure a supply of scenic and environmental public goods. However, evidence from upland areas across the UK suggests that common grazings are under threat as a result of the diminishing number of agriculturalists prepared to work in what is a strenuous, time-consuming and often poorly rewarded occupation (Burton *et al.*, 2005; Brown, 2006). Paying farmers to produce environmental public goods is seen as part of the solution to this problem – recognising the value of the non-agricultural goods produced and compensating farmers through subsidies in return for stewardship agreements. However, this chapter suggests that, in common grazing regions of exceptionally high public goods value, existing agri-environment payments may, in the long term, fail to preserve the commons.

Common grazings and public goods provision: the case of the Lake District

In 2004–5 we conducted an investigation into the social capital of hill farming in the Cumbria region of the UK. The research involved qualitative interviews with a total of forty-four farmers/farm families and was conducted in three stages. The first stage comprised eight two-hour family interviews followed by a return interview to discuss the main findings. The second stage of the research involved interviewing twelve farmers in each of the key upland massifs of Cumbria: the North Pennines (12), Orton and Howgill Fells (12) and Lake District (12) – a total of thirty-six in all (see Figure 17.1). Finally, four focus groups were held to discuss issues that arose in the earlier surveys. Interviews were transcribed in full and subject to qualitative analysis. Full details of the research process can be found in Burton *et al.* (2005).

While some issues are common across all three regions, it is the future of farmers in the Lake District – a rugged area of glaciated mountains, valleys and lakes – that is of greatest concern as the region contains some of the most scenic landscapes in the country and maintains some of the strongest remaining hefted common grazing communities. The analysis here is therefore based on the seventeen interviews that took place in this region but is supported by findings from the broader survey.

Farming in Cumbria has evolved to suit the nature of the environment. The landscape (see Figure 17.2) consists of a series of fells at a relatively high altitude (but without permanent snow), with the farms located in the surrounding valleys. One fell may thus support a number of commoners living considerable distances apart. Farms are structured to take advantage of the combination of summer grazings on the fells and low-level improved grazing in the valleys. They traditionally comprise three main management components (see Figure 17.3): 'in-bye land' – enclosed grassland used for pasture or for the production of hay or silage; 'intake land' – enclosed land used exclusively for grazing; and 'fell land' – which is covered by semi-natural upland vegetation and is generally unenclosed except along title-based boundaries. Traditionally these systems have combined sheep with some cattle, with the cattle assisting environmental management by maintaining maximum variety of sward height and by trampling bracken (Evans *et al.*, 2003).

The process of managing hefted fell land is very much a cooperative venture of the local commoners. Farmer 13 describes the process of organising the gathering on his fell:

> When it comes to gather in the fell there's a little old fellow, 65 now, and he rings round up to 10 people. 'What day of the week do you reckon?' Rings round everybody, Tuesday weather's good, everybody arrives at the fell gate, the lot. The lot goes.

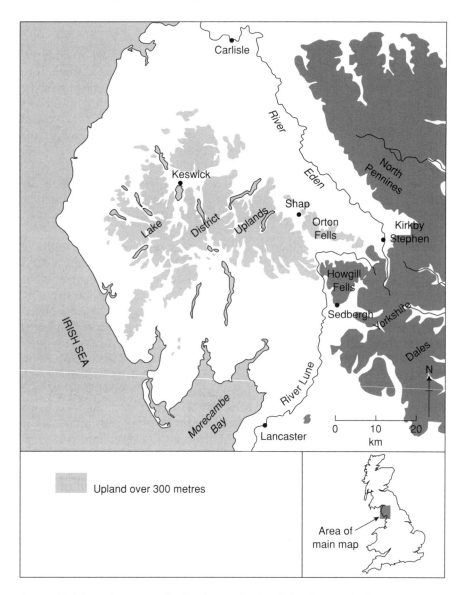

Figure 17.1 Location map of upland areas in Cumbria. (Source: L. Mansfield).

The need for strong social links between participating farmers to ensure effective farm management lies in the necessity that 'the lot' are willing to participate in this process as any holes in the gather may lead to sheep remaining on the hill. Sheep that have strayed on to an ungathered heft may act as a centre for the spread of disease or, alternatively, require the farmer to

Figure 17.2 Upland farm in Lake District (photograph: R. Burton).

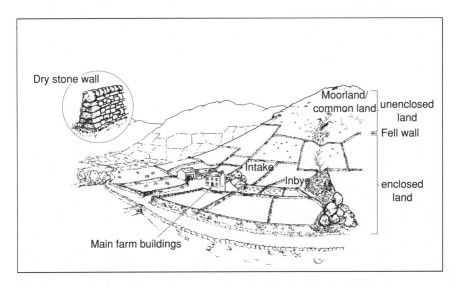

Figure 17.3 Structure of a traditional upland farm (source: L. Mansfield).

gather them again at a later date. Those that stray on to neighbouring hefts during the gather are collected by the farmer associated with that heft and then exchanged with the owner at a later time. As farmer 7 describes, 'we give them a ring and they'll probably have 4 or 5 of ours or vice-versa and we'll meet up somewhere along the road and swap them round'. Thus, maintaining friendly relations with neighbouring farmers on the commons is an important part of running an efficient business.

The effectiveness of cooperative action is also highly dependent on the number of people who are available to gather the fell relative to the area itself but independent of the number of stock on the common (IEEP, 2004). Too few people can lead to problems with fell management, for example:

> Trouble is, there was a lot more little farms 40 years ago, all had sheep on the fells and obviously there was more people to gather the fells. Whereas now it's getting more like a skeleton crew as farms have been amalgamated but we've still got the same acreage of hill to gather.
>
> (Farmer 5)

Many other farmers noted that there are problems in their commons getting enough people for the gather. Numbers have dropped significantly. For example, farmer 2 states that when his father was farming there were twenty people working the fell but now that number has dwindled to five. For farmer 6, the number of farmers working his fell has declined since 2000 from four to two. This is an interesting case of the potential 'unzipping' of the common grazings as here the retirement of one of the farmers and the pressure it placed on remaining farmers led directly to the retirement of the other. Farmer 19 tells a similar story – that the retirement of one farmer from farming on his common has led another farmer, one of the younger farmers at 40 (involved in the more strenuous work during the gather), to reconsider his position.

> It's a hard farm. And since he's turned 40, he's a fit lad, he's finding it harder. All of the sudden, there's one of the guys is going to retire, he wants out, what's going to happen to that gather?
>
> (Farmer 19)

The breakdown of the hefting system in Cumbria is already evident in some areas. While in the Lake District all seventeen farmers ran hefted flocks, for the two other massifs 25 per cent of respondents had abandoned hefting as a management tool, with some farmers now operating single enterprises within their walled commons. To ascertain how potentially serious this problem was likely to be in the future, farmers were asked whether they were likely to have a successor to take over the farm on retirement. Of the seventeen farmers interviewed in the Lake District, six were certain of having a successor, two were not sure (because their children were too young to decide) and nine were certain of having no successor. While the average age of farmers in the Lake District survey was relatively low for farming in general (approximately

55), the physically demanding nature of the work means that hill farmers have traditionally withdrawn from hill management at a younger age. Thus, combined with a lack of successors, it is possible that we could see major changes in common grazings within ten years if farms are not repopulated – a figure also suggested by the Federation of Cumbria Commoners (Federation of Cumbria Commoners, 2006).

In the Lake District, the National Trust, as a major landowner (25 per cent of land in the National Park), is likely to hold the key to maintaining farming numbers on many of the fells. Farmers in the survey observed that in the past the National Trust has been a model landlord in its concern that small farms were repopulated, rather than being split up and amalgamated with other farms. These farms acted as a 'step up the ladder' for younger farmers from the region, as farmer 20 observes:

> I think every farm in Borrowdale is owned by the National Trust. If a young lad moved into Borrowdale he would work for 3 or 4 different farms in that valley, he'd be pretty much guaranteed to get a National Trust tenancy, by the time he was mid 20s early 30s . . . and that isn't the case anymore.

A change in policy from the National Trust was also evident from the decision to divide Beatrix Potter's High Ewedale Farm between four neighbours, re-let the farm for residential purposes and transfer the flock to neighbouring farms (BBC, 2005). This is potentially a dilemma for all landowners. Letting unprofitable farms as working hill farms is clearly likely to be difficult (particularly if working the fell is a stipulation of the letting agreement); and, if the landowner also owns neighbouring farms, allowing the viability of their upland management to diminish as a result of an inability to expand is neither good business nor necessarily good for the environment.

In the case of non-National Trust farms a key factor compounding any decision on the farm's future is the exceptionally high house prices of recent years. With farming incomes currently depressed, and large farmhouses in remote and scenic areas fetching upwards of a million pounds (a figure completely disproportionate to the income of a traditional hill farm), there is clear financial pressure to divide the farm into farmhouse, outbuildings (for housing development) and land rather than selling the farm as a going concern. For example, farmer 8 moved from a farm in the Lake District to a larger farm in a cheaper region of Cumbria to enable his son to enter the business. Although he originally intended to raise the capital by selling the old farm outright, the capital raised from the house and outbuildings alone was sufficient to purchase a new farm outside the boundaries of the National Park. Even if farms are sold as a working farm, prices in the Lake District reflect the development potential of the farm – meaning that large quantities of capital would be required to purchase relatively unprofitable (and difficult) farming businesses. If a key driver of farm division is high housing prices, the question is: What drives housing prices in the region?

The issue: private accumulation of access to public goods?

In a sense, what is happening in the Lake District is that *house prices are reflecting the value of the landscape and amenity public goods produced.* Public visits to the Lake District area are based largely around activities enhanced by high public goods provision; for example hill walking, scenic driving and wildlife watching, with emphasis placed on the historical stone-walled farm landscapes and the cultural working of the land (Burton *et al.*, 2005). Researchers and local government organisations believe it is this demand that drives the housing economy in the region. For example, the Lake District National Park Authority (LDNPA, 2006) stated that quality of life and landscape are the main forces behind the 'very high level of demand' for housing in the Lake District. Similar connections between rapidly rising house prices and rugged mountain landscapes delivering scenic and recreational public goods have recently also been observed in National Parks in the USA (Smaldone *et al.*, 2005).

The problem is that, despite the popular conception of public goods as 'free for all', the distinction between public and private goods is often not as clear as portrayed (Whitby, 2000). 'Pure' public goods are goods or services that are characterised by two principles: (1) non-rivalry – an individual's consumption of the good does not reduce the access to the good for others; and (2) non-excludability – the good cannot be withheld from others by individual consumers (Pretty and Ward, 2001). While environmental goods are generally considered to be 'public goods' (Franks, 2003), in the act of consuming these goods individuals can affect their availability for others. For example, Eckton (2003: 308) observes that traffic congestion in the Lake District National Park produces an 'inherent contradiction in that the mode of transport that facilitated the tourism experience also diminishes it'. The way in which transport restricts public goods access to others is inadvertent and temporary, but within upland areas the availability of private housing enables a form of private accumulation of access to public goods that is more deliberate and permanent.

'Purchasers' of access to public goods in the region are not generally locals but incomers and second-home owners with access to capital disproportionate to the local economy – effectively disembedding the 'housing' economy from other regional economic forces. In the Lake District, external pressure on housing has long been a problem, driven by demand from the nearby industrialised areas such as Manchester, Liverpool, Birmingham and even London. Clark (1982) reported that pressure for second and retirement homes by outsiders had already been present for 'decades' with estimates of the number of second homes in 1976 at above 30 per cent for some parishes. Despite a policy of providing 'local' or 'affordable' housing in the region under section 52 of the Local Town and Country Planning Act, the situation does not appear to have improved greatly over the last three decades. Currently, the LDNPA (2006) reports that over a fifth of all houses within the National Park are second homes, although this varies, with some particularly desirable areas attracting much higher levels of second-home ownership, for example Coniston has 40 per cent of its houses as second homes.

The sale of established farm buildings as second homes may not necessarily be seen as an impediment to effective environmental public goods provision. It may be argued, as with High Yewdale Farm, that in fact increasing farm size is essential to maintain economically viable farm units to protect the natural environment. In general, improving the economic viability of farms is seen as a means of decreasing the likelihood of land abandonment, which is considered a major environmental problem for areas in Europe with low-intensity farming systems (Plieninger *et al.*, 2006). However, if countryside-based public goods are best-delivered through the traditional systems and styles of farming with which they co-evolved, then maximising public goods provision should also involve protecting the vulnerable farming systems that deliver them.

The likely alternative to a hefted common grazing system is a ranching approach by which sheep roam free over the common. Concern has recently been expressed that such 'ranchification' may occur in the Cumbria region if the decline in farming population is not halted (Alderson *et al.*, 2006, p. 266). Experience in Scotland where common grazing systems have already collapsed in many areas suggests that the grazing pattern on a 'ranched' fell is dramatically different – with reports of simultaneous under- and over-grazing on different areas of the same common grazing (Brown, 2006). Further, as Le Duc (2000, p. 158) suggests, for any restoration of heathland 'grazing can be critical'. Low initial grazing can potentially lead to an 'overshoot' of the target community and species-poor vegetation, whereas high grazing at a too early stage is likely to lead to a different, but again undesirable, plant community. Moving to a 'ranching' approach is problematic in that, if environmental degradation occurs, it may be difficult to restore the farming communities, and particularly the human and social capital necessary for effective common grazing systems.[1]

It may also be argued that the upland areas should simply modernise – for example, move away from traditional family farming systems and manage the fells through contractors or hired labour. However, one of the reasons this system has persisted is the lack of alternatives. While hired labour was used in some cases, farmers noted that this was not an ideal situation because gathering the fells is a highly skilled process. As farmer 3 observed:

> . . . somebody from outside coming in . . . well he's not going to know any of that which you know. That takes a long time to learn and probably at times could prove costly to you.

The necessity of using dogs to gather the sheep introduces further difficulties as dogs are an integral part of the hill farming system, and their experience and knowledge of the fells are essential. As farmer 18 observes:

> You have to get the dogs accustomed to the hill they are going to gather on as well. Get them used to that. You can buy a dog and get it accustomed eventually. Mostly they grow up on the farm and they know the fell that they are gathering.

An alternative solution would be mechanising the gathering process. This is possible in some fells, but for the higher, more rugged terrain (and more environmentally sensitive and scenic) it is more problematic as 'there's no flying around on motorbikes or whatever on the high fells' (farmer 5). Farmer 6 similarly comments that, while he can gather one fell with his father on bikes, for another of their fells 'it needs a team of 6 of them to gather. That's the one further up, cos it's just rock edges and all sorts.' The use of technology is already widespread in Cumbria to the extent that, without further technological developments, it seems unlikely that there is room for further mechanisation given the topography of the region.

Solving the problem: a 'commons' future for the Lake District?

While house prices in the Lake District are a driver behind the decline of the commons, it should not be imagined that tackling house prices alone would resolve the situation. In particular, if agricultural incomes are not sufficient to attract the next generation of farmers to the business, the commons will inevitably collapse even if the housing pressure is released. In some ways, we are thus reliant on the desire of farm families to 'keep farming' rather than their commercial interests to preserve important landscapes such as these. The problem is that, if farmers are only compensated for the loss of agricultural income, and yet agricultural income itself is insufficient to compete with other forms of income generation, the supply of public goods is also tied to the fate of agriculture – which appears to continue to decline. When low farming incomes are then juxtaposed with significant external economic competition for farming resources (in this case the houses and outbuildings), there can only be one outcome.

Linking farm incomes to the level of public goods supply is likely to be a difficult task. Effectively what is required is a means of transferring the value of the public goods generated back to the suppliers in a manner that discourages them from 'cashing in' their public goods access.[2] One approach would be to link agri-environmental payments to environmental goods provision rather than to agricultural income forgone. Payment-by-results schemes can be a realistic alternative to current payment systems if a close link between actions and outcomes can be established and outcomes are measurable (CRER and CJC Consulting, 2002). However, currently agri-environment payments are constrained by the requirement that payment rates should be based on income forgone or additional costs involved, as agreed by the EU within the WTO (Matthews, 2006). Perhaps the fairest solution is to ensure that those who benefit from the public goods provision – either the individuals directly or through industries dependent on the public goods supply – provide capital to ensure the continued provision.

Direct payments to farmers from the tourism industry are one possibility. The foot and mouth epidemic in Cumbria revealed that tourism in the Lake District is vastly more profitable than agriculture (Convery *et al.*, 2004); and, as some farmers in the survey pointed out, returning some of this money to the land managers seems only just. Direct payments to farmers linked to profits from tourism would break the link between public goods provision and agricultural income, and may provide a strong incentive for both maintaining farms as whole units and potential successors to remain in farming. One possible solution would be for the tourism industry itself to unify through bodies such as the Lake District Tourism and Conservation Partnership (see Garrod *et al.*, 2006) and take control over public goods provision, for example, by purchasing fell farms and acting as landlord to ensure new farmers participate in the common grazings. Such a move may also enable farmers in the region to link directly to the tourist industry and consequently benefit through direct marketing and farm tourism ventures. The problem at the moment is that, unless a direct connection between tourism profits and cooperative farming is perceived, there is little financial motivation for the tourism industry to act.

An alternative non-market solution is regulation. Measures such as preventing the use of working farm houses and outbuildings for second-home residences or ensuring that the occupant is obliged to manage a flock of fell sheep competently in addition to occupying the house would restore the balance between selling a farm in parts and selling it as a whole. This would immediately reduce both the opportunity for incomers to accumulate public goods access and the incentive for retiring farmers/landowners to capitalise on house prices – although, to ensure public goods supply and avoid fell abandonment, measures would still be required to ensure that the businesses are sufficiently lucrative to attract younger generations of farmers to the fells. Given the immediate property devaluation that would accompany such a move, measures of this kind are likely to affect opportunities to obtain investment capital from banks and the size of any anticipated 'nest-egg' for retirement, and thus may require some form of compensation. Most of all, however, they would require both a major change in attitude towards public goods provision and substantial political will.

Conclusion and outlook

There are only a limited number of remaining hefted uplands across Europe (for example, Kosovo – FAO, 1999; Ireland – Busche, 2003) for which direct lessons may be learned from the Cumbria study. Research is needed to explore whether these areas are under threat from the same processes as experienced in Cumbria. On a broader level, however, there are more general implications for common grazing policy for all areas across Europe. In particular, the study emphasises how simply providing incentives to produce public goods will not necessarily achieve the aim of preserving these fragile nor their environments. The study raises the issue of a need to examine the relationship between public and private goods in upland regions. In particular, we believe that policy is currently too focused on agri-environmental provision as an externality to agriculture (as it began) and insufficiently on public goods as part of the wider non-agricultural economy of which farm incomes are only a minor part.

In the case of the Lake District, the strength of the housing economy, the importance of common grazing systems for maintaining open and well-managed fells, and the importance of social capital within hill farming communities are issues within which both the problem and the solution must be framed. The time frame for action is very limited. As the Cumbrian Commoners Federation and the results of our survey suggest, we may only have ten to twenty years in which to deal with this issue before irreversible changes to commons management regimes occur. If we are confident that a replacement form of land management can deliver the same environmental public goods, then there is no problem with this from an environmental perspective – it could be seen as simply part of the modernisation of agriculture (although non-environmental public goods may be lost: Burton *et al.*, 2005). However, if – as seems to be recognised by the number of programmes designed to keep farmers on the fells (e.g. Rural Futures Farm Assistant Scheme, Sheep and Wildlife Enhancement Scheme) – common grazing management plays an essential part in shaping the uplands landscape, then the loss of commons may result in a long-term diminishment of environmental public goods. In this situation, planners, policy-makers and the industries that rely on the scenic value of the region could be faced with a situation irretrievable without substantial market intervention to reconstitute traditional fell farms.

Acknowledgements

We would like to thank all of the participants in our study and the International Center for the Uplands, which funded the research.

Notes

1 Please note that we are not suggesting that contemporary 'traditional' farming is entirely without negative environmental impact. Overstocking during the 'productivist' era led to some major environmental problems in hefted upland regions such as Cumbria. We simply contend that it may be easier to repair environmental damage and manage environmental public goods under traditional systems than in ranched fells.
2 Assuming there is an effective means of economically valuing public goods.

References

Alderson, A., Ellis, E., Rawling, W., Reed, J., Shaw, B. and Nicholson, K. (2006) The future of the fells index. *International Journal of Biodiversity Science and Management*, **2**, 266–8.

BBC (2005) Beatrix Potter's farm broken up. http://news.bbc.co.uk/1/hi/england/cumbria/4444780.stm

Brown, K. M. (2006) New challenges for old commons: the role of historical common land in contemporary rural spaces. *Scottish Geographical Journal*, **122**, 109–29.

Burton, R., Mansfield, L., Schwarz, G., Brown, K. and Convery, I. (2005) *Social Capital in Hill Farming*. Report for the International Centre for the Uplands, Macaulay Institute, Aberdeen. http://www.theuplandcentre.org.uk/pubs.htm

Busche, A. (2003) Sheep in Ireland shepherded from space. Australian Broadcasting Corporation. http://www.abc.net.au/science/news/stories/2003/908383.htm

Caskie, P., Davis, J. and Wallace, M. (2001) Targeting disadvantage in agriculture. *Journal of Rural Studies*, **17**, 471–9.

Clark, G. (1982) Housing policy in the Lake District. *Transactions of the Institute of British Geographers*, **7**, 59–70.

Convery, I. T., Bailey, C., Mort, M. and Baxter, J. (2004) Death in the wrong place? Emotional geographies of the UK 2001 foot and mouth disease epidemic. *Journal of Rural Studies*, **21**, 99–109.

CRER and CJC Consulting (2002) *Economic Evaluation of Agri-environment Schemes*. Report for Defra. http://statistics.defra.gov.uk/esg/evaluation/agrienv/wholerep.pdf

Eckton, G. D. (2003) Road-user charging and the Lake District National Park. *Journal of Transport Geography*, **11**, 307–17.

English Nature (2004) *Sheep and Wildlife Enhancement Scheme – Sustaining Wildlife and Sheep Farming*. Information Note 6 – The scheme in the South Pennines, 2004.

Evans, N., Gaskell, P. and Winter, M. (2003) Re-assessing agrarian policy and practice in local environmental management: the case of beef cattle. *Land Use Policy*, **20**, 231–42.

Falconer, K. and Ward, N. (2000) Using modulation to green the CAP: the UK case. *Land Use Policy*, **17**, 3–15.

FAO (1999) *Special Report: FAO/WFP Crop and Food Supply Assessment Mission to the Kosovo Province of the Federal Republic of Yugoslavia*. http://www.fao.org/docrep/004/x2901e/x2901e00.htm

Federation of Cumbria Commoners (2006) *Common Interests: A Cumbrian Perspective on Common Land and Life*. Federation of Cumbria Commoners, Newmarket, Cumbria (promotional DVD).

Franks, J. (2003) Revised agri-environment policy objectives: implications for scheme design. *Journal of Environmental Planning and Management*, **46**, 443–66.

Garrod, B., Wornell, R. and Youell, R. (2006) Re-conceptualising rural resources as countryside capital: the case of rural tourism. *Journal of Rural Studies*, **22**, 117–28.

Gray, J. (1998) Family farms in the Scottish borders: a practical definition by hill farmers. *Journal of Rural Studies*, **14**, 241–356.

Gueydon, A. and Hoffman, H. (2006) Collective alps in the alpine region of Germany. Proceedings at the IASCP Europe regional meeting 'Building the European commons: from open fields to open source'. Brescia, Italy, March 23–5.

Hodge, I. (2000) Agri-environmental relationships and the choice of policy mechanism. *The World Economy*, **23**, 257–73.

IEEP (2004) *An Assessment of the Impacts of Hill Farming in England on the Economic, Environmental and Social Sustainability of the Uplands and More Widely*. Reports of case studies. Report for Defra, London.

LDNPA (2006) *Annual Monitoring Report April 2005–March 2006*. Kendal: Lake District National Park Authority.

Le Duc, M., Pakeman, R. and Marrs, R. (2000) Vegetation development on upland and marginal land treated with herbicide, for bracken (*Pteridium aquilinium*) control, in Great Britain. *Journal of Environmental Management*, **58**, 147–60.

Matthews, A. (2006) Decoupling the Green Box: international dimensions of the reinstrumentation of agricultural support. Paper presented at the 93rd EAAE seminar 'Impacts of decoupling and cross-compliance in the enlarged EU', 22–6 September, Prague.

Mearns, R. (1996) Community, collective action and common grazing: the case of post-socialist Mongolia. *The Journal of Development Studies*, **32**, 297–339.

Niemeyer, K. and Riseth J. (2004) Impact of changing socio-economic factors on the stability of co-operative large scale grazing systems. Presentation at XI World Congress of Rural Sociology: Globalisation, Risks and Resistance in rural economies and societies. Trondheim, Norway 25–30 July. www.irsa-world.org/prior/XI/papers/9-5.pdf

Plieninger, T., Höchtl, F. and Spek, T. (2006) Traditional land-use and nature conservation in European rural landscapes. *Environmental Science and Policy*, **9**, 317–21.

Pretty, J. and Ward, H. (2001) Social capital and the environment. *World Development*, **29**, 209–27.

Short, C. (2000) Common land and ELMS: a need for policy innovation in England and Wales. *Land Use Policy*, **17**, 121–33.

Short, C. and Winter, M. (1999) The problem of common land: toward stakeholder governance. *Journal of Environmental Planning and Management*, **42**, 613–30.

Smaldone, D., Harris, C. and Sanyal, N. (2005) An exploration of place as a process: the case of Jackson Hole, WY. *Journal of Environmental Psychology*, **25**, 397–414.

Thomas, N. (1999) *Living Commons: How Improvements in Management Can Benefit Wales in the Twenty-first Century*. Sandy: Royal Society for the Protection of Birds.

Whitby, M. (2000) Reflections on the costs and benefits of agri-environment schemes. *Landscape Research*, **25**, 365–74.

18 The economic value of landscapes in the uplands of England

Nick Hanley and Sergio Colombo

Introduction

Farming plays a crucial role in maintaining the distinctive landscape and wildlife quality of many upland areas in the UK (Thompson *et al.*, 1995). Very few of our most treasured habitats can be described as 'natural', with landscapes such as heather moorland and chalk downland relying for their conservation on certain farm management regimes (typically, low-intensity livestock-grazing). This dependence of habitat quality on the maintenance of 'traditional' farming systems can also be found throughout Europe, for example on 'karst' limestone pastures in Slovenia, and in wooded meadows in Estonia. In the UK, hill farming steadily intensified throughout the twentieth century. For example, in 1975, 1995 and 2000, farms in the hill parish of Tintwistle in the Peak District were running 318 per cent, 432 per cent and 702 per cent more sheep than they ran in the mid-1930s (Anderson and Yalden, 1981).

This intensification was partly driven by production subsidies under the Common Agricultural Policy (CAP), and resulted in increasing conflicts between conservation interests and the farm lobby, as intensification became associated with declining biodiversity and undesirable changes in landscape quality (Bowers and Cheshire, 1983; Palmer, 1997; Fuller and Gough, 1999). Similar adverse effects on biological richness in semi-natural habitats from the intensification driven by the CAP and technological change have been noted throughout Europe (Buar *et al.*, 2005; Pykala *et al.*, 2005).

However, in recent years, hill-farm incomes in the UK have declined dramatically in response to falling output prices and changes in support. By 2000, average net incomes on cattle and sheep farms in Less Favoured Areas had fallen by 70 per cent from their 1995 peak (Defra, 2006). Hill-farm viability now depends on subsidy support, and many farms would have a negative income in the absence of subsidies (PDRDF, 2004; Condliffe, this volume).

At the general level of CAP support, the Single Farm Payment has recently been introduced to de-couple subsidy support from production decisions. Hill farmers have historically come to depend on additional subsidy programmes, such as agri-environment schemes and the Hill Farm

Allowance (HFA). These programmes are also in flux. The Environmentally Sensitive Areas programme and Countryside Stewardship Scheme are in the process of being replaced with the Environmental Stewardship Entry and Higher Level schemes. Indeed, throughout the EU, agri-environmental schemes are gradually becoming more important to farmers in terms of support payments. In England, the current version of the HFA programme ends in 2007, and what form any new scheme will take is subject to an ongoing policy debate in the context of the new Rural Development Regulation which covers the period 2007–13 (Defra, 2006). Reforms to the HFA will have to be in line with the current re-directing of CAP support away from production and towards environmental and rural development objectives (Latacz-Lohman and Hodge, 2003).

Since the maintenance of landscape and wildlife quality in the uplands can be presumed to be a public benefit, it seems reasonable that the public be asked to pay for this. One possibility, which has economic appeal, is to replace a production-related (and, more recently, area-related) support scheme for farmers – the HFA provisions – with a scheme which pays for these public goods. Interestingly, Defra's consultation document on reform of hill-farming support (Defra, 2006) states that 'the Government is not minded to maintain a . . . payment for the uplands which is not tied to the positive provision of public goods' (p. 11). As the market will undersupply these public goods, government has a clear role – although not by any means an exclusive one – in enhancing social welfare by setting up agri-environment schemes, so long as the social benefits exceed the social costs (for a discussion of alternative provision mechanisms for public goods in the countryside, see Hodge, 2001 and Sundberg, 2006).

This chapter focuses on determining the social benefits of a new uplands policy, which pays farmers to 'produce' environmental goods such as landscapes and wildlife habitats. In particular, it focuses on farming in upland England, and an assessment of this regional variability of preferences and willingness to pay for landscape protection and enhancement. Finding evidence of spatial variability in preferences for landscape would suggest a need for spatial targeting of policy initiatives (Latacz-Lohman and Hodge, 2003); this then requires consideration of the political economy of implementing a regionally varying subsidy scheme. The methods used here and the focus taken are appropriate to the measurement of environmental benefits from farming throughout the EU. In a sense, we use the English case study here as illustrative of the ways in which economists can estimate monetary values for the kinds of environmental output which EU agri-environment schemes can deliver.

To estimate regional willingness to pay for landscape features produced by upland farmers, we conducted 'Choice Experiment' studies in four 'SDAs': that is, areas officially designated 'Severely Disadvantaged Areas' in terms of farming activity, within which farmers are eligible for Hill Farm Allowance payments. We explain below in Box 18.1 how the Choice Experiment method works: for now, it is sufficient to understand that it is an

Box 18.1. The Choice Experiment method

The methodology we use to estimate the value of different landscape attributes is Choice Experiments, a stated preference method that is becoming increasingly popular in environmental valuation (Bennet and Blamey, 2001; Bateman *et al.*, 2002; Colombo *et al.*, 2005). In this survey-based technique, environmental goods are valued in terms of their attributes – so that, for example, the economic value of protecting forests can be represented by the values people place on characteristics such as species mix, recreational opportunities and forest biodiversity. These values are revealed by asking survey respondents to choose between different 'packages' of the environmental good, where packages vary in terms of the levels that the different characteristics take (see Table 18.2 for an example). Economists always include price as one of these attributes: that is, they include a variable which states the cost of choosing any option. By modelling these decisions the researcher can identify which attributes are important to people and calculate the WTP for different 'packages' of the environmental good. In the resulting model the coefficient of each environmental attribute represents the importance of this attribute to people. For instance, if the attribute forest biodiversity has a higher coefficient than the attribute recreational opportunities, it means that the first is more important to people than the second. By dividing the coefficient of any attribute by the coefficient of the monetary attribute, it is possible to obtain the WTP for an improvement of the quality or quantity of the attribute in question. This is for a change of only one attribute. When several attribute levels vary simultaneously WTP measures can also be obtained by using the formula described by Hanemann (1984).

For an up-to-date, accessible account of the method, see Hensher *et al.* (2005) or Louviere *et al.* (2000). A review of environmental applications of choice experiments is provided in Hanley *et al.* (2001).

economic valuation method which estimates willingness to pay on the part of some group (the general public, local residents, visitors, and so on) for changes in the characteristics of different environmental goods. The environmental good here is landscape quality, and the characteristics are the physical features within those landscapes.

Previous studies of the economic value of farm landscapes in the UK

Most previous studies of the non-market value of upland landscapes in the UK have focused on whole landscape values, rather than on the value of individual landscape features. In what follows, we focus on studies that have related upland landscapes to agricultural policy change. For a review of valuation studies related to agricultural and forest land use Europe-wide, see Swanwick *et al.*, 2007.

Willis and Garrod (1993) used the Contingent Valuation (CV) method to assess preferences for a range of different landscapes in the Yorkshire Dales which could result from future policy changes. Contingent Valuation is a method whereby respondents are directly questioned as to their Willingness to Pay (WTP) for a well-defined change in an environmental good.[1] In the Willis and Garrod study, agricultural landscapes in the Dales were described to respondents as either 'intensive and semi-intensive agricultural', 'planned', 'conserved', 'sporting', 'wild' and 'abandoned'. In this study no attempt was made to estimate WTP for separate landscape attributes, although preferences were examined by asking respondents whether they would prefer less, more or the same of these features. Bullock and Kay (1997) undertook a CV study on upland attributes in the Southern Uplands of Scotland. They estimated WTP for agricultural policies that produced landscapes associated with extensive grazing. Three policy options were presented: 'business-as-usual', 'extensive' and 'very extensive'. The results showed a clear preference for landscapes with more extensive grazing and with more tree cover than at present. Hanley *et al.* (1998) assessed the economic value of the conservation benefits of the Breadalbane Environmentally Sensitive Area (ESA) in Scotland, using both CV and Choice Experiment methods. In the choice experiment, the landscape attributes were broad-leaved woodland, moorland, wetland, drystone dikes and archaeological sites – features which farmers receiving ESA payments in this area were obliged to conserve. Respondents were keen on conserving the lansdscape showing higher WTP for greater levels of broad-leaved woodland, heather moors and wet grasslands.

Study design and conduct

Case study areas

Severely Disadvantaged Areas (SDAs) include almost all of the upland areas in the North of England (including the Pennines, the Lake District and the North York Moors), the Peak District, some of the English–Welsh border, Exmoor, Dartmoor and parts of Cornwall. The geographical focus of this paper is SDAs in England in four regions: the North West, Yorkshire and the Humber, the West Midlands, and the South West. The stated preference study was designed and implemented separately in each of the above-mentioned regions in order to estimate the economic value of upland landscapes within each region as expressed by the population of that region. We therefore implicitly ignore the value that people from outside a given region place on changes to landscape quality within that region. This is a clear limitation of the results presented here.

Table 18.1 Attributes and attribute levels used in the choice experiment.

Upland attribute	Levels
Heather moorland and bog	−12%; −2%; +5%
Rough grassland	−10%; +2%; +5%
Mixed and broadleaved woodland	+3%; +10%; +20%
Field boundaries	For every 1 km, 50 m is restored; for every 1 km, 100 m is restored; for every 1 km, 200 m is restored
Cultural heritage	Rapid decline No change Much better conservation
Increase in tax payment by your household per year	£2; £5; £10; £17; £40; £70

Survey design

The questionnaire consisted of three parts. The first part investigated attitudes to the environment and frequency of visits to the countryside. The second part contained the choice experiment exercise. Initially, fourteen landscape attributes were considered for inclusion in the choice experiment. This 'long list' of upland attributes was reduced using three focus groups undertaken in Manchester and Kendal. The final attribute list comprised heather moorland and bog, rough grassland, broad-leaf and mixed woodland, field boundaries (stone walls and hedges) and 'cultural heritage' (Table 18.1). Cultural heritage was defined to include the presence in the landscape of traditional farm buildings, the keeping of traditional livestock breeds, and traditional farming practices such as shepherding with sheep dogs. Attributes were described to respondents in the questionnaire in both words and pictures.

The selection of attribute *levels* was a hard task owing to the difficulty in making quantitative predictions of the impacts of future agricultural policy changes. These predictions were carried out by experts, based on a literature review of recent rates of change in these attributes (Cumulus *et al.*, 2005). Attribute levels finally selected are shown in Table 18.1. The questionnaire explained to respondents that higher taxes would be needed during the period 2007–13 to pay for the policy changes outlined in the choice cards. The wording used was:

> However, the government may change how it pays farmers in these hilly areas. If this happened, the main aim would be to try and reduce the bad impacts of future changes in farming on the landscape, and to increase any good impacts. However, this policy change would come at a cost to people like you, through higher national or local taxes. The government would like to know what people think of as good and bad impacts

and whether the cost of the policy change is right. This is why we are conducting this survey.

The last part of the survey contained follow-up questions on respondents' habits regarding visits to SDAs, as well as standard socio-economic characteristics.

Respondents were each presented with six choice cards, each containing three alternatives: option A, option B and a status quo. The status quo alternative in each choice set in each region represented the expected changes in the landscape attribute of SDAs by 2013 under the current policy support. A zero additional cost was attached to the status quo. Alternatives A and B then contained variations in these attribute levels, but with a positive cost, representing modification to the current policy support to SDAs. These tax increases varied between £2 and £70 per household per year – levels which were chosen based on focus group discussions and pilot testing. An example of choice card is shown in Table 18.2. Three hundred respondents in each case-study SDA region were interviewed. Each sample was chosen according to quotas for age, gender, socio-economic group, and also whether respondents resided in an urban or a rural area. The survey mode was face-to-face personal interviews.

Table 18.2 Example card – Yorkshire and Humberside sample.

	Policy Option	Current policy	Policy Option A	Policy Option B
	Change in area of Heather Moorland and Bog	A loss of 1,560 hectares (−2%)	A gain of 1,560 hectares (+2%)	A loss of 1,560 ha (−2%)
	Change in area of Rough Grassland	A loss of 17,700 ha (−10%)	A loss of 3,500 ha (−2%)	A loss of 3,500 ha (−2%)
	Change in area of Mixed and Broadleaf Woodlands	A gain of 1,000 ha (+3%)	A gain of 5,500 ha (+20%)	A gain of 2,700 ha (+10%)
	Condition of field boundaries	For every 1 km, 100 m is restored	For every 1 km, 200 m is restored	For every 1 km, 50 m is restored
	Change in farm building and traditional farm practices	Rapid decline	no change	Much better conservation
	Increase in tax payments by your household each year	£0	£20	£10

Results

Sample characteristics conformed closely with population data in terms of gender, age and location.[2] Most respondents stated that they were concerned with the environment and aware of environmental change; as a generalisation, samples with higher educational levels were more environmentally aware.

Early analysis of Choice Experiments in environmental economics made use of simple Conditional Logit or Multi-Nomial Logit models. However, whilst these are easy both to use and to interpret, they imply that we are happy with the assumption that each person in the sample has the same preferences for each attribute. A more recent development is the use of Random Parameter Logit (RPL) models, which assume that there exists a difference of tastes across people for each attribute around some mean value. For each characteristic, two statistical outputs are obtained: a mean value, which shows the mean importance of this attribute on choices; and a standard deviation for this attribute, which represents the variation in the importance this attribute has to choices across the sample of respondents. Attributes whose standard deviations are significant show that people hold heterogeneous preferences for them, in the sense that somebody may like an increase in the quality or quantity of an attribute and somebody else may prefer a reduction.

Model coefficients from the four RPL models are shown in Table 18.3, whilst Table 18.4 describes the coding used in the tables. Given the large number of coefficients, we do not provide a description of each single model but only give general findings. Concerning the interpretation of the mean coefficient values, a significant positive coefficient indicates that the likelihood of a respondent choosing an option is greater the higher the level of the variable. A significant negative coefficient (for example, on the tax attribute) indicates that, the higher the level of the variable (tax), the lower is the utility or preference associated with an option. A coefficient which is not significant indicates that it is not possible to determine how the variable affects respondents' choices. The sign and significance of the socio-economic variables reveal if respondents are more likely to choose options A or B than the status quo.

Some general findings emerge from the analysis of the model results. While the same questionnaire and the same specification of attributes are used in all regions, the factors that influence the choices that respondents make are different. The level of *heather moorland and bog* and a large improvement in *cultural heritage* are both shown to be significant factors in respondents' choices in all four regions. The amount of *broad-leaved woodland* affects choice in only two of the SDAs. On the other hand, changes in the area of *rough grassland* and *field boundaries*, and a small change in *cultural heritage* attributes, are generally not significant factors in the choice, being significant only in one of the regions. *Tax* is always significant, showing that options which attracted a higher increase in tax are less preferred by respondents.

The region that shows the highest number of significant landscape attributes is the North West. This may be because both focus groups and the

Table 18.3 Random parameters logit model coefficients for each region (coefficients found to be statistically significant at the 95 per cent level are indicated in bold).

Region	North West		Yorks and Humber		West Midlands		South West	
	Coef.	S.e.	Coef.	S.e.	Coef.	S.e.	Coef.	S.e.
Mean Values								
Const	0.337	0.933	**4.266**	1.084	**3.458**	0.801	1.463	0.957
HMB	**0.058**	0.013	**0.017**	0.010	**0.034**	0.008	**0.030**	0.009
RG	**0.056**	0.012	0.009	0.008	0.009	0.007	−0.002	0.007
BMW	**0.045**	0.010	0.006	0.010	**0.017**	0.009	0.009	0.006
FB	0.001	0.001	0.001	0.001	0.001	0.001	−0.001	0.001
CH1	0.063	0.119	0.100	0.105	0.012	0.071	**0.187**	0.083
CH2	**0.363**	0.136	**0.561**	0.116	**0.186**	0.088	**0.291**	0.108
TAX	**−0.076**	0.006	**−0.051**	0.004	**−0.041**	0.003	**−0.029**	0.003
AGE	**−0.547**	0.213	0.156	0.235	0.237	0.163	0.155	0.188
GENDER	0.038	0.276	0.402	0.267	**−0.413**	0.209	**0.903**	0.240
ENVIMP	**−0.898**	0.197	**−0.836**	0.211	**−0.468**	0.188	−0.255	0.204
VISFREQ	**0.161**	0.062	**−0.288**	0.062	**−0.201**	0.047	**−0.125**	0.047
LIVING	**−0.021**	0.009	**−0.015**	0.011	−0.010	0.007	0.003	0.008
REMAIN	**−0.216**[a]	0.126	−0.276	0.163	−0.148	0.102	−0.127	0.142
MEMBER	0.524	0.360	**0.746**	0.403	**0.574**	0.221	−0.006	0.270
EDU	**0.435**	0.100	0.234	0.131	**0.153**	0.073	**0.281**	0.105
EMPLOY	**1.573**	0.332	0.062	0.277	−0.053	0.226	−0.059	0.280
RURAL	**−1.120**	0.491	**0.880**	0.412	**−1.379**	0.386	−0.394	0.261
Standard deviations								
HMB	**0.078**	0.018	**0.067**	0.017	**0.059**	0.012	**0.062**	0.014
RG	**0.085**	0.011	**0.054**	0.010	**0.050**	0.008	**0.049**	0.009
BMW	0.010	0.031	**0.074**	0.014	**0.076**	0.011	**0.031**	0.012
FB	**0.009**	0.002	**0.005**	0.002	**0.004**	0.002	**0.008**	0.001
CH1	**0.449**	0.175	**0.773**	0.130	**0.336**	0.115	**0.471**	0.131
CH2	**0.706**	0.156	**0.886**	0.124	**0.706**	0.099	**0.900**	0.117
No. Obs.	1197		1138		1373		1135	
Log likelihood at convergence	−829.57		−963.52		−1268.62		−1032.41	
LR	948.95		573.39		479.54		429.02	
Pseudo R^2	.36		.23		.16		.17	

pilot survey were carried out in this region, so that the attributes used in the study were selected according to the preference of people of this region. In terms of socio-economic variables, several help to explain respondents' choices, as might be expected. Respondents that stated that the environmental policy is 'very important' in relation to other things that government is concerned with, such as law and order, or education, are more likely to support the public paying for hill farmers' production of environmental goods – that is, are more likely to choose either option A or B. On the same lines, the

Table 18.4 Explanation of variable abbreviations and coding in Table 18.3.

const	constant term (= 0 for the current policy, = 1 for alternatives A or B)
HMB	percentage change in area of heather moorland and bog
RG	percentage change in area of rough grassland
BMW	percentage change in area of broadleaf and mixed woodland
FB	change in the length of field boundaries (in metres restored)
CH1	small change in cultural heritage indicated (1 = yes, 0 = no)
CH2	large change in cultural heritage indicated (1 = yes, 0 = no)
TAX	tax amount indicated in pounds
AGE	respondent's age in years
GENDER	respondent's gender (1 = male, 0 = female)
ENVIMP	importance of environmental policy to respondent (1 = very important, 4 = not important)
VISFREQ	respondent's frequency of visits to severely disadvantaged areas (1 = every day, 10 = never)
LIVING	number of years respondents have been living in the region
REMAIN	respondent's expected residence in the region (1 = less than 6 month, 5 = indefinite)
MEMBER	whether respondent belongs to an environmental, recreational, etc. organization (1 = yes, 0 = no)
EDU	respondent's education level (1 = primary, 6 = higher degree)
EMPLOY	whether respondent is an active worker (1 = yes, 0 = no)
RURAL	whether respondent is a rural-dweller (1 = yes, 0 = no)

higher the level of education,[3] the more likely it is that respondents choose alternatives A or B. Place of residence (urban or rural) was also found to affect respondents' choice, although this relationship worked in different directions in different regions. In particular, in the North West and the West Midlands, urban dwellers are more likely to support changes to the hill farming scheme, whilst in the York and Humber region rural dwellers are more likely to support changes.

Inspection of the standard deviation values shows that a common characteristic amongst all regions is respondents' heterogeneity of preferences for upland landscapes. Note that in twenty-three out of twenty-four cases the parameter estimate on the standard deviation terms is statistically significant, showing that there is a lot of variability in people's preferences for landscape even within each region.

Table 18.4 shows estimates of willingness to pay (or 'implicit prices') for changes in each of the landscape attributes, along with the 95 per cent confidence intervals. In the case of the field boundaries attribute, none of these willingness-to-pay values is significantly different from zero: on this evidence, changes in this well-known landscape attribute do not impact on utility of local residents – a conclusion which seems a little surprising. In the North West region, respondents are willing to pay on average £0.75/household/year for a 1 per cent increase of the area of Heather Moorland and Bog in upland areas of the North West, and £4.75/household/year for 'much better' conservation of the cultural heritage in these areas, instead of a rapid decline. Similar valuations are observed in the West Midlands region. Important differences across regions are observed: for instance, the implicit price of the discrete change in cultural heritage from 'rapid decline' to 'much better conservation' is more than double in the York and Humber and South West regions compared to the value in the North West or the West Midlands. Respondents in the North West are the only group to have a positive WTP for improvements in rough grasslands (£0.73 household/ year for a 1 per cent increase in the amount of this habitat conserved), whilst values for broad-leaved and mixed woodland vary from £0.42 in the West Midlands to £0.58 in the North West for a 1 per cent increase in the wood-land area.

Although these implicit prices are very useful to policy-makers when defining priorities for policy design, they do not summarise the social WTP for possible future landscape scenarios, since they do not show the willing-ness to pay of individuals for multiple changes in landscape attributes. To obtain these social WTP amounts for policy change, we need to estimate 'compensating surplus' amounts, according to the Hanemann (1984) formula. This requires the definition of the policy scenarios to be appraised, which are shown in Box 18.2.

Based on these scenarios, Table 18.5 summarises the predicted percentage change of each attribute used in the choice experiment for each scenario. Compensating surplus estimates are shown in Table 18.6, along with 95 per

Table 18.5 Willingness to Pay estimates (implicit prices) and their 95 per cent confidence intervals (in bold: WTP values significantly different from zero at the 95 per cent level; HMB = heather moorland and bog, percentage increase; RG = rough grassland, percentage change; BMW = broad-leaved and mixed woodland, percentage change; FB = field boundaries, length conserved; CH1 = cultural heritage no change rather than rapid decline; CH2 = cultural heritage much better conserved rather than rapid decline).

Region	North West	Yorks and Humber	West Midlands	South West
Attribute				
HMB	**0.75**	0.33	**0.84**	**1.05**
	(0.43 1.08)	(−0.08 0.69)	(0.45 1.21)	(0.46 1.76)
RG	**0.73**	0.18	0.22	−0.07
	(0.42 1.04)	(−0.14 0.51)	(−0.10 0.52)	(−0.59 0.43)
BMW	**0.58**	0.11	**0.42**	0.31
	(0.33 0.86)	(−0.28 0.55)	(0.01 0.86)	(−0.12 0.75)
FB	0.01	0.02	0.03	−0.04
	(−0.03 0.05)	(−0.02 0.06)	(−0.01 0.06)	(−0.11 0.03)
CH1	0.82	1.96	0.30	**6.52**
	(−2.43 4.08)	(−2.13 6.16)	(−3.04 3.74)	(1.10 13.00)
CH2	**4.75**	**10.98**	**4.59**	**10.16**
	(1.57 8.12)	(6.78 15.70)	(0.47 8.93)	(3.25 17.39)

Box 18.2. Policy scenarios used in the study

Scenario 0: Baseline. Under the baseline scenario, the Hill Farm Allowance (HFA) scheme remains broadly the same as it is at present. This includes an increase in the coverage of Entry Level Stewardship to 60 per cent of all farmland by the end of 2007 and 75 per cent by 2013.

Scenario 1: Environment-agri. Under scenario 1, policy aims reflect the importance of environmental and conservation objectives and the importance of maintaining upland farming systems to achieve these objectives. This scenario is essentially a switch in emphasis from agriculture to environment compared to the baseline.

Scenario 2: Environment only. Under scenario 2, the strategic aims for upland support are focused solely on achieving environmental goals. In practice it is assumed that the funding is used for an Upland Entry Level Stewardship Scheme and would take the form of annual payments targeted at enhancing specific, valuable or threatened upland habitats.

Scenario 3: Abandonment intensification. Under scenario 3, upland support is withdrawn entirely. Existing funding of £27 million per year disappears and is 'lost' from the uplands. The CAP reform and agri-environment scheme assumptions remain the same as under the baseline scenario.

cent confidence intervals. These estimates represent respondents' average WTP to move from the state of the world given in scenario 0 (the baseline) to the state of the world given in scenarios 1, 2 or 3. Respondents show positive WTP for both scenario 1 and scenario 2, with a higher compensating surplus associated with the latter. This makes sense, since scenario 2 implies a

Table 18.6 Predictions of the change in the landscape attributes under the four policy scenarios (modified from Table 1 of Cumulus *et al.*, 2005).

Upland attribute	Scenario 0 Baseline	Scenario 1 Env-agri	Scenario 2 Env only	Scenario 3 Aband-intern
Heather moorland and bog	+1%	+3%	+5%	−2%
Rough grassland	+1%	−1%	−3%	+3%
Mixed and broadleaved woodland	+3%	+4%	+6%	+5%
Field boundaries	+5%	+6%	+10%	+2%
Cultural heritage	Rapid Decline	No change	No change	Rapid Decline

Table 18.7 Compensating surplus estimates for three policy options, relative to the baseline (£ per household per year, 95 per cent confidence intervals are shown in brackets).

Region	North West	Yorks and Humber	West Midlands	South West
Scenario 1	7.13	15.53	7.11	25.40
	(1.90 12.19)	(7.90 23.50)	(0.65 13.57)	(13.77 38.32)
Scenario 2	8.74	17.02	10.24	26.85
	(3.36 14.21)	(9.29 24.98)	(3.75 16.98)	(14.97 40.01)
Scenario 3	0.07	−1.10	−2.03	−1.61
	(−1.53 1.55)	(−3.03 0.67)	(−3.99 −0.31)	(−4.80 1.30)

higher level for each landscape attribute than scenario 1, with the exception of rough grassland. Note that there is considerable regional variation in the values attached to both scenario 1 (from £7.11/household/year in the West Midlands to £25.40 in the South West) and scenario 2 (from £8.74 in the North West to £26.85 in the South West). WTP for scenario 3 is negative or insignificantly different from zero in all regions, suggesting that respondents would not be willing to pay additional taxes for this policy option.

Household WTP estimates for scenarios 1 and 2 can be compared with the WTP obtained in other economic valuation studies, bearing in mind that considerable differences are involved in both what is being valued and how it is being valued. The range of household WTP in Table 18.7 for scenarios extends from £7.11 to £26.85/household/year. In comparison, Willis and Garrod (1993) found a WTP of £18–35/household/year for a range of alternative farmland landscape changes, ranging from intensive agriculture to wild landscape. Bullock and Kay (1997) measured a mean WTP ranging from £41 to £82 for landscape changes from the current conditions to a more extensive or very extensive grazing. Hanley *et al.* (1998) observed a WTP range of £22–7 for changes in the landscape from retaining ESA subsidies.

Finally, by aggregating the household WTP values across the relevant regional populations it is possible to obtain an aggregate WTP (social benefit) to be compared to the costs of changing support to upland farmers. A glance at the aggregate values shown in Table 18.8 reveals that in the South West region respondents are willing to pay much more than in any other region for the policy changes simulated. One reason for this is that only in this region are respondents willing to pay to avoid a 'rapid decline' of cultural heritage relative to a 'no change' situation. In addition, the parameter estimate on the tax attribute in the South West is the smallest across the four regions, implying the lowest reduction in the probability of supporting a costly policy change. This may be because in this region the abundance of the uphill landscape is quite low, being only 6 per cent of the area covered by SDA (in the North West region, 31 per cent of the area is classified as SDA), so that people are more keen on paying to conserve this scarce environmental asset.

Table 18.8 Compensating surplus aggregated across all households resident in SDA regions relative to the baseline (£ million per year, 95 per cent confidence intervals are shown in brackets).

Region	North West	Yorks and Humber	West Midlands	South West
Scenario 1	19.97	32.15	15.3	53.1
	(5.3 34.1)	(16.3 48.6)	(1.4 29.2)	(28.8 80.1)
Scenario 2	24.48	35.23	22.02	56.12
	(9.4 39.8)	(19.2 51.7)	(8.1 36.5)	(31.3 83.6)

Conclusions

Throughout the EU, fragile semi-natural environments depend for their maintenance on the practice of low-intensity traditional farming methods. These methods have produced a rich landscape and varied biodiversity over time, but the market does not reward producers for these outputs. In this paper, we have demonstrated how the Choice Experiment method can be used to value such outputs, and how these numbers could then be used to design agri-environmental schemes which replace these 'missing markets' with payment for ecological and landscape services.

In our case study, the continuation of hill farming is assumed to play an important role in maintaining landscape diversity and species conservation in upland areas of England. We investigated the economic benefits of protecting and enhancing upland landscape features, in the context of a reform of the way in which hill farmers' incomes are supported by the taxpayer. Rather than paying production-related support, as has been traditionally the case with the Hill Farm Allowance, we propose paying farmers according to the value of public goods they produce.

Our results show that many people are in favour of public support to maintain and enhance upland landscapes. More crucially, we find that environmental payments should vary both by landscape feature 'produced' and by region. Based on the public's willingness to pay, highest payments should be offered for heather moorland conservation, broad-leaved and mixed woodlands, and cultural heritage features such as old stone barns.

However, the most interesting aspect of these results is how values for given landscape features should vary regionally. Based on the figures in Table 18.5, payments for heather moorland conservation should be highest in the South West SDA, lowest in the North West SDA, and zero in Yorkshire and Humberside SDA. Clearly, there are major political economy concerns raised by such a spatial targeting of payments. Farmers in lower-payment areas may claim this is unfair relative to farmers in higher-payment areas, whilst the transactions costs of administering a regionally differentiated payment scheme will be higher than those of a uniform payments scheme. Moreover, we have not taken any account of possible regional differences in the farmers' cost of producing these landscape features. Such differences might amplify the regional re-distribution of income implicit in a regionally varying environmental payments scheme.

The aggregate social benefits associated with either of the two policy options which enhance targeting of environmental payments relative to the baseline (scenarios 1 and 2 in Tables 18.7 and 18.8) would seem to be considerable, ranging from £15 million to £56 million per annum at the regional level. Whether bringing about these landscape changes would generate additional *net* social benefits is not something we can comment on, however, since we currently have no information on the costs of producing the landscape features included in the choice experiment on a regionally disaggregated basis. This would seem to be an important focus for future research.

Finally, the question should be asked as to the usefulness of these kinds of exercise which try to quantify the economic benefits of environmental change. A key advantage of the approach is that the social costs of providing environmental goods through the public purse can be compared with the costs of provision. Given the scarcity of resources available for funding public goods, this is an important check on the prospective efficiency with which public money is spent. Second, monetary quantification of preferences and wants allows us to compare the relative benefits of providing one environmental good with another, and to assess the extent to which people are willing to give up resources in order to have more of an environmental good. All this is useful information for public policy formation. However, as is well acknowledged in the economic literature, there are significant limits to this environmental application of cost–benefit analysis principles (Hanley and Spash, 1993). Moreover, stated preference methods such as choice experiments seem susceptible to a hypothetical market bias, which leads to absolute values being overstated (Harrison, 2006). Perhaps what this research casts most light on is thus the relative values of landscape features across England, and the heterogeneity of preferences for environmental goods in the uplands.

Acknowledgements

We thank Defra for funding the empirical work on which this chapter is based, and other colleagues who worked on the Eftec project, notably Helen Johns and Alistair Hamilton. Thanks also to the editors and to three reviewers for comments on an earlier draft.

Notes

1 For a simple introduction to different environmental valuation methods, see Hanley and Spash, 1993.
2 For full details, see Eftec, 2005.
3 The income variable has been excluded from the analysis given the high number of respondents who refused to declare their income level.

References

Anderson, P. and Yalden, D. W. (1981) Increased sheep numbers and the loss of heather moorland in the Peak District, England. *Biological Conservation*, **20**, 195–213.

Bateman, I., Carson, R., Day, B., Hanemann, M., Hanley, N., Hett, T., Jones-Lee, M., Loomes, G., Mourato, S., Özdemiroglu, E., Pearce, D. W., Sugden, R. and Swanson, J. (2002) *Economic Valuation with Stated Preference Techniques*. Cheltenham: Edward Elgar.

Bennett, J. and Blamey, R. (2001) *The Choice Modelling Approach to Environmental Valuation*. Cheltenham: Edward Elgar.

Bowers, J. K. and Cheshire, P. (1983) *Agriculture, the Countryside and Land Use*. London: Methuen University Paperback.

Buar, B., Cremene, C., Groza, G., Rakozy, L., Schileyko, A., Baur, A., Stoll, P. and Erhardt, A. (2005) Effects of abandonment of subalpine hay meadows on plant and invertebrate density in Transylvania, Romania. *Biological Conservation*, **132**, 261–73.

Bullock, C. H. and Kay, J. (1997) Preservation and change in the upland landscape: the public benefits of grazing management. *Journal of Environmental Planning and Management*, **40**, 315–34.

Colombo, S., Hanley, N. and Calatrava-Requena, J. (2005) Designing policy for reducing the off-farm effects of soil erosion using Choice Experiments. *Journal of Agricultural Economics*, **56**, 80–96.

Cumulus (2005) *Assessment of the Impact of CAP Reform and Other Key Policies on Upland Farms and Land Use Implications in Both Severely Disadvantaged and Disadvantaged Areas of England*. Report to Defra, London. http://statistics.defra.gov.uk/esg/reports/cap%20uplandfarms%20report.pdf

Defra (2006) *Rural Development Programme for England 2007–2013: Uplands Rewards Structure Consultation Document*. Defra, London. http://www.defra.gov.uk/rural/uplands/consultation/rdpuplands-consultdoc.pdf

Eftec (2005) *Economic Valuation of Environmental Impacts in the Severely Disadvantaged Areas*. Report to Defra, London. http://statistics.defra.gov.uk/esg/reports/disareas/default.asp

Fuller, R. J. and Gough, S. J. (1999) Changes in sheep numbers in Britain: implications for bird populations. *Biological Conservation*, **91**, 73–89.

Hanemann, W. M. (1984) Welfare evaluations in contingent valuation experiment with discrete responses. *American Journal of Agricultural Economics*, **66**, 332–41.

Hanley, N., MacMillan, D., Wright, R. E., Bullock, C., Simpson, I., Parsisson, D. and Crabtree, B. (1998) Contingent valuation versus choice experiments: estimating the benefits of Environmentally Sensitive Areas in Scotland, *Journal of Agricultural Economics*, **49**, 1–15.

Hanley, N., Mourato, S. and Wright, R. (2001) Choice modelling approaches: a superior alternative for environmental valuation? *Journal of Economic Surveys*, **15**, 453–62.

Hanley, N. and Spash, C. (1993) *Cost–benefit Analysis and the Environment*. Cheltenham: Edward Elgar.

Harrison, G. W. (2006) Experimental evidence on alternative environmental valuation methods. *Environmental and Resource Economics*, **34**, 125–61.

Hensher, David A., Rose, John M. and Greene, W. H. (2005) *Applied Choice Analysis: A Primer*. Cambridge: Cambridge University Press.

Hodge, I. (2001) Beyond agri-environmental policy: towards an alternative model of rural environmental governance. *Land Use Policy*, **18**, 99–111.

Latacz-Lohmann, U. and Hodge, I. (2003) European agri-environmental policy for the 21st century. *Australian Journal of Agricultural and Resource Economics*, **47**, 123–39.

Louviere, J. J., Hensher, D. A. and Swait, J. (2000) *Stated Choice Methods, Analysis and Applications.* Cambridge: Cambridge University Press.

McInerney, J. (1986) Agricultural policy at the cross-roads. *Countryside Planning Yearbook* (ed. A. W. Gilg), **7**, 44–75.

Palmer, S. C. F. (1997) Prediction of the shoot production of heather under grazing in the uplands of Great Britain. *Grass and Forage Science*, **52**, 408–24.

PDRDF (2004) *Hard Times – a Report into Hill Farming and Farming Families in the Peak District.* Peak District Rural Deprivation Forum, Hope Valley, Derbyshire. http://pdrdf.org/hillfarmingreport.htm

Pykala, J., Luoto, M., Heikkinen, R. and Kontula, T. (2005) Plant species richness and persistence of rare plants in abandoned semi-natural grasslands in northern Europe. *Basic and Applied Ecology*, **6**, 25–33.

Sundberg, J. O. (2006) Private provision of a public good. *Land Economics*, **82**, 353–66.

Swanwick, C., Hanley N. and Termansen, M. (2007) *Scoping Study on Agricultural Landscape Valuation.* Report to Defra, London. http://statistics.defra.gov.uk/esg/reports/agrlandval/Mainrep.pdf

Thompson, D. B. A., MacDonald, A. J., Marsden, J. H. and Galbraith, C. A. (1995) Upland heather moorland in Great Britain: a review of international importance, vegetation change and some objectives for nature conservation. *Biological Conservation*, **38**, 439–57.

Willis, K. G. and Garrod, G. D. (1993) Valuing landscapes – a contingent valuation approach. *Journal of Environmental Management*, **37**, 1–22.

19 Landscape as an integrating framework for upland management

Carys Swanwick

Introduction

The spotlight has been on upland environments in the first decade of the new millennium. This focus has resulted from many factors, but primarily the emphasis that has been placed on developing a sustainable agricultural sector in which 'farmers continue to receive payment from the public purse, but only for public benefits that the public wants and needs' (Policy Commission on the Future of Farming and Food, 2002) and more specifically the Defra review of the system of financial support for upland farming. As the debate has evolved, it is notable that the arguments have increasingly been framed in terms of upland environments as ecosystems, with an emphasis on biodiversity values and ecosystem goods and services. This no doubt reflects current trends in environmental thinking and policy, and especially Defra's Ecosystems Approach project, which is working 'to develop a more strategic approach to policy and decision making on the natural environment' and aims to provide 'an integrated framework for looking at whole ecosystems in policy making' (Defra, 2007).

This growing emphasis on ecosystems and the biodiversity values of the uplands should not be at the expense of concern for the more socially and culturally constructed values of the uplands as landscapes. This is especially important now because of the increasing emphasis on landscape issues that has resulted from the introduction of the European Landscape Convention (ELC). The Convention (Council of Europe, 2000), now signed and ratified by many European countries, including the UK where it took effect in 2007, is the first international agreement specifically addressing landscape issues. The ELC applies equally to urban, peri-urban and rural landscapes, whether they are of high quality or are degraded. It has already had a significant effect in focusing attention on landscape matters and causing national, regional and local authorities in signatory countries to consider the steps needed to implement it.

This new emphasis is particularly important in the UK where, in the middle of the twentieth century, legislation and institutional frameworks for nature conservation and landscape conservation evolved so that these issues came to be viewed as separate from each other. This divergence, sometimes referred to as the 'great divide' (see for example Sheail, 1998), is very different from the more integrated approach, which tends to prevail in other countries in Europe and beyond. One of the results has been that for many years landscape has been interpreted mainly in terms of scenery and aesthetics, far removed from the more scientific concerns of nature conservation. This divide continued in England until 2006 when Natural England was created with a joint remit embracing both landscape and nature conservation, mirroring similar changes that had taken place rather sooner in both Scotland and Wales. In this new situation of integrated remits the ELC should play an invaluable role in helping to ensure that landscape is given equal weight to biodiversity and nature conservation issues in addressing the complex multiple values of environments such as the uplands.

This is not in any sense to imply that the landscape value of the uplands has previously been neglected. In the 1950s and 1960s the selection of National Parks, driven by the Dower Report's emphasis on extensive areas of 'beautiful and relatively wild country' (Dower, 1945), was almost exclusively concerned with upland landscapes, with nine of the ten original parks lying in the uplands. The Countryside Commission's Upland Management Experiment in the Lake District in the 1970s paved the way for a series of research studies to address the question 'What future for the uplands?', and these studies (Institute of Terrestrial Ecology, 1978; Allaby, 1983; Sinclair, 1983) as well as the many other contributions to the debate at that time (see for example contributions by Brotherton, Moggridge, Parker, Shuttleworth and Swanwick in a special edition of *Landscape Research* in 1983) put landscape at the heart of the questions about the uplands and their future management. More recently, when the uplands have been debated in multidisciplinary fora, landscape issues have often been to the fore (see for example Price and Holdgate, 2002; International Centre for the Uplands, 2005), and the Defra consultation document on upland rewards endeavoured to take a balanced approach, referring throughout to both upland landscapes and upland environments (Defra, 2006).

Nevertheless, the growing emphasis on ecosystem goods and services could signal a shift towards a more narrowly focused scientific view of the uplands, and there is still often confusion about how landscape considerations should be dealt with in practice in framing policy and designing mechanisms for intervention. Against this background, this chapter sets out the arguments for a landscape-led approach to the uplands by considering: what the concept of landscape means today; how upland landscapes can be defined and characterised; and how landscape can provide an integrating framework for considering the goods and services that uplands can provide, while also itself being one of those services or benefits. It concludes by briefly considering the drivers of change in upland landscapes.

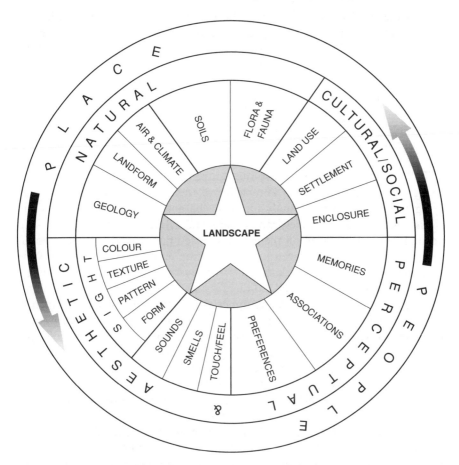

Figure 19.1 Landscape as the interaction of people and place.

The meaning of landscape

Although landscape is a complex construct with many layers of meaning and interpretation, there is generally agreement in the UK that it is concerned with the relationship between people and place. The many facets of this relationship are illustrated in Figure 19.1. Since 1985, the UK has developed a largely informal, non-statutory but increasingly coherent approach to landscape planning which is focused around the concept of landscape character – that is, what makes landscapes distinctive and different from each other. This has been expressed largely through the practice of Landscape Character Assessment, which has become a major tool to support decision-making in rural, peri-urban and urban areas (Swanwick and Land Use Consultants, 2002; Swanwick, 2004). This people-focused view of landscape and the accompanying focus on landscape character are now enshrined in the text of the ELC, which defines landscape as:

an area, as perceived by people, whose character is the results of the action and interaction of natural and/or human factors. The term 'landscape' is thus defined as a zone or area as perceived by local people or visitors, whose visual features and character are the result of the action of natural and/or cultural (that is, human) factors. This definition reflects the idea that landscapes evolved through time, as a result of being acted upon by natural forces and human beings. It also underlines that landscape forms a whole, whose natural and cultural components are taken together not separately.

Those governments that ratify the Convention are required to do several things, including: improving knowledge of their own landscapes by identifying and mapping them; analysing their characteristics, and the forces and pressures that may be transforming them; and assessing them by taking into account the value placed on them by interested parties and the wider population. The UK is well placed to achieve these requirements because of the considerable amount of work that has already taken place to map and characterise its landscapes. In England there is a hierarchy of existing assessments of landscape character, from the upper tier of the 'Character of England' with its map and accompanying descriptions of the 159 Joint Character Areas (Countryside Commission and English Nature, 1996), to a wide range of more detailed assessments of counties and districts, national parks, areas of outstanding natural beauty, and other geographical areas (Swanwick, 2004), to the even finer grain of more detailed assessments such as the work, supported by English Heritage, on Historic Landscape Character Assessment (Aldred and Fairclough, 2003; Clark *et al.*, 2004).

The emergence of Landscape Character Assessment over the last twenty years has marked a significant shift in the emphasis of landscape protection and management in this country. Since 1949 the approach in England and Wales has focused on selection of 'the best' landscapes, chosen largely, though not exclusively, from the perspective of scenery and natural beauty. These areas are then given special treatment as protected areas, notably as national parks or areas of outstanding natural beauty. In the last twenty years, however, there has been a gradual move to an approach that also emphasises 'the rest' of our landscapes, which, while still acknowledging the importance of these special highly valued landscapes, is based on the premise that all landscapes have distinctive character and sense of place, and therefore merit an approach to planning and management that recognises their particular characteristics and qualities.

Defining and characterising upland landscapes

Against this background, it is important to consider briefly how upland landscapes are defined and characterised. There is no single agreed definition for the 'uplands', although, in England, Defra suggests that areas above the upper limits of enclosed farmland containing dry and wet dwarf shrub heath species and rough grassland are referred to as such. For a landscape definition of the uplands, it is helpful – in England at least – to turn to the national level of landscape characterisation. In the early 1990s both the Countryside Commission and English Nature produced high-level national characterisations of the English countryside, resulting in the definition respectively of Countryside Character Areas and Natural Areas (Brooke, 1994; Swanwick, 2004). These were subsequently combined into the framework of Joint Character Areas (JCAs), which has been carried forward into Natural England. These frameworks all concentrated on defining areas of distinctive character and did not group them together into different types of landscape. English Nature did, however, for administrative purposes, at some point group its Natural Areas into six 'Focus Groups' (Stark and Moffat, undated), and the upland grouping was used in English Nature's *Upland Management Handbook* to help to define the extent of the uplands (Blackshall *et al.*, 2001). A total of eighteen Natural Areas were listed as having predominantly upland characteristics.

A similar but broader approach has also been taken to grouping the Joint Character Areas in an exercise carried out to assist in the development of the survey proformas for the Farm Environment Plans under Environmental Stewardship (Martin and Swanwick, 2004). In this work the Joint Character Areas were grouped together into eighteen broad landscape types, based on professional judgement, to create broad groupings of landscapes with similar geology and/or landform and/or land cover. The eighteen broad types included three categories which might reasonably be considered to represent upland landscapes, namely uplands (fifteen JCAs), moorland and moorland fringe (eight JCAs), and upland fringe (eleven JCAs). These areas are indicated in Figure 19.2, and the JCAs in these three categories are listed in Table 19.1. The upland fringe type clearly includes some landscapes that might be considered marginal in terms of their upland character. They are generally transitional between upland and lowland, but they are often inextricably linked to the adjacent uplands in terms of their social and economic systems.

Such grouping into a broad upland and moorland typology is based on the similarities between different areas of upland landscape in terms of the characteristic features that they have in common. But, while linked by their similarities, the character areas are also distinguished by their differences, with each area having its own distinct identity. No one, for example, is likely to argue that the Cumbrian High Fells of the Lake District National Park are the same as the North Pennines, or that either is the same as the Dark Peak area of the Peak District. So, at the national and regional level, upland landscapes can be construed both as high-level generic types of landscape and as individually distinctive character areas.

If the focus is refined to look at an individual upland area through Landscape Character Assessment at a more local level, it is clear that there is another level of variation in character. Most of the main upland areas,

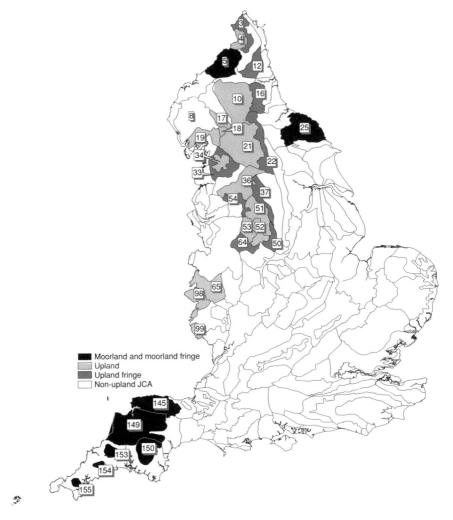

Figure 19.2 Upland, upland fringe and moorland Joint Character Areas in England
(JCA boundaries from MAGIC www.magic.gov.uk, categories based on
Martin and Swanwick, 2004).

the majority of which are either National Parks or Areas of Outstanding
Natural Beauty (AONBs), have been covered by such assessments. Most of
them identify a range of different landscape types, which vary according to
particular patterns of geology, topography and other influencing factors, but
which generally include variations on:

- moorland/upland summits, plateaux, or ridges;
- dales or valleys, sometimes sub-divided into valley/dale heads, middle
  dales and lower dales;
- moorland/upland fringes.

Table 19.1 Joint Character Areas allocated to three broad 'upland' landscape types (see Figure 19.2 for locations).

Upland Type	Moorland and Moorland Fringe Type	Upland Fringe Type
Cheviots (4)	Border Moors and	Cheviot Fringe (3)
North Pennines (10)	Forests (5)	Tyne Gap and Hadrian's
Cumbria High Fells (8)	North Yorkshire Moors	Wall (11)
Orton Fells (17)	and Cleveland Hills	Northumberland (12)
Howgill Fells (18)	(95)	Durham Coalfield Pennine
South Cumbria Low	Exmoor (145)	Fringe (16)
Fells (19)	The Culm (149)	Bowland Fringe and
Bowland Fells (34)	Dartmoor (150)	Pendle Hill (33)
Yorkshire Dales (21)	Bodmin Moor (153)	Lancashire Valleys (35)
South Pennines (36)	Hensbarrow (154)	Manchester Pennine
Dark Peak (51)	Carnmenellis (155)	Fringe (54)
White Peak (52)		Pennine Dales Fringe (22)
South West Peak (53)		Yorkshire South Pennine
Shropshire Hills (65)		Fringe (37)
Clun and North West		Derbyshire Peak Fringe
Herefordshire Hills (98)		and Lower Derwent (50)
Black Mountains and		Potteries and Churnet
Golden Valley (99)		Valley (64)

Finally, even more detailed assessments of landscape character can be carried out for smaller areas, for example to inform management planning or integrated studies of specific upland areas. Figure 19.3, for example, shows the detailed local landscape character assessment that has provided the basis for the White Peak Vision project in the area around Longstone Moor in the Peak District National Park (see Box 19.1). Historic Landscape Characterisation is another form of detailed characterisation that concentrates on the historic origins of current landscape character and is increasingly carried out in advance of, or parallel to, Landscape Character Assessments, as has been the case in the Peak District National Park for example (Barnatt, 2003).

Landscape as an integrating framework

When landscape is considered in this inclusive way, rather than simply in terms of scenery and aesthetics, its three important merits as the cornerstone of an integrated framework for policy and action become clear. First, landscape is itself an integrating concept, as Figure 19.1 shows, because by definition it embraces all the physical, natural and social/cultural influences that shape the land, together with the ways in which people interact with and perceive it to transform land into landscape. Second, the concept of landscape is also spatially comprehensive – landscape is everywhere, not just in valued landscapes that have been identified for special protection. Third, landscape

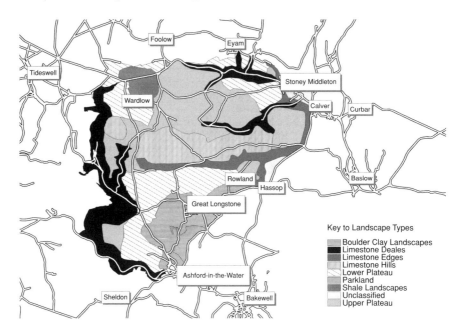

Figure 19.3 A local landscape character assessment from the White Peak Vision Project (based on information from the Peak District National Park Authority).

conceived of in this integrated and spatially comprehensive way offers scope to work at what landscape ecologists in particular frequently call the 'landscape scale'. This is in itself a complex concept. It has been argued (Burgi *et al.*, 2004; Selman, 2006) that landscape scale can be understood in terms of temporal, institutional and modification axes as well as of a spatial axis. Nevertheless, the term is most commonly used to refer to spatial scale and often tends to imply a single scale, above that of the site. In practice most landscape planning work, in England at least, uses the various different scales that can be defined through the hierarchy of landscape character assessment referred to above, to provide a spatial framework for policy and action. This approach can be used for a variety of purposes, provided that the appropriate scale and level of detail of assessment is used for the task or problem in question. For example, Joint Character Areas can be used for high-level strategic planning and management initiatives but are not suitable for use in more local initiatives, other than in providing a broad context.

Thus, there are clearly strong arguments in favour of using landscape as a framework for planning and management in upland areas and elsewhere. Selman and Knight (2006) have suggested that there are two different approaches to action at the landscape scale. There is action *for* landscape, represented by a more traditional, protectionist approach based on the singling out of the 'best' landscapes for special conservation measures; and,

Box 19.1. White Peak Vision Project

This project, run by the Peak District National Park Authority, aims to deliver landscape-scale biodiversity and associated community benefits in a key part of the National Park (PDNPA, 2006). It involves an area-based approach, using the medium of landscape character, with the aim of identifying, conserving and enhancing existing areas of high wildlife value, and linking and expanding these through a programme of habitat restoration and re-creation within a wider landscape character framework. It also aims to involve local communities through a programme of engagement and practical conservation tasks. The project area (see Figure 19.3) is centred on Longstone Moor, the largest remnant of limestone heath in the White Peak Joint Character Area, and includes a number of limestone dales. One of the key steps in the project was an assessment of landscape character, informed by work on geology and landform, historic landscape character and archaeological features, and land use. This, combined with an ecological survey, which included an assessment of site quality, led to the development of a conservation and restoration plan for the area with an emphasis on extending and linking existing high-quality sites.

From a landscape perspective the Vision Project Area was divided into three broad types of landscape, namely: limestone dales and edges; limestone plateau; and boulder clay and shale landscapes. The vision reflects the Peak District Biodiversity Action Plan and envisages, among other things, extension of daleside woodlands both up on to the limestone plateau and down into the dale bottoms; the maintenance and enhancement of the rich mosaic of dales habitats, safeguarding of flower-rich hay meadows and unimproved pastures on the plateau, and reversion of poorer grasslands to unimproved flower-rich grasslands; safeguarding of remnants of limestone heath and extension over the brow of the dales; and conservation and management of lead rakes on the plateau where these are of particular wildlife and historical importance.

In addition to its many practical benefits, the project has also provided the opportunity to explore the role of Landscape Character Assessment and its relationship to ecological land management and an insight into integrated area-based initiatives involving cross-functional team working.

increasingly relevant today, there is the idea of action *through* landscape, in which landscape offers spatial units with a degree of unity in their character, and within which data can be assembled and policies can be created and delivered. As Figure 19.4 shows, these approaches lie at opposite ends of 'a

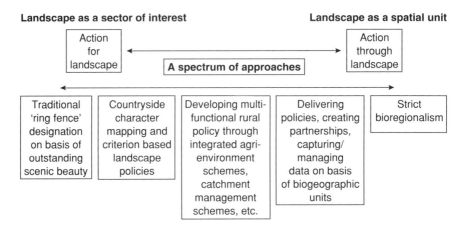

Figure 19.4 A spectrum of landscape-centred approaches (based on Selman and Knight, 2005).

spectrum of landscape centred governance, stewardship and research' (Selman and Knight, 2005). Over time the balance has shifted from an approach dominated by traditional approaches to protecting scenic beauty through designation, representing a sectoral approach to landscape, to approaches where landscape provides the spatial unit within which integrated multifunctional approaches to planning and management are adopted. This is especially appropriate in upland landscapes which are clearly multi-functional, supporting farming, forestry, water supply, and tourism and recreation, as well as various forms of development related to the needs of communities, and so demand an integrated approach.

There are many examples of initiatives that have adopted landscape units, including landscape character areas, as their starting point and reflecting this gradual shift to action through, rather than for, landscape. The first generation of National Park Management Plans offered an early example, but these were primarily sectoral, dealing with different land uses and activities separately rather than in an integrated way. The idea of more integrated approaches to management could be argued to have had its origins in the Peak District National Park with the early ideas developed by the (then) European Commission funded Peak District Integrated Rural Development Project or IRDP (Parker, 1983). This pioneering study was one of three experimental projects in the UK Less Favoured Areas and the only one to involve action research at the community level. It was based on two communities in contrasting landscapes in the park and represented an early attempt to reward farmers for achieving landscape conservation measures on their land, through measures that were tailored to the character of the area, but also included funding for community development projects.

The landscape conservation dimensions of the project provided an exemplar, which influenced the subsequent development of agri-environment schemes such as Environmentally Sensitive Areas, Countryside Stewardship and the more recent Environmental Stewardship scheme. The development of an integrated approach to rural economy and agri-environment issues in the uplands was developed further in 1998 through the Uplands Experiment which took place in Bodmin Moor and in the Forest of Bowland AONB – both upland JCAs, although they were not selected for that reason (Countryside and Community Research Unit *et al.*, 2003). Similarly, the Countryside Agency's Land Management Initiative, set up in 1999 to explore how land management and farming systems can respond to the changing demands on agriculture in ways that will maintain a healthy, attractive environment and contribute to thriving rural economies and communities (Countryside Agency, 2004), included three upland areas in National Parks – the Peak District, the North York Moors and Northumberland – in which ideas about ways of linking agricultural and environmental support with business-development support were explored.

There are still relatively few examples of comprehensive projects based on landscape as an integrating spatial framework. Outside the uplands there are some projects that are based on integrated assessments of character, and related strategies and guidelines, which bring together landscape character, biodiversity and historic environment considerations – in the South Downs for example (Land Use Consultants, 2005). English Nature has also promoted the idea of area-based projects for delivering biodiversity targets at a landscape scale. These are argued to embrace social, economic and environmental sectors, although biodiversity is still undoubtedly the main focus. The White Peak Vision Project described in Box 19.1 is one example of this approach applied to a relatively small area of upland landscape in the Peak District National Park.

Full integration of environmental measures with community development has, however, generally been slow to develop. For upland areas it is now perhaps best-exemplified by projects like the Cultural and Natural Development Opportunity (CANDO) project in the Hambleton and Howardian Hills Partnership area and the programme of sustainability projects in the Forest of Bowland Area of Outstanding Natural Beauty. These, and other similar projects, demonstrate what has been referred to (Selman and Knight, 2006) as the 'virtuous circle' that can link aspects of the different 'capitals' that are represented in landscapes, namely natural, cultural, social and economic capitals. People and place thus become mutually reinforcing in a complex system of linkages.

Ecosystem services and landscape values

In the newly emerging approach to natural resource policy in the UK, much emphasis is being placed on the idea that we value environmental features or areas for the goods, services and benefits that they provide. This approach owes much to environmental economics and is increasingly linked to the 'ecosystems approach' to resource management, promoted in particular as a result of the 1995 Convention on Biological Diversity, in which ecosystems are the 'unit' on which attention is focused, though the spatial scale of the ecosystem focus can vary. Issues relating to the application of this approach in the English policy context have been examined by Defra (Haines-Young and Potschin, 2007). In this work the emphasis is on scientific and biodiversity aspects of ecosystems, but it also acknowledges that it is appropriate to consider 'the combination of habitats found in a broad mosaic of land cover types or in distinct topographical units such as drainage basins'.

In a landscape-centred approach it can be argued that landscape units, whether they are landscape character types or landscape character areas, provide a more comprehensive framework for considering goods, services and benefits in areas such as the uplands. Landscapes embrace physical, natural, social and cultural dimensions of the environment and the interactions between them, and are arguably therefore more comprehensive in their scope than ecosystems. Any landscape will therefore provide a wide range of services and benefits including direct use through enjoyment of recreation, wildlife and biodiversity, landscape, cultural heritage and tranquillity, and indirect use – for example through environmental regulation, carbon sequestration and climate modification.

The situation is, however, complex because 'landscape' is used not only as a term describing the spatial framework for examining goods and services but also to describe one of the groups of services or benefits provided. This is closer to the sectoral approach to landscape referred to above and illustrated in Figure 19.4 – that is, action *for* landscape. Many different typologies of services and benefits have been developed in recent years, but no consistently agreed classification has emerged as yet. Most of the typologies include some form of reference to landscape services but they are described in very different ways. For example, the Millennium Ecosystem Assessment (Millennium Assessment, 2005) includes a category of cultural, non-material benefits which embraces aesthetic and sense-of-place values, which are clearly about landscape, as well as spiritual and religious, recreation and ecotourism, inspirational, educational and cultural-heritage values, all of which might be argued to overlap in part with landscape values. In economic valuation work such as the ODPM study of the value of undeveloped land (Eftec and Entec, 2002), the typology of external benefits (that is, external to the land market) lists landscape as a category and includes, first, the character of landscape and, second, visual amenity (defined as a combination of landscape character and quality) as the related benefits. The community of place-based researchers in the social sciences has developed an approach to mapping landscape values based on survey of attitudes based on a predetermined list of value statements, originally designed for forest valuation (see for example Brown *et al.*, 2002) which include aesthetic value, signified by the statement 'I value the (forest) because I enjoy the scenery, sites sounds smells' as well as spiritual, historic and therapeutic values which are also closely related to landscape.

It is, of course, not new to recognise the landscape values attached to the uplands. Yet today there is a reluctance in the policy arena to dwell on the aesthetic and perceptual values that are so important to people and little survey information to support the case for their importance. A project in the North Pennines (see Box 19.2) asked local people in three different parts of this upland Area of Outstanding Natural Beauty (Weardale, Allendale and Teesdale) why they valued both the North Pennines as a whole and individual areas identified by them as important (Land Use Consultants and University of Sheffield, 1998). The findings suggested that, for the area as a whole, the aspects of the landscape that people valued most were:

- the dramatic contrasts between the remote, wild and open character of the moorland landscapes and the enclosed, sheltered and domestic landscapes of the Dales;
- a strong sense of identity based on the particular combination of geology and landform characteristics and land use and settlement history;
- settlement features, particularly the remaining evidence of the former lead-mining industry which is an important part of the culture, history and identity of the area;
- a deeply rural remote character, contributing to feelings of peace, quiet and tranquillity, solitude and being-close-to-nature peace, all contributing to the special sense of place of the area;
- a strong sense of community and of continuity in the interactions between people and the environment over time, contributing to a sense of identity and feelings of community, and a sense of timelessness and links with the past;
- special aesthetic and perceptual qualities, notably wildness, bleakness, the challenge of upland weather, openness, big skies and the quality of light.

Perhaps what is most notable about people's responses to an upland landscape like the North Pennines, and no doubt others, is that they do not necessarily compartmentalise values into separate categories but consider the landscape as a whole. Values related to wildlife and cultural heritage are part of the experience of landscape and cannot easily be separated out in the minds of the public, who see their surroundings in an integrated way. Attempts to classify such values and to quantify them individually may therefore be doomed to failure. This is one of the particular challenges raised by the environmental economics approach to the environment, with its emphasis on services and benefits and their monetisation.

Box 19.2. North Pennines integrated management objectives

Quality of Life Assessment is a sustainability appraisal tool for maximising and integrating environmental, economic and social benefits as part of any land use or management decision.

This study (Land Use Consultants and University of Sheffield, 1998) applied the Quality of Life Capital (then called Environmental Capital) process to develop integrated management objectives for the North Pennines Joint Character Area. The work followed the following steps:

*   data collection and characterisation to identify a series of character types and areas within the North Pennines, and subsequent analysis to 'unscramble' the data set which comprised a combination of features, attributes and values;
*   evaluation of information relating to features and attributes, importance, trends and targets, and substitutability;
*   use of the results to generate a 'management profile' for each feature and attribute combination, and use of this information to prepare integrated management objectives for the whole Joint Character Area and for individual landscape character types and areas within it;
*   preparation of detailed management guidance for each feature and attribute combination, comprising measures designed to protect, manage and enhance.

The benefits of the process were found to be:

*   integration of information and management objectives;
*   formalising liaison between the four agencies on matters concerning the North Pennines;
*   providing a disciplined way of assessing data on a range of different subjects;
*   preparation of 'high level' management objectives for the Joint Character Area as a whole and for different landscapes within it and more detailed management guidance for each attribute;
*   the public participation exercise, which revealed that most people talked in terms of valued qualities and attributes rather than features.

Drivers of change in upland landscapes

There has been a great deal of interest over the years in the way that upland landscapes are changing, and the effect that change has on the way that they are perceived and valued. Several studies over the last forty years have documented such change, including the Uplands Landscape Study (Sinclair, 1983; Moggridge, 1983), the Monitoring Landscape Change in National Parks study (Countryside Commission, 1991) and the series of Countryside Surveys, notably Countryside Survey 2000 (Haines-Young *et al.*, 2000). Overall the picture in the uplands seems to be one of periods of significant change in the postwar period up to about 1980, followed by a period when rates of change have declined and the effects of environmental policies and support mechanisms have influenced trends. Upland farming and forestry have clearly been most significant in driving past change; but a recent review, based on literature and a number of upland case-study areas (IEEP *et al.*, 2004), suggests that both are now of declining economic importance in most upland areas compared with tourism, industry and the service sector. Nevertheless, hill farming is recognised as being critical to the management of upland landscapes, although it can have both positive effects, such as prevention of succession to scrub and woodland by grazing, and negative effects, such as over- or undergrazing and inappropriate management practices, especially where there is a shift towards more intensive and less environmentally benign practices.

There has been considerable interest in the future landscapes of the uplands; and, in England, a series of scenarios have been developed (Cumulus, 2005) based on possible departures from 'business as usual' – that is, the status quo with continuation of current trends. It has been reported (IEEP *et al.*, 2004) that at present there is little evidence of a risk of widespread abandonment, although the risk is greatest in the most unproductive areas. There is also, however, a growing interest in intentional re-wilding of parts of the uplands through planned withdrawal of management rather than through unplanned abandonment (for example Council for National Parks, 1997; Taylor, 2006; Worrell *et al.*, 2002). Other changes may result from other factors not linked to upland farming. A study in the Peak District (Department of Landscape and University of Sheffield, 2004) concluded that key influencing factors in the next twenty years, other than upland farming practices, were likely to be: the impact of climate change on the landscape, including growing emphasis on use of renewable energy technologies; changes in patterns of recreation and tourism and social factors which may in turn influence patterns of settlement and communications.

Research on public attitudes to change in the uplands is relatively rare. The work that has been done includes study of possible futures for the Yorkshire Dales (O'Riordan *et al.*, 1992) and of scenarios for Dartmoor, as one of six pilot countryside character areas in South West England (New Map Consortium, 1993). Both suggest a preference for the current landscape and general antipathy to change, which undermines the current valued character of these landscapes. New initiatives such as re-wilding may therefore not find favour among the public, and so managing both landscape change and public expectations is a major challenge for the future and requires integrated ways of thinking. Landscape character has a very important role to play in this, and character-based spatial frameworks offer ideal opportunities to balance different interests.

Conclusions and the future

This chapter has argued for a landscape perspective on the uplands as the best way of integrating the complex interactions between people and place, and the natural, cultural, social and economic capitals that both represent in these valued environments. It has also demonstrated that landscape can provide a valuable spatial framework that can encourage a more targeted approach to managing the full range of goods and services that the uplands offer.

Change in upland landscapes is to some degree inevitable, especially given the likely effects of climate change and the many other factors that will drive the shape of future upland landscapes. It is has been argued by many over the years (see for example Swanwick, 1983) that there should be policies for upland landscapes that are fully integrated with policies for agriculture, forestry and other land uses and that clearly recognise the multi-functional nature of such areas. Such policies need to differentiate between conservation measures in the most important and valued areas, conservation and development packages in areas where change can be accommodated alongside conservation, and creation of new upland landscapes where there is scope for significant change. Landscape strategies and guidelines developed from landscape character assessments have emerged as the most widely used approach and offer excellent opportunities for influencing the future of upland landscapes, especially now that the majority of upland areas have developed such landscape initiatives. They do, however, continue to be to some degree sectoral in their approach.

In order to recognise fully the strong link between people and place in the uplands, much more needs to be done to make such assessments fully integrated and to link environmental initiatives to economic development and community initiatives, so that they become mutually reinforcing and combine to give the uplands a more secure future. The central importance of hill farming in securing the future of these landscapes has been recognised by Defra in its consultation document on the uplands (Defra, 2006) and in its proposals for a new upland funding regime. It is to be hoped that this is not a blunt and indiscriminate instrument and that the measures can be tailored to recognise the distinctiveness and individuality of different upland landscapes, as well as reflecting the characteristics that they have in common – we do not want all our upland landscapes to become the same.

References

Aldred, O. and Fairclough, G. (2003) *Historic Landscape Characterisation: Taking Stock of the Method: The National HLC Method Review 2002.* London: English Heritage/Somerset County Council.

Allaby, M. (1983) *The Changing Uplands.* Cheltenham: The Countryside Commission.

Barnatt, J. (2003) *Landscape through Time: Historic Landscape Characterisation in the Peak Park.* Bakewell: Peak District National Park Authority/English Heritage.

Blackshall, J., Manley, J. and Rebance, M. (eds) (2001) *The Upland Management Handbook.* English Nature Science No. 6. English Nature, Peterborough.

Brooke, D. (1994) A countryside character programme. *Landscape Research*, **19**, 128–32.

Brotherton, I. (1983) Database for a debate: a review of upland research. *Landscape Research*, **8**, 30–2.

Brown, G. G., Reed, P. and Harris, C. C. (2002) Testing a place-based theory for environmental evaluation: an Alaska case study. *Applied Geography*, **22**, 49–76.

Burgi, M., Hersperger, A. M. and Schneeberger, N. (2004) Driving forces of landscape change – current and new directions. *Landscape Ecology*, **19**, 857–68.

Clark, J., Darlington, J. and Fairclough, G. (2004) *Using Historic Landscape Characterisation – English Heritage's Review of HLC Applications 2002–03.* English Heritage and Lancashire County Council. http://www.english-heritage.org.uk/server/show/nav.1293

Council of Europe (2000) The European Landscape Convention – Firenze, 20.X.2000 (ETS No. 176). Council of Europe, Strasbourg. www.coe.int/EuropeanLandscapeConvention

Council for National Parks (1997) *Wild by Design in the National Parks of England and Wales.* London: The Council for National Parks.

Countryside Agency (2004) *Experiences from the Land Management Initiatives.* Countryside Agency, Cheltenham, http://www.countryside.gov.uk/Images/CA189_tcm2-21602.pdf

Countryside Commission (1991) *Landscape Change in the National Parks.* CCP 359. Cheltenham: Countryside Commission.

Countryside Commission and English Nature (1996) *The Character of England – Landscape, Wildlife and Natural Features* (Map/Leaflet). CCX 41. Countryside Commission, Cheltenham (and the accompanying series of Countryside Commission Regional Countryside Character volumes published between 1998 *and* 2000).

Countryside and Community Research Unit, University of Gloucestershire, and ADAS Consulting Ltd (2003) *Economic Evaluation of the Upland Experiment (Bodmin Moor Project and Bowland Initiative).* Report to Defra, London. http://statistics.defra.gov.uk/esg/evaluation/upland/default.asp

Cumulus (2005) *Assessment of the Impact of CAP Reform and Other Key Policies on Upland Farms and Land Use: Implications in Both Severely Disadvantaged and Disadvantaged Areas of England.* Defra, London. http://statistics.defra.gov.uk/esg/reports/cap%20uplandfarms%20report.pdf

Defra (2006) *Rural Development Programme for England 2007–2013: Upland Rewards Structure Consultation Document.* Defra, London. http://www.defra.gov.uk/rural/uplands/consultation/rdpuplands-consultdoc.pdf

Defra (2007) *Natural Environment Policy.* Defra, London. http://www.defra.gov.uk/wildlife-countryside/natres/index.htm

Department of Landscape, University of Sheffield (2004) 2084 – Modelling sustainable landscapes for the Peak District. Unpublished report of a pilot study for the Campaign to Protect Rural England, Peak District and South Yorkshire Branch, and the Peak District National Park Authority.

Dower, J. (1945) *National Parks in England and Wales.* Ministry of Town and Country Planning. Cmnd 6628.

Eftec and Entec (2002) *Valuing the External Benefits of Undeveloped Land: Main Report.* Office of the Deputy Prime Minister. London. http://www.communities.gov.uk/documents/planningandbuilding/pdf/158136

Haines-Young, R. and Potschin, M. (2007) *The Ecosystem Concept and the Identification of Ecosystem Goods and Services in the English Policy Context.* Review paper to Defra, project code NR0107, London. http://www.defra.gov.uk/wildlife-countryside/natres/pdf/ecosys-concept.pdf

Haines-Young, R. H., Barr, C. J., Black, H. I. J., Briggs, D. J., Bunce, R. G. H., Clarke, R. T., Cooper, A., Dawson, F. H., Firbank, L. G., Fuller, R. M., Furse, M. T., Gillespie, M. K., Hill, R., Hornung, M., Howard, D. C., McCann, T., Morecroft, M. D., Petit, S., Sier, A. R. J., Smart, S. M., Smith, G. M., Stott, A. P., Stuart, R. C. and Watkins, J. W. (2000) *Accounting for Nature: Assessing Habitats in the UK Countryside.* CEH *and* DETR, London. http://www.defra.gov.uk/wildlife-countryside/cs2000/pdf/prelim.pdf

Institute for European Environmental Policy, Land Use Consultants and GHK Consulting (2004) *An Assessment of the Impacts of Hill Farming in England on the Economic, Environmental and Social Sustainability of the Uplands and More Widely.* Report for Defra, London. http://statistics.defra.gov.uk/esg/reports/hillfarming/default.asp

Institute of Terrestrial Ecology (1978) *Upland Land Use in England and Wales.* Cheltenham: Countryside Commission.

International Centre for the Uplands (2005) Future landscapes of Cumbria – an exploration of social and land management Issues. Unpublished report of a workshop. http://www.theuplandcentre.org.uk/pubs.htm

Land Use Consultants (2005) *South Downs Integrated Landscape Character Assessment.* Report for the South Downs Joint Committee and partners. http://www.southdowns.gov.uk/rte.asp?id=93

Land Use Consultants and University of Sheffield (1998) *North Pennines Environmental Capital: A Pilot Study.* Report to the Countryside Commission *and* English Nature.

Martin, J. and Swanwick, C. (2004) Pre-population of farm environment plan landscape section. Unpublished report to the Countryside Agency.

Millennium Assessment (2005) *Ecosystems and Human Well-being: A Framework for Assessment.* Washington, DC: Island Press. http://www.millenniumassessment.org/en/index.aspx

Moggridge, H. (1983) Upland landscapes: values and prospects. *Landscape Research*, **8**, 2–6.

New Map Consortium (1993) *New Map of England Pilot Project. Technical Report 2: Public Perception Study.* London: Land Use Consultants.

O'Riordan, T., Wood, C. and Shadrake, A. (1992) *Landscapes for Tomorrow: Interpreting Futures in the Yorkshire Dales National Park.* Grassington: Yorkshire Dales National Park.

Parker, K. (1983) Upland landscapes: some ideas on new policies. *Landscape Research*, **8**, 15–19.

PDNPA (2006) *The Vision for Wildlife Project.* Peak District National Park Authority, Bakewell. http://www.peakdistrict.org/index/pubs/vision-project.htm

Policy Commission on the Future of Farming and Food (2002) *Farming and Food: A Sustainable Future.* Cabinet Office, London. http://archive.cabinetoffice.gov.uk/farming/pdf/PC%20Report2.pdf

Price, M. and Holdgate, M. (2002) *Sustainable Futures for the British Uplands: Summary Statement 13.* London: Royal Geographical Society/Institute of British Geographers.

Selman, P. (2006) *Planning at the Landscape Scale.* RTPI Library Series. London: Routledge.

Selman, P. and Knight, M. (2005) Landscape as an integrating framework for rural policy and planning: review of literature and major themes. Unpublished background paper for RELU Workshop, Sheffield, 17 May.

Selman, P. and Knight, M. (2006) On the nature of virtuous change in cultural landscapes: exploring sustainability through qualitative models. *Landscape Research,* **31,** 295–307.

Sheail, J. (1998) *Nature Conservation in Britain: The Formative Years.* London: The Stationery Office.

Shuttleworth, S. (1983) Upland landscapes and the landscape image. *Landscape Research,* **8,** 7–14.

Sinclair, G. (ed.) (1983) *The Uplands Landscape Study.* Narberth: Environment Information Services.

Stark, G. and Moffat, T. (undated) *Comparing Alternative Landscape Classifications.* Working paper for Countryside Survey 2000. Grange over Sands: Institute of Terrestrial Ecology.

Swanwick, C. (1983) The seminar response – overview of a landscape research group seminar on upland landscapes held on 17th June 1983. *Landscape Research,* **8,** 20–2.

Swanwick, C. (2004) The assessment of countryside and landscape character in England: an overview. *Countryside Planning: New Approaches to Management and Conservation* (ed. K. Bishop and A. Phillips), pp. 109–24. London: Earthscan.

Swanwick, C. and Land Use Consultants (2002) *Landscape Character Assessment: Guidance for England and Scotland.* Countryside Agency, Cheltenham, and Scottish Natural Heritage, Battleby. http://www.countryside.gov.uk/lar/landscape/cc/landscape/publication/

Taylor, P. (2006) Beyond conservation: shifting the paradigm of upland land use. Unpublished paper to ESRC Trans-disciplinary Seminar Series: Sustaining Upland Landscapes, Exeter University, February.

Worrell, R., Pryor, S. N., Scott, A., Peterken, G. F., Taylor, K., Knightbridge, R. and Brown, N. (2002) *New Wildwoods in Britain: The Potential for Developing New Landscape-scale Native Woodlands.* Report to the Land Use Policy Group of the GB Statutory Conservation, Countryside and Environment Agencies (LUPG). LUPG, London. http://www.lupg.org.uk/pdf/Wildwoods.pdf

20 Using scenarios to explore UK upland futures

Kathryn Arblaster, Mark S. Reed,
Evan D. G. Fraser and Clive Potter

Introduction

Upland landscapes have been the subject of policy debates for decades. Managed under livestock-farming systems that would be uneconomic without heavy government subsidies, they are also highly valued for their biodiversity, physical beauty and recreational importance (Condliffe; Crowle and McCormack; Curry; Swanwick, all this volume). Uplands around the world have experienced significant and often rapid socio-economic change in recent years. In the EU in particular, uplands are facing an uncertain future owing to changes in national, European and international policy. For example, reforms to the European Union's Common Agricultural Policy (CAP) have 'de-coupled' subsidies from agricultural production, with perceived uncertain consequences for farmers as well as for land management and the rural environment. Significant changes in land-use practices will be required in many upland catchments if countries are to meet the requirements of the EU Water Framework Directive. The Kyoto Protocol is a potential driver that has only recently been recognised as an opportunity by policy-makers and land managers owing to the market possibilities it may create for carbon stored in soils through agricultural management (Worrall and Evans, this volume). If a link between water colour and land management practices is proved in future, water companies may require those managing their land for grouse and sheep to make significant changes to their practices. A number of conservation organisations are interested in 're-wilding' dry heath and blanket bog habitats that are currently managed for grouse and sheep, significantly reducing management inputs. The ecological consequences of such a policy are uncertain under future climate change, possibly leading to scrub and forest encroachment into marginal blanket bog habitats. In the UK, Natural England are increasingly requiring managers of blanket bog Sites of Special Scientific Interest to reduce levels of managed burning, and this may have uncertain consequences for ecology (Crowle and McCormack, this volume; Stewart *et al.*, 2005; Yallop *et al.*, this volume) and for the livelihood of those who depend on blanket bog environments (Reed *et al.*, 2005). In short, policies are being implemented in the context of ongoing socio-economic (e.g. demographic) and environmental (e.g. climate) change. Decision-makers are therefore keen to under-stand how potential future changes may affect them, and how they can best adapt to maintain upland goods and services.

As we gaze into an uncertain future that may contain a variety of envir-onmental, policy, economic and demographic surprises, traditional modelling approaches, which use past trends as the basis on which to make future pre-dictions, are proving to be a poor basis for policy (Rothman *et al.*, 2000; Morris *et al.*, 2005). As a result, scholars and policy-makers are increasingly using a process called 'scenario development' as a basis for planning. Unlike forecasts or predictions, scenarios are images of the future, or alternative futures, that present us with situations that we may need to prepare for (Berkhout *et al.*, 2001; Hubacek and Rothman, 2006; Rothman *et al.*, 2000). Scenario studies are increasingly being used to help decision-makers better understand, anticipate and respond to the sorts of dynamic and uncertain futures that uplands face. Although the number and sophistication of scen-ario methods have increased substantially in recent years, there have been few comparative analyses of outputs from such exercises. The British uplands offer a unique opportunity, owing to the significant number of scen-ario studies that have been conducted for this system. Taken separately, these studies provide a fractured picture of the future for UK uplands. However, by drawing together the results, using a combination of literature review and interviews with those involved in eight scenario studies, this chap-ter aims to provide a more coherent picture of what the future might hold. To do this, the chapter (1) evaluates which scenarios are perceived by stake-holders to be most likely and desirable, and (2) reflects on the benefits and drawbacks of the scenario methods used in the UK uplands to date.

Background: anticipating change in UK uplands

Traditional hill farming in the UK uplands typically includes grazing cattle and extensive sheep-farming, as this best suits the climate, soil fertility, depth and terrain. All UK uplands are classified as Less Favoured Areas (LFAs) under EU Directive 75/268/EEC (ADAS, 2003). Farming has significantly shaped these landscapes over the centuries, and the heritage value of features such as drystone walls, stone barns and moorlands is considerable (NFU, 2005).

Growing awareness of the environmental problems amplified by the CAP (such as overgrazing in the uplands, which has been blamed by English Nature for damaging internationally important wildlife sites among other problems [English Nature, 2003]), as well as pressure from the World Trade Organ-isation and EU enlargement, led to a series of CAP reforms which were agreed in 2003. These reforms continue a process of de-coupling CAP subsidies from production, so that farmers are now paid by area rather than, as tradition-ally, by the number of stock.

The hill farming industry is believed to be facing a number of problems including falling incomes, an ageing demographic structure, and farmland abandonment (Burton *et al.*, this volume; Burton *et al.*, 2005). This decline has been compounded by a significant reduction in the agricultural labour force owing to out-migration. This in turn is partly driven by limited non-farm employment opportunities and higher-than-average unemployment levels (Defra, 2003).

There is evidence that sheep- and cattle-grazing play an important role in maintaining upland habitats (ADAS, 2003; Burton *et al.*, 2005; Gardner *et al.*, this volume). IEEP *et al.* (2004) suggested that, without grazing and managed burning, 'all but the wettest blanket bog' would, below the tree line, naturally succeed to trees. This would dramatically change the character, value and functioning of upland landscapes. However, there is also evidence that overgrazing reduces the abundance of many important grass and heath species, reducing biodiversity. Overgrazing was cited by English Nature (2003) as the main reason for the poor condition of upland Sites of Special Scientific Interest. It can also exacerbate soil erosion and run-off, leading to water discolouration (IEEP *et al.*, 2004; ADAS, 2003).

The future of the UK uplands is a growing priority for researchers and policy-makers. There is ongoing debate about the extent to which upland farmers should be supported in the future and how far the land should continue to be farmed in order to maintain important landscape features (Burton *et al.*, 2005; Taylor, 2005). Some argue that continued public support for upland farming is essential to maintain a viable farming population in the LFAs and thus sustain biodiversity and landscape values (IEEP *et al.*, 2004; Burton *et al.*, 2005; NFU, 2005). Some of these authors also suggest that the changes taking place in the UK uplands are inevitable, that the uplands have never been static, and that alternative ways of managing these landscapes must now be considered beyond traditional hill farming (Taskforce for the Hills, 2001; ADAS, 2003; Taylor, 2005). Although the majority of scenario studies reviewed in this chapter refer to English and Welsh uplands, there are quite different issues in different parts of the UK; for example in Scotland large areas of the uplands are managed for hunting grouse and deer, with agriculture having relatively less importance.

Developing scenarios for UK uplands

Study design

We undertook a review of academic and grey literature in order to identify eight studies that had used or were using scenarios to explore UK upland change (Arblaster, 2006). These were systematically compared to elucidate methodological differences and summarise differences in the content of the scenarios they developed. Where stakeholders were consulted, the scenarios that they deemed to be most and least desirable were assessed. Alongside this analysis, nine semi-structured interviews were conducted to gain opinions on the use of scenarios and to understand better the scenarios used in each study. Interviewees were chosen on the basis of their close involvement with the scenario studies and debates surrounding upland futures.

Scenario methods evaluation

An overview of each scenario study is provided in Table 20.1. The time horizons covered by these projects ranged from less than ten years into the future in study 1, to 2030 in study 5. Although all focused on UK uplands, some were restricted in their geographical range (e.g. to England or Cumbria) and in the issues or stakeholders they targeted (e.g. effects on biodiversity conservation in study 6). Table 20.2 shows the range of different methods that were used to create the scenarios and assess their implications in these studies. Box 20.1 evaluates and compares the scenario methods used to date in UK uplands. This analysis shows how a wide range of different approaches have been used, and identifies limitations in relation to the studies that are reviewed. Although this means that it is not possible to integrate the findings of these studies, comparisons and themes can be drawn from the analysis that can provide important insights into future policy decisions for UK uplands.

UK upland futures

Table 20.3 lists the wide range of possible futures for UK uplands described in the eight studies, showing their relative desirability according to the stakeholders who were consulted in each study. Despite following very different approaches, the majority of scenarios developed in these studies fall into four key groups. Figure 20.1 shows how the scenarios differ along an environmental–economic continuum, depending on the level of support for a pro-environment policy agenda, and varying levels of financial support for farmers.

Scenario A: withdrawal of agricultural management and re-wilding

All the studies included a scenario in which financial support was withdrawn from upland agriculture, leading to the withdrawal of agricultural management and/or farm diversification (lower two quadrants in Figure 20.1). In both these scenarios, land is most likely to be abandoned on the poorest, highest and most remote land. Without alternative support, re-wilding scenarios suggest that, as the amount of land entered into agri-environmental agreements declines, farms go out of business and land is abandoned. It is anticipated under this scenario that farmland may be replaced by conservation management and/or reforestation, whether through planting or through natural regeneration.

   In studies 1, 2, 4, 6 and 7, where stakeholders were invited to express an opinion, the re-wilding scenario (without any alternative funding for conservation programmes) was deemed to be the least desirable future for UK uplands. Study 6 described this scenario (which they called 'liberalisation')

Table 20.1 Overview of UK upland scenario studies.

Project Title	Project Team & Duration	Scenario Time Horizon	Description	Reference
1. Consultation on the Future Uplands Reward Structure	Defra, 2006	2007–2013	Scenarios focussed on options for future structure of the Uplands Reward Scheme to help inform policy decisions in England and Wales	Defra, 2006
2. Economic valuation of environmental impacts in the SDAs	Eftec Consultants funded by Defra, 2005	2007–2013	Scenarios focussed on different economic effects of changes in SDA environmental characteristics arising from changes in Less Favoured Area support in England and Wales	Eftec, 2006
3. Assessment of CAP reform and other key policies on upland farms and land use implications in SDAs and DAs in England	Cumulus Consultants, IEEP and CCRU funded by Defra, 2005	2007–2013	Designed to supplement Eftec (2006) by assessing how a variety of policy scenarios might affect upland areas in England and Wales, and develop consultation options for Defra	Cumulus, 2005
4. An assessment of the impacts of hill farming in England on the economic, environment and social sustainability of the uplands and more widely	Institute for European Environmental Policy, Land Use Consultants and GHK Consulting, funded by Defra, 2003	Not specified	Used scenarios to evaluate the implications of different future hill farming activities in England and Wales	IEEP *et al.*, 2004

5. Scanning Agricultural Futures in England and Wales and Implications for the Future	Cranfield University, Silsoe Research Institute and Macaulay Land Use Research Institute, funded by Defra, 2005	2005–2030	Developed scenarios for arable and pastoral agriculture to explore possible environmental impacts and policy interventions that could promote more sustainable future agriculture in England and Wales	Morris *et al.*, 2005; Morris *et al.*, 2006
6. Bioscene	Imperial College and other partners, funded by EU FP5, 2002–2006	2005–2030	Used scenarios to evaluate effects of agricultural restructuring on biodiversity conservation in mountain areas of Europe, in order to enhance EU agri-environmental and rural development policy and implementation	Soliva *et al.*, 2007
7. Preservation and Change in the Upland Landscape: the Public Benefits of Grazing Management	Macaulay Land Use Research Institute and University of Glasgow, funded by the Scottish Office Agriculture, Environment and Fisheries Department, 1993–1994	Not specified	Evaluated Scottish public preferences for future landscapes based on willingness to pay for the subsidies that create them	Bullock & Kay (1997)
8. Sustainable Uplands	Universities of Leeds, Durham, Sheffield & Sussex with Moors for the Future and Heather Trust, funded by UK Research Councils with Defra & SEERAD, 2005–2008	2005–2025	Developing scenarios to evaluate the likely effects of key socio-economic, environmental and policy drivers and develop innovative land management adaptations, using case studies in England and Scotland	Prell *et al.*, in press a and b; Dougill *et al.*, 2006

Table 20.2 Methods used to develop and evaluate scenarios of upland change in eight UK studies.

Study Method	1. Defra	2. Eftec	3. Cumulus, IEEP & CCRU	4. IEEP et al.	5. Morris et al.	6. Bio-Scene	7. Bullock & Kay	8. Sustainable Uplands
Scenario development based on:								
Evidence from literature	X	X	X	X	X	X		X
Consultation with stakeholders	X	X			X	X	X	X
Economic valuation		X					X	
Computer simulation models					X	X		X
Scenario evaluation based on:								
Case study areas	X			X		X	X	X
Consultation with stakeholders				X			X	X
Comprehensive sustainability assessment						X		X
Visualisations						X	X	X

Box 20.1. Critical comparison of scenario methods

Stakeholder engagement in the scenario studies reviewed here typically took place during scenario development, but was also used during scenario evaluations (see Table 20.2). The choice of stakeholder selection may affect the outcome of scenario studies, especially when they are involved in both scenario development and evaluation. Although all the studies reviewed here identified farmers as pivotal stakeholders, other upland stakeholder groups appeared to be selected on an *ad hoc* basis by most research teams (only studies 6 and 8 identified stakeholders using a systematic and iterative approach). No individual study identified all the categories of upland stakeholder that had been identified in the studies taken together. Although many of the interviewees suggested that members of the general public should be involved in scenario evaluation, very few of the studies actually involved the general public. The legitimacy and importance of stakeholder involvement is discussed further in Connelly and Richardson (this volume). Few studies worked with stakeholders for both scenario development and evaluation. One of the problems of involving stakeholders in evaluating scenarios was illustrated by study 7, where respondents displayed a preference for the status quo over scenarios that involved change (c.f. Samuelson and Zeckhauser, 1988).

The depth of stakeholder consultation varied from a single workshop (e.g. studies 3 and 5) to a combination of workshops and in-depth interviews (e.g. studies 4 and 8). Economic valuation was used by studies 2 and 7 to develop scenarios with greater emphasis on economic impacts. Study 8 went a step further by using an Agent-Based Model to simulate how land managers are likely to respond to different scenarios. Such models represent human behaviour from the actual experiences, opinions and perceptions of land managers through interviews. By examining the knock-on effects of likely land manager behaviour, it should be possible to provide more realistic computational simulations of different scenarios. Study 8 was the only study to integrate simulation models with stakeholder participation (Prell, Reed and Hubacek, in press). This offers a number of advantages, as social agents are often intimately acquainted with a level of complexity and detail that is rarely represented in simulation models.

Visualisation techniques were sometimes used to communicate scenarios to stakeholders. For example, digitally manipulated photographs were used in study 6, and illustrations used in study 7, to communicate the effects of varying subsidy levels on ecological succession and biodiversity. However, visualisation techniques pose the risk of visual bias. For example, aspects of scenarios that can easily be represented visually (e.g. land cover change) may receive more attention from focus group participants than other aspects (such as cultural or demographic change).

Table 20.3 UK upland scenarios developed by eight studies, not including Business as Usual scenarios (LFA – Less Favoured Areas; SDA – Severely Disadvantaged Area; CAP – Common Agricultural Policy; ESA – Environmentally Sensitive Area. Scenarios have not yet been finalised for study 8).

	Scenario 1	Scenario 2	Scenario 3	Scenario 4	Preferred scenario	Worst scenario	Most probable
1. Defra, 2006	Abandonment-Intensification: LFA support withdrawn from uplands	Environment only: existing LFA support focussed on enhancing habitats in SDA uplands	Environment-Agri: existing LFA support focussed on producers in existing agri-environment schemes on SDA land		Mixture of 2 and 3	1	–
2. Eftec, 2006	Redistribution of support to more marginal land in LFA on condition of joining agri-environment scheme	Redistribution to agri-environment measures only	Complete withdrawal of support		2	3	–
3. Cumulus, 2005	Redistribution of support to more marginal land in LFA on condition of joining agri-environment scheme	Redistribution to agri-environment measures only	Complete withdrawal of support		2 (from environmental perspective)	3 (although possible environmental benefits)	–
4. IEEP et al., 2004	Maintain production	Reduction in hill farming: less but larger farms and remote areas abandoned	Diversification of hill farming: farming continues supported by off-farm income and increased uptake of agri-environmental agreements		3	2	1

Reference							
5. Morris et al., 2005	World Market: all financial support withdrawn, relying on markets only	Global Sustainability: support for farming based on cross-compliance with environmental measures	National Enterprise: price support and protection to serve national and local priorities (similar to pre-reform CAP)	Local Stewardship: locally defined support schemes reflect local priorities for food production, incomes & environment		Environmental = 1 & 2 Economic = 2 Social = 2, 3, 4 Overall = 2	—
6. Soliva et al., 2008	Liberalisation: all financial support withdrawn from uplands	Managed change for biodiversity: support for farming based on cross-compliance with environmental measures			2	1	1
7. Bullock & Kay (1997)	Landscape A Policy off: ESA agreements not renewed, leading to higher grazing pressure	Landscape B Policy-on-extensified: ESA support leads to lower grazing pressure in line with current trends	Landscape C Policy-on-very-extensified: ESA support leads to significant reduction in hill farming and grazing pressure		3	1	
8. Prell et al., in press a and b; Dougill et al., 2006	Farmers as ecosystem providers: a decline in levels of agricultural support leads to significant reduction in hill farming, grouse moor management and burning pressure remains constant	Blanket bog burning ban: managed burning is restricted to dry heath habitats, grouse moor management declines	Hill farming collapse: removal of agricultural support with no alternative Government funding leads to cessation of hill farming, grouse moor management remains constan	Managed retreat: provides funds to maintain fire breaks but leads to the end of hill farming and grouse moor management		—	2

	Weak environmental policy agenda	Strong environmental policy agenda
Financial support from government continuing	Continued levels of hill farming supported by pre-reform Common Agricultural Policy style subsidies **Scenario C**	Reduced levels of hill farming based on cross-compliance with environmental measures **Scenario D**
Financial support from government withdrawn	Significantly reduced levels of hill farming supported by diversification **Scenario A** **Scenario B**	Withdrawal of agricultural management and re-wilding **Scenario A**

Figure 20.1 Scenarios grouped according to levels of support for a pro-environment policy agenda and varying levels of financial support for farmers.

as 'a nightmare for biodiversity' that would be hard to reverse, with negative impacts on biodiversity, landscape amenity value and historic features. Although study 5 identified certain environmental benefits arising from this scenario, it did not identify any economic or social benefits. The lack of socio-economic benefits arising from this scenario is hardly surprising, given the current reliance of upland agriculture on subsidies and the central role that farming plays in generating income for many upland communities. However, using the HillPlan model (MLURI, 2005), study 5 predicted that a reduction in grazing pressure under this scenario may improve upland species composition in the short term, leading to an increase in heath communities and a reduction in bracken. In the long term, however, other studies recognised that a significant reduction in grazing pressure may cause many heath communities to be replaced by scrub and eventually forest. Given the international significance of these habitats for biodiversity, this was a major concern for most of the stakeholders that were consulted in the studies. In addition, during the early phases of this change, raised fuel loads may enhance the likelihood of accidental fires (Reed *et al.*, 2005). These may cause significant – sometimes long-term – damage to upland soils and plant communities.

Perhaps owing to the negative implications and the perceived political unacceptability of this scenario for many stakeholders, it was believed to be the least likely to occur. However, this view was not shared by everyone. This begs the question of whether future generations will concur with the stakeholders consulted in the studies reviewed in this chapter, given ever-increasing pressures on government to raise budgets for health, education, pensions and security. Although the socio-economic effect of withdrawing financial support is relatively clear, the environmental implications are less clear-cut. Many conservationists favour a retreat to low-impact management in certain upland habitats, particularly blanket bogs (Reed *et al.*, 2005), to maintain biodiversity and encourage certain species (e.g. raptors). Although the cessation of grazing and burning on dry heath would almost certainly increase scrub, leading to eventual reforestation, the effects are less clear-cut on blanket bog. Evidence about the effect of burning on blanket bog plant diversity is contradictory (Stewart *et al.*, 2005), and a combination of historic management and climate change may alter the future hydrology of blanket bogs, making them respond to changes in management in a similar way to dry heaths (Reed *et al.*, 2005). As such, there is an urgent need to understand the full implications of this scenario, so that upland stakeholders can adequately prepare, and so that policy-makers can better evaluate the likely implications of different policy options.

However, most studies agreed that any process of 're-wilding' would most likely consist of some form of active conservation management (including the maintenance of fire-breaks) replacing sheep or grouse management, rather than land being completely 'abandoned', and that this would need to be facilitated through some kind of alternative funding. Study 6 suggest, in their 'managed change for biodiversity' scenario, that this may be facilitated through funding equivalent to current levels, targeted at nature conservation in the form of 'cross-compliance', by which farmers would need to undertake conservation activities to continue to receive government support (Soliva *et al.*, 2008). This team estimated that such a scenario would lead to significant increases in the area of arable land, and minor increases in rough grazing and broad-leaf woodland, with minor decreases in improved grassland, wetland and heath in their Cairngorms study area, as compared to a business-as-usual scenario (Mitchley *et al.*, 2006). In terms of the quality of these habitats (using a subjective assessment), they estimated that there would be improvements for arable, heath, broad-leaf and coniferous woodland, with minor negative effects on rough grazing.

Stakeholders in study 8 perceived that a ban on burning blanket bog habitats, and hence withdrawal of active management from more limited areas, was more probable than the kind of broad-scale re-wilding described above. Such a policy would address many of the concerns and priorities of conservationists, and matches the kind of tighter regulation that English Nature lobbied for during Defra's recent review of the Heather and Grass Burning Code.

Scenario B: significantly reduced levels of hill farming supported by diversification

In the studies, re-wilding scenarios were often coupled with diversification (though they were sometimes presented separately) (bottom-left quadrant in Figure 20.1). In this scenario, it is assumed that reduced levels of hill farming are supported by a range of alternative enterprises including off-farm income. New sources of income could include for example: tourism, recreation and leisure activities (e.g. bed-and-breakfast provision); direct marketing and processing of local produce (e.g. 'fell-bred' lamb), alternative crops or other products (e.g. planting bio-energy crops in upland valleys) and new business ventures (e.g. wind farms). The associated fall in the demand for agricultural inputs and services such as feed, fertilisers, vets and auction marts would be offset to some extent by demands for alternative inputs and services associated with new enterprises and land uses in this scenario. Studies differ over the extent to which support from diversification would lead to a reduction in the number of farms and livestock in UK uplands. Where this leads to abandonment of land for agricultural purposes, afforestation and management for nature conservation would be anticipated.

Although varying levels of diversification entered many of the scenarios developed by the studies reviewed here, only study 4 developed a scenario focused specifically on the effects of diversification. Compared to the other scenarios evaluated in study 4, the diversification scenario was deemed to be most desirable, but on the assumption that it would lead to a lower impact on farm and livestock numbers than 'reduced levels of hill farming based on cross-compliance with environmental measures'. The 'local stewardship' scenario developed by study 5 included significant diversification, with agricultural support reflecting local needs, self-reliance and local social and environmental objectives. This goes beyond the diversification scenario of study 4 to suggest greater connectivity between consumers and producers through local markets and brands, and farmers' co-operatives and marketing schemes designed to add value and raise prices. This could mean that, despite reduced productivity, agricultural area could increase, with a mix of intensive and extensive systems including family farms. Although this scenario was deemed to be desirable from a social perspective, there were few perceived environmental or economic benefits from this scenario compared to others.

Scenario C: continued levels of hill farming supported by pre-reform Common Agricultural Policy-style subsidies

Although deemed unlikely, given current policy trajectories, this scenario assumes that it would be possible to halt (and possibly reverse in some areas) the existing trend towards declining upland farms. It assumes that the area of land used for hill farming and entered into agri-environmental agreements will remain largely unchanged from current levels, with minimal shifts towards alternative land uses such as forestry. Diversification into tourism and recreation would continue at current levels, with limited levels of direct marketing and processing, and the majority of farm incomes would come from agricultural production. There would be limited controls on agrochemicals and farming practices on environmental grounds. There would be a focus on commercial outputs and production with relatively intensive farming to provide self-sufficiency.

As this scenario most closely represents the status quo (as opposed to what is deemed most likely to happen), it might be expected that this would be one of the most preferred scenarios. There is a well-developed literature about 'status quo bias' that explores why most people prefer the status quo to change (Samuelson and Zeckhauser, 1988). Various arguments are proposed, including people's natural aversion to risk and the unknown. However, this bias cannot be assumed: only study 5 ranked this as a preferred scenario, and then only for social reasons (it was not deemed to have significant environmental or economic benefits).

Scenario D: reduced levels of hill farming based on cross-compliance with environmental measures

Given the range of public goods and services provided by ongoing upland management for agriculture, most of the stakeholders who were consulted believed that government financial support would continue in some form for upland farming in the future. Given the growing prominence of environmental concerns in policy-making, a scenario with reduced levels of hill farming based on cross-compliance with environmental measures was deemed by stakeholders to be the most likely to occur (top-right quadrant in Figure 20.1).

Despite a reduction in hill farm production, this scenario would contribute to local, regional and global ecosystem goods and services, including a comprehensive approach to the minimisation of diffuse pollution from agriculture and an emphasis on the multi-functionality of upland landscapes. However, there could be as much as 50 per cent fewer farms. Although there would be some amalgamation into larger farms, a limited number of family farms would remain viable. It is also assumed that large tracts of land (concentrated in the highest and most remote areas) could cease to be grazed or managed in any way for agriculture, where some afforestation and management for nature conservation may occur. The demand for agricultural inputs and services would decline, offset to an extent by demand for new goods and services to support diversification.

Most studies also agreed that some level of continued public support for hill farming would be the most desirable future scenario. Study 2 came to this conclusion on the basis of environmental criteria alone. However, other studies came to the same conclusion using broader criteria. For example, the 'global sustainability' scenario in study 5 scored highest on environmental, social and economic criteria on the basis of simulation-model outputs. Initially developed by the UK Foresight programme (OST, 2002; Berkhout and Hertin, 2002), this scenario consisted of a low-intervention, market-oriented regime, with targeted sustainability 'compliance' requirements and programmes. Similarly, study 7 found that members of the public were most willing to pay for landscapes where Environmentally Sensitive Area schemes had significantly reduced grazing levels. Like many of the scenarios in this group, these scenarios broadly match the emerging funding regime under CAP reform, with the Single Farm Payment requiring hill farmers to comply with various environmental and other standards and opportunities for additional funding linked to environmental work through the Stewardship scheme. On the other hand, study 6 estimated that this scenario (their business-as-usual scenario, assuming continuing trends) was significantly more expensive than the complete withdrawal of government support for upland agriculture. They also concluded that this scenario would provide less biodiversity bene-fits than re-wilding, whether re-wilding was supported financially through cross-compliance in their 'managed change for biodiversity' scenario or not (in their 'liberalisation' scenario).

Conclusion

Uplands around the world are facing significant socio-economic and envir-onmental change, and decision-makers need to understand better what the future may hold if they are to adapt and maintain upland goods and ser-vices. Although the impacts of such exercises on policy are notoriously hard to quantify (Phillipson and Liddon, 2007), scenario exercises of the sort explored in this chapter offer upland managers, policy-makers and stakeholders a useful tool to evaluate future practice and policy options in order to pre-pare for different futures. While the case studies reviewed in this chapter mainly focus on UK uplands, scenario development has the potential to inform pol-icy and strategy in uplands throughout the EU (see Soliva *et al.*, 2008).

Although it is difficult to compare directly the scenarios from the studies reviewed here, we can extract a number of common threads that stakehold-ers were particularly concerned about. Stakeholders agreed that the most desir-able and likely scenario would be a continuation of hill farming, albeit at reduced levels, based on compliance with environmental measures. The least desirable scenario was a complete withdrawal of government financial sup-port for hill farming. Although this was deemed by stakeholders to be the least likely scenario, it warrants close attention owing to the significance of its implications. The negative socio-economic effect of withdrawing finan-cial support is clear, but the environmental implications are less clear-cut. As such, there is an urgent need to understand the full implications of this scenario, so that upland stakeholders can adequately prepare, and so that policy-makers can better evaluate the likely implications of different policy options.

Owing to their ability to communicate a large amount of information in an easily understandable manner, scenarios are increasingly developed to engage a range of stakeholders in environmental decision-making, stimulat-ing people to evaluate and reassess their beliefs about the system under invest-igation (Peterson *et al.*, 2003; Chermack, 2004). Using a multi-stakeholder process to develop scenarios may reduce the likelihood of errors occurring in the decision-making process (Berkhout *et al.*, 2001). However, the limita-tions of scenario studies are also well documented (e.g. Berkhout *et al.*, 2001;

Hubacek and Rothman, 2006) and were emphasised by those interviewed for this research. For example, there is a danger that decisions may be biased by scenarios that lack a sufficient evidence base, that downplay uncertainty, or that do not consider sufficiently different time-horizons or perspectives. Scenarios may lack transparency if they do not make the assumptions made to create them explicit. The choice of criteria against which scenarios are evaluated may also bias the outcome, although there was no evidence that this occurred in the studies reviewed above, since those using environmental criteria alone favoured the same scenario as those using environmental, social and economic criteria.

Although it is difficult to generalise from so few studies, more in-depth participation from stakeholders appeared to broaden the scope of the scenarios developed. However, without systematic and representative stakeholder selection, there is a danger that participation may bias results (Prell, Hubacek *et al.*, in press). Although computational simulation models can enhance detail and add a predictive component to scenario development, there is a danger that these are seen as a 'black box' by stakeholders, reducing scenario credibility (Himamowa, 1975; Prell *et al.*, 2007). Moreover, while visualisation techniques can provide a powerful tool for communicating scenarios to stakeholders, they pose the risk of visually biasing scenario evaluation towards issues that are easily represented in pictures.

Acknowledgements

We are indebted to the interviewees who gave their time so generously and enthusiastically to discuss this research. Authors from the University of Leeds are funded through the Rural Economy and Land Use (RELU) programme, co-sponsored by Defra and SEERAD (project RES-224-25-0088).

References

ADAS (2003) *The Mid-Term Evaluation of the England Rural Development Programme, Hill Farm Allowance*, Wolverhampton: ADAS Consulting.

Arblaster, K. (2006) Exploring the use of scenarios as policy tools for looking at the future of the English uplands, MSc Thesis, Imperial College London.

Berkhout, F. and Hertin, J. (2002) *Foresight Futures Scenarios: Developing and Applying a Participative Strategic Planning Tool*. Science and Policy Research Unit. University of Sussex, Brighton.

Berkhout, F., Hertin, J. and Jordan, A. (2001) *Socio-economic Futures in Climate Change Impact Assessment: Using Scenarios as 'Learning Machines'*. Tyndall Centre Working Paper No. 3, University of East Anglia, Norwich.

Bullock, C. and Kay, J. (1997) Preservation and change in the upland landscape: the public benefits of grazing management. *Journal of Environmental Planning and Management*, **40**, 315–34.

Burton, R., Mansfield, L., Schwarz, G., Brown, K. and Convery, I. (2005) *Social Capital in Hill Farming*. Report for the International Centre for the Uplands, Cumbria.

Chermack, T. J. (2004) Improving decision-making with scenario planning. *Futures*, **36**, 295–309.

Cumulus, IEEP and CCRU (2005) *Assessment of CAP Reform and Other Key Policies on Upland Farms and Land Use Implications in SDAs and DAs in England.* Final report for Defra, Cumulus Countryside and Rural Consultants, Gloucestershire.

Defra (2003) *Population Changes in England's Rural Areas 1991–2001*, Rural Statistics Unit, Defra, York.

Eftec (2006) *Economic Valuation of Environmental Impacts in the Severely Disadvantaged Areas.* Defra report, Economics for the Environment Consultancy, London. http://statistics.defra.gov.uk/esg/reports/disareas/

English Nature (2003) *England's Best Wildlife and Geological Sites: The Condition of SSSIs in England in 2003*, Peterborough. www.english-nature.gov.uk/pubs/publication/PDF/SSSICondfulldoc.pdf

Himamowa, B. (1975) The Obergurgl model: a microcosm of economic growth in relation to limited ecological resources. *Nature and Resources*, **11**, 10–21.

Hubacek, K. and Rothman, D. S. (2005) *Review of Theory and Practice with Respect to Building and Assessing Scenarios.* WP 6 of RELU project 'Achieving sustainable catchment management: developing integrated approaches and tools to inform future policies' (ESRC, NERC, BBSRC: RES-224-25-0081). http://www.relu.ac.uk/research/projects/Spash.htm

IEEP, Land Use Consultants and GHK Consulting (2004) *An Assessment of the Impacts of Hill Farming in England on the Economic, Environmental and Social Sustainability of the Uplands and More Widely.* Report for Defra, Institute for European Environmental Policy, Land Use Consultants and GHK Consulting. http://statistics.defra.gov.uk/esg/reports/hillfarming/

Mitchley, J., Price, M. F. and Tzanopoulos, J. (2006) Integrated futures for Europe's mountain regions: reconciling biodiversity conservation and human livelihoods. *Journal of Mountain Science*, **3**, 276–86.

MLURI (2005) *Decision Support Tools to Link Ecology and Land Management: Development of HillPlan.* http://www.macaulay.ac.uk/hillplan/

Morris, J., Audsley, E., Wright, I. A., McLeod, J., Pearn, K., Angus, A. and Rickard, S. (2005) *Agricultural Futures and Implications for the Environment.* Technical report, Defra Research Project IS0209, Cranfield University.

NFU (2005) *Upland and Management Scheme, Policy Statement.* NFU Information and Analysis. http://www.nfuonline.com/documents/Policy%20statement%20NFUonline%20com.pdf

OST (2002) *UK Foresight Futures 2020: Revised Scenarios and Guidance.* London: Office of Science and Technology, Department for Trade and Industry. http://www.foresight.gov.uk/publications/current_round_general_publications/foresight_futures_2020_revised_scenarios_and_guidance/dti_ff_web.pdf

Peterson, G. D., Cumming, G. S. and Carpenter, S. R. (2003) Scenario planning: a tool for conservation in an uncertain world. *Conservation Biology*, **17**, 358–66.

Phillipson, J. and Liddon, A. (2007) *Common Knowledge: An Exploration of Knowledge Transfer.* Rural Economy and Land Use programme. http://www.relu.ac.uk/news/briefings/RELUBrief6%20Common%20Knowledge.pdf

Prell, C., Hubacek, K., Quinn, C. and Reed, M. S. (in press) Selecting stakeholders through social network analysis: allowing stakeholders to guide the process. *Systemic Practice and Action Research.*

Prell, C., Hubacek, K., Reed, M. S., Termansen, M., Jin, N. and Quinn, C. (2007) If you have a hammer everything looks like a nail: 'traditional' versus participatory model building. *Interdisciplinary Science Reviews*, **32**, 1–20.

Prell, C., Reed, M. S. and Hubacek, K. (in press) Social network analysis and stakeholder analysis for natural resource management. *Society and Natural Resources.*

Reed, M. S., Hubacek, K. and Prell, C. (2005) *Sustainable Upland Management for Multiple Benefits: A Multi-stakeholder Response to the Heather and Grass Burning Code Consultation.* Project report submitted to Defra's consultation on the review of the Heather and Grass (Burning) Regulations 1986 and the Heather and Grass Burning Code 1994.

Rothman, J., Asselt, M., Anastasi, C., Greeuw, S., Mellors, J., Peters, S., Rothman, D. and Rijkens, N. (2000) Visions for a sustainable Europe. *Futures*, **32**, 809–31.

Samuelson, W. and Zeckhauser, R. (1988) Status quo bias in decision making. *Journal of Risk and Uncertainty*, **1**, 7–59.

Soliva, R., Ronningen, K., Bella, I., Bezak, P., Cooper, T., Flo, B., Marty, P. and Potter, C. (2008) Envisioning Europe's upland futures: stakeholder responses to scenarios for Europe's mountain landscapes. *Journal of Rural Studies*, **24**, 56–71.

Stewart, G. B., Coles, C. F. and Pullin, A. S. (2005) Applying evidence-based practice in conservation management: lessons from the first systematic review and dissemination projects. *Biological Conservation*, **126**, 270–8.

Task Force for the Hills (2001) *Final Report.* Report to MAFF, The David Arnold-Forster Trust, Devon. http://www.hillfarming.org.uk/

Taylor, P. (2005) *Beyond Conservation: A Wildlife Strategy.* London: Earthscan.

Worrall, F., Reed, M. S., Warburton, J. and Burt, T. (2003) Carbon budget for a British upland peat catchment. *Science of the Total Environment*, **312**, 133–46.

21 Effective policy-making in the uplands

A case study in the Peak District National Park

Steve Connelly and Tim Richardson

Introduction

It is abundantly clear from other chapters in this book that upland areas provide a great diversity of services to a wide variety of stakeholders: ranging from land managers and statutory agencies to other direct users and beneficiaries to interest groups and, most diffusely, national and even global populations. Inevitably, stakeholders value these services differently, and policy-making for the uplands must mediate the conflicts between these values. The now almost mandatory response in the United Kingdom and many other places is 'stakeholder engagement' – involving stakeholders in practices ranging from informal public consultation to formal partnership working.

This sharing of responsibilities for the governance of the uplands has tangible effects. We recognise that policy outcomes depend on how different interests and values are brought together and shaped and negotiated through processes of reasoned debate or 'deliberation' (Hajer and Wagenaar, 2003). In any given situation the outcome will depend on which stakeholders were involved, which values and interests they brought into the process, and how the process was managed. This implies that governance *processes* themselves are drivers of change, which need to be understood, alongside the policy *content* discussed by Condliffe and others elsewhere in this volume.

However, despite widespread acceptance of increased stakeholder involvement, it is not clear whether such processes really are more effective in solving knotty problems of sustainable development than more 'traditional' governance by governmental bodies. In this chapter we explore this issue by introducing a framework for analysing the effectiveness of stakeholder processes, illustrated through a case study of transport policy-making in the Peak District National Park. This approach is adopted because deliberative processes can only be understood through examining real cases, but we stress that the specific details (while hopefully interesting and illuminating) are not the primary point. This is *not* an evaluation of the Peak District processes, nor are we arguing that deliberative stakeholder engagement processes are inherently misguided. All cases are different, and our specific findings are not directly generalisable to other cases. Our purpose is twofold: to present a framework for analysis which *is* widely applicable, and to draw out some issues from this case which should provoke questions and raise awareness of areas which should be of concern to anyone designing or participating in stakeholder approaches to upland policy-making.

Stakeholder involvement processes in upland management

Britain's National Parks exemplify the situation found in many upland areas, with potentially conflicting statutory purposes of conservation, amenity, and promoting the sustainable development and well-being of local communities (National Parks [Scotland] Act, 2000; Defra, 2003). This is compounded by varied demands from both local and visitor populations, and a simultaneous role in providing a range of ecosystem services to surrounding areas. National Park Authorities (NPAs) share statutory responsibilities with overlapping local authorities, part of a complex governance environment of national and regional state and quasi-statal bodies, user groups, and local and national interest groups.

NPAs have become involved in a great number of stakeholder processes, both formal and informal. These address sectoral issues such as transport (Reeves, 2006); site specific management planning for 'difficult places', typically under intense visitor pressure for multiple uses (see e.g. Croney and Smith, 2003; Guiver *et al.*, 2006); and more general tasks such as setting overall 'visions' (e.g. Dartmoor National Park Authority, 2006). NPAs also play a role in strategic regional processes associated with, for example, developing water catchment plans under the European Union (EU) Water Framework Directive (European Union, 2000).

Stakeholder engagement in upland management is a widespread phenomenon, going beyond the confines of national parks and of the UK. At the largest scale it is a prominent element of global sustainable development policy, mandated by Agenda 21 by the United Nations Conference on Environment and Development (UNCED, 1992) and translated into practical action through projects funded and developed by the UN Environmental Programme (UNEP, 2003, undated) and regional bodies such as the Himalayas International Centre for Integrated Mountain Development (ICIMOD, 2007). Practical examples abound outside the UK in the global North, with collaborative catchment management commonplace in North America (Sabatier *et al.*, 2005), alongside innovative work in more unusual policy areas such as wolf management (Todd, 2002). However, the extent to which this very consistent global message 'promoting' stakeholder involvement is turned into real programmes and projects varies enormously, depending in part on differences in national policy and political contexts. Moreover, as noted above, every process has different qualities in terms of the details of how different interests and values are brought in, whatever the context in which it takes place. Thus, stakeholder processes in the Peak District are simultaneously unique yet also typical examples of a global phenomenon, and some of their lessons have global reach.

The adoption of stakeholder engagement processes in upland management reflects a general shift in governance, from a tradition in which the state carried the primary responsibility for policy development and delivery to one in which this responsibility is shared. This development has been stimulated by the complexity and cross-sectoral nature of the problems facing policy-makers (e.g. in the field of sustainable development), the fragmentation of government, and the declining legitimacy of traditional, more hierarchical and representative government (Hajer and Wagenaar, 2003). This shift has powerful academic and policy support, with stakeholder engagement promoted as both more effective in achieving substantive outcomes and more legitimate than traditional modes of governance (Sørensen and Torfing, 2005). This position is underpinned by theories of 'deliberative democracy' in which legitimacy is grounded in the genuine reflective engagement and agreement of all affected parties (Dryzek, 2000), and often includes a commitment to building consensus (Innes, 2004).

However, empirical research on ecosystem management planning raises doubts about the impact of deliberative processes on the quality of outcomes (Brody, 2003; Sabatier *et al.*, 2005). From a theoretical perspective, a strand of critical planning literature challenges the idealism of many proponents of deliberative stakeholder processes, and argues for care in the design and execution of such processes (Huxley and Yiftachel, 2000; Flyvbjerg and Richardson, 2002). Stakeholder involvement can never achieve the claimed ideal of inclusivity (Connelly and Richardson, 2004), and it is questionable whether it can deliver the radical policy changes necessary for sustainable development. However, before exploring these issues in a real case, it is necessary to ask: What *is* 'effective deliberation'?

What is 'effective deliberation'?

We regard the 'effectiveness' of stakeholder engagement processes as having three interlinked dimensions:

- *Content sustainability*. The primary dimension is effectiveness in delivering an intended policy outcome such as sustainable upland management.

This depends on processes being effective in increasing

- *Capacity to act* – the capacity of the system of governance as a whole to take action;

and achieving

- *Legitimacy* – the recognised right to make policy.

These three are represented diagrammatically in Figure 21.1, in the ideal situation with balance and linkage between the different dimensions.

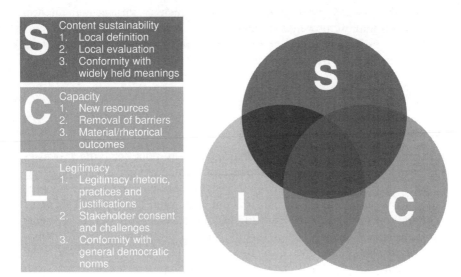

Figure 21.1 The effective deliberation framework.

The three dimensions can be analysed separately in any real situation, using the following framework.

Content sustainability

As a concept, sustainable development has a widely accepted but vague core meaning within which there are differing 'conceptions of the concept' – legitimate, yet incompatible and contested, interpretations of how the concept should be put into practice (Jacobs, 1999). We therefore expect stakeholder processes and their outcomes to be characterised by power struggles to determine a locally dominant meaning. However, stakeholder processes take place in the context of wider debates, and local constructions of 'sustainable development' can be judged against wider norms. Evaluation of content sustainability therefore asks:

- How is sustainable development defined in the process?
- How is this local definition evaluated by stakeholders?
- Does this definition conform with meanings of sustainable development in wider use?

Capacity to act

Evaluating effectiveness in increasing capacity to act is relatively straightforward, and can be approached through asking the following questions:

- Did the process generate new resources such as knowledge, finance, decision-making powers, networks?
- Did the process result in the reduction of previous barriers to achieving progress in policy-making (e.g. historical stakeholder divides)?
- Did the process result in tangible outcomes such as physical or institutional change?

Legitimacy

In the UK and elsewhere, the legitimacy of many policy-making processes traditionally rested on norms of representative democracy: decisions affecting us should be made by those we choose to represent us. Despite the purported weakening of these norms, it is not clear what has replaced them, or what are appropriate criteria for judging stakeholder processes. Proponents of stakeholder involvement claim that its legitimacy rests on deliberative democratic norms, but it is an open question as to whether these are widely accepted. Consequently, we see legitimacy as another concept whose meaning is constructed locally and can be contested. Our analysis rests on three dimensions: legality, justifiability and consent (Beetham, 1991; Parkinson, 2003). All of these have to be maintained to sustain legitimacy, and any of them is open to challenge (Connelly *et al.*, 2006).

The ability of stakeholders to act effectively rests both on how legitimate the partners and processes are within the process *and* on how successfully they can establish their legitimacy more widely. Satisfying participants does not necessarily mean that other policy actors, interest groups or the general public will view the partnership as having the legitimacy to decide.

Analysis is guided by the questions:

- What rules and practices characterise the deliberative process, and how are they justified?
- Did stakeholders consent to, or challenge, the process's legitimacy?
- Were the rules and practices, and the claims made for them, justifiable in terms of general norms of democratic process?

These questions provide a framework which can be used to analyse and compare the effectiveness of different stakeholder representation and involvement processes. We now illustrate this in an investigation of policy-making in the Peak District National Park.

The case study: Peak District National Park

As other chapters make clear, the Peak District is a typical upland area in its provision of multiple ecosystem services and its exposure to varied economic, environmental and social pressures. Transport is a useful policy issue through which to analyse the effectiveness of stakeholder involvement, because it brings up the tensions involved in planning for the sustainable provision of services particularly forcefully. On the one hand, many upland areas provide transport routes between major centres of population (e.g. transalpine roads), and transport underpins the provision of other major services such as local productive economies and leisure (see Curry, this volume). On the other hand, many upland ecosystems are sensitive to disturbance, and the provision of transport can cause damage directly through pollution and habitat fragmentation and indirectly through, for example, enabling visitor access to remote areas. These general issues are exemplified in the Peak District. Major transport challenges centre on possible controls over car-based recreation in this most accessible English National Park (with 16 million people living within one hour's drive), and on through-traffic, because of the barrier to cross-Pennine travel that its geography presents. Managing traffic flows involves balancing the regeneration interests of neighbouring conurbations, environmental protection, residents' quality of life, and the need for accessibility to support the local economy.

The Peak District National Park Authority (PDNPA) has sought to make progress in the face of longstanding stakeholder conflicts over these issues by creating new external deliberative policy arenas. Our research analysed how traffic-restraint alternatives were mediated in two of these new arenas, and compared these with processes within the PDNPA itself. The first external arena was the Stanage Forum: an inclusive, facilitated consensus-building process concerned with preparing and implementing a management plan for the small, intensively used climbing area of Stanage Edge and surrounding countryside (Croney and Smith, 2003; PDNPA, 2005a). The second arena was the Peak Park Transport Forum (PPTF), a partnership between the PDNPA, local authorities and other stakeholders established to develop a strategic approach to transport issues. Operating through separate groups of professionals and elected officials, it produced the South Pennines Integrated Transport Strategy (SPITS) in 1994 (Peak Park Transport Forum, undated) and subsequently steered this Strategy to the point of implementation. Finally, within the PDNPA, stakeholder views are represented by the Authority's members in its various committees (PDNPA, 2005b).

Our analysis of how interests were brought together and developed through deliberation within these arenas drew on Hajer's concept of 'story lines' (1995). These are simplifications of substantive issues, often to one-line slogans, which provide actors with symbolic references that suggest common understandings and form the basis for coalitions, which actors join to gain argumentative advantage. As story lines are produced and reproduced in speech, in documents and in the assumptions embodied in practices such as decision-making processes, they provide the language and ideas through which conflicts are played out. In particular they frame the nature of problems and so of appropriate and desirable solutions. Dominant story lines in the three arenas were identified, and their interactions explored to show how they became dominant through the deliberative processes. This led to the evaluation and explanation of each arena's effectiveness.

The empirical research was carried out during 2003–4 through forty in-depth interviews with participants, observation of public and 'behind-closed-doors' meetings, and examination of minutes and policy documents. Since that time some significant change, and progress, has taken place. The lessons drawn are still relevant, however, given the case's role as an illustration of stakeholder processes.

The Stanage Forum

The Forum was open to participation at any stage by anybody. It attracted a wide range of local and national recreation and conservation interest groups and local community representatives. The process was facilitated by an external consultant, whose role was to ensure that the Forum produced a consensus-based management plan (Croney and Smith, 2003).

Debate over transport was dominated by conflict between story lines of:

- *environmental limits*, i.e. the area can absorb no more private vehicles; and
- *free access*, embodying the expectation of unrestricted, cost-free public access, principally for recreation (see Curry, this volume).

Achieving consensus involved reframing the issue as a shared problem rather than as a conflict: how to allow vehicular access without having a negative impact on the environment. This generated a new, pragmatic story line centred on an integrated public transport package and limits on car-parking. Putting this into practice reopened the original conflicts, with PDNPA officials active within the Forum rejecting the proposals and key implementing organisations, such as bus companies and local transport authorities, unwilling to support the Forum's plans. This forced further deliberation, and by 2007 partial solutions were being implemented in the form of voluntary parking restrictions and a limited bus service funded by Forum partners (PDNPA, 2006).

Content sustainability

In 2004 a temporary consensus on a 'sustainable transport solution' was achieved: the acceptance of existing traffic levels while making alternatives available, underpinned by the principle of freedom of personal mobility. This 'shared understanding' was formally embodied in the Stanage Management Plan, but there was clear disquiet on the part of the PDNPA, whose attempts to prioritise the environment over access had failed. This definition of 'sustainable transport' was also at odds with wider contemporary policies, which prioritised demand management and modal shift. Outcomes were thus clearly affected by the balance of stakeholders, which favoured recreational over conservation interests.

Capacity

Producing a consensus-based management plan from a starting position of conflict between opposing groups was a considerable achievement. The process was fully inclusive and deliberative, and trust was built between formerly hostile individuals and groups, generating new, joint understandings of issues. However, consensus around transport was achieved by avoiding the issues likely to provoke most conflict, which if tackled could have yielded more radical solutions. More significantly, the Forum failed to engage external organisations with power and resources to implement its transport proposals, rendering it relatively impotent on these issues and only able to implement solutions relying on its internal resources. (This parallels the success of the Forum over other issues which fell within the power of the participants to implement, such as the concordat over protection of rare nesting birds; see PDNPA, 2006.)

Legitimacy

The Forum's legitimacy rested on its adherence to ground rules of consensual decision-making, inclusivity and open, unforced debate. While it mainly followed these principles, challenges were made internally, and other legitimising norms relied upon, as story lines competed with each other. These largely revolved around charges of self-interested behaviour, and the activities of the Forum's in-principle non-executive steering group, which increasingly took on a decision-making role. Moreover, stakeholders who were not directly involved, notably senior PDNPA managers, remained unconvinced of the Forum's legitimacy, which was contrasted unfavourably with more traditional, expert-led decision-making. From a wider perspective, the Forum was clearly experimental in terms of resting its legitimacy on consensual deliberation.

Overall, on transport issues the Forum's strong emphasis on process legitimacy came at the expense of weakly sustainable outputs and inadequate capacity to deliver on its recommendations. The effectiveness of what was potentially a powerful means of engaging stakeholders in the mediation of difficult long-term challenges was reduced by the weak institutionalisation of the Forum, and the limited acceptance of its legitimacy both within the PDNPA and among other key bodies.

The Peak Park Transport Forum

The Peak Park Transport Forum (PPTF) is a 'closed partnership' (Connelly and Richardson, 2004), initiated by the PDNPA as a means of resolving longstanding conflicts over transport strategy between itself and surrounding urban local authorities. Formally headed by a 'members' group' comprising PDNPA and local authority representatives, deliberation principally took place in closed meetings of working groups of officers from the authorities and other state transport organisations and representatives from private rail companies. The 'traffic restraint sub-group' also brought in representation from one environmental NGO, the Campaign to Protect Rural England (CPRE). The PPTF had no executive power, relying on the parent organisations to ratify and implement its principal output, the South Pennines Transport Strategy (SPITS).

The PPTF's deliberations were dominated by two mutually supportive story lines:

- improved cross-national park roads are vital for the *wider economy*, i.e. the economic health of surrounding urban areas;
- the costs and benefits of a sustainable transport 'solution' can be distributed equitably across the sub-region through a 'pragmatic compromise', i.e. traffic restraint across the national park with future growth diverted on to a single improved cross-national park road – whose environmental quality would thus be sacrificed for gains elsewhere.

The internal discussions (though not the final strategy) considered the possibility of widespread *road-user charging* as a restraint mechanism. This was a very radical idea in the 1990s and not a politically acceptable topic for public discussion.

Content sustainability

The link between cross-national park road traffic and regeneration of the neighbouring metropolitan areas was established very early in the process. Sustainable transport was subsequently framed in terms of traffic redistribution, rather than of reducing overall levels. Unlike the key stakeholders involved, the CPRE was distinctly uneasy with this definition but was unable to shift the terms of debate. Outside the PPTF processes, some PDNPA members became increasingly unhappy with the implications of a strategy which appeared to them to compromise the core national park purpose of environmental protection in order to achieve strategic agreement. This reflects the dissonance between this 'solution' and wider understandings of 'sustainable transport'.

Capacity

The PPTF built new capacity – up to a point. It allowed the PDNPA to engage successfully with key stakeholders, and demonstrated the importance of a formalised but non-executive partnership, in which time and privacy allowed exploration of new and potentially radical policy ideas. This success was manifested in the production of a joint strategy by partners with previously antagonistic viewpoints, apparently resolving a longstanding conflict over transport planning across the Pennines. The process allowed the PDNPA to influence the sub-regional transport agenda, despite its weak powers. However, by 2007 implementation of key road improvements had not begun, and the consensus appeared to be unravelling, bringing into question the longevity of the PPTF's achievement of enhanced capacity.

Legitimacy

The PPTF's claims to legitimacy rest on its institutional base in local authorities and the PDNPA, and its use of accepted representative democratic process. However, this legitimacy was very fragile. Its consensus was problematic both because it was devised by unelected officers, without broad stakeholder involvement, and because outcomes were biased towards the interests of urban authorities, with the 'compromise' being remarkably one-sided and arguably at odds with National Park purposes. Most participants saw this as unproblematic. The CPRE were again the exception, caught in the dilemma of wanting to stay involved in the transport restraint sub-group's deliberations in order to influence the process, but knowing that their involvement could help to legitimise an outcome they disagreed with. External recognition of the process's legitimacy was more conditional, and it remains to be seen whether the PPTF has sufficient legitimacy for its proposals to be implemented by its parent bodies.

While the PPTF secured a pragmatic consensus and made progress on controversial issues, the PDNPA's position on transport had become less distinct by 2004, despite its having initiated the process. Capacity was built at the cost of sustainability as judged by wider norms and on the basis of rather shaky claims to legitimacy. The interlinkage of these elements is shown by the fragility of the PPTF's capacity, and the possibility that SPITS will not be implemented.

The National Park Authority

The National Park Authority is structured like a local authority, with elected and appointed members working through committees, advised by a professional body of officers. Several competing story lines on transport emerged in the Park Management and Policy Committees and full Authority meetings, but none became dominant, reflecting the PDNPA's lack of clear policy on transport at the time. These were:

- *pragmatic compromise*, imported directly from the PPTF;

and two competitors, respectively prioritising:

- *environmental protection*
- *local needs*, i.e. local economic development rather than cross-national park transport issues.

Three 'operational' story lines also developed:

- *modal shift* away from car use by promoting public transport
- *PDNPA lack of power* to achieve modal shift
- the reconciliation of these through *road-user charging* to finance public transport improvements and to divert traffic from the national park.

The development of these story lines was linked to shifting coalitions of members and officers. *Pragmatic compromise* was promoted by a long-established grouping of transport policy officers and members. The *prioritise environmental protection* challenge came from a group of newer members with considerable influence, sharing strong environmental concerns and expertise in sustainable transport. As this story line gained ground, it threatened the PDNPA's approval of SPITS, prompting the latter's proponents to support the *road-user charging* story line, around which potentially all but the champions of local needs could coalesce. The *local needs* story line was articulated by local parish representatives and remained weak, as they were not a unified group and consequently had little impact on debates.

Content sustainability

Perhaps because of its weak statutory powers, the PDNPA had no clear, independent strategic policy on transport at the time of this research. (This was addressed in the period after this research was completed, partly in response to our findings.) Its de facto policy was imported from SPITS, with all the attendant caveats around sustainability noted above.

Capacity

In contrast to the other arenas, deliberation within the PDNPA did not appear to generate capacity to develop policy, let alone act. New ideas *were* brought into the process by local parish representatives and a new infusion of appointed 'expert' members, but this appeared to lead to disruption and fragmented debate rather than to consensus. This was perhaps a result of the absence of pressure to reach a consensus, either pragmatically in order to produce a policy or on principled consensus-seeking grounds.

Legitimacy

As the statutory authority, the legitimacy of the PDNPA was not contested from outside. However, internally there was more scope for challenge.

Although the formalities of representative democratic process were largely followed, none of the members had straightforward representative legitimacy, being either indirectly elected or appointed by a central government minister. Moreover, the ideal of open debate between equal, elected representatives was compromised as policy was developed by small groups, to whom other members deferred. Officers were very actively involved with one such group to promote SPITS within the PDNPA. This resulted in challenges prompted by concerns about outputs but articulated as criticisms of the legitimacy of the process. Unease with the implications of the *pragmatic compromise* story line for the national park's environment prompted a second expert group, along with the parish representatives, to challenge the role of the transport officers in developing and promoting this policy.

The PDNPA has had a longstanding involvement in transport issues. Yet, possibly as a result of external partnerships and complicated by a broadening of its remit in terms of local community interests, its position on transport had become less clear and less strongly articulated. Its lack of capacity in internal policy-making was tightly linked to the reduction in its capacity to defend the Park's primary conservation purpose in external arenas.

Conclusions

Stakeholder involvement in all its diversity seems likely to be an enduring element of upland management, certainly in the UK and probably elsewhere. This chapter shows that such processes matter – that how stakeholders are brought into policy-making for the uplands affects outcomes, and so needs to be considered as a potential driver of change alongside policy content and the biophysical drivers discussed elsewhere in this book.

To unpack how this happens, we used the notion of the effectiveness of deliberation, and showed that in one upland case study the working practices and combination of stakeholders present in three deliberative arenas were found to be crucial in determining their effectiveness in developing sustainable transport policies. Content sustainability, capacity and legitimacy were found to be intricately linked, and trade-offs were observed between them. For example, the Peak Park Transport Forum built most capacity to act and enabled discussion of the most radical approach to sustainable traffic management, yet its final strategy incorporates a questionable approach to sustainability, and the forum was the least legitimate arena by wider standards. The other arenas, with stronger legitimacy claims, failed to generate such capacity. The Stanage Forum, which conforms most closely to current ideals of inclusive stakeholder processes, failed in this policy area to generate ideas which were 'sustainable' against wider criteria. It also failed to influence implementing bodies, owing both to their lack of involvement in the Forum and to a related low level of legitimacy of the Forum in their eyes. Meanwhile the PDNPA's internal processes, despite their strong

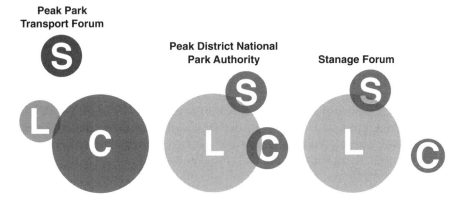

Figure 21.2 The framework applied: deliberation in practice. The sizes and over-laps of the circles give a qualitative indication of the relative salience and degree of interdependence of the components in the outcomes of the three arenas (S – content sustainability, C – capacity, L – legitimacy).

legitimacy rooted in statute and British traditions of representative local government, were weak in generating capacity to act or producing transport policies which incorporated strong sustainability principles. These variations in dimensions of effectiveness are portrayed in Figure 21.2. The ideal equal-ity between three overlapping dimensions is replaced by varying levels of achievement, with disconnection between them rather than mutual reinforcement.

These are the findings from a single UK case, yet the Peak District forums and partnerships are rather ordinary examples of very widespread processes. We thus draw two kinds of conclusion with application elsewhere in the UK and beyond. First, there are two very general points about the effectiveness of stakeholder engagement:

- Old and new forms of governance are not intrinsically so different. They share common aims of bringing together and reshaping interests through debate, and for their effectiveness rely on balancing and trading off content sustainability, creating the capacity to act, and legitimacy. Even single organisations such as a national park authority are internally diverse, and their policy-making processes demonstrate many of the same char-acteristics as processes which bring together stakeholder groups.
- This effectiveness is vulnerable to weaknesses in any one or more of these three dimensions, raising implications for the design and management of stakeholder engagement processes.

Second, our detailed findings *challenge* the received wisdom that stakeholder involvement in deliberative processes is a better way to make policy for sustainable management of the uplands. They certainly do not *negate* this claim, but should be seen as calls for caution that accepted generalisations may not be well founded, and that care is required when putting them into practice.

1. *Involving more stakeholders does not necessarily lead to more effective governance*
   Broadening the range of stakeholders does not automatically lead to increased capacity to act. The impact is context-specific, depending partly on who is involved and whether they bring decision-making resources, and partly on whether the group works together towards a substantive outcome. Nor does it necessarily increase legitimacy, because innovative stakeholder processes may win the support of participants without achieving the legitimacy held by an elected, representative body. Introducing participatory approaches alongside traditional representative practices can lead to confused claims over legitimacy.

2. *Increased deliberative democracy may not lead to stronger sustainable development*
   The often-asserted connection between widening public involvement in deliberation and achieving progress towards sustainable development is not always borne out. Bringing more voices to the debate may hamper effective decision-making, or result in power struggles leading to unsustainable outcomes. We saw in the case study that in each arena the meaning of 'sustainable transport' was weakened as non-environment interests dominated. Controversial traffic-restraint measures were difficult to sustain in debate. More generally, radical policy appears necessary for substantial progress to be made on environmental sustainability, but:

3. *Radical ideas may grow better behind closed doors*
   Public involvement, and deliberation among elected representatives, can stifle the emergence of controversial policies. The most radical proposal on sustainable transport (i.e. road-user charging) was aired in a closed partnership where sensitive issues could be tabled. This is not, however, an argument against local government or open processes, since the 'cost' of this approach was finally a *weakening* of substantive outcomes and longer-term problems for legitimacy.

4. *The 'will to consensus' can weaken the sustainability content*
   The pressure for consensus can also result in weakened 'sustainability', and raise legitimacy concerns, as difficult issues are avoided and compromises forged. The degree of consensus attained may bear little relation to sustainability of outcomes.

5. *Clear policy positions are a prerequisite for success in deliberative processes*
   In each arena, organisations which held clear positions on issues succeeded in shaping deliberation in ways which reflected their interests. The corollary is that organisations need to develop clear policies as a precondition for engagement which is effective from their perspective.

6. *Partnership working may produce policies that are not implemented*
   Individuals may work towards consensus in partnerships without the direct
   knowledge or support of their organisations. Unless a partnership has
   sufficient legitimacy in the eyes of these organisations, its hard-won policies may never be implemented. Even where legitimacy appears assured,
   changes in organisational position or personnel may weaken this commitment over time.
7. *The legitimacy of stakeholder engagement is not universally recognised*
   Despite its perceived faults, representative democracy is still very widely
   accepted by the mass of the population and by many policy-makers. In
   less democratic contexts, other traditional forms of governance may be
   viewed as legitimate. In contrast, new participatory and partnership
   approaches rely on norms of deliberation, which may only be accepted
   by (some of) the relatively limited circle of stakeholders directly involved,
   despite the global prominence of these approaches in the rhetoric of
   sustainable development.

Given all of this, it is unwise to suggest universal prescriptions for
improving the effectiveness of upland management through stakeholder
engagement processes. However, our analysis does offer reference points for
practitioners, which can support practical judgements about which deliberative approaches could be most effective in particular contexts. In deciding
whether to extend deliberation into new arenas, risks need to be balanced
against possible benefits. The effective deliberation framework enables identification of unavoidable trade-offs, and supports *appropriate* mobilisation
of new forms of deliberation between stakeholders.

All three qualities of effective deliberation are essential in constructing an
effective deliberative process. Each needs to be planned for carefully, so that:

- the substantive goals of the process are reflected in the range of interests represented (*content sustainability*);
- stakeholders have sufficient resources to enhance their collective capacity to act – including authoritative linkages to those bodies which will
  be responsible for implementation (*capacity*); and
- processes are justifiable according to established norms of legitimacy, and
  efforts are made to establish the widest possible acceptability of any new
  norms underpinning the process (*legitimacy*).

These are mutually supportive, but trade-offs between them will often be
necessary, and should be clearly identified and justified. In a certain situation it may be seen as justifiable to risk reducing legitimacy in order to enhance
capacity to act. Deliberation between stakeholders is a necessity for sustainable
upland management – but achieving *effective* deliberation is a skilled practice,
to be carried out thoughtfully and reflexively, with continuous attention to
the delicate balancing act between achieving desirable outcomes, making any
progress on difficult issues, and sustaining the legitimacy of the process.

Acknowledgements

This chapter reports on research supported by the UK Economic and Social Research Council (ESRC AWARD NO. RES000220184). Without the support of the PDNPA and the coordinators of the PPTF and the Stanage Forum, this work would not have been possible. We are very grateful for the help of all those who participated, both through giving up time for interviews and allowing us access to their meetings. We are also very grateful to Tim Miles, our research assistant who carried out the fieldwork and assisted in the analysis. While the results of the research, including the analysis presented here, have been discussed at meetings with the PDNPA and PPTF, the opinions and conclusions presented here are our own.

References

Beetham, D. (1991) *The Legitimation of Power*. Basingstoke: Macmillan.

Brody, S. D. (2003) Measuring the effects of stakeholder participation on the quality of local plans based on the principles of collaborative ecosystem management. *Journal of Planning Education and Research*, **22**, 407–19.

Connelly, S. and Richardson, T. (2004) Exclusion: the necessary difference between ideal and practical consensus. *Journal of Environmental Planning and Management*, **47**, 3–17.

Connelly, S., Richardson, T. and Miles, T. (2006) Situated legitimacy: deliberative arenas and the new rural governance. *Journal of Rural Studies*, **22**, 267–77.

Croney, M. and Smith, S. (2003) People, environment and consensus: the Stanage Forum – involving communities in protected area management. *Countryside Recreation*, **11**, 14–17.

Dartmoor National Park Authority (2006) *A Vision for the Future of Dartmoor's Moorland Unveiled*. Dartmoor National Park Authority, Bovey Tracey. http://www.dartmoor-npa.gov.uk/au_visionlaunchnews

Defra (2003) *National Parks*. Defra, London. http://www.defra.gov.uk/wildlife-countryside/issues/landscap/natparks/index.htm#purpose-np

Dryzek, J. (2000) *Deliberative Democracy and Beyond*. Oxford: Oxford University Press.

European Union (2000) COM 2000/60/EC: Directive of the European Parliament and of the Council of 23 October 2000 establishing a framework for community action in the field of water policy [the Water Framework Directive]. European Commission, Brussels. http://ec.europa.eu/environment/water/water-framework/index_en.html

Flyvbjerg, B. and Richardson, T. (2002) Planning and Foucault: in search of the dark side of planning theory. *Planning Futures: New Directions for Planning Theory* (ed. P. Allmendinger and M. Tewdwr-Jones), pp. 44–62. London: Routledge.

Guiver, J., Lumsdon, L. and Weston, R. (2006) Visitor attractions, sustainable transport and travel plans – Hadrian's Wall: a case study. *Managing Leisure*, **11**, 217–30.

Hajer, M. (1995) *The Politics of Environmental Discourse: Ecological Modernization and the Policy Process*. Oxford: Clarendon Press.

Hajer, M. and Wagenaar, H. (eds) (2003) *Deliberative Policy Analysis: Understanding Governance in the Network Society*. Cambridge: Cambridge University Press.

Huxley, M. and Yiftachel, O. (2000) New paradigm or old myopia? Unsettling the communicative turn in planning theory. *Journal of Planning Education and Research*, **19**, 333–42.

ICIMOD (2007) *Culture, Equity, Gender and Governance (CEGG).* International Centre for Integrated Mountain Development, Kathmandu. http://www.icimod.org/home/page.php?p=cegg

Innes, J. (2004) Consensus building: clarification for the critics. *Planning Theory*, **3**, 5–20.

Jacobs, M. (1999) Sustainable development as a contested concept. *Fairness and Futurity* (ed. A. Dobson), pp. 21–45. Oxford: Oxford University Press.

National Parks (Scotland) Act (2000). London: The Stationery Office.

Parkinson, J. (2003) Legitimacy problems in deliberative democracy. *Political Studies*, **51**, 180–96.

PDNPA (2005a) *Stanage Forum.* Peak District National Park Authority. Bakewell. http://www.peakdistrict.gov.uk/index/looking-after/stanage.htm

PDNPA (2005b) *The Work of the Authority.* Peak District National Park Authority, Bakewell. http://www.peakdistrict.gov.uk/index/looking-after/npa.htm

PDNPA (2006) *Report of the 8th Stanage Forum.* Peak District National Park Authority, Bakewell. http://www.peakdistrict.org/stanagereport8.pdf

Peak Park Transport Forum (undated) *SPITS: The South Pennines Integrated Transport Strategy.* Peak Park Transport Forum, Bakewell. http://www.spits.org.uk/

Reeves, R. (2006) *Tackling Traffic: Sustainable Leisure Transport in National Parks – an Overview of National Park Authority Involvement.* London: Council for National Parks. http://www.cnp.org.uk/docs/Tackling_Traffic_full_report.pdf

Sabatier, P., Focht, W., Lubell, M., Trachtenberg, Z., Vedlitz, A. and M. Matlock (eds) (2005) *Swimming Upstream: Collaborative Approaches to Watershed Management.* Cambridge, Mass.: MIT Press.

Sørensen, E. and Torfing, J. (2005) The democratic anchorage of governance networks. *Scandinavian Political Studies*, **28**, 195–218.

Todd, S. (2002) Building consensus on divisive issues: a case study of the Yukon wolf management team. *Environmental Impact Assessment Review*, **22**, 655–84.

UNCED (1992) *Agenda 21.* UN Division for Sustainable Development, New York. www.un.org/esa/sustdev/agenda21text.htm

UNEP (undated) *About UNEP: The Organization.* United Nations Environment Programme, Nairobi. http://www.unep.org/Documents.Multilingual/Default.asp?DocumentID=43

UNEP (2003) *Enhancing Civil Society Engagement in the Work of the United Nations Environment Programme: Strategy Paper.* United Nations Environment Programme, Nairobi. http://www.unep.org/civil_society/PDF_docs/Enhancing_Civil_Society_Engagement_In_UNEP.pdf

22 How class shapes perceptions of nature

Implications for managing visitor perceptions in upland UK

Natalie Suckall, Evan Fraser and Claire Quinn

Introduction

In our increasingly urbanised world, human communities have transformed natural environments. During different historical periods, this has led to a concern that natural areas are being destroyed and an impulse to protect them from development. For example, concurrent with the industrial revolution was a reaction in Britain against industrial development that romanticised the world of nature and led to significant policy changes to protect green spaces (Bunce, 1994). Many of these policies (such as establishing green belts around cities and creating national parks) have spread across the world and been strengthened in many places during the twentieth century. As a result, most Western countries today boast a system of national parks in which areas of outstanding beauty are protected from development. These parks, however, create an interesting dilemma since they are inevitably a reflection of the beliefs, values and desires of those in power at the time of their creation. In the UK, this generally means that England's national parks were established in places that affluent, university-educated white people deemed important in the middle of the twentieth century. While this may have been representative of the aims of those in power at that time, today's urbanised and multi-cultural society means that we may need to reconsider the way we think about management.

A scenario in which the UK's national parks do not reflect the beliefs and values of a multi-faceted society could pose a substantial threat to the long-term preservation of upland (and other rural) environments in the UK. Some authors are even concerned that the urbanites who live in the 'built world' and who rarely engage with the 'natural' world may develop an 'active scorn for whatever is not man-made, managed, or air-conditioned' (Orr, 1994, p. 131). This threat has been recognised by many, including Pyle (2003,

p. 209), who writes that 'people who care, may make choices to conserve; but people who don't know, don't even care'. Similarly, Rolston (2002) suggests that those people who perceive something as 'beautiful' will be more likely to feel a duty to protect it. If society no longer sees the uplands as beautiful, then the pressure to preserve them may dwindle. This hearkens back to Stendhal's (1822) comment that 'beauty is nothing other than the promise of happiness'. So, if the uplands do not deliver on that promise for many in society, their future may be uncertain.

In today's heterogeneous world, therefore, there is no guarantee that everyone will agree that uplands are worth protecting and are beautiful, or even be aware of their important ecological roles. After all, for some, areas worth protecting may be those that inspire feelings of escape or spirituality. For others, the duty to protect a landscape may be found in the feelings of belonging and elation that come from participating in a shared pursuit, regardless of where the activity takes place. For others still, people will think it is important to protect a landscape for its historic or ecological features. The UK's national parks cannot be all these things to all people. However, since they are funded by the taxpayer, and dependent on bringing visitors in, park managers have a duty to be relevant to today's changing, diverse and urban society.

This diversity of interests and values requires that we have a pluralistic understanding of the reasons people visit parks, and this needs to be included in park management strategies. For the managers of upland spaces who may be concerned that society is losing interest in protecting the landscape, a logical strategy is to use education programmes to teach this sense of duty towards protecting these environments. However, this raises another normative dilemma: Is manipulating a 'positive' relationship with nature a form of social engineering? If national park managers try to build a shared sense of 'beauty and duty' in the uplands, it is essential to understand exactly who does and does not visit natural areas, the reasons that prompt an individual to visit, and how ideas of what is beautiful play a part in deciding who visits where.

Social class and visits to national parks

In any modern heterogeneous society, some of the most obvious social divisions are based on class. Despite the classless paradigm envisaged by many British politicians (most famously British prime minister John Major in 1992), class divisions still remain firmly entrenched. The British Social Attitudes Report (Park *et al.*, 2007) found that, since the 1960s, there has been no decline in the overall proportion of people identifying themselves as belonging to a particular social class; and, in 2007, 57 per cent of people identified themselves as 'working class', compared with 37 per cent who identified themselves as 'middle class'.

Britain is not unique in this. In many economically developed Western societies, class divisions remain strong, despite a rise in income for the working class (see Goldthorpe and Lockwood, 1963). In such societies, the fact that the idea of belonging to a particular class remains is indicative of class being something other than a function of economics or income. This was reflected in the British Social Attitudes Report. Of the 57 per cent of people who identified themselves as working class, only 31 per cent were actually employed in 'blue collar' positions (Park *et al.*, 2007). So, in today's society, 'working class' is not only about jobs and income (and the associated poverty and deprivation), it is about something more than that.

The mainstream sociology literature shows that people place themselves in social classes based on a number of factors, including their type of employment and their income, but also their consumption and lifestyle patterns (Featherstone, 1991; Warde, 1994; Lamont and Molnar, 2001). Thus, class is not only about poverty or economic welfare; it is also about values, attitudes and behaviour. Perhaps, as writer and philosopher Baggini (2007) suggests, many British people are working class people with middle class money. This is not to say that poverty and deprivation are nonexistent in a prosperous consumer society such as Britain. However, poverty is no longer a defining feature of the working class.

Given that social class is such a dominant theme in the sociology literature, class divisions form a relevant basis through which to examine perceptions of natural areas and how this might affect the UK's national parks. When visitors to natural environments are examined in terms of social class a common pattern develops. Visitors are overwhelmingly from affluent, middle class backgrounds and nearly all are white (Breakell, 2002). This phenomenon has received increased recognition over the last decade (Agyeman, 1995; Agyeman and Spooner, 1997; Breakell, 2002; Pendergast, 2004). Traditionally, however, the fact that the working class are under-represented in the UK's parks has been attributed to a lack of access: in the past, generally speaking the working class were perceived to lack the leisure time or transport options that members of 'higher' classes enjoyed. However, given the increased economic affluence of the working classes, this is changing. People from across the class spectrum enjoy roughly the same means of access. For example, Suckall (2005) interviewed school children from an urban area in the north of the UK to determine if those from a working class background had the same access to transport that would take them to a local national park as children from wealthier families. This study revealed that children across the class spectrum had the same access to family cars and public transport; and all groups replied that, if they wanted to visit the park, they would be able to. This study, however, revealed significant difference in terms of those who wanted to go, with middle class children expressing more desire to go than their working class counterparts. As a result, it is important to look beyond simplistic explanations such as a lack of means to explain visitor patterns, and to explore the underlying reasons why working classes continue to stay out of the UK's parks.

For example, research on those social classes based on a shared ethnic background show that certain communities have no sense of belonging or ownership of rural space, and even feel unwelcome there (Agyeman and Spooner, 1997; Black Environment Network, 2002). This point is supported by Rose (1995), who suggests that very few people from black and minority ethnic groups are members of organisations such as the National Trust, the Ramblers' Association or the Youth Hostel Association. The likely reason for this is that these organisations have typically been the domain of the white middle classes, other groups have no sense of belonging, and images of those who enjoy the countryside as a homogenous group of middle class nature-lovers are embedded in our popular culture.

The UK is not alone in this, and Strandbu and Krange's (2003) exploration of Swedish working and middle class youths revealed some fundamental differences between the social classes in terms of attitudes towards nature. The authors examined the attitudes of members of a typically middle class environmental activism organisation and a typically working class outdoor recreation group. Although both groups had contact with nature, it was in different ways. The middle class youths saw nature as something to be protected and admired, and as a place for solitude and reflection. In contrast, the working class youths saw nature as a place for 'sensation seeking'.

The role of class identity in developing a notion of what is beautiful

In order to explore how social class shapes how visitors perceive areas like the uplands of the UK, it is necessary to explore some of the psychology literature surrounding the things we choose to consume. For example, Baudrillard (1981) points out that we do more than simply consume material items but also consume signs that reinforce our various class identities. This phenomenon was observed in Strandbu and Krange's (2003) examination of Swedish youth groups, in which the authors of the study noted that each group dressed differently. From this they concluded that there were a number of 'symbolic fences' that the working class youths had to cross in order to become members of the environmental organisation (and vice versa). These fences were related to style and identity. The sense of being aligned with a particular 'look' goes beyond fashion, and the landscape itself is one such sign that helps a person define and project their identify. For example, Schama (1995, p. 11) argues that the landscape is more than 'mere geology and vegetation . . . it is culture, convention and cognition'. From this, we can argue that specific landscapes, therefore, reinforce class identify and will be sought out by members of those classes.

Urry (2002) expands on this idea and proposes that there are at least three types of visitor to landscapes like UK uplands. First, Urry coins the phrase 'the tourist gaze' to refer to the way that transitory visitors to a region view the landscape as a curiosity to be experienced in a cursory fashion. The tourist gaze contrasts with what Urry calls the 'romantic gaze'. This is an upper- and middle class phenomenon in which the viewer emphasises 'solitude, privacy and a personal and spiritual relationship with the object of the gaze' (1990, p. 104). The visitor who looks at the landscape with a 'romantic gaze' will have a fundamentally different requirement of the landscape than the 'tourist'. The 'romantic' viewer will expect to look at the landscape privately, and the presence of other visitors intrudes upon his or her experience. Both the tourist and the romantic gaze contrast with Urry's third distinction, the 'collective gaze'. The collective gaze is less about an intrinsic value of the landscape and more about the people who are sharing the experience. The collective gazer seeks out events, amusement facilities and the presence of 'other people [to] give atmosphere or a sense of carnival to a place' (Urry, 1990, p. 45). Urry associates this gaze with more 'working class' ideas of leisure.

Overall, this example and Urry's distinction of different types of viewer reinforce Edensor's more general point that walking in nature has become an art 'bound up with notions of individuality and self development, with a retreat from the city and the urban self, and towards a freeing of the body, a rediscovery of childish sensation, and aesthetic and moral regeneration.' (2000, p. 84). These ideas fit in with the romantic perception of landscape and are firmly entrenched in middle class identities. People who grow up with working class backgrounds do not share these values.

Discussion and management implications

If our uplands are a resource to be enjoyed equally by all members of the British public, the fact that people who belong to different social classes seem to perceive upland landscapes in very different ways leads to serious management challenges. Broadly speaking, there are three strategies that can be used to address the issue of diverse visitor perceptions. First, education could be used to promote the beauty, importance and opportunities afforded by the landscape as it currently exists. Education could help build a social consensus around the need to protect places like the uplands in England. An alternative (although extreme) approach would be deregulation, by which visitors are allowed to enjoy natural areas in any way they choose, thus creating their own landscape value. A third option for management is to use legislation to protect natural areas from society's changing values.

Educational programmes are a key management strategy in many (if not all) national parks. For example, in the United States the Rocky Mountains National Park has established an ambitious interpretive education programme that exposes visitors to the important natural heritage and beauty of the site. This is done in conjunction with an outreach programme that aims to reach members of communities who may not typically participate in outdoor nature recreation. Tellingly, a major objective of the interpretive

Box 22.1. Class-based perceptions of the Peak District National Park, UK

Recent empirical evidence supports the notion that middle class visitors to rural northern England have more of a 'romantic gaze' while working class visitors have more of a 'collective gaze'. Suckall (2005) examined two socially distinct youth communities and used qualitative interviews and quantitative surveys to understand attitudes towards an upland area of the Peak District National Park (PDNP). The two youth communities were located in Sheffield, a city adjacent to parts of the PDNP. Sheffield was chosen as the study area, as the PDNP is geographically easily accessible to all of Sheffield's residents. The communities were determined by the socio-economic status of the youths' parents, and two district groups emerged: a working class group (n = 44), and a middle class group (n = 39). Suckall focused specifically on youth communities for two reasons. First, there is evidence to suggest that the frequency of enjoyable childhood visits to green spaces and natural sites is a valuable indicator for the frequency of visits later in life (Ward-Thompson, 2004). Second, attitudes held by young people are often directly related to and reflective of the attitudes of their parents. As Ritchie *et al.* (2005) state, 'parents directly determine the child's physical and social environment and indirectly influence behaviours, habits, and attitudes through socialisation processes and modelling'.

Suckall used photographs of places that were potentially easily accessible to all children in Sheffield, including the PDNP moorlands as well as a shopping mall, a botanical garden and a playground. She asked students a series of questions designed to solicit their feelings about each place, the number of times they had visited each type of place, whether they wanted to return, and whether they had access to transport to go to each place (such as an available family car or viable public transport). The findings showed that all groups had the same access to all places despite the socio-economic situation of the parents. All children said that, if they wanted to go to the moorlands, someone would take them. However, the middle class children had more positive perceptions of the moorlands than the working class children. The middle class children were enthused by the 'beauty' and 'naturalness' of the area and spoke positively of its relative isolation. By contrast, the majority of the working class children saw the area as a barren wasteland. Many of these children felt threatened by the 'loneliness' and isolation of the landscape – almost 80 per cent said they would not like to spend a day on the moorlands. This evidence was supported by analysis of the quantitative surveys. A Mann–Whitney U test revealed that the difference in perceptions of the PDNP between the two communities was statistically significant (p = 0.001). However, any difference between the communities' opinions of the botanical garden (p = 0.805), the playground (p = 0.209) and the mall (p = 0.209) were not statistically significant (Figure 22.1).

The availability of an appropriate recreational activity emerged as a fundamental factor in the decision to visit the moorlands. The middle class children considered the area an ideal place to walk and reflect – an activity which is well catered for in the PDNP. However, the majority of the working class children felt that the moorlands offered them very little in the way of recreational opportunity. As a result, they had little desire to visit the moorlands. However, many of the working class children said they would be happy to visit an urban/city park where they could participate in group activities such as boating or football. Interestingly, the middle class children also displayed an intimate knowledge of how to get to the moorlands (they were aware of local bus routes and the road network), while working class children did not have this detailed knowledge.

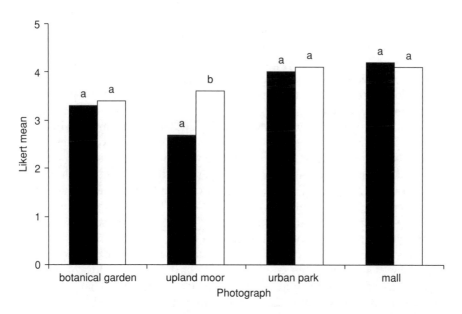

Figure 22.1 Likert mean scores assigned to groups of photographs depicting a botanical garden, a moorland, an urban park and a shopping mall by students from two economically distinct schools (n = 83). Black columns represent the working class children; white columns represent the middle class children. Higher scores indicate a more favourable overall reaction to the photograph. Columns with different letters are statistically significant (P < 0.05).

exercise is to 'share the park's values' of maintaining wilderness and finding solitude (National Park Service, 2002). Despite the park's wholesome intentions of ensuring that everyone has the opportunity to enjoy the park's solitude and aesthetic beauty, the assumption that there is only one way that nature can be perceived and enjoyed is implicit in this strategy and reinforces what Urry described as the middle class 'romantic' appreciation of the landscape.

Of course, management may decide to promote a single landscape ethic based on the values of any group in the local community – for example, the working class. However, any form of education can be considered a process of socialisation (see Durkheim, 1972). As such, a normative dilemma emerges, throwing up the spectre of social engineering (i.e. the planning and coordinating of the structure of society). At the centre of social engineering debates is the work of Hayek (1944), who asked whether in a diverse and contemporary society there can really be any fixed points to aspire to? In other words, is it essential that society shares a single landscape value (based solely on a working class or middle class perspective, but not on both), or is there room for more than one landscape ethic? If we agree with this idea of pluralism, we have a major problem in terms of management.

As an alternative to using education to create a single landscape value, it is possible for management to respond to a number of different landscape values. One way to do this would be to develop a more laissez-faire attitude towards natural areas through deregulation. However, aside from the obvious threat of environmental degradation, there is likely to be discontent among those who already enjoy natural areas for their tranquil and solitary characteristics. Through creating opportunities for increased visits by previously absent groups, managers would open the door to changing the meaning of a natural area for those who already enjoy it. This issue emerged in work done by Fraser and Kenney (2000) that explored conflicts over a shade tree protection programme in Toronto. This study found that cultural identity played a significant role in how people perceived shade trees, with British residents promoting shade trees while Italian residents argued that shade trees prevented them from planting vegetable gardens. One possible response to this would be simply to allow the owner of each home to decide what they wanted in their own backyards rather than trying to force a mature canopy of shade tree on the entire city. In this case a laissez-faire approach would have been easy to administer but would probably have involved a loss of the ecological benefits of having mature trees in a city. On the other hand, such an approach would have increased the amount of food produced locally.

A third approach could involve strengthening legislation to protect natural areas. In many national parks across the world, building and development is prohibited or strictly controlled. Legislation could take this further still, ensuring the long-term conservation of national parks by eradicating any direct human influence. In extreme cases all humans, including the local community, could be excluded from national parks. Any opportunity for re-creation in parks would be removed, and the parks would exist solely for the purposes of conservation (and perhaps profit through strictly man-aged recreational activity). For example, in 1988, local communities in the Mkomazi Game Reserve in north-eastern Tanzania were expelled by the gov-ernment in an effort to preserve the biodiversity of the land. Only a handful of paying tourists are now allowed into the area. This totalitarian approach to land management was based on the principle of conservation over com-munity, fundamental to which was the belief that local communities and tra-ditional management inevitably led to environmental degradation (see Quinn and Ockwell, in press). However, recent research has suggested that the link between human pressures and the loss of biodiversity was unsub-stantiated and the biodiversity has not returned to the region despite these efforts (Homewood and Brockington, 1999). As such, this policy undermined the conservation goal as well as the local people's needs.

In reality, of course, a combination of legislation, deregulation and edu-cation will be needed, and there are a number of examples of this sort of mixed-management approach in action. For example, Ingar, a popular tourist area in the Blue Mountains National Park, New South Wales, Australia, offers the park's users unregulated access and use. Group bike tours are commonplace, and visitors enjoy swimming in the creek and pitching tents amongst the trees. As a result, the environmentally sensitive area has suf-fered significant deterioration including erosion and compaction of soil, death of mature trees, lack of regeneration and pollution of the creek (New South Wales National Parks and Wildlife Service, 2001). Within the same national park, restrictions and controls are placed on land near water storage areas. There are two water quality protection zones: Schedule One land prohibits all access, either on foot or by vehicle, and including motorcycles, bicycles and horses. However, walkers are able to pass through the land on specially designated walking tracks. Schedule Two land permits exploration but bans swimming, horse riding, fishing, cycling and boating (Sydney Catchment Authority, 2007). Although these regulations exist primarily for the protec-tion of water catchments, an indirect effect is to preserve the tranquillity and solitude of the area and create conservation benefits.

Conclusion

In a world in which society is rapidly changing and urbanisation threatens natural areas, managers of national parks must respond to ensure that parks reflect a diversity of needs. Current models of promoting a single land-scape value, such as the middle class idea that a national park is a place of wilderness and solitude, serve to alienate those who do not share this value. In making parks more inclusive for all of society, managers automatically face a challenge of how to incorporate pluralistic views of landscape without alienating those who already enjoy the park. Although there will always be tension between different landscape values, a mixed-management approach might well be the way to make national parks more inclusive while still preserving some aspects and qualities that are the desire of the middle classes.

Acknowledgements

The authors would like to thank Jessica Robinson for helping with interviews, and the staff and students at Waltheof and Tapton schools. Thanks also to the Moors for the Future Partnership for funding this work. The views expressed here do not necessarily reflect those of the funding body.

References

Agyeman, J. (1995) Environment, heritage and multiculturalism. *Interpretation: A Journal of Heritage and Environmental Interpretation*, **1**, 5–6.

Agyeman, J. and Spooner, R. (1997) Ethnicity and the rural environment. *Contested Countryside Cultures: Otherness, Marginalisation and Rurality* (ed. P. Cloke and J. Little) pp. 197–217. London: Routledge.

Baggini, J. (2007) *Welcome to Everytown: A Journey into the English Mind*. London: Granta Publications.

Baudrillard, J. (1981) *Simulacra and Simulation: The Body in Theory*. Ann Arbor, Mich.: University of Michigan Press.

Black Environment Network (2002) Are open spaces representative of users – how is ethnic diversity expressed? *Green Spaces* Issue No. 2. http://www.ben-network. org.uk/participation/green_spaces/issues/q2_issue.htm

Breakell, B. (2002) Missing persons: who doesn't visit the people's parks? *Countryside Recreation*, **10**, 13–17.

Bunce, M. (1994) *The Countryside Ideal*. London: Routledge.

Durkheim, E. (1972) *Education and Society*. (Trans. A. Giddens) Cambridge: Cambridge University Press. (Original work published 1922.)

Edensor, T. (2000) Walking in the British countryside: reflexivity, embodied practices and ways to escape. *Body and Society*, **6**, 81–106.

Featherstone, M. (1991) *Consumer Culture and Postmodernism*. London: Sage.

Fraser, E. D. G. and Kenney, A. (2000) Cultural background and landscape history as factors affecting perceptions of the urban forest. *Journal of Arboriculture*, **26**, 107–13.

Goldthorpe, J. and Lockwood, D. (1963) Affluence and the British class structure. *Sociological Review*, **11**, 133–63.

Hayek, F. A. (1944) *The Road to Serfdom*. Chicago, Ill.: University of Chicago Press.

Homewood, K. and Brockington, D. (1999) Biodiversity, conservation and development in Mkomazi Game Reserve, Tanzania. *Global Ecology and Biogeography*, **8**, 301–13.

Lamont, M. and Molnar, V. (2001) How Blacks use consumption to shape their collective identity: evidence from marketing specialists. *Journal of Consumer Culture*, **1**, 31–45.

National Park Service (2002) *Backcountry/Wilderness Management Plan, Rocky Mountain National Park, Colorado.* http://www.nps.gov/archive/romo/planning/wilderness_mgmt_plan/wilderness_mgmt_plan.htm

New South Wales National Parks and Wildlife Service (2001) *Blue Mountains National Park: Plan of Management.* http://www.nationalparks.nsw.gov.au/pdfs/pom_final_bluemountains.pdf

Orr, D. (1994) *Earth in Mind: On Education, Environment, and the Human Prospect.* Washington, DC: Island Press.

Park, A., Curtice, J., Thomson, K., Phillips, M. and Johnson, M. (eds) (2007) *British Social Attitudes: The 23rd report – Perspectives on a Changing Society.* London: Sage.

Pendergast, S. (2004) *Social Inclusion: Involving People from Ethnic Minorities in the Peak District National Park.* http://www.openspace.eca.ac.uk/conference/proceedings/PDF/Pendergast.pdf

Pyle, R. M. (2003) Nature matrix: reconnecting people and nature. *Oryx,* **37**, 206–14.

Quinn, C. H. and Ockwell, D. (in press) The link between ecological and social paradigms and the sustainability of environmental management: a case study of semi-arid Tanzania. *Handbook for Environmental Management* (ed. J. C. Lovett and D. Ockwell). Cheltenham: Edward Elgar.

Ritchie, L., Welk, G., Styne, D., Gerstein, D. and Crawford, P. (2005) Family environment and pediatric overweight: what is a parent to do? *Journal of the American Dietetic Association,* **105**, 70–9.

Rolston, H. (2002) From beauty to duty: aesthetics of nature and environmental ethics. *Environment and the Arts: Perspectives on Environmental Aesthetics* (ed. A. Berleant), pp. 127–42. Aldershot/Burlington, Vt: Ashgate.

Rose, G. (1995) Place and identity: a sense of place. *A Place in the World? Places, Cultures and Globalisation* (ed. D. Massey and P. Jess), pp. 87–118. New York: Oxford University Press.

Schama, S. (1995) *Landscape and Memory.* New York: Alfred A. Knopf.

Stendhal (1983) *On Love: The Classic Analysis of Romantic Love.* Cambridge, Mass.: Da Capo Press. (Original work published 1822.)

Strandbu, A. and Krange, O. (2003) Youth and the environmental movement – symbolic inclusions and exclusions. *The Sociological Review,* **51**, 177–98.

Suckall, N. (2005) An analysis of access to the Peak District moors by disadvantaged youths from Sheffield. Unpublished Master of Arts thesis, University of Leeds.

Sydney Catchment Authority (2007) Access in special areas. http://www.sca.nsw.gov.au/catchments/accessrestrictions.html

Urry, J. (1990) *The Tourist Gaze: Leisure and Travel in Contemporary Societies.* London: Sage.

Urry, J. (2002) Mobility and proximity. *Sociology,* **36**, 255–74.

Ward-Thompson, C. (2004) *Playful Nature(s).* http://www.openspace.eca.ac.uk/conference/proceedings/PDF/Ward.pdf

Warde, A. (1994) Consumption, identity-formation and uncertainty. *Sociology,* **28**, 877–98.

23 Moorland wildfire risk, visitors and climate change

Patterns, prevention and policy

Julia McMorrow, Sarah Lindley, Jonathan Aylen, Gina Cavan, Kevin Albertson and Dan Boys

Introduction

Wildfires are of increasing concern in a range of ecosystems and cultural landscapes. Variously known as bushfires or wildland fires, wildfires are vegetation fires, which can occur accidentally, as a result of arson or prescribed burns which escape. Although often associated with Mediterranean climates and forest habitats, severe wildfires are also common in the UK in drought years, especially on moorlands and heaths. Although fire is also used as a traditional management tool to maintain the character of UK moorlands (Froyd, 2006; Sotherton *et al.*; Yallop *et al.*, both this volume), uncontrolled wildfires in the uplands can be highly damaging, dangerous, and expensive to extinguish (Burnett, 2004). They pose a serious threat to the delivery of ecosystem goods and services, such as carbon retention, erosion prevention, or provision of habitat for biodiversity, as well as threats to human settlements in some locations. Wildfire frequency and magnitude are likely to increase with climate change (Solomon *et al.*, 2007).

This chapter reviews the wildfire problem in UK moorlands and heaths. It uses the Peak District National Park (PDNP) as a detailed case study to examine the spatial pattern and timing of wildfire occurrence, as well as associated policy implications.

Causes of wildfires

Wildfires may be natural or caused by humans, and can be accidental or malicious (arson). Human negligence causes 80 per cent of wildfires in the USA (Goldammer, 2001). According to the EU Global Vegetation Fire Inventory, 52 per cent of UK fires with a recorded cause in 2003 were arson, with negligence accounting for all but a fraction of the rest (Global Fire Monitoring Centre [GFMC], 2007a). Managed fires only occasionally become wildfires; and natural wildfires, caused by lightning or sunlight magnified by broken glass, are rare in the UK (Bruce, 2002).

Wildfire hazard and risk

The complex interplay between biophysical and socio-economic factors determines the risk of wildfires occurring and influences effectiveness of management response. Biophysical conditions such as summer drought create *fire hazard*, but in most cases it is humans who create *fire risk* by providing ignition sources, such as high fuel loads in vegetation (Scottish Wildfire Forum [SWF], 2006). The UK Met Office (2005), however, defines fire risk as the risk of occurrence of an ignition source together with the likelihood of a fire spreading. As settlement worldwide has expanded into vulnerable rural areas, communities have become more exposed to wildfires and with it the demand for fire suppression. Paradoxically, perceived fire risk leads to demand for fire suppression, which can exacerbate risk (Miller *et al.*, 2000; Dombeck *et al.*, 2004). Management response in the US and in southern Europe until the early 1990s was an attempt to suppress wildfires completely, which only increased fuel load and the risk of more severe fires (Legg *et al.*, 2005; Deutsches Zentrum für Luft- und Raumfahrt [DLR], 2007). There is now a more enlightened approach of 'learning to live with fire'. Prescribed burns are used to manipulate natural fire regimes (e.g. Tàbara *et al.*, 2003) as burning reduces fuel load and future wildfire hazard (Davies, Legg, Hamilton and Gray, 2006). However, increased fire occurrence is not solely attributable to fuel build-up due to land-use management. Severe hotter, drier weather ('fire weather') associated with suspected climate change adds to the hazard. This is evidenced by the sudden marked increase in large, long-lived wildfires in parts of the Rockies, USA, where fire suppression (e.g. by removing undergrowth) has not been practised (Westerling *et al.*, 2006).

Magnitude and frequency of wildfires in Europe

Wildfires are monitored globally by satellites (Chuvieco, 2003), supplemented by ground reporting. Many organisations maintain fire atlases, for example the Global Fire Monitoring Centre (GFMC, 2007b), or early-warning systems such as the European Forest Fire Information System (EFFIS) (Joint Research Centre [JRC], 2006). Each year in Europe, an average of approximately 500,000 ha is lost to wildfire in the EU's five Southern Member States (JRC, 2006). Between 1980 and 2005, there were over 1.3 million fires, which burnt 12.3 million ha in these five states, two-thirds in Portugal and Spain alone. Fire frequency increased steadily during the 1990s.

Wildfires in the UK

Wildfires occur annually in the UK. Between 1974 and 2005 the Fire Service attended on average 71,700 vegetation fires a year (Home Office, 1990; Office of the Deputy Prime Minister [ODPM], 2007). Fires are far more frequent in years of exceptional summer drought (Asken Ltd, 2004), such as

1995 and 2003 when some 174,600 and 152,700 fires respectively were recorded. Government data on UK wildfires are currently poor, do not differentiate by vegetation type and are likely to underestimate occurrence (Bruce, 2002). Most vegetation fires are not primary fires – those involving casualties, rescues or attendance by five or more appliances (Communities and Local Government [CLG], 2007) – so data are not available on size, duration and impact, which could provide an indication of relative fire severity and other aspects of the fire. This should improve with the introduction of the new electronic Incident Recording System (IRS) from July 2007 (CLG, 2006). Bruce (2002) asserts that the large fires usually occur on moorlands because, unlike the situation with forest, it is not economic to dedicate permanent fire cover. Furthermore, moorlands are vulnerable because grass and heather are fine 'one-hour fuels' which dry quickly and whose continuity allows fire to spread horizontally and vertically (Bruce, 2002; Murgatroyd, 2002).

Peatlands are particularly vulnerable because, once ignited, peat fires can burn for days underground, making them difficult to detect and extinguish. Fires in tropical peatlands have received most attention (e.g. Page *et al.*, 2002), but there is growing concern for boreal and temperate peatlands under climate change and human pressure (Poulter *et al.*, 2006). Severe wildfires on peat in the UK are not new, with reports of particularly severe fires in 1871, 1949 and 1959 (Astbury, 1958; Radley, 1965). Recently, some 844 ha of peat moorland were burnt in a single fire on the Bleaklow plateau in the PDNP over the Easter bank holiday weekend 2003 (Baynes and Bostock, 2003). Increased fire incidents during that year were also recorded for the ecologically rare Dorset heaths, the whole of north-west England and Scotland (see Burnett, 2004; SWF, 2006).

Effect of fires on moorland ecosystem services

Fire plays a key role in carbon and nutrient budgets, landscape, biodiversity, erosion, water balance and water quality (Davies, Legg, Hamilton and Gray, 2006). Not all of its impacts are negative. Fire ecology recognises the beneficial role of managed and naturally ignited wildfire as an agent of natural disturbance in heather and other ecosystems worldwide (e.g. Legg *et al.*, 1992; Davies, Legg, Hamilton and Gray, 2006; Davies, Legg, Smith and MacDonald, 2006). Prescribed rotational burns are used in UK uplands between 1 October and 15 April to manage blanket bog for red grouse, deer, sheep and cattle (Yallop *et al.*, this volume). These 'muirburns' promote the germination of fire-tolerant species such as heather at the expense of less palatable species such as purple moor grass *Molinia caerulea* (Gimmingham, 1972). Fire is used to prepare land for re-afforestation (Legg *et al.*, 2005). If poorly controlled, managed fires can become wildfires, but normally wildfire risk is reduced by lowering fuel load. This is especially important for fine fuels like heather and grass (Bruce, 2002).

Severe wildfires threaten moorland ecosystem services, especially those of peatlands. Deep-seated summer fires expose peat, creating long-lived fire scars, initiating gully erosion and requiring costly restoration (Anderson *et al.*, this volume). Dry, burnt peat is difficult to re-wet, making it vulnerable to erosion. Much peat erosion can be traced back to exceptional events, especially fires (Tallis, 1987). Fire disturbs or kills ground-nesting birds and small mammals (Anderson, 1986). Smoke from fires can lead to road and airport closure, and have health impacts.

Perhaps the greatest concern is the threat of wildfire on the carbon budget of peatlands. UK Peatlands are a huge carbon store, holding more carbon than UK forests (Worrall and Evans, this volume). Carbon is lost not only in combustion, but also in decomposition of the exposed peat and export of particulate and dissolved organic carbon in eroding streams (Evans, this volume). The eroded peat is deposited in reservoirs where it reduces water-storage capacity and discolours drinking-water supply. Yallop *et al.* (this volume) raise concerns about the impact of managed burns on water quality, which could also apply to wildfire. Heavy metals deposited from airborne industrial pollution in previous centuries are disturbed by burning and leach into water catchments from exposed peat (Rothwell *et al.*, 2007).

Wildfire management costs

It is difficult to calculate the real cost of wildfire incidents, especially costs to ecosystem services. Vegetation fires are combined with other outdoor fires in UK government estimates of economic costs (ODPM, 2006). Extra costs are imposed on emergency services by the need to deploy, use and retrieve equipment from incidents, then to repair and maintain it. Indirect costs include re-positioning back-up crews to provide station cover, and providing police assistance. Analysis of a sample of recent wildfires in the PDNP suggests costs of wildfire control ranged from £8,500 for a small fire close to an urban area to £132,000 for a fire in a remote location on Bleaklow Moor (Aylen *et al.*, 2007). This excludes longer-term costs to landowners of loss of revenue and loss of ecosystem services.

Modelling the timing, location and behaviour of fire risk

Modelling wildfire in the UK context is relatively new. Three types of modelling – temporal, spatial, fire behaviour – analyse the 'when and where' of wildfire risk and how fire spreads. The type and the method used depend on the aims of the work and the data available.

Temporal models use daily weather data to predict when wildfire hazard or risk is highest. Statistical versions, like the one presented for the PDNP, address wildfire risk. They establish a customised mathematical relationship between past fires and local weather, so tacitly include weather–visitor relationships, taking these to be constant over time. Physical models such as the UK Met Office Fire Severity Index (MOFSI) address the biophysical hazard. MOFSI uses operational meteorological data in a generic model linking past weather with moisture status at three levels in the soil/biomass (Met Office, 2005). It uses local weather stations, so is spatially distributed on a coarse grid, but does not allow for non-weather factors or fire–visitor –weather relationships contributing to actual fire risk. MOFSI forecasts the likelihood of a severe fire daily on a five-point scale up to five days ahead and is available online as interactive 10 km grid maps. Closure of Access Land to prevent fire is activated at level 5 under the Countryside and Rights of Way (CROW) Act 2004.

Spatial models use Geographic Information Systems (GIS) to analyse the distribution of wildfire hazard or risk (Chuvieco and Salas, 1996; Perry, 1998). Modelling risk of occurrence requires incorporation of socio-economic factors, however challenging (Romero-Calcerrada and Millington, 2007). Some spatial models, like that presented for the PDNP, map only the risk of reported fire occurrence, using statistical relationships between mapped factors and an archive of historic fires. Spatial modelling approaches vary from Multi-Criteria Evaluation (MCE) (Chuvieco and Salas, 1996; Setiawan *et al.*, 2004) to geographically weighted regression and kernel density (Romero-Calcerrada and Millington, 2007). MCE is valuable because it facilitates the involvement of stakeholders at various stages of the research process. An insight into causes of wildfires can be obtained by inspecting the relative importance of factors in a validated spatial model (Allgöwer *et al.*, 2002). This also applies to statistically based temporal models.

Fire behaviour models are used to estimate wildfire spread (Perry, 1998; Venevsky *et al.*, 2002). The most sophisticated, such as FARSITE, combine spatial data on topography and fuels with temporal data on weather and wind to map the rate of spread of fire over a landscape over time (Stratton, 2006). Remote sensing may contribute meteorological data and near-real-time monitoring of fuel moisture content (e.g. Danson and Bowyer, 2004).

Climate change and wildfire risk

The UK Climate Impacts Programme (UKCIP) 2002 (Hulme *et al.*, 2002) provides the most current, detailed and reliable climate change scenarios for the UK. The four UKCIP02 scenarios (Figure 23.1) describe alternative future climates based on potential world development and greenhouse-gas emissions (Climate Change and the Visitor Economy [CCVE], 2005). They suggest that there is likely to be a warming of summer average temperatures in the UK between 1–5°C by the 2080s (Hulme *et al.*, 2002; see also Caporn and Emmett, this volume).

Hot, dry summer spells like those in 2003 are likely to be more frequent under UKCIP02 climate change scenarios. This will have a disproportionately large effect on the probability of wildfire for the UK (McEvoy *et al.*,

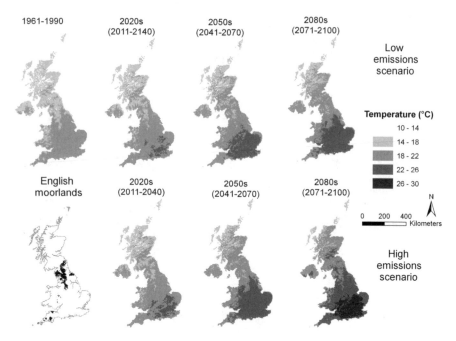

Figure 23.1 Climate scenarios for summer maximum temperature for the UK. Data from UKCIP (Hulme *et al.*, 2002). Figure at bottom left shows distribution of English moorlands.

2006; McMorrow *et al.*, 2006). This operates through the combined impact of climate change on environmental capacity and visitor numbers, with complex feedback relationships (Figure 23.2).

Environmental capacity is reduced by higher evapotranspiration, increasing soil moisture deficit and plant stress, and increased flammability of above-ground green biomass. Warmer winters and summers are likely to lead to a significant lengthening of the thermal growing season for plants, producing more biomass to burn (Crimmins and Comrie, 2004; Running, 2006). Climate change therefore threatens to increase the length of the fire season (Wotton and Flannigan, 1993; McKenzie *et al.*, 2004), shifting it into the autumn, as soil moisture will take a longer time to restore after increasingly hot, dry summers.

Feedback relationships between climate, vegetation and fire risk on a longer timescale are more complex. Changes in the structure and composition of plant communities, driven by changes in climate, will affect fire risk by altering the physical properties and availability of fuels (Ryan, 1991). Changes in fire regimes will also modify vegetation by encouraging fire-tolerant species and directly affect the atmosphere by emitting gases and particulate matter. In the USA, fire regimes are predicted to change quicker than vegetation can respond to climate alone. The combined effects of fire and

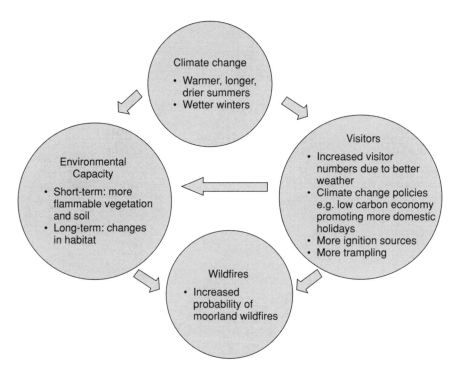

Figure 23.2 Conceptual model of the relationships between climate change, visitors, ecosystems and wildfires.

climate change will encourage invasive species such as in annuals and weeds at the expense of fire-sensitive species and specialist species of restricted range (McKenzie *et al.*, 2004).

In England and Wales blanket bog is particularly sensitive, with increases in mean temperature of around 3°C potentially resulting in a reduction of 25 per cent in current extent (Bardgett *et al.*, 1995). The current extent of heather moorland is less sensitive to the likely mean increases in temperature, but there may be changes in its distribution. Loss of blanket bog, together with an increase in oxidation of peat soils, is likely to result in a change in vegetation type to dry heath and acid grassland. These possible changes in vegetation are likely to increase fire risk.

Relationships between climate change, visitors and fire

Weather can also be expected to exert a strong influence on visitor demand (Figure 23.2). Warmer temperatures encourage more visitors. Since visitors are the main ignition source of wildfires due to negligence or arson, this adds to the risk of outbreaks. Non-climatic drivers such as national and interna-

tional policies can also indirectly increase wildfire risk. Climate change policies, such as promotion of a low-carbon economy and subsequent increases
in fuel tax may increase fire risk by encouraging more domestic holidays which
will increase visitor numbers.

Modelling wildfires in the Peak District National Park

Overview

Accidental summer fires are potentially the single biggest threat to the
fragile ecosystem of the Peak District moors (PDNPA, 2005). The PDNP is
an excellent case study for many reasons. It is the most visited National Park
in the UK. Ecologically, it is very vulnerable to climate change, with many
northern blanket bog species already at their south-easterly limit. These two
factors make it a good analogue for future wildfire risk in more northerly
peatlands under the combined effects of climate change and increased visitor pressure. Third, the PDNP has pioneered the partnership approach to
wildfire management in the UK with the formation in the mid-1990s of the
Peak District Fire Operations Group (FOG) and the former Fire Advisory
Panel (FAP). Finally, the Peak District is unusual in having an unbroken
record of 353 wildfires recorded in the PDNPA Rangers' Fire Log from 1976
to 2004. These fires are spatially and temporally clustered (Figures 23.3, 23.4),
prompting questions about the factors underlying moorland fire risk.

The fire database was used with weather data, spatial map layers and stakeholder input to model the timing and spatial pattern of fire occurrence in
the PDNP. The material draws on the results of the 'Climate Change and
the Visitor Economy' project (www.snw.org.uk/tourism) and close collaboration with FOG and the Moors for the Future Partnership (McEvoy *et al.*,
2006; McMorrow *et al.*, 2006; Aylen *et al.*, 2007; McMorrow and Lindley,
2007).

Climate change in the Peak District

Climate scenarios for the PDNP show spatial variation in likely changes (Figure
23.3). Rainfall patterns follow relief, with the high Dark Peak area in the
north receiving the most rainfall in summer – around 400 mm. By the 2020s,
average summer rainfall is likely to decrease by about 10 per cent; and, by
the 2080s, a decrease of between 23 per cent and 45 per cent is expected in
the Peak District. These changes in rainfall will have significant consequences for many habitats such as blanket bog, which require a high number
of rain days and total rainfall. In contrast, winter precipitation is expected
to increase, with a 12–23 per cent increase likely by the 2080s. Summer maximum temperature is likely to increase by 3–5.5°C by the 2080s, extending
the growing season significantly. Warmer winters will cause significant reductions in snowfall (50–90 per cent less by the 2080s).

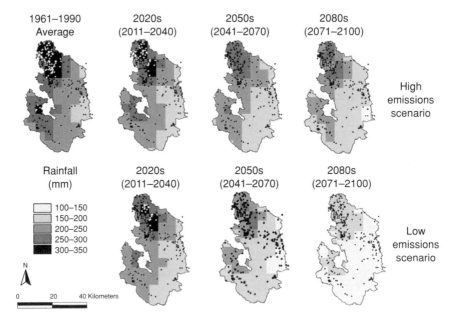

Figure 23.3 Climate scenarios for summer rainfall for the PDNP, with 1978–2004 wildfires overlaid (black dots). Data derived from UKCIP02 climate change scenarios (Hulme *et al.*, 2002). Top row shows current situation based on average of 1961–90 records and high carbon emissions scenario for three time periods, 2020s, 2050s and 2080s. Bottom row shows low carbon emissions scenarios for the three time periods.

Modelling the timing of moorland wildfires in the PDNP

Since wildfire events occur in response to hot dry periods, or relative rainfall 'deficit' (Anderson, 1986), weather can be used to estimate the timing of wildfire risk. Using the PDNPA Rangers' Fire Log and daily weather records for Buxton, a non-linear probability model of reported fires in the PDNP was developed to predict the chance of a fire breaking out on a particular day. Although appropriate data on visitor numbers were not available, known events such as weekends, bank holidays and Easter were used as a proxy for visit levels. The model allows assessment of the risk of wildfire for given climatic and visitor conditions, and forecasting of risk of moorland fire under climate change scenarios. Unlike MOFSI, actual local fire occurrence was used, so results are customised for the PDNP and indirectly include the effect of varying visitor levels with weather. The method is transferable to other areas.

Observed fires are not distributed evenly throughout the year or across years. April–May and July–August are more risky, reflecting the interplay between visitor numbers and the changing flammability of moorland

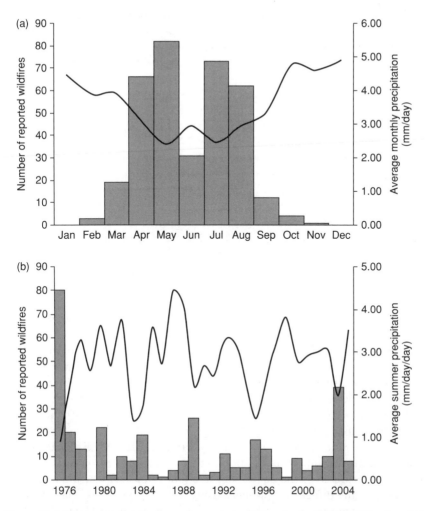

Figure 23.4 Temporal distribution of reported wildfires in the PDNP (Nfires) and its relationship to precipitation: (*a*) Seasonal distribution of Nfires, showing a spring peak in April–May and a summer peak in July–August. Solid line shows average monthly precipitation for Buxton (mm/day); (*b*) Intra-annual distribution of Nfires, showing the disproportionate influence of drought years, notably 1976, 1988 and 2003, August. Solid line shows average summer precipitation for Buxton (mm/day/day).

vegetation. Spring and summer peaks (Figure 23.4a) correspond to the combination of dry, warm weather and build-up of brown biomass. The spring greening-up lowers fire hazard in June, a pattern repeated in other UK moorlands (FireBeaters, personal communication) and in the USA. The dry years of 1976 and 2003 had a disproportionately high number of fires (Aylen *et al.*, 2007) (Figure 23.4b).

The relationship between fire probability on any given day and the set of explanatory variables was obtained using two non-linear techniques: Poisson and Probit regression (Albertson *et al.*, submitted). Probit performed better. The performance of models was evaluated by their degree of fit to the sample data. The model (Table 23.1) was refined by removing explanatory variables whose coefficients were insignificantly different from zero (Gilbert, 1986). To incorporate build-up of soil moisture deficit, temperature and precipitation deficits were specified for lag periods from seven to fifty-six days. For example, the variable P21 represents the difference between the precipitation that actually occurred over the previous three weeks and that which might have been expected, based on long-term averages. Persistence of rainfall and temperature deficits were represented using indicator variables. For instance, IT7 captured the persistence of the effects of a very warm period (average weekly temperatures in the highest decile for the time of year). It might be expected that the risk of fire is increased by a fire outbreak in the recent past, as the factors which gave rise to a fire might persist for some time, or there may be a recurrence of a fire. Therefore, the variable FIREWEEK was used to capture the number of fires in the previous seven days.

Final model coefficients (Table 23.1) show the relative significance of variables in explaining the outbreak of a reported fire. Signs show the direction of the relationship. They confirm what might be expected: that hotter, drier weather contributed to the risk of a moorland wildfire. The implication of the significant dummy variables, FRIDAY, SATURDAY, SUNDAY and BH (bank holiday), was that visitor activity increased the chance of a moorland wildfire occurring, although decreasing it on Fridays. Probability was increased further if it was APRIL or MAY. School holidays did not prove to be a significant variable. The dummy variable FIREWEEK was significant, reflecting the importance of fire occurrence over the previous week. This could be interpreted as the persistence of circumstances favouring a fire over the week, or the difficulty of fully dousing a deep peat fire so that the same fire flares up again near to previous incidents on successive days (Albertson *et al.*, submitted).

To test the model, fire risk was forecast for an independent period, June 1976 to May 1977, with good overall performance (Table 23.2). For illustration, a cautious 'threshold' of fire risk greater than 5 per cent was used. A higher risk threshold would mean fewer false alarms (false positives), but more fires remaining unforecast (false negatives). In fire management terms, there is a trade-off between unanticipated wildfires and the cost of keeping crews on standby. Consider the performance in the test set (Table 23.2b): if fire crews were alerted to stand by on the basis of these forecasts, typically for thirty-six 'high risk' days a year, they would anticipate nearly two-thirds of the fires (63 per cent). Note, however, that the classification of a day as 'high risk' does not mean that a fire will necessarily occur. In fact, we see fires on fewer than half (45 per cent) of 'high risk' days in this model.

Table 23.1 Probit estimation results for Peak District National Park reported moorland wildfires. Sample period 1 February 1978 to 1 August 2004. Daily observations from February to October (No. of observations = 7,287; Log likelihood = −614.1; Likelihood Ratio $\chi^2(14)$ = 525.4; Prob > χ^2 = 0.0000; Pseudo R^2 = 0.2996; base month October; base day Wednesday).

Variable	Definition	Coefficient	Standard error	z	Pr > |z|
FIREWEEK	Incidence of fires in the previous 7 days	0.463	0.107	4.31	0.000
PPT	Daily precipitation, mm	−0.080	0.023	−3.47	0.001
TMIN	Daily minimum temperature, °C	−0.082	0.016	−5.21	0.000
TMAX	Daily maximum temperature, °C	0.108	0.013	8.51	0.000
BH	Dummy variable: Bank holiday (1/0)	0.606	0.158	3.85	0.000
FRIDAY	Dummy variable (1/0)	−0.300	0.142	−2.11	0.035
SATURDAY	Dummy variable (1/0)	0.250	0.104	2.42	0.016
SUNDAY	Dummy variable (1/0)	0.280	0.101	2.76	0.006
APRIL	Dummy variable (1/0)	0.592	0.116	5.10	0.000
MAY	Dummy variable (1/0)	0.442	0.103	4.30	0.000
P21	Actual precipitation over previous 21 days minus that which might have been expected	−0.101	0.037	−2.74	0.006
P56	Actual precipitation over the previous 56 days minus that which might have been expected	−0.111	0.046	−2.43	0.015
IT7	Persistence of effects from a period of very dry weather. 1 if either: the week's rainfall was in the lowest decile for the time of year; or the previous day, and this week's rainfall was < median for the time of year	0.237	0.092	2.57	0.010
T28	TMAX observed in the preceding 28 days minus that which might be expected in a typical year	0.094	0.027	3.46	0.001
Constant		−3.51	0.164	−21.5	0.000

Table 23.2 Contingency table for Peak District National Park moorland wildfires temporal model for: (a) probit model training data (25/11/1977–11/8/2004: 9,747 days with 190 'fire days') and; (b) test data (1/6/1976–31/5/1977: 365 days with 40 'fire days'). The left-hand tables (a1) and (b1) relate to the forecast; e.g. in (b1) on 45 per cent of days on which a high risk was forecast, a fire occurred. The right-hand tables relate to whether a fire was observed; e.g. on 63 per cent of days when fires occurred, the forecast risk was high (F – days with five recorded; NF – days with no fire recorded; pF – days on which the Probit function indicates there was a significant [greater than 5 per cent] probability of a fire; pNF – days on which the Probit function indicates that there was not a significant probability of fire).

a1) *Forecast*	pF	pNF	a2) *Actual*	pF	pNF
F	14	1	F	71	29
NF	86	99	NF	9	91

b1) *Forecast*	pF	pNF	b2) *Actual*	pF	pNF
F	45	5	F	63	38
NF	55	95	NF	9	91

The test set period includes the very hot summer of 1976. This was a tough but realistic test as, if climate change scenarios are realised, such summers will become more common. To illustrate their impact, the probability of a moorland wildfire on a 'typical' Spring Bank Holiday Monday was calculated, holding all variables at their average levels, but allowing an increase in daily maximum and minimum temperature.

The average temperature for Spring Bank Holiday Monday for the model data was 15°C and a fire (or fires) occurred on 8 per cent of all days between 1977 and 2004. Importantly, as temperature rises, the risk of a wildfire increases disproportionately. The hottest Spring Bank Holiday in the sample (1978) had a temperature of 22.5°C. This increases the probability of a fire to 20 per cent, more than twice the typical fire risk for the time of year. In fact, seven fires were reported that day. Climate change scenarios estimate such very warm weather will become more common. The model suggests that a Spring Bank Holiday of 30°C would have a 40 per cent probability of wildfire (Figure 23.5).

Climate change may bring more clement weather, benefiting UK tourism as a whole, but the combination of more visitors on the moors with a drier, more flammable environment will increase the risk of wildfire.

Modelling the spatial distribution of moorland wildfires in the PDNP

An empirically informed and stakeholder-guided MCE methodology was used to estimate the likelihood of wildfire occurrence based on relationships

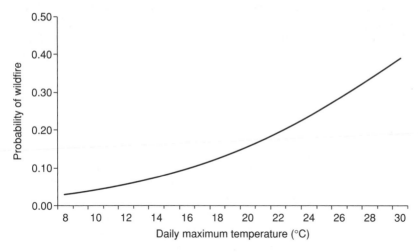

Figure 23.5 Relationship of probability of a wildfire in the Peak District National Park on a Spring Bank Holiday Monday and daily maximum temperature (°C).

between spatially explicit wildfire indicators and previously reported wildfire events. The study area covered 480 km², and a spatial risk model was generated for an average year. A stakeholder-informed risk map of wildfire occurrence in the PDNP was produced for use in strategic management responses, involving representatives of the PDNP FOG group and Moors for the Future.

Individual factors affecting wildfire risk of occurrence were mapped as separate geospatial data layers (Amatulli *et al.*, 2007). Layers can be viewed either as representing structural indices which have relative long-term stability, or as dynamic indices which show a more rapid change with time (Iliadis, 2005). The former can include factors such as population, road density, soil type and topography (e.g. slope elevation, aspect, surface roughness). The latter can include climate parameters (e.g. wind speed, precipitation) and land-cover characteristics (e.g. land-cover classes or biomass) (e.g. Iliadis, 2005; Nadeau and Englefield, 2006). Once the factors were decided, zones within each of the data layers were scored according to estimates of the relative degree of wildfire occurrence at that location. Final risk scores for each zone were calculated as the sum of all of the scores from the individual factor layers multiplied by any Boolean (binary) constraint layers (e.g. open water). Since not all factors were of equal importance, layers were weighted differentially to represent their relative contribution to overall wildfire likelihood. Stakeholder input was used to help develop an approved set of layers, scores for each layer and an appropriate weighting scheme using an online survey and an in-depth follow-up workshop.

Table 23.3 shows the geospatial data layers developed to represent the various factors considered to affect the likelihood of moorland wildfire. All data were mapped on to a 50 metre raster grid. Initial factor-based risk scores for each 50 metre cell were generated by empirical assessment of the frequency of fires on land areas with different characteristics (e.g. habitat type), or the frequency of fire occurrence with distance from features (e.g. paths). Empirical analysis used a 60 per cent 'training' sub-set of the full wildfires database (n = 128).

Habitat was used as an indicator of the likelihood of fire occurrence by approximating the potential vegetative fuel loading and the type and wetness of substrate. In the full empirical analysis, three classes recurrently emerged as being associated with a higher than predicted number of wildfires: bare peat, eroding moor and (inorganic) bare ground (Figure 23.6a). Stakeholders also showed very good agreement over the importance of bare peat, and the medium importance of grassland. However, views on the relative importance of other habitats, especially bilberry and heather moor, were more mixed (Figure 23.6b). The differences in the perception of the importance of heather moor in wildfire risk compared to the empirical results are probably due to stakeholders correctly associating it with a larger number of wildfires (and perhaps confusing wildfires with managed fires), but without taking into account its large areal coverage. A reason for the relatively low empirical risk on heather moor may be that managed fires reduce subsequent fuel load for wildfires. The database also did not allow fire intensity or fire hazard to be modelled, only the risk of fire occurrence, whereas stakeholders may have been influenced by the higher fire hazard presented by fine fuels like heather.

Wildfires in the Peak District are believed to be primarily caused by accidental and deliberate fire setting (CCVE, 2005). Workshop discussions suggested that accidental fires may be most strongly related to access by foot (e.g. walkers and rough campers), whereas arson may be most strongly associated with vehicular access.

The Pennine Way – a major long-distance footpath – was consistently reported as the most influential anthropogenic factor determining wildfire risk. Risk was also considered to be directly proportional to the popularity of footpaths. Empirical analysis backed up these views. Other factors were included on the basis of evidence from both stakeholder views and empirical analysis (Table 23.3). In some cases, empirical analysis did not support stakeholder views, such as on car parks. It is possible that certain car parks have a strong influence, but across the entire study area this effect is lost. Indeed, one limitation of the current study was the use of a single function to represent factors where processes may differ spatially across the Park.

Model outputs were tested using the remaining 40 per cent (n = 84) of the fires database. Mann–Whitney significance tests of model performances identified two models with similar robustness, both of which used a heavier weighting for habitat factors than the original stakeholder weights. Other

Table 23.3 Factors and associated datasets considered in the Multi-Criteria Evaluation spatial model of the risk of wildfire occurrence in the Peak District National Park.

Factor Group	Factor	Dataset and comments	Modelled?
Land cover	Habitat	Dark Peak and Southwest Peak Environmentally Sensitive Area (ESA) habitat maps 1991 36 classes. Class grouping informed by stakeholder workshop	Yes – evidence from empirical analysis
Foot access*	Distance to major footpaths	Data representing the path covered by the Pennine Way as the major public footpath in the area was taken from the Moors for the Future (MFF) Public Rights of Way (PROW) dataset	Yes – evidence from empirical analysis
	Distance to other Public Rights of Way	MFF PROW dataset, excluding the Pennine Way	Yes – evidence from empirical analysis
	Distance to other waylines	MFF wayline dataset showing eroded and trampled paths, generated from interpretation of aerial photography. Data were cross checked against PROW data to avoid double counting	Yes – evidence from empirical analysis
Vehicular access	Distance to major roads	Ordnance Survey (OS) data representing A roads and primary routes	No – no empirical relationships found
	Distance to minor roads	OS data representing B and other roads. Included after stakeholder workshop	Yes – evidence from empirical analysis
	Distance to vehicle tracks	MFF vehicle track data	Yes – evidence from empirical analysis
	Distance to car parks	MFF car park location data. Car park size was also considered	No – no empirical relationships found
	Distance to settlements	Geometric centroids of population centres defined as urban from an analysis of Enumeration Districts developed from the UK Census of Population for 1991	Yes – evidence from empirical analysis
Topographic	Aspect	Generated from OS 50 m Digital Terrain model data	No – inconclusive survey findings
	Slope	Generated from OS 50 m Digital Terrain model data	No – inconclusive survey findings
	Elevation	Generated from OS 50 m Digital Terrain model data	No – inconclusive survey findings

* Relative path popularity was also assessed for all path layers through use of MFF Visitor Survey data.

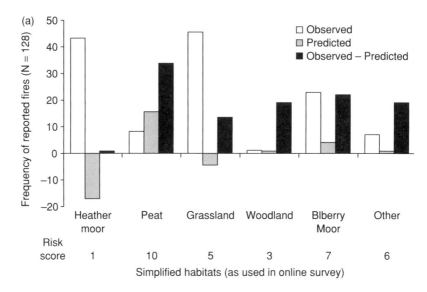

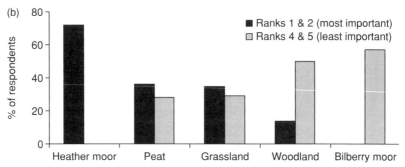

Figure 23.6 (*a*) Example of derivation of empirical habitat scores for PDNP MCE model. For simplicity, only six generalised habitats classes are shown, five of which were used in the online survey; 'Other' was added for the empirical analysis. The Peat class included 'bare peat' and 'eroding moor'. Differences between predicted and observed numbers of fires were used to derive the empirical fire risk scores. Scores are shown on the bottom line; 10 highest risk for peat to 1 lowest risk for heather moor. (*b*) Stakeholder views from the online survey of the importance of five broad habitats for explaining fire risk in the PDNP. The main differences from the empirical rankings derived from (*a*) are that heather moor was ranked by stakeholders as most important in explaining wildfire risk, but had the lowest empirical score, whereas there was agreement on peat.

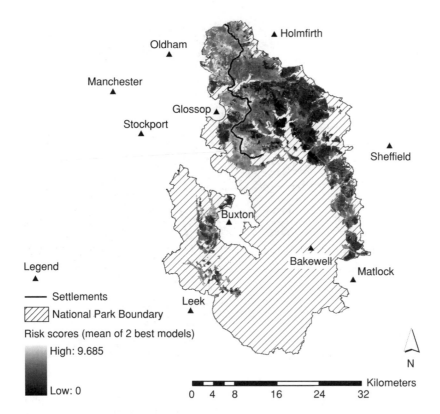

Figure 23.7 Average wildfire risk-of-occurrence scores for the two most statistically robust wildfire models. Hatched area shows the Peak District National Park. © Crown Copyright Ordnance Survey.

studies have also found the influence of vegetation to be dominant (Venevsky *et al.*, 2002). For the purposes of this chapter, risk scores from these two 'best' models have been averaged (Figure 23.7). The findings clearly highlight a number of areas of elevated wildfire risk (see also McMorrow and Lindley, 2007).

The spatial risk model can also be used to test what-if scenarios and provide decision support, such as effects of land-cover changes or other fire-risk mitigation strategies (Iliadis, 2005). For example, Figure 23.8 shows the potential impact on fire risk of relocating part of the Pennine Way. Some reduction in risk scores is demonstrated, which may help to make the remaining area of high risk more manageable, especially in conjunction with other strategies such as targeted habitat recovery.

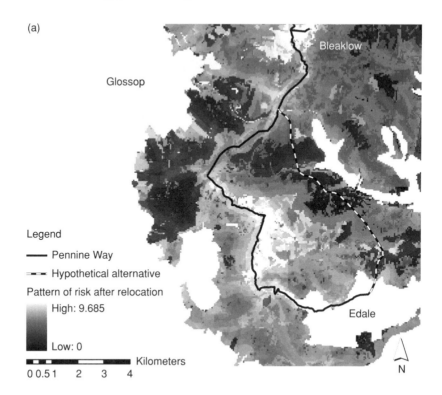

Figure 23.8 Results of 'what-if' scenario for relocation of the southern portion of the Pennine Way in the PDNP: (*a*) current position. (*b*) after hypothetical relocation. All risk scores are generated from an average of the two most statistically robust wildfire models. © Crown Copyright Ordnance Survey.

Management options: preparation, prevention and control

The main driver of wildfire risk management is the need to minimise damage to human life, to the environment, and the wider potential for disruption and economic loss. There are three aspects to wildfire management: preparation, prevention and control.

Preparation involves creating fire plans, staff training and equipment provision. In the PDNP, preparation is coordinated by FOG, which has operational Fire Plans and a spatial database to ensure equipment is available. FOG is a very successful partnership between land managers, water utilities, the PDNPA and fire services. It has been hugely influential in the development of similar groups elsewhere, for instance in Northumberland and in parts of Scotland. It coordinates responses to wildfires, and negotiates compatibility of equipment and joint specialist training (PDNPA, 2005).

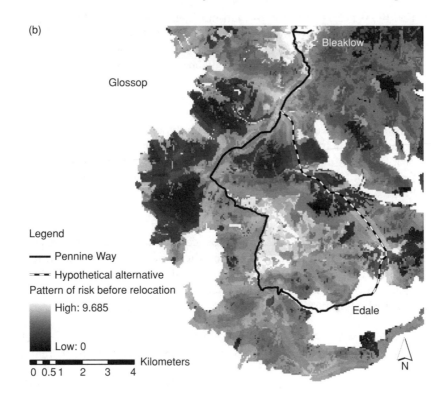

Figure 23.8 (cont'd)

Prevention aims to reduce the risk of a wildfire outbreak, including:

1. Controlling access to moorland. To date there is no statistical evidence that the number of fires reported is significantly different between periods of closure and when the moors are open, perhaps because of continued access through Public Rights of Way footpaths. Indeed, closure may mean fewer visitors to report fires when they do break out.
2. Awareness-raising aimed at walkers and picnickers, including warning signs, leaflets and ashtray pouches for cigarettes.
3. Fire watching at high-risk times. Rangers and volunteers armed with binoculars located at key sites indicated from the risk map and a digital elevation model can identify and report the exact location of fires, which helps rapid deployment of fire-fighting resources. Firewatchers may also tackle small fires.
4. Controlled burning, grazing or cutting to reduce fuel load is an effective management solution, since managed heather moorlands in the PDNP are statistically less prone to wildfire.

5. Fire breaks can be natural or man-made, created by ploughing or burning vegetation. They should be 6–10 metres wide and at least 2.5 times the flame height to be effective (Murgatroyd, 2002). Natural breaks, such as rocks, cliff edges or drystone walls are more effective.
6. Preventive wetting of dry vegetation; but this requires a lot of water, and vegetation close to a fire very quickly re-dries. Dry peat is also very difficult to re-wet (it is hygrophobic).
7. Raising water levels in blanket bog. Gully-blocking (Anderson *et al.*, this volume) can help locally to maintain high water levels in peat. Keeping peat moist reduces flammability and encourages re-vegetation.
8. Erection of temporary Flexi-dams – temporary, open-top ponds of rubberised canvas filled with water, located in areas of high fire risk and prior to MOFSI level 5.

Management control, or fire suppression, concentrates on fighting fires once started, and reacting to the consequences after a fire is extinguished. It tackles the 'fire triangle' by reducing fuel, oxygen and heat (Murgatroyd, 2002). Fighting moorland wildfires is very different from fighting city fires, requiring specialist equipment and training. Potential resources include:

1. *Mobile vehicles:* All-terrain vehicles (ATV) and other specialised vehicles reduce access time to fires and carry heavy equipment to remote fire sites.
2. *Helicopters on standby for fire-fighting:* Helicopters are ideal for investigating smoke reports, assessing fire sites, deployment of personnel and equipment and swift dousing of remote fires. If available, they are highly cost effective, especially in rapid aerial response with a dousing bucket. Despite helicopters being expensive to deploy and costly to keep on standby, two of the major landowning bodies in the PDNP, the National Trust and United Utilities, operate a zero-tolerance policy to wildfires based on rapid response by helicopter.
3. *Static fire-fighting resources:* Steep-sided ponds containing clean water are ideal for fire-fighting, as equipment may be clogged by vegetation in natural ponds, but may be less suitable for wildlife and public safety. Ensuring a permanent water supply is problematic, as water is needed in spring and summer when ponds are likely to dry up. Flexi-dams are a reliable source of water at high-risk times and were deployed in the PDNP in 2006 by the National Trust. They are best-placed in high-risk areas identified by the spatial risk map which also fall outside a critical four-minute helicopter flight turnaround from existing water sources (mainly reservoirs within the lower-altitude moors).
4. *Post-fire management of fire site:* Management once a fire is extinguished includes re-seeding and re-planting. Such restoration lowers wildfire risk by re-vegetating high-risk bare peat habitat but requires considerable resources and time (Anderson *et al.*, this volume).

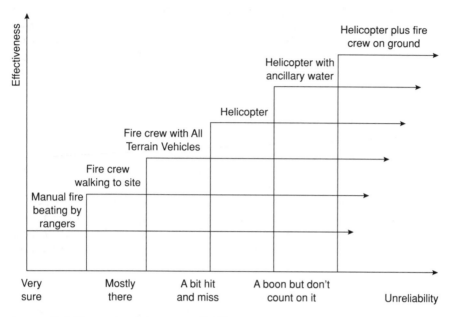

Figure 23.9 The trade-off between reliability and effectiveness of fighting moorland wildfires.

With all management options, there is a trade-off between effectiveness and reliability (Figure 23.9), reflecting access to the fire, availability of water and equipment at the time, size of fire when detected and weather conditions.

Conclusions

The increase in severe fire weather implied by climate change models, coupled with greater access of visitors (increasing sources of ignition), is likely to increase the risk of moorland wildfires precisely when water supplies will be more scarce. A greater number of severe fires may occur, but they may be concentrated in a few years, or even days. The policy implication is that we should assume that fire risk follows established patterns for day-to-day operational management, but plan for the possibility of a catastrophic fire in order to prevent it (Aylen *et al.*, 2007).

There will be additional pressure on fire-fighting resources and increased management costs. More frequent wildfires may mean that some fires grow into severe incidents. There is a strong case for central government funding of rapid-response helicopter fire-fighting to prevent catastrophic losses of the soil carbon store and to protect other moorland ecosystem services. Furthermore, Fire Service integrated risk management planning and fire prevention measures need to be extended to wildfires (Burnett, 2004; SWF, 2006).

The temporal and spatial models developed for the PDNP demonstrate how fire risk varies markedly with time of year, week and day, and with geographical location. They show that fire outbreaks are influenced not just by climate-drivers, but also by the combination of weather conditions, vegetation and its management, and proximity access points. They complement MOFSI to forecast the likely timing and location of fires and identify high-risk locations and times for deploying fire-fighting resources. They are also valuable for modelling 'what-if' climate change and management scenarios.

It is assumed that warmer, drier summers will mean more visitors, but moorland visitor–weather relationships require quantitative and qualitative investigation. Daily, long-run data sets of moorland visitor numbers are needed for statistical analysis (McMorrow et al., 2006). Better public fire awareness is needed, although some fear this may actually encourage arson (CCVE, 2005). Examples include the interactive web-mapping for the Dorset Heath project in the UK (Dorset County Council, 2007) and the American 'Living with Fire' educational game (United States Department of Agriculture [USDA] Forest Service, 2005).

Conclusions regarding land management are controversial and echo the fire paradox approach now common in the USA and in southern Europe (e.g. McKenzie et al., 2004). Spatial analysis for the PDNP shows that heather moorlands are less prone to reported wildfire outbreaks (McMorrow et al., 2006; McMorrow and Lindley, 2007). It may be that small escaped fires on heather are dealt with by land managers and so are not reported, but large escaped fires are unlikely to remain unnoticed. Burning to reduce the fuel load could therefore be seen as an effective, if controversial, management solution on heather moors (burning on UK blanket bog is normally not permitted). Grazing or cutting may in some circumstances be an alternative, as controlled burning is restricted to certain vegetation types and its effects on ecosystem services are disputed. A consistent method of monitoring and forecasting moorland fuel loads is required, especially on blanket peat and where grazing has been reduced. Moorland restoration theoretically lowers fire risk by re-vegetating bare peat and raising water tables, but fuel load build-up by excluding grazing could threaten investment if not carefully monitored.

Moorland wildfire risk cannot be successfully managed in a policy vacuum. Wildfire has repercussions for all moorland land-users and ecosystem services. Equally, decisions in other policy arenas will impact on moorland wildfire risk if they result in a change of land cover, grazing pressure, level of human use (ignition sources) or public attitude to fire. Lack of consistent national and local databases hinders assessment of the scale of the wildfire problem in the UK and international comparison. The UK's new electronic incident-reporting system should help provide the evidence required. The value of local databases like the PDNPA Rangers' Fire Log has been demonstrated. They should be maintained and improved, and the Fire and Rescue Services' incident report number included to allow cross-referencing to that database. Fire group partnerships between the Fire Service and land managers should be encouraged. The new English Wildfire Forum is a welcome innovation for the uplands. Joined-up thinking on wildfire risk is urgently needed at a national level to protect upland ecosystem services.

Acknowledgements

The authors would like to thank all those who gave time, expertise, data or financial support. They include the Peak District Fire Operations Group, especially Ian Hurst and Sean Prendergast, Moors for the Future, stakeholder and online survey participants, Geoff Eyre, Karl Hennermann and John Handley.

References

Albertson, K., Aylen, J., Cavan, G. and McMorrow, J. (subm.) Forecasting the outbreak of moorland wild fires in the English Peak District. *International Journal of Environmental Management.*

Allgöwer, B., Calogine, D., Camia, A., Cuiñas, P., Fernandes, P., Francesetti, A., Hernando, C., Kötz, B., Koutsias, N., Lindberg, H., Molina, D., Morsdorf, F., Ribeiro, L. M., Rigolot, E. and Séro-Guillaume, O. (2002) *Methods for Wildland Fuel Description and Modelling: A State of the Art.* EUFIRELAB: Euro-Mediterranean Wildland Fire Laboratory, a 'wall-less' laboratory for wildland fire sciences and technologies in the Euro-Mediterranean region. Deliverable D-02-01. http://www.eufirelab.org/prive/directory/units_section_2/D-02-01/D-02-01.pdf

Amatulli, G., Peréz-Cabello, F. and de la Riva, J. (2007) Mapping lightning/human-caused wildfires occurrence under ignition point location uncertainty. *Ecological Modelling*, **200**, 321–33.

Anderson, P. (1986) *Accidental Moorland Fires in the Peak District: A Study of Their Incidence and Ecological Implications.* Peak District Moorland Restoration Project, PDNPA, Bakewell.

Asken Ltd (2004) *Fire Outbreaks in Spring 2003.* Report prepared for the Countryside Agency, Countryside Council for Wales and the Forestry Commission. Asken, Kendal.

Astbury, A. K. (1958) *The Black Fens.* Golden Head Press, Cambridge. http://www.cam.net.uk/home/greg/local/fenfire.htm

Aylen, J., Cavan, G. and Albertson, K. (2007) *Identifying the Best Strategy for Mitigating Moorland Wildfire Risk.* Small grant project report for Moors for the Future, Edale.

Bardgett, R. D., Marsden, J. H., Howard, D. C. and Hossell, J. E. (1995) The extent and condition of heather in moorland and the potential impact of climate change. *Heathland and Moorland, Cultural Landscapes* (ed. D. B. A. Thompson, A. J. Hester and M. B. Usher), pp. 43–50. Edinburgh: Scottish Natural Heritage.

Baynes, T. P. and Bostock, S. N. (2003) *Burning Issues.* Presented at the Wildfire event, Otterburn, August. http://www.moorlandassociation.org/burn.doc

Bruce, M. A. (2002) Country report for the United Kingdom. Baltex Fire 2000. The Second Baltic Seminar and Exercise in Forest Fire and Information and Resources Exchange 2000. http://www.fire.uni-freiburg.de/iffn/country/gb/gb_2.htm

Burnett, G. (2004) *Report to Scottish Wildfire Forum*. Her Majesty's Fire Service Inspectorate for Scotland. http://www.scotland.gov.uk/Topics/Justice/Fire/15130/wildfireforum

Carlson, J. D. and Burgan, R. E. (2003) Review of users' needs in operational fire danger estimation: the Oklahoma example. *International Journal of Remote Sensing*, **24**, 1601–20.

CCVE (2005) *Risk Workshop: Moorland Wildfires in the Peak District*. Technical Report. Centre for Urban and Regional Ecology, University of Manchester, 2005. http://www.snw.org.uk/tourism/downloads/PD_workshop_report.pdf

Chuvieco, E. (ed.) (2003) *Wildland Fire Danger Estimation and Mapping: The Role of Remote Sensing Data*. Singapore: World Scientific Publishing.

Chuvieco, E. and Salas, J. (1996) Mapping the spatial distribution of forest fire danger using GIS. *Geographical Information Systems*, **10**, 333–45.

CLG (2006) *New Incident Recording System (IRS)*. http://www.communities.gov.uk/fire/fireandresiliencestatisticsandre/firestatistics/newincidentrecording/

CLG (2007) *Fire Statistics, United Kingdom, 2005*. http://www.communities.gov.uk/documents/fire/pdf/320258

Countryside Agency (2007) The Met Office Fire Severity Index. http://www.openaccess.gov.uk/wps/portal/!ut/p/.cmd/cs/.ce/7_0_A/.s/7_0_G3/_s.7_0_A/7_0_G3

Crimmins, M. A. and Comrie, A. C. (2004) Interactions between antecedent climate and wildfire variability across south-eastern Arizona. *International Journal of Wildland Fire*, **13**, 455–66.

Danson, M. and Bowyer, P. (2004) Estimating live fuel moisture content from remotely sensed reflectance. *Remote Sensing of Environment*, **92**, 309–21.

Davies, G. M., Legg, C. J., Hamilton, A. and Gray, A. (2006) The future of fire management in the uplands. *The Future of Biodiversity in the Uplands*. Conference Proceedings, Battleby, Perth, 8 December. http://www.cms.uhi.ac.uk/conferences/upland_biodiversity_Dec2006/toc.htm

Davies, G. M., Legg, C. J., Smith, A. and MacDonald, A. (2006) Developing shrub fire behaviour models in an oceanic climate: burning in the British uplands. *Forest Ecology and Management*, **234**S: S107.

DLR (2007) Wild Fires and their impact on nature and human well being: fire ecology. Zentrum für satellitengestüzte KrisenInformation http://www.zki.caf.dlr.de/fireModis/fireinfo_de.html

Dombeck, M. P., Williams, C. A. and Wood, C. A. (2004) Wildfire policy and public lands: integrating scientific understanding with social concerns across landscapes. *Conservation Biology*, **18**, 883–9.

Dorset County Council (2007) Scalable vector graphics. Urban heaths project. http://www.dorsetforyou.com/index.jsp?articleid=342642

Froyd, C. A. (2006) Holocene fire in the Scottish Highlands: evidence from macroscopic charcoal records. *The Holocene*, **16**, 239–45.

GFMC (2007a) Europe and temperate-boreal Asia fires statistics. http://www.fire.uni-freiburg.de/inventory/gvfi/eurasia_stat.htm

GFMC (2007b) Activity of the UN International Strategy for Disaster Reduction (ISDR) http://www.fire.uni-freiburg.de/

Gilbert, C. L. (1986) Professor Hendry's econometric methodology. *Oxford Bulletin of Economics and Statistics*, **48**, 283–307.

Gimmingham, C. H. (1972) *Ecology of Heathlands*. London: Chapman & Hall.

Goldammer, J. (2001) *Global Forest Fire Assessment 1990–2000.* Rome, Forest Resources Assessment WP 55. http://www.fao.org/docrep/006/ad653e/ad653e00.htm

Home Office (1990) Summary fire statistics 1989. *Statistical Bulletin,* **38/90.** http://www.homeoffice.gov.uk/rds/pdfs2/hosb3890.pdf

Hulme, M., Jenkins, G. J., Lu, X., Turnpenny, J. R., Mitchell, T. D., Jones, R. G., Lowe, J., Murphy, J. M., Hassell, D., Boorman, P., McDonald, R. and Hill, S. (2002) *Climate Change Scenarios for the United Kingdom: The UKCIP02 Scientific Report.* United Kingdom Climate Impacts Programme, Oxford.

Iliadis, L. S. (2005) A decision support system applying an integrated fuzzy model for long-term forest fire risk estimation. *Environmental Modelling and Software,* **20,** 613–21.

JRC (2006) *Forest Fires in Europe 2005.* European Commission Directorate-General Environment, Institute for Environment and Sustainability, Land Management and Natural Hazards Unit, EUR 22312, European Communities. http://www.fire.uni-freiburg.de/programmes/eu-comission/EU-Forest-Fires-in-Europe-2005.pdf

Legg, C. J., Bruce, M. and Davies, G. M. (2005) Country report for the United Kingdom. Unpublished summary of the status of wildland fire in the UK. http://firebeaters.geos.ed.ac.uk/UserFiles/File/Country%20Report%20for%20the%20United%20Kingdom%

Legg, C., Maltby, E. and Proctor, M. C. F. (1992) The ecology of severe moorland fire on the North York Moors: seed distribution and seedling establishment of *Calluna vulgaris. Journal of Ecology,* **80,** 737–52.

McEvoy, D., Handley, J., Cavan, G., Aylen, J., Lindley, S. and McMorrow, J. (2006) *Climate Change and the Visitor Economy: Challenges and Opportunities for England's Northwest.* Final Report. Sustainability Northwest, Manchester and UKCIP, Oxford. http://www.snw.org.uk/tourism/downloads/CCVE_Challenges_And_opportunities.pdf

McKenzie, D., Gedalof, Z. E., Peterson, D. L. and Mote, P. (2004) Climatic change, wildfire and conservation. *Conservation Biology,* **18,** 890–902.

McMorrow, J., Aylen, J., Albertson, K., Cavan, G., Lindley, S., Handley, J. and Karooni, R. (2006) *Moorland Wildfires in the Peak District National Park, Peak District Case Study,* Technical Report 3, Climate Change and the Visitor Economy, CCVE, Centre for Urban and Regional Ecology, Manchester University. http://www.snw.org.uk/tourism/downloads/Moorland_Wildfires_Final_Report.pdf

McMorrow, J. M. and Lindley, S. J. (2007) *Modelling the Spatial Risk of Moorland Wildfire.* Small grant project report for Moors for the Future, Edale, and Peak District Fire Operations Group.

Met Office (2005) *The Met Office Fire Severity Index for England and Wales.* Prepared for the Countryside Agency, Countryside Council for Wales and the Forestry Commission. Met Office ref: M/BO/P87. Met Office, Exeter. http://www.openaccess.gov.uk/wps/portal/!ut/p/.cmd/cs/.ce/7_0_A/.s/7_0_G3/_s.7_0_A/7_0_G3

Miller, C., Landres, P. B. and Laaback, P. B. (2000) Evaluating risks and benefits of wildland fire at landscape scales. *Crossing the Millenium: Integrating Spatial Technologies and Ecological Principles for a New Age in Fire Management: Proceedings, Joint Fire Sciences Conference and Workshop; June 15–17, 1999* (technical eds L. F. Neuenschwander and K. C. Ryan). Boise, Idaho: University of Idaho. http://www.treesearch.fs.fed.us/pubs/23564

Murgatroyd, I. (2002) *Forest and Moorland Fire Suppression*. Forestry Commission Technical Note, September.

Nadeau, L. B. and Englefield, P. (2006) Fine-resolution mapping of wildfire fuel types for Canada: fuzzy logic modeling for an Alberta pilot area. *Environmental Monitoring and Assessment*, **120**, 127–52.

ODPM (2006) *The Economic Cost of Fire: Estimates for 2004*. http://www.communities.gov.uk/documents/fire/pdf/144524

ODPM (2007) *Fire Statistics 2005*. http://www.communities.gov.uk/documents/fire/doc/firestatsuk

Page, S. E., Siegert, F., Rieley, J. O., Boehm, H.-D. V., Jayak, A. and Limink, S. (2002) The amount of carbon released from peat and forest fires in Indonesia during 1997. *Nature*, **420**, 61–5.

PDNPA (2005) Preventing and fighting wild moorland fires. http://www.peakdistrict.gov.uk/index/looking-after/rangers/fire.htm

Perry, G. L. W. (1998) Current approaches to modelling the spread of wildland fire: a review, *Progress in Physical Geography*, **22**, BP 222–45.

Poulter, B., Christensen, N. L. and Halpin, P. N. (2006) Carbon emissions from a temperate peat fire and its relevance to interannual variability of trace atmospheric greenhouse gases. *Journal of Geophysical Research*, **111**, D06301, doi:10.1029/2005JD006455.

Radley, J. (1965) Significance of major moorland fires. *Nature*, **215**, March 27, 1254–9.

Romero-Calcerrada, R. and Millington, J. D. A. (2007) Spatial analysis of patterns and causes of fire ignition probabilities using logistic regression and weights-of-evidence based GIS modelling. *Geophysical Research Abstracts*, **9**, 01337, SRef-ID: 1607-7962/gra/EGU2007-A-01337.

Rothwell, J. J., Evans, M. G. and Allott, T. E. H. (2007) Lead contamination of fluvial sediments in an eroding blanket peat catchment. *Applied Geochemistry*, **22**, 446–59.

Running, S. W. (2006) Is global warming causing more, larger wildfires? *Science*, **313**, 927–8.

Ryan, K. C. (1991) Vegetation and wildland fire: implications of global climate change. *Environment International*, **17**, 169–78.

Setiawan, I., Mahmud, A. R., Mansor, S., Mohamed Shariff, A. R. and Nuruddin, A. A. (2004) GIS grid-based and multi-criteria analysis for identifying and mapping peat swamp forest fire hazard in Pahang, Malaysia. *Disaster Prevention and Management*, **13**, 379–86.

Solomon, S., Qin, D., Manning, M., Marquis, M., Averyt, K., Tigor, M. M. B., LeRoy Miller, H. and Chen, Z. (eds) (2007) *Climate Change 2007: The Physical Science Basis*. Contribution of Working Group 1 to the Fourth Assessment Report of the Intergovernmental Panel on Climate Change. IPCC, Geneva. http://news.bbc.co.uk/1/shared/bsp/hi/pdfs/02_02_07_climatereport.pdf

Stratton, R. D. (2006) *Guidance on Spatial Wildland Fire Analysis: Models, Tools, and Techniques. Gen. Tech. Rep. RMRS-GTR-183*. USDA Forest Service, Rocky Mountain Research Station, Fort Collins, Colo. http://www.firemodels.org/downloads/farsite/publications/stratton_rmrs_gtr_183_v16.pdf

SWF (2006) *Scottish Wildfire Forum Annual Report 2005*. http://www.scotland.gov.uk/Resource/Doc/1100/0024206.pdf

Tabara, D., Saur, D. and Cerdan, R. (2003) Forest fire risk management and public participation in changing socio-environmental conditions: a case study in a Mediterranean region. *Risk Analysis*, **2**, 249–60.

Tallis, J. H. (1987) Fire and flood at Holme Moss: erosion processes in an upland blanket mire. *Journal of Ecology*, **75**, 1099–129.

USDA Forest Service (2005) *Living with Fire, Public Simulator*. http://www.fs.fed.us/ rm/fire_game/

Venevsky, S., Thonicke, K., Sitch, S. and Cramer, W. (2002) Simulating fire regimes in human-dominated ecosystems: Iberian peninsula case study. *Global Change Biology*, **8**, 984–98.

Westerling, A. L., Hidalgo, H. G., Cayan, D. R. and Swetnam, T. W. (2006) Warming and earlier spring increase western US forest wildfire activity. *Science*, **313**, 940–3.

Wotton, B. M. and Flannigan, M. D. (1993) Length of the fire season in a changing climate. *The Forestry Chronicle*, **69**, 187–92.

24 Moorland restoration: potential and progress

Penny Anderson, Matt Buckler and Jonathan Walker

Introduction

Moorlands are open upland areas usually on podsols or peat covered in blanket bog, dwarf shrub, bracken and other associated vegetation types. Moorlands have faced a catalogue of pressures (Crowle and McCormack, this volume), resulting in degradation of moorland vegetation, animal communities and hydrological systems leading to loss of ecosystem functioning. Ecological restoration assists the recovery of a degraded, damaged or destroyed ecosystem to re-create a naturally functioning self-sustaining system (Wheeler and Shaw, 1995). Restoration has the potential to enhance ecological character and nature conservation value, to improve carrying capacity for agriculture and recreation/tourism, as well as to increase the carbon sequestration potential and to reduce the discharge of dissolved organic carbon (DOC) that affects water quality.

Causes of degradation

Degradation is driven by several factors. Air pollution (Caporn and Emmett, this volume) has resulted in the loss of bryophytes and lichens close to urban areas (Skeffington *et al.*, 1997). This reduces biodiversity, but also removes early colonisers of damaged ground. The Peak District, the South Pennines and South Wales have been the most severely affected moorland areas in the UK; some of the degradation commenced as long ago as the fourteenth century. Significant increases in grazing-animal numbers – especially sheep at the expense of cattle (which may be historic in some areas; see Shimwell, 1974), and the way they are managed on the moor (Anderson and Yalden, 1981; Backshall, 1996), often combined with increased use of managed fire, has resulted in large-scale changes of vegetation types. Some of these changes have been driven by government policy and agricultural economics (Condliffe, this volume), others by management for red grouse *Lagopus lagopus scoticus*. In some areas, years of regular (often annual) managed burning on a large scale for sheep, and with no cattle to graze the re-growing vegetation, has resulted in large blocks of dominating purple moor grass *Molinia caerulea* on wet ground or mat grass *Nardus stricta* in drier areas.

Extensive excavation of drains (grips), grant-aided last century in Britain, has damaged the hydrological integrity of blanket bogs in particular. It was initiated to increase dwarf shrub cover for grouse or to reduce the wetness for more effective sheep-grazing, but is contributing to increasing DOC in streams from enhanced peat decay, reduction in bog wetness (Holden and Burt, 2003), and vegetation dominated by species preferring drier conditions. Grips with sufficient runoff generate considerable erosion, that can cut down into the underlying substrate below the peat (Holden, this volume). The density of grips across the North Pennines and Yorkshire Dales is probably greater than in any other part of England.

Burning for red grouse management has contributed to increased heather dominance replacing other dwarf shrubs and blanket bog species on a widespread scale (Crowle and McCormack, this volume). Accidental wildfire in drought periods, if the root mat is destroyed, can result in extensive bare ground, especially on blanket peat (McMorrow *et al.*, this volume). Bare mineral ground might re-colonise naturally, but erosion and gullying develop where fragile peats are exposed, where soil acidity has increased from air pollution and where early colonising bryophytes have been lost. This is especially prevalent in the Peak District where over 33 km^2 of bare or partly bare and eroding ground was identified (Phillips *et al.*, 1981). Smaller areas occur in the South Pennines, the North York Moors (Maltby *et al.*, 1990), the North Pennines, and on blanket bog in Wales (Yeo, 1997) and Scotland. Bared peat leads to increased sediment into rivers and reservoirs (Phillips *et al.*, 1981), increased gullying, increased DOC (Allott, this volume), and greater vulnerability to further fires due to the drying of the surrounding peat (McMorrow *et al.*, this volume).

A final driver of damage is trampling by visitors, although this is usually small-scale compared with the other drivers. However, erosion and soil collapse, rill formation and more severe erosion can develop on the more sensitive routes or areas (McEvoy *et al.*, 2006).

Understanding restoration

The first step in any restoration project is to understand and assess the current situation. Only then can restoration targets be set. These need to reflect stakeholder priorities, such as biodiversity, soil carbon retention, drinking-water provision, sporting interests, farming, recreation/amenity, and so on, funding and timescales, and success measured against these outcomes.

Rebuilding functioning moorland ecosystems

When moorlands lose resilience, they become vulnerable to perturbations previously absorbed without changes in function or structure. However, when the length, intensity, scale or nature of the pressure causes it to pass an ecological threshold (the level of an environmental pollutant, the loss of a species or a species invasion), it can 'flip' to an alternative equilibrium or stable state from which natural recovery of the original ecosystem is generally not possible, or only possible in an unacceptable timescale, for example bare, eroding peatlands, or extensive stands of native species such as purple moor grass (Holling, 1973; Walker *et al.*, 1981). In this scenario, innovative management that addresses the constraints of the degraded system is required to restore the original habitat (Suding *et al.*, 2004). Controlling the driver may not be enough to dislodge this equilibrium, and more significant intervention is required, like removal of invasive or introduced species, substrate stabilisation and (re-)introductions.

The choice of approach

The choice is whether control or manipulation of the drivers is sufficient, and thus recovery of the ecosystem facilitated, or whether larger-scale intervention is needed reflecting exceedence of ecological thresholds resulting in an irreversible state. In many instances a different driver from that which produced the original damage (e.g. wildfire) is controlling the restoration process – frost heave (Tallis and Yalden, 1983), acidic substrates or lack of available nutrients on blanket peat (Phillips *et al.*, 1981).

The resilience of moorland is its capacity to retain the same function, structure, identity and feedbacks following or during disturbance (Holling, 1973; Walker *et al.*, 2004). If the tolerance levels of this natural resilience are exceeded, restoration would rely on greater intervention to re-establish ecosystem functioning (Peterson *et al.*, 1998) including hydrology, soil health and species diversity.

Intervention can be a costly approach, with complex solutions and practical issues that require significant understanding. Timescales can be long (five to ten or more years), and management input continuous. Controlling drivers to enable repair within the natural resilience of the ecosystem would be much more cost-effective and achievable on a shorter timescale. Understanding the effectiveness and demands of different approaches is therefore critical for planning restoration programmes and costings. Integral to this is a full appreciation of local site conditions (climate, hydrology), the species' autecology, the restoration capacity (e.g. potential seed banks), the local air quality and nutrient loading (Mitchell *et al.*, 2000), and how these interact with the management options. Most methods focus on restoration of the dominant moorland plant under the assumption that other plant (and animal) species will eventually colonise from elsewhere (Littlewood, Pakeman and Woodin, 2006).

Restoration in practice

The different moorland restoration approaches, working from the simplest and cheapest to the complex options that address the more challenging restoration problems, are addressed below and summarised in Table 24.1.

Table 24.1 Upland management problems and some solutions.

Restoration problem	Problem type	Possible Driver/Cause	Treatment	Treatment type	Required Knowledge
Overgrazing	Loss of biodiversity, Reduction in ecosystem function	Excessive/inappropriate stock numbers	Stock reduction	Remove driver	Preferential grazing patterns by stock concerned
Invasive species – native (e.g. Molinia, Pteridium, Betula)	Loss of biodiversity, Loss of ecosystem function	Excessive grazing, inappropriate burning	Stock reduction, alteration of burning management, possible chemical/mechanical control to reduce dominance	Remove driver	Understanding of ecology of invasive species
			Introduction of desired species	Rebuilding biodiversity	Ecology of desired species/community
Invasive species – introduced (e.g. Rhododendron, ponticum)	Significant loss of biodiversity	Inappropriate introductions, inappropriate management	Chemical, biological/mechanical control to eradicate species	Remove driver	Impact of biological controls
			Re-introduction of desired species	Rebuilding biodiversity	Ecology of desired species/community
Invasive species – conifers	Significant loss of biodiversity, Loss of ecosystem function	As above plus significant drainage	Removal of conifers	Remove driver	Desired hydrology
			Restoration of hydrology		
			Re-introduction of desired species	Rebuilding biodiversity	Ecology of desired species/community
Desiccation	Loss of ecosystem function	Drainage/climate change	Grip/gully blocking	Remove driver; Large scale repair	Hydrology
Bare peat restoration	Loss of biodiversity, loss of ecosystem function	Wildfire/historic/over-grazing/	Stock exclosure & Wildfire prevention	Remove driver	
			Peat Stabilisation (Nurse crop, geo-textiles, heather brash etc.)	Large scale repair	Indirect impact of techniques, site parameters
			Re-introduction of desired species	Rebuilding biodiversity	Ecology of desired species/community

Severity & Cost →

Controlling or managing the driver to achieve recovery

If the resilience of the system is relatively intact, and it has not flipped into another stable but undesirable state, the immediate action required for restoration is the control or management of the driver that has effected change. This represents sustainable, informed management that alleviates further pressure and degradation of the habitat, allowing system recovery through natural succession to the target state. Examples are managing grazing and burning regimes, blocking grips and removing planted or invasive species.

Managing grazing regimes

It has been estimated that 80 per cent of English and Welsh moors that deteriorated after about 1950 would benefit from reduced or altered grazing pressure (Thompson *et al.*, 1995; Gardner *et al.*, this volume). The agri-environment schemes have helped to produce significant recovery in places. However, recovery is often slow and patchy, even with stock excluded, on blanket bog and on steep mineral slopes (Anderson and Radford, 1994). It can take twenty years or more for the desired species mixture and a complete vegetation cover to re-establish (Anderson *et al.*, 1997). Where dwarf shrubs have been suppressed, they can benefit more rapidly from reduced grazing pressure (Hulme *et al.*, 2002; Pakeman *et al.*, 2003), provided that there are colonisation gaps still present for re-colonisation of desirable species (Gardner *et al.*, this volume).

Managing burning regimes

There are growing concerns about effects of managed burning on heather moors on podsols and blanket peat on bryophytes, especially *Sphagnum* species, and on the storage and release of carbon (Backshall *et al.*, 2001; Crowle and Cormack; Yallop, both this volume). Management options are to identify 'no burn' sensitive areas, to stop or reduce the burning cycle on blanket bog, and to use cool burning techniques that have less impact on mosses. More research is needed on these aspects.

Blocking grips

Extensive grip-blocking is being undertaken in several projects in the UK uplands, often using methods adapted from drain-blocking in lowland valley and raised mires (Wheeler and Shaw, 1995; Brooks and Stoneman, 1997). Grip-blocking techniques are fairly new, and there is not yet sufficient experience of them to be confident of their long-term efficacy. Some experience has been gained from United Utilities' Sustainable Catchment Management Programme project and projects in Geltsdale, Northumberland and the Yorkshire Dales (MFF/NE, in press). Grip-blocking to repair the hydrology relies usually on natural colonisation to restore the moorland vegetation.

Monitoring blocking reveals a locally raised water table in the peat for a longer period in the year. This can facilitate colonisation by mire species like *Sphagna*, and thus improve the vegetation's ecological quality. Grip-blocking can also contribute to reducing the DOC levels (Wallage *et al.*, 2006), although extended data runs for this are not yet available.

Removing conifers

Restoring dwarf shrub heathland and blanket mire from conifer plantations, as in the Flow Country in Scotland, has been attempted in uplands and lowlands. Removing conifers can involve grinding out stumps and removal of brash and timber, although chipping on site has also been used (Webb, 2001). Felled trees have been used to track on the mire surface to access trees, and to block drains established for conifer-planting. Where there are sufficient vestiges of the previous moorland vegetation, its recovery can be rapid, such as the re-colonisation of *Sphagnum* species in the Kielder Forest (Webb, 2001). Where these are lacking, other measures may be needed (see below).

Controlling the driver plus other restoration measures

Assuming that relevant factors such as grazing, wildfire, managed burning or conifers have been controlled or removed, desired plant species do not always colonise naturally even though the ecosystem has not switched to an alternative stable state. It is worthwhile first testing the seed bank (Gilbert and Anderson, 1998), to see whether the species required are present. This will also reveal potentially undesirable species. Major seed banks of rush (*Juncus*) species, for example, could cause problems and should not be disturbed (Gilbert and Anderson, 1998).

It is also important to understand which species produce viable seed that survives in seed banks. For example, cottongrass, bilberry and crowberry seeds are rare in seed banks, whereas heather, bell heather and cross-leaved heath can be more abundant (Anderson *et al.*, 1997; Pywell *et al.*, 1997). If desirable species are present but do not germinate, the lack of establishment needs investigating. Many species cannot establish in dense vegetation, so colonisation gaps may be needed. Creating these is not easy on moorland, and may involve cutting or burning the vegetation, scarification or manipulation of grazing (Anderson *et al.*, 1997; Gilbert and Anderson, 1998). If seed is not present, species may need to be introduced (see Box 24.1).

However, to establish only one species, most commonly and feasibly heather (*Calluna vulgaris*), does not necessarily restore the wider plant community, which can be very variable. Littlewood, Dennis *et al.* (2006) found that the success of eight restored sites in Scotland and England ranged from 5.6 per cent to 96.4 per cent (mean 60.5 per cent) as measured against

---

Box 24.1. Introducing plants into moorland restoration sites

Potential methods

- Harvesting heather seed using special harvesters (Robinson, 2001; 2002; Gilbert and Anderson, 1998) – only useful where the species occur in monocultures and are accessible.
- Hand collection of seed for scarcer species, such as bell heather *Erica cinerea*.
- Cut whole heather plants with the seed still in the capsules in autumn to 'thatch' bare peat patches within blanket bog. This is successful in small areas of bare peat on its own, but needs a nurse crop on large areas of bare peat. Can be spread manually, using muckspreader or similar.
- Double chop forage harvested heather (see Box 24.2). Very successful for small- and large-scale restoration of bare peat. Spread as for cut whole heather plants, or can be spread by helicopter.
- Plants grown from local cuttings to supplement heather seeding, such as crowberry *Empetrum nigrum*, cross-leaved heath *Erica tetralix* and bilberry *Vaccinium myrtillus* (Anderson *et al.*, 1997) or the cottongrasses. Except for cross-leaved heath, these do not readily establish from seed.

Note that *Calluna vulgaris* is mostly used, as it is harvestable on a sufficient scale.

'target' communities nine to sixteen years after initiation of restoration. The most 'successful' sites benefited from just grazing exclusion (compared with treatment by herbicides, scarification, and re-seeding in other plots), indicating that, for rehabilitation of the whole plant community, grazing exclusion might be preferable where feasible.

Controlling invasive species

Invasive species are a concern on many upland sites. They may establish as a result of direct introduction or through moorland degradation that either increases species' competitive ability or offers novel colonisation opportunities. Examples in the UK are bracken *Pteridium aquilinum*, *Molinia caerulea* and rhododendron *Rhododendron ponticum*.

Decisions are needed on whether the dominance of an invasive species warrants retention or restoration to a more useful vegetation type. For example, tall, dense bracken with a thick litter layer on steep slopes may be best retained as it protects the soils and will probably quickly re-colonise after treatment in areas where it grows well. Similarly, dense *Molinia* may also protect peaty soils holding carbon and provide a good habitat for voles and their predators.

On the other hand, both species have invaded other moorland communities, and these could be restored. The removal of the blanketing vegetation, usually with its accumulated litter and brash, is necessary before reversion to other moorland vegetation (Backshall *et al.*, 2001). Where bare ground is generated as a result, seeding may be needed to avoid erosion, or grazing controlled to accelerate regeneration. Control of bracken and rhododendron are well rehearsed elsewhere (Backshall *et al.*, 2001; Symes and Day, 2003).

The same principles apply to *Molinia* control. It is not actively controlled by grazing exclusion (e.g. Todd *et al.*, 2000), although summer grazing can reduce its extent (Hulme *et al.*, 2002), more particularly using cattle (Gardner *et al.*, this volume). Small-scale trials showed that treatment with herbicide (glyphosate) consistently controlled dense, homogenous *Molinia*, with little impact on other moorland species (Milligan *et al.*, 2003; Marrs *et al.*, 2004). Large-scale herbicide application, subsequent removal of the litter and tussocks through burning, burying and/or demolishing, with heather and other seed applied subsequently, have resulted in increased diversity (Anderson, 2002; Ross *et al.*, 2003).

Larger-scale intervention

Where degraded sites have changed from their original state so that primary succession is a prerequisite for restoration, additional measures are needed. This is exemplified on bare, eroding moorland peat, which shares some restoration requirements with mined lowland raised mires. Restoration success may depend on manipulation of altered biophysical conditions back within the tolerance of target communities.

Moorland restoration ecology in these circumstances follows the general trend with increased emphasis on directing ecological succession (Byers *et al.*, 2006) such as the re-introduction of key functional species or using nurse plants that moderate local environmental conditions. Nurse crops can improve resource availability, reduce soil water evaporation, lower soil and air temperature, decrease radiation reaching seedlings (protection), reduce frost injuries and protect against herbivory, thereby improving the establishment of target plants by mimicking a natural process (Padilla and Pugnaire, 2006). Similar successional facilitation has been found in the restoration of cut-over peatland where cottongrass tussocks may offer a variety of micro-sites for colonisers with varying ecological requirements (Tuittila *et al.*, 2000).

This experience is mirrored in upland bare peat restoration where environmental conditions are severe and the peat is a poor growing medium owing to elevated acidity, mobility in wind, rain, frosts and lack of nutrients (Tallis and Yalden, 1983). Just adding mire species such as heather seed or brash

Box 24.2. Large-scale re-vegetation of bare peat in the Peak District

Restoration works

The Moorland Management Project, an eighteen-year partnership project, examined the extent and causes of bare ground, and trialled methods for its restoration (Anderson *et al.*, 1997). Moors for the Future (MFF), a major corporate partnership project (Bonn, Rebane and Reid, this volume), is applying the research findings on a larger scale.

Since 2003, it has restored 6 km^2 of the most degraded moors in the Peak District. The task is considerable. The legacy of very low pH (between 2.8 and 3.5) and very high heavy metal concentrations (Rothwell *et al.*, 2006) inhibits nutrient uptake.

The process commences with exclusion of livestock and the addition of lime to raise the pH to above 4. Without lime application, root development is insufficient in the Peak District conditions (Caporn *et al.*, 2007). The next step is to apply fertiliser several weeks after the lime – P$_2$O$_5$ at 120 kg/ha at seeding and 60 kg/ha during the following two years, N at 30 kg/ha and K at 60 kg/ha for three years to allow rapid growth and flowering of the sown grasses.

A nurse crop of agricultural and amenity grasses and locally collected wavy-hair grass *Deschampsia flexuosa* is sown. Each species acts as nurse for heather, which in turn facilitates colonisation by cotton grasses, crowberry and bilberry over ten to twenty years.

The sides of deep erosion gullies, peat banks and other actively eroding slopes are stabilised using geojute (jute mesh used as a geotextile) with heather brash on tops and gentle slopes of peat domes. A total of 11 ha of geojute were placed in 2003–7.

Heather brash also supplies significant seeds and other vascular plants and mosses. It may also act as a means of inoculating ericaceous mycorrhizae. MFF has applied over 1,000 tonnes of heather brash, sourced from moors within the Peak District National Park, and is adding plug plants. MFF sourced over 100,000 plug plants, propagated by micro-propagation from material collected locally, to increase the range of species. Trials to add *Sphagnum* species are underway.

Monitoring results

The reduction in the area of bare peat 2003–7 has been highly significant, with an average 45 per cent cover in vegetation achieved within three years of restoration, while control areas have remained bare peat (Figure 24.1; Buckler *et al.*, in press). Once re-vegetated, there is a significant reduction in sediment reaching the streams and reservoirs, but restoration of the hydrological integrity of the bog is absent if large gullies remain (see Box 24.3).

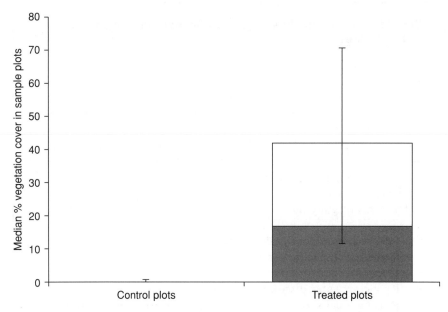

Figure 24.1 Vegetation cover on Bleaklow Plateau (Peak District National Park) in 2006 on unrestored site and a site restored three years previously (grey – nurse crop species; white – other plant species). Values presented are median (±quartiles) values within 226 vegetation plots. There is a significant difference in vegetation cover between the restored and unrestored sites (Mann–Whitney U = 486.0, n = 226, P < 0.001).

(see Box 24.1) is not necessarily sufficient, and nurse species as well as surface stabilisers are added to ensure succession and long-term survival (see Box 24.2).

Ideally, in such conditions moorland restoration should make use of ecosystem engineer plants such as *Sphagnum* species (Rochefort, 2000) that exert large influences on the abiotic environment and thus create or modify habitats to facilitate subsequent changes in species composition (Byers *et al.*, 2006). Furthermore, *Sphagnum* is also one of the most important groups of carbon-sequestering plants in temperate and northern bog ecosystems (Berendse *et al.*, 2001). *Sphagnum* re-introduction on cut-over raised bogs, however, was found to be efficient only after pioneer vascular species were established (Sliva and Pfadenhauer, 1999).

Experience from the restoration of cut-over (worked) peatlands in Canada shows that collecting material from intact peatland and spreading it in the restoration site (diaspore transfer) is more successful compared with the other commonly used method of 'hay' transfer (Rochefort and Lode, 2006). However, translation of these proven restoration methods from mined lowland mires to the uplands presents significant logistical and legal constraints.

Box 24.3. Gully-blocking to restore blanket bog vegetation and hydrology

Erosion gullies in blanket peat lead to desiccation of the peat body. This results in accelerated peat decomposition, leading to discolouration of local water sources, the release of greenhouse-gas emissions into the atmosphere and DOC into the stream network. Substantial sediment transport in streams (up to 267 t/km² per year in some catchments: Evans *et al.*, 2006) and water discolouration are of increasing concern for water companies. Blocking erosion channels can aid the long-term recovery of degraded moorlands, as explored by the National Trust in the Peak District.

The aims of gully-blocking include

- Controlling further gully erosion
- Reducing sediment loss from peatlands
- Promoting re-vegetation
- Reducing water discolouration of streams
- Raising local water table to increase saturation of peat domes.

Combined evidence from naturally re-vegetated sites and analysis of the existing gully blocks leads to the following key recommendations for blocking (Evans *et al.*, 2005):

- Gully-blocking works need to suit the sites and gully types. On intact domes of peat on shallow gradients with minimal gullying, the focus is on water-holding techniques to raise water levels, for example using plastic piling. On heavily degraded moorlands, the goals are re-vegetation and peat stabilisation by using semi-permeable dams made of wood, stone, or brash.
- Information on hill-slope saturation derived through analysis of high-resolution topographical data (LiDAR) and aerial-photograph interpretation can aid restoration priority-setting.
- Blocking should start at the head of the gully system to prevent further erosion into intact areas of blanket bog. Block width and spacing should not exceed 4 m, and blocks should be placed on slopes <7° and not into bedrock.

The difficulties in terms of cost, efficacy of measures, long-term commitments needed, erosive forces in gullies and the extent of gullies should not be underestimated.

Successful but more labour-intensive options include plug plants or laying turfs (Anderson *et al.*, 1997; Box 24.2).

Gully-blocking

Dense gully systems, eroding deep down into blanket peat, can be found throughout the Pennines, but more particularly in the Peak District. The water table within the adjoining peat is reduced alongside the gullies (Bell and Tallis, 1974), and the edges can dry out and collapse. Older gullies are at an advanced state of erosion, with substantial sediment loss (Evans and Warburton, 2005). Natural re-vegetation may occur when the sides collapse, and trap water and sediment (Evans *et al.*, 2005), but often does not occur, and the ecosystem passes beyond its natural restorative capability.

Controlling these effects is the goal of the experimental gully-blocking (Evans *et al.*, 2005; Box 24.3). Owing to the size (depth and width) of some gullies, recent attempts have been made in the Peak District to re-profile instead of blocking them. A shallow depression is created, and the surface is restored using vegetation recovered from the area re-profiled and bare peat re-vegetation restoration techniques. These can be created with or without embedded plastic piling to block partially the new profile (J. Stewart, personal communication). Upland gully-blocking techniques are fairly new, and there is not yet sufficient experience to be confident of their relative efficacy.

Constraints and future challenges to moorland restoration

Tong *et al.* (2006) note that ecological restoration often tends to be focused towards site-specific objectives, rare species or a community based on conservation status. However, restoration objectives in a wider landscape context are needed. Considerable advances are being achieved in the Peak District (Box 24.2). Landscape-scale working has involved research and development of novel techniques in moorland restoration, from the utilisation of helicopters to the development of special bulk seed-collection machinery and seed-delivery systems. These systems include seed treatment such as prilling (combining seed with a material such as clay to form a larger seed unit for sowing) and design and use of hoppers for helicopters.

Restoration actions in themselves can have negative environmental impacts, and these need to be identified and addressed. Raising peat pH using lime for nurse crop establishment, for example, can lead to increased carbon emissions in the short term (Caporn *et al.*, 2007). Building in robust monitoring of restoration success is fundamental, and should include capacity to quantify both positive and negative outcomes.

Whilst most moorland restoration work has involved re-establishing vegetation, it can benefit animal communities. Littlewood, Dennis *et al.* (2006) show how reversion of *Molinia*-dominated vegetation could add diversity to the moorland Hemiptera and Lepidoptera assemblages. Substantial increases in moorland breeding birds have been reported on land where *Molinia* has been treated on a large scale (Anderson, 2002; G. Eyre, personal communication). On the other hand, there are some invertebrates that favour bare ground, and their long-term survival could be threatened if all the moorlands were restored.

There are also several common features in the moorlands which are not fully understood, and their successful restoration is still outstanding. A key feature is peat pipes (sub-peat tunnels at the interface between the base of the peat and the underlying mineral substrate). These are not mapped; their significance, in terms of drainage of blanket bogs, is not fully appreciated, although research is being conducted (Holden, this volume) and no methods have yet been trialled to attempt to block any.

No trials have been set up, either, on reverting extensive mat grass and heath rush *Juncus squarrosus* species-poor plant communities to a more diverse state. They are of little grazing value; have little to offer with respect to biodiversity; and their restoration would have less potential adverse impact on peat soils compared to high-level intervention blanket bog restoration as they occur more on mineral soils.

Future moorland restoration: the influence of climate change

Possibly the greatest question for the success of current and future moorland restoration is climate change. Peatlands have become drier over the last forty years, with these changes primarily driven by summer temperature changes. Given the predicted future climate change scenarios (Caporn and Emmett, this volume), further water-table declines will follow, so that current intervention activities are unlikely to restore mires to their former condition (Hendon and Charman, 2004). Harris *et al.* (2006) recommend the need to look outside historic conditions and species compositions to a wider consideration of proper ecosystem functioning. The key consideration should be building ecosystem-functioning resilience to future change into restoration. An example they cite is using plant material derived from locations adapted to predicted future climatic conditions rather than locally sourced (and locally adapted).

The importance and potential of upland peatlands in locking up carbon (Worrall and Evans, this volume) will significantly affect moorland restoration targets and practices. This will bring new challenges as restoration outcomes are potentially increasingly targeted towards carbon storage in addition to existing priorities, and restoration methods will be required to become more 'carbon efficient'. The impact of these changes is yet to be seen, but is already igniting considerable interest. Research and development is underway into a new wave of moorland restoration best practice that ultimately will have to balance rebuilding past systems, resilient systems for the future and their carbon storage potential.

References

Anderson, P. (2002) Diversity from *Molinia* moorlands. *Enact*, **10**, 4.

Anderson, P. and Radford, E. (1994) Changes in vegetation following reduction in grazing pressure on the National Trust's Kinder Estate, Peak District, Derbyshire, England. *Biological Conservation*, **69**, 55–63.

Anderson, P., Tallis, J. H. and Yalden, D. W. (1997) *Moorland Management Project Phase III Report.* Bakewell: Peak Park Joint Planning Board.

Anderson, P. and Yalden, D. W. (1981) Increased sheep numbers and the loss of heather moorland in the Peak District. *Biological Conservation*, **10**, 195–214.

Backshall, J. (1996) *A Literature Review of the Historical Effects of Burning and Grazing on Blanket Bog and Wet Heath.* English Nature Research Report 172 Peterborough: English Nature.

Backshall, J., Manley, J. and Rebane, M. (eds) (2001) *Upland Management Handbook.* English Nature. http://www.english-nature.org.uk/pubs/handbooks/upland.asp?id=1

Bell, J. N. B. and Tallis, J. H. (1974) The response of *Empetrum nigrum* L. to different mire water regimes, with special reference to Wybunbury Moss, Cheshire and Featherbed Moss, Derbyshire. *Journal of Ecology*, **62**, 75–95.

Berendse, F., Van Breemen, N., Rydin, H., Buttler, A., Heijmans, M., Hoosbeek, M. R., Lee, J. A., Mitchell, E., Saarinen, T., Vasander, H. and Wallen, B. (2001) Raised atmospheric CO_2 levels and increased N deposition cause shifts in plant species composition and production in *Sphagnum* bogs. *Global Change Biology*, **7**, 591–8.

Brooks, S. and Stoneman, R. (1997) *Conserving Bogs: The Management Handbook.* Edinburgh: The Stationery Office.

Buckler, M., Walker, J. and Bonn, A. (in press) *Bare Peat Restoration on Peak District Moorlands: Nurse Crop Establishment and Plant Succession.* Moors for the Future Report No. 14, Edale.

Byers, J. E., Cuddington, K., Jones, C. G., Talley, T. S., Hastings, A., Lambrinos, J. G., Crooks, J. A. and Wilson, W. G. (2006) Using ecosystem engineers to restore ecological systems. *Trends in Ecology and Evolution*, **21**, 493–500.

Caporn, S., Sen, R., Field, C., Jones, E., Carroll, J. and Dise, N. (2007) *Consequences of Lime and Fertiliser Application for Moorland Restoration and Carbon Balance.* Report to Moors for the Future. Manchester Metropolitan University.

Evans, M., Allott, T., Holden, J., Flitcroft, C. and Bonn, A. (eds) (2005) *Understanding Gully Blocking.* Moors for the Future Report No. 4, Edale. http://www.moorsforthefuture.org.uk/mftf/main/Publications.htm

Evans, M. and Warburton, J. (2005) Sediment budget for an eroding peat moorland catchment in northern England. *Earth Surface Processes and Landforms*, **30**, 557–77.

Evans, M., Warburton, J. and Yang, J. (2006) Sediment budgets for eroding blanket peat catchments: global and local implications of upland organic sediment budgets. *Geomorphology*, **79**, 45–57.

Gilbert, O. and Anderson, P. (1998) *Habitat Creation and Repair.* Oxford: Oxford University Press.

Harris, J. A., Hobbs, R. J., Higgs, E. and Aronson, J. (2006) Ecological restoration and global climate change. *Restoration Ecology*, **14**, 170–6.

Hendon, D. and Charman, D. J. (2004) High-resolution peatland water-table changes for the past 200 years: the influence of climate and implications for management. *Holocene*, **14**, 125–34.

Holden, J. and Burt, T. P. (2003) Runoff production in blanket peat covered catchments. *Water Resources Research*, **39**, 1191.

Holling, C. S. (1973) Resilience and stability of ecological systems. *Annual Review of Ecology and Systematics*, **4**, 1–23.

Hulme, P. D., Merrell, B. G., Torvell, L., Fisher, J. M., Small, J. L. and Pakeman, R. J. (2002) Rehabilitation of degraded *Calluna vulgaris* (L.) Hull-dominated wet heath by controlled sheep grazing. *Biological Conservation*, **107**, 351–63.

Littlewood, N. A., Dennis, P., Pakeman, R. J. and Woodin, S. J. (2006) Moorland restoration aids the reassembly of associated phytophagous insects. *Biological Conservation*, **132**, 395–404.

Littlewood, N. A., Pakeman, R. J. and Woodin, S. J. (2006) A field assessment of the success of moorland restoration in the rehabilitation of whole plant assemblages. *Applied Vegetation Science*, **9**, 295–306.

McEvoy, D., Handley, J. F., Cavan, G., Aylen, J., Lindley, S., McMorrow, J. and Glynn, S. (2006) *Climate Change and the Visitor Economy: The Challenges and Opportunities for England's Northwest*. Sustainability Northwest and UKCIP, Manchester, Oxford. http://www.snw.org.uk/tourism/downloads/CCVE_Challenges_And_Opportunities.pdf

Maltby, E., Legg, C. J. and Proctor, M. C. F. (1990) The ecology of severe moorland fire on the North York Moors: effects of the 1976 fires, and subsequent surface and vegetation development. *Journal of Ecology*, **78**, 490–518.

Marrs, R. H., Phillips, J. D. P., Todd, P. A., Ghorbani, J. and Le Duc, M. G. (2004) Control of *Molinia caerulea* on upland moors. *Journal of Applied Ecology*, **41**, 398–411.

Milligan, A. L., Putwain, P. D. and Marrs, R. H. (2003) A field assessment of the role of selective herbicides in the restoration of British moorland dominated by *Molinia*. *Biological Conservation*, **109**, 369–79.

Mitchell, R. J., Auld, M. H. D., Hughes, J. M. and Marrs, R. H. (2000) Estimates of nutrient removal during heathland restoration on successional sites in Dorset, Southern England. *Biological Conservation*, **95**, 233–46.

Moors for the Future and Natural England (in press) *Moorland Restoration Manual for England.* Moors for the Future/Natural England.

Padilla, F. M. and Pugnaire, F. I. (2006) The role of nurse plants in the restoration of degraded environments. *Frontiers in Ecology and the Environment*, **4**, 196–202.

Pakeman, R. J., Hulme, P. D., Torvell, L. and Fisher, J. M. (2003) Rehabilitation of degraded dry heather [*Calluna vulgaris* (L.) Hull] moorland by controlled sheep grazing. *Biological Conservation*, **114**, 389–400.

Peterson, G., Allen, C. R. and Holling, C. S. (1998) Ecological resilience, biodiversity, and scale. *Ecosystems*, **1**, 6–18.

Phillips, J., Yalden, D. and Tallis, J. (eds) (1981) *Moorland Erosion Study: Phase 1 Report*. Bakewell: Peak Park Joint Planning Board.

Pywell, R. F., Webb, N. R. and Putwain, P. D. (1997) A comparison of techniques for restoring heathland on abandoned farmland. *Journal of Applied Ecology*, **32**, 400–11.

Robinson, T. (2001) Options for seed harvesting techniques: part one. *Enact*, **9**, 4–8.

Robinson, T. (2002) Options for seed harvesting techniques: part two. *Enact*, **10**, 4–8.

Rochefort, L. (2000) New frontiers in bryology and lichenology – *Sphagnum* – a keystone genus in habitat restoration. *Bryologist*, **103**, 503–8.

Rochefort, L. and Lode, E. (2006) Restoration of degraded boreal peatlands. *Boreal Peatland Ecosystems* (ed. R. K. Wieder and D. H. Vitt), pp. 381–422. Berlin: Springer.

Ross, S., Adamson, H. and Moon, A. (2003) Evaluating management techniques for controlling *Molinia caerulea* and enhancing *Calluna vulgaris* on upland wet heathland in northern England, UK. *Agriculture Ecosystems and Environment*, **97**, 39–49.

Rothwell, J. J., Robinson, S. G., Evans, M. G., Yang, J. and Allott, T. E. H. (2005) Heavy metal release by peat erosion in the Peak District, South Pennines, UK. *Hydrological Processes*, **19**, 2973–89.

Shimwell, D. (1974) Sheep grazing intensity in Edale, 1692–1747, and its effect on blanket peat erosion. *Derbyshire Archaeological Journal*, **94**, 35–40.

Skeffington, R., Wilson, E., Maltby, E., Immirzi, P. and Putwain, P. (1997) Acid deposition and blanket mire degradation and restoration. *Blanket Mire Degradation – Causes, Consequences and Challenges* (ed. J. H. Tallis, R. Meade and P. D. Hulme), pp. 29–37. Aberdeen: Macaulay Land Use Research Institute.

Sliva, J. and Pfadenhauer, J. (1999) Restoration of cut-over raised bogs in southern Germany: a comparison of methods. *Applied Vegetation Science*, **2**, 137–48.

Suding, K. N., Gross, K. L., and Houseman, G. R. (2004) Alternative states and positive feedbacks in restoration ecology. *Trends in Ecology and Evolution*, **19**, 46–53.

Symes, N. and Day, J. (2003) *A Practical Guide to the Restoration and Management of Lowland Heathland*. Sandy: Royal Society for the Protection of Birds.

Tallis, J. H. and Yalden, D. W. (1983) *Peak District Moorland Restoration Project. Phase 2 Report: Re-vegetation Trials.* Bakewell: Peak Park Joint Planning Board.

Thompson, D. B. A., MacDonald, A. J., Marsden, J. H. and Galbraith, C. A. (1995) Upland heather moorland in Great Britain: a review of international importance, vegetation change and some objectives for nature conservation. *Biological Conservation*, **71**, 163–78.

Todd, P. A., Phillips, J. D. P., Putwain, P. D. and Marrs, R. H. (2000) Control of *Molinia caerulea* on moorland. *Grass and Forage Science*, **55**, 181–91.

Tong, C., Le Duc, M. G., Ghorbani, J. and Marrs, R. H. (2006) Linking restoration to the wider landscape: a study of a bracken control experiment within an upland moorland landscape mosaic in the Peak District, UK. *Landscape and Urban Planning*, **78**, 115–34.

Tuittila, E. S., Rita, H., Vasander, H. and Laine, J. (2000) Vegetation patterns around *Eriophorum vaginatum* L. tussocks in a cut-away peatland in southern Finland. *Canadian Journal of Botany*, **78**, 47–58.

Walker, B., Holling, C. S., Carpenter, S. R. and Kinzig, A. (2004) Resilience, adaptability and transformability in social-ecological systems. *Ecology and Society*, **9**: Article 5 (online) http://www.ecologyandsociety.org/vol9/iss2/art5/main.html

Walker, B. H., Ludwig, D., Holling, C. S. and Peterman, R. M. (1981) Stability of semi-arid savanna grazing systems. *Journal of Ecology*, **69**, 473–98.

Wallage, Z. E., Holden, J. and McDonald, A. T. (2006) Drain blocking: an effective treatment for reducing dissolved organic carbon loss and water discolouration in a drained peatland. *Science of the Total Environment*, **367**, 811–21.

Webb, S. (2001) Life after conifers. *Enact*, **9**, 18–22.

Wheeler, B. D. and Shaw, S. C. (1995) *Restoration of Damaged Peatlands*. London: The Stationery Office.

Yeo, M. (1997) Blanket mire degradation in Wales. *Blanket Mire Degradation, Causes, Consequences and Challenges* (ed. J. H. Tallis, R. Meade and P. D. Hulme), pp. 101–15. Aberdeen: Macaulay Land Use Research Institute.

25 Ecosystem services

A new rationale for conservation of upland environments

Aletta Bonn, Mick Rebane and
Christine Reid

Introduction

The challenge for the conservation of upland environments is to increase understanding and awareness that their protection and enhancement is relevant to people. Then society can take actions that shape sustainable solutions for society and the natural environment. We also need to understand what the most appropriate actions to take are, and how to align different societal pressures and choices to achieve the best solutions for the environment and for society (MacDonald *et al.*, 2007). This book has identified the many benefits healthy upland environments can provide, and how these benefits can be easily diminished. Choices about land use and management that focus consistently on resolving the existing pressures and stresses faced by upland ecosystems and communities will help them to adapt more readily and successfully to future pressures, especially those brought about by climate change. Many different sectors of society, such as agriculture, tourism and recreation, management for game, forestry, industry, transport and others, have an impact on the uplands either directly or indirectly through their decisions and actions. We argue here that by adopting a more holistic ecosystem approach to decision-making, whereby the consequences of actions on all aspects of the ecosystem are fully considered, we could help to avoid unintended negative environmental consequences and better secure the value of the uplands for both their tangible benefits to society and their intrinsic worth.

The state of the uplands and present challenges

Globally, uplands are often places of exceptional scenic beauty and harbour hotspots of biodiversity owing to high local variation in topography, climatic extremes or habitat heterogeneity (e.g. Kerr and Packer, 1997; Davies *et al.*, 2007), and are sometimes regarded as some of the last areas of 'wilderness'. This has long been recognised by national and international conservation designations. For example, within the UK, uplands in Wales and Scotland are renowned for their spectacular scenery, and in England over 50 per cent of nationally important wildlife sites lie within the 12 per cent of the country that is classed as upland. Furthermore, uplands hold a rich cultural heritage and are major contributors of biodiversity and vital ecosystem services for society. Ecosystem services are defined as the benefits society derives from the natural environment. The UN Millennium Ecosystem Assessment (MA, 2005) categorised ecosystem services in four broad groups: provisioning, regulating, cultural and supporting services (see Figure 1.1, introductory chapter, Bonn *et al.*, this volume). Functioning upland ecosystems provide ecosystem services and benefits to wider society well beyond their boundaries (Beniston, 2000), such as water provision, flood mitigation, climate regulation through carbon storage and sequestration in peat soils and upland woodlands, as well as opportunities for recreation and educational experiences.

Despite their remote nature, however, many upland areas in Europe and worldwide have been shaped by centuries of human activity, with land management leading to significant habitat changes over centuries (Bevan, this volume). Some of these changes have become valued components of the suite of 'semi-natural' upland habitats, such as the creation of alpine meadows with the lowering of the tree line (Beniston, 2000). Other changes induced by land management – and the social and economic conditions driving it – can threaten the continued provision of upland ecosystem services and biodiversity. Intensive land use, such as overgrazing and trampling by high numbers of livestock, inappropriate burning, drainage, deforestation and afforestation practices, have damaged upland habitats (Crowle and McCormack; Gardner *et al.*; Pearce-Higgins *et al.*, all this volume). In combination with additional pressures from atmospheric deposition and other diffuse pollution, wildfires and visitor pressures, these have led to upland ecosystem disservices to society, such as severe soil erosion and associated loss of carbon, reduction in water quality, decreased water-storage potential and increased flood risk, as well as to damage of distinctive upland wildlife communities (Allott; Caporn and Emmett; Holden; McMorrow *et al.*; Worrall and Evans; Yallop *et al.*, all this volume). Table 25.1 illustrates the range of ecosystem services provided by the uplands, and examples of the opportunities and risks to upland environments.

Future challenges for the upland environment

In the twenty-first century, given current trends, the resilience of many ecosystems is likely to be exceeded by an unprecedented combination of climate change and its knock-on effects, such as flooding, drought and wildfire, and global change drivers, such as land-use change, pollution, further fragmentation of natural ecosystems, and overexploitation of resources (Schröter *et al.*, 2005; IPCC, 2007). Global market forces, such as food prices or production incentives (e.g. for biofuel crops), exert a strong steer as indirect drivers on these threats (see Condliffe; Hubacek *et al.*, both this volume). A key challenge for society will be to understand how to work effectively

Table 25.1 Ecosystem services provided by the uplands.

Ecosystem services	UK upland examples	Opportunities and risks for upland environments
Provisioning services		
Food (livestock, crops)	Dramatic increases in sheep numbers from 1950–1990s (250–400% in Devon and Derbyshire) and a decrease since late 1990s (Condliffe, this volume). Cereal and other crop production is of little importance in UK uplands today.	Livestock farming (sheep and cattle) has shaped and maintained semi-natural open moorland habitats. However, overgrazing has been a major reason for upland habitat deterioration and is linked to flood risk increase (Crowle & McCormack; Holden, both this volume). Burning and drainage for livestock management have also caused habitat deterioration and soil carbon loss. Grazing pressure is driven by a mix of agricultural policy, market forces, livestock disease, social values and 'tradition' (Condliffe, this volume). Potential opportunities exist for niche markets from sale of traditional breeds, or new uses for wool, supported through agri-environment schemes that could allow more sustainable grazing levels to be maintained. Opportunities for 'wilding' may exist where withdrawal of formal agriculture is happening. With agricultural changes in the lowland and milder climates, crop production may become attractive in uplands with both positive (e.g. for farmland birds) and negative (e.g. for water quality) consequences depending on management.
Fibre (timber, wool)	Deforestation of UK upland started in prehistoric times. Some ancient woodlands remained, mainly for charcoal and tannin production. From 1920 onwards, woodland grant schemes encouraged afforestation, mainly with conifer plantations. Sheep provide wool.	In the past, inappropriate afforestation and associated drainage has led to habitat loss, landscape despoliation, soil compaction, and increased run off or peat decomposition. The Biodiversity Action Plan process has recently promoted the regeneration and expansion of native woodland in the uplands, supported by grant aid, for species such as black grouse, and more widely to increase habitat heterogeneity, and to improve flood amelioration and carbon sequestration. Trends for rising timber prices may make it more economically viable to restore peat bogs by removing conifers for sale, and to manage and create more native woodlands for sustainably managed timber.

Minerals	Building stone, aggregates and lime	Inappropriate mineral extraction can cause deterioration of landscape value and wildlife habitat, as well as increased traffic, noise and air pollution loads. However many extant permissions for quarrying remain, often providing a useful source of employment in upland areas, as well as stone for vernacular buildings that re-affirm local landscape character. Geological exposures as a result of quarrying can have scientific and educational value.
Energy provision	Due to their topography and climate the uplands have been harnessed as sources of hydro-electric power and wind energy. Peat cuttings can provide fuel (non-renewable energy source). Wood fuel can be derived from forests.	The uplands clearly have potential to provide renewable energy. They can thereby mitigate the impacts of climate change and help reach current UK national targets of 15% energy provision from renewable sources by 2015/16. Benefits have to be weighed up against trade-offs on other ecosystem services. For example wind farm construction and maintenance can result in biodiversity loss, peat loss and soil compaction, release of soil carbon and alteration of hydrological regime (through associated drainage), impact on scenic beauty and wilderness feeling, and wildlife disturbance. This is a particular issue on blanket bog habitats.
Fresh water provision	70% of UK drinking water flows from upland catchments. For example, the Peak District uplands provide 450M litres of water per day to surrounding conurbations.	Land management and water quantity and quality are closely linked. Often, improvements to water quality and storage potential (e.g. through blocking artificial land drains and reducing grazing and burning pressure on upland catchments) will have beneficial impacts on wildlife and landscape. Water provision may alter in reliability with climate change (longer dry spells, earlier snow melting, floods). This may lead to increased needs for water storage (reservoirs) or water abstraction.

Table 25.1 (cont'd)

Ecosystem services	UK upland examples	Opportunities and risks for upland environments
Regulating services		
Climate regulation: Carbon storage and sequestration	Uplands can serve an important function in global climate regulation. Peatlands are the single largest carbon reserve in the UK with 40–50% UK soil carbon stored in ca 8% of its land area. Upland peat bogs in England and Wales could absorb around 400,000 t carbon per year if in active condition (Worrall & Evans, this volume). Upland woodlands also contribute to carbon sequestration.	Degraded upland peatlands are at risk of turning from carbon sinks to carbon sources with resulting increasing fluvial and atmospheric carbon emissions of up to 381,000t carbon per year (Worrall & Evans, this volume). Around 55% of upland blanket bogs are estimated to be degraded due to intensive land use, industrial acidification, wildfires and are under further threat with climate change (Crowle & McCormack, this volume). Opportunities exist to undertake peatland restoration works and sensitive woodland planting schemes to improve carbon storage and sequestration potential. 'Carbon off-setting schemes' could be developed to fund these activities. Hotter drier summers and warmer wetter winters predicted for the coming decades may make peat restoration work more difficult (more wildfires, greater soil erosion) but these impacts may be offset by adapted land management practices.
Air quality regulation	Uplands contribute to air cooling. Uplands are main areas for atmospheric deposition of pollutants due to higher levels of precipitation and cloud deposition, thereby 'cleaning' the air (Caporn & Emmett, this volume).	Due to high levels of atmospheric deposition from industry and traffic emissions, many UK upland soils and headwaters exceed critical levels of acidification (Caporn & Emmett; Allott, this volume). This can impact on plant species composition and may in turn affect the provision of other ecosystem services, such as carbon sequestration from functioning peatlands and water quality.

Water quality regulation	Clean water is a valuable good to all consumers, but often taken for granted. Treatment costs can be substantial. The EU Water Framework Directive sets strict targets to reach good chemical and ecological status of all water bodies by 2015.	Efforts to improve water quality have addressed upland soil erosion, soil and water acidification, heavy metal leaching, contamination with pesticides and livestock bacteria from run-off, and reduced filtration capacity – associated with intensive land use and diffuse pollution by agriculture and industry. The aim is to reduce sediment loads and associated contaminants as well as water discolouration (from peat), that is affecting the supply of acceptable potable water and fisheries (Allott; Holden, both this volume). Environmentally sustainable land management across catchments is increasingly seen as a realistic alternative to end-of-pipe purification costs (e.g. the Loch Lomond Catchment management plan or the SCaMP programme in the South Pennines).
Flood risk prevention	Uplands will always be a source of water. Vegetation type and land management influence run-off patterns and thereby ameliorate or exacerbate effects of extreme weather events on downstream settlements (Holden, this volume).	Intensive land management leading to vegetation removal, soil compaction, desiccation and drainage of peat bogs can result in reduced infiltration and increased local water flows. Altered land management can reduce these effects and may also reduce the severity of downstream flooding, although more extreme weather events might not be buffered by such activity. More research is needed in this area (Holden, this volume).
Wildfire risk prevention	Wildfires are natural processes in many ecosystems. Healthy ecosystems with habitat mosaics and high water tables are less prone to exacerbated levels of wildfires.	Degraded and desiccated peatlands with low water tables and areas of dense biomass are at high risk of accidental wildfires. Fires severely damage carbon stocks, water quality and wildlife habitat. Fire fighting costs the UK economy more than a million pounds each year. With climate change, habitat vulnerability and visitor numbers are expected to increase, leading to increased wildfire risk (McMorrow et al., this volume). Restoration and sustainable land management, informed fire management and improved understanding of the risks by countryside users may ameliorate this.

Table 25.1 (cont'd)

Ecosystem services	UK upland examples	Opportunities and risks for upland environments
Cultural services		
Recreation, tourism, education	Uplands are among the most popular tourist destinations with 69.4M visitor days per year to the English upland national parks. Tourism is one of the main income streams to upland communities (see also Curry, this volume). In the Peak District National Park tourism accounts for 27% of employment. Uplands also provide a resource for outdoor education. Wildlife watching is a source of enjoyment for many people.	Climate change and socio-cultural changes will have implications for recreational use. Warmer, drier summers may increase the summer tourism season and vitally support local economies. Warmer winters may lead to a shift in activities, incl. motorised activities that may conflict with other visitor uses and wildlife. High visitor pressure can lead to disturbance of wildlife, local erosion risk and increased wildfire risk (McMorrow *et al.*, this volume). As most tourist activities are largely restricted to 'honey-pot' areas or popular routes, management can target these and many upland areas may remain unaffected. There is increasing interest in environmentally responsible low-impact tourism, seeking out a high quality environmental experience. Opportunities exist to improve understanding of the values and fragility of the uplands through visitor information and education programmes. Development of innovative economic tools can help to link the maintenance of upland landscapes by farmers/wardens/rangers with the tourism economy e.g. through 'tax' schemes or promotion of environmentally-friendly local products.
Field sport recreation/ game management	In England, 74% of upland Special Protection Areas (SPAs) are managed as grouse moors. Deer shooting and fisheries are also sources for recreation. As game in the UK is mainly managed for recreational field sports than for food supply, this is classed as cultural service.	Grouse moor management has, along with grazing, been responsible for shaping heather moorland habitats. Sensitive management grouse moors can form an important landscape management tool and provide local employment (Sotherton *et al.*, this volume). Drainage and inappropriate burning practices on grouse moors can lead to deterioration in habitat structure, species composition and water quality (Crowle and Cormack; Yallop *et al.*, both this volume), carbon stores can also be affected. Illegal control of birds of prey to maximise grouse populations is also of long-standing concern. Overgrazing by deer can deteriorate plant communities, in particular limiting tree regeneration.

Landscape aesthetics: tranquillity, scenic beauty, sense of wilderness	Uplands have concentrations of landscapes of national significance, e.g. 50% of the English uplands are designated as National Park. Scenic beauty, 'ruggedness' and tranquillity (CPRE, 2006) are the main reasons mentioned for visiting Peak District uplands (Davies, 2006).	Although most UK uplands are cultural landscapes shaped over centuries by people (Swanwick, this volume), they are often cherished for their 'wilderness' by visitors. The concept of wilderness is shaped by perception and can be experienced in remote Scottish highlands as well as in tranquil cultural landscapes in the Peak District. Risks to these wilderness qualities can arise e.g. from development, traffic, intensified and altered land use, or wind power generation. However, the high landscape value is one of the main reasons that people are willing to protect and maintain uplands as areas for 'escape' (e.g. through agri-environment schemes or National Park designations). With increasing urbanisation, maintaining wilderness areas may become more important to people and to local tourism economy. This may create opportunities for 're-wilding' in some uplands (Yalden, this volume).
Cultural heritage	Sites of archaeological and vernacular interest, spiritual places, traditions and customs in communities, e.g. well-dressing, as well as local dialects and languages.	The rich past and present cultural heritage of the uplands is highly regarded (Bevan, this volume), and receives public support through agri-environment schemes e.g. stonewall or barn restoration. It can be at risk from inappropriate land management damaging archaeological features or out-migration leading to loss of local customs. Maintenance of cultural features can in some cases conflict with nature conservation objectives. The Dartmoor Vision project is one example of addressing this issue through a spatial mapping and prioritisation approach.
Biodiversity	Biodiversity has intrinsic and bequest values for many people.	Biodiversity may not only support other ecosystem services, but similar to landscape aesthetics or cultural heritage, carries intrinsic values. Even if not experienced directly through wildlife watching, many people value biodiversity, as evidenced by e.g. membership in conservation organisations. Species distribution and survival may be supported or threatened by land management and climate change.

Table 25.1 (cont'd)

Ecosystem services	UK upland examples	Opportunities and risks for upland environments
Health benefits	Outdoor recreation and experience of nature provides measurable physical and mental health benefits (Pretty et al., 2007; SDC, 2008). Due to their steep slopes and weather conditions uplands also provide a significant degree of challenge, physically and mentally.	There are huge potential health benefits available in the uplands, but some significant challenges to realising these. The appetite for countryside recreation for many people is decreasing as over 40% of the adult population in England never visited the countryside during 2005 (Natural England, 2006) and recreation patterns change (Curry; Suckall et al., this volume). Access barriers can by physical (e.g. transport to remote areas) or psychological, such as insufficient knowledge, lack of experience and socio-cultural trends. Sports and health programmes are already harnessing the physical and inspirational qualities of upland recreation to address national goals of tackling obesity and (mild) depression.
Supporting Services		
Nutrient cycling, water cycling, soil formation	Support for all of the above services.	The recognition that protection of natural resources (soil/water/air) support all other benefits derived from uplands is becoming more 'mainstream'. The English agri-environment programme has included natural resource protection as an explicit objective since 2005. Legislation such as the over-grazing rules and the recently revised Heather and Grass burning regulations are also intended to address intensive and inappropriate land use and management that threatens the continued provision of these fundamental processes.
Habitat provision for wildlife	Uplands are the largest remaining tracts of un-fragmented semi-natural habitats of national and international importance in the UK. In England uplands cover 12% total land and contain 53% of the SSSI area (419,000 ha) (see Crowle and McCormack, this volume).	Most key ecosystem services for the wider society are under-pinned by ecosystem processes and habitat structure in the uplands. Degradation, conversion and fragmentation that threaten the provision of valuable wildlife habitat, also threaten the provision of associated ecosystem goods and services and consequently human health and well-being. More research is needed to fully understand the links between service provision and habitat quality, and the long-term sustainability of land management practices that impact upon them.

together to address these pressures. Below we focus on the challenges associated with climate change, as a major driver of change, on the uplands.

The fourth assessment report of the Intergovernmental Panel on Climate Change (IPCC, 2007) identifies the uplands as one of the habitats most sensitive to climate change owing to their vulnerability to warming (see also Caporn and Emmett, this volume). Rising temperatures, changes in rainfall regimes, and increases in extreme weather events will affect snow and glacier cover, water availability and erosion patterns. Changes to other aspects of climate such as wind speeds and cloud cover are more difficult to predict. All will affect biodiversity and alter the delivery of vital ecosystem services. Importantly, these impacts act in addition to the existing and historical pressures affecting upland environments.

Risks associated with various forms of extreme weather events, such as floods, storms, wildfire, landslides or avalanches, may increase in the future and have an impact on human lives and livelihoods, and lead to high damage cost for society (Beniston, 2007). Earlier snow-melts and decreased rainfall in summer may lead to water shortages with effects on drinking-water provision, agriculture (irrigation in southern latitudes) and wildfire (McMorrow *et al.*, this volume). Sediment loads derived from increased erosion processes will affect water quality and sedimentation rates in reservoirs and fish spawning beds (Holden; Worrall and Evans, both this volume). Deterioration of water quality and water provision will be felt by all consumers.

There is a growing body of observed changes in biodiversity and ecosystems with climate change (for reviews, see Parmesan and Yohe, 2003; Thomas *et al.*, 2004; Hopkins *et al.*, 2007; Mitchell *et al.*, 2007; Royal Society, 2007). Globally, the rate of species extinction may increase by up to 30 per cent with a 2°C rise in temperature. Changes in distribution and abundance of species are expected, with altitudinal and latitudinal movements upwards and northwards (Walmsley *et al.*, 2007). In the uplands, arctic alpine plants and birds such as ptarmigan *Lagopus mutus* will be at risk of (local) extinctions (Huntley *et al.*, 2007). New species will arrive from the lowlands and southern habitats (Walmsley *et al.*, 2007). Changes in species phenology, the seasonal timing of events, may lead to decoupling of important species interactions, such as predator–prey relationships, as predicted for golden plovers *Pluvialis apricaria* and their tipulid prey (Pearce-Higgins *et al.*, 2005). Changes in water availability may actually dictate growth patterns and survival rates to a greater extent than temperatures. This may have an impact on higher decomposition rates in peatlands or changed growth rates in forests – both important factors in climate regulation.

Upland crop productivity may alter as a result of climate change, and agriculture and forestry may become financially viable in higher altitudes again. Changes in economic pressures, global food markets, and technology may also result in altered agricultural patterns, such as shifts in type and intensity of crop and livestock production, afforestation or habitat restoration to improve water and carbon storage capacities. This may provide opportunities to integrate biodiversity and economic interests. While increases in vector-borne diseases (transmission usually via insects that depend on water and warm winters) are mainly a problem in the tropics and sub-tropics, upland farming in northern latitudes could be affected by an increase in blue tongue disease transmitted via midges or in tick-borne diseases.

The tourism industry in the uplands may experience costs and benefits with climate change. While winter ski tourism may decline owing to reduction in reliable snow coverage (66 per cent in the Alps, in the worst scenario; see Beniston, 2000), ski resorts at higher altitudes may experience increased demand with greater pressures on sensitive ecosystems. At lower altitudes recreation activities may shift away from skiing to other forms of recreation, such as mountain biking, and summer seasons may be extended. Health-related visits to the uplands may become more popular to escape hot city climates, too, and potential rises in aviation fuel prices may lead to higher visitor pressures in local uplands, potentially resulting in increased wildfire risks (McMorrow *et al.*, this volume). Changed visitor patterns will impose increased stress on ecosystems and biodiversity if not managed in sustainable ways.

Climate change may result in further societal pressures, such as human migration to cooler climates. This might result in increased movement to northern countries and into uplands, and possibly migration into higher altitudes. Urban populations might prefer cooler climates, and an increased pressure on local housing markets may affect local upland communities and social capital (see Burton *et al.*, this volume).

Opportunities: valuing ecosystem services

The ecosystem service concept can provide a useful tool to help understand and communicate the importance and relevance of ecosystems to people. Better understanding and transparency of the nature, extent and value of upland ecosystem service provision and the number of stakeholders affected can support informed decision-making by natural-resource managers, politicians and the public (see Box 25.1).

The benefits of maintaining healthy ecosystems can become more tangible to land managers, companies, politicians and society when portrayed in economic terms and through the number of beneficiaries. Cost–benefit analyses, including non-market values, can enhance the understanding of trade-offs between competing uses of ecosystems and management strategies (Naidoo and Ricketts, 2006). Investment in natural capital and conservation can then become attractive for corporate businesses and government (Balmford *et al.*, 2002). For example, the protection of some highly valued services, such as clean water, through conservation of ecosystems is increasingly viewed as an alternative to end-of-pipe solutions and expensive engineering projects. In the UK, up to 70 per cent of water is provided by upland catchments. Treatment costs for removing dissolved organic carbon derived from peat soil erosion or pesticides applied in farming practices are directly

Box 25.1. Benefits of greater understanding of the extent and value of ecosystem services

Making decisions based on a fuller appreciation of the value of ecosystem services (see also Daily, 1997; MA, 2005; Chan *et al.*, 2006; EFTEC, 2006; Rodriguez *et al.*, 2006; Defra, 2007a, b; Egoh *et al.*, 2007) can:

Enhance communication and participation

- communicate the relevance of nature conservation to land managers, industry, policy and the general public by illustrating the high dependency of society on its ecological base;
- convey the associated benefits and risks from good or poor land management to the continued provision of upland ecosystem services;
- identify and involve all stakeholders and beneficiaries affected;
- form partnerships to improve communication between all sectors.

Develop understanding and direction

- inform choice between competing land-use, e.g. estimate synergies and trade-offs among management strategies that maximise different environmental goods and services;
- advise land and water managers on the economic case for sustainable management of their resources;
- develop more focused research and monitoring to understand effects of land management on ecosystem service delivery;
- devise best practice of maintenance of ecosystem services, based on scientific evidence, local knowledge and adaptive management.

Inform costs of, and incentives for, land management

- inform and raise real costs of (un)sustainable activities by internalising costs and benefits;
- support development of economic market incentives for land managers and business such as payment for ecosystem services (e.g. through stewardship reward schemes through agri-environment schemes), certification of sustainable production, emission charges, offset policies and liability charges.

Inform policy

- inform evaluation of policy interventions by providing evidence of the full range of benefits and costs of policy impacts on upland environments and society;
- develop a policy development framework for planning for ecosystem services (especially regulating services);
- prioritise public funds and policies towards approaches that generate highest net benefits for society.

shared by consumers through water prices, and proactive upland catchment management could reduce these costs. Although there are limits to the valuation of ecosystem services, owing to their complexity and uncertainty, considering the 'cost of inaction' is becoming an increasingly important tool in environmental decision-making (Defra, 2007b; EEA, 2007).

Ecosystem service provision does not only affect upland communities, but also has significant impacts for the lowlands (Beniston, 2000). Issues of scale and interdependency become apparent when considering that upland ecosystems are globally the source for over 50 per cent of all rivers, and changes in hydrology in the uplands will have wide-ranging effects in spatially distant locations (Beniston, 2000; Orr *et al.*, 2008). Clearly, the majority of people benefiting from these goods and services do not live in the uplands and may rarely or never visit the uplands. Today, the majority of people live in urban settings – 50 per cent globally (UNFPA, 2007) and 73 per cent in the UK (2001 Census data, UK National Statistics). Only 1 per cent of England's population live in the uplands. Being so far removed from nature, the relevance and importance of biodiversity and ecosystems is difficult to realise for many people (Gutman, 2007), and a recent survey reported that 66 per cent of people give little or no thought to the loss of biodiversity in the UK (Defra, 2007d). Evaluating the provision of ecosystem services from the uplands may therefore raise their relevance to society and aid conservation and decision-making in upland management.

The ecosystem approach

The Convention on Biological Diversity (CBD, www.cbd.int) and the Millennium Ecosystem Assessment (MA, 2005) both identify the interdependency between biodiversity and human well-being through the perspective of ecosystem services. The CBD endorses the ecosystem approach with twelve principles (Box 25.2).

The ecosystem approach (see also Haynes-Young and Potschin, 2008) forms a strategy for the integrated management of land, water and living resources that promotes conservation and sustainable use in an equitable way. While, traditionally, short-term local benefits of provisional services have been favoured (e.g. timber extraction, livestock sales), the ecosystem approach will enable longer-term perspectives at greater scales such as water catchments, with regard to regulating (e.g. water purification), cultural (e.g. enjoyment) and supporting services (e.g. soil health), and within acceptable environmental limits. Its importance for the UK government is reflected in the new cross-government Public Service Agreement (PSA) target to 'secure a healthy natural environment for today and the future' by embedding an ecosystems approach in policy-making and delivery (Defra, 2007c).

A key challenge for upland conservation is therefore to understand how to align the enhancement of upland ecosystem services and the protection of uplands for biodiversity to optimise benefits to society. To implement

Box 25.2. The principles of the ecosystem approach.
Adopted by the Conference of the Parties to the Convention on Biological Diversity at Its Fifth Meeting, Nairobi, 15–26 May 2000. Decision V/6, Annex 1. CBD COP-5 Decision 6 UNEP/CBD/COP/5/23 (www.cbd.int/decisions/?lg=0&m=cop-05&d=06, see also Defra, 2007a, c)

1. The objectives of management of land, water and living resources are a matter of societal choice.
2. Management should be decentralised to the lowest appropriate level.
3. Ecosystem managers should consider the effects (actual or potential) of their activities on adjacent and other ecosystems.
4. Recognising potential gains from management; there is usually a need to understand and manage the ecosystem in an economic context. Any such ecosystem-management programme should:

   (a) reduce those market distortions that adversely affect biological diversity;
   (b) align incentives to promote biodiversity conservation and sustainable use;
   (c) internalise costs and benefits in the given ecosystem to the extent feasible.

5. Conservation of ecosystem structure and functioning, in order to maintain ecosystem services, should be a priority target of the Ecosystem Approach.
6. Ecosystems must be managed within the limits of their functioning.
7. The Ecosystem Approach should be undertaken at the appropriate spatial and temporal scales.
8. Recognising the varying temporal scales and lag-effects that characterise ecosystem processes, objectives for ecosystem management should be set for the long term.
9. Management must recognise that change is inevitable.
10. The Ecosystem Approach should seek the appropriate balance between, and integration of, conservation and use of biological diversity.
11. The Ecosystem Approach should consider all forms of relevant information, including scientific and indigenous and local knowledge, innovations and practices.
12. The Ecosystem Approach should involve all relevant sectors of society and scientific disciplines.

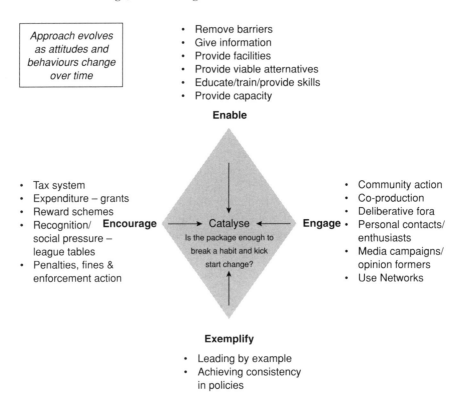

Approach evolves as attitudes and behaviours change over time	• Remove barriers • Give information • Provide facilities • Provide viable alternatives • Educate/train/provide skills • Provide capacity

Enable

• Tax system
• Expenditure – grants
• Reward schemes
• Recognition/ **Encourage** social pressure – league tables
• Penalties, fines & enforcement action

Catalyse
Is the package enough to break a habit and kick start change?

Engage

• Community action
• Co-production
• Deliberative fora
• Personal contacts/ enthusiasts
• Media campaigns/ opinion formers
• Use Networks

Exemplify

• Leading by example
• Achieving consistency in policies

Figure 25.1 Strategies to deliver visions (source: UK Sustainable Development Strategy, SDU 2005).

the ecosystem approach, informed decision-making is needed. The UK Sustainable Development Strategy (SDU, 2005) promotes a framework which can help society to make better long-term choices and act on them (Figure 25.1). We apply this approach to the uplands below.

Implementing the ecosystem approach

Engage: shared understanding and partnerships

Both the Convention on Biological Diversity and the Millennium Ecosystem Assessment agree on the importance of involving local communities and all relevant stakeholders to formulate visions and to translate the ecosystem approach into action in the uplands. Baseline information, a shared understanding of the issues affecting the uplands, the true value of a healthy upland environment, a willingness to engage and finding a common language is required in the development and delivery of visions.

Innovative partnerships between different interest groups – government agencies, NGOs, community-level organisations, and industries, as well as individual stakeholders outside organisations – can form effective ways forward to manage change and identify, promote and deliver visions across administrative and organisational boundaries. Successful partnerships can achieve change by mobilising substantial resources to fund joint capital investment to implement improvement projects. These can include large-scale land-management projects, new buildings, education programmes, or communication and networking opportunities. Partnerships are often a prerequisite for major grants or other funding applications.

Collaboration through joint projects, workshops and networks can overcome traditional sectoral thinking and create new opportunities to find innovative solutions to managing change. Collective resources are best-maximised in acknowledging respective strengths, sharing expertise and knowledge, and building up evidence together. Koontz and Bodine (2008) identify cultural and socio-political factors as the greatest barriers to ecosystem management, not necessarily scientific knowledge. A willingness to share decisions is needed, to allow change and to innovate as well as to be prepared to 'think outside the box' in bigger pictures. Inclusive and open partnerships can help to channel energies, deflect antagonisms and enhance synergies between stakeholders to form collective visions forward. In the long term, partnerships can also arrive at institutional change by relationship-building, advocacy and capacity-building through development of best practice to change attitudes and policies.

Enable: information, skills and capacity-building

In the upland conservation context, ensuring that people have information about the existing condition of the environment and the successfulness of conservation measures (e.g. designated sites or agri-environment programmes) has been important in targeting and promoting future action. Living with environmental change and promoting effective conservation will require an articulate vision for landscape conservation and quantifiable objectives that offer unambiguous signposts for measuring progress (Lindenmayer *et al.*, 2008). Equipping people with the right information, skills and facilities will inspire and enable them to take action. This includes inspiring young people through innovative media campaigns and outdoor activities, to enable a culture of valuing ecosystem services and sustainable management into the future.

The CBD explicitly requires regular reporting of outputs to provide a strategic assessment of progress made, as well as identifying challenges and obstacles (Mace and Baillie, 2007). Biodiversity Action Plans (BAPs) form an important vehicle to create biological inventories for selected species and habitats (e.g. upland heathland or blanket bog), to assess the conservation status of species, to create measurable targets for conservation and restoration, and to set up budgets, timelines and institutional partnerships for implementing the BAP. In the UK, the development of the Common Standard Monitoring by the Joint Nature Conservancy Council (JNCC) and the country agencies has highlighted the poor condition of many upland habitats (Crowle and McCormack, this volume). Based on this information, the recent UK government PSA target to achieve favourable condition of Sites of Special Scientific Interest (SSSIs) in England by 2010 has been a strong driver in promoting action through Natural England to restore designated sites to or towards favourable condition (Anderson *et al.*, this volume). Public expenditure on improving the condition of designated sites is constantly under review, e.g. by the National Audit Office. Better information about the ecosystem services provided by improvements to these areas would provide further justification of the value of this resource and its management.

Advice and advocacy are needed to aid further practical action on the ground. For example, to meet Water Framework Directive requirements, the Department for Environment, Food and Rural Affairs (Defra) is developing measures to tackle diffuse water pollution from agriculture within the Catchment Sensitive Farming programme (http://www.defra.gov.uk/farm/environment/water/csf/delivery-initiative.htm). To enable a strategic, proactive and risk-based approach to flood risk management, the Environment Agency works through Catchment Flood Management Plans (CFMPs, http://www.environment-agency.gov.uk/subjects/flood/1217883/1217968/907676) with key decision-makers across England and Wales.

Conservation action needs to be based on the best available scientific evidence. To understand the importance of upland ecosystem services more widely, how to improve their provision and how to facilitate societal choice, we need a transdisciplinary approach to research. This involves joint working between natural and social scientists, practitioners and policy-makers to

- understand where and how they are supplied (Balvanera *et al.*, 2001);
- identify best management regimes to support the delivery of ecosystem services (e.g. which land management practices can best deliver water quality in which habitats?);
- understand synergies and trade-offs between management for different services and biodiversity;
- assess the range and size of stakeholders affected and the extent to which they are affected;
- define acceptable environmental, social and economic limits;
- develop methods for and apply mapping of ecosystem services and benefit flows to improve the targeting of actions (see Chan *et al.*, 2006).

Scientific evidence of the links between biodiversity and ecosystem services is not always clear (Kremen, 2005) and is still being developed. But research suggests that more diverse ecosystems are also more effective in delivering ecosystem services (Balvanera *et al.*, 2006). While many upland habitats, such as blanket bogs, are naturally species-poor, spatial heterogeneity and structural diversity with different age stands of vegetation, water pools and *Sphagnum* moss carpets can provide both habitat for wildlife (see Pearce-Higgins *et al.*, this volume) and a range of services, such as carbon sequestration or water retention. At the regional scale, a representation of a range of habitats (see Table 8.1, Crowle and McCormack, this volume), especially on the moorland fringes, such as a mix of blanket bog, dwarf shrub, aquatic communities and clough woodland habitats, instead of large-scale monoculture habitats, can contribute to similar goals. An understanding of how to conserve biodiversity and provide services that are environmentally sustainable is vital for future generations.

Encourage: policy drivers, protected areas and incentives

While the ecosystem approach needs to be led by societal choice, a sustainable policy, legal and financial framework will be required to support the achievement of goals. Conservation of resilient upland ecosystems and their services is already at the heart of national and international agreements for protecting soil carbon (Kyoto Protocol, proposed EU Soil Framework Directive), water bodies (EU Water Framework Directive, WFD) and biodiversity (CBD) that promote sustainable development and integrated catchment management, and manifested in the recent UK cross-government PSA target. In many cases, funding of current conservation projects has been enabled by finding solutions to challenges created by new policies or legislation, government PSA targets (Walker *et al.*, 2008), and business interests. This is encouraging, especially as policy, and particularly agricultural policy (Condliffe, this volume), has been a driver for over-exploitation and deterioration of upland environments in the past.

Ecosystem management is often hindered by legal barriers owing to complicated ownerships or law suits (Walker *et al.*, 2008; Koontz and Bodine, 2008). This may impede management at appropriate scales, e.g. across whole water catchments, or restrict actions owing to legal objections to unwelcome associated effects on neighbouring landholding conditions. Partnership working and sharing information may contribute to overcoming these difficulties.

Protected areas

Protected areas constitute a legally defined backbone to biodiversity and landscape conservation in all its manifestations from genes to species, habitats and ecosystems as required by the UN Convention on Biological Diversity. In the EU, the Natura 2000 network with Special Areas of Conservation (SAC, Habitats Directive 92/43/EEC) and Special Protected Areas (SPA, Birds Directive 79/409/EEC) forms a centrepiece of biodiversity policy to meet the European Council's goal of halting biodiversity decline within the EU by

2010. These are complemented by national designations, and today Natura 2000 sites cover about 20 per cent of EU territory, and in the UK 50 per cent of the uplands are subject to conservation designations. However, a static representation of contemporary patterns of biodiversity cannot be a sustainable aim. Biodiversity is dynamic in time and space as a result of both natural processes and anthropogenic activity (Pressey *et al.*, 2007). Ecological and evolutionary processes should be an integral part of protected area conservation (Balmford *et al.*, 1998; Cowling *et al.*, 1999). The goal is to develop ecologically resilient and flexible networks of protected areas or landscapes (see also Opdam and Wascher, 2004; Hopkins *et al.*, 2007) that can maintain their functions and characteristics after being disturbed or damaged and can adapt to future changes. This can be achieved by reducing existing sources of harm to ecosystem functioning and by promoting improved species dispersal within and between upland sites, to allow altitudinal or latitudinal migration with climate change. High habitat heterogeneity with different microclimates on south- and north-facing slopes, short and tall vegetation swards, will facilitate local adaptation for species to find suitable climatic envelopes within existing sites. Locally, this may mean that some protected areas may need to accept loss of some species, and may need to consider welcoming and protecting newcomers. Flexibility in approach may include incorporating (natural levels of) biophysical processes into spatial planning such as erosion, succession or flooding, and species processes, such as predation by birds of prey or large mammals, succession, migration and dispersal, (local) extinction and speciation. Protected areas may contribute core areas for both biodiversity and ecosystem service provision. However, conservation targets centred solely on biodiversity may be challenged by the ecosystem approach to meet multiple benefits across landscapes and not only within designated sites.

Incentives: payment for ecosystem services and biodiversity conservation

Currently the major source of public funding for positive environmental management of the countryside is through the EU Rural Development Programme, part of the Common Agriculture Policy (CAP), in particular agri-environment schemes. To ensure that agri-environment payments provide 'value for money', their effectiveness at delivering their objectives must be carefully monitored. Ecosystem services have, to date, not been an explicit element of many agri-environment programmes; however, investigations are currently underway to examine how provision of environmental services could be better-rewarded (Land Use Policy Group, personal communication, http://www.lupg.org.uk).

New avenues for funding upland conservation may arise if beneficiaries of upland ecosystem services are willing to pay for land management that benefits them. For example:

- water companies may fund integrated upstream land management to reduce 'end of pipe' water treatment costs;
- upland restoration may benefit from carbon off-setting schemes, when a suitable verification process has been achieved;
- tourists may be willing to pay for the maintenance of the countryside they enjoy, for example through a tax on tourist accommodation, which feeds back into support for sustainable land management (note: agri-environment schemes are already supported by public tax);
- renewable energy schemes are likely to generate income opportunities in uplands;
- consumers may choose to buy sustainably produced upland products promoted through local environmental marketing initiatives;
- public health initiatives may promote the provision of recreation opportunities in inspirational landscapes to improve physical and mental health (Pretty, 2007; SDC, 2008).

While beneficiaries often display a theoretical willingness to pay (Bramwell and Fearn, 1996; Pearce, 2007; Hanley and Colombo, this volume), these schemes need to be accompanied by innovative awareness-raising programmes, in order to be accepted.

Exemplify

Successful conservation partnerships in the UK uplands include for example the Moors for the Future Partnership (see Box 25.3), the Sustainable Catchment Management Programme (SCaMP) and the Peatscapes project among others. It is likely that in future the ecosystem services approach will allow more people and organisations to see the relevance of conservation to their individual agendas, and thus further partnerships will emerge.

Policy needs to lead by example and promote best practice in all the above areas, including cross-discipline and interagency collaboration, willingness to innovation and change, and providing adequate policy and finance frameworks. The new UK government PSA target to endorse the ecosystem approach will hopefully enable holistic and innovative avenues to safeguard upland environments and their benefits to society and wildlife as well as to integrate societal choice into conservation.

Benefits of taking an ecosystem services approach for conservation

The ecosystem services concept is clearly centred on society, and concerns have been raised that this could disregard intrinsic values of biodiversity and 'sell out nature' (McCauley, 2006). However, the following examples illustrate that an ecosystem service framework can reinforce biodiversity concerns and form powerful avenues to safeguard ecosystems (Daily, 1997).

Box 25.3. The Moors for the Future Partnership

The Moors for the Future Partnership in the English Peak District (www.moorsforthefuture.org.uk) is a public–private upland partnership between local government (Peak District National Park Authority, Sheffield City Council, Derbyshire County Council), government agencies (Natural England, Environment Agency), non-government organisations (National Trust, Moorland Association), water industries (United Utilities, Yorkshire Water, Severn Trent Water) and private landowners, supported by the Heritage Lottery Fund in the first phase of the £4.7 million project.

The partnership aims to reverse the degradation of moorland landscape, to improve access for visitors whilst conserving sensitive areas, and to establish a learning centre to widen people's understanding of how to protect moorlands. Strong policy drivers (e.g. PSA targets, CBD, WFD) and business interests have enabled funding commitments. Building on the original targets of conservation and recreation, adaptive management and learning have enabled a widening of the agenda. Ecosystem service arguments are now central in promoting the project with partners, landowners and the general public. For example, the restoration of over 6 km^2 of bare peat to vegetated moorland and 22 km^2 of footpaths since 2003 has reduced soil erosion and improved habitat provision for wildlife (soil and habitat as supporting service), enhanced soil carbon storage and sequestration potential, thus aiding climate change mitigation efforts and improved downstream water quality (regulating services). Restoration might also aid flood mitigation capacity (regulating service), although evidence is yet to be established (see Holden, this volume). Footpath restoration and enhanced interpretation can enhance visitor experience (cultural service). It is because of the wide relevance of the aims of this partnership for different sectors of society that support for it has been widely forthcoming.

The varied partnership network has been involved in joint meetings, site visits and specific projects. This has enabled the development of a widely supported land management strategy with common goals, helped secure funding for the project, enabled collaboration to undertake practical land-restoration tasks and to develop new technologies for achieving this, and engaged in innovative strategies to deal with conflict situations (e.g. dogs and wildlife) and environmental risk (e.g. wildfire watch). Wider awareness-raising and engagement beyond the core partners has been developed to engender a sense of social ownership and responsibility for the moorland landscape. This has been delivered through 'lifelong learning' programmes including art projects, development of interpretation tools, self-guided audio trails, curriculum-based school programmes, website resources, as well as two new buildings – a visitor centre and a learning base centre.

A strong multi-disciplinary research component within the partnership provides a scientific evidence base for informed planning and management. Embedded in collaborations with surrounding research institutes, the partnership has been fortunate in providing a networking platform for knowledge exchange between the science and user community with annual conferences, specialist workshops, field trips as well as individual meetings. Thereby it helps to scope research needs of practitioners and policy-makers, such as understanding of changes to carbon budgets, hydrology, wildfire risk and biodiversity through upland restoration and management, and facilitates new research to develop understanding of social and environmental adaptation to change in uplands. This book has been motivated by this upland research forum.

To address climate change

As discussed above, climate change is one of the biggest challenges facing society and the upland environment. However, there is still time to avoid the worst impacts of climate change, if we take strong action now (Stern, 2006; IPCC, 2007). This will require significant investment, but costs of inaction will be far greater (Stern, 2006; EEA, 2007). Taking an approach that values ecosystem services provided by the uplands, and shows how these might be affected by climate change or indeed mitigate climate change, can provide powerful and persuasive arguments to fund and implement appropriate mitigation and adaptation activities and provide opportunities for biodiversity conservation, too.

The UK Government Stern Review (Stern, 2006) recommends that land managers can play a vital role in mitigating climate change by improving the ecosystem service of carbon cycling. At a global level, land management could contribute to around 10 per cent of the annual greenhouse gas emissions reductions required to keep global temperature rise at a relatively safe level. Uplands offer significant carbon storage and capture potential (see also Worrall and Evans, this volume), and land managers can enhance this by:

- conservation of existing carbon pools in peat soils (restoration to reduce soil erosion and drainage, land management following codes of best practice);
- improving carbon sequestration from the atmosphere (peatland protection and restoration, afforestation of lower slopes with native tree species, wetland creation);

- uptake of renewable energy schemes in appropriate locations (wind, hydro, wood fuel and biogas generation with careful evaluation of environmental, economic and social costs and benefits).

Taking an ecosystem approach, these actions are aimed at multiple benefits for a range of ecosystem services and biodiversity, with climate change mitigation as the primary focus. They could for example lead to improved drinking-water quality through reduced soil erosion and grazing pressure, potentially increased water storage and thus flood mitigation potential, enhanced inspirational qualities of upland landscapes, and improved provision of habitat for wildlife.

To address conservation designations

Clearly making the links between the beneficiaries of upland ecosystem services and upland management will be vital for maintaining healthy upland environments and its wildlife. Applying an ecosystem approach to protected area management may challenge the rationale for conservation designations. A greater emphasis on upland ecosystem services, such as protecting and enhancing carbon stores, provision of clean drinking water and flood mitigation, or enhancement of inspirational qualities for enjoyment such as sense of wilderness, may become of greater interest to society alongside current biodiversity and landscape designations. However, this might also be embraced as an opportunity for the development of 'wild' places, where natural succession can take place, providing habitat for wildlife, including larger predators (Yalden, this volume). These 'wilded' landscapes, although not possible everywhere, may be attractive for people to visit and experience, while providing a range of other ecosystem services.

Conclusions

Conservation of upland biodiversity and ecosystems needs to embrace the ecosystem services framework, to improve its relevance to society and provide a strong rationale for continued conservation action. The Millennium Ecosystem Assessment, the IPCC report and the Stern Review provide clear guidance to take action now, as society cannot afford to wait. Awareness-raising of the importance of uplands beyond their boundaries to all society is needed to build public support and find expenditures to achieve sustainable solutions. Development of shared visions and actions through innovative partnerships can promote progress. Essentially, conservation needs to find ways to clarify, promote and support the role of land managers who deliver environmentally sustainable upland management. In addition, innovative economic tools are required to promote the role of a high-quality environment that provides ecosystem services, for sustaining viable rural businesses.

Only through integrated approaches can we hope to secure the long-term well-being of upland environments and the people that benefit from it.

Acknowledgements

We are grateful to Robert Bradburne, Matt Buckler, Alison Holt, Dave Raffaelli, Steve Redpath, David Thompson and Des Thompson for constructive comments that helped to improve the chapter.

References

Balmford, A., Bruner, A., Cooper, P., Costanza, R., Farber, S., Green, R. E., Jenkins, M., Jefferiss, P., Jessamy, V., Madden, J., Munro, K., Myers, N., Naeem, S., Paavola, J., Rayment, M., Rosendo, S., Roughgarden, J., Trumper, K. and Turner, R. K. (2002) Economic reasons for conserving wild nature. *Science*, **297**, 950–3.

Balmford, A., Mace, G. M. and Ginsberg, J. R. (1998) The challenges to conservation in a changing world: putting processes on the map. *Conservation in a Changing World* (ed. G. M. Mace, A. Balmford and J. R. Ginsberg), pp. 1–28. Cambridge: Cambridge University Press.

Balvanera, P., Daily, G. C., Ehrlich, P. R., Ricketts, T. H., Bailey, S. A., Kark, S., Kremen, C. and Pereira, H. (2001) Conserving biodiversity and ecosystem services. *Science*, **291**, 2047.

Balvanera, P., Pfisterer, A. B., Buchmann, N., He, J. S., Nakashizuka, T., Raffaelli, D. and Schmid, B. (2006) Quantifying the evidence for biodiversity effects on ecosystem functioning and services. *Ecology Letters*, **9**, 1146–56.

Beniston, M. (2000) *Environmental Change in Mountains and Uplands.* London: Arnold.

Beniston, M. (2007) Linking extreme climate events and economic impacts: examples from the Swiss Alps. *Energy Policy*, **35**, 5384–92.

Bramwell, B. and Fearn, A. (1996) Visitor attitudes to a policy instrument for visitor funding of conservation in a tourist area. *Journal of Travel Research*, **35**, 29–33.

Chan, K. M. A., Shaw, M. R., Cameron, D. R., Underwood, E. C. and Daily, G. C. (2006) Conservation planning for ecosystem services. *Plos Biology*, **4**, 2138–52.

Cowling, R. M., Pressey, R. L., Lombard, A. T., Desmet, P. G. and Ellis, A. G. (1999) From representation to persistence: requirements for a sustainable system of conservation areas in the species-rich Mediterranean-climate desert of southern Africa. *Diversity and Distributions*, **5**, 51–71.

CPRE (2006) *Campaign to Protect Rural England: Saving Tranquil Places.* http://www.cpre.org.uk/library

Daily, G. C. (1997) *Nature's Services: Societal Dependence on Natural Ecosystems.* Washington, DC: Island Press.

Davies, R. G., Orme, C. D. L., Storch, D., Olson, V. A., Thomas, G. H., Ross, S. G., Ding, T. S., Rasmussen, P. C., Bennett, P. M., Owens, I. P. F., Blackburn, T. M. and Gaston, K. J. (2007) Topography, energy and the global distribution of bird species richness. *Proceedings of the Royal Society, B, Biological Sciences*, **274**, 1189–97.

Defra (2007a) *Conserving Biodiversity – the UK Approach.* http://www.defra.gov.uk/wildlife-countryside/pdfs/biodiversity/ConBioUK-Oct2007.pdf

Defra (2007b) *An Introductory Guide to Valuing Ecosystem Services.* http://www.defra.gov.uk/wildlife-countryside/natres/pdf/eco_valuing.pdf

Defra (2007c) *Securing a Healthy Natural Environment: An Action Plan for Embedding an Ecosystems Approach.* http://www.defra.gov.uk/wildlife-countryside/natres/pdf/eco_actionplan.pdf

Defra (2007d) *Survey of Public Attitudes and Behaviours toward the Environment.* http://www.defra.gov.uk/environment/statistics/pubatt/index.htm

EEA (2007) *Climate Change: The Cost of Inaction and the Cost of Adaptation.* European Environment Agency, Rep. No. 13/2007, Copenhagen. http://reports.eea.europa.eu/technical_report_2007_13/en

Eftec (2006) *Valuing Our Natural Environment.* Defra, London. http://www.defra.gov.uk/wildlife-countryside/natres/pdf/nr0103-full.pdf

Egoh, B., Rouget, M., Reyers, B., Knight, A. T., Cowling, R. M., van Jaarsveld, A. S. and Welz, A. (2007) Integrating ecosystem services into conservation assessments: a review. *Ecological Economics,* **63**, 714–21.

Gutman, P. (2007) Ecosystem services: foundations for a new rural–urban compact. *Ecological Economics,* **62**, 383–7.

Haynes-Young, R. and Potschin, M. (2008) England's terrestrial ecosystem services and the rationale for an ecosystem-based approach. Full technical report to Defra, project code NR0107. http://www.ecosystemservices.org.uk/reports.htm

Hopkins, J. J., Allison, H. M., Walmsley, C. A., Gaywood, M. and Thurgate, G. (2007) *Conserving Biodiversity in a Changing Climate: Guidance on Building Capacity to Adapt.* Published by Defra on behalf of the UK Biodiversity Partnership. http://www.ukbap.org.uk/Library/BRIG/CBCCGuidance.pdf

Huntley, B., Green, R. E., Collingham, Y. C. and Willis, S. G. (2007) *A Climatic Atlas of European Breeding Birds.* Barcelona: Lynx Edicions.

IPCC (2007) *Intergovernmental Panel on Climate Change: Fourth Assessment Report.* http://www.ipcc.ch

Kerr, J. T. and Packer, L. (1997) Habitat heterogeneity as a determinant of mammal species richness in high-energy regions. *Nature,* **385**, 252–4.

Koontz, T. M. and Bodine, J. (2008) Implementing ecosystem management in public agencies: lessons from the US Bureau of Land Management and the Forest Service. *Conservation Biology,* **22**, 60–9.

Kremen, C. (2005) Managing ecosystem services: what do we need to know about their ecology? *Ecology Letters,* **8**, 468–79.

Lindenmayer, D., Hobbs, R. J., Montague-Drake, R., Alexandra, J., Bennett, A., Burgman, M., Cale, P., Calhoun, A., Cramer, V., Cullen, P., Driscoll, D., Fahrig, L., Fischer, J., Franklin, J., Haila, Y., Hunter, M., Gibbons, P., Lake, S., Luck, G., MacGregor, C., McIntyre, S., Nally, R. M., Manning, A., Miller, J., Mooney, H., Noss, R., Possingham, H., Saunders, D., Schmiegelow, F., Scott, M., Simberloff, D., Sisk, T., Tabor, G., Walker, B., Wiens, J., Woinarski, J. and Zavaleta, E. (2008) A checklist for ecological management of landscapes for conservation. *Ecology Letters,* **11**, 78–91.

MA (2005) *Millennium Ecosystem Assessment. Ecosystems and Human Well Being; Synthesis.* Washington, DC: Island Press. http://www.millenniumassessment.org

McCauley, D. J. (2006) Selling out on nature. *Nature,* **443**, 27–8.

MacDonald, D. W., Collins, N. M. and Wrangham, R. (2007) Principles, practice and priorities: the quest for 'alignment'. *Key Topics in Conservation Biology* (eds D. W. MacDonald and K. Service), pp. 271–90. Oxford: Blackwell.

Mace, G. M. and Baillie, E. M. (2007) The 2010 biodiversity indicators: challenges for science and policy. *Conservation Biology*, **21**, 1406–13.

Mitchell, R. J., Morecroft, M. D., Acreman, M., Crick, H. Q. P., Frost, M., Harley, M., Maclean, I. M. D., Mountford, O., Piper, J., Pontier, H., Rehfisch, M. M., Ross, L. C., Smithers, R. J., Stott, A., Walmsley, C., Watts, O. and Wilson, E. (2007) *England Biodiversity Strategy – towards Adaptation to Climate Change*. London, Defra. http://www.defra.gov.uk/wildlife-countryside/resprog/findings/ebs-climate-change.pdf

Naidoo, R. and Ricketts, T. H. (2006) Mapping the economic costs and benefits of conservation. *PLOS Biology*, **4**, 2153–64.

Opdam, P. and Wascher, D. (2004) Climate change meets habitat fragmentation: linking landscape and biogeographical scale level in research and conservation. *Biological Conservation*, **117**, 303–9.

Orr, H. G., Wilby, R. L., McKenzie-Hedger, M. and Brown, I. (2008) Climate change in the uplands: a UK perspective on safeguarding regulatory ecosystem services, *Climate Research*, **37**, 77–98.

Parmesan, C. and Yohe, G. (2003) A globally coherent fingerprint of climate change impacts across natural systems. *Nature*, **421**, 37–42.

Pearce, D. (2007) Do we really care about biodiversity? *Environmental and Resource Economics*, **37**, 313–33.

Pearce-Higgins, J. W., Yalden, D. W. and Whittingham, M. J. (2005) Warmer springs advance the breeding phenology of golden plovers *Pluvialis apricaria* and their prey (*Tipulidae*). *Oecologia*, **143**, 470–6.

Pressey, R. L., Cabeza, M., Watts, M. E., Cowling, R. M. and Wilson, K. A. (2007) Conservation planning in a changing world. *Trends in Ecology and Evolution*, **22**, 583–92.

Rodriguez, J. P., Beard, T. D., Bennett, E. M., Cumming, G. S., Cork, S. J., Agard, J., Dobson, A. P. and Peterson, G. D. (2006) Trade-offs across space, time, and ecosystem services. *Ecology and Society*, **11**, 28.

Royal Society (2007) *Biodiversity – Climate Interactions: Adaptation, Mitigation and Human Livelihoods. Report of an International Meeting Held at the Royal Society 12–13 June 2007*. http://www.royalsociety.org/document.asp?tip=0andid=6830

Schröter, D., Cramer, W., Leemans, R., Prentice, I. C., Araujo, M. B., Arnell, N. W., Bondeau, A., Bugmann, H., Carter, T. R., Gracia, C. A., de la Vega-Leinert, A. C., Erhard, M., Ewert, F., Glendining, M., House, J. I., Kankaanpaa, S., Klein, R. J. T., Lavorel, S., Lindner, M., Metzger, M., Meyer, J., Mitchell, T. D., Reginster, I., Rounsevell, M., Sabate, S., Sitch, S., Smith, B., Smith, J., Smith, P., Sykes, M. T., Thonicke, K., Thuiller, W., Tuck, G., Zaehle, S. and Zierl, B. (2005) Ecosystem service supply and vulnerability to global change in Europe. *Science*, **310**, 1333–7.

SDC (2008) *Health, Place and Nature. How Outdoor Environments Influence Health and Well-being: A Knowledge Base*. Sustainable Development Commission report. http://www.sd-commission.org.uk/publications/downloads/Outdoor_environments_ and_health.pdf

SDU (2005) *Securing the Future – UK Government Sustainable Development Strategy*. Norwich: The Stationery Office. http://www.sustainable-development.gov.uk/ publications/uk-strategy/index.htm

Stern, N. (2006) *The Economics of Climate Change: The Stern Review*. Cabinet Office–HM Treasury. http://www.sternreview.org.uk

Thomas, C. D., Cameron, A., Green, R. E., Bakkenes, M., Beaumont, L. J., Collingham, Y. C., Erasmus, B. F. N., de Siqueira, M. F., Grainger, A., Hannah,

L., Hughes, L., Huntley, B., van Jaarsveld, A. S., Midgley, G. F., Miles, L., Ortega-Huerta, M. A., Townsend Peterson, A., Phillips, O. L. and Williams, S. E. (2004) Extinction risk from climate change. *Nature*, **427**, 145–8.

UNFPA (2007) *State of World Population 2007: Unleashing the Potential of Urban Growth*. United Nations Population Fund, New York. http://www.unfpa.org/upload/lib_pub_file/695_filename_sowp2007_eng.pdf

Walker, J., Holden, J., Evans, M. G., Worral, F., Davison, S. and Bonn, A. (2008) A compendium of UK peat restoration and management projects. Final Report to Defra, project code SP0556.

Walmsley, C. A., Smithers, R. J., Berry, P. M., Harley, M., Stevenson, M. J. and Catchpole, R. (eds) (2007) *MONARCH: Modelling Natural Resource Responses to Climate Change – a Synthesis for Biodiversity Conservation*. UKCIP, Oxford. http://www.eci.ox.ac.uk/research/biodiversity/monarch.php

26 Conclusions

Managing change in the uplands – challenges in shaping the future

Aletta Bonn, Tim Allott, Klaus Hubacek and Jon Stewart

Introduction

Change in the uplands is occurring at an accelerating pace. Over the coming decades, contemporary drivers of widespread change such as land use, diffuse pollution and demographic challenges are likely to be exacerbated by climate change and associated socio-economic pressures. The underlying health of upland ecosystems and their component habitats and biodiversity, and their ability to supply vital ecosystem services such as food, water, climate regulation, opportunities for recreation and businesses for thriving communities, will therefore be subject to increasing pressures and choices. The value of some of these services, e.g. carbon storage or flood control, may become more important to society and political agendas. The chapters of this book draw out and discuss a wide range of environmental, social, economic and political drivers of change in upland environments and demonstrate their inter-relatedness. Both natural and anthropogenic drivers act over a range of spatial and temporal scales, and owing to the complex inter-relationships there are no easy solutions for managing change. We can, however, draw some overarching conclusions from the contributions to this volume that could help us develop more effective approaches to making decisions for maintaining both healthy upland environments and communities that can continue to benefit from their services.

We have sought to set these out in the hope of stimulating thought and debate but ultimately informed action. Does the ecosystem services concept work for the uplands? Can it help our understanding and inform sustainable management? How can science help us move forward? How do we advance with only partial understanding of complex systems, and with numerous and varied interested parties – many with important stakes in the uplands that sometimes conflict? What are the big issues and questions we still need to answer, and can they help us manage land-use conflicts and develop a shared vision?

A sustainable future for the uplands relies on creating support for shared visions, adoption of a holistic approach, tackling both ecological and social issues at appropriate scales, building on cross-disciplinary understanding, and creating effective partnerships between science, policy and management.

Drivers of change and their effects on upland ecosystem services

This volume has used the ecosystem service concept (MA, 2005) as a framework for exploring a wide range of environmental, economic and social issues in upland environments. This approach offers new angles for linking cross-cutting drivers and widening the boundaries of interdisciplinary research. Fundamentally, the distribution and the quality of all upland ecosystems services are initially determined and constrained by natural drivers, such as climate and geophysical processes, together with the underlying supporting services of upland habitats, biodiversity, soil formation and nutrient cycling (see Evans, this volume). Climatic events, especially severe weather events such as heavy rainfalls or droughts, continue to be natural drivers of change, and resulting floods or fires are often vital components and determinants of ecosystems. However, anthropogenic drivers now exert a more dominant control on upland environmental change, with associated impacts on ecosystem services. Anthropogenic processes also modify natural drivers, for example by increasing the wildfire vulnerability of damaged upland habitats (see McMorrow *et al.*, this volume).

When considering the impacts of drivers on ecosystem services, the three types of service – provisioning, regulating and cultural (see Figure 1.1, Table 25.1, this volume) – act at different scales. Our understanding and capacity to actively manage their provision is not uniform across services. Provisioning services, such as food or timber production, are frequently directly driven through intentional management that seeks to optimise their value (Zhang *et al.*, 2007a). Owing to their local distribution and associated market value, people can actively alter the production processes across space and time. For example, whilst the provision of crops, but also water and energy, is governed primarily by natural climatic drivers, their delivery for human benefits is often facilitated by technology and engineering such as agricultural practices, water abstraction, dams or, recently, renewable energy schemes. Provisioning services are strongly demand-led by external markets and policies, in particular food security. Striking examples are the fluctuation of UK upland livestock numbers in response to national and EU agricultural policy over the past fifty years (see Condliffe, this volume) or in response to global food markets following the crash in New Zealand sheep flocks recently. Another socio-economic driver, demographics, may have an impact on upland community structures and thereby alter the continued management of provisioning services leading to altered ecosystems properties (Burton *et al.*, this volume). Depending on the state of the ecosystem, impacts may be quickly reversible within years or decades, through agriculture, forestry or natural succession, as experienced by natural afforestation

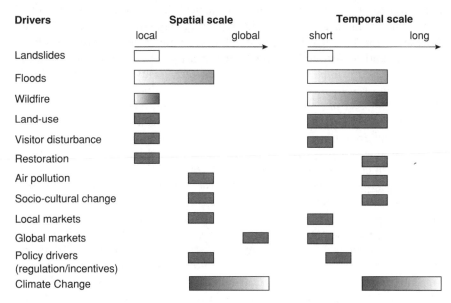

Drivers	Spatial scale	Temporal scale
	local global	short long

Figure 26.1 Temporal and spatial effects of selected drivers of environmental change in uplands. Natural drivers are represented in white, anthropogenic drivers in grey. Some direct drivers are local and can be controlled through local management; other indirect drivers originate outside the upland system and may have immediate to longer-term effects on upland ecosystems and communities. Anthropogenic intervention in upland ecosystems can alter the effect size of drivers, for example damaged blanket bogs or homogeneous even-age forest stands can become more vulnerable to (larger) wildfires, visitors may increase wildfire risk through arson and effects are likely to persist for longer. In turn, the rate of climate change is affected by anthropogenic emissions, and effects may be exacerbated or ameliorated through land use at a regional scale.

of former grazing pastures after land abandonment in the Alps and Mediterranean garigue uplands (Gehrig-Fasel *et al.*, 2007). However, if land management has structurally altered the supporting services, such as soil formation and nutrient cycles, long-term effects can persist and may be irreversible. For example, the deforestation of the British uplands over many centuries has led to the formation of blanket bog landscapes (although natural climax vegetation type in some areas; see Evans, this volume) – a process not reversible in the medium term.

Direct drivers for regulating services, such as flood regulation, water quality and carbon storage, are generally less well understood than those for provisioning services despite being fundamental to human well-being. These drivers and their effects act at large spatial scales, are strongly influenced by climate, and cannot normally be controlled by actions of individual land managers, although cumulatively land managers can exert a strong influence.

It is important to recognise that management for provisioning services is one of the main drivers of change affecting regulating services and biodiversity with significant trade-offs. Land management practices such as drainage and controlled burning, for example, affect carbon storage, hydrology and water regulation, soil properties and plant and wildlife communities (Holden; Crowle and Cormack; Gardner *et al.*; Yallop *et al.*; Pearce-Higgins *et al.*, all this volume). Drivers and effects, as well as costs and benefits, are often spatially divorced. For example, the cumulative effects of upstream land use, such as drainage, burning or pesticide release – often influenced by proximate market or policy drivers – may be felt by downstream communities through altered water quality. An additional scale problem relates to these services as 'classic' public goods (see Hanley and Colombo, this volume). Managing regulatory ecosystem services is often not attractive for individual land managers, as the wider beneficiaries and society in general are not, or are not perceived as, contributing directly to the costs of their provision. Management strategies for the maintenance of regulating services have often been technological and reactive (e.g. through building downstream flood defences or water treatment works), and legally implemented through environmental standard regulations in response to known drivers, such as 'acid rain' (e.g. the Gothenborg Protocol; see Caporn and Emmett, this volume). Nevertheless, following environmental degradation the quality of service provision is not always easily reversed, as illustrated by the slow recovery of upland waters from acidification and metal pollution (Allott, this volume). The challenge for the future is to understand better the coupled indirect and direct human-environment drivers and their impacts on ecosystems (Turner *et al.*, 2007). Then we can identify proactive management, as illustrated for managing wildfire risk by McMorrow *et al.* and for reinstating lost ecosystem functions through restoration by Anderson *et al.* (both this volume).

Drivers for cultural services of upland environments, such as opportunities for recreation, inspiration and aesthetic enjoyment, are particularly hard to quantify (see also Van Jaarsfeld *et al.*, 2005). Landscape aesthetics and distinctiveness (Swanwick, this volume) may vary locally with topography and with land use. Preferences for landscapes may vary among stakeholders from different geographical areas (Hanley and Colombo, this volume). In the UK and many other countries, the supply of recreation opportunities may not be limited, for example in England after the provision of statutory open access across mountain, moor, heath and down through the Countryside and Rights Of Way Act 2000. Rather, socio-cultural drivers may affect the demand for services, such as shifts in leisure patterns and class-mediated preferences (Curry; Suckall *et al.*, both this volume). That is, a majority of people may not choose to take up opportunities for upland recreation, as falling visitor numbers suggest (Natural England, 2006). Nevertheless, the strong cultural bond of many people to 'upland heritage' and first-hand outdoor experiences may be key drivers of environmental awareness and the value placed on continued protection of upland environments. There is still a strong tourism market in the uplands that is based on 'selling' the special qualities of these areas. A major proportion of upland economies is founded on tourism through catering, hotel business and other service providers (Curry; Hubacek *et al.*, both this volume). However, in general, little direct economic benefit occurs to local landowners and managers through recreation and tourism, with the exception of land management businesses that have diversified. Recreation itself can be a driver for disturbance of livestock, game and wildlife, through dogs or wildfire (McMorrow *et al.*, this volume). Furthermore, the value of the landscape and amenity public goods produced may be reflected in rising local house prices (e.g. Luttik, 2000) and thereby threaten the social fabric and alter socio-demographics as discussed by Burton *et al.* (this volume). Looking to the future, targeted public health programmes to promote physical and mental benefits from outdoor activities (Pretty *et al.*, 2007) may become drivers for more upland recreation, and climate change is likely to alter visitor patterns and activities.

In summary, it is clear that seeking to understand the way drivers of change in the uplands influence and affect ecosystem services takes us towards a more holistic analysis that should help us make wise decisions on how we manage the uplands. However, it creates a complicated multi-dimensional picture upon which we need to bring different approaches to bear.

Applying science in the uplands

The complexities inherent in making decisions based on an ecosystems approach (see Bonn, Rebane and Reid, this volume) in the uplands call for well-thought-out and fit-for-purpose science. A number of themes have emerged from the papers in this volume and the implications that flow from their findings.

Importance of baseline data and long-term monitoring

Effectively to detect, understand and evaluate the impact of environmental and social change, high-quality baseline data are crucial (Parr *et al.*, 2003; Allott; Caporn and Emmett; Crowle and McCormack; Evans; Holden; Worrall and Evans, all this volume). Long-term data from palaeo-ecological studies or monitoring networks such as the Environmental Change Network (www.ecn.ac.uk; see also Caporn and Emmett, this volume), and continuous data from air- and space-borne sensors, allow the identification of baseline conditions as well as the detection of detrimental changes (Turner *et al.*, 2007). They also facilitate the testing of hypotheses for the drivers of such change. Long-term monitoring often has additional value beyond that originally envisaged. Data from the UK Acid Waters Monitoring Network (www.ukawmn.ucl.ac.uk), for example, have underpinned our understanding of recovery from acidification but have also been central to the detection and evaluation of recent trends of rising dissolved organic carbon (DOC) in upland waters (Evans *et al.*, 2005; see Allott, this volume). Without baseline and long-term monitoring data, management decisions cannot be made in the context of realistic ecosystem health. Environmental change can be slow, and responses to direct and indirect drivers may be gradual and subject to time-lags or obscured by yearly variations due to weather or population cycles. Even when drivers are removed, recovery may be slow (see Allott, this volume) and desired effects not achieved over short time periods. Long-term monitoring programmes therefore need to be protected and new ones created, and the length of such studies needs to match the timescales of ecological and social processes.

Importance of scale

Ecological experiments at the right spatial and temporal scale are required to test hypotheses (Sutherland and Watkinson, 2001). As drivers of environmental change in uplands and their effects on ecosystem services act at a variety of scales, approaches to address these solely with small-scale field trials within for example 1–100 m^2 plots or laboratory experiments are likely to fall short in providing answers of policy relevance. While these approaches are important to identify intricate singular relationships within ecosystems and have high statistical power owing to replication, multidisciplinary experiments focusing on policy questions are also needed at a variety of scales (see Figure 26.2). In particular, more experiments are needed at the catchment or landscape scale to investigate the effects of upland management intervention on reinstating ecosystem services, such as bare peat re-vegetation, drainage channel blocking and woodland regeneration for climate and water regulation. A key challenge is to reconcile both scales of approach addressing the problem of up-scaling from plot scales to landscapes (e.g. Zhang *et al.*, 2007b).

Understanding the interactive effects of drivers of change

Until relatively recently, upland environmental science has focused on evaluating the influence of individual drivers – e.g. climate, air pollution, or land use – on ecosystem health and change. However, predictions of future climate change have increased attention on the interactive effects of different drivers (see Caporn and Emmett, this volume). The importance of such interactive effects has long been recognised, represented for example by research on the enhancement of acid deposition following upland conifer afforestation, but climate changes are likely to result in complex interactions with other drivers, and there is uncertainty over the extent to which their impacts will be reinforced or counteracted. For example, McMorrow *et al.* (this volume) argue that recreational pressures will reinforce the role of climate change

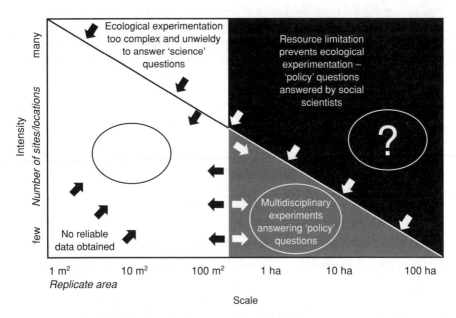

Figure 26.2 Constraints to experimental design. Experiments to answer policy-relevant questions may need to be conducted at larger scales using a multidisciplinary approach. However, resource limitation restricts the intensity of studies at a catchment scale. (Idea and design by Matt Walker based on discussions with Alastair Fitter, Phil Ineson and John Forrester; reproduction by kind permission by UKPopNet, www.ukpopnet.org.)

in significantly increasing future wildfire risk in the UK uplands. Conversely, Caporn and Emmett (this volume) provide examples of interactions which can counteract ecosystem damage, including increased CO_2 concentrations reducing the effects of ozone pollution on upland vegetation. There is clearly an imperative for fuller evaluation of the complex interactions between climate change and other environmental and social drivers (Turner *et al.*, 2007), including assessment of the overall cumulative effects and their incorporation into models of future upland ecosystem change.

Importance of trans-disciplinary approaches

As the issues of upland natural resource management and their implications for society are multi-faceted and complex, they cannot be adequately addressed by a single discipline. Truly trans-disciplinary approaches (Max-Neef, 2005) are needed to investigate biophysical, socio-economic and sustainable development relationships within the uplands and across their boundaries with lowlands. Trans-disciplinary research involves natural and social scientists and stakeholders from fields such as ecology, hydrology, geography, engineering, economics, planning, law and public health working together on cross-disciplinary projects such as upland water catchment management. Although the need for interdisciplinary projects has been widely recognised, truly novel approaches are seldom funded, as they rarely fit into 'calls' from research councils or agencies, cannot provide proven track records, and reviewers have difficulties appreciating or judging unconventional research proposals. Despite these comments, there have been some recent promising developments, such as interdisciplinary research council initiatives in the UK, for example the Rural Economy and Land Use programme (RELU, www.relu.ac.uk/), or the UK government's Foresight programme (www. foresight.gov.uk/) and knowledge exchange initiatives.

Living with uncertainty and an incomplete scientific understanding

While the scientific case for accelerating change in uplands due to climate change and land-use pressures is irrefutable, there is considerable uncertainty connected with predicting the exact nature of change and managing this change. Although there is growing information on the source and effect of drivers of upland change, as outlined in the chapters of this book, insufficient knowledge of causalities and interactions can present obstacles to effective policy responses and management strategies. It is also clear that we are only likely to have partial answers at any point in time from scientific investigations owing to the complexities involved and the time taken for studies to report set against the imperative to develop policy to implement adaptation strategies. Predictive scenario modelling and evaluation may help to forecast and explore change and allow us to go beyond what can be studied in the field (Soliva *et al.*, 2008; Arblaster *et al.*; Hanley and Colombo, both this volume). However, even with well-conceived studies and models, uncertainties ultimately arise because key drivers, such as climate, technology or global market change, are unpredictable and may change non-linearly (Walker *et al.*, 2002).

Managers and policy-makers may be less willing to act on the information because of the uncertainty connected to some of the scientific evidence. Here, scientists need to find a balance to express the degree of uncertainty and to formulate clear messages from their research results. Nonetheless, the absence of complete understanding should not be used as an excuse for inactivity (Brooker and Young, 2006). Owing to imperfect understanding of the functioning of upland ecosystems, we need to accept that initial management choices and conservation policy tools may be sub-optimal, and mistakes may be made. This should not prevent action and development of visions based on the best available evidence but should happen within a framework that supports mutual learning and feedback mechanisms to ensure continuous improvements in decision-making.

Adaptive management

Adaptive management is about learning to live with variability of natural conditions or societal changes through the implementation of policies or strategies, or in simple terms through learning by doing. To take advantage of this on-going learning process, we need a system of iterative management practice and policy development, that is review known evidence – consult – implement management practice – monitor outcomes – assess outcomes and review new evidence – share experience – consult – refine management practice, and so on (see Brooker and Young, 2006). This requires flexibility and the willingness to take risks and adapt once new evidence becomes available. This process has been refined in a series of on-the-ground applications in problems of forestry, fisheries, national parks, and river systems (e.g. Gunderson and Holling, 2002; Walker *et al.*, 2002) and lends itself well to the uplands.

Common themes that seem to emerge from the experiences of these studies (Johnson, 1999; Brooker and Young, 2006; Fraser and Hubacek, 2007) are the need

- to see management agencies not as providers of solutions, but as facilitators and partners with citizens;
- to involve stakeholders in decision-making and find ways to incorporate non-scientific knowledge and data that stakeholders can bring into the adaptive management process;
- to embrace fully the notions of flexibility, risk, change, adaptation, and cooperation as part of management. A 'no blame' culture should be adopted to allow and accept mistakes during the process and to find best solutions in iterative optimisation;
- to monitor change effectively and include feedback at all stages of the process. When implementing land-management change or restoration, this includes monitoring of controls, before the start of management intervention, during and after interventions. Current funding streams, however, seldom allow for these vital information feedback loops.

Ultimately, adaptive upland management should aim to maintain resilience in socio-ecological systems. Resilience refers to sustaining both the natural environment and the well-being of communities and their economies depending on these services (Folke *et al.*, 2004). Resilience management (Walker *et al.*, 2002) therefore aims to prevent the system undergoing irreversible undesired change in the face of stresses and disturbance, such as climate change, and to foster key functions that enable renewal and reorganisation following a substantive change, such as a wildfire. In the uplands, this is to maintain the continued delivery of vital ecosystem services, the capacity for provision of wildlife habitat, water purification, climate regulation or aesthetic beauty for enjoyment. In the face of uncertainty, management can aim to reduce pressures from existing direct land-use drivers and provide buffers to allow for change.

Partnerships between science, policy and management

To achieve the successful incorporation of the scientific evidence base into policy and management, more effort is required to exchange knowledge and expertise between and within the scientific and user communities with innovative knowledge exchange programmes. Close collaborations between scientists, land managers, policy-makers, landowners, industry (agriculture, water, tourism, energy) and other stakeholders can ensure that science addresses policy-relevant questions and that users can translate the evidence base into action to improve the effectiveness of land management, public services and policy. Truly trans-disciplinary approaches involve stakeholders in problem-solving from the outset of the research. This can help to define locally relevant questions, find synergies and integrate different types of knowledge (Parkes and Pannelli, 2001; Dougill *et al.*, 2006) and, moreover, enable stakeholders to transfer research results into action better (ERFF, 2007).

Collaboration between different disciplines or between the science and the user communities, however, takes commitment, time and effort on all sides. Exchange and learning within trans-disciplinary teams is not always simple, and tackling barriers in language, conceptual models, style or convention can be difficult. Indeed, knowledge-exchange activities are not always highly regarded or rewarded within scientific communities; and, conversely, some policy-makers use science rather 'the way a drunk uses a lamppost – more for support than for illumination' (King and Thomas, 2007, p. 1702). An important message is that willingness is required by both the science and the user communities to break down complex questions into tenable projects and then to re-package the results to provide answers to generic issues that will be of use in a policy context (Sutherland *et al.*, 2006).

To address this, adequate funding for time and resources is needed to ensure effective science–user partnerships. Recent knowledge-exchange initiatives from UK research councils are very encouraging. Next to funding for workshops and opportunities to meet, it may be beneficial to involve facilitators, who can 'translate' and move between the research and the user base, and enhance communication between the academic and the policy/management community. Funding for secondments between the research base and user organisations can increase understanding and facilitate ongoing and future collaborations.

Finally, research output needs to be in accessible formats (Sutherland *et al.*, 2006; ERFF, 2007; King and Thomas, 2007). Research results only published in scientific journal articles are not easily accessible for many stakeholders. Imaginative dissemination formats are needed. An example developed as part of the UK Government Office for Science Foresight programme is Floodranger, an interactive, educational computer-based flood simulator that explores strategies for flood defence along coasts and rivers (www.discoverysoftware.co.uk/FloodRanger.htm). User involvement is important in defining what knowledge is needed and what formats are most useful. Creativity is essential.

Public participation in decision-making

The big-tent philosophy can be extended, and conflicts potentially be better managed, by widening participation in the decision-making process beyond the professionals. Practical examples of the participatory processes can include collaborative environmental management and citizen advisory committees or panels, but there can often be difficulties with such approaches. In this volume, Connelly and Richardson explore the effectiveness of stakeholder involvement for different contexts. They argue that broadening the range of stakeholders does not necessarily lead to more effective governance or more sustainable development. They voice concerns that involving more people can impede decision-making owing to the pressure for consensus-building or potential power struggles. Effective stakeholder deliberation is therefore a skilled practice with continuous attention to the delicate balancing act between achieving desirable outcomes, making progress on difficult issues, and sustaining the legitimacy of the process.

In order to facilitate informed decision-making by society, we need inspirational ways for promoting awareness of the value of ecosystem services and biodiversity and how to safeguard them. Knowledge itself is important, but not always enough to inform attitudes and behaviour to promote sustainable management. For 'winning hearts and minds', we should not forget the importance of emotional and spiritual qualities in both experiencing nature and environmental decision-making. To facilitate a sense of ownership, social belonging and responsibility for upland environments, active involvement is needed. To quote Pyle (2003), 'people who care, may make choices to conserve; but people who don't know, don't even care' (see also Suckall *et al.*, this volume).

Resolving land use conflicts and developing shared visions

The ecosystem approach clearly acknowledges that 'the objectives of management of land, water and living resources are a matter of societal choice' (Malawi Principle No. 1, Convention of Biological Diversity; see Box 25.2, this volume). Thus, land use planning and decision-making processes should be receptive to different values and knowledge bases. This requires representation of the various ways in which the environment matters to people, and different sections of society will have different priorities and values, according to their social, economic and cultural background. This may present serious challenges to current upland management and changes to it.

For example, current conservation and recreation management in upland National Parks, promoting low-impact recreation and notions of tranquillity and solitude, may not match the diversity of interests in society, as discussed by Curry and Suckall *et al.* in this volume. Incorporating pluralistic views of recreation opportunities in management, for example by providing adventure playgrounds, off-road mountain-bike trails or events, such as live music concerts (as promoted by the Forestry Commission), may be controversial and not suitable for all areas. But this may offer novel opportunities to include more sections of society benefiting from uplands and possibly increasing their environmental awareness, while avoiding damaging practices (cf. McMorrow *et al.*, this volume).

Wildlife conservation conflicts represent another contentious issue. As debated by Pearce-Higgins *et al.* and Sotherton *et al.* in this volume, views on the relative benefits of birds of prey in areas of grouse moor, and of the impacts of grouse moor management on upland bird communities of conservation concern (waders), are divided. Illegal persecution has led to declines of upland raptors, and raptor conservation programmes meet with mixed responses (Redpath *et al.*, 2004), and diversionary feeding has been identified as a potential compromise. Certainly, grouse moor management illustrates an important point about the impact of land management driven by one main objective. It is possible to maximise a species population and in so doing elevate the populations of other species that require similar conditions. However, this can be at the expense of other ecosystem services or biodiversity. Rather than maximising certain populations, including those subject to conservation designations or special protection, should we be looking for sustainable populations that allow other features and species to flourish? Such an approach could have an impact on sites. If grouse moor shoots were to become economically less viable owing to decreased grouse population densities in response to predation or altered management, would a compensatory payment be a solution? Would a change in expectations and the nature of the sporting recreation activity resolve issues or would the cultural service of opportunities for field sport recreation be lost?

We can try to anticipate future land-use conflicts. The notion of maintaining the status quo in landscape and habitat composition may have to be challenged in order to promote other services. For example, to mitigate climate change, society might foster carbon sequestration through increased woodland cover on foot slopes and land management that optimises the ability of (semi-)natural habitats such as blanket bog and heath, as well as more intensively managed farmland, to store carbon and produce a reliable water supply of high quality. Do we need the continued maintenance of cultural landscapes, such as grouse moors, hay meadows or dry grassland pastures for conservation, landscape aesthetics, recreational or cultural heritage reasons? As agricultural management for some of these habitats may become financially unviable, are conservation payments justified to maintain these? Can we allow some areas to undergo 're-wilding' or low-impact management (Yalden, this volume)? There is increasing interest in and attempts to implement the concept of re-wilding even in a densely populated country like England. What will be the opportunities and threats for the delivery of other ecosystem services, such as aesthetic or adventurous enjoyment, wildfire risk prevention, water regulation, and biodiversity? Answers to these questions will be facilitated by better understanding the costs and benefits of changes in natural resource management for ecosystem service delivery and biodiversity, and the associated geographic variation. However, it is worth noting that uplands are inherently low-productivity systems, and resource exploitation over the last century or two has in parts of the world led to diminishing capacity to provide all services. In order to provide a balanced suite of ecosystem services, it may now be appropriate to move in general to lower-intensity management irrespective of wilderness debates.

In the uplands, as well as elsewhere, we are going to be increasingly challenged to resolve conflicts between conservation values such as landscape character and renewable energy as we seek means of mitigating some of the effects of climate change (Bergmanna, 2008). Whilst this volume has not covered the potential for renewable energy in the uplands in any detail, it is pertinent to decision-making particularly given the huge reserves of potential wind and water power as well as biomass energy that could be marshalled at local, regional or national scales. There are clear conflicts with landscape aesthetics, wilderness and potentially biodiversity interests that call for imaginative solutions and perhaps some hard decisions.

Ultimately, making decisions in favour of some ecosystem services will mean conflict with others, hence the importance of inclusive, well-informed participatory processes in arriving at decisions. The holy grail of sustainable upland management would seem to be about identifying and justifying a suite of mutually beneficial and reinforcing services and supporting systems at appropriate scales and management intensities that produce an argument for their delivery and development that outweighs any impingement upon or loss of other services. In so doing, the costs and benefits and therefore the rewards of any public financial support would be drawn out. The process of identifying them requires the development of shared and, as far as possible, inclusive visions and answers to – or at least illumination of – the questions below.

Towards a fuller understanding: reinforcing the evidence base

This volume has brought together a range of contributions from natural and social scientists, policy-makers and practitioners. The evidence base provided by these and other studies is crucial for the effective management of upland environments. Although we have a sound knowledge base for some issues, many important questions remain only partially understood or unresolved. Some of the overarching issues for sustainable management of the uplands identified in this volume are encapsulated in the following questions: How does the natural environment contribute to human well-being, and how can these benefits be evaluated? What are sustainable environmental and social limits? How can management and policy develop proactive responses? These issues can be broken down into a number of components of strong relevance to the uplands as set out in Box 26.1. This list of questions is certainly not intended to be exhaustive, but the answers are crucial for informed sustainable management and policy development in the uplands in the context of their drivers of change.

Box 26.1. Reinforcing the evidence base for decision-making: some key research questions

What are the internal and trans-boundary ecosystem service flows in upland systems? How can targeted management alter these?

- Which are optimal levels of land management to increase the carbon storage and sequestration potential of upland habitats? Do effects differ over space and time? Which locations offer the greatest net gains?
- How can uplands be managed to optimise their role in reducing flood risk? Can a change in management regime, restoration or land cover change, e.g. burning, grazing or cutting, gully/grip blocking, re-vegetation or afforestation, increase water retention capacity and reduce downstream flooding?
- How can water quality be safeguarded? How can the rising trends of dissolved organic carbon (DOC) in streams be halted or managed? How can sensitive farming management contribute to reduction in contaminant (pesticides, bacteria) and sediment loads?
- Which renewable energy schemes are most efficient in their carbon balance, cost-effectiveness and least impact on other ecosystem services and biodiversity? In what locations can they be best deployed?

What are the synergies and trade-offs of management for different ecosystem services and biodiversity (Van Jaarsfeld *et al.*, 2005; Chan *et al.*, 2006; Kareiva *et al.*, 2007)?

- How does management for one set of ecosystem services affect other services and biodiversity?
- Can we find an optimal geographic configuration for managing different services in different areas that maximises overall benefits?
- How do we understand and reconcile the ecosystem services approach to conserving biodiversity with non-utilitarian rationales for biodiversity conservation such as intrinsic value?
- How do we reach agreement over establishing sustainable rather than maximum populations of target species?

How can we most effectively evaluate the costs and benefits of upland ecosystem services (Turner *et al.*, 2003)?

- What are the economic and social cost–benefit relationships of services? How can costs for (un)sustainable management be internalised and stewardship for ecosystem services be rewarded?
- Which management is most cost-effective for delivering services? Does it vary geographically?
- How can evaluation inform the development of novel economic tools for incentives or payments for ecosystem service management?
- How do people value ecosystem services? How do attitudes and experience shape values and choices in relation to ecosystem services? Do they vary geographically or across sectors of society?

How do ecosystem services contribute to human well-being?

- How is well-being, for example security, safety and health, influenced through ecosystem services and disservices? How can we measure and quantify links?
- Who are the beneficiaries? Can we identify and map distribution and inequalities? How can these be addressed?

How will future drivers affect ecosystem service provision and biodiversity (see also Sutherland *et al.*, 2008)? How can impacts be mediated?

- How can we deal with current diffuse air pollution impacts and the legacy of historical air pollution in some uplands?
- How can upland environments be managed in the face of climate change to increase resilience and safeguard existing services and biodiversity?
- How will likely changes in global markets influence decision-making in upland natural resource management and thereby influence services?
- How can we encourage traditional land managers to become suppliers of a wider range of ecosystem services and derive professional satisfaction from so doing, for example farming for carbon storage?
- How will demand for renewable energies affect semi-natural habitats, and how can we quantify the impact of location and scale of schemes?
- How can re-wilding be accommodated where there are competing demands for land use? Can it support carbon storage, water supply and flood management services?

Box 26.2. The Peak District and other National Parks as test beds for the upland ecosystem approach?

This book is partly drawn from experiences within the Peak District National Park in the UK providing case studies for many issues. As an upland landscape that is surrounded by large conurbations, with 16 million people living within a one-hour drive, it continues to be subject to immense social and environmental drivers of change. Being situated at the southern climatic edge of upland blanket bog within the UK, it is particularly susceptible to the effects of climate change. The Peak District therefore offers a great opportunity to help understand the effects of change and how people can adapt to live with changing environmental conditions. It can serve as an important model region to help develop policy and management tools for sustainable natural resource management and community governance. The strong links with surrounding cities also clearly manifest the trans-boundary effects of upland ecosystem service delivery and widen the range of beneficiaries and stakeholders. The surrounding urban populations will directly experience any future alterations to the delivery of upland ecosystem services. While this highlights the potential extent of future problems, it also presents opportunities for novel solutions. In the last century, the social tension experienced around the burgeoning birth cities of the Industrial Revolution, Manchester and Sheffield, and the Peak District led to a challenge of existing legal and political frameworks. Working class people from the cities valued the health benefits of fresh air and the inspiration they found in the uplands (see Bevan, this volume), and took action to demand change. This has ultimately led to the creation of the National Parks in Britain.

Hopefully, the Peak District and other National Parks can continue to play a leading role and become showcases and test beds (ENPAA, 2008) for new ways to value upland environments and to adapt to change. National Parks can foster and promote the ecosystem approach through holistic decision-making involving all relevant stakeholders through innovative partnerships. They can take leadership in best-practice upland management for carbon storage and sequestration, water quality and flood risk management at a landscape scale. To mitigate climate change, they can develop and promote energy conservation and micro-generation in the context of iconic landscapes. By welcoming and fostering research, they can endorse learning and adaptive management. Finally, National Parks have the opportunity to communicate with millions of visitors each year the value and relevance of upland ecosystem services, to raise understanding of how to safeguard them and to promote sustainable choices and actions (see ENPAA, 2008).

Outlook

In the face of global change we need concerted action for upland environments now. The challenge is to understand more fully the nature of the socio-economic and environmental benefits accruing from the various ecosystem services to enable more informed decision-making by policy-makers and land managers. Political will (Koontz and Bodine, 2008) and effective partnerships between policy, science and management are required to integrate and align interests to find sustainable solutions to safeguard uplands and the services they provide. Bridging the gap between science, local knowledge and policy is essential to move towards sustainable upland environments. Partnerships are vital to explore the challenges, costs, and benefits of upland research and resource management. Based on the ecosystem services concept, viewpoints may be broadened and responsibilities redefined. With the understanding that there is uncertainty rather than perfect information, successful answers to change require collaboration, adaptive management, consensus-building and social learning.

We need to find new mechanisms to provide continued and enhanced delivery of upland ecosystems services and at the same time maintain vibrant rural communities. As we look towards a future full of uncertainty, we need to devise land-use systems that work within the constraints of local nutrient cycles and disturbance regimes, and are based on an understanding of ecosystem relationships and environmental limits. We need to restore healthy constituent habitats of ecosystems to build robustness and thus maximise their chances of adapting to changing environmental conditions.

There is currently much interest in developing more sustainable approaches to upland management (e.g. English Nature, 2001; RSPB, 2007; Natural England, in press). We need to find places to develop these ideas and approaches, and in Box 26.2 we illustrate how an area like the Peak District National Park could contribute to the goals.

Understanding the different scales and interactions of drivers, approaches to decision-making and action will need to operate across administrative boundaries and scientific disciplines. Taking an ecosystem approach, we need institutions that will take a locally grounded understanding of ecosystem relations and develop strong incentives for land managers and national and international policy-makers to promote public goods as well as privately profitable commodities.

Let's continue the dialogue!

References

Bergmanna, A., Colombo, S. and Hanley, N. (2008) Rural versus urban preferences for renewable energy developments. *Ecological Economics*, **65**, 616–62.

Brooker, R. and Young, J. (2006) Climate change and biodiversity in Europe: a review of impacts, policy responses, gaps in knowledge and barriers to the exchange of information between scientists and policy makers. Final report for Defra research contract CRO326. http://www.defra.gov.uk/wildlife-countryside/resprog/findings/climatechange-biodiversity/report.pdf

Chan, K. M. A., Shaw, M. R., Cameron, D. R., Underwood, E. C. and Daily, G. C. (2006) Conservation planning for ecosystem services. *PLOS Biology*, **4**, 2138–52.

Dougill, A. J., Fraser, E. D. G., Holden, J., Hubacek, K., Prell, C., Reed, M. S., Stagl, S. and Stringer, L. C. (2006) Learning from doing participatory rural research: lessons from the Peak District National Park. *Journal of Agricultural Economics*, **57**, 259–75.

English Nature (2001) *State of Nature – the Upland Challenge.* Peterborough: English Nature. http://naturalengland.communisis.com/naturalenglandshop/docs/CORP1.8.pdf

ENPAA (2008) *English National Park Authorities Association. Ministerial seminar on National Park Authorities contribution to addressing climate change.* 27 March 2008, London. http://www.nationalparks.gov.uk/enpaa/whatsnew/enpaa-climatechange-seminar.htm

ERFF (2007) *Environment Research Funders Forum. Using research to inform policy: the role of interpretation.* http://www.erff.org.uk/reports/reports/reportdocs/interpretstudy070919.pdf

Evans, C. D., Monteith, D. T. and Cooper, D. M. (2005) Long-term increases in surface water dissolved organic carbon: observations, possible causes and environmental impacts. *Environmental Pollution*, **137**, 55–71.

Folke, C., Carpenter, S., Walker, B., Scheffer, M., Elmqvist, T., Gunderson, L. and Holling, C. (2004) Regime shifts, resilience, and biodiversity in ecosystem management. *Annual Review of Ecology, Evolution, and Systematics*, **35**, 557–81.

Fraser, E. and Hubacek, K. (2007) The challenge of land use change: international dimensions. *The Economics of Sustainable Development: International Perspectives* (ed. K. Steininger and M. Cogoy), vol. 55. Cheltenham: Edward Elgar.

Gehrig-Fasel, J., Guisan, A. and Zimmermann, N. E. (2007) Tree line shifts in the Swiss Alps: climate change or land abandonment? *Journal of Vegetation Science*, **18**, 571–82.

Gunderson, L. H. and Holling, S. S. (eds) (2002) *Panarchy, Understanding Transformations in Human and Natural Systems.* Washington, DC: Island Press.

Johnson, B. L. (1999) Introduction to the special feature: adaptive management – scientifically sound, socially challenged? *Conservation Ecology*, **3**, 10.

Kareiva, P., Watts, S., McDonald, R. and Boucher, T. (2007) Domesticated nature: shaping landscapes and ecosystems for human welfare. *Science*, **316**, 1866–9.

King, D. A. and Thomas, S. M. (2007) Taking science out of the box: foresight recast. *Science*, **316**, 1701–2.

Koontz, T. M. and Bodine, J. (2008) Implementing ecosystem management in public agencies: lessons from the US Bureau of Land Management and the Forest Service. *Conservation Biology*, **22**, 60–9.

Luttik, J. (2000) The value of trees, water and open space as reflected by house prices in the Netherlands. *Landscape and Urban Planning*, **48**, 161–7.

MA (2005) *Millennium Ecosystem Assessment. Ecosystems and Human Well-being: Synthesis.* Washington, DC: Island Press. http://www.millenniumassessment.org/

Max-Neef, M. A. (2005) Foundations of transdisciplinarity. *Ecological Economics*, **53**, 5–16.

Natural England (2006) *England Leisure Visits: Report of the 2005 Survey.* Cheltenham: Natural England. http://www.naturalengland.org.uk/leisure/recreation/dayvisits05.pdf

Natural England (in press) *Principles for Sustainable Upland Management.* Peterborough: Natural England.

Parkes, M. and Panelli, R. (2001) Integrating catchment ecosystems and community health: the value of participatory action research. *Ecosystem Health,* **7,** 85–106.

Parr, T. W., Sier, A. R. J., Battarbee, R. W., Mackay, A. and Burgess, J. (2003) Detecting environmental change: science and society – perspectives on long-term research and monitoring in the 21st century. *Science of the Total Environment,* **310,** 1–8.

Pretty, J., Peacock, J., Hine, R., Sellens, M., South, N. and Griffin, M. (2007) Green exercise in the UK countryside: effects on health and psychological well-being, and implications for policy and planning. *Journal of Environmental Planning and Management,* **50,** 211–31.

Pyle, R. M. (2003) Nature matrix: reconnecting people and nature. *Oryx,* **37,** 206–14.

Redpath, S. M., Arroyo, B. E., Leckie, F. M., Bacon, P., Bayfield, N., Gutiérrez, R. J. and Thirgood, S. J. (2004) Using decision modelling with stakeholders to reduce human–wildlife conflict: a raptor–grouse case study. *Conservation Biology,* **18,** 350–9.

RSPB (2007) *The Uplands – Time to Change?* Sandy: Royal Society for the Protection of Birds. http://www.rspb.org.uk/Images/uplands_tcm9-166286.pdf

Soliva, R., Ronningen, K., Bella, I., Bezak, P., Cooper, T., Flo, B. E., Marty, P. and Potter, C. (2008) Envisioning upland futures: stakeholder responses to scenarios for Europe's mountain landscapes. *Journal of Rural Studies,* **24,** 56–71.

Sutherland, W. J., Armstrong-Brown, S., Armsworth, P. R., Brereton, T., Brickland, J., Campbell, C. D., Chamberlain, D. E., Cooke, A. I., Dulvy, N. K., Dusic, N. R., Fitton, M., Freckleton, R. P., Godfray, H. C. J., Grout, N., Harvey, H. J., Hedley, C., Hopkins, J. J., Kift, N. B., Kirby, J., Kunin, W. E., Macdonald, D. W., Marker, B., Naura, M., Neale, A. R., Oliver, T., Osborn, D., Pullin, A. S., Shardlow, M. E. A., Showler, D. A., Smith, P. L., Smithers, R. J., Solandt, J. L., Spencer, J., Spray, C. J., Thomas, C. D., Thompson, J., Webb, S. E., Yalden, D. W. and Watkinson, A. R. (2006) The identification of 100 ecological questions of high policy relevance in the UK. *Journal of Applied Ecology,* **43,** 617–27.

Sutherland, W. J. *et al.* (2008) Future novel threats and opportunities facing UK biodiversity identified by horizon scanning. *Journal of Applied Ecology,* doi: 10.1111/j.1365-2664.2008.01474.x.

Sutherland, W. J. and Watkinson, A. R. (2001) Policy making within ecological uncertainty: lessons from badgers and GM crops. *Trends in Ecology and Evolution,* **16,** 261–3.

Turner, R. K., Paavola, J., Cooper, P., Farber, S., Jessamy, V. and Georgiou, S. (2003) Valuing nature: lessons learned and future research directions. *Ecological Economics,* **46,** 493–510.

Turner, B. L., Lambin, E. F. and Reenberg, A. (2007) The emergence of land change science for global environmental change and sustainability. *Proceedings of the National Academy of Sciences of the United States of America,* **104,** 20666–71.

Van Jaarsveld, A. S., Biggs, R., Scholes, R. J., Bohensky, E., Reyers, B., Lynam, T., Musvoto, C. and Fabricius, C. (2005) Measuring conditions and trends in ecosystem services at multiple scales: the Southern African Millennium Ecosystem Assessment (SAfMA) experience. *Philosophical Transactions of the Royal Society,* B, *Biological Sciences,* **360,** 425–41.

Walker, B., Carpenter, S., Anderies, J., Abel, N., Cumming, G. S., Janssen, M., Lebel, L., Norberg, J., Peterson, G. D. and Pritchard, R. (2002) Resilience management in social-ecological systems: a working hypothesis for a participatory approach. *Conservation Ecology*, **6**, 14.

Zhang, W., Ricketts, T. H., Kremen, C., Carney, K. and Swinton, S. M. (2007a) Ecosystem services and dis-services to agriculture. *Ecological Economics*, **64**, 253–60.

Zhang, N., Yu, Z. L., Yu, G. R. and Wu, J. G. (2007b) Scaling up ecosystem productivity from patch to landscape: a case study of Changbai Mountain Nature Reserve, China. *Landscape Ecology*, **22**, 303–15.

List of acronyms

ANC	Acid Neutralising Capacity
AONB	Area of Outstanding Natural Beauty
API	Aerial Photographic Interpretation
AWMN	Acid Waters Monitoring Network
B&B	Bed and Breakfast
BAP	Biodiversity Action Plan
BP	Before Present (meaning years before 1950)
CAP	Common Agricultural Policy
CBD	Convention on Biological Diversity
CCW	Countryside Council for Wales
CFCs	Chlorofluorocarbons
CFMP	Catchment Flood Management Plan
CHUM	CHemistry of the Uplands Model
CROW Act	Countryside and Rights of Way Act
CPRE	Campaign to Protect Rural England
CS	Countryside Stewardship (Scheme)
CSM	Common Standards Monitoring
CV	Contingent Valuation
DA	Disadvantaged Area (of LFA)
DEFRA	Department for Environment, Food and Rural Affairs
DETR	Department of the Environment, Transport and the Regions
DIC	Dissolved Inorganic Carbon
DOC	Dissolved Organic Carbon
DoE	Department of the Environment
EC	European Commission
EEC	European Economic Community
ELC	European Landscape Convention
ELS	Entry Level Stewardship (Environmental Stewardship)
EN	English Nature
ESA	Environmentally Sensitive Area
ESRC	Economic and Social Research Council
ESS	Environmental Stewardship Scheme
EU	European Union

FAB	Fire Advisory Panel
F&CGS	Farm and Conservation Grant Scheme
FOG	Fire Operations Group (in the Peak District)
GATT	General Agreement on Tariffs and Trade
GHG	Greenhouse Gas
HFA	Hill Farm Allowance
HLCA	Hill Livestock Compensatory Allowance
HLS	Higher Level Stewardship (Environmental Stewardship)
IEEP	Institute for European Environmental Policy
IPCC	Intergovernmental Panel on Climate Change
IRDP	Integrated Rural Development Project
JCA	Joint Character Area
JNCC	Joint Nature Conservation Committee
LAF	Local Access Forum
LFA	Less Favoured Areas
LiDAR	Light Detection and Ranging (remote sensing technology)
MAFF	Ministry of Agriculture, Fisheries and Food
MAGIC	Model of Acidification of Groundwaters in Catchments
NAO	National Audit Office
NCC	Nature Conservancy Council
NEE	Net Ecosystem Exchange of CO_2
NFU	National Farmers' Union
NGO	Non-Governmental Organisation
NNR	National Nature Reserve
NPA	National Park Authority
NVC Code	National Vegetation Classification Code
OELS	Organic Entry Level Stewardship (Environmental Stewardship)
PDNP	Peak District National Park
PDNPA	Peak District National Park Authority
PDRDF	Peak District Rural Deprivation Forum
POC	Particulate Organic Carbon
PPTF	Peak Park Transport Forum
PSA	Public Service Agreement
RDP	Rural Development Programme
RDPE	Rural Development Programme for England
RDR	Rural Development Regulation
RPL	Random Parameter Logit (model)
SAC	Special Area of Conservation (EU Habitats Directive)
SCI	Sites of Community Importance (EU Habitats Directive)
SDA	Severely Disadvantage Area (of LFA)
SPA	Special Protection Area (EU Birds Directive)
SPITS	South Pennines Integrated Transport Strategy
SPS	Single Payment Scheme
SSSI	Site of Special Scientific Interest

UAA	Utilisable Agricultural Area
UELS	Upland Entry Level Stewardship Scheme
UK	United Kingdom
UN	United Nations
VOCs	Volatile Organic Compounds
WAO	Welsh Audit Office
WES	Wildlife Enhancement Scheme
WFD	Water Framework Directive
WHI	Way to Health Initiative
WHO	World Health Organisation
WTO	World Trade Organisation
WTP	Willingness to Pay

Index

Page numbers in *Italics* represent Tables and page numbers in **Bold** represent Figures

Abbey Brook: tresspassing 272
access resource: growth 277; nature of 276–8
acid flushes 41
acid neutralising capacity (ANC): South Pennines (UK) **146**
acid rain 34, 48
acidification 38–41; aquatic biota 136–7; critical loads 137–9; first-order acidity balance (FAB) 137; lakes and streams 16; nitrate 142; palaeo-limnological techniques 136; Peak District 140; Salamonid fish 136–7; soil 53; steady-state water chemistry (SSWC) 137; surface-water 135–7, 139–46, 142
Acreman, M.: and Bullock, A. 114
acrotelmcatotelm model 116
Adamson, J.: and Worrall, F. 103–4
Aerts, R.: and Ludwig, F. 105
afforestation 102–3, 217–19; hydrological impact 126–7; impacts *216*
agri-environment: strategy 82; subsidies 240; uptake 83
agri-environment schemes 87, 204; growth 74; obligatory 73; uptake of *84*
agricultural practices: rational 265
agriculture 60–6, 69–70, 76–9; European policy *61*; management 361–9
Agriculture Act (1947) 65–6
air pollution: climate change 48–54; dry deposited 38; ecological response 55; photochemical 38–41; road

traffic 39; role 54; transport and transformation 38; wet deposited 40–1
air quality: climate change 47–54
annual average temperature: Central England Temperature data **47**
anthropogenic emissions: greenhouse gases 41–7
anthropological drivers 476
aquatic biota: acidification 136–7
areas of outstanding beauty (AOB) 293–304
Areas of Outstanding Natural Beauty (AONB) 60, 69, 344
Armstrong, A. 101–2
atmospheric deposition: nitrogen 107–8; sulphur 104–5
atmospheric sources: pollution 146–7
attribute levels: selection groups 327

back-firing: burning 177
Baudrillard, J. 396
behaviour models: fire risk 408
Bellamy, P. 302
berry crops: moorland 215–17
biodiversity 466–7; conservation 243–5; deer 233; grouse management 245–53; human well-being 460; impacts 368
Biodiversity Action Plans (BAPs) 244; ecosystem approach 463–4
biological recovery: processes 143
bird population 209–11, *210*; Breeding Bird Survey (BBS) 211; Common Bird Census (CBC) 211; conclusions 220; drivers of change 211–12;

estimates 211; grazing 213; outlook 220; predator control 215–16; trends 211
bird species: breeding ranges 251–2; habitat associations 250; Peak District 250; upland *214*
birds: breeding **247**; British specialist 230; burning 215; grouse management 245; heather 213–14; moorland 215–17, *218*, *249*, *250*; moorland berry crops 215; vegetation structure 214–15
birds of prey 253–4; hen harrier 253
blanket bog 165, 182, 358; burning 179, 180, 369; landscapes 477; management 219
blanket peat: carbon store 168; erosion **26**
blocking grips 436–7
Boatman, N. 191
Bodine, J.: and Koontz, T. 463
bog: dry 182; recoverable 182
bracken: control 439
breeding: birds **247**
Breeding Bird Survey (BBS): bird populations 211
British Social Attitude 394
Brotherton, I. 340
budgets: leisure-time 280
Bullock, A.: and Acreman, M. 114
Bullock, C.: and Kay, J. 326
Burbage: moors 269–70
burning: back-firing 177; birds 215; blanket bog 179, 180, 369; *Calluna vulgaris* **176**; cool 165; ecological effects 177–81; ecology 171–82; frequency 178–9; grouse management *176*, 177–81; heather 215, 242–3, 244–5; hot 165; management **174**, **175**; moorland **164**; Peak District **178**; prehistory 171–2; recent history 172; red grouse management 433; regimes 436; site condition 164–6; woodland colonisation 171
Burning Regulations and Codes of Practice 254
Burt, T.: and Holden, J. 22, 119
business income: farm **86**
butterfly: mountain ringlet 50

Cairngorm mountains: Scotland 41
Calluna: moncultures 182; phasal development 172, *173*
Calluna vulgaris: burning **176**

capacity: National Park Authority 386
capacity to act 379–80
carbon balance 302; estimation 96; peatlands 219
carbon budget: Moor House 97–8; peats *98*; wildfires 407
carbon cycle: disruption 36; upland peats 94
carbon dioxide 42; elevated atmospheric 99–100; soil respiration 106; uptake 106
carbon pool: peatlands 128
carbon storage: Peak District 7
carbon store: blanket peat 168; peatland 106–7
carbon-sequestering: plants 441
Carlsen, J.: and Getz, ?. 282
Castleton commons 267–8
catchment: habitat disturbance 148–50, *149*; vegetation cover 24
Catchment Flood Management Plans (CFMPs) 464
Catchment Sensitive Farming Programme 152
catotelm hydraulic conductivities 22
cattle: grazing 360
Central England Temperature data: annual average temperature **47**
change: migration 107
Character of England 342
chemical evolution of lake basins: Glacier Bay **16**
chemistry trends: streamwater 145
Chemistry of the Upland Model (CHUM) 143, 147
Chiverell, R. 17–18
Choice Experiment: method 324–5, 335
Clark, G. 280
Clark, J.: *et al.* 99
class divisions: strength 394
clean air legislation 139
climate: hypotheses 150; predictions 46–7
climate change 3, 99–101, 172, 236, 369, 457–8, 469–70; air pollution 48–54; air quality 47–54; directional 151; ecological response 48; fire risk 408, 409, 410; greenhouse gases 41–2; hydrological impact 127–9; land use 219, 220; man-made *xxvi*; rapid 35; scenarios *46*; societal pressures 458; stream biology 151; visitors and fire 410–23; water balance 128
Climate Impacts Programme (UK) 46

climate variables: comparison *44*
climax: soils 17; vegetation cover 17
cloud cover: significance 41
cloud droplets: orographic 41
coastal access 278
cold-niche specialist organisms: threat 48
collective gaze: Urry, J. 397
colonisation: woodland 171
commodity: land 265
Common Act (2006) 80
Common Agricultural Policy (CAP) 73, 81; livestock 189; production subsidies 323; Rural Development Regulation 83; Single Farm Payment 323
Common Bird Census (CBC): bird populations 211
common councils: establishment 80
common grazings 310; Lake District 311
common land: reform 79, 79–80
Common Standards Monitoring (CSM) 157–8, 161–2, 168
Common Standards for Monitoring of Upland Habitats 182
commons: loss of 320
community: involvement 277–8
compensating surplus: aggregate *335*; estimates *334*
compounds: nitrogen 38, **40**
concentrations: ozone **39**
condition monitoring: habitats 161–2; interest features 157; upland habitats 162–8
coniferous afforestation: reduction 126
conifers: removing 437
conservation 466; biodiversity 243–5; designations 470; gamekeeping 181–2; landscape 237; partnerships 467; scientific evidence 464–5
conservation management: active 369
construction: hydrological impact 127
content sustainability: evaluation 379; National Park Authority 386; Stanage Forum 382–3
Contingent Valuation: research methods 326
Convention on Biological Diversity (CBD) 74–5, 460
Convention Council of Europe (2000) 339
Cork Declaration 76
Cotton grass: spread 26–7

countryside: England *280*
Countryside Act (1968) 69
Countryside Agency 71
Countryside Commission 69
Countryside and Rights of Way Act (2000) 13, 277, 478
Countryside Stewardship scheme: environmentally sensitive areas (ESA) 74; launch 74
Countryside Surveys 353
County War Agricultural Committees 60
Critical load concept **138**; approaches 146; models 139
Crowe, S. 27
cryptosporidium 149
cultural heritage: Peak District 7
Cumbrian Commoners Federation 320
Curry Commission 79

damage: remediation 197
Daniels, S. 102
Daplyn, J.: and Ewald, J. 245–9
decadal climatic oscillations 151
decision-making: evidence base 488–9; public participation 485
deep-seated summer: wildfires 407
deer: biodiversity 233; grazing 212–15; grouse 300–1; sheep 212–15
deforestation: uplands 477
degradation: causes 432–3
deliberation: effective 390; effectiveness 387
deliberative democracy 389; theories 378
demographic drivers 476
Department for the Environment, Food and Rural Affairs (Defra) 59, 78, 79, 80, **82**, 156, 464
deposition: nitrogen 142, 143
deregulation 397; natural areas 400
developing countries: pollutants 34
direct drivers: change 4–5
direct marketing: farm produce 296
dissolved inorganic carbon (DIC) 95
dissolved organic carbon (DOC) 95, 179, 180
diversification 370; hill farming 369; tourism 370
diversity: loss 165
domestic grazing: mammals 235–7
Doomsday Book 260, 261
Dowers Report 340

drainage 101–4, 107; land 120; peat 101; prediction and effect 121; site condition 167, 168; upland 120

drinking-water: faecal contamination 149; Peak District 147

drivers: change 99–105; external and long-term 5

drought 100–1; summer increase 128

dry heath 358

dwarf shrub heath: nitrogen **49**

dynamic equilibrium: upland landscapes **18**

ecological response: air pollution 55; climate change 48

ecological restoration: benefits 432

ecology: burning 171–82

economic base theory 303

economic sectors: ecosystem service 302–3

economic viability: farms 317

ecosystem approach 461, 462–7, 465, 467–9, 490; Biodiversity Action Plans (BAPs) 463–4

ecosystem engineer: plants 441

ecosystem service 349–52, 449–71, *450*; definition 449; economic sectors 302–3; lowlands 460; providers 303–4; provision 304; uplands 476–9; valuing 458–60; wildfires 406–7

ecosystems: economic and social value *xxvii*; freshwater 151–2; services 5–6, 254; source 1

Ecosystems Approach Project 339

ecosytems: good and services 283

education: social consensus 397

Educational Programmes 397

effective deliberation: definition 378–9

elevated atmospheric: carbon dioxide (CO_2) 99–100

emission trends: pollutants 36–7

enclosure 267–9; movement boundaries 268; parliamentary walls 268

energy crops: forestry 299–300

England: countryside *280*

England Leisure Visits Survey 279

English Environmental Stewardship (ESS) 189, 190–1, 195, 196–7, 203

English Nature 71

English Wildfire Forum 427

Engstrom, D. 16–17

Entry Level Scheme (ELS) 83

Entry Level Stewardship Scheme 79

environment 69, 70; upland 449–59

environmental awareness: action 60–6

environmental capacity: reduction 409

environmental change: direct effects 50–3; interactive effects 53–4

environmental obligations 74–5

Environmental Quality Mark 303

Environmental Stewardship Scheme 324, 343, 349

Environmentally Sensitive Areas (ESA) 60, 70–1; Countryside Stewardship scheme 74; payments 235

erosion: blanket peat **26**; peat 104; peatlands 23; sedimentation 149

estate management: Duke of Devonshire 263; moorland 263

Europe: wildfires 405

European Economic Community (EEC) 66

European Landscape Convention 339

European policy: agriculture *61*

European Union (EU): Habitats and Species Directive 156; Water Framework Directive 358

European Water Framework Directive 27

eutrophication 38–41, 48; Lake District 148; nutrient enrichment 148

Evans, C 150–1

Evans, C.: and Monteith, D. 105

Evans, M.: *et al.* 24–5; and Warburton, J. 24

Ewald, J.: and Daplyn, J. 245–9

extinction: species 457

faecal contamination: drinking-water 149

farm: business income **86**

Farm Business Survey 85

Farm and Conservation Grant Scheme (F&CGS) 71

Farm Environment Plans 343

farm incomes: public goods supply 318

farm landscapes: economic value 325–6

farm produce: direct marketing 296

farmers: changing role 85–7; decline 85; declining network 296; social links 312–13; tourism industry 319

Farmers' Voice: postal survey 190

farming 298–9

farms: economic viability 317

Favourable Conservation Status 168

fell management: problems 314

field: moor 261

fire risk: behaviour models 408; climate change 408, 409, 410; modelling 407–8; physical models 408; spatial models 408

fire-fighting: wildfires 426

first-order acidity balance (FAB): acidification 137

flood risk 113

flooding 127; valley 169; water quality *xxvii*

focus groups 327

food and fibre: provision 7

Food from Our Own Resources: White Paper 66

foot-and-mouth disease 13, 78, 279; economic consequence 283; rural tourism 282

footloose economy 304

forest: post-glacial 174

forestry: development 270; energy crops 299–300

Forestry Commission: creation 66; establishment 270

Fraser, E.: and Kenny, A. 400

freedom to roam: walking 272–3

Freeman, C. 150

freshwater: ecosystems 151–2; monitoring schemes 135; South Pennines (UK) 144

Frolking, S. 97

Fuller, R.: and Gough, S. 190

game: hunting 268; management 240

gamekeepers: effects of absence 254; importance 242; mammals 233–4; role of 233–4

gamekeeping: conservation 181–2; sporting interest 240

Garnett, M. 103

Garrod, G.: and Willis, K. 326

gaseous ammonia 38

General Agreement on Tariffs and Trade (GATT) 73

Getz, and Carlsen, J. 282

Gimmingham, C.: and Hobbs, R. 177; and Kinako, P. 104

Glacier Bay: chemical evolution of lake basins **16**

glacier meltwater 127

glaciers: retreat 269

Glaves, D. 103

global change 491

global market forces 449

global sustainability 371

global warming 42–5; mountain regions 43

Good Farming Practice 77

Gorham, E. 93

Gothenburg Protocol 138

Gough, S.: and Fuller, R. 190

government: landscapes 324; role landscapes 324

government intervention: first examples 60

grazing 104; bird populations 213; cattle 360; control 243; deer 212–15; hill scheme 192; impact 196; moorland 189–90, 204; regime 203; sheep 212–15, 360; vegetation condition 166

grazing regimes *188*; managing 436

Great Britain: night satellite imagery **8**; rainfall 45; total emission **37**

great divide 340

Green Box payments 73

green environmental spaces: mental health 285; physical inactivity 285; Walking the Way to Health Initiative (WHI) 285, 286

greenhouse effect 41–2

greenhouse gases: anthropogenic emissions 41–7; climate change 41–2; increases 34

grouse: deer management 300–1; management 241–2, 256–7, 257; moorland 241; nematode gut parasite (*Trichostrongylus*) 242; shooting 268

grouse management 241–2, 256–7, 257; biodiversity 245–53; birds 245; burning *176*, 177–81; conservation objectives 256; ecological effects 177–81; fire use 172–7; impacts *216*; moorland 253; purposes 256

grouse moor: costs *256*

gully drainage 28

gully erosion: Peak District **125**

gully-bank collapse 27

gully-blocking 27, 442, 443

gunring: managed 358

habitat disturbance: catchment change 148–50

habitats: condition monitoring 161–2

Habitats Directive 74–5

Habitats and Species Directive: European Union (EU) 156; interest features 157

Hajer, M.: story lines 381

Hall, D.: and Roberts, L. 282
Harris, J. 444
Hartley, S.: and Mitchell, R. 197
Harvey, A. 17
Hayek, F.: social engineering 400
health: benefits 285; walking 284–6, 285
heather 243–4; birds 213–14; burning 215, 242–3, 244–5; burning rotation 243; cover percentage **244**
Heather and Grass Burning Code for England 165, 173, 179
heavy metal: pollution 146–8
hefting system: breakdown of 314–15
hefts: advantages 310; definition 310
hen harrier: birds of prey 253
Hetherington, D. 236
High Ewdale Farm: Potter, B. 315
Higher Level Scheme (HLS) 83, 189, 192, 203
Hill Farm Allowance (HFA) 77, 309; replacement scheme 85
hill farmers: subsidy systems 149
hill farming 323, 335, 353, 359–60; diversification 369; importance 354; public support 371; reduced levels 369; strategies *191*
Hill Farming Act 65
Hill and Livestock Compensatory Allowance (HLCA) 72
Hill Plan model 368
hillslope hydrology 115–19
Historic Landscape Characterisation 345
Hobbs, R.: and Gimmingham, C. 177
Hodge, I. 309
Holcene change: landscapes *14*
Holden, J. 101–2, 123; and Burt, T. 22, 119; and Holden 168
Holocene timescales 14
house prices: high 315; rising 316
Hudson, P. 254–6
Huggett, R. 18
Hughes, S. 101
human well-being: biodiversity 460
hunting: forests 261; game 268
hydrological characteristics *124*
hydrological impact: afforestation 126–7; climate change 127–9; construction 127; severe degradation 125–6; upland burning 121–3; vegetation cover 125–6
hydrological processes 150

ICP Waters Programme (UN) 142
Incident Recording System (IRS): wildfires 406
income: livestock 73; tourism 276; visitors 301
income leakage: rural tourism 282
indirect drivers: change 5
industrial mills 269
industrial restructuring: effects 139
infiltration-excess overland flow: water 11–16
Ingar: New South Wales 401
intake enclosure 261–2
interactive effects: environmental change 53–4
interest features *158*; condition monitoring 157; Habitats and Species Directive 157
intervention 434; large scale 439–43
invasive species: controlling 438–9
investment: natural capital 458

Joint Character Areas (JCAs) 342, 343, *345*, 346
Joint Nature Conservancy Council (JNCC) 464
Joint Raptor Study (JRS) 253–4
Jones, V. 149–50

Kay, J.: and Bullock, C. 326
Kenney, A.: and Fraser, E. 400
Kinako, P.: and Gimmingham, C. 104
Kinder Mass Tresspass 272
Kinder Scout 272; tresspassing 276
Knight, M.: and Selman, P. 346, 349
Koontz, T.: and Bodine, J. 463
Krange, O.: and Strandbu, A. 396

Laiho, R. 103
Lake District: case study 311; common grazings 311; commons future 318; eutrophication 148; medieval settlement history 262; nutrient enrichment 148; public goods model 311–15; research methods 311; traffic congestion 316
lakes: acidification 16
land: commodity 265; drainage 120
land management: drainage 101–4; soil hydrological process 130; totalitarian approach 401; uplands 129, 130
land-based extractive sectors 303
land-based sectors 297–303

land-use: climate change 219, 220; conflicts 486; drivers 219–20; futures 486

landscape *14*, 323–36, **477**; attributes *333*; conservation 237; integrating framework 344–9; meaning of 341–2; re-wilding 126; restoration 27; upland 342–5

Landscape Character Assessment 341, 342, 343–4

landscape diversity: maintaining 335

landscape scale: definition 346

legislation: natural areas 401

legitimacy: National Park Authority 386

leisure: consumption 280; lifestyle 280–1; opportunities 279–80

leisure patterns shifts 278

Less Favoured Area (LFA) 66–9, 297, 349; rural employment 255; spatial coverage in England **68**

Less Favoured Area Directive 60; livestock 189

Lewin, J.: and Macklin, M. 18

lifestyle: leisure 280–1

light penetration: ultraviolet (UV) 151

Lindsay, R. 21–2

livestock: Common Agricultural Policy (CAP) 189; density decline 219; income 73; Less Favoured Areas (LFA) Directive 189; moorland 186–204; subsidy payments 73; vegetation 186

Local Access Forum (LAFs) 277–8

long-term changes: upland landscapes 14–21

Lovat, L. 172–3, 177

low population density 294–5

lowlands: ecosystem services 460

Ludwig, F.: and Aerts, R. 105

McDonald, A.: and Mitchell, G. 101

Macklin, M.: and Lewin, J. 18

Major, J. 394

mammal groups: phylogenetic analysis 229

mammals 227–37; communities 229–30; domestic grazing 235–7; domination 235; field vole (*Microtus agrestis*) 235; gamekeepers 233–4; international context 227–8; mink (*Mustela vison*) 234, 235; montane fauna 227–8; mountain hare (*Lepus timidus*) 230–2; overgrazing 230;

pigmy shrew (*Sorex minutus*) 235; predatory 233–5; refugia 233; smaller montane 229; threats to 0; water vole (*Arvicola terrestris*) 234

management 484; blanket bog 219; burning 107; grouse 241–2; patch dynamics 29

Manchester Society for the Preservation of Ancient Footpaths 271

marginal economic performance 293–304

Maskell: *et al.* 295

medieval wastes 261–2

mental health: green environmental spaces 285

metal concentrations: Peak District 147

methane (CH_4) 94, 106

Meyles, E. 123

migration: change 107

migration patterns: explanations 294–5

Millennium Ecosystem Assessment 350, 460, 470

Millennium Greens 278

Ministry of Agriculture and Fisheries 65

mink (*Mustela vison*): mammals 234, 235

minor components 96

Mitchell, G.: and McDonald, A. 101

Mitchell, R.: and Hartley, S. 197

monasteries 262

moncultures: *Calluna* 182

monitoring schemes: freshwater 135

mono-agriculture 269

Montane: Wales 41

montane fauna: mammals 227–8

montane zone 157

Monteith, D. 151; and Evans, C. 105

moor: field 261

Moor House: carbon budget 97–8; location **97**; Trout Beck catchment *84*

Moore, T. 107

moorland: berry crops 215–17; birds 215–17, *218*; burning **164**; ecosystems 433–4; enclosing 263–71; estate management 263; government support 186; grazing 189–90, 204; grouse 241; grouse management 253; livestock 186–204; local gentry 263; mapping 263; Peak District 240; rambling 271–3; red grouse **246**; resilience 434; restoration 434–43, 437, 437–8, 443–4; Sheffield Clarion

Ramblers 271–2; social hierarchy 263; vegetation **248**; wildfire 404–27; wildfires 404–27, 406–7, 412–17, *415*, 417, 426

moorland management: grouse 253; red grouse 241

Moorland Scheme 75–6; polluter pays principle 75

moors: Burbage 269–70

Moors for the Future Partnership 468–9

Morgan-Davies, C.: and Waterhouse, A. 194–5

mountain hare (*Lepus timidus*) **232**; mammals 230–2

mountain regions: global warming 43

mountain ringlet: butterfly 50

Mountains and Moorlands (Pearsall) *xxvi*

National Audit Office 464

National Nature Reserves (NNR) 69

National Park: Peak District 7–9

National Park Authority (NPA) 377; capacity 386; content sustainability 386; legitimacy 386; Peak Park Transport Forum (PPTF) 385–7; South Pennines Transport Strategy (SPITS) 387

National Park Management Plans 349

National Parks 69, 344; formation 273; foundation 265; social class 394–6

National Parks and Access to Countryside Act (1947) 69

National Trust: major landowner 315

National Vegetation Classification (NVC) 157

natural areas: deregulation 400; legislation 401

natural capital: investment 458

natural changes: classification 14; definition 14

natural processes: peatland systems 21–7; upland management 27–8

natural re-vegetation: peatlands 25–6

natural system recovery 29

nature: romanticising 393; urbanites 393

Nature Conservancy 69, 156

nematode gut parasite (*Trichostrongylus*): grouse 242

net ecosystem exchange (NEE) 94

New Labour: re-election 78–9

New South Wales: Ingar 401

Nilson, E. 236

nitrate: acidification 142

nitrogen: atmospheric deposition 107–8; compounds 38, **40**; deposition 142, 143; dwarf shrub heath **49**

nitrogen cycle: disruption 35–6

North Pennines: management objectives 351–2

North York Moors National Park 85–6

nutrient enrichment 148; eutrophication 148; Lake District 148

organic carbon: dissolved 150–1

Organic Entry Level Scheme (OELS) 83

overgrazing: cross-compliance 72; mammals 230; problems *xxvi*

ozone 39; concentrations **39**; pollutants 38

palaeo-limnological techniques: acidification 136

Parish Paths Partnership 278

parliamentary walls: enclosure 268

particulate organic carbon (POC) 95, 106

partnerships 491

patch dynamics: management 29

payments-by-results scheme 318–19

Peak District: acidification 140; bird species 250; burning **178**; carbon storage 7; cultural heritage 7; drinking water guidelines 147; grouse moor estate 255–6; gully erosion **125**; metal concentrations 147; moorland 240; National Park 7–9; re-vegetation 28; recreational value 7; Special Area of Conservation (SAC) 241; studies 261

Peak District Moorland Stream Survey (PD-MSS) **141**

Peak District National Park 293, 349, 398–9; case study 380–7; transport policy 380–1; wildfires 411–25

Peak District National Park Authority (PNPA) 381

Peak District Sustainable Tourism Strategy (2000) 301–2

Peak Park Transport Forum (PPTF) 381; capacity 384–5; content sustainability 384; legitimacy 385; National Park Authority 385–7; Stanage Forum 383–5

Pearce-Higgins, J. 248–50
Pearsell, W. 15–16
peat: bog 172; drainage 101; erosion 104; impacts 302; re-vegetation 440–1; relative age dating 96
peat development: onset of 17
peat erosion: wildfires 407
peat-cutting 267
peatland systems: natural processes 21–7
peatlands: carbon balance 219; carbon pool 128; carbon store 93, 106–7; catchments 114, **114**; erosion 23; gullying of 21; natural re-vegetation 25–6; rewetting 103; sediment delivery **25**; wildfires 6
peats: carbon budget *98*
Pennines: pollution 25
permafrost 44–5
phasal development: *Calluna* 172
phenology: changes 50; species 457
Philips, H. 279
phosphorus loadings: increased 148
photochemical: air pollution 38–41
phylogenetic analysis: mammal groups 229
physical inactivity: green environmental spaces 285
physical models: fire risk 408
pigmy shrew (*Sorex minutus*): mammals 235
plantation forestry: expansion 149
plants: carbon-sequestering 441; ecosystem engineer 441
policy 484; clear positions 389; partnership working 390
policy making processes: legitimacy 380
pollutant concentrations: rainwater **52**
pollutants: developing countries 34; emission trends 36–7; ozone 38; primary 38; primary and secondary *36*; secondary 38
pollution: airbourne industrial 407; atmospheric sources 146–7; heavy metal 146–8; Pennines 25; snowfall 41
post glacial spread: upland tree taxa **15**
Potter, B.: High Ewdale Farm 315
precipitation: variations 127–8
predation experiment 251, **252**
predator control 242; bird population 215–16
predictive scenario modelling 482
pristine state: upland landscapes 27

production subsidies: Common Agricultural Policy (CAP) 323
protected areas 465–6
provision: food and fibre 7; water 7
public goods model 309; Lake District 311–15; provision 316; purchasers of access 316
public goods supply: farm incomes 318
Public Service Agreement (PSA) 460; targets 80–1
purchasers of access: public good model 316
purple moor grass 196
Pwllpieran 197, *201*; Redesdale *202*
Pyle, R. 393

radiative forcing: global warming potential *42*
rainfall 100; Great Britain 45; increase 45; inputs 96; UK changing patterns 45
rainwater: pollutant concentrations **52**
rambling: moorland 271–3; Ward, B. 272
ranchification 317
Random Parameter Logit (RPL) 329
raptors: persecution 217
rates of carbon accumulation (RCA) 93–4
re-vegetation: Peak District 28; peat 440–1
re-wilding 361–9; landscape 126
re-wilding experiment: Rum 236
recreation: national outdoor 278; outdoor 176
recreational disturbance 212
recreational value: Peak District 7
red grouse: moorland management 241; moorlands **246**
red grouse management: burning 433
Redesdale 197, **200**, **201**; Pwllpieran 197, *202*
reform: common land 79, 79–80
refugia: mammals 233; uplands 233
regulation 319
relative age dating: peat 96
remediation: damage 197
renewable energy 487
research methods: Contingent Valuation 326; Lake District 311
research questionnaire 327
reservoirs: creation 269
residential development 271

restoration: landscape 27; moorland 434–43, 437, 437–8, 443–4; techniques 108; understanding 433–4
retirement homes 316–17
reversability: service provision 479
rewetting: peatlands 103
rewilding 237
rhododendron: control 439
River Basin Management Plans 152
river flow 114–15
road traffic: air pollution 39
Roberts, L.: and Hall, D. 282
romantic gaze: Urry, J. 397
Rose, G. 396
Royal Forest of the Peak: records 262
Rum: re-wilding experiment 236
rural areas: decline in services 297; income levels 297; social relationships 295–6
Rural Development Programme for England (RDPE) 83
Rural Development Regulation (RDR) 76–7
Rural Economy and Land Use: programme 483
rural employment: Less Favoured Areas (LFA) 255
rural leisure: consumption 279; value of consumption 276
rural space 396
Rural Task Force 78
rural tourism 281–3; benefit 281; economic effects 281; economic limitations 282; foot-and-mouth disease 282; income leakage 282

Saarnio, S. 105
Salamonid fish: acidification 136–7
Sanson, A. 124, 166
scale: importance 480
scenario development 359
scenario research: methods evaluation 361; study design 360–1
scenario studies 372–3; critical comparison 365; evaluation methods *364*; uplands 362–3, *366–7*
science 484; uplands 479
science-user partnerships: funding 484
Scotland: Cairngorm mountains 41
scrub invasion 13
second homes 316–17; owners 304
sediment delivery: peatlands **25**
sedimentation: erosion 149
seeder-feeder scavenging 41

selection groups: attribute levels 327
self-sufficiency: drive for 60–6
Selman, P.: and Knight, M. 346, 349
service provision: reversability 479
severe degradation: hydrological impact 125–6
Severely Disadvantaged Areas (SDAs) 324, 326
shared visions: developing 485–7
sheep: deer 212–15; grazing 212–15, 360; rise in 166; stocking rates 189
sheep dogs 317
Sheep National Envelope 81
sheep tracks: role 124
Sheffield Clarion Ramblers: moorland 271–2
Short, C.: and Winter, M. 310
Silvola, J. 105
Single Farm Payment 372; Common Agricultural Policy (CAP) 323
Single Payment Scheme (SPS) 189–90; introduction 202–3
site condition: burning 164–6; drainage 167, 168
Sites of Special Scientific Interest (SSSIs) 156, *166*, 464; reasons for adverse conditions **164**; upland habitat **162**, **163**
slutch caves 118
smaller montane: mammals 229
snow cover 44
snowfall: pollution 41
social class 395, 396; national parks 394–6
social consensus: education 397
social engineering: Hayek, F. 400
social hierarchy: moorland 263
social relationships: rural areas 295–6
socio-economic patterns: changing 293
soil: acidification 53; climax 17; pipes 118–19; upland 118–19
soil hydrological process: land management 130
soil respiration: carbon dioxide 106
South Pennines Transport Strategy (SPITS): National Park Authority 387
South Pennines (UK): acid neutralising capacity (ANC) **146**; freshwaters 144
spatial distribution: wildfires 417–23
spatial models: fire risk 408
Special Areas of Conservation (SACs) 75, 156; Peak District 241
Special Protection Areas (SPAs) 75, 241

species: distribution and abundance 457; extinction 457; phenology 457
sphagnum: increase of species **52**
sporting interest: gamekeeping 240
spring melt: earlier 44
stakeholder: involvement 389
stakeholder engagement: effectiveness 389, 389–90
Stanage Forum 382–3, 387–8; capacity 383; content sustainability 382–3; environmental limits 382; free access 382; legitimacy 383; Peak Park Transport Forum (PPTF) 383–5
steady-state water chemistry (SSWC): acidification 137
Stern Review 469, 470
Strandbu, A.: and Krange, O. 396
stream biology: climate change 151
streams: acidification 16
streamwater: chemistry trends 145
stress factors: natural 54
structural disadvantages: upland farming 287
sub-montane zone 157
subsidy payments: livestock 73
subsidy systems: hill farmers 149
sulphur: atmospheric deposition 104–5
sulphur emission: decline 37
surface-water: acidification 135–7, 139–46, 142
sustainable approaches: upland management 491
synthetic industrial compound: release 36

Tallis, J. 23
Task Force for the Hills 77
temperature: increase in 99; uplands 127
threshold effects 143
throughflow pathways **115**
totalitarian approach: land management 401
tourism 301–2; diversification 370; income 276; sustainable 283
tourism industry: farmers 319; uplands 458
tourism market: upland 479
tourist gaze: Urry, J. 397
traffic congestion: Lake District 316
trans-disciplinary approaches 481–2
transport policy: Peak District National Park 380–1

tresspassing 272; Abbey Brook 272; Kinder Mass Tresspass 272; Kinder Scout 276
Trout Beck catchment: Moor House *95*

UK Acid Rain Monitoring Network 50
UK Acid Waters Monitoring Network 142–3, 479
UK Climate Impacts 142
UK upland economies: characteristics and trends 293–7
ultraviolet (UV): light penetration 151
UN Millennium Ecosystem Assessment 80, 449
upland: adaptive management 483–4; benefits 1; bird species *214*; changing minds 475–91; definitions 4; deforestation 477; drainage 120; drivers change 475; ecosystem services 476–9; environment 449–59; futures 361–72; land management 129; landscape 342–5; management problems *435*; scenario studies *362–3*; science 479; state 448–9; temperature 127; threats 1; tourism industry 458; tourism market 479; uncertain futures 358
upland burning: hydrological impacts 121–3
upland economy: composition 296–7
upland farmers: subsidies 71
upland farming: structural disadvantages 287
upland grazing: hydrological impact 123–4
upland habitat: condition Monitoring 162–8; Sites of Special Scientific Interest (SSSIs) **162**, **163**
upland landscapes: drivers of change 352–4; dynamic equilibrium **18**; long-term changes 14–21; pristine state 27
upland management: changes 113; natural processes 27–8; stakeholder involvement 377–8; sustainable approaches 491
upland peats: carbon cycle 94
upland scenarios *366*; overview *362*
upland tree taxa: post glacial spread **15**
uplands systems: changing 6
Upper Derwent: ownership and land use 264
Upper Wharfdale *117*

urbanites: nature 393
Urry, J. 396, 400; collective gaze 397; romantic gaze 397; tourist gaze 397

valley: flooding 169
variability: weather 45
vegetation: change 196–202, 210–12; livestock 186; moorland **248**
vegetation condition: grazing 166
vegetation cover: catchment 24; climax 17; hydrological impact 125–6
vegetation structure: birds 214–15
veterinary intervention 236
visitors: income 301

Wales: Montane 41
walking: freedom to roam 272–3; health 284–6, 285
Walking the Way to Health Initiative (WHI): green environmental spaces 285, 286
Wallage, Z. 101
Warburton, J.: and Evans, M. 24
Ward, B.: rambling 272
water: baseflow 115; changes 457; infiltration-excess overland flow 11–16; need for 269; provision 7; throughflow 115–16
water balance: climate change 128
water colour: trends 150–1
Water Framework Directive 84, 152
water quality: benefits 303; flooding *xxvii*
water vole (*Arvicola terrestris*): mammals 234
water-table: depth 117, **117**, **122**; lowered 102

Waterhouse, A.: and Morgan-Davies, C. 194–5
weather: variability 45; wildfires 426
White Paper: *Food from Our Own Resoucres* 66
White Peak Vision: project 345, 347
wildfires 236; carbon budget 407; causes 404; control 423–5; deep-seated summer 407; ecosystem services 406–7; Europe 405; fire-fighting 426; hazard and risk 405; Incident Recording System (IRS) 406; managed 405; management costs 407; modelling the timing 412–17; moorland 404–27, 406–7, 412–17, *415*, 417, 426; Peak District National Park 411–25; peat erosion 407; peatlands 6; preparation 423–5; prevention 423–5; spatial distribution 417–23; uncontrolled 404; United Kingdom 405; weather 426
Wildlife and Coutryside Act (1981) 70
Wildlife Enhancement Scheme (WES) 75
will to consensus 389
Willis, K.: and Garrod, G. 326
Wilson, A. 253
Wilson, C. 236
Winter, M.: and Short, C. 310
woodland: clearance 171, 261; colonisation 171
woodland colonisation: burning 171
working classes 395
World Trade Organisation (WTO) 73
Worrall, F. 96–7, 97, 101–2, 302; and Adamson, J. 103–4; *et al.* 99